# Ireland For Dummies
## 3rd Edition

D0405017

## The Ring of Kerry

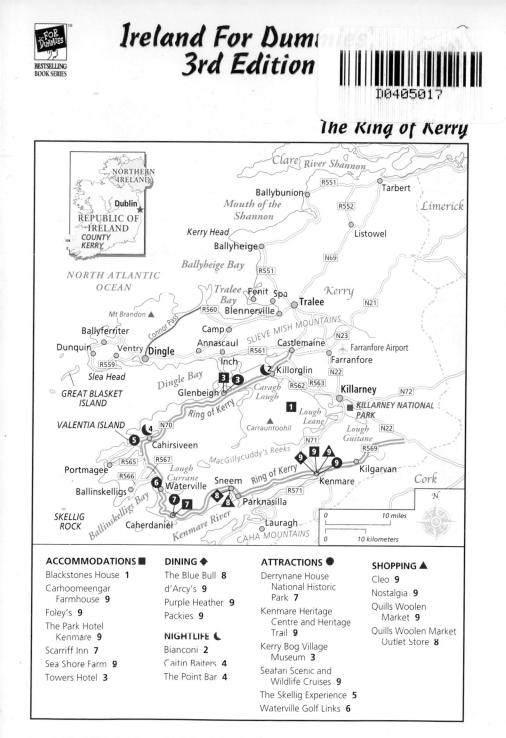

**ACCOMMODATIONS** ■
Blackstones House **1**
Carhoomeengar
 Farmhouse **9**
Foley's **9**
The Park Hotel
 Kenmare **9**
Scarriff Inn **7**
Sea Shore Farm **9**
Towers Hotel **3**

**DINING** ◆
The Blue Bull **8**
d'Arcy's **9**
Purple Heather **9**
Packies **9**

**NIGHTLIFE** ☾
Bianconi **2**
Caitin Baiters **4**
The Point Bar **4**

**ATTRACTIONS** ●
Derrynane House
 National Historic
 Park **7**
Kenmare Heritage
 Centre and Heritage
 Trail **9**
Kerry Bog Village
 Museum **3**
Seatari Scenic and
 Wildlife Cruises **9**
The Skellig Experience **5**
Waterville Golf Links **6**

**SHOPPING** ▲
Cleo **9**
Nostalgia **9**
Quills Woolen
 Market **9**
Quills Woolen Market
 Outlet Store **8**

# Learning the Lingo

Refer to this helpful list of lingo while touring Ireland.

| | | | |
|---|---|---|---|
| **An Lar** | city center | **lift** | elevator |
| **bonnet** | car hood | **mna** | women (Gaelic) |
| **boot** | car trunk | **off-license** | liquor store |
| **Bord Fáilte** | Irish Tourist Board (Gaelic) | **press** | cabinet |
| **cheers** | thanks | **petrol** | gas |
| **crack, craic** | good times, fun | **quay** | waterfront (pronounced *key*) |
| **creche** | day care | **quid or bob** | pounds or money |
| **deadly, brilliant** | great, excellent | **sláinte** | cheers or goodbye (Gaelic — pronounced *schlancha*) |
| **fáilte** | welcome (Gaelic) | | |
| **fir** | men (Gaelic) | **take-away** | fast food, to go |
| **footpath** | sidewalk | **tins** | canned goods |
| **garda** | policeman | | |

# Ireland Mileage Guide

Use this mileage chart to help plan your itinerary.

| Belfast | | | | | | | | | | |
|---|---|---|---|---|---|---|---|---|---|---|
| 264 | **Cork** | | | | | | | | | |
| 73 | 266 | **Derry** | | | | | | | | |
| 112 | 250 | 43 | **Donegal** | | | | | | | |
| 104 | 160 | 147 | 138 | **Dublin** | | | | | | |
| 190 | 130 | 169 | 127 | 136 | **Galway** | | | | | |
| 271 | 54 | 274 | 235 | 192 | 120 | **Killarney** | | | | |
| 201 | 65 | 204 | 184 | 123 | 65 | 69 | **Limerick** | | | |
| 128 | 209 | 84 | 41 | 135 | 86 | 213 | 144 | **Sligo** | | |
| 207 | 78 | 238 | 222 | 98 | 137 | 120 | 80 | 182 | **Waterford** | |
| 192 | 116 | 235 | 231 | 88 | 157 | 158 | 118 | 191 | 39 | **Wexford** |

# FOR DUMMIES

## The fun and easy way™ to travel!

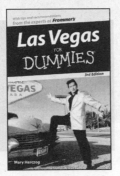

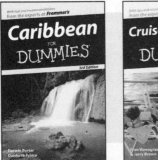

# Ireland
## FOR
# DUMMIES®
### 3RD EDITION

by Liz Albertson

**WILEY**

Wiley Publishing, Inc.

**Ireland For Dummies®, 3rd Edition**
Published by
**Wiley Publishing, Inc.**
111 River St.
Hoboken, NJ 07030-5774
www.wiley.com

WILEY

# About the Author

**Liz Albertson** worked as an editor for Frommer's Travel Guides for four years before making the leap to the other side of the computer as the author of *Ireland For Dummies*. When she wasn't researching and writing, Liz spent her time sitting in on traditional music sessions across Ireland, fiddle in hand. She is currently pursuing her master's degree in Middle School Education and Museum Education while working as a freelance writer, editor, actor, and fiddler based in Brooklyn, NY. Liz welcomes feedback and suggestions for the next edition of the book at ejalbertson@yahoo.com.

# Dedication

For Hugh.

# Author's Acknowledgments

The deepest of thank yous to Christine Ryan, for giving me the wonderful opportunity to work on this book and for being a patient and meticulous editor. Big thanks also to Helen and Richard Albertson (also known as mom and dad) for being terrific travel companions on the Northern Ireland leg of my research trip. And to all of the following for their travel tips, encouragement, and excitement on my behalf: Lauren Weintraub, Kendra Falkenstein, Nina Rubin, Nick Trotter, Nellie Zupancic, Marisa Suescun, Suzanne Grossman, Noah Lansner, Caroline Sieg, John Nevin and the whole Dempsey's bunch, Mara McCarthy, Raihan Majid, Catherine Scott, Greg Whalen, Alison Root, Liz Strickland, Lisa Goldstein, Lisa Farber, Kelly Regan, Trina Fischer, Cara Hirsch, and Shannon Woolley, and last, but certainly not least, Hugh Crowl, travel companion, price converter, and boyfriend extraordinaire.

# Publisher's Acknowledgments

We're proud of this book; please send us your comments through our Dummies online registration form located at www.dummies.com/register/.

Some of the people who helped bring this book to market include the following:

## Editorial

**Editors:** Kathleen A. Dobie and Christine Ryan

**Cartographer:** Nick Trotter

**Editorial Manager:** Michelle Hacker

**Editorial Supervisor:** Carmen Krikorian

**Editorial Assistant:** Nadine Bell

**Senior Photo Editor:** Richard Fox

**Cover Photos:** Front: SIME s.a.s./ eStock Photo; Back: Irish Image Collection/Premium/Panoramic Images

**Cartoons:** Rich Tennant, www.the5thwave.com

## Composition

**Project Coordinator:** Ryan Steffen

**Layout and Graphics:** Lauren Goddard, Barry Offringa, Melanee Prendergast, Julie Trippetti

**Proofreaders:** Laura Albert, Jessica Kramer, Carl Pierce, TECHBOOKS Production Services

**Indexer:** TECHBOOKS Production Services

---

### Publishing and Editorial for Consumer Dummies

**Diane Graves Steele,** Vice President and Publisher, Consumer Dummies

**Joyce Pepple,** Acquisitions Director, Consumer Dummies

**Kristin A. Cocks,** Product Development Director, Consumer Dummies

**Michael Spring,** Vice President and Publisher, Travel

**Brice Gosnell,** Associate Publisher, Travel

**Kelly Regan,** Editorial Director, Travel

### Publishing for Technology Dummies

**Andy Cummings,** Vice President and Publisher, Dummies Technology/ General User

### Composition Services

**Gerry Fahey,** Vice President of Production Services

**Debbie Stailey,** Director of Composition Services

# Contents at a Glance

# Maps at a Glance

# Table of Contents

# Introduction

. . . . . . . . . . . . . . . . . . . . . . . . . . . . . . . . . . . . . . . .

*R*elatively tiny Ireland (84,434 sq. km/32,600 sq. miles) offers travelers a surprisingly diverse range of experiences. You find landscapes that range from those famed rolling green hills to stark, rugged cliffs; restaurants that serve the best in modern fusion cuisine and pubs that serve Irish stew made from a recipe that's hundreds of years old; theaters showcasing the best in contemporary dance and festivals devoted to traditional Irish music. This guide highlights the best of Ireland's diverse offerings so that you can plan the trip of your dreams.

## About This Book

This guide is designed to help you travel smarter, with a concise, savvy approach that helps you get to the heart of what you're looking for. It's a quick reference guide that includes need-to-know information, from the best online bargains and package deals to helpful tips on how to organize and maximize your time in a destination. Each destination features a selective, streamlined choice of hotels and restaurants in all price ranges. I weeded out the clunkers to focus on the best choices, whether you're looking to splurge on a luxury resort or find an affordable place for a family of four.

I tried to anticipate every question you may have about traveling to Ireland and provide the answers. If you've never been to the country before, I show you what to expect and how to plan for it. If you're an old Ireland hand, you probably bought this book because you don't want to waste a lot of time sorting through a billion different hotels, restaurants, and attractions trying to find the absolute best ones. You want a quick and easy, yet comprehensive, source of information, and that's exactly what I give you here.

Of course, you don't have to read the whole book. And you don't have to start at the beginning, either. This is a reference book. Check out the table of contents and then read the parts that answer your specific questions.

Please be advised that travel information is subject to change at any time — this is especially true of prices. You may want to write or call ahead for confirmation when making your travel plans.

---

# Dummies Post-it® Flags

As you read this book, you'll find information you want to reference as you plan or enjoy your trip — whether it be a new hotel, a must-see attraction, or a must-try walking tour. Mark these pages with the handy Post-it® flags included in this book to help make your trip planning easier!

---

## Conventions Used in This Book

In this book, I include descriptions of the best sights in Ireland; reviews of the best hotels, restaurants, shops, pubs, and more; and all sorts of tips for planning your visit to the Emerald Isle. I employ a few conventions designed to convey critical information in a simple, straightforward manner.

### Money matters

For this edition of *Ireland For Dummies*, I used the currency exchange rates of $1.15 to every €1 and $1.85 to every £1. Exchange rates fluctuate all the time; check www.xe.com for up-to-date exchange rates.

All prices given here over ten euro, dollars, or pounds are rounded to the nearest euro, dollar, or pound. All prices are, of course, subject to change.

In the accommodations sections, the listed price is a *rack rate* (the official rate published by the hotel) for one night in a double room (one room accommodating two people); the actual prices you'll pay are often less than the rack rate.

Each accommodation and dining review is accompanied by a dollar-sign designation designed to help you get a sense of the price category of the lodging or restaurant at a glance. The following table gives you the key to the dollar-sign designations for accommodations and restaurants.

| Accommodation Category | Euro | British Pound | U.S. Dollar |
|---|---|---|---|
| $ | €70 | £44 | $80 or less |
| $$ | €71–€130 | £44–£81 | $81–$125 |
| $$$ | €131–€190 | £81–£118 | $126–$225 |
| $$$$ | €191 or more | £119 or more | $226 or more |

| Restaurant Category | Euro | British Pound | U.S. Dollar |
|---|---|---|---|
| $ | € 10 | £6.20 | $12 or less |
| $$ | €11–€17 | £6.85–£11 | $13–$20 |
| $$$ | €18–€24 | £11–£15 | $21–$28 |
| $$$$ | €25 or more | £16 or more | $29 or more |

## Other matters

I provide an entry called *Suggested visit* at the end of each attraction listing. This is my estimate of how much time you should budget to do and see most of what's available at each attraction. This length of time is just a suggestion — you may find you need more or less time, depending on your interests.

The following is a list of the credit card abbreviations used in the listings in this book:

AE  American Express

DC  Diners Club

MC  MasterCard

V  Visa

In the dining sections, the listed prices are the range of prices for dinner main courses, unless otherwise noted.

And just in case you're not familiar with the term *en suite,* it means a room with a bathroom connected. In some B&Bs especially, you may be expected to share a bathroom with other guests, so ask for a room en suite if a private bath is important to you.

# Foolish Assumptions

In this book, I make some assumptions about you and your needs as a traveler. I assume you are one of the following:

- ✔ An inexperienced traveler looking for guidance when determining whether to travel to Ireland and how to plan for it
- ✔ An experienced traveler who hasn't yet visited Ireland and wants expert advice on where to go and what to see
- ✔ A traveler looking for a book that focuses on only the best and most essential Irish sights, tastes, and experiences

If you fit any of these criteria, *Ireland For Dummies,* 3rd Edition, gives you the information you're looking for.

# How This Book Is Organized

This book is divided into seven parts. Parts I and II whet your palate and get you ready to go, and Parts III through VII deal with what you can see and do while you're there. Be aware that each section in the regional chapters has a Fast Facts portion at the end, listing addresses and contact information for visitors' bureaus and tourism offices, Internet cafes, hospitals, local genealogical resources, and post offices.

## Part 1: Introducing Ireland

This part introduces you to the splendor of Ireland and helps you get an idea of what you'd like to see and where you'd like to go. The book starts with a chapter devoted to the very best that Ireland has to offer. Chapter 2 includes all sorts of information about Ireland, from a look at the island's history to translations of local lingo to culinary information. Chapter 3 provides brief descriptions of the regions covered in this guide so that you get a sense of where you'd like to go. In Chapter 3, I also discuss various approaches to touring the country, and hash out the pros and cons of visiting during different seasons. I also give you a rundown of the many festivals, events, and celebrations held in Ireland throughout the year. In case you'd like some guidance on how to plan your itinerary, I offer outlines for four different suggested itineraries in Chapter 4.

## Part 11: Planning Your Trip to Ireland

Part II answers all your practical questions about planning and getting ready for a trip to Ireland. Chapter 5 deals with money, providing rough guidelines on what things cost, helping you decide how to carry your money, and listing 21 (count 'em: 21) money-saving tips. Chapter 6 outlines the different ways to get to Ireland, and Chapter 7 deals with the various options for getting around the island. After you plan how to get there, you can turn to Chapter 8, which gives you the lowdown on the different types of accommodations in Ireland, plus tips on how to save on lodging costs. Chapter 9 includes tips for travelers with special needs and interests, including seniors, travelers with disabilities, gay and lesbian travelers, outdoorsy travelers, and more. Before you go start buying your travel-size toothpaste, check out Chapter 10 for information on getting a passport, figuring out your insurance, packing your bags, and staying in touch once you get to Ireland.

## Part 111: Dublin and the East Coast

Part III is dedicated to Dublin and the surrounding counties: Meath and Louth to the north and Wicklow, Wexford, Waterford, Kilkenny, and Tipperary to the south.

Chapter 11 covers Dublin, the Republic of Ireland's bustling, vibrant capital city. This fat chapter is packed with information on the best restaurants, hotels, attractions, shopping, and nightlife in the city. If the choices overwhelm you, check out the one-, two-, and three-day itinerary suggestions I provide.

Counties Meath and Louth, just north of Dublin, are home to a treasure trove of prehistoric sights, including the remarkable burial mounds at Knowth and Newgrange, and the storied Hill of Tara, ancient seat of the Irish high kings. Chapters 12, 13, and 14 cover the beautiful southeastern counties of Wicklow, Kildare, Wexford, Waterford, Kilkenny, and Tipperary. These counties offer a diverse array of attractions, including some of Ireland's most beautiful gardens, medieval towns, stunning mountain and coastal scenery, and the popular Waterford Crystal Factory.

## Part IV: Counties Cork and Kerry

Part IV covers only two counties, Cork and Kerry, which together attract the lion's share of visitors to Ireland, who come for the stunning mountain and coastal scenery in these parts. Chapter 15 gives you the inside track on Cork City and its terrific culinary and arts scenes. The gorgeous sea- and landscapes, and the cute towns of West are covered in Chapter 15, while Chapter 16 features the best of beautiful Killarney National Park and the breathtaking Ring of Kerry and Dingle Peninsula.

## Part V: The West and the Northwest

This part bundles the entire western and northwestern areas of Ireland into one neat package that incorporates a tremendous variety of landscapes and towns. Chapters 17 through 20 are filled with information on gorgeous natural wonders, including the sheer Cliffs of Moher and Slieve League cliffs; the rocky, wildflower-studded Burren; the beautiful Aran Islands; the wild landscape of Connemara; and much more. You get the lowdown on some of the best cities and towns in this area, including the sweet Mayo town of Westport, artsy Sligo Town, and the it's-so-great-why-doesn't-everyone-live-here city of Galway.

## Part VI: Northern Ireland

Part VI covers the separate country of Northern Ireland, which may be last in this book but is not least in terms of natural beauty and interesting cities. Chapters 21, 22, and 23 guide you to the most beautiful natural wonders, including the Mourne Mountains and the hexagonal basalt columns of the Giant's Causeway. They also give you all the information you need to explore the hot-and-happening city of Belfast and the up and-coming historic city of Derry.

## Part VII: The Part of Tens

The Part of Tens chapters feature some fun extras, such as Irish food and drink that you shouldn't miss during your trip, and my top ten suggestions of what to buy in Ireland.

You also find another element near the back of this book. I include an appendix — your "Quick Concierge" — containing lots of handy information you may need when planning your trip.

## Icons Used in This Book

Keep an eye peeled for these icons, which appear in the margins:

This icon highlights money-saving tips and/or great deals.

This icon highlights the best the destination has to offer in all categories: hotels, restaurants, attractions, activities, shopping, and nightlife.

This icon gives you a heads-up on annoying or potentially dangerous situations, such as tourist traps, unsafe neighborhoods, rip-offs, and other things to beware of.

This icon highlights attractions, hotels, restaurants, or activities that are particularly hospitable to children or people traveling with kids.

This icon points out useful advice on things to do and ways to schedule your time.

## Where to Go from Here

Now you're ready to go! Put a Chieftains CD on the stereo; pour yourself a glass of Guinness; and get ready to fling yourself headlong into the historic, friendly, beautiful experience that is Ireland today.

# Part I

# Introducing Ireland

©RICH TENNANT

WHILE ON VACATION IN IRELAND, BILL AND DENISE WATCH A LOCAL FAMILY WORKING ON THE TRADITIONAL THATCHED ROOF COTTAGE, THATCHED ROOF SATELLITE DISH, AND THATCHED ROOF JEEP CHEROKEE.

# In this part . . .

*I*reland is a traveler's dream, with diverse and spectacular scenery, vibrant towns and cities humming with activity, a culinary scene that makes the most of the country's delicious fresh produce, a wide array of attractions, and more than its share of superb accommodations, from upscale hotels to cozy B&Bs. Chapter 1 whets your appetite with brief descriptions of some of Ireland's best scenery, restaurants, accommodations, and more.

Read through Chapter 2 for background information on Ireland, including looks at Irish history, Irish cuisine, and local lingo, plus a list of some fun and interesting Irish books, movies, and music.

In Chapter 3, I provide brief descriptions of the regions covered in this guide, discuss various approaches to touring the country, and hash out the pros and cons of visiting during different seasons. I also include a calendar of events so that you can schedule your trip to coincide with the festivals and celebrations that interest you.

Overwhelmed by the wealth of things to see and do in Ireland? Chapter 4 includes some suggestions for itineraries.

# Chapter 1

# Discovering the Best of Ireland

*T*his chapter gives you the lowdown on the very best that Ireland has to offer, from the best food on the island to the most gorgeous seascapes to the best spots to hear traditional Irish music. The nearby "Ireland" map gives you an overview of the terrain.

## The Best Travel Experiences

With all that Ireland has to offer, it's tough to come up with a list of favorite experiences. But here are some of the adventures I keep daydreaming about long after I'm home.

✓ **Listening to traditional Irish music:** What could be better (or more Irish) than relaxing to live traditional music in an atmospheric pub? The Traditional Irish Musical Pub Crawl (see Chapter 11) is a terrific introduction to the musical style. If you're in the groove after the pub crawl, head to the Cobblestone (also in Chapter 11), which hosts exceptional musicians.

✓ **Taking in the Book of Kells:** This ninth-century book of the four gospels glows with ornate Latin script and stunning Celtic knots and designs. The exhibit about the making of the book is fascinating. See Chapter 11.

✔ **Filing into Newgrange Tomb:** You'll feel like a lucky explorer as you descend into the cool, dim chamber of this 5,000-year-old *passage tomb* (an underground chamber thought to have had religious or ceremonial importance), where you find ancient geometric rock carvings. See Chapter 12.

✔ **Strolling through Powerscourt Gardens:** These gardens have many facets, including a mossy grotto, a formal garden with an impressive fountain and statuary, a rose garden that bursts into a riot of color in season, and peaceful woodlands. See Chapter 13.

✔ **Touring the Waterford Crystal Factory:** A fascinating tour takes you behind the scenes to watch the evolution of Waterford Crystal pieces, from their beginnings as molten crystal through to finished product. Naturally, there is a giant retail space on site. See Chapter 14.

✔ **Eating your way through Kinsale:** Not only is Kinsale the picture of charm, with a beautiful harbor and an adorable town center, but it's also Ireland's gourmet capital, so you find loads of excellent restaurants here. See Chapter 15.

✔ **Exploring Killarney National Park:** Use a bike, horse, jaunting car, or your own two feet to explore the silver streams, sapphire lakes, dense woodlands, and heather-covered mountains here. See Chapter 16.

✔ **Driving the Ring of Kerry and the Dingle Peninsula:** Driving along both of these peninsulas, you'll encounter vista after vista, each more spectacular than the one before it. Seascapes, cliffs, and mountain views are the order of the day on the Ring of Kerry, while the Dingle Peninsula is all vibrant green hills, sandy beaches, craggy cliffs, and more seascapes. See Chapter 16.

✔ **Walking through the Burren:** Walking is the ultimate way to see this strange and gorgeous rocky plateau, filled with wildflowers poking up through cracks in the rock, shallow lakes and rivers springing up from below, and ruins from the Stone Age through medieval times. See Chapter 17.

✔ **Exploring the Aran Islands:** Taking the ferry out to the three Aran islands is part of the adventure. The other part is exploring these peaceful islands, with their small fields surrounded by stone walls, by bike or by foot. See Chapter 18.

✔ **Gazing awestruck at the Cliffs of Moher:** Tuck your extra rolls of film into your backpack before you head up to these breathtaking cliffs, which plummet down to the Atlantic 288m (760 feet) below. The vistas are stunning — you can see all the way to the Aran Islands in Galway Bay when the weather is clear. See Chapter 17.

✔ **Clambering around the Giant's Causeway:** You can climb around this natural wonder — a stretch of tightly packed six-sided basalt columns of varying heights — like you're on a Stairmaster gone crazy. See Chapter 22.

*Ireland*

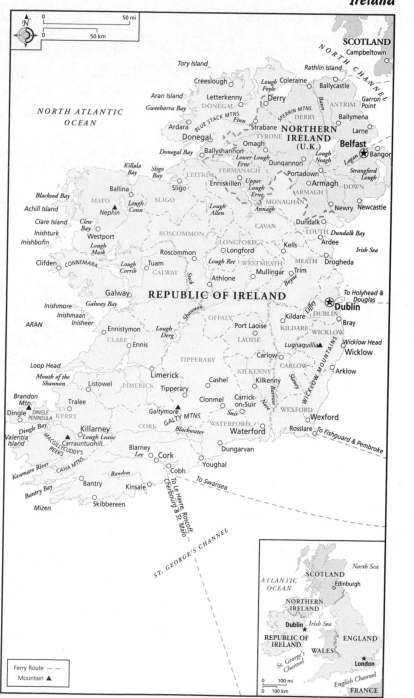

# The Best Hotels

The following hotels made my list of favorites because they offer a unique atmosphere, outstanding service, uncommon luxury, a particularly Irish flavor, or perhaps all of the above.

- ✔ **Number 31 (Dublin):** A country-chic oasis with gorgeous modern accents, this small hotel is a calm retreat in the middle of Georgian Dublin. Good luck pulling yourself away from the delicious breakfast. See Chapter 11.

- ✔ **Waterford Castle (Waterford):** Don your crown and head to this castle on its own island, with an interior boasting tapestries, antiques, and stone fireplaces. See Chapter 14.

- ✔ **Butler House (Kilkenny):** The decor here is a gorgeous marriage of old and new; service is spot-on; and many of the spacious rooms have views of Kilkenny Castle that are so beautiful, they look like storybook illustrations. See Chapter 14.

- ✔ **The Old Presbytery (Cork):** The only way that this place could be more relaxing would be if a masseuse came with each room. The huge beds are filled with snow-white blankets and pillows, many rooms have tubs or Jacuzzis, and the staff is among the friendliest and most helpful around. See Chapter 15.

- ✔ **Killarney Park Hotel (Kerry):** Luxury, luxury, and more luxury are on tap at this hotel, with a gorgeous Victorian-style lobby and spacious guest rooms furnished with antiques and lush fabrics. See Chapter 16.

- ✔ **Adare Manor Hotel & Golf Resort (Limerick):** You'll want for nothing at this castle-like manor house. The public rooms are grand and luxurious, and the bedrooms are filled with opulent fabrics and carved wood and stone. The grounds feature a trout-filled river, sweeping parklands, and a Trent Jones–designed golf course. See Chapter 17.

- ✔ **Ashford Castle (Mayo):** Live out a fairy tale with a stay in this luxurious castle. Public rooms hold large gilt-framed oil paintings, medieval coats of armor, and oak paneling, while antiques and carved wood furniture are the order of the day in guest rooms. The forested grounds are the perfect place for a walk after dinner. See Chapter 19.

- ✔ **The McCausland Hotel (Antrim):** I challenge even the grouchiest traveler to find fault with this trendy boutique hotel, where service is extraordinarily friendly, and the warm, spacious rooms are designed to cater to every need. See Chapter 22.

# The Best B&Bs

I love bed-and-breakfasts because you get the company and advice of a friendly local along with a homey, comfortable room — and often a good bargain to boot. Here are some of my favorites:

- **McMenamins Townhouse (Wexford):** Kind hosts, soothing rooms, a central location, and a spectacular breakfast make this place one of Ireland's best B&Bs. See Chapter 14.

- **Foxmount Country House (Waterford):** It's easy to feel like the lord or lady of this manor as you stroll the stunningly landscaped grounds and settle down in your cozy, elegant room. See Chapter 14.

- **Ballymakeigh House (Cork):** Dine on a five-course meal made from the freshest of produce before stumbling upstairs to your comfortable room overlooking the surrounding dairy farm. See Chapter 15.

- **Dowling's Leeside (Kerry):** Friendly and generous hostess Maura Dowling offers rooms at her bright, cheerful B&B for bargain prices. See Chapter 16.

- **Berry Lodge (Clare):** The views of farmland and sea are gorgeous, and the bedrooms are comfy and bright, but the real reason to stay here is the unbelievably delicious dinners served downstairs. See Chapter 17.

- **The Merchant's House (Derry):** Slip back in time with a stay at this beautifully restored Georgian B&B, featuring high ceilings, intricate plasterwork, and a museum-quality Georgian-style dining room. See Chapter 21.

- **Ash-Rowan Town House (Antrim):** This serene B&B is a welcome oasis after a long night in Belfast's pubs or a long day exploring the city. Rooms are decorated with country-style furniture, Victorian antiques, and fresh flowers from the garden in back. See Chapter 22.

## The Best of the Irish Awards

As you make your way around Ireland, you discover that the Irish absolutely love awards. Almost every restaurant and lodging has some sort of sign or sticker indicating that the place is lauded by one organization or other. In fact, there are even awards for the best public bathrooms in each county. You heard it here first: One of Ireland's top toilets is in Lismore, in County Cork. The esteemed public bathroom is located at the foot of the road leading toward the castle. As you enter towns and villages in each county in the Republic, you often see awards for the Tidiest Town, presented by the environmental council. If you feel like planning an itinerary through Ireland's tidiest towns, check out www.tidytowns.ie.

✔ **Slieve Croob Inn (Down):** You can't beat the location of this comfortable inn, nestled in rolling green hills a few minutes away from the Mourne Mountains. Walking trails start practically at the front door. See Chapter 23.

## The Best Restaurants

Feel like sitting down to an elegantly prepared seafood entrée? Or is meat-and-potatoes comfort food more your style? Perhaps you'd like a fusion meal, featuring ingredients and cooking techniques from all over the world? No matter what you're craving, you won't go hungry in Ireland. Following are my favorite places to dig in.

✔ **Mermaid Café (Dublin):** Fresh Irish ingredients and innovative dishes characterize the menu at this buzzy, warm, modern restaurant. See Chapter 11.

✔ **The Tea Room (Dublin):** Inexpensive, it ain't, but the daring dishes served at this hip, celebrity-frequented restaurant — for example, caramelized monkfish with Serrano ham — are worth the big bucks (or euro, in this case). See Chapter 11.

✔ **Ristorante Rinuccini (Kilkenny):** Open the door and slip into Florence at this romantic Italian restaurant. The homemade pasta is excellent. See Chapter 14.

✔ **Jacob's On the Mall (Cork):** Settle down in this airy cathedral of a restaurant for fresh, creative dishes such as crisp vegetable and duck confit spring rolls. See Chapter 15.

✔ **Fishy Fishy Café (Cork):** Come here for sparkling fresh fish prepared beautifully and served in a bright, sea- and sky-blue room. See Chapter 15.

✔ **Man Friday (Cork):** There's no fancy footwork at this seafood-and-meat restaurant, just excellent ingredients cooked in a way that allows their flavor to shine, such as the black sole cooked on the bone. The interior is warm, romantic, and cozy, lit by lantern-style lamps. See Chapter 15.

✔ **Packies (Kerry):** You can't go wrong with any of the dishes at this hip and lively restaurant, from the simple crab claws in garlic butter to the adventurous plaice with orange, lime, and cilantro. See Chapter 16.

✔ **Out of the Blue (Kerry):** In a sea of seafood restaurants, Out of the Blue stands out, offering some of the freshest fish in town in a cheerful, Mediterranean-style restaurant. See Chapter 16.

✔ **The Wild Geese (Limerick):** Dishes at this candlelit restaurant, all made with local ingredients, are daring, modern, and absolutely delicious, such as the onion-and-Parmesan tartlet studded with raisins. In addition, service is some of the most gracious and attentive in Ireland. See Chapter 17.

✔ **Nimmo's Wine Bar (Galway):** The inventive dishes here make use of herbs and spices from all over the world to complement the flavors of the fresh main ingredients. The restaurant overlooks the River Corrib and has a cozy, eclectically decorated interior with a nautical bent. See Chapter 18.

✔ **Brown's Bar and Brasserie (Derry):** How does honey-glazed lamb with mint jus and a tomato, mint, and mozzarella tart sound? This sleek, modern restaurant has a menu full of dishes like these — imaginative creations that take advantage of local ingredients. See Chapter 21.

✔ **Cayenne (Antrim):** There's a reason that all those decked-out folks are crowded into the entranceway of this restaurant: The fusion cuisine here is daring and luscious, featuring bold dishes such as an appetizer of cinnamon quail with carrot, honey, and ginger salad. See Chapter 22.

✔ **Zen (Antrim):** Though I've tried to rein myself in, you'll probably notice my passion for sushi as you read this guide. Boy, was I happy to find this excellent restaurant, where delicious Japanese dishes (sushi and others) are served in ultra-dramatic surroundings. See Chapter 22.

# The Best Castles

You can step back in time and unleash your inner lord or lady at any of the following castles.

✔ **Cahir Castle (Tipperary):** This 13th- to 15th-century defensive castle, the setting for the movie *Excalibur,* is one of the best-preserved medieval castles in Ireland. See Chapter 14.

✔ **Kilkenny Castle (Kilkenny):** A storybook-castle exterior, a beautiful interior boasting 1830s furnishings, and expansive grounds are the charms of this medieval castle. See Chapter 14.

✔ **Blarney Castle (and Stone) (Cork):** Does this place really need an introduction? You can explore the impressive grounds and well-preserved ruins of this 15th-century castle. And, of course, you can kiss the famed hunk of rock. See Chapter 15.

✔ **King John's Castle (Limerick):** One of the finest examples of a fortified Norman structure in Ireland, King John's Castle boasts weapons of defense in the courtyard and a fully restored interior that's open to the public. See Chapter 17.

✔ **Bunratty Castle and Folk Park (Clare):** Built in 1425, and featuring an interior that's furnished as it was in the 15th century, Bunratty Castle is one of Ireland's most popular attractions. For the full castle experience, book a seat at one of the medieval banquets held here. See Chapter 17.

## Travel: A study in serendipity

This is probably the most difficult chapter to write, because some of my Ireland "bests" are one-of-a-kind moments, which lack admission fees and open hours — a late-night Irish music session, a great conversation with a Dublin taxi driver, the sun breaking out of the clouds to illuminate a faraway hill. You will have these "bests" too, experiences unique to your trip. Dog-ear this book, mark off everything you want to experience, and make reservations for the best restaurants, but don't forget to be open to those serendipitous experiences that make travel so magical.

✔ **Dunguaire Castle (Galway):** Each floor of 16th-century Dunguaire Castle is furnished to reflect a different era in its history. The view of Connemara and Galway Bay from the top of the battlements is incredible. The castle hosts excellent medieval-style banquets. See Chapter 18.

✔ **Dunluce Castle (Antrim):** Perched over the crashing waves of the ocean, the stone ruins of 17th-century Dunluce Castle are some of the most picturesque in Ireland. Window openings and doors frame the sea and sky, and you can still see the remains of the giant stone fireplaces. See Chapter 22.

## *The Best Ruins and Archeological Sites*

History buffs will have a field day at any of the following attractions:

✔ **Newgrange (Meath):** Check out the stones carved with geometric designs before entering the passageway of this 5,000-year-old burial chamber. See Chapter 12.

✔ **Glendalough (Wicklow):** A monastic community founded in the sixth century, Glendalough functioned as a community of learning for almost 900 years. As you gaze at the remains of a cathedral, graveyard, and remarkably well-preserved round tower, you can almost hear the passionate exchange of ideas. See Chapter 13.

✔ **Jerpoint Abbey (Kilkenny):** One of the best-preserved monastic ruins in the country, this 15th-century Cistercian Abbey is home to Celtic crosses and stone carvings of knights and dragons. See Chapter 14.

✔ **Rock of Cashel (Tipperary):** Once the province of the high kings of Munster, many of the ruins on this limestone outcropping are tied to St. Patrick, who is said to have explained the Holy Trinity to pagans on this site. See Chapter 14.

✔ **Lough Gur (Limerick):** Evidence shows that this Stone Age settlement was occupied from neolithic times to medieval times. You can explore diverse ruins here: burial mounds, a wedge tomb, and the impressive 4,000-year-old Great Stone Circle. See Chapter 17.

✔ **Dún Aengus (Galway):** Set on a sheer cliff overlooking the Atlantic Ocean, this giant, well-preserved prehistoric stone fort stretches over 4.4 hectares (11 acres). See Chapter 18.

✔ **Carrowmore Megalithic Cemetery (Sligo):** More than 60 megalithic passage tombs have been discovered at this site, and many have been excavated, including one that dates back 7,400 years, making it older than Newgrange. See Chapter 19.

## The Best Scenic Drives

Ireland's landscape is so stunning that almost every drive is a scenic drive. Here's a list of my favorite excursions:

✔ **Cooley Peninsula Drive:** This drive, along the rough Irish Sea and pretty Carlingford Lough, travels past *dolmen* (neolithic tombs), forests, mountains, rivers, and quaint fishing villages. See Chapter 12.

✔ **South East Coastal Drive:** Fishing villages, seaside towns, and coastal vistas are the highlights of this drive. See Chapter 14.

✔ **The Vee:** This drive provides panoramas of lush mountains and the farmland laid out like a quilt below. See Chapter 14.

✔ **The Coastal Drive from Skibbereen to Mizen Head:** Cliffs and seascapes are the stars of this drive, which ends at wild-and-wooly Mizen Head, where the Atlantic waves crash on Ireland's most southwestern point. See Chapter 15.

✔ **The Ring of Kerry:** Give yourself at least a whole day for this winding drive, because you'll be pulling over every other minute to take pictures. The ever-changing seascapes and mountain views are very photogenic, as are the charming villages along the way. I recommend getting off the Ring drive at some point to explore the beautiful mountains in the interior. See Chapter 16.

✔ **Slea Head tour on the Dingle Peninsula:** This round-trip circuit will make your jaw drop. Highlights include the towering cliffs of Slea Head, incredible views of the Atlantic Ocean and the nearby Blasket islands, and rolling farmland. See Chapter 16.

✔ **Galway Bay Coast and Connemara Drive:** The drive west from Galway tracing the Galway Bay Coast is spectacular, featuring amazing views of the Aran Islands and passing through some adorable seaside towns. Join up with N59 in Maam Cross, and head out to the west and then up to Leenane. This part of your journey affords amazing views of the silent bogs, lush woodlands, and glistening lakes of Connemara. See Chapter 18.

✔ **Drive around Lough Gill:** Take along a book of Yeats's poems as you make the drive around this peaceful blue lake. The lake itself and its many islands (including the famed Lake Isle of Innisfree) feature prominently in the poet's works. See Chapter 19.

✔ **The A2 along the Antrim coast:** The A2 winds along the Antrim coast, past cliffs, beautiful seascapes, and small seaside towns. See Chapter 22.

## The Best Golf Courses

Ireland likes to take credit for starting the sport of golf and boasts over 250 courses within its borders (not bad for such a small country). Following are some of the best:

✔ **Portmarnock (Dublin):** A rugged natural course, Portmarnock has been home to a number of championships. See Chapter 11.

✔ **Kildare Country Club (Kildare):** This tough (and expensive) course was designed by Arnold Palmer himself. See Chapter 13.

✔ **Old Head Golf Links (Cork):** This is a challenging course with breathtaking views of the surrounding Atlantic Ocean. See Chapter 15.

✔ **Ballybunion Golf Club (Kerry):** This seaside club features two excellent 18-hole, par-71 courses. See Chapter 16.

✔ **Royal County Down Golf Club (Down):** The two tough courses here are full of sand dunes, but if you get frustrated with how your game is going, you can distract yourself with the surrounding views of the Mourne Mountains. See Chapter 23.

## The Best Natural Wonders

The sites on this list should inspire even the most reluctant outdoorspeople to strap on some sturdy walking shoes and explore:

✔ **The Wicklow Mountains (Wicklow):** If you want green, point yourself towards the lush and rolling Wicklow Mountains. You find leafy woodlands, shimmering lakes, verdant fields, and plenty of walking trails on which to enjoy the surroundings. See Chapter 13.

✔ **The Burren (Clare):** This vast expanse of limestone is a strange and stunning place. Though it looks like a forbidding habitat, the Burren supports a wide variety of flora and fauna. A dazzling rainbow of wildflowers pushes up through the cracks, and the diverse array of plants includes species that are usually seen only in the Arctic or Mediterranean. Twenty-six species of butterfly — plus lizards, badgers, frogs, and birds — call this place home. See Chapter 17.

✔ **The Cliffs of Moher (Clare):** These sheer cliffs rise more than 213m (700 feet) above the crashing Atlantic, providing spectacular views of the Clare coast; the Aran Islands; and, on a clear day, mountains as far away as Kerry and Connemara. See Chapter 17.

✔ **Connemara (Galway):** Still glacial lakes, stands of evergreens, towering mountains, quiet boglands, and granite moorlands compose the hauntingly beautiful area of Connemara, populated by rugged Connemara ponies. See Chapter 18.

✔ **Glenveagh National Park (Donegal):** Lace up your walking shoes to explore this gorgeous national park, offering valleys and glens; pristine lakes; dense woodlands; alpine gardens; and the highest mountain in Donegal, Mount Errigal. See Chapter 20.

✔ **Slieve League (Donegal):** The cliff of Slieve League are the highest in all of Europe, towering over the turbulent Atlantic. You can take in their grandeur from a viewing area or experience it yourself with a walk along the ridge. See Chapter 20.

✔ **The Giant's Causeway (Antrim):** This place practically defines the term *natural wonder.* The landscape is made up of natural six-sided basalt column of varying heights, cascading down into the sea. See Chapter 22.

## The Best Pubs

It's no secret that the Irish have a bit of a reputation for being enthusiastic drinkers. Check out a few of these inviting pubs, and maybe you'll understand why:

✔ **Cobblestone (Dublin):** This is the real deal — a cozy pub filled with locals and boasting traditional Irish music played by excellent musicians. See Chapter 11.

✔ **Jack Meade's (Waterford):** Crackling fires, loud laughter, a warren of small rooms, and terrific pub food conspire to make Jack Meade's a gem in the Waterford countryside. See Chapter 14.

✔ **The Long Valley (Cork):** Belly up to the long bar here to drink pints, munch on giant sandwiches, and shoot the breeze with the friendly regulars. See Chapter 15.

✔ **The Bulman (Cork):** This pub has it all — crackling fires, good company, live traditional Irish music, great seafood dishes, and a view of beautiful Kenmare Bay. See Chapter 15.

✔ **Dick Mack's (Kerry):** One of Ireland's quaintest pubs, Dick Mack's used to double as a cobbler's shop, and one side of the place still holds the leatherworking tools of the trade. The interior hasn't changed in years, which pleases the many locals who frequent this place. See Chapter 16.

✔ **Durty Nelly's (Clare):** This pub has been around since 1620, and not much has changed since. Settle in to enjoy traditional Irish music sessions surrounded by sawdust-strewn floors and lanterns casting a warm glow. See Chapter 17.

✔ **Crane Bar (Galway):** In a city full of excellent traditional Irish music, this is the place to go for the very best. See Chapter 18.

✔ **Hargadon (Sligo):** This is quite an atmospheric bar, with dark wood walls, stone floors, lots of colored glass, and plenty of little snugs (alcoves). Check out the shelves, lined with old goods from the time when the pub also functioned as a grocery store. See Chapter 19.

✔ **Crown Liquor Saloon (Antrim):** This is one of the most beautiful pubs in all of Ireland, outfitted with carved wood, brass fittings, and gas lamps. You'll be drooling into your Guinness. See Chapter 22.

## *The Best Literary Sights*

Bring a journal and some nice pens, because you're sure to be inspired by the sights associated with Yeats, Joyce, and the other literary stars of Ireland.

✔ **James Joyce Centre (Dublin):** Explore exhibits featuring some of Joyce's possessions, the real people who inspired characters in *Ulysses,* and a library of Joyce's works. See Chapter 11.

✔ **Dublin Writers Museum (Dublin):** Biographies, works, personal effects, letters, portraits, and photographs of Ireland's literary luminaries are on display here, along with text about Ireland's literary movements. A terrific audio guide complements the exhibits, relating intriguing facts and presenting snippets of literature and conversations read by actors. See Chapter 11.

✔ **Abbey Theater (Dublin):** Founded by writers and literature-lovers W. B. Yeats and Lady Gregory, the Abbey Theater presents some of the finest in Irish drama. There are frequent productions of the works of Sean O'Casey and John Millington Synge, two pillars of the Irish theater. See Chapter 11.

✔ **Joyce Tower and Museum (Dublin):** This round tower is the setting for the first scene of *Ulysses* and features Joyce's walking stick, cigar case, and some correspondence, among other objects. See Chapter 11.

- **Blasket Centre (Kerry):** The Blasket Islands, located a few miles out from the Dingle Peninsula, were home to a hearty, close-knit community of farmers and fisherfolk until the 1950s. This fascinating heritage center explores all the facets of Blasket Island life, with particular attention paid to the storytelling traditions of the Islanders and the published authors who emerged from this community. See Chapter 16.

- **Angela's Ashes Walking Tour (Limerick):** Fans of Frank McCourt's beautiful and harrowing tale of growing up poor in Limerick City will want to tour the Limerick sites mentioned in the book. See Chapter 17.

- **Coole Park (Galway):** These grounds once belonged to Lady Gregory, a writer and literary patron who co-founded the Abbey Theater. Be sure to check out the Autograph Tree, where you find the carved initials of such famous wits and writers as George Bernard Shaw, Oliver St. John Gogarty, Sean O'Casey, and W. B. Yeats. See Chapter 18.

- **Thoor Ballylee (W. B. Yeats's Summer Home) (Galway):** Yeats's poems "The Winding Stair" and "The Tower" were both inspired by this stone house, which has views of the surrounding fields and forests. The house contains a museum devoted to Yeats's life and work. See Chapter 18.

- **Lough Gill or Lake Isle of Innisfree Cruise (Sligo):** Yeats wrote poems inspired by both of these lakes. You can take in his inspired words, read by an actor, as you cruise either one. See Chapter 19.

- **The Verbal Arts Centre (Derry):** Devoted to the spoken and written word, The Verbal Arts Centre presents readings, classes, and performances. Check out the glass sculpture in the lobby, which contains poems and prose written by some of Ireland's top authors. See Chapter 21.

# Chapter 2

# Digging Deeper into Ireland

· · · · · · · · · · · · · · · · · · · · · · · · · · · · · · · · · · · · ·

## In This Chapter

▶ Taking a short course in Irish history
▶ Discovering the mythology, saints, and literary giants of Ireland
▶ Noting language differences
▶ Eating and drinking your way through Ireland
▶ Getting the lowdown on pubs
▶ Appreciating Irish music
▶ Absorbing books and movies about Ireland

· · · · · · · · · · · · · · · · · · · · · · · · · · · · · · · · · · · · ·

**S**ure, you need reviews of hotels, restaurants, and attractions when you travel. But for a rich experience, you also need to know about the history and culture of your destination. This chapter gives you the lowdown on Irish history, language, food and drink, music, sports, and other facets of Irish culture.

## History 101: The Main Events

Ireland has one of the most intriguing and complex histories of any nation; it stretches back to the prehistoric period and is fraught with invasions, battles, and rebellions.

### Invaders welcome

From the beginning, Ireland put out a doormat welcoming invaders, or so it seems. Ireland was first inhabited by Mesolithic hunters and fishermen who appeared in the country around 7500 B.C., most likely hailing from Scotland. They were followed by a wave of Neolithic farmers, also from Scotland, who arrived around 3500 B.C. Around 450 B.C., or perhaps even earlier, the Celts arrived from Europe, conquering the earlier settlers and spreading the Gaelic culture and language that still thrives today. In the fifth century A.D., Christian missionaries, including St. Patrick, arrived in Ireland from various parts of Europe and converted much of the Irish population to Christianity.

Beginning in the eighth century, Norse Vikings began to raid and plunder Ireland, setting up coastal bases that evolved into the country's first cities: Dublin, Wexford, Waterford, Cork, and Limerick. The Vikings were

# Irish history timeline

✓ 7500 B.C.: First human presence in Ireland.

✓ 3500 B.C.: Neolithic farmers arrive in Ireland.

✓ 450 B.C.: The Celts arrive in Ireland and spread Gaelic culture and language.

✓ A.D. 432: St. Patrick and other Christian missionaries arrive and convert many Irish.

✓ 700s: Norse Vikings plunder Ireland and found coastal cities.

✓ 1014: High Gaelic King Brian Boru drives out the Norse Vikings.

✓ 1169: Anglo-Normans, led by Strongbow, conquer much of Ireland and intermarry with the Celts.

✓ 1541: Henry VIII of England proclaims himself king of Ireland.

✓ 1558–1603: Elizabeth I sends troops to conquer Ireland and sends English to settle on Irish land.

✓ 1601: British troops, under Lord Mountjoy, triumph over a combined Gaelic and Spanish army and introduce English law to much of Ireland.

✓ 1649: Cromwell leads a bloody campaign through Ireland, gaining control over most of the island.

✓ 1690: Catholic King James II is defeated by Protestant King William of Orange at the Battle of the Boyne, ensuring British control over Ireland.

✓ 1700s: British introduce Penal Laws in Ireland, heavily restricting the rights of both Gaelic and Old English Catholics.

✓ 1783: Penal Laws begin to be repealed.

✓ 1796–1798: Irishman Theobald Wolfe Tone leads unsuccessful rebellion against the British with the help of French forces.

✓ 1828: Catholic Emancipation Act is passed, allowing Catholics to sit as members of the British Parliament. Daniel O'Connell sits as part of Parliament, fighting for the rights of Irish Catholics.

✓ 1845–1848: Over two million Irish die or emigrate during the Great Famine. O'Connell dies in 1847.

✓ 1870s–1880s: Parnell makes progress in fighting for home rule (Ireland would have its own parliament but still be part of Britain). Headway is stalled when Parnell is accused of adultery.

✓ 1914: John Redmond, supported by many nationalists, passes a Home Rule bill. Redmond promises that nationalist Ireland will help the British fight in WWI, which some of his previous supporters ardently disagree with.

*(continued)*

*(continued)*

📌 1916: Padraig Pearse and James Connolly lead the Easter Uprising, an armed rebellion proclaiming an independent Irish Republic. British troops conquer the uprising and execute 15 of the movement's leaders.

📌 1918–1919: Political party Sinn Fein wins seats in the British Parliament but declares itself an independent Irish parliament, igniting the War of Independence in 1919.

📌 1921: The Anglo-Irish Treaty puts an end to the war, giving home rule to 26 of Ireland's 32 counties, though they are still part of the British Commonwealth. The remaining eight counties — Northern Ireland — remain under the British government.

📌 1922–1923: Civil war breaks out between those who are willing to accept the treaty as is and those who want complete independence for the 26 counties. The side that wants full independence wins.

📌 1937: The Republic of Ireland adopts its own constitution.

📌 1948: The Republic of Ireland cuts its final ties with Britain.

📌 1969: Violence between Protestants and Catholics begins in Northern Ireland — the start of the Troubles.

📌 1998: Belfast Agreement (Good Friday Agreement) is signed by all parties, a plan for peace in Northern Ireland, involving the creation of a new Northern Irish government.

📌 2000: British rule is restored to Northern Ireland because the IRA (Irish Republican Army) fails to decommission its weapons.

📌 2004: Peace process is stalled, with both sides failing to honor the plans set out in the 1998 Belfast Agreement.

defeated in 1014 by the armies of High King Brian Boru, who was the first leader to preside over all of Ireland. After the Vikings were defeated, Ireland experienced a period of relative peace.

But that peace didn't last long. In 1169, Diarmuid MacMurrough, the dethroned king of Leinster (the southeastern portion of Ireland), called on the Anglo-Normans, under the leadership of Strongbow, to help him recover his kingdom. The Anglo-Normans were Vikings who had settled in Normandy and had control over most of Britain. With their superior military, they had no trouble capturing much of Ireland for themselves.

## Rebels with a cause

In the 14th and 15th centuries, the Celts (also called the Gaels) rose up against both the British and the Anglo-Norman invaders. They succeeded in containing the British in an area around Dublin known as The Pale, but they had no luck in ridding the island of the powerful Norman overlords. In fact, through intermarriage and the adoption of Irish language and culture, the Normans were becoming as Irish as the Irish themselves.

In the 16th century, the British launched a reconquest of Ireland under Henry VIII, who declared himself king of Ireland and forced the Irish chieftains to acknowledge his sovereignty. Though Henry VIII did not introduce British colonists to Ireland, his daughter Mary encouraged colonialism after his death, and her sister, Queen Elizabeth I, sent a steady flow of British settlers into Ireland. Due to Henry VIII's split with the church in Rome, Catholics began to be persecuted in Ireland.

In 1601, Irish Gaelic troops joined with a Spanish army to try to squelch the English army, but the English forces triumphed under Lord Mountjoy, and English law was introduced to much of the island, including Ulster, previously the most Irish Gaelic part of Ireland. Defeated, many of the O'Neills and O'Donnells, the most powerful Irish Gaelic clans in Ulster, left Ireland. The English government pronounced the O'Neill and O'Donnell lands forfeit to the crown and sent Protestant English and Scottish settlers to develop farms and towns in the area. Naturally, the Irish Catholic inhabitants of Ulster strongly resented the imposition of these Protestant settlers, and thousands were massacred when the Catholics rebelled in 1641. The bitterness between the Protestant settlers and the Catholic natives that developed during the 17th century is one of the roots of the modern Troubles in Northern Ireland.

In 1649, the ruthless Puritan English leader Oliver Cromwell arrived in Ireland, with the goal of taking the whole of Ireland under English control. Cromwell's army raged through Ireland, butchering thousands, and by 1652 controlled the country. Cromwell dispossessed every Catholic landowner east of the River Shannon, whether Irish or Old English. Connacht and County Clare, west of the Shannon, were used as a reservation for Catholics who had not fled the country. Though Catholics caught a glimpse of hope when Catholic King James II came to the throne, it was a brief peek that ended as the Glorious Revolution brought Protestant William of Orange to the throne. James struck back in Ireland, launching the unsuccessful siege of Protestant Derry. In what is arguably the most important battle in Irish history, James was defeated by William at the Battle of the Boyne in 1690, giving Protestant England complete control over Ireland.

What followed was almost 100 years of Penal Laws that forbade both Gaelic and Old English Catholics from owning land, practicing law, holding public office, bearing arms, and even practicing Catholicism (though this last tenet was not strictly enforced). These laws were repealed in 1783 as a result of unrest in rural areas of the country, the need for Irish Catholic recruits to fight in the American War of Independence, and the liberal philosophies of the European Enlightenment.

The French Revolution in 1789 threw kindling on the fire of rebellious feelings that were already smoldering among the Catholics, and in 1798, war between Britain and France gave Ireland a window of opportunity for another rebellion. Irishman Wolfe Tone conspired with the French to drive the British out of Ireland, but his rebellion failed, claiming more that 30,000 Irish lives. Captured by British forces, Tone slit his own throat rather than face execution by his enemies.

In 1828, Daniel O'Connell ran for a Member of Parliament position, even though, as a Catholic, he would not be able to sit as part of the Parliament. O'Connell was elected by a landslide, and the British prime minister, striving to avert a civil war in Ireland, passed the Catholic Emancipation Act, allowing Catholics to sit as Members of Parliament. O'Connell spent his time in Parliament fighting for the rights of Catholics, earning him the nickname *The Great Liberator.* O'Connell also strove to dissolve the union between Ireland and Britain. The progress that O'Connell was making was stopped in its tracks when the Great Famine struck in 1845. O'Connell's health failed, and he died in 1847.

The population of Ireland, over 8 million in 1841, depended on the potato as its main diet staple. When a fungus killed off potato crops for five successive years, beginning in 1845, the island was thrown into turmoil. More than one million people died as a result of starvation, and another million left Ireland for the shores of the United States and other countries, beginning a flow of Irish emigration that would keep up until the 1930s. While famine tore through the rest of Ireland, Protestant Ulster began to experience an Industrial Revolution, and Belfast blossomed from a small town into an industrial city. Both Catholics and Protestants joined the working class in Belfast, and riots between the two groups, spurred by their rancorous history, were common.

Exhausted by the famine, Ireland didn't see a new leader until the 1870s and 1880s, when Charles Stewart Parnell showed up on the scene. Parnell, Ireland's representative to the British Parliament, succeeded in uniting different factions of Irish nationalists and began the legislative struggle for home rule (Ireland would have its own parliament while still being part of Britain). Parnell was well on his way to realizing this goal when the news broke in 1890 that he was living with the estranged wife of one of his followers. The Irish Catholic hierarchy turned against him as an adulterer, as did his fellow nationalist Members of Parliament. Parnell never regained his popularity and died in 1891.

# The Irish flag

Ireland's flag — three thick vertical strips of green, white, and orange — first flew publicly over Dublin's General Post Office during the Easter Rising of 1916. The green represents Ireland's Catholics, the orange represents Protestants (symbolic of William of Orange, a 17th-century king of Britain), and the white stands for the hoped-for peace between them.

In the 1900s, nationalists reunited under leader John Redmond, who managed to pass a Home Rule bill in 1914. However, Redmond promised that nationalist Ireland would support the English in World War I. Although some of his followers agreed with this plan, others did not and broke away to create the separatist Irish Volunteers. The Volunteers staged Ireland's most famous rebellion: On Easter Monday in 1916, 1,500 freedom fighters, led by Patrick Pearse and James Connolly, seized Dublin's General Post Office. They hoisted the tricolor flag from the roof of the post office, and Pearse read the Proclamation of the Irish Republic from the front steps. This rebellion led to swift retaliation by the British, who sailed gunboats up the River Liffey and heavily shelled the city. After six days of battle, the rebels were overwhelmed. Connolly, Pearse, and 13 other leaders of the Rising (as the rebellion was called) were taken to Kilmainham Gaol (jail), tried, and shot. The Irish were outraged at the savage executions, especially that of Connolly, who had been so badly injured in the fighting that he couldn't stand and had to be tied to a chair to face the firing squad. The murdered patriots became martyrs in Ireland, and the Irish commitment to fight for freedom was bolstered.

In 1918, the nationalist party of Sinn Fein (pronounced *shin fane*) won the General Election in Ireland. But instead of taking their seats in the British Parliament, they declared an independent Irish parliament. The British were not pleased with this turn of events, and Ireland plummeted into a civil war for independence, led by Michael Collins. A truce was reached in 1921, followed by the Anglo-Irish Treaty, which gave autonomy to 26 of Ireland's 32 counties. The remaining six counties remained part of the United Kingdom (U.K.) and became known as Northern Ireland. Many Irish, eager to finally reach peace, accepted the accord for the Irish Free State, even though it kept Ireland in the British Commonwealth. Others, led by Eamon de Valera, wanted to sever all ties with Britain. Another civil war broke out, claiming Michael Collins as one of many victims, but de Valera's side eventually triumphed, officially cutting all ties with Britain when the Republic of Ireland Act was passed in 1948.

There was a nervous peace in Northern Ireland for the first half of the 20th century. However, in the late 1960s, Catholics in Northern Ireland began to campaign against religious discrimination in jobs, politics, and housing. Civil-rights meetings deteriorated into violence and opened the door to the Irish Republic Army (IRA), a nationalist paramilitary group that organized a number of terror attacks. Violence continued on both sides up until the Belfast Agreement (also known as the Good Friday Agreement) of 1998, when the Irish voted to make a fresh start with a new government in Belfast. Unfortunately, the new government was suspended because paramilitary groups did not agree to disarm (and still have not). As this book goes to press, the peace process is at an impasse. Happily, there has been little violence since 1998. For the most up-to-date news on the political situation in Northern Ireland, visit www.politicsni.com.

# Who's Who in Irish Mythology

Some of the folks I describe in this section lived more verifiably real lives than others, but all have entered the mythology to such an extent that you're almost sure to hear them mentioned at some point in your trip.

- ✔ **Children of Lir:** In this legend, the wicked new wife of King Lir (pronounced *leer*) puts a spell on his children to turn them into swans for 900 years. She later regrets her evil deed but can't reverse the spell, so she gives the birds the gift of song. A beautiful sculpture depicting the Children of Lir is the centerpiece of Dublin's Garden of Remembrance, and today it is illegal to kill a swan in Ireland.

- ✔ **Cuchulainn (pronounced coo-*cul*-in):** The famous Celtic warrior of ancient myth, Cuchulainn can grow to such enormous size and strength that he can kill scores of men with one swing of a sword. Many legendary stories are told of his feats. A statue stands in Dublin's General Post Office depicting Cuchulainn in bloody action.

- ✔ **Queen Medb or Maeve (pronounced mave):** Cuchulainn's enemy, whom legend credits with stealing the prize bull of Ulster and killing Cuchulainn, among other exploits.

- ✔ **Finn MacCool:** An Irish hero immortalized in poems by his son Osian and in many *Fenian ballads,* named after the Fenians (or Fianna), professional fighters whom Finn was said to have led in the third century. Finn and his men defended the country from foreign aggressors and hunted for food; these two activities are the main subjects of the stories about him. He is often portrayed as a giant with supernatural powers and is frequently accompanied by his pet hound, Bran.

- ✔ **Osian (pronounced o-*sheen*):** Finn MacCool's son, a great leader and warrior, as well as a talented poet. The name means "fawn," and legend says that his mother spent part of her life as a deer.

# Who's Who among Irish Saints

Getting your Patricks and your Brigids mixed up? Here's a primer on three of Ireland's most important saints:

- ✔ **St. Brigid:** Known for her compassion and generosity, Brigid is probably the best-known saint in Ireland after Patrick. She founded a convent in Kildare and became an abbess there, holding the same rank as a bishop. Her convent became a monastic city of learning, home to a famous school of metalwork and manuscript illumination. Brigid is renowned for her miracles, especially in the realm of healing. Her feast day is February 1.

✔ **St. Columcille (St. Columba):** This saint's pious nature as a young boy earned him the nickname *Columcille,* which means "dove of the church." Columcille was a busy guy, founding dozens of monasteries, including the monastery in Derry and the monastery on the island of Iona, in Scotland, and converting many of the inhabitants of Northern Scotland to Christianity. A great lover of books and a bard himself, Columcille copied hundreds of manuscripts. His feast day is June 9.

✔ **St. Patrick:** The patron saint of Ireland. Brought to the country as a teenage slave, Patrick later escaped, only to return to Ireland with the goal of converting the Irish to Christianity. Though he was not the first Christian missionary, Patrick was perhaps the most influential. In addition to converting a large percentage of the Irish populace, Patrick succeeded in converting several of the Celtic high kings. His feast day is March 17 (sound familiar?).

## Who's Who in Irish Literature

The Irish are fiercely proud of their rich literary tradition, and many writers have places of honor around the country. You can't go to County Sligo without tripping over sights related to poet W. B. Yeats, and repeated references to the novels of James Joyce fill Dublin. The walls of theaters around Ireland resonate with the words of playwrights O'Casey, Shaw, Synge, Beckett, and other Irish wordsmiths.

Following are some bite-size bios of the literary wonders you're most likely to hear about:

✔ **Brendan Behan (1923–1964):** Behan's youth was full of run-ins with the law, including a stint with the Irish Republican Army in his teens. The playwright, columnist, and novelist is perhaps most famous for *The Borstal Boy,* a novel based on his experiences in jail and reform school; *The Quare Fellow,* a play that draws on his experiences in prison; and *The Hostage,* a play about the events surrounding an IRA member's execution.

✔ **Samuel Beckett (1906–1989):** A playwright and novelist, most of Beckett's work deals with lonely and bewildered people in search of an unknown something. The best-known and most performed of his plays is *Waiting for Godot,* which centers on two men waiting endlessly for the arrival of a mysterious character named Godot.

✔ **James Joyce (1882–1941):** Though he moved to Continental Europe at age 22, Joyce's four major works — *Portrait of the Artist As a Young Man, Dubliners, Finnegan's Wake,* and *Ulysses* — are all set in Dublin. Joyce is known for his experimentation with language, and his books are rich in puns, metaphor, and wordplay.

✔ **Sean O'Casey (1880–1964):** This famous playwright shocked theatergoers with controversial plays based on his early, poverty-stricken days and the fight for Irish home rule. Best known are *Juno and the Paycock,* the story of a poor family during the 1916 Rising, and *The Plough and the Stars,* which deals with different perspectives on the 1916 Rising.

✔ **George Bernard Shaw (1856–1950):** In his works, Socialist Shaw explored moral and social problems with wit and intellect. His most famous plays include *Pygmalion,* the story of plucky Eliza Doolittle; *Major Barbara,* which centers on a Salvation Army major questioning charity and capitalism; and *St. Joan,* about Joan of Arc.

✔ **John Millington Synge (1871–1909):** A noted Abbey Theatre playwright, Synge is best remembered for plays that explore the rural life of western Ireland. *Riders to the Sea* explores life in a fishing community on the Aran Islands, where the threat of drowning looms over all residents; in *Shadow of the Glen,* a man fakes his death in order to find out if his wife is cheating on him; and in *Playboy of the Western World,* a man is celebrated as a hero for killing his father.

✔ **W. B. Yeats (1865–1939):** Poet and playwright Yeats cofounded Dublin's Abbey Theatre. Many of his poems take the landscapes and mythology of Ireland as their themes, while others riff on the struggle for Irish home rule and on love and romance.

## *Word to the Wise: The Local Lingo*

Sure, English is the main language in use in Ireland, but between slang words and the accent, it can sound like a foreign language at times. Read these handy glossaries so that you don't have to have one of those polite but puzzled smiles on your face while talking with locals.

## The Irish language in contemporary Ireland

Irish Gaelic (also called Irish) and English are the official languages of Ireland. Almost the entire population speaks English, and about 95% of the population use English as their primary language. About a million of Ireland's 5 million residents can speak at least a few words of Irish Gaelic (the language is now taught in all public schools), and about 600,000 people use Gaelic as their first language. Gaelic-speaking areas are called *Gaeltacht* (pronounced *gwale*-tokt) and are concentrated in the west of Ireland, though they are found all over the island.

## Getting the lingo

Some of the following terms are slang or just Irish usage, and some are authentic Irish Gaelic:

- **An Lar:** City center (Gaelic)

- **Bonnet:** Car hood

- **Boot:** Car trunk

- **Bord Fáilte (pronounced bord *fal*-cha):** Irish Tourist Board (Gaelic)

- **Cheers:** Thanks

- **Crack, craic (pronounced crak):** Good times, fun (Gaelic)

- **Creche:** Day care

- **Deadly, brilliant:** Great, excellent

- **Fáilte (pronounced *fal*-cha):** Welcome (Gaelic)

- **Fir:** Men (Gaelic, sometimes used on bathroom doors)

- **Footpath:** Sidewalk

- **Garda:** Police officer

- **Grand:** Great (as in "Would you like some more Guinness?" "Thanks, that'd be grand")

- **Hash:** Pound sign (on telephone keypads and the like)

- **Lads:** A group of people, regardless of gender. Often used to address a group, like "y'all" in the American south.

- **Lift:** Elevator

- **Mna (pronounced just like it's spelled: muh-*nah*):** Women (Gaelic, sometimes used on bathroom doors)

- **Off-license:** Liquor store

- **Petrol:** Gasoline

- **Press:** Cabinet

- **Stroke:** Slash (as in "girls/women")

- **Quay (pronounced key):** Waterfront

- **Quid, sterling, or bob:** Pounds, or money

- **Slainte! (pronounced *slon*-cha):** Cheers! (Gaelic)

- **Take-away:** Fast food; to go

- **Till:** Cash register

- **Tins:** Canned goods

- **Windscreen:** Windshield

# Having the craic!

No, silly, that chatty group you met at the pub aren't a bunch of drug pushers. The Gaelic word "craic" (pronounced *crak*) means a great time, and is most often used to describe that alchemy of convivial friends, laughter, good music, flowing conversation, and great drinks that you'll find in pubs all over Ireland.

## Avoiding misunderstandings

In Ireland (especially Northern Ireland), holding your pointer and middle fingers up in a *V* with your palm facing inward is the same as raising your middle finger to someone. Careful when ordering two pints!

Curses are used rather liberally in Ireland (makes me homesick for Brooklyn!), and you'll probably encounter people saying "shite" as they drop something or "for feck's sake" (the equivalent of "for God's sake") when their favorite football team misses a goal.

The following words and phrases have definitions that are quite different in Ireland than they are in other parts of the world:

- **Cute hoor (pronounced like *whore*):** Boy, does this one have a different meaning than it does in many other countries. In Ireland, *cute* is often used to mean someone who is sly or devious, and a *cute hoor* is a devious person. The phrase is almost always used to describe a man, rather than a woman, and is often used to describe politicians.

- **Fag:** Cigarette.

- **Fanny:** Female genitalia.

- **Ride:** Sex or an attractive person. So ask for a lift if you're looking for someone to drive you somewhere.

- **Take the piss out of** (as in: "We were just taking the piss out of him"): Messing with you, teasing you. Another phrase for this is "slagging you."

## Translating Irish Gaelic place names

You're passing through a quaint town with an even quainter name. Wonder what it means? Use the following list to mix and match parts of names to get their Irish Gaelic meaning. For example, Tullamore translates into Great Small Hill (tul + mor). Sounds better their way, huh?

- **Ard:** Height, hill
- **Aw, ow:** River
- **Bal, bally:** Town

- **Bawn:** White
- **Beg:** Small
- **Carrick, carrig:** Rock
- **Cloch:** Stone
- **Derg:** Red
- **Doo, du:** Black
- **Drom, drum:** Ridge
- **Dun:** Fort
- **Glen, glas:** Valley
- **Innis, ennis, inch:** Island
- **Kil, kill:** Church
- **Knock:** Hill
- **Lis, liss:** Fort
- **Lough:** Lake
- **Mone, mona:** Bog
- **Mor:** Great, large
- **Owen, avon:** River
- **Rinn, reen:** A point
- **Ross:** Peninsula
- **Shan, shane:** Old
- **Tra, traw:** Beach
- **Tul, tulagh:** Small hill

# Taste of Ireland: Irish Cuisine and Dining

If you think of shepherd's pie, Irish stew, and mashed potatoes when you think of Irish cuisine, you're right. But that's only half the story: In the past few decades, Ireland has seen huge changes on the food scene. A stroll down a row of restaurants is like paging through a book about the world's cuisines. Especially in larger towns and cities, you can find everything from Italian restaurants that would make the *Sopranos* proud, to Indian restaurants serving fiery curries, to minimalist temples to sushi.

Along with these ethnic eateries is a bevy of restaurants creating innovative dishes that showcase the best of Ireland's sparkling fresh produce and incorporating international influences. Typical dishes? How about fresh Irish salmon served with wasabi-infused mashed potatoes or local free-range beef with a Thai curry sauce?

# Are you getting fresh?

Ireland is full of fresh food. A feast of seafood is pulled from the sea, and fresh lamb and beef come from farm to table with only a few stops in between. The island produces quite a few delicious farmhouse cheeses, and opting for a cheese course after dinner rather than a dessert isn't exactly making a sacrifice. Homemade bread, baked daily, is everywhere, and although considered a humble food, it's one of the country's most delicious (and addictive) offerings. More and more farms are beginning to produce a wide array of fresh vegetables, many organically grown. If you are in Ireland in the summer and see a roadside stand selling Wexford strawberries, hit the brake and buy a few bags of these sweet, juicy rubies.

If you're in the market for traditional Irish dishes, your best bet is a pub, where you find hearty offerings such as Irish stew, thick vegetable soups, and ploughman's lunches (cheese, pickles, and bread). Pub grub hasn't escaped the influences of the last few decades. The dishes are better than ever, many chefs use as much local produce as possible, and international influences are found in many dishes (who knew that chili jam would go so well with Gubbeen, a West Cork cheese?). And you'd better sit down for what I'm going to say next: Many traditional pubs now squeeze salads and other healthy options onto the menu.

If you want something quick and inexpensive, try a pub or head for one of the loads of small cafes and lunch counters that offer soups and sandwiches. Even more plentiful are *chippers* and *take-aways*, fast-food places where you can get, among other things, traditional fish and chips.

 If you have your heart set on eating at a posh restaurant in one of the larger cities during the summer or on a weekend (or on a summer weekend!), make reservations. For the poshest of the posh restaurants, it's a good idea to make reservations no matter what time of year it is.

See Chapter 24 for my top ten traditional Irish meal and beverage suggestions.

## Checking out meal prices

You probably won't have to pay for breakfast, which comes standard with almost every hotel and B&B room and is often quite comprehensive. Lunch typically sets you back around €10 ($12) if you eat in a restaurant or as little as €5 ($5.75) if you have fast food or carry-out, like the ubiquitous fish and chips.

Dinner is more expensive, with entrees ranging from €11 ($13) to €14 ($16) on the low end to €18 ($21) and way up on the high end. After you factor in wine and service, the tab can get rather high. See the introduction for the price scale used in this book.

Many restaurants offer early-bird (usually about 5:30 p.m. to about 7:30 p.m.) fixed-price multi-course dinners that are terrific bargains, and several top-of-the-line restaurants offer great fixed-price lunch deals as well. In both cases, the dishes are often the same as those you'll see for much higher prices on the a la carte dinner menu. I include other dining-related money-saving tips in Chapter 5.

## Minding your manners: Irish meal times and dining customs

The lowdown on Irish dining habits: You may notice that the Irish, like many Europeans, keep the knife in their right hand and lift food on the fork with the left hand. Table settings are the same, except that a large soup spoon often lies across the top of your place setting.

In Ireland, breakfast begins around 7 a.m. and finishes at 10 or 11 a.m. Lunch goes from noon to about 3 p.m., with 1 to 2 p.m. being the busiest time. Dinner is usually served from about 6 to 10 p.m., sometimes going until 11 p.m. on weekends.

Your server won't bring the check until you ask for it.

For information on tipping, see Chapter 5.

## Deciphering the menu

Here are a few foreign food terms you may run up against:

- ✔ **Aubergines:** Eggplants.
- ✔ **Barn brack:** A cake-like bread.
- ✔ **Boxty:** Potato pancakes filled with meats and vegetables.
- ✔ **Chipper:** Fast-food fish-and-chips shop.
- ✔ **Chips:** French fries.
- ✔ **Coriander:** Cilantro.
- ✔ **Courgette:** Zucchini.
- ✔ **Crisps:** Potato chips.
- ✔ **Dublin coddle:** A thick stew made with sausages, bacon, onions, and potatoes.
- ✔ **Mange tout:** Snap peas.
- ✔ **Mash:** Mashed potatoes.
- ✔ **Minerals:** Soft drinks.
- ✔ **Ploughman's lunch:** A lunch of cheese, bread, and pickles.
- ✔ **Prawns:** Shrimp.

- **Rasher:** Bacon. If you want American-style bacon, ask for streaky bacon.

- **Rocket:** Arugula (a gourmet salad green).

- **Salad:** Aside from its universal meaning, salad also indicates a garnish of lettuce and tomato on a sandwich.

- **Sambo:** Slang for sandwich.

- **Shepherd's pie:** Ground beef and vegetables topped with mashed potatoes.

- **Sultanas:** Similar to raisins.

- **Take-away:** Carry-out or take-out food.

# Living the Pub Life

Visiting Ireland without stepping foot into a pub would be like going to Egypt and missing the pyramids. Pubs serve as the beating heart of communities around Ireland, offering witty conversation; laughter; fabulous music (often traditional Irish); great pub food; and, of course, drinks. If you want to find out who's dating who, you go to the pub. If you're upset and need a shoulder to cry on, drag yourself to the pub. If you are keen to discuss current politics, existential philosophy, or anything in between, get thee to a pub. And if you want groceries? Well, in the past (and still today in some tiny towns), many pubs had two or even three extra functions on top of providing liquor: serving as grocery stores, post offices, blacksmith shops, undertakers, and so on.

Pubs originated centuries ago, when groups of friends would gather in someone's living room or kitchen to chat and perhaps play some music and drink some home-brewed liquor. Word of the friendliest places spread, attracting more and more people, and the houses gradually became known as *public houses,* shortened to *pubs.*

There is as wide a variety of pubs as there are folks who drink in them: music pubs; literary pubs (both those that appear in literature and those that writers frequented and still frequent); sports pubs; actors' pubs; even political pubs, where revolutionaries met in secret to plan uprisings. Pub designs also run the gamut. Most familiar are those shiny Victorian dark-wood pubs that show up in cities around the world. But there are also pubs that look like someone's well-loved living room, with tattered, mismatched furniture and dusty books — and, on the other end of the spectrum, modern, streamlined pubs that look an awful lot like clubs.

In many pubs, you may notice small partitioned areas called *snugs.* These small compartments are great places for quiet conversation or to get away from the crowd. But that's not what they were for originally. Until the late 1960s, it was impolite for women to drink in public, so they were confined to the snugs. The barman would pass drinks (only half-pint glasses, of course!) through a small opening.

# There are worse things than being locked in a pub

Very occasionally, a publican decides to allow patrons to stay in a pub after closing hours. This is called a *lock-in* because the doors are locked and the curtains pulled (and the lights are sometimes dimmed) so that no one else can come in. Locks-ins are great fun and an excellent way to get to know locals, as the wee hours are filled with lively conversation, laughter, and often rollicking traditional Irish music. One of my best nights (mornings?) in Ireland was spent in pub in a tiny Clare town, learning new Irish tunes from several fantastic musicians until about 5 a.m. Lock-ins are much more common in small towns and rural pubs than in big-city pubs.

## Figuring out pub hours and drink prices

Most pubs open at 10:30 a.m. Monday through Saturday for you go-getters. Pubs usually close about an hour after last call, which is 11:30 p.m. Monday through Wednesday, 12:30 a.m. Thursday through Saturday, and 11:00 p.m. Sunday. Clubs and late bars can get special licenses to stay open as late as 3 a.m.

Wondering what a night in a pub will run you? Ballpark figures are about €2.50 ($2.90) for a pint in a small town to as much as €3.50 ($4) in the city. The price for a glass of liquor (called a *short*) ranges from €2.75 ($3.15) on the low end to €3.70 ($4.25) for the more expensive areas. Nondrinkers may be shocked to discover that a small bottle of soda costs nearly the same as a pint of Guinness.

## Paying attention to pub etiquette

If you're drinking with a group, think rounds. Everyone (including guests) takes turns buying drinks for the group.

The larger size glass is called a *pint,* and the smaller one (which measures a half-pint) is called a *glass.* If you're ordering hard cider, you may be asked if you want a glass of ice with it. Contrary to what I first thought, this is not a joke and actually makes the drink even more refreshing.

Bartenders do not expect a tip unless they have provided table service. Instead, it is customary to buy the bartender a drink every once in a while.

The Irish version of "cheers" is *slainte!* — pronounced *slon*-cha and meaning "health."

If you're hanging out in a traditional music session, and someone asks you to perform, they usually really mean it. If you're up for it, recite a poem or sing a song — doesn't matter if it's not Irish.

Finally, if you order a mixed drink (a vodka tonic, for instance), don't be surprised if the barkeep hands you a glass with ice and liquor and a bottle of tonic.

## Savoring the black stuff: Guinness

The pints of Guinness in Ireland taste nothing like Guinness elsewhere. Call it the home-court advantage, or credit the fact that the stuff is as fresh as all get-out in Ireland, but it's a fact that the Guinness you drink in Ireland is a high cut above the Guinness anywhere else.

When Arthur Guinness took over a small brewery in Dublin, he had fantastic foresight. He may not have known then that his brew would account for one of every two pints sold in Ireland or would be sold in more than 150 countries, but he definitely was going for longevity — in 1759, he signed a 9,000-year lease on the brewery's site!

I want to clear up a few misconceptions about Guinness. One misconception is that it has a huge number of calories. Actually, a pint of Guinness has about as many calories as a pint of orange juice — around 260. Another misconception is that Guinness is a particularly heavy drink, an idea that probably comes from the look of it. Really, Guinness is very easy to drink and refreshing — don't let the thick head scare you.

 Finally, five words to live by: A good pint takes time. Barkeeps draw the pint about three-quarters and let it sit for about two minutes. Then, by pushing the tap forward so the stout comes out even more slowly than the first draw, they fill the glass the rest of the way (some fill the glass in a three-step process). This slowness isn't cruel taunting; it's how a real pint is pulled and is how you get the best creamy, white head on top. Even when you finally get the pint in your hands, don't drink just yet. Wait until it has settled completely and has turned a deep ruby, almost black. A good test is to take a coin and tap it against the glass, working upward. When the coin makes a heavy thud throughout the glass, rather than a tinny tap, your brew is ready. You can also tell a good pint of Guinness by the circle of foam that it leaves on the inside of the glass with each sip.

# Guinness versus Murphy's

Wondering what the difference is between Guinness and Murphy's Stout? Well, employees at St. James's Gate, where Guinness is brewed, have an idea. According to rumor, a drawing inside the brewery shows a donkey drinking from a trough labeled "Guinness." Behind the donkey is another trough, into which the animal is urinating. This trough, of course, is labeled "Murphy's." I assume Murphy's has its own ideas about its rival.

## Sampling other Irish brews

As hard is it may be to believe, Guinness doesn't have a complete monopoly on Irish beer. Some of the other popular brews are Harp, a light lager that's good for people who aren't into dark beers; Caffrey's, an ale that settles like a stout; Smithwick's, a dark ale; Kilkenny, a red ale with a sweet malty taste and a creamy head like Guinness; Murphy's Amber, a light ale; Murphy's Stout, which is a bit sweeter than Guinness; and Bulmers Cider, a sweet, entirely too drinkable hard cider.

## Sipping some Irish whiskey

Monks did a lot for Ireland. They painstakingly crafted the Book of Kells. They protected Irish antiquities in their round towers during invasions. But ask your average man on an Irish street, and he may say that the best thing monks did for Ireland was invent whiskey.

You read that right — monks invented whiskey. In about the sixth century, missionary monks brought the secret of distillation home from the Middle East, forever changing the face of Ireland. Irish whiskey is known all over the world for its smoothness and quality, and it has brought Ireland huge revenues over the centuries. The original Gaelic term for whiskey, *uisce beatha* (pronounced *ish-ka ba-*ha) means "water of life." Even today, every European country that distills a native spirit refers to theirs as the water of life: *eau de vie* in France, *akvavit* in Scandinavia, *Lebenswasser* in Germany, *agua de la vida* in Spain, and *aqua della vita* in Italy.

Whiskey became more than just a home brew in 1608, when the world's first distillery license was given to Old Bushmills Distillery. Next came John Jameson & Son in 1780 and John Powers & Son in 1791. These licenses blew open the whiskey export trade in Ireland, and the world's love affair with Irish whiskey began. By the end of the 19th century, more than 400 brands were available in America alone.

The money stopped rolling in when Prohibition was introduced in the United States in 1919. Bootleggers began distributing lousy liquor under the respected name of Irish whiskey, destroying its reputation. Meanwhile, Ireland and England were engaged in an economic war and stopped buying each other's products completely. With Irish whiskey out of the picture, Scotch jumped in to fill the void. Only recently has Irish whiskey become internationally popular again.

Irish whiskey has a distinctive smoothness, which results from triple-distillation (American whisky is distilled only once and Scotch, twice).

If you're interested in the distillation of Irish whiskey, three historic and popular distilleries are open for tours: **The Old Bushmills Distillery,** County Antrim (☎ **028-207-31521**); **The Old Jameson Distillery,** Dublin (☎ **01-807-2355**), and **The Old Midleton Distillery,** Cork (☎ **021-461-3594**).

### Comparing Scotch and whiskey

Irish whiskey and Scotch whisky have always been in healthy competition, but it was the Irish who taught the Scottish how to make the spirit. Distillation of Scotch began around the 13th century, making Irish whiskey nearly twice as old. (Note that Scotch whisky is spelled without the letter *e*.)

### Sampling poteen

You may have heard of a potent potable called poteen and wondered just what it is. Well, *poteen* (or potcheen or poitín) is unlawfully distilled clear whiskey, banned since 1661. Basically, it's the Irish equivalent of moonshine, originally made from potatoes. Recently, some companies have started to produce a legal poteen (which still contains a huge amount of alcohol), so you may see it around Ireland.

## Appreciating Irish Music

This should say something about the importance of music in Ireland: It's the only nation in the world with a musical instrument as a national symbol. The Tara Harp appears on all official documents of the Irish government. You can see the oldest harp in Ireland on display in the Old Library of Trinity College in Dublin (see Chapter 11).

Traditional Irish music (often called *trad*) has been around for centuries and is an integral part of Irish culture, woven into the daily lives of many Irish people. In fact, you'd be hard-pressed to find an Irish person who doesn't know at least a few tunes or songs. Irish traditional music is a living tradition, and new tunes and songs are constantly incorporated into the repertoire, from a snappy new fiddle tune called "Millennium Eve" to a song about the war in Iraq. Trad has been enjoying a huge surge in international popularity since the late 1960s and the 1970s, when traditional groups such as the Clancy Brothers, the Dubliners, and the Wolfe Tones began to tour. The music has become hotter and hotter, with international superstars like Solas, Altan, and the Corrs playing to sold-out audiences all over the world.

## Turlough O'Carolan

Turlough O'Carolan (sometimes called "Carolan") is a famous harper and composer. After smallpox blinded him in his teens, he learned to play the harp and for the rest of his years traveled throughout Ireland as an itinerant musician and bard, composing tunes for patrons across Ireland. He wrote more than 200 compositions that are still played today, more than 300 years later.

The best place to hear Irish music is in a pub. Offerings range from scheduled ballad singers to pick-up traditional instrumental *sessions*, open to anyone who shows up. Ballad singers sing a range of Irish songs, accompanying themselves on guitar, from upbeat tunes about a night of boisterous drinking to slow songs about the death of a Irish freedom fighter. Instrumental session can range from small, planned, miked sessions to giant acoustic sessions open to anyone who wants to play. In instrumental sessions, you often find tin whistles (also called *penny whistles* — thin, recorder-type instruments), wooden Irish flutes, fiddles (the same as violins; just played differently), bodhráns (handheld goatskin drums; pronounced *bow-*rons), mandolins, uilleann pipes (the Irish version of bagpipes; pronounced *ill-*un), concertinas (small accordion-type instruments), and accordions. Other instruments that show up include bones (animal bones used for rhythmic accompaniment), guitars, harmonicas, bouzuki, and harps.

If you have been turned on to Irish traditional music and want to find sessions near your home, check out the geographic search feature on www.thesession.org.

# Background Check: Recommended Books and Movies

Ireland has produced a wealth of wonderful literary figures and has its share of great filmmakers. The books and movies in the following sections should enhance your appreciation and understanding of the island. Also see "Who's Who in Irish Literature," earlier in this chapter.

## Fiction

For a look at Dublin in the beginning of the 20th century, written with an incredible command of language, wrap your mind around the novels of James Joyce, including *A Portrait of the Artist As a Young Man, Finnegan's Wake,* and *Ulysses,* and Joyce's short story collection, *Dubliners.*

Roddy Doyle offers a funny and sometimes poignant look at contemporary Ireland in his novels, which include *Paddy Clarke Ha Ha Ha; A Star Called Henry;* and the trilogy *The Commitments* (the basis of the movie), *The Snapper,* and *The Van.*

Other novels to check out include:

- *Juno and Juliet,* by Julian Gough, is a beautifully written contemporary novel about a pair of twins away for college in Galway.
- *Finbar's Hotel,* edited by Dermot Bolger, is composed of seven intertwining short stories by seven well-known Irish novelists.
- Niall Williams' *Four Letters of Love* is a mystical, poetic, romantic novel set in Galway.

---

# Starting your Irish music collection

The following six CDs are a great beginning — or addition — to your musical library:

- ✔ **Eileen Ivers: Wild Blue (1995):** Fiddler Ivers is an innovator, incorporating influences from rock to jazz to classical to blues to Eastern European into her interpretations of classic and modern Irish tunes.

- ✔ **From the Beginning: The Chieftains 1 to 4 (1999):** Like the Bothy Band, The Chieftains are responsible for popularizing traditional Irish music. The musicians are top-notch, playing a gorgeous collection of tunes on these four compilation CDs.

- ✔ **Live in Seattle: Martin Hayes & Dennis Cahill (1999):** Fiddler Martin Hayes and guitar player Dennis Cahill are an unbelievable pair. Hayes is a virtuoso known for his breathtaking improvisations and ornaments on traditional tunes, and Cahill provides the perfect back-up.

- ✔ **Music at Matt Molloy's (1992):** This CD is as close as you can get to an Irish music session in your living room without inviting a bunch of musicians over. Crack open a can of Guinness and listen to the wild reels, jigs, and songs, all recorded live in Matt Molloy's Pub in Westport, County Mayo.

- ✔ **Solas (1996):** This CD features some of the most beautiful and spirited playing of Irish supergroup Solas. Singer Karan Casey's voice is as clear and pure as spring water, giving life to the English and Gaelic songs that pop up between the instrumental tunes.

- ✔ **The Best of the Bothy Band (1988):** One of the first traditional Irish bands with mass appeal, the Bothy Band was composed of superb musicians playing with a fiery style.

---

## Autobiography

If you haven't read it yet, pick up *Angela's Ashes,* Frank McCourt's wrenching novel about growing up in poverty in Limerick.

Written by former IRA member Ernie O'Malley, *On Another Man's Wound: A Personal History of Ireland's War of Independence* is a fascinating collection of memoirs about Ireland's fight for independence between 1916 and 1921.

Great Blasket Island, off the coast of the Dingle Peninsula, was home to a small and very traditional Irish community up until the 1950s. An island of storytellers, Great Blasket produced several excellent writers. In *Peig: The Autobiography of Peig Sayers of the Great Blasket Island,* the eponymous author relates the hardships and joys of life on the island. *Twenty Years A-Growing,* by Maurice O'Sullivan, is a beautifully written, innocent book about growing up on Great Blasket.

*McCarthy's Bar: A Journey of Discovery in the West of Ireland,* by Pete McCarthy, is a hilarious travelogue about journalist Pete McCarthy's ramblings around Ireland.

## Poetry

Poetry is where you hit the jackpot in Ireland. The gorgeous, mystical poems of W. B. Yeats are a wonderful introduction to the mythology, history, and landscapes of Ireland. *Collected Poems: 1909-1962* is the best anthology.

For beautifully spun poems about farming, rural life, and the Irish landscape, pick up Patrick Kavanagh's *Collected Poems.*

Seamus Heaney's poems about the land are rhythmic and powerful, sounding like music when read aloud. *Opened Ground: Selected Poems 1966-1996* is a great sampler of his poems, and *The Haw Lantern, Death of A Naturalist,* and *The Spirit Level* — all collections — are gems.

## History and politics

*A Short History of Ireland,* by John O'Beirne Ranelagh, gives an overview of Irish history from pre-Christian times to 1998. If you'd like something more comprehensive, pick up the *Oxford History of Ireland* by R. F. Foster. For a look at Irish nationalism, check out *The Green Flag* by Robert Kee.

There are quite a few books out about the political situation in Northern Ireland. Among the best are *We Wrecked The Place,* by Jonathan Stevenson, which features interviews with both Loyalist and Unionist militants, and *The Troubles: Ireland's Ordeal 1966–1996 and the Search for Peace,* by Tim Pat Coogan, a history with a Republican slant.

*How the Irish Saved Civilization,* by Thomas Cahill, is a lively history of how Irish monks and scribes preserved the great written works of the West when the rest of Europe was immersed in the Dark Ages.

## Movies

*The Quiet Man* (1952) is a version of *The Taming of the Shrew* set in a small Irish village. John Wayne plays a boxer returning to the village to woo beautiful Maureen O'Hara.

On the comedy front, *The Commitments* (1990) is the often-humorous story of a motley crew of working-class Dubliners who form a soul band. You'll laugh through *Waking Ned Devine* (1998), which captures a tiny Irish village turned upside down when one of their own wins the lottery and then promptly dies.

A magical film that both kids and adults enjoy, *The Secret of Roan Inish* (1996) centers on a *selkie* — a half-woman–half-seal creature from Celtic mythology — and her impact on an Irish family. In the same magical realism vein, *Into the West* (1992) tells the story of two Irish gypsy boys who travel from the slums of Dublin to the west of Ireland in pursuit of their lost horse.

Quite a few excellent movies have been made about Irish politics. *Michael Collins* (1996) depicts the life of Collins, leader of the Irish Republican Army (IRA), from the Easter Uprising of 1916 to his assassination six years later. *In The Name of the Father* (1993) deals with a man convicted for an IRA bombing that he didn't commit. *The Boxer* (1997) is the story of an ex-IRA man and former boxer building a new life in Belfast.

# Chapter 3

# Deciding When and Where to Go

*W*ould you rather gaze at the rainbows that show up during the spring in Ireland, or enjoy the solitude of the countryside during the winter? Do you want to experience Galway's Arts Festival in July, or Cork City's Jazz Festival in October? Should you base yourself in one place and take day trips, or go the nomadic route? This chapter can help you decide when to take your trip and gives you tips for planning your itinerary.

## Going Everywhere You Want to Be

Should you fly into Shannon or Dublin? Do you want to see the Ring of Kerry or Donegal? Is Northern Ireland worth a visit? The information in this section is a quick primer on the various regions of the island so you can make informed choices about where to spend your precious vacation time. The "Ireland's Regions" map shows the breakdown of the areas I talk about in the following sections.

### Experiencing the vibrant Dublin area

People often fly into Dublin airport and set off for the western part of the country, with its dramatic scenery, before their plane even comes to a complete stop. Unless you know there's an honest-to-goodness pot o' gold waiting for you out west, there's no reason to rush away. **Dublin,** with its big-time hotels, restaurants, shops, clubs, pubs, and museums, is a vibrant city with plenty to hold your attention (Chapter 11 covers this city). South of the city, the counties **Wicklow** and **Kildare** (see Chapter 13) offer green hills, loads of outdoor activities, and some of the

## Ireland's Regions

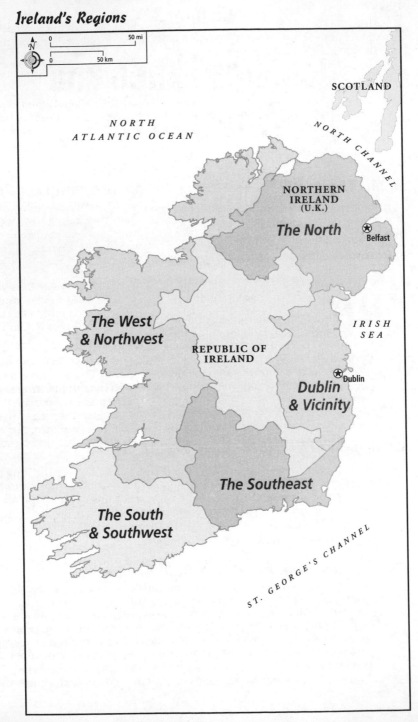

0 50 mi

0 50 km

SCOTLAND

*NORTH ATLANTIC OCEAN*

*NORTH CHANNEL*

NORTHERN IRELAND (U.K.)

**The North**

⍟ Belfast

**The West & Northwest**

*IRISH SEA*

REPUBLIC OF IRELAND

⍟ Dublin

**Dublin & Vicinity**

**The Southeast**

**The South & Southwest**

*ST. GEORGE'S CHANNEL*

most beautiful gardens in Ireland. And just north of Dublin are **Meath** and **Louth counties,** which contain magnificent prehistoric ruins and which I tell you about in Chapter 12.

## Touring the southeastern counties

The southeastern counties of **Wexford, Waterford, Kilkenny,** and **Tipperary** offer the famous Waterford Crystal Factory, the bustling harbor town of Wexford, the medieval streets and storybook castle of Kilkenny Town, verdant farmland, the historic Rock of Cashel, and more. Sound good? It is — read Chapter 14 to find out more.

## Swinging by the southern and southwestern counties

Cork City is a bustling place with terrific restaurants and a healthy arts scene, plus an array of diverse attractions nearby, including a wildlife park and the Blarney Stone. West Cork County offers quaint towns, including **Kinsale,** the gourmet capital of Ireland, plus stunning cliff, beach, and island scenery.

If the southern counties of Ireland were a high school, **County Kerry** would be the prom queen. It's long been Ireland's hottest tourist spot, offering awe-inspiring vistas of the sea, cliffs, and green mountains (most commonly viewed on a drive around the Ring of Kerry), plus a number of lively towns and a rich offering of Gaelic culture.

## Wandering the western counties

The west of Ireland offers the wonderful city of **Galway,** with its great restaurants, excellent pubs (including plenty with traditional Irish music), and hot arts scene. Then there's the incredible scenery of the West, including the beaches and sheer **Cliffs of Moher** in **Clare;** the wild, mountain-filled landscape of **Connemara;** the woods, lakes, and beaches of **Sligo;** and the craggy coastline of **Donegal.**

## Rambling through Northern Ireland

When you cross that invisible border between the Republic and Northern Ireland, the first thing you're likely to notice is that you don't notice anything different. The landscape is as green, and the people are as friendly. Highlights are the rolling **Mourne Mountains,** the spectacular **North Antrim** coast, and the hopping cities of **Belfast** and **Derry.**

# Scheduling Your Time

You can put together your own custom trip in numerous ways, but the two easiest methods for seeing Ireland on your own are the base-camp approach and the nomadic approach. Check out Chapter 4 for some suggested itineraries.

### Settling on the base-camp approach

For this approach, pick two or three cities or towns, and make day-trips out from them. Base yourself in lovely cities like **Cork** or **Kenmare** (to explore the South), **Galway** (for the West), **Dublin** (for Dublin City and the areas south and north), and **Belfast** (for the North). If you have only one week, and you've never been to Ireland before, you may want to plant yourself in Dublin for a couple days and then stay in a large town in the west, such as **Kenmare** or **Killarney,** for a few more nights.

Many top sights are within an easy drive of these base-camp towns. By staying a couple of nights in the same place, you save the time and hassle of switching hotels every day and worrying about check-in and check-out times.

Self-catering accommodations (lodgings with kitchens and laundry facilities) are a cost-efficient option that families and groups choosing the base-camp approach may want to consider. For more information, check out Chapter 8.

### Opting for the nomadic approach

I recommend touring Ireland with a car and moving from place to place over the course of your vacation. I laid out this guidebook to introduce areas in a counterclockwise direction from Dublin City. If you take the nomadic approach, plan your itinerary so that you make some sort of circuit, starting and then finishing in the city where you arrive and depart Ireland.

It's sometimes better to forgo seeing a few places than to try to cram everything in, because Ireland is a country that invites lingering over meals, spending late nights in the pub, and just parking the car and taking an impromptu ramble.

## Revealing the Secrets of the Seasons

For those of you lucky enough to have the luxury of traveling whenever you want to, this section presents the highlights and drawbacks of the four seasons.

### Summer

The most popular and arguably the best time to tour Ireland is the summer.

Summer is great because

- ✔ Ireland is just plain gorgeous during this time of year. Just think of your hotel's high-season rates as a cover charge for the great weather. Temperatures stay comfortably warm and breezy during the day and drop to that perfect light-sweater temperature at night.

Don't hold me to this forecast — you'll still get caught in the rain, but it will be a bearable, if not pleasant and refreshing, experience.

✔ It is the busiest tourist season by far, which can be a good thing. Towns that are lonely during the rest of the year bustle with visitors in summertime.

✔ Summer is when all attractions are open and offer the longest hours; some attractions (mostly in smaller towns) abbreviate their hours or close completely during the off season.

But keep in mind

✔ Every major attraction, hotel, and restaurant is likely to be jampacked. If you'd rather escape crowds, this is not the time to go.

✔ Lodging prices are at their highest during this time.

## Fall

Fall is probably the most underrated time to visit Ireland — days are mild, with not too much rain, and daylight lasts until nearly 9 p.m., which is great for marathon sightseeing.

Fall is great because

✔ In late September or early October, hotel prices start to drop. Even some restaurants offer menus with lower prices.

✔ Plenty of people still travel the country during the fall, so Ireland certainly isn't a desolate place. Plus you're more likely to have the chance to hang out with the Irish folks, because they're back from their summer holidays.

But keep in mind

✔ Honestly, I can't think of any downside to visiting Ireland in the fall.

## Winter

Okay, if I didn't love Ireland so much, I'd probably tell you to hightail it down to the warm and sunny Caribbean for your winter vacation. But I'm such an unabashed Celtophile that although winter is not the ideal time to travel to Ireland, I'm still pointing out the benefits of going in this harsh season.

Winter is great because

✔ Prices are at their lowest all across the country, and you're likely to find the cheapest fares of the year to get to the country.

✔ You're liable to have the run of the country. And the landscape is still beautiful — winter doesn't take as hard a toll on Ireland's plants and trees as it does in many areas of North America.

But keep in mind

- ✔ Ireland is spared snow, for the most part, and the temperature doesn't dip to extreme lows, but the forecast is often cold, rainy, and windy.

- ✔ Lots of places close for the season, including many attractions and some small hotels and B&Bs. If they don't close, attractions often have much shorter hours.

## Spring

Many argue that spring is the perfect time to travel in Ireland.

Spring is great because

- ✔ The warmer temperatures, flower-filled scenery, and longer days combine to make wonderful circumstances for touring the country.

- ✔ The locals are fresh from their own break from tourists and are ready to start playing host.

But keep in mind

- ✔ This is the beginning of the high season, so prices go up starting around March, and plenty of people visit during spring, so you won't exactly have the run of the country (though it's not as crowded as in the summer).

- ✔ The weather's pretty rainy in the spring, but often, the rain showers last only part of the day, opening up the sky to sun and yes, even rainbows.

- ✔ A few attractions are not open yet, and some still have abbreviated hours.

# Walking on Sunshine and Singing in the Rain: Ireland's Climate

Ireland actually has a pretty moderate climate, and it's rare to get a scorching summer day or a bitterly cold winter day. Table 3-1 lists the average temperature of each month.

 The key to dressing for Ireland is layers, because as the Irish like to say, you often end up getting all four seasons in one day.

From the true-stereotypes file: It rains often. No matter what time of the year you go, chances are slim that you'll make it back without having an encounter with a shower, so pack a raincoat or umbrella.

Rain falls heavier and more often during certain times of the year —
winter especially. Also, certain places on the island see more rain than
others. The southwest of the country (Counties Limerick, Clare, and
Kerry) tends to get more rain all year round.

| Table 3-1 | Average Monthly Temperature in Ireland | |
| --- | --- | --- |
| Month | Temp (F) | Temp (C) |
| January | 34–46 | 1–8 |
| February | 35–47 | 2–8 |
| March | 37–51 | 3–10 |
| April | 39–55 | 4–13 |
| May | 43–60 | 6–15 |
| June | 48–65 | 9–18 |
| July | 52–67 | 11–20 |
| August | 51–67 | 11–19 |
| September | 48–63 | 9–17 |
| October | 43–57 | 6–14 |
| November | 39–51 | 4–10 |
| December | 37–47 | 3–8 |

Weather and temperature aren't the only factors involved in deciding
when to go. The amount of daylight varies greatly from season to
season. Ireland is situated at such a high latitude that summer days are
blissfully long (sunset as late as 11:00 p.m.), but winter days are short
(sunset as early as 4:30 p.m.). Remember, the more daylight there is, the
more sights you get to see.

The best site on the Web for Ireland's weather forecasts is www.ireland.
com/weather.

# Perusing a Calendar of Festivals and Events

Just about any time you visit Ireland, some sort of event or festival is
sure to be going on. About a zillion events are held each year, of all
kinds. I've sorted through and picked the highlights. You may notice the

absence of January and February on the list below. These two months are the slowest in Ireland in terms of festivals and events.

Dates often fluctuate from year to year, so I generally list roughly the time of the month when the event occurs, rather than the specific dates. For dates, call the event's number or visit its Web site.

Attention, sports fans: Check out the golf, horse racing, hiking, and fishing sections in Chapter 9 for events of particular interest to you.

## March

The feast day of the patron saint of Ireland is celebrated at the **St. Patrick's Day Dublin Festival** (☎ 01-676-3208; www.stpatricksday. ie), a four-day festival of music, street theater, and fireworks, with a huge parade down O'Connell Street. March 17.

## April

The **Pan-Celtic Festival** (☎ 056-51-500; www.panceltic.com) in Kilkenny celebrates all the Celtic nations and features music, dancing, sports, parades, and more. Early April.

Irish dancers from around the world compete in the **World Irish Dancing Championships** (☎ 01-475-2220). Location varies. Mid-April.

**The Dublin Film Festival** (☎ 01-679-2937) features the best of Irish and world cinema, as well as seminars and lectures on filmmaking. Mid- to late April.

## May

During the **County Wicklow Gardens Festival** (☎ 0404-66-058; www. wicklow.ie/tourism/events), many beautiful private gardens and estates open to visitors on select dates. Throughout May.

**Murphy's Cat Laughs Comedy Festival,** in Kilkenny (☎ 056-63-416; www.thecatlaughs.com) features stand-up comedians from all over the world. Late May.

## June

**Diversions Temple Bar** in Dublin (☎ 01-677-2255; www.temple-bar. ie) is a free outdoor program offering dance, music, film, theater, and visual arts. June to August.

Classical music by internationally renowned musicians is presented in beautiful buildings and mansions during the **Music Festival in Great Irish Houses,** in Dublin, Wicklow, and Kildare (☎ 01-278-1528). Mid-June.

**Bloomsday,** in Dublin, (☎ 01-878-8547; www.jamesjoyce.ie) commemorates Leopold Bloom, the main character in James Joyce's 900-plus page novel *Ulysses,* which takes place in Dublin on June 16, 1904. Restaurants and pubs do everything to look the part, and there are guided walks of Joyce-related sights. June 16.

Overlapping with the famous Bloomsday celebration, the **Dublin Writers Festival** (☎ **01-671-3639;** www.dublinwritersfestival.com) honors writers from all over the world with readings by Irish and visiting writers; a poetry slam; a jazz and poetry night; and events planned specifically for children, including workshops with children's poets and writers. Most of the events are free to the public. Mid-June.

Held in the Curragh, County Kildare, **The Budweiser Irish Derby,** Kildare, (☎ **045-441-205;** www.curragh.ie) is Ireland's version of the Kentucky Derby. Book tickets as far in advance as possible. Last Sunday in June or first Sunday in July.

## *July*

Stand rough side to the world's most famous masters at **The Irish Open** (☎ **01-662-2433**). This golf championship attracts the best of the best, and each year, one of the country's top courses plays host. Because the venue changes from year to year, contact the organizers for more information. First week of July.

**Galway Arts Festival and Races,** Galway City (☎ **091-566-577;** www.galwayartsfestival.ie) is two weeks of terrific music, theater, visual arts, and more. The famous Galway horse races follow the Arts Festival. Second half of July.

The **Lughnasa Fair,** Antrim (☎ **028-4336-6455**) is a medieval fair with crafts, entertainment, and costumes, all set inside and on the grounds of the 12th-century Carrickfergus Castle. Last Saturday of July.

## *August*

The **Kilkenny Arts Festival** (☎ **056-52-175;** www.kilkennyarts.ie) features all sorts of music, films, readings, visual arts, and more. Early to mid- August.

The **Rose of Tralee Festival,** Tralee (☎ **066-712-1322;** www.roseoftralee.ie), consists of five days of concerts, entertainment, horse races, and a beauty pageant to pick the new "Rose of Tralee." Late August.

The **Lisdoonvarna Matchmaking Festival, Lisdoonvarna** (☎ **065-707-4005;** www.matchmakerireland.com) is a huge singles festival, featuring lots of music; dancing; and, of course, matchmaking. Late August to early September.

The **Puck Fair** (www.puckfair.ie) in Killorglin is three days of parades, concerts, street entertainment, and general debauchery in the small town of Killorglin. The festivities center around the crowning of "King Puck" — a local goat. August 10 to 12.

## September

Tickets to the live matches of the **All-Ireland Hurling and Football Finals,** held at Croke Park in Drumcondra, outside Dublin, are virtually impossible to get, but the games are televised, and the excitement shouldn't be missed. Get thee to a pub. Mid-September.

Besides eating, events at the **Galway Oyster Festival** (☎ 091-52-2066; www.galwayoysterfest.com) include dancing, an oyster-shucking competition, a golf tournament, and a yacht race. Late September.

## October

The **Kinsale International Gourmet Festival** (☎ 021-477-4026), held in the foodie town of Kinsale, features special menus at local restaurants, plus visiting star chefs. Mid-October.

A wide array of films are shown all over Cork City during **Murphy's Cork International Film Festival** (☎ 021-427-1711; www.corkfilmfest.org). You can also find numerous film-related events. Mid-October.

The popular **Wexford Opera Festival,** Wexford Town (☎ 053-22-400; www.wexfordopera.com) features performances of 18th- and 19th-century operas, plus classical concerts. Mid- to late October.

The **Guinness Cork Jazz Festival,** in Cork City (☎ 021-427-8979; www.corkjazzfestival.com), has an excellent lineup of top jazz musicians. Late October.

**Halloween (Samhain)** is celebrated with fireworks, bonfires, and the eating of monkey nuts (peanuts in the shell). If you're in the country at the end of October and want to find out where the party's going to be, just look for the field or lot where kids are stacking up wood scraps. October 31.

The **Belfast Festival at Queen's** (☎ 028-9066-7687; www.belfastfestival.com) is an all-out arts festival hosted by Queen's University, featuring ballet, dance, film, opera, jazz, and traditional and classical music. Late October and early November.

## December

On **St. Stephen's Day,** boys all over the country dress up as *Wren boys* (chimney sweeps) and sing carols for charity. December 26.

# Chapter 4

# Following an Itinerary: Four Great Options

*I*reland is a jewel box, filled with vibrant cities, charming towns, and stunning landscapes and seascapes. If you're overwhelmed by the bounty of choices and the different routes around the country, the four itineraries in this chapter may help provide some structure.

These itineraries are intended for travelers with a car, but the first three can easily be followed by bus as long as you keep on top of the schedules.

## Seeing Ireland's Highlights in One Week

This tour guides you to many of the country's highlights while still giving you time to relax and have a pint between attractions.

### Day 1: Dublin

Fly into **Dublin** (most flights arrive in the morning). Get settled in your hotel or B&B and then visit the **Dublin Tourism Centre** if you'd like to scope out some free literature on day trips, tours, and so on. Head over to **Trinity College** to see the **Book of Kells** and explore the campus. If you like, take the **Historical Walking Tour** that leaves from the front gates of Trinity. Grab a quick lunch of fish and chips at **Beshoff** and then catch the **Hop On Hop Off** bus, a bus tour with narration that hits the top sights in Dublin. As the name implies, you can hop off the bus to explore an attraction and then continue your journey on a later bus. Highlights of the bus tour include the **Guinness Brewery**, the **National Museum**, and **St. Stephen's Green**. After your bus tour, have dinner

## Suggested Itineraries

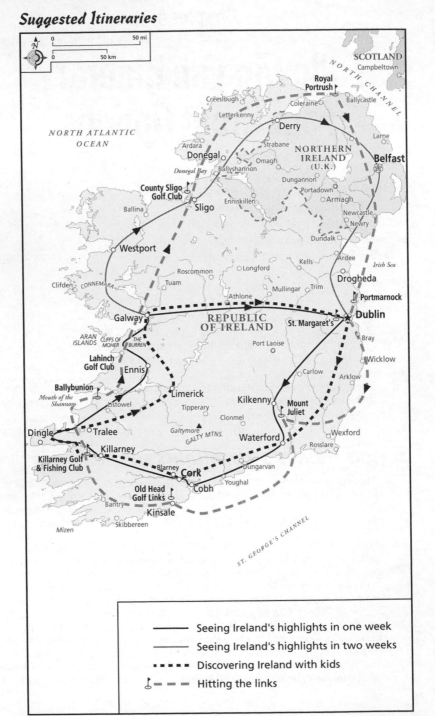

**Legend:**

— Seeing Ireland's highlights in one week

— Seeing Ireland's highlights in two weeks

• • • • Discovering Ireland with kids

⚑ – – – Hitting the links

before heading to Oliver St. John Gogarty's Pub for the **Musical Pub Crawl** or to Duke's Bar to begin the **Literary Pub Crawl**. See Chapter 11 for more information on Dublin.

## Day 2: Dublin to Kilkenny

Walk off your traditional Irish breakfast by visiting some of the Dublin landmarks you missed yesterday, such as **Merrion Square** or the **Grafton Street** area for shopping. Then pick up your rental car and head south through Wicklow, perhaps stopping to take in beautiful **Powerscourt Gardens** and peaceful **Glendalough.** Make your way to the medieval city of **Kilkenny,** check into your hotel (**Butler House** is a great choice), explore the town if it's still early, and treat yourself to a nice dinner after a long drive. See Chapter 13 for more information on Wicklow and Chapter 14 for more on Kilkenny.

## Day 3: Kilkenny to Cork City

If you didn't get to look around much yesterday, spend the first part of the day visiting the highlights of Kilkenny, including **Kilkenny Castle** and the **Design Centre.** Then head south toward Waterford City to take the tour of the **Waterford Crystal Factory.** After that, drive west along the coast towards Cork City, stopping at the quaint harbor town of **Cobh.** Definitely plan to be in **Cork City** by dinner so that you can eat at one of the city's many excellent restaurants; then take in a concert or play at one of the arts venues, or do a pub-crawl around the city. If you want to stay right in the city, **Garnish House** is a great choice. If you're looking for the peace of the country, go for **Ballymakeigh House.** You can read up on Waterford in Chapter 14; I cover Cork in Chapter 15.

## Day 4: Cork City to Killarney

Explore the Cork City area for a few hours in the morning, perhaps buying some car-picnic fixings at the **English Market,** saying hello to the giraffes at **Fota Wildlife Park,** taking in some art at the **Crawford Municipal Gallery,** or puckering up for the Blarney Stone at **Blarney Castle.** Have lunch at one of the restaurants in Ireland's gourmet haven of **Kinsale** before heading to Killarney via the coastal route that takes in the spectacular West Cork coastline. Check into your hotel and then set out to explore gorgeous **Killarney National Park.** Back in the town of Killarney, you may want to finish your day with a visit to **The Laurels,** where you can always hear someone singing an Irish ballad. For more on County Kerry, including Killarney, turn to Chapter 16.

## Day 5: Killarney to Ennis

Get up really early so that you can drive at least part of the **Dingle Peninsula,** County Kerry's lesser-known (and therefore less crowded) driving tour. (Competing with the tour buses driving the popular Ring of Kerry is not for the faint of heart.) Plan on a late lunch in Dingle Town. If you have time, head to **Limerick City** to stretch your legs and visit the

**Hunt Museum** or **King John's Castle,** or take your break from driving in the village of **Adare,** with its thatched-roof cottages. You may want to grab an early dinner in Adare at **The Wild Geese** before heading on to **Ennis** to spend the night. Before flopping into bed, check out the traditional music scene in town; **Cruises** is always a good bet. For information on Ennis and the rest of County Clare, as well as the city and county of Limerick, see Chapter 17.

### Day 6: Ennis to Galway City

Right after breakfast, make your way west, and hold onto your hat (it's really windy!) at the **Cliffs of Moher.** Then drive up through **the Burren** to **Galway City,** stopping perhaps for a walking tour of the Burren and getting some background on the area at **Burren Exposure.** Get into Galway City in time for dinner at one of the city's fabulous restaurants (**Nimmo's** is my favorite) and some excellent traditional Irish music at **The Crane Bar.** Find out more about Galway in Chapter 18.

### Day 7: Galway City to Dublin

Head back to Dublin today. Even though driving through the midlands can be a bit of a yawn, your adventure doesn't have to end. If you still have the stamina, drive north of the city to see the **Newgrange,** a prehistoric burial site, and the **Hill of Tara** before heading back to Dublin (I cover both sights in Chapter 12). When you get there, you may be tempted to get a good night's sleep for your flight the next morning. Nonsense. Treat yourself to dinner at the **Mermaid Café** or **The Tea Room** and then pub-crawl through trendy **Temple Bar.** You can sleep on the plane.

## Touring the Best of Ireland in Two Weeks: A Whirlwind Tour

This tour is for those who want to cram in visits to as many places as possible and don't mind spending significant chunks of time in the car each day.

For the first ten days, follow the itinerary for a week in Ireland, which I lay out in the preceding section, adding a second day to take in more of Dublin's sights and adding two days between Days 5 and 6, one to see the **Ring of Kerry** and one to see the **Dingle Peninsula.** Ignore Day 7, because it outlines the trip back to Dublin from Galway.

### Day 10: Galway City to Connemara

Have a leisurely morning in **Galway City** and then set out to drive around **Connemara,** visiting **Connemara National Park.** Make your way up to the cute and bustling town of **Westport** in County Mayo for the night. Drop in to **Matt Molloy's** for traditional Irish music. Read up on Connemara in Chapter 18 and Westport in Chapter 19.

# Discovering the magic of Ireland off the beaten path

Some of the most magical moments of your trip to Ireland may be those times when you turn down that little road toward a tiny farming village, or when you happen into a roadside pub, where fires are roaring and fiddles are tuning up for an evening of music, or when you spontaneously decide take a stroll down to a glimmering lake for a picnic.

This book can help you discover the highlights of the country, but I can't emphasize enough the wonderful rewards that often result from following your instincts in getting off the well-trodden path.

## Day 11: Connemara to Sligo

Head up toward **Sligo** today, passing through beautiful Yeats country. Take a cruise on Lough Gill or the Lake Isle of Innisfree, and visit the **Sligo County Museum and Library,** the **Niland Gallery,** and **Sligo Abbey.** I cover Sligo in Chapter 19.

## Day 12: Sligo to Derry

Head up through Donegal today, making a circuit around the coast and leaving plenty of time to ramble around **Glenveagh National Park** and to check out the art at **Glebe House.** End your day by crossing the border into Northern Ireland and staying in **Derry** for the night. **The Merchant's House** and **The Saddler's House** are great places to stay, and you can't go wrong with a meal at **Brown's Bar and Brasserie.** See Chapter 20 for more on Donegal and Chapter 21 for information on Derry.

## Day 13: Derry to Belfast

Leave Derry early to head up to Antrim, where stops at **Dunluce Castle, Giant's Causeway,** and the **Carrick-A-Rede Rope Bridge** are musts. Trace the gorgeous coast down to Belfast, where you may want to indulge in a gourmet dinner at **Cayenne** or **Michael Deane,** and then check out the hot club scene. I cover County Antrim, including Belfast, in Chapter 21.

## Day 14: Belfast to Dublin

Head back toward Dublin today, stopping at the prehistoric tomb of **Newgrange** before you hit the city (see Chapter 12). Treat yourself to dinner at the **Mermaid Café** or the **Tea Room** in Dublin and then hit the pubs for your last night in Ireland.

# Discovering Ireland with Kids

Ireland is a family-friendly place, and with a little planning, you can have a terrific time with your children. In this itinerary, I pulled together some of the most kid-friendly sights, hotels, and restaurants.

## Day 1: Dublin

Fly into **Dublin** (most flights arrive in the morning), and head to your hotel or B&B. Your best option for a hotel is **Jury's Christchurch Inn,** which has family-friendly rates and is within walking distance of most sites and restaurants. Kids will love **Dvblinia,** a hands-on museum about Dublin during medieval times. For lunch, head to **Elephant & Castle,** with its great burgers and omelets. In the afternoon, explore **Phoenix Park and Zoo** if it's nice out or hit the **National Museum.** A fun dinner pick is the **Bad Ass Café.** Turn to Chapter 11 for more information on these and other kid-friendly picks in Dublin.

## Day 2: Dublin to Waterford City

Get rid of excess energy before your car trip with a good walk around Dublin, visiting some of the city's landmarks like the **Ha'Penny Bridge** and **St. Stephen's Green.** As you make your way to **Waterford City,** play some good car games, like Count the Sheep!, and stop to stroll around **Powerscourt Gardens.** Get your bearings in Waterford with a short walk before dinner. Kids should enjoy eating on a boat cruising down a river, so check out the **Galley Cruising Restaurant.** You can find more on Waterford in Chapter 14.

## Day 3: Waterford City to Cork City

Take the time to see **Reginald's Tower** before you leave Waterford; it's a fun climb. Then head to the **Waterford Crystal Factory.** Next stop: **Cork City.** You'll have plenty of time to visit **Blarney Castle** on the way, as well as the exotic animals at **Fota Wildlife Park.** In Cork, **Pizza Republic** is a cute spot with a tremendous selection of pizzas. See Chapter 15 for more on Cork.

## Day 4: Cork to Killarney

Head out to **Killarney National Park** for lakes, waterfalls, and plenty of scenery to keep young travelers happy. Be sure to visit the **Muckross Traditional Farm.** Back in town, your little princes or princesses will likely enjoy eating at the **Killarney Manor Banquet.** Read up on Killarney and the rest of County Kerry in Chapter 16.

## Day 5: Killarney to Limerick City

If you get up early enough, you can stick around County Kerry long enough for an excursion to the **Dingle Peninsula.** Kids (and parents) may want to have an extended leg stretch with a walk down **Inch Strand.** Then head to **Limerick City** for a visit to **King John's Castle,** and end your day with dinner at **Nestor's.** See Chapter 17 for more on Limerick.

## Day 6: Limerick City to Galway City

On the way to **Galway City,** drive through the **Burren.** If your kids are old enough, a walk is a great idea. In the Burren, kids should enjoy the **Burren Experience, Poulnabrone Dolmen,** and **Aillwee Cave.** Get into Galway City early enough for dinner at **Couch Potatas,** an all-baked-potato eatery. Your best bet for a hotel is the **Galway Great Southern Hotel,** which has an indoor pool and special kids' rates. I cover Galway in Chapter 18.

## Day 7: Galway City to Dublin

You have to hit the road early to get back to Dublin, but try to take a walk around Galway before you go, and make a fun stop in the nearby resort and amusement park town of **Salthill.** If you still have the stamina after you reach Dublin, drive a little north of the city to see the ancient burial sites of **Newgrange** and the **Hill of Tara** (see Chapter 12 for more information). By the time you get back to Dublin, the whole family will be tuckered out.

# Emerald green on the silver screen

If you're a diehard movie buff, you can plan your itinerary around locations from some of your favorite films. Here are several areas and the movies that were filmed there:

- ✔ **Aran Islands:** *Man of Aran*
- ✔ **Belfast:** *The Boxer*
- ✔ **Cahir, County Tipperary:** *Excalibur* (Cahir Castle)
- ✔ **Cong, County Mayo:** *The Quiet Man*
- ✔ **Cork City:** *Angela's Ashes*
- ✔ **Dingle:** *Far and Away*
- ✔ **Donegal:** *Dancing at Lughnasa*
- ✔ **Dublin:** *Michael Collins, The General, Angela's Ashes, Into the West, In the Name of the Father* (Kilmainham jail), *Educating Rita* (Trinity College), *An Awfully Big Adventure* (Olympia Theatre)
- ✔ **Limerick:** *Angela's Ashes*
- ✔ **County Galway:** *The Lion in Winter*
- ✔ **Counties Kildare and Meath:** *Braveheart*
- ✔ **County Wexford:** *Saving Private Ryan*
- ✔ **County Wicklow:** *Zardoz*

# Hitting the Links: The Nine-Day, All-Golf Ireland Tour

This ultimate tour for golf-lovers lets you play through nine of the country's best courses.

## First hole: St. Margaret's

One of the hosts of the Irish Open, St. Margaret's is a challenging and exciting course of the highest standard, with an infamously difficult finishing hole. Located in Stephubble, St. Margaret's, County Dublin (☎ 01-864-0400; www.stmargaretsgolf.com). Par: 73. Fees: €65 ($75) weekdays, €80 ($92) weekends. Visitors welcome daily.

## Second hole: Portmarnock

This course was the home of the first Irish Open in 1889 and was renovated and reopened in the early 1990s. It's a natural golf course, incorporating the rugged landscape of the region. Located 25 minutes from Dublin's city center, Portmarnock, County Dublin (☎ 01-846-2968; www.portmarnockgolfclub.ie). Par: 72. Fees: €163 ($187) weekdays, €190 ($219) weekends. Visitors welcome every day except Wednesday.

## Third hole: Mount Juliet

This Jack Nicklaus Signature course was host of the Irish Open from 1993 to 1995. The lakes and waterfalls make a picturesque backdrop to this course, called the "Augusta of Europe" and voted the best inland course in Ireland. Located on the N9 Waterford-Dublin Road, Thomastown, County Kilkenny (☎ 056-24-455; www.mountjuliet.com). Par: 72. Fees: €135 ($155) weekdays, €150 ($173) weekends. Visitors welcome daily.

## Fourth hole: Old Head Golf Links

Located on a stunning outcrop of land and surrounded by the Atlantic, the Old Head Links was a cooperative project, built by the top golfers of the country. It can be challenging and is very expensive. Located in Kinsale, County Cork (☎ 021-477-8444; www.oldheadgolflinks.com). Par: 72. Fees: €250 ($288). Visitors welcome daily.

## Fifth hole: Killarney Golf and Fishing Club

Home of the 1991 and 1992 Irish Open Championship, the three courses here are nestled among the beautiful lakes of Killarney and below the majestic MacGillycuddy's Reeks Mountains. Located at Mahony's Point, Killarney, County Kerry (☎ 064-31-034; www.killarney-golf.com). Par: 72. Fees: €75 ($86) on Killeen and Mahony's, and €50 ($58) on Lackbane. Visitors welcome every day except Sunday.

## Sixth hole: Ballybunion

This seaside club has two fine 18-hole courses. The Old Course is the more challenging of the two; the newer Cashen course was fashioned by the legendary Robert Trent Jones. Located on Sandhill Road, Ballybunion, County Kerry (☎ 068-27-611; www.ballybuniongolfclub.ie). Par: 71 and 72. Fees: €75 ($86) Cashen course; €110 ($127) Old course; €135 ($155) for both on the same day. Visitors welcome weekdays.

## Seventh hole: Lahinch Golf Club

High elevations provide amazing views of the sea and valleys below, and local goats are known to cross the fairway. The club has two 18-hole courses; one is a championship course. Located in Lahinch, County Clare (☎ 065-81003; www.lahinchgolf.com). Par: 71 and 70. Fees: €110 ($127) Old Course; €50 ($58) Castle course.

## Eighth hole: County Sligo Golf Club

This difficult course challenges top players, but dabblers have fun playing it too. The course is set between striking Atlantic beaches and the hill of Benbulben. Located in Rosses Point, County Sligo (☎ 071-77-186; www.countysligogolfclub.ie). Par: 71. Fees: April through October €65 ($75) weekdays, €80 ($92) weekends; November through March €50 ($58) weekdays, €65 ($75) weekends. Visitors welcome daily.

## Ninth hole: Royal Portrush

The two excellent 18-hole courses here all offer amazing seaside views of the northern Antrim Coast. Located on Dunluce Road, Portrush, County Antrim (☎ 028-7082-2311; www.royalportrushgolfclub.com). Par: 72 and 70. Fees: Dunluce £85 ($157), Valley £30 ($56) weekdays. Visitors welcome weekdays.

# Part II
# Planning Your Trip to Ireland

The 5th Wave    By Rich Tennant

"This afternoon I want everyone to go on line and find all you can about Native American culture, history of the old west, and discount airfares to Ireland for the two weeks I'll be on vacation."

# In this part . . .

**B**efore you can start planning your trip to Ireland, you'll want to do some legwork. How much will it cost? What are your options for getting there? What about your options for getting around? What kinds of accommodations are available? The chapters in this part give you the answers to all these questions and more.

Of course, there's the bottom line. Chapter 5 features information on currency in Ireland, planning your budget, what things cost, and how to save money.

Chapter 6 gives you the lowdown on how to get to Ireland, and Chapter 7 covers the nitty-gritty of getting around the country.

After you figure out how you're getting to Ireland, turn to Chapter 8 for tips on booking accommodations.

Seniors, students, disabled travelers, families, outdoorsy folks, and other travelers should consult Chapter 9 for tips specific to them, and everyone should have a look at Chapter 10 for information on tying up loose ends before you leave.

# Chapter 5

# Managing Your Money

C an you visit Ireland for $5 a day? Maybe in 1965, but not now. How about $30 a day? Yes, if you don't mind hostel bunk beds and grocery-store dinners. If you want hotels or B&Bs and restaurant meals, you should figure on spending at least $65 to $100 per person per day — not including a rental car and airfare. Ireland has become much more expensive in the past few years. In fact, the price of a restaurant meal is now about 50% more than what you'd pay in the United States. And you should expect to pay top price in Dublin. But fret not, because this guide — and this chapter in particular — give you lots of money-saving tips, and subsequent chapters offer accommodation and dining selections that won't tap your wallet like a keg of Guinness on St. Patrick's Day. Read on for tips on creating a budget and cutting costs.

## Planning Your Budget

Generally speaking, you should factor the following into your budget:

▶ **Airfare:** Airfare to and from Ireland varies depending on where you're flying from, the time of year, and the totally arbitrary whims of the airline gods. On average, airfare from New York to Ireland and back runs about $700. See Chapter 6 for tips on getting the best airfare deals.

▶ **Transportation:** Transportation costs vary depending on whether you're busing or training it or renting a car. Driving — the transportation choice for most tourists — costs around $50 a day, plus an additional $15 in gas. Bus fares can cost anywhere from $1 to $20, depending on your destination. The train is slightly more expensive. See Chapter 7 for more information.

✔ **Lodging:** An average double room runs about $80, rooms on the low end go for about $60, and those on the high end about $130 to $180.

✔ **Meals:** This is one area where it's difficult to save money; even a simple pub lunch can cost about $10. A good per-person allowance for lunch is $12, and for dinner, between $15 and $30. Breakfast is included with most accommodations, so you don't have to figure that into your daily costs.

✔ **Attractions:** A fair amount to budget for sights is $15 per day. Buying a Heritage Card is worth it if you're planning to see a lot of sights (for more information on the Heritage Card, see "Cutting Costs — But Not the Fun," later in this chapter).

✔ **Shopping:** Are you planning to buy clothes, jewelry, Waterford crystal, and antiques or just a few postcards, a snow globe, and some other inexpensive souvenirs? A modest piece of Waterford crystal can set you back $80; a nice Guinness sweatshirt is about $50. Gauge your buying tendencies and factor them in. A perk of buying in Ireland: You can get the value-added tax (VAT) on your purchases refunded (I explain how under "Getting your VAT refund," later in this chapter).

✔ **Nightlife:** Pubs are the most popular place to spend the evening, and they are as free as the air you breathe, except for all those pints of Guinness (about $3.50).

Table 5-1 offers the average costs of some common items.

### Table 5-1     What Things Cost in Ireland

| Item | Cost in U.S. Dollars |
|---|---|
| Pint of Guinness | $3.50 |
| Soda in a restaurant | $2.85 |
| Chocolate bar | 90¢ |
| Double room at an expensive hotel | $220 |
| Double room at a moderate hotel | $150 |
| Double room at a B&B | $75 |
| Lunch for two at most pubs | $20 |
| Dinner for two at an expensive restaurant (with wine) | $95 |
| Walking tour | $8 |

*Note:* Prices for food and accommodations in Dublin will be slightly higher than the prices given here.

# The ins and outs of tipping

Some restaurants include a service charge (tip) of 10% to 15% in their bill, while others leave the tip up to you. The service charge is different from the VAT (13.5% in the Republic of Ireland and 17.5% in Northern Ireland), which is always included. Many restaurants note their service-charge policies on the menu; if you can't figure out whether the service charge has been included, just ask. If no service charge has been added, tip up to 15%. If a service charge has been added, but it is less than 15%, it is customary to leave a tip that rounds the charge up to 15%. Bartenders do not expect a tip for dispensing drinks.

## Cutting Costs — But Not the Fun

Worried you won't be able to afford your trip? Well, you can rent *Far and Away,* read *Angela's Ashes,* listen to a Chieftains CD, and just pretend you're in Ireland, but what fun is that? Instead, make your vacation a bargain by cutting a few corners. I scatter various money-saving tips throughout this book, but I also present a list of 21 general money-savers in one place, organized by category:

✔ **Accommodations:** Cut some corners in the lodging department with these tips:

- **Stay in B&Bs.** I can't emphasize enough how wonderful the bed-and-breakfast experience is. Not only are B&Bs usually a third cheaper than staying in a hotel in the same area, but you also frequently get a friendly insider perspective from the folks running these places.

- **Check out self-catering accommodations.** By renting an apartment or house (called *self-catering accommodations* in this guide) for a week or more, you can save money overall on accommodations (especially if you're traveling with a group) and on food because you can prepare your own meals in the kitchen. (See Chapter 8.)

- **Get out of town.** In many places, hotels just outside the most popular areas can be a great bargain. You may be able to find a great deal just a short cab, bus, or car ride away. And as an extra bonus, hotels that are off the beaten path may even offer free parking. The rooms may not be as fancy, but they're often just as comfortable and a whole lot cheaper.

- **Ask if your kids can stay in your room with you.** Although many accommodations in Ireland charge by the head, some allow kids to stay for free. Even if you have to pay $10 or $15 for a rollaway bed, in the long run you'll save hundreds by not booking two rooms.

- **Share a bathroom.** Rooms without a bathroom are always cheaper. (See Chapter 8 for more tips on saving on accommodations.)

- **Skip the fantabulous views.** Rooms with great views are the most expensive rooms in any hotel, but you probably won't be hanging out in your room all day, so why pay the price?

- **Never make a phone call from a hotel.** The marked-up fees that hotels charge are scandalous. Walk to the nearest coin or card phone for calls in and out of the country.

✔ **Attractions:** Save money as you tour Ireland's sights:

- **Get your hands on a Heritage Card.** A Heritage Card gives you free admission to more than 65 attractions throughout Ireland. You can buy the card at any participating attraction, purchase it over the phone with a Visa or MasterCard (☎ 1-800-600-601 in Ireland [yes, Ireland has 800 numbers] or ☎ 01-647-2461 outside of Ireland), or purchase it on the Internet at www.heritageireland.com.

- **Pick up those free, coupon-packed visitor pamphlets and magazines.** Detailed maps, feature articles, dining and shopping directories, and discount and freebie coupons give these pocket-size giveaways a good wallop. Especially popular and reliable are *Visitor, Discover Ireland, Ireland,* and *Southeast Holiday Guidebook.*

✔ **Food:** Grab your grub for less with these suggestions:

- **Take advantage of free breakfasts.** Most accommodations include a substantial free Irish breakfast, so don't oversleep. If you have a big breakfast and then wait to have a late lunch or early dinner, you'll save the cost of a meal a day. If the breakfast is buffet-style, stash away a piece of fruit for an afternoon snack.

- **Try expensive restaurants at lunch or pre-theater times.** Lunch and pre-theater tabs (often between 5:30 p.m. and 7:30 p.m.) instead of at regular dinner times are usually a fraction of what a meal would cost at a top restaurant during regular dinner hours, and the menu often boasts many of the same specialties.

- **Look before you tip.** Many restaurants in Ireland add a service fee (gratuity) to the bill. Always check, or you may pay a double tip by mistake (see the sidebar "The ins and outs of tipping," earlier in this chapter).

- **Picnic.** A fancy restaurant may have an indoor waterfall, but can that beat dining near a real waterfall on a warm day? Grab some food from a market or grocery store, and set up camp outside.

✔ **Special prices:** Taking advantage of discounts and group rates can cut your costs substantially:

- **Always ask for discount rates.** Membership in AAA, frequent-flier plans, trade unions, AARP, or other groups may qualify you for savings on car rentals, plane tickets, hotel rooms, and even meals. Students, teachers, youths, and seniors are also often entitled to discounts (see Chapter 9). Ask about discounts; you may be pleasantly surprised.

- **Take advantage of group and family prices.** For travel packages and admission to individual attractions, group rates are a fantastic way to save money, and you don't necessarily have to travel with a busload of other people to get them. Sometimes, a group is as few as three people, so always ask. You and the folks behind you might even be able to form a makeshift group to get the discounted price. Most attractions in Ireland offer significantly reduced family rates for parents and up to four kids. Look for family prices on the rate board at attractions, or just ask.

- **Try a package tour.** For many destinations, you can book airfare, hotel, ground transportation, and even some sightseeing just by making one call to a travel agent or packager for a much lower price than if you put the trip together yourself. (See Chapter 6 for more on package tours.)

✔ **Ground transportation:** Getting around Ireland can be cheaper than you think:

- **Book your rental car at weekly rates, when possible.** Doing so often saves you money over daily rates.

- **Don't rent a gas-guzzler.** Renting a smaller car is cheaper, and you save on gas to boot. For more on car rentals, see Chapter 7.

- **Walk.** You can easily explore all the cities in Ireland and Northern Ireland by foot, even Dublin and Belfast. So save the bus and cab fare (or, worse, the rental-car fees) and hoof it to save a few extra pounds or euro. As a bonus, you'll get to know your destination more intimately, because you'll be exploring at a slower pace.

✔ **Travel costs:** Getting to Ireland can eat up a large chunk of change, but planning ahead can ease the financial bite:

- **Go in the off season.** Traveling between November and April saves you a lot on your airfare and the cost of accommodations. Christmas week is the exception — it's when many Irish in other countries come home to visit, and the airlines cash in. (See Chapter 6 for more information on airfares.)

- **Travel midweek.** If you can travel on a Tuesday, Wednesday, or Thursday, you may find cheaper flights to your destination. When you ask about airfares, see if you can get a cheaper rate by flying on a different day.

# Making Sense of the Currency in Ireland

The Republic of Ireland uses the euro currency, which is the currency of many countries across Europe. Euro notes come in denominations of €5, €10, €20, €50, €100, €200, and €500. The euro is divided into 100 cents. The coins come in 1¢, 2¢, 5¢, 10¢, 20¢, 50¢, €1, and €2 pieces. The word *euro* is always used in the singular, so €30 is *30 euro.*

Northern Ireland is part of the United Kingdom, which uses the pound sterling as its currency. Pounds used in Northern Ireland are found in notes of £5, £10, £20, £50, and £100. The pound is divisible by 100 pence (abbreviated as *p*). Coins in circulation are 1p, 2p, 5p, 10p, 20p, 50p, and £1.

The exchange rate fluctuates daily by small amounts, but Tables 5-2 and 5-3 give you an idea of what to expect. For up-to-the-minute currency conversions, visit www.xe.com.

| Table 5-2 | Republic of Ireland Exchange Rates |
|---|---|
| *Home Currency* | *Euro* |
| $1 U.S. | €0.87 (€1 = $1.15 U.S.) |
| $1 Canadian | €0.63 (€1 = $1.60 Canadian) |
| £1 British | €1.51 (€1 = £0.66) |
| $1 Australian | €0.59 (€1 = $1.71 Australian) |
| $1 New Zealand | €0.52 (€1 = $1.91 New Zealand) |

| Table 5-3 | Northern Ireland Exchange Rates |
|---|---|
| *Home Currency* | *British Pound* |
| $1 U.S. | £0.54 (£1 = $1.85 U.S.) |
| $1 Canadian | £0.41 (£1 = $2.42 Canadian) |
| $1 Australian | £0.39 (£1 = $2.59 Australian) |
| $1 New Zealand | £0.35 (£1 = $2.89 New Zealand) |

# Handling Money

Credit cards, bank cards, traveler's checks, and cash are all easy to use in Ireland. The very best way to get cash in Ireland is from ATMs, which are available in all but the tiniest villages. You may want to change $100 or so before departing for Ireland just so you have enough money to tide you over. All the airports have ATMs, though, so you can take out money as soon as you land.

## Using ATMs and carrying cash

The easiest and best way to get cash away from home is from an ATM, called a "cash point" in Ireland. The **Cirrus** (☎ 800-424-7787; www. mastercard.com) and **PLUS** (☎ 800-843-7587; www.visa.com) networks span the globe and are all over Ireland; look at the back of your bank card to see which network you're on and then call or check online for ATM locations at your destination. Be sure you know your personal identification number (PIN) before you leave home; almost all Irish ATMs accept four- to six-digit PINs, but the keys often lack letters, so make sure you know your PIN as a number. In addition, be sure to find out your daily withdrawal limit. Finally, keep in mind that many banks impose a fee every time your card is used at a different bank's ATM, and that fee can be higher for international transactions (up to $5 or more) than for domestic ones (where they're rarely more than $1.50). You can ask your bank for its international withdrawal fees. On top of this, the bank from which you withdraw cash may charge its own fee. The best way to beat the system is to take out a lot of cash at each ATM visit, so that you reduce the number of fees over the course of your vacation.

## Charging ahead with credit cards

Credit cards are a safe way to pay your expenses: They also provide a convenient record of all your expenses, and they generally offer relatively good exchange rates. You can also withdraw cash advances from your credit cards at banks or ATMs, provided you know your PIN. If you've forgotten yours, or didn't even know you had one, call the number on the back of your credit card and ask the bank to send it to you. It usually takes 5 to 7 business days, though some banks will provide the number over the phone if you tell them your mother's maiden name or some other personal, identifying information.

Keep in mind that when you use your credit card abroad, most banks assess a 2% fee above the 1% fee charged by the credit card company for currency conversion on credit charges. But credit cards still may be the smart way to go when you factor in things like exorbitant ATM fees and higher traveler's check exchange rates (and service fees).

Some credit card companies recommend that you notify them of any impending trip abroad so that they don't become suspicious and block your charges when the card is used numerous times in a foreign destination. Even if you don't call your credit card company in advance, you can always call the card's toll-free emergency number if a charge is refused — a good reason to carry the phone number with you. But perhaps the most important lesson here is to carry more than one card with you on your trip; a card may not work for any number of reasons, so having a backup is the smart way to go.

Visa and MasterCard are the most widely accepted credit cards in Ireland, with American Express coming in at second place, and Diner's Club following at a very distant third (you rarely find a B&B that accepts Diner's Club). Discover is accepted very rarely in Ireland.

 Some restaurants and hotels put your credit card transaction through in your home currency. This often results in an unfavorable exchange rate and a higher service charge, so ask establishments to put your charges through in euro in the Republic of Ireland and pounds in Northern Ireland.

## Exchanging money

You get the best exchange rates by using an ATM, though exchanging cash is also easy in Ireland. You can exchange money anywhere you see a Bureau de Change sign, but you get the best rates and the most inexpensive exchange fees at banks. The major banks to look for in Ireland are the **Allied Irish Bank,** the **Bank of Ireland, National Irish Bank,** and **Ulster Bank.**

## Toting traveler's checks

These days, traveler's checks are less necessary because most towns and cities have 24-hour ATMs that allow you to withdraw cash as needed. However, keep in mind that you will likely be charged an ATM withdrawal fee if the bank is not your own, so if you're withdrawing money every day, you may be better off with traveler's checks — provided that you don't mind showing identification every time you want to cash one. You can cash traveler's checks at the Bureau de Change counter in banks all over Ireland. The vast majority of merchants, restaurants, and lodgings **do not** accept traveler's checks as payment.

You can get traveler's checks at almost any bank. **American Express** (Amex) offers denominations of $20, $50, $100, $500, and (for cardholders only) $1,000. You pay a service charge ranging from 1% to 4%. You can also get American Express traveler's checks over the phone by calling ☎ **800-221-7282;** Amex gold and platinum cardholders who use this number are exempt from the 1% fee.

**Visa** offers traveler's checks at Citibank locations nationwide, as well as at several other banks. The service charge ranges between 1.5% and 2%; checks come in denominations of $20, $50, $100, $500, and $1,000. Call ☎ **800-732-1322** for information. AAA members can obtain Visa checks

without a fee at most AAA offices or by calling ☎ **866-339-3378.**
**MasterCard** also offers traveler's checks. Call ☎ **800-223-9920** for a
location near you.

 If you choose to carry traveler's checks, be sure to keep a record of their
serial numbers separate from the checks themselves in the event that
they are stolen or lost. You'll get a refund faster if you know the numbers.

## Taking Taxes into Account

All prices for consumer items in Ireland (except books and children's
clothing) include a *value-added tax* (VAT) of about 17%. Happily, travelers who are not citizens of the EU are entitled to a refund of this tax.

Here's how it works: Many stores have stickers reading "Tax Free for
Tourists," indicating that they are part of the Global Refund network
(www.globalrefund.ie). When you make a purchase in one of these
stores, get a refund check, fill it out, and then hand in your completed
checks at the VAT-refund counter in the airport (in the departure hall in
Dublin and the arrivals hall in Shannon). If you are running late, you can
get the checks stamped by customs officials and then send them in to
Global Refund. If you forget to get your checks stamped while in Ireland,
a notary public or police officer can stamp them for you when you get
home. You can also get the VAT refunded by stores that aren't part of
the Global Refund network; just get a full receipt that shows the shop's
name, the address, and the VAT paid, and get the receipt stamped at the
Customs Office when you are leaving Ireland. You can then mail the
receipts back to the store where you made the purchase, and it will
refund your VAT with a check sent to your home.

## Dealing with a Lost or Stolen Wallet

Be sure to contact all of your credit card companies the minute you discover your wallet is gone and file a report at the nearest police precinct.
Your credit card company or insurer may require a police report number
or record of the loss.

Most credit card companies have an emergency toll-free number to call if
your card is lost or stolen; they may be able to wire you a cash advance
immediately or deliver an emergency credit card in a day or two. Call the
following emergency numbers in Ireland:

- ✔ **American Express:** ☎ 00-1-336-393-1111 (dial collect)

- ✔ **Diner's Club:** ☎ 303-799-1504 (call collect) from the Republic of
  Ireland or ☎ 0-800-46-0800 in Northern Ireland

✔ **MasterCard:** ☎ 1-800-55-7378 in the Republic or ☎ 0800-96-4767 in Northern Ireland

✔ **Visa:** ☎ 1-800-55-8002 in the Republic or 0800-89-1725 in Northern Ireland

If you need emergency cash over the weekend, when all banks and American Express offices are closed, you can have money wired to you via **Western Union** (☎ 800-325-6000; www.westernunion.com).

Identity theft or fraud are potential complications of losing your wallet, especially if you've lost your driver's license along with your cash and credit cards. Notify the major credit-reporting bureaus immediately; placing a fraud alert on your records may protect you against liability for criminal activity. The three major U.S. credit-reporting agencies are **Equifax** (☎ 800-766-0008; www.equifax.com), **Experian** (☎ 888-397-3742; www.experian.com), and **TransUnion** (☎ 800-680-7289; www.transunion.com).

Finally, if you've lost all forms of photo ID, call your airline and explain the situation; it might allow you to board the plane if you have a copy of your passport or birth certificate and a copy of the police report you filed.

# Chapter 6

# Getting to Ireland

• • • • • • • • • • • • • • • • • • • • • • • • • • • • • • • • • • • • • • • • • •

## In This Chapter

▶ Going by air
▶ Ferrying your way to Ireland
▶ Selecting an escorted tour
▶ Picking a package deal

• • • • • • • • • • • • • • • • • • • • • • • • • • • • • • • • • • • • • • • • • •

*B*ecause those jet-packs that we've been promised still haven't mate-
rialized, you need to begin your vacation in Ireland with a flight or
a ferry crossing. This chapter explores the ins and outs of selecting a
flight or a ferry trip. In addition, I cover package and escorted tour
options.

## Flying to Ireland

The sections here offer tips on winging your way over to the Emerald
Isle.

When you book your flight, let the ticket agent know the ages of any children coming along. Some airlines offer child-companion fares and have a
special kids' menu upon request. Flight attendants are usually happy to
warm up baby food and milk if you ask.

### Picking an arrival airport

Your options for major international airports in the Republic of Ireland are
**Dublin Airport** (☎ 01-814-1111; www.dublin-airport.com), located
11km (7 miles) outside Dublin on the East Coast of Ireland (via the N1),
and **Shannon Airport** (☎ 061-71-2000; www.shannonairport.com),
located 24km (15 miles) west of Limerick, on the West Coast (via the N18).

In Northern Ireland, **Belfast International Airport** (☎ 028-9448-4848;
www.belfastairport.com) is located 31km (19 miles) west of the city.

Choose your arrival airport based on fares and on the proximity of the
airport to the starting point of your itinerary.

## *Finding out which airlines fly to Ireland*

In addition to Aer Lingus (which is Irish Gaelic for — guess what? — *airline*), a few U.S. airlines fly to Shannon and Dublin airports. Getting fares from more than one airline to compare prices is a good idea.

Many U.S. airlines fly to England, where you can catch a connecting flight to Ireland (see the list of airlines with flights from Ireland to England later in this section). Many North American travelers take advantage of this option, because a flight to England and a connecting flight to Ireland are often cheaper than a direct flight to Ireland.

The major airlines that fly from the United States and Canada to England are:

- ✓ **Air Canada** (☎ 888-247-2262; www.aircanada.ca)
- ✓ **American Airlines** (☎ 800-443-7300; www.aa.com)
- ✓ **British Airways** (☎ 800-247-9297; www.britishairways.com)
- ✓ **Continental Airlines** (☎ 800-231-0856; www.continental.com)
- ✓ **Delta Airlines** (☎ 800-241-4141; www.delta.com)
- ✓ **Northwest Airlines** (☎ 800-447-4747; www.nwa.com)
- ✓ **United Airlines** (☎ 800-538-2929; www.united.com)
- ✓ **Virgin Atlantic** (☎ 800-862-8621; www.virgin-atlantic.com)

Here's a list of the major airlines that fly direct to Ireland from North America:

- ✓ **Aer Lingus** (☎ 800-474-7424; www.aerlingus.com): Out of Boston to Shannon, Dublin, and Belfast; out of Chicago to Shannon and Dublin; out of New York to Shannon, Dublin, and Belfast; and out of L.A. to Dublin and Shannon.
- ✓ **American Airlines** (☎ 800-433-7300; www.aa.com): Out of New York and Chicago to Dublin and Shannon.
- ✓ **Continental** (☎ 800-231-0856; www.continental.com): Out of Newark, New Jersey, to Shannon and Dublin.
- ✓ **Delta Air Lines** (☎ 800-241-4141; www.delta.com): Out of Atlanta to Shannon and Dublin.

Some major airlines that fly direct to Ireland from England are:

- ✓ **Aer Lingus** (☎ 800-474-7424 in the U.S. or ☎ 020-8899-4747 in Britain; www.aerlingus.com)
- ✓ **British Midland** (☎ 800-788-0555 in the U.S. or 0870-607-0555 in Britain; www.flybritishmidland.com)
- ✓ **CityJet** (☎ 0345-445-588 in Britain)

✔ **Lufthansa** (☎ 800-645-3880 in the U.S.; www.lufthansa.co.uk)

✔ **Ryanair** (☎ 0541-569-569 in Britain; www.ryanair.com)

## Getting the best deal on your airfare

Competition among the major U.S. airlines is unlike that of any other industry. Every airline offers virtually the same product (basically, a coach seat is a coach seat is a . . .), yet prices can vary by hundreds of dollars.

Business travelers who need the flexibility to buy their tickets at the last minute and change their itineraries at a moment's notice — and who want to get home before the weekend — pay (or at least their companies pay) the premium rate, known as the *full fare*. But if you can book your ticket far in advance, stay over Saturday night, and are willing to travel midweek (Tues, Wed, or Thurs), you can qualify for the least expensive price — usually a fraction of the full fare. On most flights, even the shortest hops within the United States, the full fare is close to $1,000 or more, but a 7- or 14-day advance purchase ticket may cost less than half of that amount. Obviously, planning ahead pays.

The airlines also periodically hold sales, in which they lower the prices on their most popular routes. These fares have advance purchase requirements and date-of-travel restrictions, but you can't beat the prices. As you plan your vacation, keep your eyes open for these sales, which tend to take place in months of low travel volume: late fall, winter, and early spring for Ireland. You almost never see a sale around the peak summer vacation months of July and August, or around Thanksgiving or Christmas, when many people fly, regardless of the fare they have to pay.

**Consolidators,** also known as *bucket shops,* are great sources for international tickets, although they usually can't beat the Internet on fares within North America. Start by looking in Sunday newspaper travel sections; U.S. travelers should focus on the *New York Times, Los Angeles Times,* and *Miami Herald.* For less-developed destinations, small travel agents who cater to immigrant communities in large cities often have the best deals.

Bucket shops can offer great savings, but be careful — tickets are usually nonrefundable or rigged with stiff cancellation penalties, often as high as 50% to 75% of the ticket price, and some consolidators put you on charter airlines with questionable safety records.

Reliable consolidators include **Ireland Consolidated** (☎ 888-577-2900; www.ukair.com), which sells discounted tickets to Ireland on already-scheduled major flights. Several other reliable consolidators serve customers worldwide and are accessible on the Internet. **STA Travel** (☎ 800-781-4040; www.statravel.com), the world's leader in student travel, offers good fares for travelers of all ages. **ELTExpress** (☎ 800-TRAV-800; www.flights.com) started in Europe and has excellent fares worldwide but particularly to that continent. Flights.com also has "local"

Web sites in 12 countries. **FlyCheap** (☎ **800-FLY-CHEAP;** www.1800fly cheap.com) is owned by package-holiday megalith MyTravel and so has especially good access to fares for sunny destinations. **Air Tickets Direct** (☎ **800-778-3447;** www.airticketsdirect.com) is based in Montreal and leverages the currently weak Canadian dollar for low fares.

## *Booking your flight online*

The big three online travel agencies — **Expedia** (www.expedia.com), **Travelocity** (www.travelocity.com), and **Orbitz** (www.orbitz.com) — sell most of the air tickets bought on the Internet. (Canadian travelers should try www.expedia.ca and www.travelocity.ca; U.K. residents can go for expedia.co.uk and opodo.co.uk.) Each has different business deals with the airlines and may offer different fares on the same flights, so shopping around is wise. Expedia and Travelocity will also send you an **e-mail notification** when a cheap fare becomes available to your favorite destination.

Of the smaller travel agency Web sites, **SideStep** (www.sidestep.com) receives good reviews from users. It's a browser add-on that purports to "search 140 sites at once" but in reality beats competitors' fares only as often as other sites do.

Great **last-minute deals** are available through free weekly e-mail services provided directly by the airlines. Most of these deals are announced on Tuesday or Wednesday and must be purchased online. Most are valid only for travel that weekend, but some (such as Southwest's) can be booked weeks or months in advance. Sign up for weekly e-mail alerts at airline Web sites or check mega-sites that compile comprehensive lists of last-minute specials, such as **Smarter Living** (www.smarterliving.com). For last-minute trips, www.site59.com in the United States and www.last minute.com in Europe often have better deals than the major-label sites.

If you're willing to give up some control over your flight details, use an opaque fare service such as **Priceline** (www.priceline.com) or **Hotwire** (www.hotwire.com). Both offer rock-bottom prices in exchange for travel on a mystery airline at a mysterious time of day, often with a mysterious change of planes en route. The mystery airlines are all major, well-known carriers — and the possibility of being sent from Philadelphia to Chicago via Tampa is remote. But your chances of getting a 6 a.m. or 11 p.m. flight are pretty high. Hotwire tells you flight prices before you buy; Priceline usually has better deals than Hotwire, but you have to play their "name our price" game. *Note:* In 2004, Priceline added non-opaque service to its roster. You now have the option to pick exact flights, times, and airlines from a list of offers — or opt to bid on opaque fares as before.

Great last-minute deals are also available directly from the airlines themselves through a free e-mail service called *E-savers.* Each week, the airline sends you a list of discounted flights, usually leaving the upcoming Friday or Saturday and returning the following Monday or Tuesday.

You can sign up for all the major airlines at one time by logging on to **Smarter Living** (www.smarterliving.com), or you can go to each individual airline's Web site. Airline sites also offer schedules, flight booking, and information on late-breaking bargains.

# Getting to Ireland by Ferry

Ferries are not the fastest or cheapest way to get to Ireland, but they're still popular because they can be a more interesting and relaxing way to travel than by air — getting there becomes part of the adventure. Ferry service to Ireland leaves from the U.K. and France and brings you within striking distance of Cork, Dublin, or Belfast. When you arrive, public transportation is available from the ferry terminals to the city. You can bring a car onto all of these ferries.

Note that the Irish Sea can be rough, so you should take a pill or patch if you're prone to seasickness.

**Irish Ferries** (☎ 08705-171717 in the U.K. or ☎ 01-638-3333 in Ireland; www.irishferries.com) travels to Dublin from Holyhead, Wales, and to Rosslare in County Wexford from Pembroke, Wales, and from Roscoff and Cherbourg, France. **Stena Line** (☎ 888-274-8724 in the U.S. or ☎ 01233-647-022 in Britain; www.stenaline.com) travels from Holyhead, Wales, to Dun Laoghaire (a few miles south of Dublin, pronounced *leer*-ee); from Fishguard, Wales, to Rosslare; and from Stranraer, Scotland, to Belfast. Brittany Ferries (☎ 021-427-7801; www.brittany-ferries.com) sails from Holyhead, Wales, to Dublin; from Fishguard and Pembroke in Wales to Rosslare; from Roscoff, France, to Cork; and from Stranraer, Scotland, to Belfast. **P& O Ferries** (☎ 561-563-2856 in the U.S., ☎ 01-638-3333 in Ireland; www.poferries.com) travels from Cherbourg, France, to Rosslare; Liverpool to Dublin; and Cairnryan, Scotland, to Larne, Northern Ireland. **Seacat Scotland** (☎ 800-551-743 in Britain, ☎ 01-874-1231 in Ireland; www.seacat.co.uk) goes from Liverpool to Dublin and from Heysham and Troon, in Scotland, to Belfast. **Norse Merchant Ferries** (☎ 0870-600-4321 in Britain, ☎ 01-819-2999; www.norsemerchant.com) travels from Liverpool to Dublin and Belfast.

# Joining an Escorted Tour

You may be one of the many people who love escorted tours. The tour company takes care of all the details and tells you what to expect at each leg of your journey. Also, you know your costs up front, and you don't have to spend time driving. Escorted tours can take you to the maximum number of sights in the minimum amount of time with the least amount of hassle. If your mobility is limited, if you like the ease and security of an escorted tour, or if you're just the sociable type who likes to travel in a group, an escorted tour may be for you. However, you should know that traveling on your own in Ireland is both rewarding and easy, particularly if you don't mind driving. So if you've been thinking about going it on your own on vacation, this may be the place to give it a try.

If you decide to go with an escorted tour, I strongly recommend purchasing travel insurance, especially if the tour operator asks you to pay up front. But don't buy insurance from the tour operator! If the tour operator doesn't fulfill its obligation to provide you the vacation you paid for, there's no reason to think that it'll fulfill its insurance obligations, either. Get travel insurance through an independent agency. I tell you about the ins and outs of travel insurance in Chapter 10.

When choosing an escorted tour, along with finding out whether you have to put down a deposit and when final payment is due, ask a few simple questions before you buy:

- ✔ **What is the cancellation policy?** Can they cancel the trip if they don't get enough people? How late can you cancel if you are unable to go? Do you get a refund if you cancel? If they cancel?

- ✔ **How jam-packed is the schedule?** Does the tour schedule try to fit 25 hours into a 24-hour day, or does it give you ample time take a walk around town or shop? If getting up at 7 a.m. every day and not returning to your hotel until 6 or 7 p.m. sounds like a grind, certain escorted tours may not be for you.

- ✔ **How large is the group?** The smaller the group, the less time you spend waiting for people to get on and off the bus. Tour operators may be evasive about this, because they may not know the exact size of the group until everybody has made reservations, but they should be able to give you a rough estimate.

- ✔ **Is there a minimum group size?** Some tours have a minimum group size and may cancel the tour if they don't book enough people. If a quota exists, find out what it is and how close they are to reaching it. Again, tour operators may be evasive in their answers, but the information may help you select a tour that's sure to happen.

- ✔ **What exactly is included?** Don't assume anything. You may have to pay to get yourself to and from the airport. A box lunch may be included in an excursion but drinks may be extra. Beer may be included but not wine. How much flexibility do you have? Can you opt out of certain activities, or does the bus leave once a day, with no exceptions? Are all your meals planned in advance? Can they accommodate special diets? Can you choose your entree at dinner, or does everybody get the same chicken cutlet?

- ✔ **What does double occupancy mean in this case?** Some tours offer rooms with two twin beds, while others set travelers up in rooms with one queen- or king-size bed. If this is important to you, ask the tour operator to clarify.

If you do decide to join an escorted tour, you have a lot to choose among. Most of them are priced all-inclusively, which means you pay one price and don't have to worry about paying your hotel bill or tipping your bus driver. Always remember to check whether your airfare is included in the price — some tour operators include it with their quoted prices and some don't.

Depending on your recreational passions, I recommend one of the following tour companies. For companies that run escorted golf tours, see Chapter 2.

- ✔ **Brian Moore International Tours** (☎ 800-982-2299; www.bmit.com): Many of these tours take in Ireland's most popular attractions. The ten-day Enchanting Ireland Tour travels from east to west across Ireland and cost $1,129 to $1,369 (airfare not included) in 2004. Walking and biking tours are also on offer.

- ✔ **CIE Tours International** (☎ 800-CIE-TOUR; www.cietours.com): CIE offers a large selection of tours. The 14-day Irish Classic makes a circuit around the country; it cost $2,087 to $2,646 (airfare included) in 2004.

- ✔ **Cosmos** (☎ 800-276-1241; www.cosmosvacations.com). The budget arm of Globus offers a slightly less upscale and less expensive version of Globus trips. In 2004, the ten-day Irish Explorer tour cost $1,533 to $1,843 (airfare included).

- ✔ **Destinations Ireland** (☎ 800-832-1848; www.Destinations-Ireland.com) offers an eight-day guided pony trek across Connemara ($2,589 to $2,669 without airfare).

- ✔ **Globus** (☎ 866-755-8581; www.globusjourneys.com). Globus offers a variety of upscale tours. The eight-day Introduction to Ireland tour cost $1,506 to $1,796 in 2004.

- ✔ **Tauck Worldwide Tours** (☎ 800-214-8809; www.tauck.com) offers deluxe tours of Ireland that house you in the finest hotels in the Emerald Isle. The eight-day A Week In Ireland tour cost $2,590 in 2004.

# Choosing a Package Tour

Package tours are a way to buy your airfare, accommodations, and other elements of your trip (such as car rentals and airport transfers) at the same time — one-stop vacation shopping. In many cases, a package tour that includes airfare, hotel, and transportation to and from the airport costs less than an independently booked hotel room. That's because packages are sold in bulk to tour operators, who resell them to the public. It works on a buy-in-bulk principle — the tour operator is the one who buys the 1,000-count box of garbage bags and resells them 10 at a time at a cost that undercuts the local supermarket.

Package tours can vary quite a bit. Some offer a better class of hotels than others; others provide the same hotels for lower prices. Some book flights on scheduled airlines; others sell charters. In some packages, your choice of accommodations and travel days may be limited. Some let you choose between escorted vacations and independent vacations; others allow you to add on just a few excursions or escorted day trips (also at discounted prices) without booking an entirely escorted tour.

Most package tours in Ireland are of the self-drive, B&B or hotel variety; Airfare and a rental car are included, as are vouchers good at thousands of B&Bs. The length of the car rental and number of vouchers are usually not flexible (most of the package tours cover seven or eight days), but your itinerary is completely up to you.

To find package tours, check out the travel section of your local Sunday newspaper or the ads in the back of national travel magazines such as *Travel & Leisure, National Geographic Traveler,* and *Condé Nast Traveler.* **Liberty Travel** (call ☎ 888-271-1584 to find the store nearest you; www. libertytravel.com) is one of the biggest packagers in the Northeast, and usually boasts a full-page ad in Sunday papers.

Another good source of package deals is the airlines themselves. **Aer Lingus** (☎ 800-495-1632; www.aerpackages.com) offers some excellent air/land packages, as do most major airlines, including **American Airlines Vacations** (☎ 800-321-2121; www.aavacations.com), **Delta Vacations** (☎ 800-221-6666; www.deltavacations.com), **Continental Airlines Vacations** (☎ 800-301-3800; www.covacations.com), and **United Vacations** (☎ 888-854-3899; www.unitedvacations.com). In addition, several big **online travel agencies** — Expedia, Travelocity, Orbitz, Site59, and Lastminute.com — also do a brisk business in packages. If you're unsure about the pedigree of a smaller packager, check with the Better Business Bureau in the city where the company is based, or go online at www.bbb.org. If a packager won't tell you where it's based, don't fly with it.

The following operators offer the best package tours in the business:

  ✔ **Brendan Worldwide Vacations** (☎ 800-421-8446; www.brendan vacations.com): Brendan's Go-As-You-Please tours included airfare, car rental, and seven days of B&B vouchers for $659 to $978 in 2004.

  ✔ **Brian Moore International Tours** (☎ 800-982-2299; www.bmit. com): Brian Moore's Ireland's Friendly B&Bs included airfare, car rental, and eight days of B&B vouchers for $699 to $1,219 in 2004. The company also offers walking and biking tours.

  ✔ **CIE Tours International** (☎ 800-CIE-TOUR; www.cietours.com): CIE's Go-As-You-Please tours included airfare, car rental, and seven days of B&B vouchers for $525 to $995 in 2004.

# Chapter 7

# Getting around Ireland

* * * * * * * * * * * * * * * * * * * * * * * * * * * * * * * * *

## In This Chapter

▶ Renting a car in Ireland
▶ Taking the bus
▶ Traveling by train

* * * * * * * * * * * * * * * * * * * * * * * * * * * * * * * * *

*Y*our choices for transportation in Ireland are trains, buses, or a car. For most trips, I recommend renting a car, because you can get to the less accessible area of Ireland, and you can tour at your own pace. In addition, if you are traveling in a group, renting a car can be the most economical option. For those who would rather not drive the winding roads, buses are a great option — they're cheap, run frequently, and have big windows so you can see the country rolling by.

## Seeing Ireland by Car

I think the best way to see Ireland is by car. No timetables, plenty of leg room, and control over the music — what more could you want? However, I want to mention that driving in Ireland can be harrowing at times, due to the narrow width of some roads and the fact that the Irish drive on the left side of the road, which can take some getting used to.

When planning your car trips, check out the handy mileage chart I provide on the tear-out card in the front of this book. Check out www. aaireland.ie for route-planning help and specific driving directions.

### Booking a rental car

In the off season (between Oct and Mar), you should have little difficulty getting a car on short (or no) notice. Booking anything during the summer, however, is a different story. To stay on the safe side, book any time from a few weeks to a month in advance.

Because prices are bound to increase based on demand, the earlier you book your car, the better your chance of getting a deal. Major rental car companies operating in Ireland are **Auto-Europe, Argus, Avis, Budget, Dan Dooley, Hertz, Murrays Europcar,** and **National.** The toll-free numbers and Web sites for these companies are listed in the appendix.

If you fly into Dublin and plan to spend some time there, wait to get a car until you're ready to head out to the countryside. Dublin is relatively walkable, and the bus system in the city is excellent, so you don't need a car — and with the lack of parking, you won't want one. However, if you're planning to leave town straightaway, or if you fly into Shannon airport, getting the car upon arrival is a good idea.

Most rental-car companies allow you to drop off cars at places other than where you picked them up, and most do not charge a drop-off fee (but some do, so be sure to ask). However, some companies don't allow you to pick up a car in the Republic and drop it off in Northern Ireland, or vice versa.

### Saving money on your rental

Rental-car costs can add up quickly, but these few budget-saving tips can help:

- ✔ **Go for the package rate.** Weekend rates may be lower than weekday rates. If you're keeping the car five or more days, a weekly rate may be cheaper than the daily rate. Ask whether the rate is the same for pickup Friday morning as it is Thursday night.

- ✔ **Ask for the advertised rate.** If you see an advertised price in a newspaper, be sure to ask for that specific rate; otherwise, you may be charged the standard (higher) rate.

- ✔ **Mention membership in AAA, AARP, and trade unions.** A membership can entitle you to discounts ranging from 5% to 30%.

- ✔ **Check your frequent-flier accounts.** Most airlines send discount coupons to frequent fliers and add at least 500 miles to your account for car rentals.

- ✔ **Use the Internet.** The Internet can make comparison shopping for a car rental much easier. You can check rates at most of the major agencies' Web sites. Also, all the major travel sites — **Travelocity** (www.travelocity.com), **Expedia** (www.expedia.com), **Orbitz** (www.orbitz.com), and **Smarter Living** (www.smarterliving.com), for example — have search engines that can dig up discounted car-rental rates. Just enter the car size you want, the pickup and return dates, and location, and the server returns a price. You can even make the reservation through any of these sites.

### Considering your rental options

You can choose among three levels of rental cars: economy (small), compact (medium), and intermediate (large). You may think you want a larger vehicle, but keep in mind that most roads are nail-bitingly narrow; winding down a street lined with cars and filled with oncoming traffic, you'll appreciate driving a mini-mobile. So try to get the smallest car you think you'll be comfortable in. Another thought: Smaller is cheaper.

# Meeting car agency age limits

If you're under 25 or over 70, you may have trouble renting a car in Ireland. The following lists age limits for various rental companies:

✓ **Argus:** In most cases, you must be at least 25; the maximum age is 70. Age limits vary across Ireland, so call or visit www.argusrentals.com for specifics.

✓ **Auto Europe:** Must be at least 23; maximum age is 75.

✓ **Avis:** Must be at least 23; maximum age is 74.

✓ **Budget:** Must be at least 23; maximum age is 75.

✓ **Dan Dooley:** Must be at least 21; maximum age is 75; extra fee applies to drivers between 21 and 24, and over 70.

✓ **Hertz:** Must be at least 21; €25 ($29) a day extra up to age 24; maximum age is 74 (up to 79 in special cases).

✓ **Murrays Europcar:** Must be at least 24; maximum age is 69.

✓ **National:** Must be at least 24, extra €10 ($12) for drivers up to 26; maximum age is 74.

Expect a stick shift. Unlike the United States, where it's standard for rental cars to have an automatic transmission, the standard in Ireland is a manual transmission. You can get an automatic — but it costs you. Prices vary widely, so if you're sure you want an automatic, shop around for the best deal.

Because the driver's side is on the right side of cars in Ireland, the stick shift is controlled by your left hand, not your right. Sounds wacky and hard to do, but you should get the hang of it in no time.

## Paying for a rental car

Some companies require a deposit when you make your reservation, generally on a credit card. If you book by phone, you may be asked for a deposit.

Don't be shocked if the rental company charges you a gas deposit on your card, too. Just be sure to fill the tank before drop-off, and the deposit will be taken off (good thing, because the deposit is always way higher than the actual cost of the gas).

Gas, called *petrol* in Ireland, is costly. The prices that petrol stations advertise may seem decent until you realize that they're priced per liter, not gallon. So in essence, you're paying three to four times what you would in the United States. This is another good reason to get a smaller car: better gas mileage.

# Boots, bonnets, and other brouhaha

To save you confusion about the words and phrases that the Irish have for car-related things, here's a list of the most commonly used (and most commonly confused):

✔ **Bonnet:** Hood

✔ **Boot:** Trunk

✔ **Footpath:** Sidewalk

✔ **Gear stick:** Stick shift

✔ **Motorways:** Highways

✔ **Petrol:** Gasoline

✔ **Roundabout:** Traffic circle (or a rotary, if you're from New England). These are common, especially entering and leaving cities. Make sure you go left and yield to the right!

## *Getting the scoop on driver's licenses and insurance*

If you are from the United States, Canada, or an EU country, all you need to legally drive a car in Ireland is a valid driver's license from your country of residence. If you are not from one of these countries, you should obtain an International Driving Permit. These are usually available from automobile associations in your home country.

Your personal auto insurance doesn't extend to rental cars in Ireland. You must get a Collision Damage Waiver (CDW), which is included in the price of the rental. Once in a blue moon, credit card companies will pay for the CDW, so check with your credit card company and with the rental car company.

If you plan on taking the car into Northern Ireland, be sure to inform the rental company, and ask whether additional insurance is required.

## *Figuring out the rules of the road*

Here are some important traffic rules and laws that will help you get around safely and legally:

✔ The general speed limit is 60 mph (96 km/h) unless otherwise posted. Standard 60-mph signs are indicated only by a black circle with a slash through it. When the speed limit is other than 60 mph, there'll be a sign with a red circle and the limit written inside in black. You often see these signs when entering small towns, where you should reduce speed to 30 mph. On motorways (highways), the speed limit is generally 67 mph.

✔ A sign that is a red circle with a red X through the middle means no stopping or parking during posted hours.

✔ A flashing yellow light means yield to pedestrian traffic, but proceed with caution if it's clear.

✔ Yield to traffic coming from your right.

✔ Seat belts must be worn by drivers and front-seat passengers. If your car has back seat belts, they must be worn as well.

✔ Drinking and driving is a serious offense and is dealt with harshly. Do not drink and drive under any circumstances.

An arcane law in Northern Ireland prohibits a driver from going around a roundabout more than three times. So no getting yourself dizzy just for kicks when you're up north.

If you have any further questions about traffic laws, you can call the **National Safety Council** in Dublin at ☎ **01-496-3422**.

### Driving on the left side of the road

To get an idea of what driving in Ireland is like, simply imagine driving in North America and then turn that image upside down. The steering wheel is on the right side, and the gearshift is on the left (the positions of the gas, clutch, and brake are the same). This causes most people an initial fright. Fortunately, it's a temporary feeling, and soon you'll be sailing down the roads.

# How do I find a place when there's no #&@*$! address!?

Welcome to one of the facts of life in Ireland: Outside of the major cities, American-style street names and addresses simply aren't used. As you leaf through this book, you'll often see the name of a B&B listed with just the town name after it. This is just the way it works. In fact, if you were to write a letter to the place, you'd address it the very same way, with just its name and the town.

I know what you're thinking: "How am I supposed to find any of these places?!" Fear not: It's not as hard as it seems. Often, these places are right on the town's main thoroughfare (such as R236 or the Dublin-Waterford road), and in these cases, if you drive into the town, you can't miss them. Other places are near the town's main street and have signs directing you toward them from the center of town. Of course, there are also several places that are nowhere near the main part of town. In these cases, I include specific directions.

# Funny, there aren't any road signs (Or they're facing the wrong way)

One of the biggest complaints visitors have about traveling around Ireland is the lack of road signs. The reason for this is somewhat surprising: They get stolen! Pub owners and, yes, tourists steal signs as decorations and souvenirs, especially if the signs have a family name or ancestral town name on them. You know the kind: white, arrow-shaped signs that you've undoubtedly seen in Irish bars in the United States. And you thought they were reproductions!

If you see a sign pointing in the opposite direction of what your map says, trust your map. Sign-twisting is a popular pastime in some areas.

In highway traffic, you merge to the right while slower traffic stays on the left. Roundabouts are tricky, and you'll probably pop a few curbs while making sharp lefts, but don't get discouraged. Driving in Ireland just takes practice, practice, practice.

## Understanding parking rules and regulations

First, there's no law that prohibits you from parking a car facing into traffic. You will often see cars on one side of the road parked in both directions, which makes it tough to tell if you're going the wrong way on a one-way street.

In larger towns, there are some, but not many, parking garages. Street parking is fine, but don't think that parking is free just because there are no meters. In Ireland, you have to buy *parking disks,* which are paper disks that indicate how long you've been in the spot. You can buy disks at machines marked *P.* Purchase a disk and then display it in the window. Residential neighborhoods and some towns require disks but have no parking-disk machines. In those cases, local corner shops usually sell the disks.

# Traveling by Bus

Buses are a pretty great way to see Ireland for a variety of reasons: They make many more stops than trains, you get a great view of the countryside from the huge windows, they're comfortable, and they're pretty inexpensive. On the other hand, you're not free to stop whenever you want, and most buses don't have toilets. The nearby "Irish Bus Routes" map shows where you can go.

## Getting to know the major bus companies

**Bus Éireann** is the country's principal public coach line, with a vast network of routes that web through all the major towns of Ireland and into

*Irish Bus Routes*

Northern Ireland. Bus Éireann is pretty much a tool of transportation rather than tourism, so it doesn't always stop right near popular sights. The trick is to get to a town near the attraction that you want to see and then take local transportation from there. Prices, schedules, routes, and other information can be found at Bus Éireann on Store Street, Dublin 1 (☎ 01-836-6111; www.buseireann.ie).

In Northern Ireland, **Ulsterbus** is the area bus service, with routes that include stops at or near the region's attractions. The two stations in Belfast are Europa Bus Station on Glengall Street and Oxford Street Bus Station. Call the timetable hot line at ☎ 028-9066-6630. You can also find information online at www.ulsterbus.co.uk.

## Finding bus packages and tours

Bus Éireann offers guided sightseeing tours that cover a number of top attractions. Routes become more limited in the off season, so call ahead to find out when each tour is offered. The major day-trips out of Dublin are:

 ✔ Glendalough and Wicklow (see Chapter 13)

 ✔ Newgrange and Boyne Valley (see Chapter 12)

 ✔ Kilkenny City, Jerpoint Abbey, and the Nore Valley (see Chapter 14)

 ✔ Ballykissangel and Wicklow Mountains (see Chapter 13)

 ✔ Powerscourt Gardens and Wicklow (see Chapter 13)

 ✔ Waterford Crystal and River Barrow Cruise (see Chapter 14)

 ✔ The Mountains of Mourne (see Chapter 23)

You can also book seasonal trips out from Cork, Galway, and Sligo. For more information, visit www.buseireann.ie or call ☎ 01-836-6111.

# Riding the Rails

Ireland has an excellent rail system that connects the major cities of the Republic and Northern Ireland; the "Irish Rail Routes" map shows the system. The advantages of train travel are that it's fast and very comfortable. On the downside, trains are more expensive and travel to fewer destinations than buses, and you have to be ready to jump off with all your luggage, because trains pull into the station and stop for half a second before flying on to the next stop.

Trains between major cities run three to five times daily and are reliable. During low season, you should have no problem buying tickets a half-hour before departure, but during the high season, calling the day before to confirm availability is advisable. For information about destinations, times, and fares, call **Iarnród Éireann** (Irish Rail) at ☎ 1850-366-222

## Irish Rail Routes

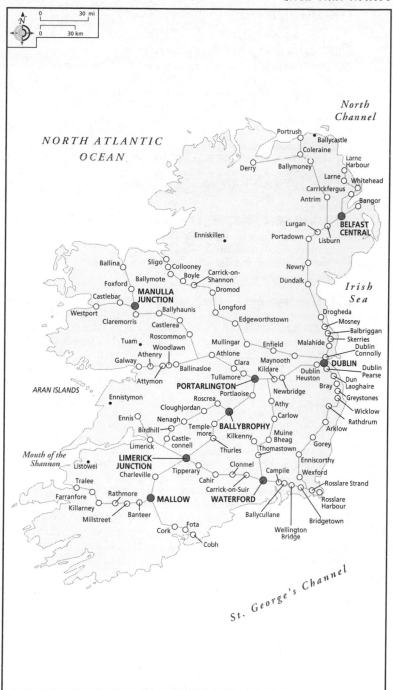

(www.irishrail.ie). In Northern Ireland, **NI Railways** information is
☎ **028-9024-2420** (www.nirailways.co.uk).

## Finding train packages and tours

Excellent packages combine train travel to a destination with a bus tour
that explores non-rail-accessible destinations such as the Burren, Connemara, and the Ring of Kerry. Some of these offerings include hotel
accommodations. **Railtours Ireland,** at Dublin Tourism Centre (☎ **01-
856-0045;** www.railtours.ie), is one of the best private tour operators.

**Iarnród Éireann** (Irish Rail) offers a number of rail tours, from single-
day to multiple-day tours that include accommodations. Contact the
**Travel Centre** at 35 Lower Abbey St., Dublin 1 (☎ **01-703-4070;** www.
irishrail.ie — click on <u>Breaks and Trips</u>), for more information.

## Bus and rail passes for extended travel

The following bus and rail deals are available through **Iarnród Éireann**
(Irish Rail) (☎ **01-703-4070;** www.irishrail.ie/home/international_
visitors.asp). For a flat price, you get a pass allowing you unlimited use
of trains and buses.

- ✔ **Irish Explorer:** Five days out of 15 consecutive days, rail only
  (includes Intercity, DART, and Suburban Rail): €116 ($133) adult,
  €59 ($67) under 12. Eight days out of 15 consecutive days, com-
  bined rail and bus (includes Intercity, DART, and Suburban Rail;
  Bus Éireann Expressway; Provincial Bus; and city buses in Cork,
  Limerick, Galway, and Waterford): €176 ($202) adult, €88 ($101)
  under 12.

- ✔ **Irish Rover:** Five days out of 15 consecutive days all-Ireland rail
  only (includes Intercity, DART, Suburban Rail, and Northern Ireland
  Railways): €143 ($164) adult, €72 ($82) under 12.

- ✔ **Emerald Card:** Eight days out of 15 consecutive days combined rail
  and bus (covers Intercity; DART; Suburban Rail; Northern Ireland
  Railways; Bus Éireann Expressway; Provincial Bus; Ulsterbus
  Provincial Services; and city buses in Belfast, Cork, Limerick,
  Galway, and Waterford): €198 ($228) adult, €99 ($114) under 12.
  Fifteen days out of 30 consecutive days: €341 ($392) adult, €171
  ($196) under 12.

- ✔ **Irish Rambler:** Three days out of eight consecutive days, 8 days out
  of 15 consecutive days, or 15 days out of 30 consecutive days bus
  (covers Bus Éireann Expressway and Provincial Services, and Bus
  Éireann City Services in Cork, Limerick, Galway, and Waterford.)
  Three-day is €53 ($61) adult, €32 ($37) under 12; 8-day is €116
  ($133) adults, €74 ($85) under 12; 15-day is €168 ($193) adult, €105
  ($121) under 12.

# Chapter 8

# Booking Your Accommodations

**A**re B&Bs the best value? Where can you find discounts on lodging? How much does a swanky hotel cost? Read on for answers to all your burning accommodations questions.

## *Knowing Your Options*

From grand manor houses to cute and charming B&Bs (bed-and-breakfasts), Ireland has accommodations for a range of budgets and tastes. Anywhere you stay, you're likely to encounter the warmth and friendliness that the Irish are so famous for. It's not a myth; people here take a lot of pride in their hospitality. **Gulliver (☎ 011-800-668-668-66** from the U.S., ☎ 00800-668-688-6 from Ireland and Northern Ireland; www.gulliver.com) has a tremendous database of lodgings and allows you to reserve with a credit card. You can find and book hotels and guest-houses through www.irelandhotels.com. The tourist boards of the Republic of Ireland (☎ **01-60-24-00;** www.ireland.ie) and Northern Ireland (☎ **028-9023-1221;** www.discovernorthernireland.com) can also help you find and book a room.

### *Opting for hotels*

Among hotels, the range of accommodations is wide — from castles on down to small family-run lodges. Though you can assume that many of the larger and chain hotels provide fitness equipment, room service, and in-house pubs and restaurants, don't count on these amenities in smaller independent hotels.

*Be Our Guest* is the **Irish Hotel Federation's** guide to hotels, manor houses, inns, and castles. Contact the Irish Tourist Board for a copy (☎ **1850-230-3300;** www.tourismireland.com) or check it out online at www.irelandhotels.com.

The Irish Tourist Board and the Northern Ireland Tourist Board rank hotels from one to five stars based on the amenities and facilities offered. These ratings give you a rough idea of what you can expect in terms of room service, dataports, and so on, but they don't say much about the character and decor of the places or about the owners and staff.

The following chains have quality hotels in major cities throughout the country. I list them here starting with the most upscale:

  ✔ **Great Southern:** ☎ **01-214-4800;** www.gshotel.com (Parknasilla, Killarney, Galway, Rosslare, Cork Airport, Dublin Airport, Shannon Airport, Derry)

  ✔ **Tower:** ☎ **071-44-000;** fax 071-46-888; www.towerhotelgroup.com (Dublin, Waterford, Killarney, Sligo)

  ✔ **Jurys:** ☎ **01-607-0070;** www.jurys.com (Dublin, Waterford, Cork, Galway, Limerick, Belfast)

  ✔ **Travelodge:** ☎ **0870-191-1600;** www.travelodge.co.uk (Dublin, Waterford, Cork)

If you're looking for fancy manor houses and castles, check out **Ireland's Blue Book** (☎ **01-662-7166;** www.irelands-blue-book.com). For upscale manor houses and guesthouses, including some of the most beautiful and oldest houses in Ireland, contact **The Hidden Ireland** (☎ **800-688-0299** in the U.S., ☎ 01-662-7166 in Ireland; www.hidden-ireland.com).

# Getting the best room

After you make your reservation, asking one or two more pointed questions can go a long way toward making sure you get the best room in the house:

  ✔ Always ask for a corner room. These rooms are usually larger, quieter, and have more windows and light than standard rooms, and they don't always cost more.

  ✔ Ask if the hotel is renovating. If it is, request a room away from the renovation work.

  ✔ Inquire, too, about the location of the restaurants, bars, and discos in the hotel — all sources of annoying noise.

And if you aren't happy with your room when you arrive, talk to the front desk. If they have another room, they should be happy to accommodate you, within reason.

## Staying in casual comfort: Choosing B&Bs

Though they're not for everyone, I think that bed-and-breakfasts (B&Bs) are the best lodging option in Ireland. Because they're small, they give you an opportunity to get to know the owners, who much more often than not are friendly and knowledgeable about the area. Another big advantage of choosing a B&B over a hotel is the price. The cost of a double room is usually much lower than at a hotel, averaging between €45 ($52) and €90 ($104).

Keep in mind that many B&Bs don't accept credit cards, so make sure you have enough cash on hand when it's time to check out.

Most B&Bs have between four and ten rooms only, so the better ones fill up quickly during the high season. You should book at least a week in advance of your trip — even sooner if possible.

Some B&B rooms are not *en suite,* meaning that they don't have a private bathroom. If you don't want to share facilities with other guests, make sure you ask for a room with its own bathroom, keeping in mind that you'll probably pay more for privacy.

If you'd like a booklet of the 2,000 or so B&Bs in Ireland, write to or call the Irish Tourist Board (☎ 1850-230-3300; www.tourismireland.com). For Northern Ireland, ask the Northern Ireland Tourist Board (☎ 028-9023-1221; www.discovernorthernireland.com) for the free *Bed & Breakfast* brochure (on the Web site, click on the <u>Maps & Brochures</u> link in the menu on the main page). For upscale B&Bs, including some of the most beautiful and oldest houses in Ireland, contact The Hidden Ireland (☎ 800-688-0299 in the U.S., ☎ 01-662-7166 in Ireland; www.hidden-ireland.com).

## Enjoying self-catering accommodations

Self-catering accommodations are a place for you to drop your bags, settle in, and do things family-style, including cooking your own meals and making your own beds. If you're making the trip with children, this may be a perfect option, both in terms of convenience and cost.

With self-catering, you pay one price, generally for the week. (Some rent for two to three days.) Compared to the amount of money you pay for hotels and B&Bs on a nightly basis, the price is usually a bargain. Food costs decrease when you're buying your own and cooking it, too.

The drawback is location. Although some self-catering cottages and apartments are in *great* locations, the trouble is that they don't move: Rent one and you're in one place for the whole week; to see the sights around the country, you have to drive to them and then drive "home" again Of course, this is fine if you intend to spend all your time in one area. But making day-trips to sights in far-flung parts of the country may be tough.

The variety of self-catering options is as diverse as types of hotels. You can stay in actual thatched-roof cottages or completely modernized units. All of these accommodations are registered with the tourism authorities and are rated from one star to four (four being the best).

As with any place to stay, all you have to do is call the tourist board in the area you want to visit, and the staff there will help you with bookings. To get you started, the following organizations deal solely with self-catering accommodations:

- **Irish Cottage Holiday Homes Association** (☎ 01-205-2777; www. irishcottageholidays.com) rents vacation cottages in the Republic of Ireland.

- **Northern Ireland Self-Catering Holidays Association** (☎ 028-9077-6174; www.nischa.com) rents cottages in Northern Ireland.

- **Rent an Irish Cottage** (☎ 061-41-1109; www.rentacottage.ie) organizes self-catering in cottages all over Ireland.

- **Self-Catering Ireland** (☎ 053-33-999; www.selfcatering-ireland.com) is the most comprehensive reservation service, offering 3- and 4-star self-catering apartments throughout Ireland and Northern Ireland.

- **Trident Holiday Homes** (☎ 01-668-3534; fax 01-660-6465; www. thh.ie) offers a good selection of rentals near the coasts.

## Staying at a hostel

Hostels have a reputation for being the accommodation of choice for the micro-budgeted, and if you have the image in your head of hostels full of young, tireless travelers who don't mind going long stretches without showers or food, you're partly right — though only partly. Today, hostels serve all kinds of independent travelers who cherish flexibility and are adding more facilities to accommodate couples and families.

Some Irish hostels offer community kitchens, and many sleep people dorm-style, with anywhere from four to dozens of people per room. Some hostels have separate dorm rooms for women and men, but others have mixed dorms. Many hostels have been adding double and family rooms, and even private single rooms, so you may not need to share a room with other travelers.

 Hostels provide a blanket and pillow, and some beds have sheets, but to be safe, bring your own *sleep-sack* — two twin sheets sewn together.

 You may wonder how safe your luggage will be in a hostel, because your personal belongings most likely sit at the foot of the bed. Theft is not a major problem, but it is something to consider. Many hostels provide security lockers (ask when you reserve if it's important to you), but if not, take some precautions: Make your luggage as difficult to get into as possible by, for instance, stacking bags on top of one another, with the most valuable at the bottom. Also, bring your wallet, passport, purse, and other important personal belongings to bed with you for safekeeping and under no circumstances leave important documents or money in your room.

As for bathrooms, think of high-school gym restrooms — cold tiles, a row of small sinks and toilets, and shower stalls. You may not love it, but you can get the job done in it.

I can't vouch for every hostel in Ireland, but if there's one undeniable fact, it's that they're cheap. You can get a warm bed for under €20 — sometimes way under. And you meet people from all over the world doing the same thing as you. Sure, you run into your share of hostels that don't exactly disinfect the toilet daily, but on the whole, Irish hostels are the cleanest I've seen anywhere.

Some hostels take reservations. Others are first-come, first-sleep. If you're planning to do a hostel tour of Ireland, you'll really benefit from joining **Hostelling International** (www.hiayh.com in the U.S., www.hihostels.com in Canada, www.yha.org.uk in the U.K. , www.yha.com.au in Australia, and www.yha.org.nz in New Zealand) before you depart. Fees are about $25 a year. With a membership card, you get discounts at places affiliated with the group.

To find hostels in the Republic of Ireland, check out **An Óige**, the Irish Youth Hostel Association (☎ **01-830-4555**; fax 01-830-5808; www.irelandyha.org). For hostels in Northern Ireland, contact or visit **YHANI** (Youth Hostels Association of Northern Ireland), also called HINI, (☎ **028-9032-4733**; fax 028-9043-9699; www.hini.org.uk).

### Seeking out alternatives

If you're looking for something a little different from the usual hotel or B&B, try one of these options:

- ✔ **Caravans (trailers/motorhomes):** For information on renting or buying a caravan or trailer, contact **Irish Caravan & Camping Council** (fax 011-353-98-28237; www.camping-ireland.ie).

- ✔ **Farmhouse accommodations:** For information on staying on a farm, visit the **Irish Farm Holidays Association** (www.irishfarmholidays.com).

- ✔ **University housing:** Check with local tourist boards or directly with universities to find out whether they have unused dorm space in campus housing to rent. Cities with large universities include Dublin, Galway, Cork, and Limerick. Housing is usually available only during the summer and Christmas holidays.

## Figuring Out Accommodation Prices

To make it easy for you to quickly gauge the price of each lodging in this guide, in Table 8.1, I list the cost of a *double room* for each option — the cost for two people to stay in one room together. The range given typically indicates the lowest price for the room during the low season up to the highest price during the high season. The range also takes into account (no pun intended) the difference in price for a room with a view, a larger room, and so on. If you're traveling alone, count on paying a bit more than half the price listed for a double.

Almost every place I list in the book includes a full Irish breakfast.

| Table 8.1 | | Key to Hotel Dollar Signs |
|---|---|---|
| Dollar Sign(s) | Price Range | What to Expect |
| $ | Up to $80 | Small bed-and-breakfasts often fall into this category, offering cozy rooms and homemade breakfasts. You may miss high-end amenities (there is usually no pool, restaurant, or the like), but you're sure to appreciate the friendly hosts and hostesses who operate these spots. |
| $$ | $81–$125 | B&Bs and hotels both fall into this price range. The more expensive B&Bs are often a bit classier and refined than those in the preceding category, with gourmet breakfasts, prime locations, antique-filled rooms, and so on. Hotels in this range are usually stylish and offer extras such as hair dryers, irons, and microwaves. |
| $$$ | $126–$225 | Higher-class still, these accommodations are pretty plush. Think grand manor houses, castles, and top-tier business hotels, boasting perks such as fine linens, hand-carved furniture, antiques, excellent in-house restaurants, and polished service. |
| $$$$ | $226 and up | These top-rated accommodations (most often manors, castles, and hotels) come with luxury amenities such as golf courses, spas, and in-room hot tubs and CD players. |

# Finding the Best Room Rate at Hotels

The **rack rate** is the maximum rate a hotel charges for a room. It's the rate you get if you walk in off the street and ask for a room for the night. You sometimes see these rates printed on the fire/emergency exit diagrams posted on the back of your door.

Hotels are happy to charge you the rack rate, but you can almost always do better. Perhaps the best way to avoid paying the rack rate is surprisingly simple: Just ask for a cheaper or discounted rate. You may be pleasantly surprised.

In hotels and larger guesthouses, the rate you pay for a room depends on many factors — chief among them being how you make your reservation. A travel agent may be able to negotiate a better price with certain hotels than you can get by yourself. (That's because the hotel often gives the agent a discount in exchange for steering business to that hotel.)

 Reserving a room through the hotel's toll-free number may also result in a lower rate than calling the hotel directly. On the other hand, the central reservations number may not know about discount rates at specific locations. For example, local franchises may offer a special group rate for a wedding or family reunion, but they may neglect to tell the central booking line. Your best bet is to call both the local number and the toll-free number, and see which one gives you a better deal.

Room rates (even rack rates) change with the season, as occupancy rates rise and fall. In most of Ireland, hotels charge the highest rate during the high season of June through August and the lowest during the low season of November through March (the prices during April, May, Sept, and Oct usually depend on the weather in the specific location). In Dublin, all bets are off because the city receives a high volume of visitors all year, and most rates don't go down during the winter. See Chapter 3 for more on the seasons in Ireland. Know that even within a given season, room prices are subject to change without notice, so the rates quoted in this book may be different from the actual rate you receive when you make your reservation.

 Weekends are often the cheapest time to stay at hotels in major cities. These hotels thrive on business travelers, who go home on the weekends. Hotels are eager to keep the house full, so some offer great deals to tourists. It's worth asking.

Be sure to mention membership in AAA, AARP, frequent-flyer programs, any other corporate rewards programs you can think of — or your Uncle Joe's Elks lodge, in which you're an honorary inductee, for that matter — when you call to book. You never know when an affiliation may be worth a few dollars off your room rate.

See Chapter 6 for information on package tours, which often include airfare and accommodations sold together for a deeply discounted price.

## Surfing the Web for Hotel and B&B Deals

Shopping online for hotels is generally done one of two ways: by booking through the hotel's own Web site or by booking through an independent booking agency (or a fare-service agency such as Priceline). These Internet hotel agencies have multiplied in mind-boggling numbers of late, competing for the business of millions of consumers surfing for accommodations around the world. This competitiveness can be a boon to consumers who have the patience and time to shop and compare the online sites for good deals — but shop you must, for prices can vary considerably from site to site. And keep in mind that hotels at the top of a site's listing may be there for no other reason than that they paid money to get the placement, so be sure to scroll down.

Of the major booking sites, **Expedia** (www.expedia.com) offers a long list of special deals and virtual tours or photos of available rooms so you can see what you're paying for (a feature that helps counter the claims that the best rooms are often held back from bargain-booking Web sites). **Travelocity** (www.travelocity.com) posts unvarnished customer reviews and ranks its properties according to the AAA rating system. Also reliable are **Hotels.com** and **Quikbook.com.**

Another booking site, **Travelweb** (www.travelweb.com), is partly owned by the hotels it represents (including the Hilton, Hyatt, and Starwood chains) and is therefore plugged directly into the hotels' reservations systems — unlike independent online agencies, which have to fax or e-mail reservation requests to the hotel, a good portion of which get misplaced in the shuffle. More than once, travelers have arrived at the hotel only to be told that they have no reservation. To be fair, many of the major sites are undergoing improvements in service and ease of use, and Expedia will soon be able to plug directly into the reservations systems of many hotel chains — none of which can be bad news for consumers. In the meantime, it's a good idea to **get a confirmation number** and **make a printout** of any online booking transaction.

An excellent free program, **TravelAxe** (www.travelaxe.net), can help you search multiple hotel sites at once, even ones you may never have heard of — and conveniently lists the total price of the room, including the taxes and service charges.

In the opaque Web site category, **Priceline** (www.priceline.com) and **Hotwire** (www.hotwire.com) are even better for hotels than for airfares; with both, you're allowed to pick the neighborhood and quality level of your hotel before offering up your money. Priceline's hotel product even covers Europe and Asia, though it's much better at getting five-star lodging for three-star prices than at finding anything at the bottom of the scale. On the downside, many hotels stick Priceline guests in their least desirable rooms. Be sure to go to the **BiddingforTravel** Web site (www.biddingfortravel.com) before bidding on a hotel room on Priceline; it features a fairly up-to-date list of hotels that Priceline uses in major cities. For both Priceline and Hotwire, you pay up-front, and the fee is nonrefundable. *Note:* Some hotels do not provide loyalty program credits or points or other frequent-stay amenities when you book a room through opaque online services.

# Chapter 9

# Catering to Special Travel Needs and Interests

*A*lthough every traveler has different needs, some special cases are common enough that special travel services are set up around the world just for them. In this chapter, I run through some services, give some tips, and note some challenges of travel in Ireland. I also offer resources for travelers with special interests such as genealogy research, golfing, hiking, biking, and fishing.

## Traveling with the Brood: Advice for Families

If you have enough trouble getting your kids out of the house in the morning, dragging them thousands of miles away may seem like an insurmountable challenge. But family travel can be immensely rewarding, giving you new ways of seeing the world through smaller pairs of eyes.

**Familyhostel** (☎ 800-733-9753; www.learn.unh.edu/familyhostel) takes the whole family, including kids ages 8 to 15, on moderately priced domestic and international learning vacations. Lectures, field trips, and sightseeing are guided by a team of academics.

You can find good family-oriented vacation advice on the Internet from sites such as the **Family Travel Forum** (www.familytravelforum.com), a comprehensive site that offers customized trip planning; **Family Travel Network** (www.familytravelnetwork.com), an award-winning site that offers travel features, deals, and tips; **Traveling Internationally with Your Kids** (www.travelwithyourkids.com), a comprehensive site offering sound advice for long-distance and international travel with children; and **Family Travel Files** (www.thefamilytravelfiles.com), which offers an online magazine and a directory of off-the-beaten-path tours and tour operators for families.

Most attractions and some public transportation companies in Ireland and Northern Ireland offer reduced fees for children. And most attractions have family group prices (usually for two adults and two or three children) that are a great bargain. Be sure to ask. (See more money-saving tips in Chapter 5.)

Car-rental companies provide necessary car seats, and all vehicles have rear seatbelts. The law requires that children always buckle up.

For a small additional fee, you can sometimes add a cot to your room at a hotel, guesthouse, or B&B so that your child can stay in the same room as you. Check with the concierge or manager.

Throughout this book, I point out kid-friendly accommodations, dining options, and attractions — just look for the Kid Friendly icon.

## Making Age Work for You: Advice for Seniors

Mention the fact that you're a senior citizen when you make your travel reservations — many hotels offer discounts for seniors. The **Irish Tourist Board** (☎ 01-60-24-00; www.ireland.ie), publishes a list of discount hotel packages for seniors, called *Golden Holidays/For the Over 55s.*

In Ireland, people over the age of 60 qualify for reduced admission to theaters, museums, and other attractions, as well as for discounted fares on public transportation.

Members of **AARP** (formerly known as the American Association of Retired Persons), 601 E St. NW, Washington, DC 20049 (☎ 888-687-2277 or 202-434-2277; www.aarp.org), get discounts on hotels, airfares, and car rentals. AARP offers members a wide range of benefits, including *AARP: The Magazine* and a monthly newsletter. Anyone over 50 can join.

Many reliable agencies and organizations target the 50-plus market. **Elderhostel** (☎ 877-426-8056; www.elderhostel.org) arranges study programs for those age 55 and over (and a spouse or companion of any age) in the United States and in more than 80 countries around the world. Most courses last five to seven days in the United States (two to four weeks abroad), and many include airfare, accommodations in university dormitories or modest inns, meals, and tuition. **ElderTreks** (☎ 800-741-7956; www.eldertreks.com) offers small-group tours to off-the-beaten-path or adventure-travel locations, restricted to travelers 50 and older. American tour operator **CIE Tours** (☎ 800-CIE-TOUR; www.cietours.com) gives substantial discounts to seniors. In addition,

SAGA Tours (☎ 800-343-0273; http://holidays.saga.co.uk/travel) operates tours to Ireland specifically for seniors.

Recommended publications offering travel resources and discounts for seniors include the quarterly magazine *Travel 50 & Beyond* (www. travel50andbeyond.com); *101 Tips for Mature Travelers,* available from Grand Circle Travel (☎ 800-221-2610 or 617-350-7500; www.gct. com); and *Unbelievably Good Deals and Great Adventures That You Absolutely Can't Get Unless You're Over 50* (McGraw-Hill), by Joan Rattner Heilman.

# Accessing Ireland: Advice for Travelers with Disabilities

A disability shouldn't stop anyone from traveling. There are more options and resources out there than ever before.

 Ireland has accessibility regulations for public areas, though they're not as comprehensive as in the United States. Most sidewalks have ramps, and many accommodations are wheelchair-accessible. Getting around in cities and towns isn't hard, but some of Ireland's attractions are not very accessible. Not every museum has closed captions for video presentations, and not every castle has an entrance ramp. Calling ahead to find out about accessibility at attractions and at B&Bs (many of which aren't disability-friendly) is always a good idea, but you can feel fairly confident that most restaurants and newer hotels are entirely accessible. An excellent resource is www.disability.ie (click on Holidays), which offers advice on traveling in Ireland with a disability and lists companies that specialize in helping travelers with disabilities.

For further information, the Access Department of the **National Rehabilitation Board,** 24-25 Clyde Rd., Dublin 4 (☎ 01-608-0400) publishes several guides for travelers with disabilities, listing wheelchair-friendly attractions, restaurants, and accommodations. For tips on travel in the North, contact **Disability Action** (☎ 028-9029-7880; www.disabilityaction.org). The Northern Ireland Tourist Board (☎ 028-9023-1221; www.discovernorthernireland.com) publishes an *Information Guide to Accessible Accommodation.*

Free wheelchairs for travelers in Ireland are available from the **Irish Wheelchair Association** (☎ 01-833-8241; www.iwa.ie). The association has offices in Dublin, Kilkenny, Cork, Limerick, and Galway.

Many travel agencies offer customized tours and itineraries for travelers with disabilities. **The Guided Tour, Inc.** (☎ 215-783-5841; www.guided tour.com) conducts annual trips to Ireland for mentally challenged travelers. **Flying Wheels Travel** (☎ 507-451-5005; www.flyingwheelstravel. com) offers escorted tours and cruises that emphasize sports and private tours in minivans with lifts. **Access-Able Travel Source** (☎ 303-232-2979; www.access-able.com) offers extensive access information and advice for traveling around the world with disabilities. **Accessible Journeys** (☎ 800-846-4537 or 610-521-0339; www.accessiblejourneys.com) offers wheelchair travelers and their families and friends resources for travel.

Organizations that offer assistance to disabled travelers include **MossRehab** (www.mossresourcenet.org), which provides a library of accessible-travel resources online; **SATH (Society for Accessible Travel and Hospitality)** (☎ 212-447-7284; www.sath.org; annual membership fees: $45 adults, $30 seniors and students), which offers a wealth of travel resources (including *Open World Magazine,* with subscription rates of $13 per year, $21 outside the U.S.) for all types of disabilities and informed recommendations on destinations, access guides, travel agents, tour operators, vehicle rentals, and companion services; and the **American Foundation for the Blind** (AFB) (☎ 800-232-5463; www.afb.org), a referral resource for the blind or visually impaired that includes information on traveling with guide dogs.

For more information specifically targeted to travelers with disabilities, the community Web site **iCan** (www.icanonline.net/channels/travel/index.cfm) has destination guides and several regular columns on accessible travel. Also check out the quarterly magazine *Emerging Horizons* ($14.95 per year, $19.95 outside the U.S.; www.emerging horizons.com).

## Studying Up on Ireland: Advice for Students

With half of its population under 25, Ireland is accustomed to catering to students. Most attractions have student admission prices that are significantly lower than the usual prices, and many transportation companies offer students discounts. Some attractions and companies require the presentation of an official student ID card (instead of your regular university ID), so check out the ISE Card (International Student Exchange Card) at www.isecard.com or the ISIC (International Student Identity Card) at www.isiccard.com.

In the United States, **Council Travel** (☎ 800-226-8624; www.council travel.com) offers information on all sorts of student travel discounts. In Canada, **Travel CUTS** (☎ 800-667-2887 or 416-614-2997; www.travel cuts.com) does the same.

In Ireland, check out Council Travel's affiliate **USIT** (☎ 01-679-8833 in Ireland, ☎ 028-9032-4073 in Northern Ireland; www.usitnow.ie). There is also a branch of USIT in New York at 891 Amsterdam Ave. (☎ 212-663-5435).

# Following the Rainbow: Advice for Gay and Lesbian Travelers

Ireland is becoming more and more gay-friendly. Though some of the smaller towns may still have a negative reaction to homosexuality, the larger towns and cities — especially Dublin, Cork, and Galway — actively support their gay population and make gay visitors feel especially welcome.

Dublin in particular has a pretty thriving gay scene, with hotels, pubs, and clubs geared toward gay men and lesbians. **George,** 89 S. Great George's St. (☎ 01-478-2983), a huge pub and nightclub, is *the* place for gay men to gather.

Your guide to all things gay and lesbian is the *Gay Community News,* a free monthly newspaper devoted to the gay community. The paper is available in gay-oriented venues, especially bookshops, all over Ireland. In Dublin, the city's event listing guide has several pages listing gay events, organization, clubs, and the like.

**Gay Ireland** (www.gay-ireland.com) and **Outhouse** (www.outhouse.ie) are the best online resources for gay events, organizations, and information in Ireland.

The following organizations (all located in Dublin) offer all sorts of information for gay men and lesbians:

- ✔ **Outhouse,** 105 Capel St., Dublin 1 (☎ 01-873-4932; www.outhouse.ie)

- ✔ **Gay Switchboard Dublin** (☎ 01-872-1055; www.gayswitchboard.ie)

- ✔ **LOT (Lesbian Organizing Together),** 5 Capel St., Dublin 1 (☎ 01-872-7770)

**The International Gay and Lesbian Travel Association (IGLTA)** (☎ 800-448-8550 or 954-776-2626; www.iglta.org) is the trade association for the gay and lesbian travel industry and offers an online directory of gay- and lesbian-friendly travel businesses.

Many agencies offer tours and travel itineraries specifically for gay and lesbian travelers. **Above and Beyond Tours** (☎ 800-397-2681; www.abovebeyondtours.com) is the exclusive gay and lesbian tour operator for United Airlines. **Now, Voyager** (☎ 800-255-6951; www.nowvoyager.com) is a well-known San Francisco–based gay-owned and operated travel service. **Olivia Cruises & Resorts** (☎ 800-631-6277 or 510-655-0364; www.olivia.com) charters entire resorts and ships for exclusive lesbian vacations and offers smaller group experiences for both gay and lesbian travelers.

These travel guides are available at most travel bookstores and gay and lesbian bookstores, or you can order them from **Giovanni's Room** bookstore, 1145 Pine St., Philadelphia, PA 19107 (☎ **215-923-2960**; www. giovannisroom.com): *Frommer's Gay & Lesbian Europe* (Wiley) is an excellent travel resource (www.frommers.com); *Out and About* (☎ **800-929-2268** or 415-644-8044; www.outandabout.com) offers guidebooks and a newsletter ($20/yr; 10 issues) packed with solid information on the global gay and lesbian scene; *Spartacus International Gay Guide* (Bruno Gmünder Verlag; www.spartacusworld.com/gayguide/) and *Odysseus* (Damron Co.) are both good, annual English-language guidebooks focused on gay men; and the *Damron* guides (www.damron. com), with separate annual books for gay men and lesbians.

# Exploring Your Special Interests

Whether your tastes run to tracing family history or casting a line for salmon, here are some suggestions for travelers with special interests.

## Doing genealogy research

The Irish Tourist Board publishes a book called *Tracing Your Ancestors in Ireland,* which is available free from any Irish Tourist Board office. The best online sites to begin your search for records pertaining to your Irish ancestors are the **Irish National Archives** (www.nationalarchives.ie), which has a database of many of Ireland's records, and the **Irish Family History Foundation** (www.irishroots.net), where you can sift through records for free or hire a researcher to help you out.

You can dig through records in Ireland at the **Manuscripts Reading Room** in the National Library, Kildare St., Dublin 2 (☎ **01-603-0200**; www.nli.ie), and at **The National Archives,** Bishop Street, Dublin 8 (☎ **01-407-2333**). In Northern Ireland, hit **The Public Record Office of Northern Ireland,** 66 Ballmoral Ave., Belfast BT9 (☎ **028- 9025-1318**; www.proni.gov.uk).

You can also hire someone to research your roots for you. **Hibernian Research Co.,** P.O. Box 3097, Dublin 6 (☎ **01-496-6522**), and **ENECLANN,** Trinity College Resource Center, Pearse Street, Dublin 2 (☎ **01-671-0338**; www.eneclann.ie), are two of the finest family-research agencies.

See the Fast Facts listings in each chapter for genealogy services specific to that region.

## Rambling your way around Ireland by foot

Hiking (usually called *walking* or *hill-walking* in Ireland) is one of the very best ways to soak up the beauty of Ireland and Northern Ireland, whether you take off on a weeklong trek or go for an afternoon stroll. For detailed information on Ireland's long-distance marked trails (many of which are composed of a series of day hikes), visit **Walkireland**

# Connecting names and counties

Here are just a few popular Irish surnames and the counties where they originated. Many of these families later spread throughout the island and beyond. Each name has plenty of variations; for instance, FitzGerald has derivations of Fitzpatrick, Flanagan, Flynn, Fogarty, Foley, and Gaffney.

**Ahearne:** Clare, Limerick

**Butler:** Kilkenny

**Donoghue:** Cork, Kerry

**FitzGerald:** Cork, Kerry, Kildare

**MacCarthy:** Munster

**Maguire:** Ulster

**Martin:** Connaught

**Murphy:** Sligo, Tyrone, Wexford

**O'Brien:** Clare, Limerick

**O'Donnell:** Donegal

**O'Keeffe:** Cork

**O'Kelly:** Galway

**O'Neill:** Ulster

**O'Sullivan:** Tipperary

**Power:** Waterford, Wicklow

**Regan:** Dublin, Meath

**Ryan:** Limerick, Tipperary

**Walsh:** Dublin, Kilkenny, Leitrim, Waterford, Wicklow

What's in a name? Ages ago, the prefixes of Irish last names signified a great deal. *Mc* or *Fitz* meant "son of," and *O* before a name meant "grandson of" or "from the family of." So the name O'Brien means "ancestors of the Brien family" (in this case, the ancestors of Brian Boru, the most famous of the high kings of Ireland). You also occasionally see a name with an *Ní* prefix (such as Ní Dhomhnaill), but this configuration is, for the most part, archaic. Literally, it means "formerly of," as in Triona Briain Ní Dhomnaill, the name Triona might go by if she were a proud Dhomnaill who married a Briain.

(Waymarked Ways) at www.irishsportscouncil.ie/walkireland/. For information on walking and hiking in Northern Ireland, visit **Northern Ireland's Tourist Board** Web site (www.discovernorthern ireland.com), click on <u>Walking</u> under the Quick Activities Guide, then visit the walking and hiking page.

 *Walking Ireland — The Waymarked Ways* is a complete guide to walking trails in the country. You can pick it up at the Dublin Tourism Centre and other tourism offices for routes to the Wicklow Way, Royal Canal Way, Grand Canal Way, and 22 other trails throughout the country. The Northern Ireland Tourist Board's *An Information Guide to Walking* is another great resource. In addition, the **National Sports Council** (☎ 01-873-4700) has information on long-distance walking routes in the Republic, and the **Sports Council of Northern Ireland** (☎ 028-9038-1222) puts out Ulster Way leaflets detailing walking routes in the North.

You can also get hold of a number of excellent walking guidebooks, such as *Walking In Ireland* (Lonely Planet) and *Best Irish Walks* (McGraw-Hill). Good guides are also available from **An Óige**, the Irish Youth Hostel Organization, 61 Mountjoy St., Dublin 1 (☎ 01-830-4555; www.anoige. ie), and **YHANI**, Northern Ireland's Youth Hostel Association, 22 Donegal Rd., Belfast BT12 5JN (☎ 028-9031-5435). For detailed maps and route guides, contact **East West Mapping** (☎ and fax 054-77-835; homepage.eircom.net/~eastwest).

A number of companies offer hiking vacation packages. **Hidden Trails** (☎ 888/9-TRAILS; www.hiddentrails.com) offers weeklong guided and self-guided hiking tours in several regions in Ireland. For a guided hiking tour of the Burren, contact **Burren Walking Holidays** (☎ 065-707-4036). In the southwest, **SouthWest Walks Ireland** (☎ 066-712-8733) offers guided hiking vacations. For a full hiking package in County Clare and Connemara or County Kerry, contact **BCT Scenic Walking**, 227 North El Camino Rd., Encitas, CA 92024 (☎ 800-473-1210; www.bct walk.com).

Finally, there are a couple of walking festivals you can take part in. **The Wicklow Mountains Autumn Walking Festival** organizes day and night excursions for hikers of all abilities. The festival takes place in West County Wicklow toward the end of October. For more information, contact the **Wicklow County Tourism Office** in Kilmantin Hill, Wicklow (☎ 0404-20-070; www.wicklow.ie/tourism). The town of **Kenmare** in County Kerry usually holds a walking festival in May, with guided hikes through the Cork and Kerry Mountains. At press time, it is not clear whether this festival will take place. Call ☎ 064-42-639 to confirm.

## Teeing off on the greenest greens

Golf is the biggest sporting attraction in Ireland. To get a feel for the different courses and options, visit www.golf.travel.ie. For detailed information on 105 of Ireland's golf courses, visit www.golfcourse.com. You can find more golfing information at the Golfing Union of Ireland's Web site, www.gui.ie. (And for an itinerary of nothing but golf, see Chapter 4.)

**Specialty Ireland**, Castlemeadows, Murrintown, County Wexford (☎ 053-39-962; www.specialtyireland.com), can arrange itineraries that include visits to any of 27 championship golf courses and more than 400 other courses.

Many U.S. companies plan golf packages, including Atlantic Golf Company (☎ 800-542-6224 or 203-454-1086; www.atlanticgolf.com), Emerald Isle Golf Tours (☎ 800-446-8845 or 847-446-7885; www.emeraldislegolf tours.com); Golf International (☎ 800-833-1389 or 212-986-9176; www. golfinternational.com), and Wide World of Golf (☎ 800-214-4653 or 831-625-9671; www.wideworldofgolf.com).

## Bicycling around Ireland

Stunning scenery, short distances between towns, and many flat roads make Ireland a wonderful place for cycling. **Backroads** (☎ 800/GO-ACTIVE or 510/527-1555; www.backroads.com) and **VBT** (☎ 800/BIKE-TOUR; www.vbt.com) — both based in the United States — offer package bike vacations that include bikes, gear, luggage transportation, food, and accommodations. **Irish Cycling Safaris** (☎ 01-260-0749; www.cyclingsafaris.com) plans and outfits trips all over Ireland. **Irish Cycling Tours** (☎ 095-42-302; www.irishcyclingtours.com) offers both guided and self-guided tours in the West of Ireland.

If you want to create your own itinerary, you can rent a bike from an Irish company that permits one-way rentals. **Eurotrek Raleigh,** Longmile Road, Dublin 12 (☎ 01-465-9659; www.raleigh.ie), and **Rent-A-Bike Ireland,** 1 Patrick St., Limerick (☎ 061-416-983; www.irelandrentabike.com), are two reliable options. For independent cycling in southeast Ireland, contact **Celtic Cycling** (☎ 053-75-282; www.celticcycling.com).

## Fishing Ireland's waters

Ireland may be the best place in Europe to cast your line for salmon, sea trout, and brown trout. Salmon season is January 1 to September 30, brown-trout season is February 15 to October 12, and sea-trout season is June 1 to September 30. Course fishing and sea angling take place all year. Find details about fishing in Ireland at www.angling.travel.ie, and pick up the brochure *Angling in Ireland* from the Angling Information Office at the **Central Fisheries Board** (☎ 01-837-9206; www.cfb.ie), which also has information about fishing licenses. Check out **The Great Fishing Houses of Ireland** (www.irelandfishing.com) for information on hotels that have private lakes and ponds and offer fishing equipment and guides.

In Northern Ireland, you must get a rod license and often need a permit: Contact the **Department of Culture, Arts and Leisure,** Interpoint Center, York Street, Belfast BT4 3PW (☎ 028-9052-3434) for details. *An Information Guide to Game Fishing,* by the Northern Ireland Tourist Board, is full of useful suggestions.

## Sailing the Irish seas

Ireland's clear waters and Gulf Stream winds rival the Caribbean, so if you want to do some sailing, you're in luck. Contact or visit the Web site of the **Irish Sailing Association,** 3 Park Rd., Dun Laoghaire, County Dublin (☎ 01-280-0239; www.sailing.ie), for a list of approved teaching schools that rent boats.

The charming fishing village of Kinvarra, County Galway, hosts **Cruinniú na mBad** (literally, "Gathering of the Boats") at the end of August. The festival focuses on races among the majestic hooker sailboats that used to carry turf from port to port. Contact the **Galway Tourist Office** for information (☎ 091-53-77-00), or visit www.kinvara.com.

## Horseback riding

What could be more romantic than clip-clopping through the Irish countryside on horseback? For a list of horseback-riding outfitters, contact or visit the Web site of the **Association of Irish Riding Establishments,** 11 Moore Park, Newbridge, County Kildare (☎ 045-43-1584; www.aire.ie), in the Republic, or the **British Horse Society,** House of Sport, Upper Malone Road, Belfast (☎ 028-92-683-801; www.bhsireland.co.uk), in Northern Ireland. For a selection of horseback-riding vacation outfitters, visit the Web site of **Equestrian Holidays Ireland** at www.ehi.ie.

## Spectator sports

Spectator sports are hugely popular in Ireland. Many pubs, especially in larger cities, have the local game on — whether it's football (soccer), Gaelic football, hurling, or horse racing. Seeing a live sporting event is a quintessential Irish experience.

### Horse racing

Steeplechases are run year-round. The flat season (races without hurdles) is from mid-March to early November. The Irish Tourist Board draws up an Irish Racing Calendar every year. Here are some of the highlights:

- ✔ **The Dublin Horse Show:** The Horse Show is held during the first two weeks in August at the Royal Dublin Society (RDS) Showgrounds, Ballsbridge, Dublin 4. One of the biggest social and sporting events in the country, this show features the best show horses, riders, and jumpers in Ireland and awards the prestigious Aga Khan Trophy. See www.dublinhorseshow.com for more information.

- ✔ **Christmas Horse Racing Festival:** This late-December festival encompasses three days of Thoroughbred racing at Leopardstown Racetrack, in Dublin. Call ☎ 01-289-3607 for information or visit www.leopardstown.com.

- ✔ **Irish Grand National:** Three days of racing take place at Fairyhouse in County Meath. For information, call ☎ 01-825-6167 or visit www.fairyhouseracecourse.ie.

- ✔ **The Budweiser Irish Derby:** Three days of races are held in the Curragh, County Kildare, on the last Sunday in June or the first weekend in July. For information, contact the Curragh Racecourse Office at ☎ 045-441-205 or visit www.curragh.ie.

### Greyhound racing

Greyhound racing takes place around the country, usually Monday through Saturday at 8 and 10 p.m. The largest racetracks are the

Shelbourne Park Stadium in Dublin and Kingdom Greyhound Stadium in Tralee. For more information, visit the Irish Greyhound Board (www. igb.ie).

## Rugby, soccer, hurling, and Gaelic football

These four sports are played throughout the country. You're probably familiar with the first two, so I explain only the Ireland-specific sports. *Gaelic football* is a rough-and-tumble sport that combines the best aspects of American football, soccer, and rugby. *Hurling* is a fast-paced and thrilling game akin to field hockey or lacrosse played with a stick called a *hurley stick*. The game is traced to the pre-Christian folk hero Cuchulainn.

Big matches are played in Croke Park in Dublin City (north of O'Connell Street). You can get Gaelic-football and hurling schedule information from the Gaelic Athletic Association (GAA) at ☎ 01-836-3222 (www. gaa.ie). Soccer is called "football" in Ireland. You can get schedules and information for soccer from the Football Association of Ireland, 80 Merrion Sq., Dublin 2 (☎ 01-703-7500; www.fai.ie). For rugby schedules and information, go to www.irishrugby.ie or call ☎ 01-647-3800.

# Chapter 10

# Taking Care of the Remaining Details

● ● ● ● ● ● ● ● ● ● ● ● ● ● ● ● ● ● ● ● ● ● ● ● ● ● ● ● ● ● ● ● ● ● ● ● ● ● ● ● ● ● ● ●

## In This Chapter

▶ Figuring out passports

▶ Looking at travel and health insurance

▶ Keeping in touch with friends and family at home

▶ Bringing the correct electrical adapters

▶ Knowing what to expect regarding airline security

● ● ● ● ● ● ● ● ● ● ● ● ● ● ● ● ● ● ● ● ● ● ● ● ● ● ● ● ● ● ● ● ● ● ● ● ● ● ● ● ● ● ● ●

*N*ow that you're all excited to go to Ireland, here are some final tips on things like passports, insurance, and bringing the right electrical adapters.

## Getting a Passport

A valid passport is the only legal form of identification accepted around the world. You can't cross an international border without it. Getting a passport is easy, but the process takes some time.

### Applying for a U.S. passport

If you're applying for a first-time passport, follow these steps:

1. Complete a **passport application** in person at a U.S. passport office; a federal, state, or probate court; or a major post office. To find your regional passport office, check the **U.S. State Department** Web site, http://travel.state.gov/passport/index.html, or call the **National Passport Information Center** (☎ 877-487-2778) for automated information.

2. Present a **certified birth certificate** as proof of citizenship. (Bringing along your driver's license, state or military ID, or Social Security card is also a good idea.)

3. Submit **two identical passport-size photos,** measuring 2 by 2 inches. You often find businesses that take these photos near a

passport office. *Note:* You can't use a strip from a photo-vending machine because the pictures aren't identical.

4. Pay a **fee.** For people 16 and over, a passport is valid for ten years and costs $85. For those 15 and under, a passport is valid for five years and costs $70.

Allow plenty of time before your trip to apply for a passport; processing normally takes three weeks but can take longer during busy periods (especially spring).

If you have a passport in your current name that was issued within the past 15 years (and you were over age 16 when it was issued), you can renew the passport by mail for $55. Whether you're applying in person or by mail, you can download passport applications from the U.S. State Department Web site at http://travel.state.gov/passport/index. html. For general information, call the **National Passport Agency** (☎ 202-647-0518). To find your regional passport office, check the U.S. State Department Web site or call the **National Passport Information Center's** toll-free number (☎ 877-487-2778) for automated information.

## Applying for other passports

The following list offers more information for citizens of Australia, Canada, New Zealand, and the United Kingdom:

- ✔ **Australians** can visit a local post office or passport office, call the **Australia Passport Information Service** (☎ 131-232 toll-free from Australia), or log on to www.passports.gov.au for details on how and where to apply.

- ✔ **Canadians** can pick up applications at passport offices throughout Canada; at post offices; or from the central **Passport Office, Department of Foreign Affairs and International Trade,** Ottawa, ON K1A 0G3 (☎ 800-567-6868; www.ppt.gc.ca). Applications must be accompanied by two identical passport-size photographs and proof of Canadian citizenship. Processing takes five to ten days if you apply in person or about three weeks by mail.

- ✔ **New Zealanders** can pick up a passport application at any New Zealand Passports Office or download it from the office's Web site. For information, contact the **Passports Office** or download it from the office's Web site. Contact the **Passports Office** at ☎ 0800-225-050 in New Zealand or 04-474-8100, or log on to www.passports. govt.nz.

- ✔ **United Kingdom** residents can pick up applications for a standard ten-year passport (5-yr. passport for children under 16) at passport offices, major post offices, or a travel agency. For information, contact the **United Kingdom Passport Service** (☎ 0870-521 0410; www.ukpa.gov.uk).

# Playing It Safe with Travel and Medical Insurance

Three kinds of travel insurance are available: trip-cancellation insurance, medical insurance, and lost-luggage insurance. The cost of travel insurance varies widely, depending on the cost and length of your trip, your age and health, and the type of trip you're taking, but expect to pay between 5% and 8% of the vacation itself. Here is my advice on all three:

✔ **Trip-cancellation insurance** helps you get your money back if you have to back out of a trip, if you have to go home early, or if your travel supplier goes bankrupt. Allowed reasons for cancellation can range from sickness to natural disasters to the U.S. State Department's declaring your destination unsafe for travel. (Insurers usually don't cover vague fears, though, as many travelers discovered who tried to cancel their trips in October 2001 because they were wary of flying.)

A good resource is **Travel Guard Alerts,** a list of companies considered high-risk by Travel Guard International. You can find the list on the company's Web site (www.travelguard.com). Protect yourself further by paying for the insurance with a credit card — by law, consumers can get their money back on goods and services not received if they report the loss within 60 days after the charge is listed on their credit card statement.

*Note:* Many tour operators, particularly those offering trips to remote or high-risk areas, include insurance in the cost of the trip or can arrange insurance policies through a partnering provider, a convenient and often cost-effective way for the traveler to obtain insurance. Make sure the tour company is a reputable one, however: Some experts suggest you avoid buying insurance from the tour or cruise company you're traveling with, saying it's better to buy from a third-party insurer than to put all your money in one place.

✔ For domestic travel, buying **medical insurance** for your trip doesn't make sense for most travelers. Most existing health policies cover you if you get sick away from home — but check before you go, particularly if you're insured by an HMO.

For travel overseas, most health plans (including Medicare and Medicaid) do not provide coverage, and the ones that do often require you to pay for services up front and reimburse you only after you return home and file the necessary paperwork with your insurance company. As a safety net, you may want to buy travel medical insurance, particularly if you're traveling to a remote or high-risk area where emergency evacuation is a possible scenario. If you require additional medical insurance, try **MEDEX Assistance** (☎ **410-453-6300;** www.medexassist.com) or **Travel Assistance International** (☎ **800-821-2828;** www.travelassistance.com; for general information on services, call the company's Worldwide Assistance Services, Inc., at ☎ **800-777-8710**).

✔ **Lost-luggage insurance** is not necessary for most travelers. On domestic flights, checked baggage is covered up to $2,500 per ticketed passenger. On international flights (including U.S. portions of international trips), baggage coverage is limited to approximately $9.07 per pound, up to approximately $635 per checked bag. If you plan to check items more valuable than the standard liability, see whether your valuables are covered by your homeowner's policy, get baggage insurance as part of your comprehensive travel-insurance package, or buy Travel Guard's BagTrak product. Don't buy insurance at the airport — it's usually overpriced. Be sure to take any valuables or irreplaceable items with you in your carry-on luggage, as many valuables (including books, money, and electronics) aren't covered by airline policies.

If your luggage is lost, immediately file a lost-luggage claim at the airport, detailing the luggage contents. For most airlines, you must report delayed, damaged, or lost baggage within four hours of arrival. The airlines are required to deliver luggage, once found, directly to your house or destination free of charge.

For more information, contact one of the following recommended insurers: **Access America** (☎ **866-807-3982;** www.accessamerica.com), **Travel Guard International** (☎ **800-826-4919;** www.travelguard.com), **Travel Insured International** (☎ **800-243-3174;** www.travelinsured.com), and **Travelex Insurance Services** (☎ **888-457-4602;** www.travelex-insurance.com).

## Staying Healthy When You Travel

Getting sick will ruin your vacation, so I strongly advise against it (of course, last time I checked, the bugs weren't listening to me any more than they probably listen to you).

For domestic trips, most reliable health-care plans provide coverage if you get sick away from home. For travel abroad, you may have to pay all medical costs up front and be reimbursed later. For information on purchasing additional medical insurance for your trip, see the previous section.

Talk to your doctor before leaving on a trip if you have a serious and/or chronic illness. For conditions such as epilepsy, diabetes, or heart problems, wear a **MedicAlert identification tag** (☎ **888-633-4298;** www.medicalert.org), which immediately alerts doctors to your condition and gives them access to your records through Medic Alert's 24-hour hotline. Contact the **International Association for Medical Assistance to Travelers (IAMAT)** (☎ **716-754-4883** or, in Canada, 416-652-0137; www.iamat.org) for tips on travel and health concerns in the countries

## Avoiding economy-class syndrome

**Deep vein thrombosis** or, as it's known in the world of flying, *economy-class syndrome,* is a blood clot that develops in a deep vein. Symptoms include leg pain or swelling — even shortness of breath. This potentially deadly condition can be caused by sitting in cramped conditions — such as an airplane cabin — for too long.

During a flight (especially a long-haul flight), get up, walk around, and stretch your legs every 60 to 90 minutes to keep your blood flowing. Other preventive measures include frequent flexing of the legs while sitting, drinking lots of water, and avoiding alcohol and sleeping pills.

If you have a history of deep vein thrombosis, heart disease, or any other condition that puts you at high risk, some experts recommend wearing compression stockings or taking anticoagulants when you fly; always ask your physician about the best course for you.

you're visiting and lists of local English-speaking doctors. The United States **Centers for Disease Control and Prevention** (☎ 800-311-3435; www.cdc.gov) provides up-to-date information on health hazards by region or country and offers tips on food safety.

## *Communicating with the Folks Back Home*

This section helps you figure out the best ways to stay in touch while you're away from home.

### *Using a cellphone abroad*

The three letters that define much of the world's **wireless capabilities** are GSM (Global System for Mobiles), a big, seamless network that makes for easy cross-border cellphone use throughout Europe and dozens of other countries worldwide. In the United States, T-Mobile, AT&T Wireless, and Cingular use this quasi-universal system; in Canada, Microcell and some Rogers customers are GSM, and all Europeans and most Australians use GSM.

If your cellphone is on a GSM system, and you have a world-capable multi-band phone (such as many Sony Ericsson, Motorola, or Samsung models), you can make and receive calls across civilized areas on much of the globe, from Andorra to Uganda. Just call your wireless operator, and ask to have international roaming activated on your account. Unfortunately, per-minute charges can be high — usually $1 to $1.50 in Western Europe and up to $5 in places like Russia and Indonesia.

That's why it's important to buy an unlocked world phone from the get-go. Many cellphone operators sell *locked* phones that restrict you from using any other removable computer memory phone chip card (called a *SIM card*) other than the ones they supply. Having an *unlocked* phone allows you to install a cheap, prepaid SIM card (available at a local retailer) in your destination country. (Show your phone to the salesperson; not all phones work on all networks.) You get a local phone number — and much, much lower calling rates. Getting an already locked phone unlocked can be a complicated process, but it can be done; just call your cellular operator, and say you'll be going abroad for several months and want to use the phone with a local provider.

For many, **renting** a phone is a good idea. While you can rent a phone from any number of overseas sites, including kiosks at airports and at car-rental agencies, I suggest renting the phone before you leave home. That way, you can give loved ones and business associates your new number, make sure the phone works, and take the phone wherever you go — especially helpful for overseas trips through several countries, where local phone-rental agencies often bill in local currency and may not let you take the phone to another country.

Phone rental isn't cheap. You usually pay $40 to $50 per week, plus airtime fees of at least a dollar a minute. If you're traveling to Europe, though, local rental companies often offer free incoming calls within their home country, which can save you big bucks. The bottom line: Shop around.

Two good wireless rental companies are **InTouch USA** (☎ **800-872-7626**; www.intouchglobal.com) and **RoadPost** (☎ **888-290-1606** or 905-272-5665; www.roadpost.com). Give them your itinerary, and they'll tell you what wireless products you need. InTouch will also, for free, advise you on whether your existing phone will work overseas; simply call ☎ **703-222-7161** between 9 a.m. and 4 p.m. EST, or go to http://intouchglobal.com/travel.htm. In Ireland, **Rent A Phone Ireland** (www.rentaphone-ireland.com) will send a phone to the first B&B or hotel you're staying in, so you can get it as soon as you get to Ireland.

## Using pay phones

You can find two types of pay phones in Ireland: coin phones and card phones. Both kinds of phones are spread throughout the country, and you may even see them side by side.

If you use a coin phone, read the directions before you start feeding in coins. Some phones require putting the coins in before you dial; others have you put in the coins after the other party answers. Have change in hand while you're on your call — the phone gives an extremely short warning before disconnecting.

Got no calling card? Got no change? Got no problem. The Irish have phone cards that work the same as those in the United States, like a debit card, and you can get one in many shops or at a post office. Phone cards come in varying denominations. What's different about the Irish version is that you use the phone card in its own phone booth, designated by the sign *Cardphone.* When you enter the booth, slide the card in the slot like you would a credit card. There's a screen on the phone that says how many units the card has left. The units decrease while you're on the phone, so you know how much time is left before you're hung up on. No more "Time'supI'lltalktoyoulatergoodb–."

Numbers beginning with 800 within Ireland are called *Freephone numbers* and are toll-free, but calling a toll-free number in the United States from Ireland is not free. In fact, doing so costs the same as a regular overseas call.

Making calls before or after Irish business hours (8 a.m. to 6 p.m.) is much cheaper. This is sometimes tough to finesse when calling North America because of the time difference, but it will save you some bucks if you can swing it. (Ireland is five time zones ahead of the U.S. East Coast, so when it's noon in New York, it's 5 p.m. in Ireland, and when it's noon in Los Angeles, it's 8 p.m. in Ireland.)

## Using a U.S. calling card

AT&T, MCI, and Sprint calling cards all operate worldwide, so using any of them in Ireland is no problem (though hotel rooms sometimes block these numbers, so you may need to call via pay phone). Each card has a local access number, which saves you the cost of dialing directly to the United States. When you want to use your card in the Republic of Ireland, just call ☎ 1800-55-0000 for **AT&T,** ☎ 1800-55-1001 for **MCI,** and ☎ 1800-55-2001 for **Sprint.** In Northern Ireland, call ☎ 0500-89-0011 for **AT&T,** ☎ 0800-89-0222 for **MCI,** and ☎ 0800-89-0877 for **Sprint.** The operator will then explain how to make the call.

If you have a calling card with a company other than one of the three I named, contact the company before you go on the trip to see whether it has a local access number in Ireland. Whatever card you have, call the company before you go on your trip to see whether it has a discount plan for calling overseas.

## Accessing the Internet

Travelers have any number of ways to check their e-mail and access the Internet on the road. Of course, using your own laptop — or even a PDA (personal digital assistant) or electronic organizer with a modem — gives you the most flexibility. But even if you don't have a computer, you can still access your e-mail and even your office computer from a cybercafe.

It's hard nowadays to find a city that *doesn't* have a few cybercafes. Although there's no definitive directory for cybercafes — these are independent businesses, after all — two places to start looking are www.cybercaptive.com and www.cybercafe.com.

Aside from formal cybercafes, most **youth hostels** nowadays have at least one computer you can use to get to the Internet. And most **public libraries** across the world offer Internet access free or for a small charge. Avoid **hotel business centers** unless you're willing to pay exorbitant rates.

Most major airports now have **Internet kiosks** scattered throughout their gates. These kiosks, which you also see in shopping malls, hotel lobbies, and tourist information offices around the world, give you basic Web access for a per-minute fee that's usually higher than cybercafe prices. The kiosks' clunkiness and high price mean they should be avoided whenever possible.

To retrieve your e-mail, ask your **Internet service provider (ISP)** if it has a Web-based interface tied to your existing e-mail account. If your ISP doesn't have such an interface, you can use the free **mail2web** service (www.mail2web.com) to view and reply to your home e-mail. For more flexibility, you may want to open a free, Web-based e-mail account with **Yahoo! Mail** (http://mail.yahoo.com). (Microsoft's Hotmail is another popular option, but Hotmail has severe spam problems.) Your home ISP may be able to forward your e-mail to the Web-based account automatically.

If you need to access files on your office computer, look into a service called **GoToMyPC** (www.gotomypc.com). The service provides a Web-based interface for you to access and manipulate a distant PC from anywhere — even a cybercafe — provided your target PC is on and has an always-on connection to the Internet (such as with Road Runner cable). The service offers top-quality security, but if you're worried about hackers, use your own laptop rather than a cybercafe computer to access the GoToMyPC system.

If you're bringing your own computer, the buzzword in computer access to familiarize yourself with is *Wi-fi* (wireless fidelity), and more and more hotels, cafes, and retailers are signing on as wireless hotspots from where you can get high speed connection without cable wires, networking hardware, or a phone line. You can get Wi-fi connection in one of several ways. Many laptops sold in the past year have built-in Wi-fi capability (an 802.11b wireless Ethernet connection). Mac owners have their own networking technology, Apple AirPort. For those with older computers, an 802.11b/Wi-fi card (around $50) can be plugged into your laptop.

You sign up for wireless access service much as you do cellphone service, through a plan offered by one of several commercial companies that have made wireless service available in airports, hotel lobbies, and coffee shops, primarily in the United States (followed by the U.K. and Japan). **Boingo** (www.boingo.com) and **Wayport** (www.wayport.com) have networks in airports and high-end hotel lobbies. iPass providers (www.ipass.com) also give you access to a few hundred wireless hotel lobby setups. Best of all, you don't need to be staying at the Four Seasons to use the hotel's network; just set yourself up on a nice couch in the lobby. The companies' pricing policies can be byzantine, with a variety of monthly, per-connection, and per-minute plans, but in general you pay around $30 a month for limited access — and as more and more companies jump on the wireless bandwagon, prices are likely to get even more competitive.

Some companies provide **free wireless networks** in cities around the world. To locate these free hotspots, go to www.personaltelco.net/index.cgi/WirelessCommunities.

If Wi-fi is not available at your destination, most business-class hotels throughout the world offer dataports for laptop modems, and a few thousand hotels in the United States and Europe now offer free high-speed Internet access using an Ethernet network cable. You can bring your own cables, but most hotels rent them for around $10. Call your hotel in advance to see what your options are.

In addition, major ISPs have **local access numbers** around the world, allowing you to go online by simply placing a local call. Check your ISP's Web site or call its toll-free number, and ask how you can use your current account away from home and how much it will cost.

If you're traveling outside the reach of your ISP, the **iPass** network has dial-up numbers in most of the world's countries. You have to sign up with an iPass provider, which then tells you how to set up your computer for your destination(s). For a list of iPass providers, go to www.ipass.com, and click on <u>Reseller Locator</u>. One solid provider is **i2roam** (www.i2roam.com; ☎ **866-811-6209** or 920-235-0475).

Wherever you go, bring a **connection kit** of the right power and phone adapters, a spare phone cord, and a spare Ethernet network cable — or find out whether your hotel supplies them to guests. I talk more about electrical current later in this chapter.

## Sending and receiving snail mail in the Republic and Northern Ireland

You do know you'll be hard-pressed to get someone to pick you up at the airport if you don't send home any postcards, right? Post offices in the Republic are called *An Post* (www.letterpost.ie for general information) and are easy to spot: Look for a bright green storefront with the name across it. Ireland's main postal branch, the **General Post Office (GPO)**, on O'Connell Street, Dublin 1 (☎ **01-872-6666**), is in the heart of Dublin and is the hub of all mail activity. Its hours are 8 a.m. to 8 p.m. Monday through Saturday and 10:30 a.m. to 6:30 p.m. Sunday (for stamps only). Major branches, located in the bigger towns and cities, are open 9 a.m. to 5:30 p.m. Monday through Friday and 9 a.m. to 1:30 p.m. Saturday. Minor branches, which are in every small town, are open 9 a.m. to 1 p.m. and 2:30 to 5:30 p.m. Monday through Friday, and 9 a.m. to 1 p.m. Saturday. Irish post offices sell phone cards and lottery tickets, and you can even change money at main branches.

From the Republic, mailing an air-mail letter or postcard costs €.57 (66¢). It usually takes mail about a week to get to the United States. If you plan to mail packages, you can save money by sending them economy, or surface, mail. This idea comes in handy when mailing things to yourself.

Sending mail from Northern Ireland is just as easy. Up north, the post offices are called Post Offices, and the offices and post boxes are bright red. The general hours are the same as those of An Post, too. The cost to send a letter is 39p (72¢); the cost to send a postcard is 34p (63¢).

If you need mail sent to you while on your trip in Ireland, no problem. Just have the sender address the mail with your name, care of the General Post Office, Restante Office, and the town name (for instance, Joe Smith, c/o General Post Office, Restante Office, Galway, Ireland). Your mail will be held there for you to pick up for 30 days. Only larger post office branches provide this service.

## Figuring Out Electricity in Ireland

Electricity in the Republic of Ireland operates on 220 volts with a three-pronged plug, and electricity in Northern Ireland operates on 250 volts. To use American 110-volt appliances, you need a transformer and a plug adapter (a three-pronged adapter for the Republic and a two-pronged one for the North).

Some travel appliances, such as shavers and irons, have a nice feature called *dual voltage* that adapts to the change, but unless your appliance gives a voltage range (such as 110v to 220v), don't chance it. Most laptop computers have this feature, but always check with the manufacturer as a precaution. Plug adapters are not hard to find; your local hardware store or even the airport should have what you need. For more information, check out www.walkabouttravelgear.com or call the **Franzus Corporation** (☎ 203-723-6664) for its pamphlet on foreign electricity. Many laptops have transformers built in, so check before you buy one.

 If you plan on bringing a video camera, bring enough battery packs and also enough videotape. VHS cassette tapes in Ireland look identical to the ones from home, but they won't work in your camera.

# Keeping Up with Airline Security

With the federalization of airport security, security procedures at U.S. airports are more stable and consistent than ever. Generally, you'll be fine if you arrive at the airport **1 hour** before a domestic flight and **2 hours** before an international flight; if you show up late, tell an airline employee, and she'll probably whisk you to the front of the line.

Bring a **current, government-issued photo ID** such as a driver's license or passport. Keep your ID at the ready to show at check-in, the security checkpoint, and sometimes even the gate. (Children under 18 do not need government-issued photo IDs for domestic flights, but they do for international flights to most countries.)

In 2003, the TSA (Transportation Security Administration) phased out gate check-in at all U.S. airports. And **E-tickets** have made paper tickets nearly obsolete. Passengers with E-tickets can beat the ticket-counter lines by using airport **electronic kiosks** or even **online check-in** from your home computer. Online check-in involves logging on to your airlines' Web site, accessing your reservation, and printing out your boarding pass — and the airline may even offer you bonus miles to do so! If you're using a kiosk at the airport, bring the credit card you used to book the ticket or your frequent-flier card. Print out your boarding pass from the kiosk, and simply proceed to the security checkpoint with your pass and a photo ID. If you're checking bags or looking to snag an exit-row seat, you can do so by using most airline kiosks. Even the smaller airlines are employing the kiosk system, but always call your airline to make sure these alternatives are available. **Curbside check-in** is also a good way to avoid lines, although a few airlines still ban curbside check-in; call before you go.

Security checkpoint lines are getting shorter than they were during 2001 and 2002, but some doozies remain. If you have trouble standing for long periods of time, tell an airline employee; the airline will provide a wheelchair. Speed up security by not wearing metal objects such as big belt buckles. If you've got metallic body parts, a note from your doctor can prevent a long chat with the security screeners. Keep in mind that only ticketed passengers are allowed past security, except for folks escorting disabled passengers or children.

Federalization has stabilized what you can carry on and what you can't. The general rule is that sharp things are out, nail clippers are okay, and food and beverages must be passed through the X-ray machine — but that security screeners can't make you drink from your coffee cup. Bring food in your carry-on rather than checking it, as explosive-detection machines used on checked luggage have been known to mistake food (especially chocolate, for some reason) for bombs. Travelers in the United States are allowed one carry-on bag, plus a personal item such as a purse, briefcase, or laptop bag. Carry-on hoarders can stuff all sorts of things into a laptop bag; as long as it has a laptop in it, it's still considered a personal item. The Transportation Security Administration (TSA) has issued a list of restricted items; check its Web site (www.tsa.gov/public/index.jsp) for details.

Airport screeners may decide that your checked luggage needs to be searched by hand. You can now purchase luggage locks that allow screeners to open and re-lock a checked bag if hand-searching is necessary. Look for Travel Sentry certified locks at luggage or travel shops and Brookstone stores (you can buy them online at www.brookstone.com). These locks, approved by the TSA, can be opened by luggage inspectors with a special code or key. For more information on the locks, visit www.travelsentry.org. If you use something other than TSA-approved locks, your lock will be cut off your suitcase if a TSA agent needs to hand-search your luggage.

# Part III
# Dublin and the East Coast

The 5<sup>th</sup> Wave                          By Rich Tennant

"OK—we got one cherry lager with bitters and a pineapple slice, and one honey malt ale with cinnamon and an orange twist. You want these in steins or parfait glasses?"

# In this part . . .

**D**ublin City and the surrounding areas offer attractions that run from quiet mountain towns to hot, trendy clubs. Vibrant Dublin City is home to several excellent museums, an array of fabulous restaurants serving everything from fish and chips to gourmet fusion meals, and a varied and hopping nightlife scene. Just north of the city are Counties Meath and Louth, where you find some of Ireland's most magnificent ancient ruins (see Chapter 12). To the south are Wicklow and Kildare, two counties filled with gardens and estates, mountains, horses (especially in Kildare), and loads of that gorgeous Irish green. You won't want for outdoor activities in these parts. See Chapter 13 for more.

The southeastern counties of Wexford, Waterford, Tipperary, and Kilkenny offer an array of places to see and things to do. Some highlights are driving along the coast and through sweet fishing villages in Wexford; watching Waterford Crystal being created; exploring the Rock of Cashel in Tipperary; and wandering the medieval streets of Kilkenny. See Chapter 14 for more information.

# Chapter 11

# Dublin

. . . . . . . . . . . . . . . . . . . . . . . . . . . . . . . . . . . . . . . . . .

. . . . . . . . . . . . . . . . . . . . . . . . . . . . . . . . . . . . . . . . . .

*W*alking down a street in Dublin (see the nearby "Dublin and the East Coast" map) filled with hip young things heading for an after-work pub visit, you could be in any cosmopolitan city in the world. Dublin has undergone major changes in the past 15 years or so. The strong software and communications economy (dubbed the Celtic Tiger by locals) pumped money into the city, and the European Economic Community (now the European Union) showered grants on Ireland and on Dublin in particular. Though the Celtic Tiger's roar has died down to a purr, the economic pendulum is still on the upswing, and Dublin remains one of Europe's trendiest cities. Dublin's population has gotten younger, and the twenty-something and thirty-something Dubs are helping create and support vibrant, cutting-edge arts, dining, clubbing, and shopping scenes. Many of the hot restaurants, hotels, pubs, theaters, galleries, and clubs that opened in the nineties and early naughts are still going strong, the streets are bustling, and the city continues to change at a breakneck speed — just count the number of building cranes on the horizon.

But Dublin is not all new, new, new. Spend a few hours strolling the heart of Dublin, and you start to feel a palpable sense of the city's thousand-year history. Those hip young things are crowding into pubs that natives from two centuries ago would recognize; walking down cobblestone streets as they talk on their cellphones; and sitting on benches in Trinity College, which was founded in 1591, as they sip their organic smoothies. You may also start to feel that Dublin is more of a lively and bustling large town than a city. The heart of the city is small, the entire greater Dublin area is home to only 1.5 million people, and the Dubs themselves are often friendly and helpful in a way that you might expect in a small town — directing travelers to bus stops; striking up chats in a pub.

## County Dublin and the East Coast

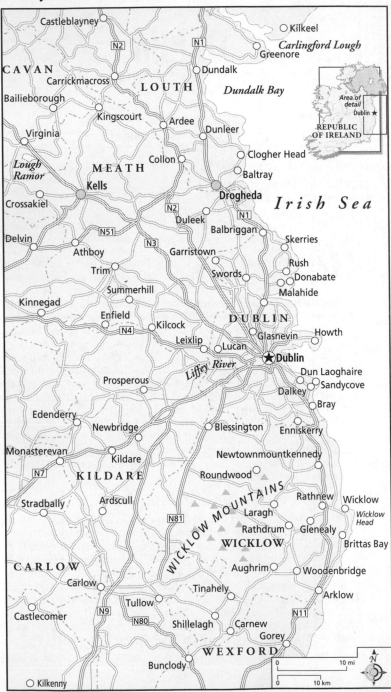

Castleblayney
Kilkeel
N2
N1
*Carlingford Lough*
Greenore
CAVAN
Dundalk
Carrickmacross
LOUTH
*Dundalk Bay*
Bailieborough
Kingscourt
Ardee
Dunleer
Virginia
Clogher Head
Collon
MEATH
Baltray
*Lough Ramor*
Kells
Crossakiel
Drogheda
*Irish Sea*
N2
Duleek
Delvin
N51
Balbriggan
N1
Athboy
N3
Garristown
Skerries
Trim
Rush
Summerhill
Swords
Donabate
Kinnegad
Malahide
Enfield
N4
Kilcock
DUBLIN
Leixlip
Glasnevin
Howth
Lucan
*Liffey River*
★Dublin
Prosperous
Dun Laoghaire
Dalkey
Sandycove
Bray
Edenderry
Blessington
Enniskerry
Newbridge
Monasterevan
Newtownmountkennedy
Kildare
N7
Roundwood
KILDARE
Stradbally
Ardscull
Rathnew
Wicklow
N81
Laragh
*Wicklow Head*
Rathdrum
Glenealy
Brittas Bay
WICKLOW
CARLOW
Aughrim
Woodenbridge
Carlow
Tinahely
Arklow
Tullow
N9
N11
Castlecomer
N80
Shillelagh
Carnew
Gorey
WEXFORD
Bunclody
0        10 mi
Kilkenny
0        10 km
N

Area of detail
Dublin ★
REPUBLIC OF IRELAND

This coexistence of old and new is part of Dublin's appeal. You can explore some of the city's many historical attractions — the Book of Kells, Trinity College, Christ Church Cathedral, and many more — by day and then sit down to a fusion cuisine meal at a hot restaurant before joining the hordes of glittery pub- and club-crawlers.

# Getting to Dublin

Dublin is one of Ireland's two main international gateways, so if you're flying to the country, there's a good chance you'll be touching down here. Dublin is also well connected to the rest of the country by bus, train, and ferry routes.

## By plane

**Dublin International Airport** (☎ 01-814-1111; www.dublin-airport. com) is 11km (7 miles) north of the city, about a 25-minute to 45-minute drive from the city center (*An Lar* in Gaelic). Aer Lingus, Continental, Delta, and American fly directly into Dublin from the United States. British Midlands, Aer Lingus, CityJet, Lufthansa, and Ryanair have regular flights from England. See Chapter 6 for more on flights into Ireland.

In the Arrivals Concourse, you'll find an excellent Travel Information Desk that can help you figure out how to get to your destination, desks for the major car-rental companies listed in Chapter 7, and ATMs.

Taxis are available outside the arrival terminal's main entrance — just look for the signs. The fare to downtown Dublin is about €13 to €19 ($15 to $22), and the trip takes 20 to 40 minutes, depending on traffic. You should tip between 10% and 15%.

**AirCoach** (☎ 01-844-7118; www.aircoach.ie) runs at 15-minute intervals every 24 hours from Dublin airport to various stops in Dublin's city center and south side. The fee is €6 ($6.90) one-way. **Dublin Bus** (☎ 01-872-0000; www.dublinbus.ie) has several routes between the airport and the city center; check with the Travel Information Desk in the Arrivals Concourse to figure out which one to use. If you are looking to catch a bus or train out of Dublin immediately, the **Airlink Express Coach** (☎ 01-873-4222) travels to the city bus station and the two city train stations. The Airlink runs every 20 to 30 minutes daily from 7 a.m. to 11 p.m. (Sun 7:30 a.m.–8:30 p.m.) and costs €5 ($5.75) adults, and €2 ($2.30) children under 12. Finally, some of the larger hotels offer an airport pickup service for guests.

## By ferry

A number of ferry companies have routes to Dublin from harbors in Wales and England. Ferries dock either at **Dublin Ferryport** (☎ 01-855-2222) or at **Dun Laoghaire** (pronounced dun *leer*-ee) **Ferryport**, less than 13km (8 miles) from Dublin. Public transportation into the city is available from both ports. See "Getting to Ireland by Ferry" in Chapter 6 for a listing of ferry companies and the ports that they serve.

## By train

Iarnród Éireann (pronounced ee-*arn*-rod *air*-an), or **Irish Rail** (☎ 01-836-6222; www.irishrail.ie), runs between Dublin and the major towns and cities of Ireland, including Belfast in Northern Ireland. Trains arrive at one of three stations: Connolly Station on Amiens Street (serving trains from the North and Northwest, including Northern Ireland); Heuston Station on Kingsbridge, off St. John's Road (serving trains from the South, Southwest, and West); and Pearse Station on Westland Row, Tara Street (serving trains from the Southeast). The **DART** (Dublin Area Rapid Transit) (☎ 01-836-6222; www.irishrail.ie) commuter train connects the city to the suburban towns north of Dublin City (as far as Balbriggan) and south of the city (as far as Greystones).

## By bus

Ireland's bus system, **Bus Éireann** (☎ 01-836-6111; www.buseireann.ie), runs between Dublin and most cities and towns in the Republic. The city's bus terminal, called **Busaras,** is on Store Street, three blocks east of O'Connell Street, north of the river behind the Trading House building.

## By car

N1, N2, and N3 lead into Dublin from the North; N4 and N7 lead in from the West, and N11 leads into the city from the South. The M50 is Dublin's beltway, surrounding three sides of the city and linking most major routes into and out of town. Once you get into Dublin, you should return your rental car or leave it in your hotel parking lot, and use your feet, public transportation, and taxis to see the city.

# Orienting Yourself in Dublin

The thin ribbon of the River Liffey divides Dublin into north and south sides. On the north side, the main thoroughfare is wide O'Connell Street, which leads up to Parnell Square. Along the river on the south side is hopping Temple Bar, which is filled with pubs, arts venues, and restaurants. Nearby Nassau Street runs along the Trinity College campus and intersects with Grafton Street, a bustling pedestrian street that leads up to St. Stephen's Green, a popular park. See the neighborhood breakdown in this section for more details.

A few words on street names: They have a tendency to change when you least expect it. One minute, you're on Aungiers Street; the next, you're on South Great George's Street. Did you make a turn without knowing it? No, that's just how the streets are in Dublin, so trust your sense of direction.

All Dublin address include a digit after the word *Dublin,* as in *General Post Office, O'Connell Street, Dublin 1.* These numbers are postal codes, similar to American zip codes. Most of central Dublin is located within postal codes 1, 2, and 8. Odd numbers are north of the River Liffey, and even numbers are south of it.

## Introducing the neighborhoods

Here is a breakdown of Dublin's central city neighborhoods, from trendy Temple Bar to posh Merrion and Fitzwilliam squares:

- **O'Connell Street Area (north side of the Liffey):** Although this area once thrived as the most fashionable part of the city, it's now something of an aging starlet, with many of its buildings in need of repair. Between stately buildings such as the **General Post Office** and **Gresham Hotel** are fast-food joints, movie theaters, and souvenir shops. However, efforts are being made to rejuvenate this area, and the silvery sky-scraping **Millennium Spire** (affectionately called "the stiletto in the ghetto") is a reminder that things are changing. O'Connell Street's center median is home to impressive statues of noted Irishmen, and at the top of the street, you find the serene **Garden of Remembrance,** the excellent **Hugh Lane Municipal Gallery of Modern Art,** and the interesting **Dublin Writers Museum.** A few blocks to the east of O'Connell Street are the famous **Abbey Theatre** and the well-done **James Joyce Centre;** to the west are the bustling shopping streets of Henry, Moore, and Abbey.

- **Trinity College Area (south side):** Just across O'Connell Bridge on the south side of the River Liffey stands **Trinity College.** This sprawling campus of green lawns and old buildings sits in the heart of the city and is surrounded by classy bookstores and shops.

- **Temple Bar (south side):** Tucked into a spot between Trinity and Dublin Castle is the funky and fashionable Temple Bar, where you find hip shops, pubs, and arts venues along cobbled alleys. This area is always bustling and hosts a number of excellent weekend markets, including a book market, a fashion market, and an organic food market.

- **Old City–Historical Area (south side):** This historical area boasts narrow streets and ancient buildings, some dating as far back as Viking and medieval times. Some highlights are **Dublin Castle, Christ Church Cathedral, St. Patrick's Cathedral,** and the **old city walls.** A bit further on is the **Guinness Storehouse** (described later in this chapter in the "Exploring Dublin" section).

- **St. Stephen's Green and Grafton Street (south side):** This area begins at the bottom of the pedestrian Grafton Street, with its many trendy clothing stores and its variety of street performers, and finishes up in St. Stephen's Green — Dublin's favorite park. This pretty part of town has plenty of upscale shops and cafes, and is always teeming with people.

✔ **Merrion and Fitzwilliam squares (south side):** These two square parks are surrounded by some of Dublin's most beautiful Georgian townhouses, each with a distinctive, brightly colored door. Some were once the homes of Dublin's most famous citizens, but today, many of them house professional offices. Some big names from Dublin's past lived on Merrion Square, including the poet W. B. Yeats, Irish nationalist leader Daniel O'Connell, and writer Oscar Wilde.

## Finding information after you arrive

**Dublin Tourism** (☎ 01-605-7700; www.visitdublin.com) runs four walk-in visitor centers around the center of the city. The largest and best is on Suffolk Street, Dublin 2, and is open September to June Monday through Saturday 9 a.m. to 5:30 p.m., and July and August Monday through Saturday 9 a.m. to 7 p.m. and Sunday 10:30 a.m. to 3 p.m. The others are at the **Arrivals Hall** at the Dublin airport (open daily 8 a.m. to 10 p.m.); at **Exclusively Irish** at O'Connell St., Dublin 1 (open Mon to Sat 9 a.m. to 5 p.m.; closed Sun); and **Baggott Street Bridge**, Baggott Street, Dublin 2 (open Mon to Fri 9:30 a.m.–noon and 12:30–5 p.m.; closed weekends).

For information on events once you get to Dublin, pick up a copy of the *InDublin* magazine or *The Event Guide* newspaper, available at the visitors' centers and around Dublin.

# Getting Around Dublin

The best way to see Dublin is to lace up a good pair of shoes and hoof it. The center of the city is compact and easily walkable. For attractions that are not within walking distance, take advantage of the excellent bus network. Even if you ignore the rest of this book, heed these words: Don't explore Dublin by car. The slow traffic and confusing streets are a study in frustration, and parking is expensive and out of the way.

Remember that the Irish drive on the left side of the road, so look right first before stepping into the street.

## By bus

**Dublin Bus,** 59 Upper O'Connell St., Dublin 1 (☎ 01-872-0000; www.dublinbus.ie), operates double-decker buses, regular buses, and *imps* (minibuses) throughout Dublin city and its suburbs, with fares under €2 ($2.30). The destination and bus number are posted in the windshield; buses going towards the city center read *An Lar,* which is Irish Gaelic for "center city." You find bus stops every two or three blocks, and most bus routes pass down O'Connell Street, Abbey Street, and Eden Quay on the north side of the river and down Westmoreland Street, Nassau Street, and Aston Quay on the south side. Buses run every 10 to 15 minutes Monday through Saturday 6 a.m. to 11:30 p.m. and Sunday 10 a.m.

to 11:30 p.m. A late-night bus service runs on a limited route Thursday, Friday, and Saturday from midnight to 3 a.m.

 The buses accept exact change only, so have your loose change at the ready. If you pay more than the required amount, you get a coupon for a refund that you can redeem at the Dublin Bus headquarters at 59 Upper O'Connell St. Discount one-day, three-day, five-day, and seven-day passes are available at Dublin Bus headquarters.

## By taxi

To get a taxi in Dublin, go to a taxi rank, where cabs line up along the street, or hail a cab by sticking out your arm. If the cab's roof light is on, it means that the cab is unoccupied and ready to pick up passengers. If possible, take a cab with a meter and a roof sign; unmarked cabs may overcharge you. There are taxi ranks at large hotels, train stations, the bus station, the O'Connell Street median near the General Post Office, opposite St. Stephen's Green shopping center, and near Trinity College on Dame Street. You can also call a cab; reliable companies include **Cab Charge** (☎ 01-677-2222), **Co-op** (☎ 01-676-6666), and **VIP Taxis** (☎ 01-478-3333).

 In Ireland, passengers usually sit up front with the driver, rather than in the back seat chauffeur-style.

## By train

The **DART** commuter train (☎ 1850-366-222; www.irishrail.ie) connects the city to suburbs and coastal towns both north (as far as Balbriggan) and south (as far as Greystones), and is quite a bargain for a day-trip to a nearby town. The three stops in Dublin's city center are Connolly Station, Pearse Street Station, and Tara Street Station. It's not usually worth it to take the DART within the city center, because the three stops are within such easy walking distance of one another. The DART runs every 5 to 20 minutes from 6:30 a.m. to 11:45 p.m. Monday through Saturday and from 9 a.m. to about 11:00 p.m. Sunday. Tickets are on sale in each station. See the Cheat Sheet in the front of this book for a DART map. The shortest journeys come in at €1 ($1.15) each way, with trips to nearby seaside towns costing around €2.10 ($2.40) each way.

## By car

If you are completely ignoring me and driving in Dublin anyway, remember to avoid parking in bus lanes or along curbs with double yellow lines — these are easy ways to get your tires clamped by parking officials. To park on the streets in Dublin, buy parking discs at one of the black vending machines along the street, and display a disc in the window of your car. There are parking lots (called *car parks*) at Kildare Street, Lower Abbey Street, Marlborough Street, and St. Stephen's Green West.

# Spending the Night in Dublin

As Dublin becomes more and more hip and cosmopolitan, trendy (and expensive) hotels are springing up to cater to the likes of Gwyneth Paltrow, Cate Blanchett, and Julia Roberts, all regular visitors to the city. If you're looking for luxury, Dublin offers an embarrassment of riches. If that trust fund hasn't turned up yet, your accommodation options are more limited, because central Dublin lacks the cozy, inexpensive B&Bs found in abundance across the rest of Ireland. But fear not: This section points you to some of the best lodging deals in the city — check the "Dublin Accommodations and Dining" and "Temple Bar" maps for locations.

 Unlike accommodations in the rest of the country, Dublin hotels don't significantly lower prices during the off season (Oct through April). However, many lodgings offer weekend or midweek packages, so ask. See Chapter 8 for more tips and information on finding and booking various types of accommodations.

Many of the accommodations listed here have free or discounted parking, and all include breakfast in their prices unless otherwise noted.

 ### Ariel House

**$$    Ballsbridge, Dublin 4**

Sure, it's located in a leafy residential area that's about a 20-minute walk from the center of the city (or a super-quick ride on the DART), but this romantic hotel is worth any tradeoff in convenience. Rooms in the 1850s house are spacious and gorgeously furnished. You could spend hours gazing at the beautiful details of each room, from the Victorian and Georgian antiques to the luxurious, period-style wallpaper and fabrics to the canopy beds that grace some of the rooms. The drawing room is elegant and welcoming — you may be inspired to take out your quill pen and write some postcards in front of the crackling fire. Ariel House's beauty is more than skin deep; the staff are some of the friendliest and most knowledgeable in Dublin, making this hotel, like Kilronan House (reviewed later in this section), one of the best choices for first-time Dublin visitors.

*52 Lansdowne Rd.* ☎ *01-688-5845. DART: Lansdowne Road. Rates: €80–€150 ($92–$173). MC, V.*

### Avalon House

**$    Old City, Dublin 2**

This funky hostel, which plays host to a mix of travelers from teens to young families to older groups of friends, is legendary among backpackers for its friendliness, clean rooms, and sense of community. The atmosphere of the hostel can be summed up in the fact that you can rent an acoustic guitar at the front desk with a €20 ($23) deposit. Avalon House offers singles, twins, quads, and dorm-style rooms, some with bathrooms and some without. Rooms are pretty cramped and get a zero on the decor scale (they're pretty sparse), but that probably won't matter, because you can chill out in the self-catering kitchen or in the airy Avalon Café, which offers hot drinks and pastries and often hosts free live entertainment. The young staff can tell you about the hottest and hippest places in Dublin, and can arrange all sorts of excursions and tours. Note to performers: If you agree to perform in the Avalon Café, your stay is free.

*See map p. 138. 55 Aungier St.* ☎ *1-800-AVALON or 01-475-0001. Fax: 01-475-0303.* www.avalon-house.ie. *DART: Tara Street Station. Bus: 16, 16A, 19, or 22. Rates: €28–€35 ($32–$40) double. MC, V.*

### The Clarence

$$$$    Temple Bar, Dublin 2

This high-class hotel has a lot to offer, including a terrific location at the doorstep of the lively Temple Bar area, an elegant modern look, and superior service. It's even touched by fame: The hotel is partly owned by Bono and The Edge of the Irish rock band U2. You may not want to leave your enormous bed, where you can bliss out to CDs on the room's stereo. Decor is simple and chic, with vivid colors gracing each room. The classy Octagon bar and the wonderful Tea Room restaurant (reviewed in the "Dining in Dublin" section later in this chapter) are downstairs. The Clarence is the Jackie O of the city's top hotels — not as supertrendy as The Morrison and not as posh as The Shelbourne, but just plain classy.

*See map p. 144. 6–8 Wellington Quay.* ☎ *01-407-0800. Fax: 01-407-0820.* www.the clarence.ie. *DART: Tara Street Station. Bus: 51, 51B, 68, 68A, 69X, 78A, 79, 90, 210. Valet parking. Rates: €315–€335 ($362–$385) double. Breakfast not included. AE, DC, MC, V.*

### Grafton Guesthouse

$$   Old City, Dublin 2

This guesthouse is an incredible value, offering bright, cute, decent-size rooms at ridiculously low prices. Rooms are decorated with kitschy touches such as wallpaper with bright flowers and mod lamps. The kicker is that this place is in a central location, on hip Great Georges Street, right near Grafton Street and Trinity College. Service is a little rushed but still friendly. Vegetarians should appreciate the vegetarian version of the traditional Irish breakfast, complete with nonmeat sausages.

*See map p. 138. 26–27 S. Great Georges St.* ☎ *01-679-2041. Fax: 01-6779715. E-mail:* graftonguesthouse@eircom.net. *DART: Tara Street Station. Bus: 50, 50A, 54, 56, 77. Rates: €100 ($115) double. MC, V.*

### Jurys Inn Christchurch

$$   Old City (near Temple Bar), Dublin 8

You can't beat Jurys for value if you're traveling as a family: This hotel group is one of the few in Ireland that doesn't charge extra if more than two people share a room. The rooms here are large and modern, with the

## Dublin Accommodations and Dining

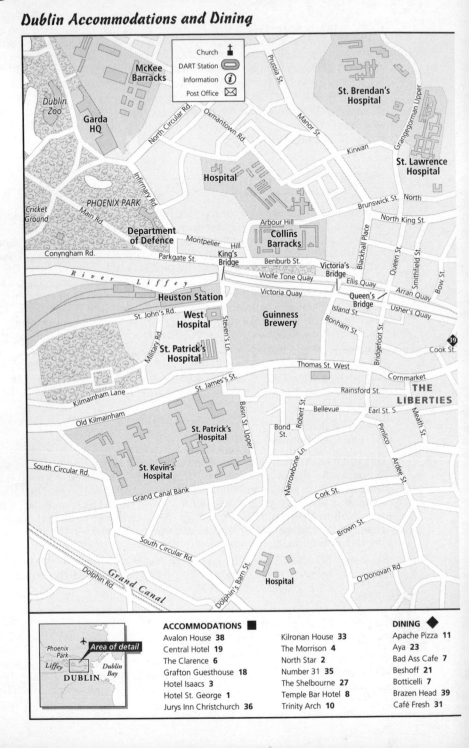

| ACCOMMODATIONS ■ | | DINING ◆ |
|---|---|---|
| Avalon House 38 | Kilronan House 33 | Apache Pizza 11 |
| Central Hotel 19 | The Morrison 4 | Aya 23 |
| The Clarence 6 | North Star 2 | Bad Ass Cafe 7 |
| Grafton Guesthouse 18 | Number 31 35 | Beshoff 21 |
| Hotel Isaacs 3 | The Shelbourne 27 | Botticelli 7 |
| Hotel St. George 1 | Temple Bar Hotel 8 | Brazen Head 39 |
| Jurys Inn Christchurch 36 | Trinity Arch 10 | Café Fresh 31 |

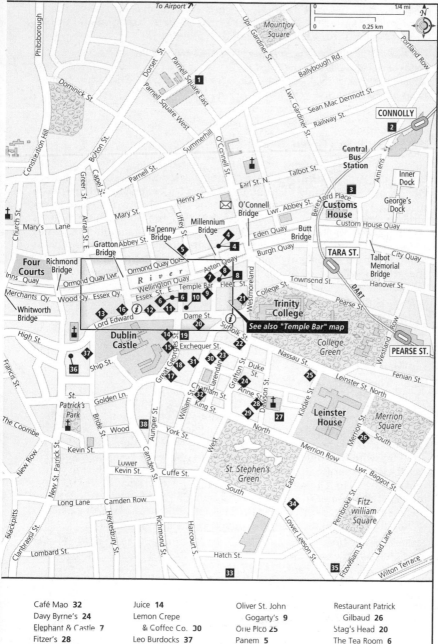

Café Mao **32**
Davy Byrne's **24**
Elephant & Castle **7**
Fitzer's **28**
Halo **4**
Il Posto **29**
Jaipur **17**

Juice **14**
Lemon Crepe
 & Coffee Co. **30**
Leo Burdocks **37**
The Mermaid Café **12**
Nude **22, 34**
Oliver Goldsmith's **8**

Oliver St. John
 Gogarty's **9**
One Pico **25**
Panem **5**
Poco Loco **16**
Queen of Tarts **13**

Restaurant Patrick
 Gilbaud **26**
Stag's Head **20**
The Tea Room **6**
Yamamori Noodles **15**

standard hotel decor of floral fabrics. There's a lively pub downstairs, and the hotel offers babysitting services. Christchurch Inn is centrally situated at the top of Dame Street, right near Christ Church Cathedral and Dublin Castle (ask for a room with a view of the cathedral).

*See map p. 138. Christ Church Place.* ☎ *800-44-UTELL toll-free from the United States, or 01-454-0000. Fax: 01-454-0012.* www.jurys.com. *DART: Tara Street Station. Bus: 21A, 50, 50A, 78, 78A, 78B. Rates: €99–130 ($114–$150) for up to three adults or two adults and two children. AE, DC, MC, V.*

### Kilronan House
$$$  St. Stephen's Green, Dublin 2

This small family-run hotel, with only 15 rooms, is one of the best places to stay if this is your first visit to Dublin. Terry Masterson, the hotel's friendly proprietor, makes a point to sit down with each guest to help plan an itinerary and to field questions about the city. Located on a quiet street within a ten-minute walk of St. Stephen's Green, the Georgian townhouse features many original details, such as beautiful ceiling molding, large bay windows, Waterford chandeliers, and hardwood floors. The spacious rooms are modern, brightly painted, and filled with natural light — ask for one with a skylight. An excellent full Irish breakfast is served in the elegant dining room.

*See map p. 138. 70 Adelaide Rd.* ☎ *01-475-5266. Fax: 01-478-2841.* www.dublinn. com/kilronan.htm. *DART: Pearse St. Bus: 10, 10A, 11, 13B, 20B. Rates: €152–€170 ($175–$196) double. AE, MC, V.*

### The Morrison
$$$$  North Liffey, Dublin 1

This top-notch hotel, in league with the Clarence and the Shelbourne, is a utopia for those who love modern, minimalist style. Public spaces are a visually pleasing mix of high ceilings, stone floors, and modern art. The elegant, uncluttered bedrooms are decorated in cream, black, and cocoa, and are filled with amenities, including a state-of-the-art sound system. The service is pampering and flawless. Halo, the hotel's hip Asian-fusion restaurant (reviewed in "Dining in Dublin," later in this chapter), serves fabulous food in stylish, modern surroundings. Though The Morrison is located on the less-happening north side of the Liffey, it is within easy walking distance of Temple Bar, Dublin Castle, and many other top attractions.

*See map p. 138. Ormond Quay (in front of the Millennium Bridge).* ☎ *01-887-2400. Fax: 01-878-3185.* www.morrisonhotel.ie. *DART: Connolly Station. Rates: €270–€445 ($311–$512) double. AE, DC, MC, V.*

### Number 31
$$$  St. Stephen's Green, Dublin 2

You know how guidebooks always say that certain hotels are "an oasis in a busy city"? Well, Number 31 really is. Designed by Sam Stephenson, one of Ireland's most famous modern architects, this guesthouse is tucked away behind a vined wall on a peaceful little lane about a ten-minute walk from St. Stephen's Green. The style inside is a marriage of modern design and country chic. The spacious rooms have intentionally weathered white wood country furniture and cozy quilts, plus little modern surprises such as a burnished gray mirrored wall or a sunken bathtub created with turquoise mosaic tiles. Sitting in the glass-walled conservatory; munching on fresh-baked cranberry bread and delightful hot breakfast dishes (I loved the eggs with salmon); and chatting with Deirdre and Noel Comer, your warm hosts, you may want to move in permanently. Be sure to say hi to Homer, the resident Golden Labrador.

*See map. p. 138. 31 Lower Leeson Close, Lower Leeson St.* ☎ *01-676-5011.* www. number31.ie. *Bus: 11, 11A, 11B, 13, 13A, 13B. Rates: €175 ($201) double. AE, DC, MC, V.*

### The Shelbourne
$$$$ **St. Steven's Green, Dublin 2**

Don your celebrity-spotting glasses, because this is the place to see and be seen for writers, politicians, businesspeople, actors, and other rich and/or famous people. Since it opened in 1824, this luxurious hotel has seen its fair share of history — it was one of the first buildings in Dublin to have electric lights; Room 112 is the Constitution Room, where Michael Collins and others drafted the constitution of the Irish Free State in 1922; and JFK and Jackie stayed here during a visit in 1957. The many public rooms are decorated with rich reds, greens, and yellows, and boast sumptuous fabrics, chandeliers, and Victorian and Georgian antiques. The hotel has a range of restaurants and bars, from the grand Lord Mayor's Lounge — *the* spot in Dublin for afternoon tea — to the bistro-style Side Door restaurant. The health club is one of the finest in Dublin, with a full range of fitness classes and a large swimming pool. Rooms range from sleek and modern to classic, so specify your desire when you book. Surprisingly, rooms are not as opulent as the rest of the hotel, though they are squeaky clean and nicely decorated. It's worth it to ask for a room overlooking beautiful St. Stephen's Green.

*See map p. 138. 27 St. Stephen's Green.* ☎ *01-663-4500. Fax: 01-661-6006.* www. shelbourne.ie. *DART: Tara Street Station. Bus: 32X, 39X, 41X, 66X, 67X. Rates: €199–€235 ($229–$270) double. Breakfast not included. AE, DC, MC, V.*

### Temple Bar Hotel
$$$ **Temple Bar, Dublin 2**

This hotel has everything: a terrific location in the heart of Temple Bar, a welcoming and helpful staff, an airy Art Deco lobby, and a nice restaurant serving light fare under the glow of skylights. In fact, the only drawback to the hotel is the small size of the bedrooms, which feature mahogany furniture, deep green and burgundy colors, and firm double beds. Ask for a room off the street if you're a light sleeper.

See map p. 144. Fleet St. ☎ *01-677-3333.* Fax: 01-677-3088. www.templebar hotel.com. DART: Tara Street Station. Bus to Fleet St.: 51, 51B, 68, 68A, 69X, 78A, 79, 90, 210. Rates: €170–€190 ($196–$219) double. AE, DC, MC, V.

### Trinity Arch
**$$ Temple Bar, Dublin 2**

It's all about location for a reasonable price at this place: Occupying an 18th-century building, this hotel is on the edge of Temple Bar and smack-dab between Trinity College and Dublin Castle, a position central to most of the city's attractions. The decent-size rooms are simple, clean, and brightly painted, with good-size bathrooms. The elegant **Oliver Goldsmith's Bar** is right downstairs, serving tasty pub snacks at low prices. Request a room off the street if you don't want to hear post-pub-closing conversations from below. This hotel and Grafton Guesthouse are very similar, so if one is booked, try the other.

See map p. 144. 46 Dame St. ☎ *01-679-4455.* Fax: 01-679-4511. www.trinity archhotel.com. DART: Tara Street Station. Bus: 51, 51B, 68, 68A, 69X, 78A, 79, 90, 210. Rates: €100–€140 ($115–$161) double. AE, DC, MC, V.

## Runner-up hotels

### Central Hotel
**$$ Old City, Dublin 2** This hotel is very accurately named, located just a stone's throw from Grafton Street, Temple Bar, and Trinity College. Bedrooms are spacious and bright, and public rooms have a Victorian look. See map p. 138. 1–5 Exchequer St. ☎ *800-780-1234* in the U.S. or 01-679-7302. Fax: 01-679-7303. www.centralhotel.ie. DART: Tara Street Station. Bus: 22A. Rates: €120–€170 ($138–$196) double. AE, DC, MC, V.

### Hotel Isaacs
**$$–$$$ O'Connell Street Area, Dublin 1** This moderately priced hotel is right across the street from the Bus Éireann station, close to Dublin's main shopping area and a mere five-minute walk from the city center. The building is a restored wine warehouse, and much of the original brickwork is still visible, giving it a lot of character. Rooms are modern and tastefully furnished. Il Vignardo, an Italian restaurant, is downstairs. See map p. 138. Store St. ☎ *01-855-0067.* Fax: 01-836-5390. www.isaacs.ie. DART: Connolly Street Station. Bus: 90. Rates: †110–†170 ($127–$196) double. AE, MC, V.

### Hotel St. George
**$$ O'Connell Street Area, Dublin 1** One in a row of classic Georgian townhouses, the Hotel St. George sits at the top of O'Connell Street on the north side of the Liffey, a nice location if you're planning to visit the Abbey, Peacock, or Gate theaters; the Writers Museum; the Hugh Lane Gallery; or the James Joyce Centre. The bustling shopping area around Henry Street is also close by. The rooms are large and grand, with high ceilings and

antiques. *See map p. 138. 7 Parnell Sq.* ☎ *01-874-5611. Fax: 01-874-5582.* indigo. ie/~hotels/george.htm. *DART: Connolly Street Station. Bus: 1. Rates:* €*105–*€*130 ($121–$150) double. MC, V.*

### North Star

$$ **O'Connell Street Area, Dublin 1**   This family-owned hotel is right near the Connolly rail and DART station on the north side of the River Liffey, close to the new financial-services district. The large, clean, reasonably priced rooms make this a great place to stay if you have business in the area — and even if you don't. *See map p. 138. Amien St.* ☎ *01-836-3136. Fax: 01-836-3561.* www.regencyhotels.com. *DART: Connolly Street Station. Bus: 90. Rates.* €*130–*€*150 ($150–$173) double. AE, MC, V.*

# Dining in Dublin

You can't swing a cat in Dublin (not that you'd want to) without hitting a pleasant place to eat. The city is chock-full of great restaurants for all budgets and tastes. Being a diverse city, Ireland's capital is home to eateries that offer cuisines from across the globe. Looking for Indian or Mediterranean? You've got it. Or is it French, Tex-Mex, or Creole that's tempting your taste buds? No problem. And, of course, there are Dublin's myriad pubs, many of which offer tasty Irish fare — stew, sandwiches, shepherd's pie — for low prices.

You don't usually need reservations to dine out in Dublin, especially during the off season or during the week. However, if you plan on dining somewhere posh and popular, phone ahead a couple of days, especially on weekends or during the summer. I indicate when reservations are necessary in the following listings.

Dublin diners tend to dress in smart casual clothes when going out to a fancy restaurant. At all but the most chi-chi places, even a nice pair of jeans is fine.

## Lunch on the move

Need to grab a bite between attractions? Hit **O'Brien's Irish Sandwich Bar,** which offers prepackaged sandwiches, beverages, and salads; or **Nude,** which sells pasta, salads, sandwiches, and other quick bites made with organic ingredients. You find branches of O'Brien's all over town; some of the most popular locations are 63 Dame Street, 23 Dawson Street, 34B Grafton Street, and 14 Merchants Arch in Temple Bar (see the "Temple Bar" map). The two Nudes in Dublin are at 103 Leeson Street and 21 Suffolk Street. On the north side of the Liffey, **Panem,** Ha'penny Bridge House, 21 Ormond Quay Lower, Dublin 1 (☎ 01-872-8510), is a popular spot for a lunch of soup or pasta of the day. The baked goods are a big draw, and the coffee and hot chocolate are delicious. Finally, I can't think of a better sightseeing pick-me-up than a freshly made crepe folded around banana slices and Nutella or around cheese and eggs.

## Temple Bar

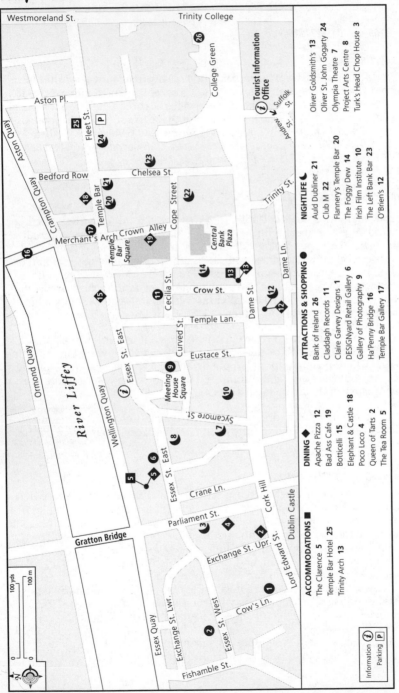

Westmoreland St.

Trinity College

College Green

Aston Pl.

Aston Quay

Crampton Quay

Bedford Row

Fleet St.

Chelsea St.

Temple Bar

Merchant's Arch  Crown  Alley

Cope  Street

Central Bank Plaza

Temple Bar Square

Cecilia St.

Crow St.

Curved St.

Temple Lan.

Eustace St.

Sycamore St.

Essex St. East

Meeting House Square

Essex Quay

Ormond Quay

Wellington Quay

River Liffey

Essex St. East

Crane Ln.

Parliament St.

Gratton Bridge

Essex St. Lwr.

Exchange St. Lwr.

Exchange St. Upr.

Essex St. West

Cow's Ln.

Cork Hill

Lord Edward St.

Dublin Castle

Fishamble St.

Dame St.

Dame Ln.

Trinity St.

Trinity St.

Suffolk St.

Andrew St.

Tourist Information Office

100 yds
100 m

N

**ACCOMMODATIONS ■**
The Clarence **5**
Temple Bar Hotel **25**
Trinity Arch **13**

**DINING ◆**
Apache Pizza **12**
Bad Ass Cafe **19**
Botticelli **15**
Elephant & Castle **18**
Poco Loco **4**
Queen of Tarts **2**
The Tea Room **5**

**ATTRACTIONS & SHOPPING ●**
Bank of Ireland **26**
Claddagh Records **11**
Claire Garvey Designs **1**
DESIGNyard Retail Gallery **6**
Gallery of Photography **9**
Ha'Penny Bridge **16**
Temple Bar Gallery **17**

**NIGHTLIFE ◆**
Auld Dubliner **21**
Club M **22**
Flannery's Temple Bar **20**
The Foggy Dew **14**
Irish Film Institute **10**
The Left Bank Bar **23**
O'Brien's **12**

Oliver Goldsmith's **13**
Oliver St. John Gogarty **24**
Olympia Theatre **7**
Project Arts Centre **8**
Turk's Head Chop House **3**

Information ⓘ  Parking Ⓟ

Follow the crowds to **Lemon Crepe & Coffee Co.,** 68 South William St., Dublin 2 (☎ **01-672-9044**).

## Pub grub

Pubs are a great place to get a good, relatively cheap lunch or dinner. Most serve real stick-to-the-ribs Irish options, such as stew, shepherd's pie, and beef in Guinness, along with a few lighter options such as salads and sandwiches. Some of your best bets for good food are:

- **Brazen Head,** 20 Lower Bridge Street, Dublin 8 (☎ **01-679-5186**)

- **Davy Byrne's,** 21 Duke Street, Dublin 2 (☎ **01-677-5217**)

- **Oliver Goldsmith's,** Trinity Arch Hotel, 46 Dame St., Dublin 2 (☎ **01-679-4074**)

- **Oliver St. John Gogarty,** 58 Fleet Street, Temple Bar, Dublin 2 (☎ **01-671-1822**)

- **Stag's Head,** 1 Dame Court (off Dame Street ), Dublin 2 (☎ **01-679-3701**)

# Dublin's Top Restaurants A to Z

### Apache Pizza
$   Temple Bar, Dublin 2   PIZZA

Located in the heart of the city, Apache is a perfect stop for some quick chow or a postbar bite. You can get pizza by the pie or slice, or try a famous Totem Roll: pizza ingredients stuffed into a hoagie bun and baked. There's a fabulous jukebox to sort through while waiting for your order.

*See map p. 144. 58 Dame St., at Eustace St.* ☎ *01-677-8888. DART: Tara Street Station. Bus to Fleet St.: 46, 46A, 46B, 63, 150. Main courses: €2.25–€5 ($2.60–$5.75). No credit cards. Open: Mon–Wed noon–12:30 a.m., Thurs and Sun noon–1:30 a.m., Fri noon–3 a.m., Sat noon–3:30 a.m.*

### Aya
$$–$$$$   Grafton Street Area, Dublin 2   JAPANESE

This place bears a striking resemblance to my idea of heaven, with an endless parade of sushi and other Japanese treats traveling before your eyes courtesy of a refrigerated conveyor belt. Here's how it works: You take a seat at the conveyor belt, and grab whatever looks good. The four different colors of the plates correspond to different prices, and your server calculates your bill based on the number and colors of the plates that you stack up. The restaurant offers a number of deals, including the popular *55 Time* special (Sun–Wed and Fri from 5 p.m. on), which allows you to eat all you can from the conveyor belt in 55 minutes for €25 ($29), and my personal favorite, *Last Call,* from 10 p.m. to 11 p.m. Sunday to Wednesday and

10:30 p.m. to 11:30 p.m. Thursday through Saturday, when every plate is €1 ($1.15). I particularly recommend the raw tuna slices bathed in spicy sauce, the shrimp tempura maki rolls, the edamame (steamed soybeans), and the rich caramel-and-banana dessert. The only dud I encountered was the salmon sashimi, which didn't taste like much of anything. The modern decor is simple and chic, but it probably won't matter, because you'll be hypnotized by the conveyor belt. The restaurant also offers fine pan-Asian sit-down meals.

*See map p. 138. 49–52 Clarendon St.* ☎ *01-677-1544. DART: Tara St. Bus: 16A, 19A, 22A, 55, or 83. Main courses (including a conveyor-belt meal): €10–€25 ($12–$29). AE, MC, V. Open: Mon–Thurs 12:30–10:30 p.m., Fri and Sat 12:30–11 p.m., Sun 1–10:30 p.m.*

### Bad Ass Cafe

**$–$$   Temple Bar, Dublin 2   PIZZA-AMERICAN**

No, you don't have to be tough to come here (the name refers to the restaurant's donkey mascot), but you do have to be hungry. This Dublin institution occupies an old warehouse and has a fun, casual, airy look and feel, with cash shuttles that whisk your money across the room to the cashier, bright colors, and windows looking out to the teeming streets of Temple Bar. Some of the best pizza in the city is served here, including the delicious *Kitchensinkio,* which sports every topping you can think of. Pastas (including Mickey Rooney Macaroni), burgers, and other basic dishes round out the menu, and the salads are fresh and delicious. The whole menu is kid-friendly, especially the bottom portion, which lists the sundaes and other desserts.

*See map p. 138. 9–11 Crown Alley.* ☎ *01-671-2596.* www.badasscafe.com. *DART: Tara Street Station. Bus to Fleet St.: 46, 46A, 46B, 63, 150. Main courses: €7.30–€18 ($8.40–$20). AE, MC, V. Open: Mon–Wed noon–9 p.m., Thurs noon–10 p.m., Fri and Sat 9 a.m.–11 p.m.*

### Beshoff

**$   Trinity Area, Dublin 2   FISH AND CHIPS**

If there were an Olympic category for best *chipper* (fish-and-chips shop), and I were the judge, Beshoff would get the gold. The fish here, and there's quite a variety (cod is the classic), is as fresh as can be, its juices sealed in by a fried golden-brown crust; the *chips* (fries) are cut fresh each day and are thick and deliciously dense. If you like salt and vinegar to begin with, you'll love how they complement fish and chips, so ask for them. If you feel the same way about fish that my friend Shannon does — "If it comes from the sea, let it be" — take heart and order the chicken option. Beshoff has seating, so you can pick up your food downstairs and then climb the stairs to find a table overlooking busy Westmoreland Street. However, these meals tend to taste best when carried across the street to the cricket *pitch* (field) or the garden at Trinity College (walk straight through the Trinity gate, walk past the Old Library, and make a right at the pretty little garden with benches). There is another branch of Beshoff at 6

Upper O'Connell St., Dublin 1. Beshoff's rival is **Leo Burdocks,** at 2 Werburgh St., Dublin 8 (☎ 01-454-0306). I think Beshoff is better, but let me know your vote, and I'll tally them up.

*See map p. 138. 14 Westmoreland St.* ☎ *01-677-8026. DART: Tara Street Station. Bus: 7A, 8, 15A, 15B, 15C, 46, 55, 62, 63, 83, 84. Main courses: €5–€8.50 ($5.75–$9.80). No credit cards. Open: Mon–Sat 10 a.m.–10 p.m., Sun 11 a.m.–10:30 p.m.*

### Botticelli
**$$   Temple Bar, Dublin 2   ITALIAN/PIZZA**

This restaurant, run by Italians, serves food for people who know and love their Italian cuisine. It's frequented by groups of locals, making it hard to get into on weekends, but the gnocchi, huge variety of pizzas, and tiramisu make it worth the wait. The interior is casual, with warm lighting and blue tablecloths. Save room for the delicious gelato served up at the storefront next door, run by the same folks. Come here for a casual Italian meal; if you're looking for something more formal, try Il Posto (reviewed later in this section).

*See map p. 144. 3 Temple Bar Rd.* ☎ *01-672-7289. DART: Tara Street Station. Bus to Fleet St.: 46, 46A, 46B, 63, 150. Main courses: €8.50–€19 ($9.80–$22). AE, DC, MC, V. Open: Daily 10 a.m.–midnight.*

### Café Fresh
**$   Trinity Area, Dublin 2   VEGETARIAN**

Fennel, leek, and goat-cheese lasagna; Thai green curry; Moroccan lentil soup — the tasty dishes at this inexpensive vegetarian cafe even make omnivores forget to miss meat. Housed in a refurbished 18th-century mansion that now accommodates an upscale shopping center, Café Fresh is one of Dublin's top choices for a casual lunch. The kitchen works to accommodate people with various food allergies.

*See map p. 138. Unit 25 I Powerscourt Townhouse Centre, top floor.* ☎ *01-671-9669. DART: Tara Street Station. Bus to Fleet St.: 10, 16, 22, 46, 46A. Main courses: €3–€8.95 ($3.45 $10). MC, V. Open: Mon–Sat 10 a.m.–6 p.m. and Thurs until 8 p.m.*

### Café Mao
**$$   Grafton Street Area, Dublin 2   ASIAN FUSION**

Take a seat outside or in the airy interior of this excellent restaurant, and settle down for a long, casual meal and some great people-watching. The menu roams Asia and is full of flavorful dishes, including tender salmon with sweet sauce and vegetables, Malaysian chicken curry, and the popular tofu-and-pumpkin curry served on jasmine rice. Don't miss the excellent pumpkin spring rolls, served with a sweet and zingy plum sauce.

*See map p. 138. 2–3 Chatham Row.* ☎ *01-670-4899. DART: Pearse Street Station. Bus: 10, 11A, 11B, 13, or 20B. Main courses: €9.95–€18 ($11–$21). AE, MC, V. Open: Mon–Sat noon–10:30 p.m., Sun 1–10:30 p.m.*

### Elephant & Castle
$–$$    **Temple Bar, Dublin 2**    AMERICAN

Locals and visitors alike pile into this immensely popular, buzzing joint in the heart of Temple Bar, which serves exceptional burgers, salads, omelets, and other American diner fare. Burger-slingers around the world should cross their fingers that Elephant & Castle doesn't open a branch in their town, because these juicy, flavorful burgers are some of the best I've ever tasted. Garlic-philes must try the garlic burger, with roasted garlic cloves, garlic butter, and aioli; another winner is the burger with horseradish, black pepper, and sour cream. Or go for a tasty omelet or a fresh, generous salad. And don't miss the beverage list, which offers everything from elderflower soda to fresh limeade. This warm, relaxed restaurant, with its wood booths and funky paintings and photos (my favorite is a painting of a sign shop, reading "Advertise with SIGNS. We make them."), is the perfect place to watch the crowds of people who parade down Temple Bar.

*See map p. 144. 18 Temple Bar St. ☎ 01-679-3121. DART: Tara Street Station. Bus to Fleet St.: 46, 46A, 46B, 63, 150. Main courses: €7.25–€14 ($8.35–$16). AE, DC, MC, V. Open: Mon–Fri 8:00 a.m.–11:30 p.m., Sat 10:30 a.m.–11:30 p.m., Sun noon–11:30 p.m.*

### Fitzer's
$$–$$$    **St. Stephen's Green Area, Dublin 2**    INTERNATIONAL

Owned by the Fitzpatricks of Dublin, a family that began as fruit and vegetable merchants in the city, Fitzer's cafes use some of the freshest produce around. From creative and filling salads to innovative pasta dishes to lamb tandoori, Fitzer's menu features a variety of delicious, simply prepared dishes from around the world. The surroundings are casual and airy, the atmosphere is classy without being unapproachable, and the staff is friendly. You'd never guess, but Fitzer's is a chain. There are three locations in the city, each with different menus and prices. The one located on Dawson Street, just blocks from Grafton Street, is the one I recommend. Just for the record, though, the other locations are The Millennium Wing of the National Gallery, Merrion Square, Dublin 2 (☎ 01-663-3500), and 42 Temple Bar Square, Dublin 2 (☎ 01-679-0440).

*See map p. 138. 51 Dawson St. ☎ 01-677-1155. DART: Tara Street Station. Bus: 10, 11A, 11B, 13, 20B. Main courses: €14–€20 ($16–$23). AE, DC, MC, V. Open: Daily 11:30 a.m.–11 p.m.*

### Halo
$$$$    **North Liffey, Dublin 1**    FUSION/NEW IRISH

Though it's not a white-hot as it was when it first opened, this beautiful minimalist cathedral of a restaurant is still one of the most popular places for an indulgent lunch or dinner. Don your hippest clothes, and dig into creative ultramodern dishes such as duck fillet with sweet potato fondant, red onion compote, and pinot noir sauce. If you want something distinctively local, go for the starter of Irish marinated salmon — both smoked and seared, with scallion blinis and lime and wasabi fromage frais.

*See map p. 138. Ormond Quay (in the Hotel Morrison in front of the Millennium Bridge).* ☎ *01-887-3421. Reservations required. DART: Connolly Station. Main courses: €21–€33 ($24–$38). AE, DC, MC, V. Open: 7–10:30 p.m.*

## Il Posto
**$$–$$$    Dublin 2    ITALIAN**

Everything about this place is warm, inviting, and elegant, from the friendly service to the orange-and-cream paintings on the wall to the candles on each table. The delicious and filling food, served in giant portions, just adds to the general feeling of ease and comfort. The all-Italian menu features many excellent standards, such as the delicious Spaghetti Bolognese, plus a few surprises, including a sautéed breast of chicken with pepperoni, lentils, crushed truffles, and new potatoes, served with stir-fried vegetables. The seafood dishes, including braised tilapia with roasted garlic and fresh tomatoes, are especially delicious.

*See map p. 138. 10 St. Stephen's Green.* ☎ *01-679-4769. Reservations recommended. Main courses: €13–€23 ($14–$26). AE, DC, MC, V. Open: Daily 6–11 p.m. and Mon–Sat 11 a.m.–3 p.m.*

## Jaipur
**$$    Grafton Street Area, Dublin 2    INDIAN**

You know you're in for a delicious Indian meal as soon as you take a bite of the complimentary airy pappadum, which are served with a trio of sauces: a sweet pineapple chutney, a tangy cilantro sauce, and a spicy red sauce. The atmosphere is refined and romantic, with exotic fresh flowers on each table and candlelight casting a golden glow on the faces of the couples and small groups of friends dining here. The menu is filled with great options, from traditional Indian favorites such as Chicken Tikka Masala to more unusual choices such as Nalli Gosht — tender roast lamb in a hot broth with the chef's special spices. Be sure to order the Pulao Rice — fluffy, spiced basmati rice — to complement your main dish.

*See map p. 138. 41 South Great Georges St.* ☎ *01-677-0999. Reservations recommended. DART: Tara Street Station. Bus: 50, 50A, 54, 56, 77. Main courses: €16–€19 ($18–$22). AE, MC, V. Open: Thurs–Sat 12:30–3 p.m. and daily 5–11 p.m.*

## Juice
**$–$$    Old City, Dublin 2    GLOBAL/VEGETARIAN**

Juice is a casual, friendly little slice of health-conscious California in the heart of Dublin. Small groups of friends and solo diners drop in to chat, flip through the newspaper, or write in their journals over generous portions of vegetarian and vegan dishes that take their inspiration from cuisines all over the planet. You find everything from miso soup to spicy bean burgers to crepelike pancakes served with organic maple syrup shot through with mango puree. And as the name not-very-subtly suggests, you also find all kinds of juices, which are so fresh, they taste like you just inserted a straw directly into the fruit or vegetable. High ceilings, curved walls, a metal panel covered with Christmas lights, and candy-colored glass flower vases and votive holders give this place a warm, funky air that invites lingering, especially on a cool, rainy day (not that Dublin has any of those).

*See map p. 138. 73–83 South Great Georges St.* ☎ *01-475-7856. DART: Tara Street Station. Bus: 50, 50A, 54, 56, 77. Main courses: €5.75–€16 ($6.60–$18). AE, MC, V. Service Charge of 10% added. Open: Mon–Wed noon–10 p.m., Thurs and Fri noon–11 p.m., Sat 11 a.m.–11 p.m., Sun 11 a.m.–10 p.m.*

### The Mermaid Café
**$$–$$$$    Dublin 2    NEW IRISH**

This is my favorite restaurant in Dublin, because it serves innovative dishes made with some of the freshest, most flavorful ingredients around. The menu changes seasonally, offering the likes of Irish Angus ribeye steak with sage-and-mustard mashed potatoes and garlicky beans; yellowfin tuna with plum tomatoes, capers, mint, and wasabi mayonnaise; and a salad of asparagus and quail eggs with shaved parmesan and greens. The crowd is always buzzy and chic; businesspeople descend on the restaurant at lunch, while dinner sees more couples and small groups. The surroundings are cozy and modern, featuring contemporary art, white wood walls, high-backed pine chairs, and solid pine tables. Save room for the unbelievable desserts, including pecan pie served with maple ice cream.

*See map p. 138. 70 Dame St.* ☎ *01-670-8236. Reservations recommended. DART: Tara Street Station. Bus: 50, 50A, 54, 56A, 77. Main courses: €16–€29 ($18–$33). MC, V. Open: Mon–Sat 12:30–3:30 p.m. and 6–11 p.m., Sun noon–3:30 p.m. and 6–9 p.m.*

### One Pico
**$$$–$$$$    Grafton Street Area, Dublin 2    CONTINENTAL-NEW IRISH**

This is my number-one pick for sealing a business deal in Dublin. A classy crowd (including quite a few businesspeople) fills this elegant restaurant, decorated with browns and golds, to sample star chef Eamon O'Reilly's creations. Like the chefs at **The Tea Room, Halo,** and **Mermaid Café** (all reviewed in this section), O'Reilly creates adventurous dishes with fresh Irish produce, though his menu seems to have more of a French influence than the menus at those three restaurants. The starter of seared rare tuna with black sesame seeds, coriander (cilantro) puree, and red onion crème fraiche, served alongside a fennel, pear, and cucumber salad, is a delight, as is the Irish Angus beef fillet with artichoke puree, boiled asparagus, Pomme Anna (thinly sliced potatoes layered with butter), and cabernet sauvignon sauce. Whatever you do, be sure to try the Cookies & Cream dessert, a haute re-creation of some of the world's favorite cookies. The prix-fixe lunch here is a nice deal, at €25 ($29) for two courses or €30 ($35) for three.

*See map p. 138. 5–6 Molesworth Place, Schoolhouse Lane.* ☎ *01-676-0300. Reservations recommended. DART: Pearse. Bus: 10, 11A, 11B, 13, or 20B. Main courses: €20–€30 ($22–$34). AE, DC, MC, V. Open: Mon–Sat 12:30–2:30 p.m. and 6–11 p.m.*

### Poco Loco
**$–$$   Dublin 2   TEX-MEX**

If you're looking for some filling, inexpensive, authentic-tasting Tex-Mex food, this is the place. Some things belie the fact that you're not in a cantina in Austin, such as the absence of jalapenos, but when it comes to burritos and enchiladas smothered in cheese, tacos stuffed with spicy beef, and fab nachos, Poco Loco is on the mark. It's small and dim, with painted wooden tables, and you may hear Elvis crooning in the background.

*See map p. 144. 32 Parliament St.* ☎ *01-679-1950. DART: Tara Street Station. Bus to Fleet St.: 46, 46A, 46B, 63, 150. Main courses: €8–€15 ($9.20–$17). AE, MC, V. Open: Mon–Wed 5–11:30 p.m., Thurs–Sat 5 p.m. to midnight., Sun 5–10 p.m.*

### Queen of Tarts
**$   Dublin 2   BAKERY/CAFE**

If I lived near this bakery, I'd weigh about 900 pounds, and that would be tragic, because then I might not be able to fit through the door to sample more of their incredible desserts. Savory lunch tarts (such as an onion, potato, rosemary, and cheddar combo) and toothsome homemade soups attended by a thick slice of brown bread are served in a cheerful, casual yellow room. But the excellent lunch fare is just the opening act for the glorious desserts, including a tangy blackberry-and-apple crumble offset by sweet cream that I could eat every day.

*See map p. 144. 4 Corkhill (part of Dame St. across from Dublin Castle).* ☎ *01-670-7499. DART: Tara Street Station. Main courses and baked goods: €1.50–€7.95 ($1.75–$9.15). No credit cards. Open: Mon–Fri 7:30 a.m.–6 p.m., Sat 9 a.m.–6 p.m., Sun 10 a.m.–6 p.m.*

### Restaurant Patrick Guilbaud
**$$$$   Dublin 2   FRENCH**

Some of the finest cuisine in Dublin is served in this bright, cream-colored room, which sports abstract paintings. Dishes combine fresh Irish and French ingredients with French cooking techniques for some real stunners, such as the Connemara lobster in coconut cream sauce and the pan-fried fillet of black sole served with duck confit. Desserts are appropriately complex and impressive; a recent menu listed a plate of eight different dark chocolate confections. The €30 ($35) three-course lunch is a fabulous deal.

*See map p. 138. In the Merrion Hotel, 21 Upper Merrion St.* ☎ *01-676-4192. Reservations required. DART: Westland Row. Bus: 10, 11A, 11B, 13, or 10B. Main courses: €31–€48 ($36–$55). AE, DC, MC, V. Open: Tues–Sat 12:30–2 p.m. and 7:30–10:15 p.m.*

### The Tea Room
**$$$–$$$$    Temple Bar, Dublin 2    NEW IRISH**

It's quite a feat to divide your attention between the sophisticated, adventurous dishes served here and the hip clientele, which frequently includes at least one celebrity. Chef Antony Ely takes advantage of Ireland's bounty of fresh ingredients in the creation of his dazzling, up-to-date dishes. Though some dishes are relatively simple, such as the roast organic Glenarm salmon served with pot-roasted root vegetables and a lentil and red-wine jus, most fall into the daring category — a lunch entrée of loin of Finnebrogue venison with celeriac puree, roast parsnips, and chocolate sauce; or an appetizer of butternut squash soup with Lyonnaise sausage and deep-fried quail eggs. The wine list is incredible (though pricey), and service is gracious and professional. Housed in the fabulous Clarence Hotel (reviewed in "Spending the Night in Dublin," earlier in this chapter), The Tea Room has an airy, pared-down look, with soaring ceilings and windows and lots of blond wood. The prix-fixe lunch is a good deal, at €26 ($30) for two courses and €30 ($35) for three.

*See map p. 144. In the Clarence Hotel, 6-8 Wellington Quay.* ☎ *01-407-0820. Reservations required. DART: Tara Street Station. Bus: 51, 51B, 68, 68A, 69X, 78A, 79, 90, 210. Main courses: €19–€36 ($22–$41). AE, DC, MC, V. Open: Sun–Fri 12:30– 2:30 p.m.; Mon–Sat 6:30–10:30 p.m., Sun 6:30–9:30 p.m.*

### Yamamori Noodles
**$$    Old City, Dublin 2    NOODLES/JAPANESE**

If you're craving Japanese noodle dishes and soups, and a boisterous atmosphere, Yamamori is your place. In a large, simply furnished space decorated with white lanterns and a glass panel sandwiching delicate cherry-blossom-shaped lights, groups of friends talk and laugh over superfresh sushi, bowls of ramen big enough (and delectable enough) to drown in, and other Japanese noodle dishes, such as wok-fried noodles; rare tuna loin served with a trio of soba, rice, and green tea noodles; and various teriyaki plates. Try the sushi handrolls — cones of delicate seaweed wrapped around warm vinegared rice and the fresh filling of your choice. This place is a bit pricey for a noodle joint, but for some of the best noodles in town, I think it's worth it.

*See map p. 138. 71–72 South Great Georges St.* ☎ *01-475-5001. DART: Tara Street Station. Bus: 50, 50A, 54, 56, 77. Main courses: €13–€18 ($14–$20). AE, MC, V. Open: Sun–Wed noon–11 p.m., Thurs–Sat noon–11:30 p.m.*

## Exploring Dublin

Dublin is packed with things to see (use the "Dublin Attractions" map to locate them). An exploration of the city is like a journey through history as you discover medieval churches, Viking ruins, an 18th-century college campus, and museums containing artifacts such as 3,000-year-old Celtic gold jewelry. Modern Dublin is evident in sights ranging from a recent portrait of U2 singer Bono to the über-trendy shops that popped up in the wake of the economic boom of the 1990s.

As you explore Dublin, keep an eye out for brass plaques laid into the ground with passages from Joyce's *Ulysses* that relate to that site.

If you're in Dublin for a short time, one of the best ways to take in as many attractions as possible is to use the Hop On Hop Off Tour bus. The bus visits nineteen of Dublin's most popular attractions, and as the name indicates, you can hop off the bus to see an attraction and then pick up another bus when you're finished. See the review in "Seeing Dublin by Guided Tour," later in this chapter, for more details.

Dublin is relatively compact, but it still makes sense to look at a map and plan to see attractions in the same area in the same day.

No need to break the bank sightseeing; all the parks in Dublin are free, as are many other attractions listed here. You can also get combined tickets to some attractions, which could save a few euro (see reviews for further information).

Families should be aware that most attractions in Dublin and the rest of Ireland offer family rates — low flat rates that usually cover two adults and up to four children.

**The Dublin Pass,** available at any Dublin tourism office or at www. dublinpass.com, offers a terrific deal. You pay a flat price and get free admission to tons of Dublin and Dublin-area attractions, plus discounts on several tours and at some restaurants. The pass is €29 ($33) adults and €19 ($22) for kids 17 and under for one day; €49 ($56) adults and €34 ($39) kids 17 and under for two days; €59 ($68) adults and €39 ($45) kids 17 and under for three days; and €89 ($102) adults and €49 ($56) kids 17 and under for six days. If you know that you're going to do a lot of sightseeing, the Dublin Pass may be perfect for you.

## The top attractions

### Chester Beatty Library
**Dublin 2**

The Chester Beatty Library is one of those gems that often gets overlooked in favor of the more flashy attractions of Dublin. But this extensive collection of books, artwork, manuscripts, and religious objects from around the world is worth at least a few hours of precious vacation time. On the first floor, you find a diverse collection of works, from Chinese scroll paintings to a tenth-century Persian illustration of astronomy knowledge to a large Northern Italian book of choir music from 1450. Narrated videos of craftspeople at work are found throughout the gallery, illuminating crafts such as bookbinding, papermaking, and printmaking. The second floor is dedicated to books and objects from many of the world's religious traditions. A beautifully created audiovisual explores religious practices and

## Dublin Attractions

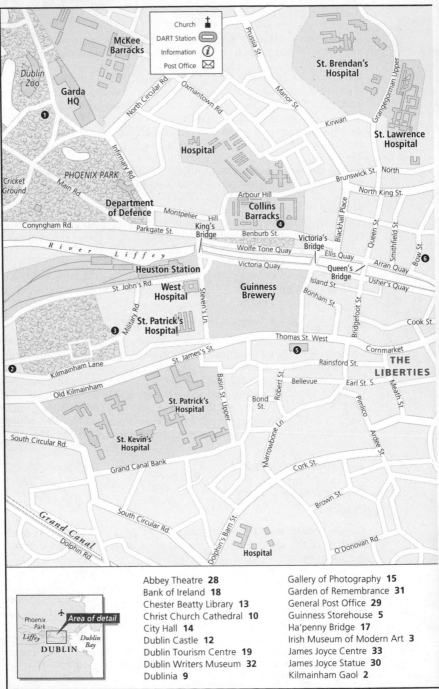

| | |
|---|---|
| Church | ✝ |
| DART Station | ⬭ |
| Information | ⓘ |
| Post Office | ✉ |

Abbey Theatre **28**
Bank of Ireland **18**
Chester Beatty Library **13**
Christ Church Cathedral **10**
City Hall **14**
Dublin Castle **12**
Dublin Tourism Centre **19**
Dublin Writers Museum **32**
Dublinia **9**

Gallery of Photography **15**
Garden of Remembrance **31**
General Post Office **29**
Guinness Storehouse **5**
Ha'penny Bridge **17**
Irish Museum of Modern Art **3**
James Joyce Centre **33**
James Joyce Statue **30**
Kilmainham Gaol **2**

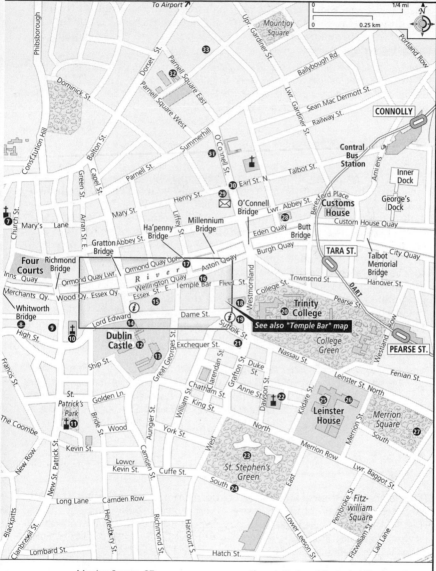

Merrion Square **27**
The Millennium Spire **29**
Molly Malone Statue **21**
National Gallery **26**
National Museum of
   Decorative Arts & History **4**
National Museum of Ireland **25**
Newman House **24**
Old Jameson Distillery **6**

Phoenix Park and Zoological Gardens **1**
St. Ann's Anglican Church **22**
St. Audoen's Church **8**
St. Michan's Church **7**
St. Patrick's Cathedral **11**
St. Stephen's Green **23**
Temple Bar Gallery **16**
Trinity College and the
   Book of Kells **20**

belief systems around the world. The treasures on this floor are numerous, including a Hindu cosmological painting from 18th-century Nepal; a standing Tibetan Buddha; and some of the earliest New Testament and Gospel texts, including the Gospel of St. John, written on Greek papyrus, circa 150 to 200.

*See map p. 154. Dublin Castle.* ☎ *01-407-0750.* www.cbl.ie. *Bus: 50, 50A, 54, 56A, 77, 77A, 77B. Free admission. Open: May–Sept Mon–Fri 10 a.m.–5 p.m., Sat 11 a.m.–5 p.m., and Sun 1 p.m.–5 p.m.; Oct–Apr Tues–Fri 10 a.m.–5 p.m., Sat 11 a.m.–5 p.m., and Sun 1 p.m.–5 p.m. Suggested visit: 1 ½–2 hours.*

### Christ Church Cathedral
**Dublin 8**

Christ Church Cathedral, an Anglican/Episcopal church, has existed in various forms in this spot for almost a thousand years. The Vikings built a simple wood church at this location in 1038. In the 1180s, the original foundation was expanded into a cruciform, and the Romanesque cathedral was built in stone. The church you see today is the result of restoration and rebuilding on the 1180s building during the 1870s. The cathedral provides an informative self-guided tour brochure when you enter. Don't let all the soaring architecture above you make you forget to look down at the beautiful tile floor. On your way to the Peace Chapel of Saint Laud, check out the mummified rat and cat found in a pipe of the organ in the late 1860s. Your ticket also covers admission to the crypt, which houses the cathedral's Treasury. Visitors are welcome at services; just call ahead for times. Note that admission is reduced if you visit Dublinia (reviewed later in this section) first.

*See map p. 154. Christ Church Place.* ☎ *01-677-8099. DART: Tara Street Station. Bus: 50, 50A, 78, 78A. Admission: €5 ($5.75) adults, €2.50 ($2.90) students and seniors, free for children accompanied by a parent. Open: Mon–Fri 9:45 a.m.–5 p.m. (last admission at 4:30 p.m.), Sat 10 a.m.–5 p.m. (last admission at 4:30 p.m.), Sun 12:45 p.m.–4:45 p.m. Suggested visit: 45 minutes.*

### Dublin Castle
**Dublin 2**

This is not your typical storybook castle. It originally was built in the 13th century, but many additions were made over the following 800 years. Today, the castle looks like an encyclopedia of European architectural styles, from the 13th-century Norman Record Tower to the Church of the Holy Trinity, designed in 1814 in Gothic style. The castle now hosts official state functions such as the president's inauguration, and the clock tower is home to the excellent Chester Beatty Library (reviewed earlier in this section). Forty-five-minute guided tours take you through the many of the impressively furnished State Apartments, including the Drawing Room, which features a breathtaking Waterford Crystal chandelier; the Throne Room, which holds what is believed to be an original seat of William of

# Exploring Temple Bar

In the 1970s, artists of all kinds began setting up shop in Temple Bar, and the area, which had hitherto been in decline, became a hotbed for cutting-edge visual and performing arts. Though the 1980s were rough for Temple Bar, the area rallied during the economic boom of the early 1990s. The result of this boom money is that Temple Bar is now both bohemian *and* upscale, much like Manhattan's SoHo — you can get a gorgeous one-of-a-kind handmade dress, but it certainly won't be a bargain.

Temple Bar is especially fun to visit when the Food Market, Book Market, and Cow's Lane Fashion & Design Market are taking place (see the "This little traveler went to market" sidebar in the "Shopping in Dublin" section, later in this chapter).

Check out a few of my favorite spots in Temple Bar (shown in the "Temple Bar" map):

- ✔ The **Gallery of Photography,** Meeting House Square (☎ 01-671-4654), has a great permanent exhibit of early-20th-century Irish photography and also puts on excellent temporary exhibits by contemporary Irish and international photographers.

- ✔ **The Irish Film Institute,** 6 Eustace St., (☎ 01-679-5744), is one of the hippest places in Dublin, showing a terrific selection of old and independent films. The cute café there serves the best nachos in Dublin. During the summer, they project films on an outdoor screen in Meetinghouse Square on Saturday nights.

- ✔ **Temple Bar Gallery,** 5-9 Temple Bar (☎ 01-671-0073), exhibits new works by up-and-coming artists.

- ✔ **Project Arts Centre,** 39 East Essex St. (☎ 01-679-6622), presents new and often avant-garde art exhibits, theater, and dance.

Drop into the **Temple Bar Information Centre,** 12 East Essex St.. (☎ 01-677-2397; www. visit-templebar.com) for all sorts of information on Temple Bar, including the lowdown on the area's many free outdoor events. The Information Centre is open Monday to Friday 9 a.m. to 6 p.m. all year, and on Saturdays and Sundays during the summer, and offers tours of Temple Bar daily at 11 a.m., 1 p.m., and 3 p.m.

Orange; and Patrick's Hall, which boasts the banners of the knights of St. Patrick and historical ceiling paintings. Don't miss the Church of the Holy Trinity, with its beautiful carved oak panels and stained-glass windows. Note the statue of Justice in the courtyard. See how she faces away from the city? Cynical Dubliners will tell you that was intentional. During state occasions, the State Apartments may be closed.

*See map p. 154. Cork Hill, off Dame St. ☎ 01-677-7129. Bus: 50, 50A, 54, 56A, 77, 77A, 77B. Admission: €4 ($4.60) adult, €3.50 ($4.05) students and seniors €1.50 ($1.75) under 12. Guided tours are obligatory. Open: Mon–Fri 10 a.m.–5 p.m., Sat and Sun 2–5 p.m. Suggested visit: 45 minutes.*

## Dublinia
### Dublin 8

Try on some chain mail, rummage through the apothecary's drawers to find a cure for what ails you, and sniff through the spice merchant's wares at the Medieval Fayre, one of several exhibits at Dublinia, a well-done hands-on museum that illustrates life in medieval Dublin from 1170 to 1540. Though the wall text is comprehensive and geared to adults, kids will love the activities and the walk-through scenes, including a stunning room in which you seem to be standing on the deck of a ship as it approaches one of Dublin's quays. Other highlights include a scale model of Dublin in medieval times, costumed musicians playing instruments of the times (check out the hand-cranked hurdy-gurdy), a woodworking demonstration, artifacts from Dublin's medieval city, and the beautiful view from the top floor of the museum. Adults without kids shouldn't write this one off; four other adults and I had a ball.

*See map p. 154. St. Michael's Hill, High St, (next to Christ Church).* ☎ *01-679-4611.* www.dublinia.ie. *Bus: 50, 78A. Admission: €5.75 ($6.60) adults, €4.75 ($5.45) students and seniors, €4.25 ($4.85) child over 5, €15 ($17) family of 2 adults and 2 children; free for children under 5. Open: April–Sept daily 10 a.m.–5 p.m., Oct–March Mon–Sat 11 a.m.–4 p.m., Sun 10 a.m.–4:30 p.m. Suggested visit: 1½ hours.*

## Guinness Storehouse
### Dublin 8

Though the actual Guinness Brewery is closed to the public, the Guinness Storehouse will fill you in on everything you've ever wanted to know about "black gold." This temple to Guinness is housed in a 1904 building that was used for the fermentation process — when yeast is added to beer. The core of the building is a recently created seven-level, pint-shaped structure that could hold approximately 14.3 million pints of Guinness. The Storehouse explores every facet of Ireland's favorite beverage, from the ingredients that go into each batch to the company's advertising campaigns to the role of Guinness in Irish culture. Though there is a sense of unabashed propaganda to the whole attraction, the exhibits are beautifully done in a cool, modern design. There is a lot to see, but you'll definitely want to make time for the ingredients exhibit, which features a veritable beach of barley and a waterfall of Irish water; the intriguing exhibit about the Guinness and Irish pubs around the world (did you know that the first Irish pub in Abu Dhabi opened in 1995?); and the fascinating display of Guinness advertisements through the years. The top-floor Gravity Bar is (literally) the Storehouse's crowning glory, offering 360-degree views of Dublin through floor-to-ceiling glass walls, and dispensing a free pint of black stuff to every visitor over the age of 18.

*See map p. 154. St. James's Gate.* ☎ *01-408-4800.* www.guinness-storehouse. com. *Bus: 51B, 78A, 123. Admission: €14 ($16) adults, €12 ($14) seniors, €9 ($10) students, €3 ($3.45) children 6–12, free for children under 6. Price includes a free pint of stout or a soda. Open: Sept–June daily 9:30 a.m.– about 6:30 p.m. (last admission 5 p.m.), July–Aug daily 9:30 a.m.– about 10 p.m. (last admission at 9 p.m.). Suggested visit: 2 ½ hours.*

## The Ha'Penny Bridge
**Dublin 1 and 2**

This famous footbridge — the only pedestrian-only bridge across the River Liffey — has connected the north side of the river directly to Temple Bar since 1816. Its name comes from the half-penny toll that it once cost to cross the bridge. (The poet W. B. Yeats and others were not fans of the toll and walked down to O'Connell Bridge to avoid it). You can't miss the bridge — it's bright white and arches high over the River Liffey, and at night, it's festooned with cheerful lights. The bridge offers views up and down the River Liffey. If you want a view of the Ha'Penny Bridge stretching over the Liffey, walk to the Millennium Bridge, a shimmery little wisp of a bridge directly west of the Ha'Penny. You'll find a peaceful boardwalk along the north side of the river.

*See map p. 144. Over the River Liffey between O'Connell and Millennium bridges, across from Liffey St. Lower on the north side. Suggested visit: 5 minutes.*

## Kilmainham Gaol
**Dublin 8**

From the 1780s to the 1920s, many Irish rebels against the British crown were imprisoned at Kilmainham Gaol (pronounced *jail*), some for years and others only for the short period before they met the firing squad. Used as the set for the 1993 Daniel Day Lewis film *In the Name of the Father,* the jail has been restored and offers excellent tours, plus intriguing exhibits about the political history of Ireland and the fascinating history of the jail. Peering into the dank cells, you can practically see the figures of the famous patriots who were imprisoned here, among them Charles Stewart Parnell, Joseph Plunkett, and James Connolly. A short movie about the jail is shown in the chapel where Plunkett was allowed to marry Grace Gifford just hours before being shot for his part in the 1916 Rising. Perhaps the most haunting part of the tour is the visit to the stark courtyard where firing squads executed many of the rebels from the 1916 Rising, including Connolly, who was so badly injured during the fighting that he couldn't stand up by himself and had to be strapped into a chair to be shot.

*See map p. 154. Inchicore Rd., Kilmainham. ☎ 01-453-5984. Bus: 51, 51A, 79. Admission: €5 ($5.75) adult, €3.50 ($4.05) seniors, €2 ($2.30) students and children. Open: Apr–Sept daily 9:30 a.m.–6 p.m. (last admission 4:45 p.m.), Oct–March Mon–Sat 9:30 a.m.–5:30 p.m. (last admission 4 p.m.), Sun 10 a.m.–6 p.m. (last admission 4:45 p.m.). Tours leave every hour on the hour. Suggested visit: 2 hours.*

## Merrion Square
**Dublin 2**

This is my favorite of Dublin's parks. Thick with old trees and brilliant, splashy flowers during the warm months, Merrion Square's park is filled with little nooks and paths that make it seem many times larger than it is. Take one path, and you're walking in a lush, dense forest filled with birdsong; make a turn, and there's a sun-dappled field with school kids kicking around a soccer ball; turn again, and you're greeted by a couple picnicking on a bench in a formal garden area. Lining the square are textbook Georgian row houses, characterized by their brightly painted doors, elegant brass door knockers, and *fanlights* — half-moon-shaped windows over the doors. Around the square are plaques that identify the former homes of poet W. B. Yeats (No. 82), playwright Oscar Wilde (No. 1), and Catholic liberator Daniel O'Connell (No. 58). On Sundays, the city's top artists hang their works for sale from the rails surrounding the square.

*See map p. 154. Merrion Square takes up the block directly behind the National Gallery. Take Nassau St. on the south side of Trinity College and continue east for a few blocks until it becomes Merrion Square North. DART: Pearse Street Station and head south on Westland Row and Merrion St. Lower. Bus: 5, 7A, 8 Admission: Free. Open: Daylight hours. Suggested visit: 20 minutes.*

## The National Gallery
### Dublin 2

This fine collection of Western European art (mostly paintings) from the Middle Ages through the 20th century is often overlooked by visitors planning their itineraries in Dublin, which is a shame, because the collection is varied and interesting. The museum has an extensive collection of Irish works from the 18th century through today and boasts 17th-century treasures such as Caravaggio's *The Taking of Christ*, Vermeer's *Lady Writing a Letter*, and Rembrandt's *Rest on a Flight Into Egypt*. A gem of the museum is a large room (No. 21) devoted to the works of the Yeats family, with a focus on the mystical, vivid paintings of Jack Yeats (brother of W. B.). The star of the Portrait Gallery just may be a recent portrait of U2 singer Bono. The minimalist cafe is a great spot to rest your museum-weary feet and indulge in a cup of sweet hot chocolate. If you're in the museum on Saturday or Sunday, take advantage of the free guided tours.

*See map p. 154. Merrion Square West. ☎ 01-661-5133. DART: Pearse Street Station and head south on Westland Row and Merrion St. Lower. Bus: 5, 7A, 8, 44, 47, 47B, 48A, 62. Admission: Free, although special exhibits may have a cost. Open: Mon–Wed and Fri–Sat 9:30 a.m.–5:30 p.m., Thurs 9:30 a.m.–8:30 p.m., Sun noon–5:30 p.m. Free guided tours available 3 p.m. Sat and 2, 3, and 4 p.m. Sun. Suggested visit: 1 ½ hours.*

## National Museum of Ireland
### Dublin 2

This grand museum, featuring a huge rotunda and beautiful mosaics, is home to many of Ireland's most dazzling and important artifacts from 7000 B.C. to the present. The stars of the museum's collection are in The Treasury, where you find the gorgeous Tara Brooch and Ardagh Chalice, plus masterpieces of craftsmanship from Ireland's Iron Age; and in Ireland's Gold, where elegant gold ornaments dating from 7000 to 2000 B.C. are displayed. The other exhibits, including Prehistoric Ireland, The Road to Independence (featuring uniforms and other objects from the nationalist struggle of the early 20th century), Viking Ireland, Medieval Ireland, and the somewhat-out-of-place Ancient Egypt also boast interesting and beautifully presented objects.

*See map p. 154. Kildare and Merrion streets.* ☎ *01-677-7444. DART: Pearse Street. Bus: 7, 7A, 8, 10, 11, 13. Admission: Free. Open: Tues–Sat 10 a.m.–5 p.m., Sun 2–5 p.m. Guided tours available. Suggested visit: 2 hours.*

### St. Patrick's Cathedral
**Dublin 8**

St. Patrick's Cathedral, the national cathedral of the Church of Ireland, derives its name from the belief that in the fifth century, St. Patrick baptized converts to Christianity in a well that once existed on this land. Though there have been churches on this spot since the fifth century, the glorious church that stands today was built in the early 13th century, with restorations to the west tower in 1370 and the addition of a spire in 1749. Volunteers provide an informative map pamphlet that guides you through the church, explaining the highlights of the interior. You can visit the moving memorial of author and social critic Jonathan Swift, who served as the dean of the cathedral and is buried next to his beloved friend Stella, and pay your respects to the monument of Turlough O'Carolan (1670–1738), one of Ireland's finest and most prolific harpers and bards, who composed many tunes that are still played by Irish musicians today. Don't miss the Choir, which is adorned with colorful medieval banners and helmets. Beautiful matins (Sept–June Mon–Fri 9:40 a.m.) and evensongs (Mon–Fri 5:45 p.m.) are sung here.

*See map p. 154. Patrick's Close.* ☎ *01-475-4817. DART: Tara Street Station. Bus: 50, 54A, 56A. Admission: €4.20 ($4.85) adults, €3.20 ($3.70) students and seniors, services free. March–Oct daily 9 a.m.–6 p.m.; Nov–Feb Mon–Fri 9 a.m.–6 p.m., Sat 9 a.m.–5 p.m., Sun 10 a.m.–3 p.m. Suggested visit: 45 minutes.*

### St. Stephen's Green and Newman House
**Dublin 2**

Sitting in this beautiful, centrally located park on a sunny Saturday, you'll probably see about half of Dublin's population promenading by, pushing strollers, lugging shopping bags, munching on sandwiches, and so on. The 27-acre park encompasses several different landscapes, from a large duck pond shaded by the trailing leaves of a weeping willow to formally laid-out flower gardens to open green spaces that beg you to settle down for a picnic. During the summer months, you can enjoy the frequent lunchtime concerts. Newman House, on the south side of the green, was once home to the Catholic University of Ireland. You can take a guided tour of the house, which is filled with some gorgeous examples of Georgian furniture and interior design.

*See map p. 154. St. Stephen's Green takes up the block at the top of Grafton St.; Newman House is located at 85–86 St. Stephen's Green, between Harcourt St. and Earlsfort Terrace. Take Grafton St. away from Trinity College.* ☎ *01-706-7422. DART: Tara Street Station. Bus: 10, 11, 13, 14, 14A, 15A, 15B. Admission: Green: Free;*

*Newman House: €4 ($4.60) adults, €2.50 ($2.90) students and seniors. Green Open: Daylight hours. Newman House tours run June–Sept Tues–Fri at noon, 2 p.m. 3 p.m., and 4 p.m.; Sat and Sun 11 a.m., noon, and 1 p.m. Only open to groups Oct–May. Suggested visit: About 1 hour.*

### Trinity College and the Book of Kells
### Dublin 2

Trinity College, founded in 1592 by Elizabeth I, looks like the ideal of an impressive, refined, old-world college, with Georgian stone buildings and perfectly manicured green lawns. The campus sits in the middle of the busy city, but within its gates, everything is composed and quiet. As you enter the main gate, look to your left to see the cross-denominational Christian chapel. Directly opposite, on your right, is the college exam hall. If you're passing through during exam time, you may see students sprinting from chapel to exam hall, having just offered up a prayer for a good mark. On your left next to the chapel is the dining hall. As you wander the cobbled paths around Trinity, you can imagine the days when former students Oscar Wilde, Samuel Beckett, Jonathan Swift, and Bram Stoker (a great athlete at Trinity) pounded the same pavement on their way to class. During nice weather, students lounge on the well-kept greens or on benches for picnics or studying. There is nothing finer than taking a picnic lunch (try fish and chips from nearby Beshoff, reviewed earlier in this chapter, in the "Dining in Dublin" section) to Trinity's little hidden garden or cricket and rugby pitch (walk past the Old Library, and make a right at the pretty little garden with benches).

The jewel in Trinity College's crown is the **Book of Kells** along with its attending exhibit, housed in the Old Library. This manuscript of the four gospels of the Bible was painstakingly crafted by monks around A.D. 800. The gospels are written in ornate Latin script, and the book is filled with stunning, vivid illustrations, including intricate Celtic knots and fantastical animals. The engaging exhibit that leads to the Book of Kells (and three other ancient Irish religious texts) explains the historical context in which the books were created and reveals the techniques used in the creation of the books. You get to see only one page of the Book of Kells on each visit (they turn a page each day).

You may be tempted to turn around and leave the exhibit after you've seen the Book of Kells. Don't. Instead, go upstairs to the Long Room, which has gallery bookcases filled with Trinity's oldest books and is lined with marble busts of dead white men (I mean that in the most affectionate way) from Shakespeare to Swift. This room, used as a model for the Hogwarts dining hall in the Harry Potter movies, also boasts the oldest known harp in Ireland, made of oak and willow.

*See map p. 154. Main entrance on College St. at the eastern end of Dame St. Walk two blocks south of the River Liffey from O'Connell Street Bridge; entrance is on your left. Walk through the front entrance arch, and follow signs to the Old Library and Treasury. ☎ 01-677-2941 for Trinity College information or 01-608-2308 for Book of Kells information. DART: Tara Street Station. Bus: 15, 15A, 15B, 83, 155. Admission:*

*College grounds: Free; Old Library and Book of Kells: €7.50 ($8.65) adults; €6.50 ($7.50) students, children 12–17, and seniors 60 and over; free under 12. Open: June–Sept Mon–Sat 9:30 a.m.–5 p.m., Sun 9:30 a.m.–4:30 p.m.; Oct–May Mon–Sat 9:30 a.m.–5 p.m., Sun noon to 4:30 p.m. Closed for ten days during Christmas holiday. Suggested visit: 2½ hours.*

## More cool things to see and do

The following sections list other great attractions in Dublin, including churches, museums, and historic buildings.

### More landmarks and historic buildings

✔ **The Bank of Ireland:** Once the Parliament House, the Bank of Ireland is a striking 18th-century building. The Irish House of Lords chamber, where Parliament sat before being merged with England's Parliament, features Irish oak woodwork, period tapestries, and an awesome Irish crystal chandelier dating back to 1765. One thing you'll notice right away: There aren't any windows in the Bank of Ireland. This isn't for security reasons; rather, when it was built, England levied a hefty property tax that increased drastically with each window built. To save money, the building was constructed with a single atrium for light and no windows. Ever heard of the phrase "daylight robbery"? You guessed it — it comes from the government's charging for daylight.

Location: 2 College Green, Dublin 2 (see map p. 144). ☎ 01-661-5933, ext. 2265. Free admission. Open: Monday through Wednesday and Friday from 10 a.m. to 4 p.m., Thursday from 10 a.m. to 5 p.m. Guided 15-minute tours of the House of Lords chamber are given Tuesdays at 10:30 a.m., 11:30 a.m., and 1:45 p.m. Suggested visit: 15 minutes.

✔ **General Post Office:** The bullet holes scarring the pillars of the General Post Office (GPO) testify to the violent battle between Irish patriots (also called Republicans) and English forces during the Easter Rising of 1916. The Republicans commandeered the building, and leader Pádraig Pearse read the Proclamation of the Irish Republic from the front steps. The patriots held their ground for a week before shelling from the British forces drove them to surrender. Thirteen of the Republican leaders were executed shortly thereafter, and the interior of the post office was burned to the ground. Rebuilt in 1929, this is now Dublin's main post office. Inside, lining the walls, is an evocative series of paintings depicting the 1916 Rising — a visual history lesson. You can also find a statue of the ancient mythic Irish hero Cuchulainn, dedicated to those who died during the Rising.

Location: North of the River Liffey, halfway up the left side of O'Connell Street, Dublin 1 (see map p. 154). ☎ 01-705-8833. Free admission. Open: Monday through Saturday from 8 a.m. to 8 p.m., Sunday from 10:30 a.m. to 6:30 p.m. Suggested visit: 30 minutes.

✔ **Glasnevin Cemetery:** This primarily Catholic cemetery, founded in 1832, is the final resting place of many famous Irish citizens, including political heroes Michael Collins and Charles Stewart Parnell, and playwright Brendan Behan. There are many stunning Celtic crosses throughout the cemetery. There's a heritage map that lists who is buried where (pick one up for a small fee at the flower shop at the cemetery entrance), and the guided walking tour is filled with interesting information that gives a face to many parts of Irish history.

Location: Finglas Road (see map p. 169). ☎ **01-830-1133;** www. glasnevin-cemetery.ie. Bus: 19, 19A, or 13 (from O'Connell St. to Harts Corner, a 5-minute walk from the cemetery) or 40, 40A, 40B, or 40C (from Parnell St. to the main cemetery entrance). Free admission and tours. Open: Daily from 8 a.m. to 4 p.m. Tours meet at the main entrance of the cemetery at 2:30 p.m. on Wednesday and Friday.

✔ **James Joyce Statue:** This statue pays homage to the wiry, bespectacled man whose inspired words have become the essence of Dublin in the "auld times."

Location: Halfway up O'Connell Street, just at the top of Earl Street North, Dublin 1 (see map p. 154). Suggested visit: A few seconds, unless you decide to recite a sentence or two from *Finnegan's Wake,* which could take a month.

✔ **The Millennium Spire:** This 120m (394-ft.) high spike of stainless steel is meant to represent 21st-century Dublin. The spire replaces Nelson's Pillar, which was erected during the British occupation of Ireland.

Location: O'Connell Street, Dublin 1 (in front of the main post office; see map p. 154). Suggested visit: Time enough to gaze up in vertiginous awe and snap a photo.

✔ **Molly Malone Statue:** Sing along, now: "In Dublin's fair city, where the girls are so pretty, there once was a girl named sweet Molly Malone . . . " Inspired by the traditional song "Cockles and Mussels," this statue is a tribute to the fictional Molly Malone, who represents all the women who hawked their wares on Dublin's busy streets in the past. Affectionately known as "The Tart with the Cart," Molly welcomes shoppers at the head of Grafton Street.

Location: Corner of Nassau and Grafton streets (see map p. 154). Suggested visit: About 30 seconds, unless you take time to sing the whole song.

## More museums

✔ **Dublin's City Hall: The Story of the Capital:** Located in Dublin's beautiful city hall, this exhibit gives a good overview of Dublin history through audiovisuals, text, and objects.

Location: Dame Street near Dublin Castle (see map p. 154). ☎ 01-72-2204. Bus: 54, 50, 56A, 77, 77A, 123, and 150. Admission: €4 ($4.60) adults, €2 ($2.30) seniors and students, €1.50 ($1.75) children. Open: Monday to Saturday from 10 a.m. to 5:15 p.m., Sunday from 2 p.m. to 5 p.m. Suggested visit: 45 minutes.

✔ **Dublin Writers Museum:** Who said to U.S. Customs officials: "I have nothing to declare — except my genius?" That would be witty Oscar Wilde. Wilde's life and literature are presented at this museum, along with the biographies, works, personal effects, letters, and portraits and photographs of Ireland's literary luminaries from ancient times through the 20th century. Exhaustive and interesting text on the walls relates the biographies of the writers and explains Ireland's literary movements. If you're lacking time, you can just read the two- or three-line summary posted at the bottom of the text panel. The audio tour gives brief descriptions of the writers and includes snippets of text read by actors and music appropriate to the display that you're looking at (don't be cowed by the listening device; it takes everyone a few minutes to master it). Lectures, actors portraying writers, readings, and children's programs are on offer (call for details). You can contemplate the words of the literary giants over a snack in the tranquil Zen Garden or have a complete meal at the museum's excellent restaurant, Chapter 1. Kids under 10 or 11 will probably be bored at this museum.

Location: 18 Parnell Square North, Dublin 1 (see map p. 154). ☎ 01-872-2077. DART: Connolly Station. Bus: 10, 11, 11A, 11B, 13, 16, 16A, 19, 19A, 22, 22A, 36. Admission: €6.25 ($7.20) adult, €5.25 ($6.05) 18 and under, and seniors, €3.75 ($4.30) under 12. Open: June to August, Monday through Friday from 10 a.m. to 6 p.m., Saturday from 10 a.m. to 5 p.m., and Sunday from 11 a.m. to 5 p.m.; September to May, Monday through Saturday from 10 a.m. to 5 p.m., Sunday from 11 a.m. to 5 p.m. Suggested visit: 2 hours if you want to read all the text, 45 minutes if you want to zip through.

✔ **Irish Museum of Modern Art:** Sitting grandly at the end of a tree-lined lane, this is one of Ireland's most magnificent 17th-century buildings, built in 1680 as a hospital for injured soldiers. The building is so impressive that when it was finished, many lobbied to use it as the campus for Trinity College. Be sure to check out the Baroque chapel, with its wood carvings and stained glass. The permanent collection includes a small but exciting array of Irish and international works, and the museum hosts frequent temporary exhibitions.

Location: Military Road, Kilmainham, Dublin 8 (see map p. 154). ☎ 01-612-9900. www.modernart.ie. Bus: 79, 90. Admission: Free. Open: Tuesday through Saturday from 10:00 a.m. to 5:30 p.m., Sunday from noon to 5:30 p.m. Suggested visit: 1 hour.

✔ **James Joyce Centre:** This one is for Joyce fans. The Centre has a comprehensive library and archives, plus exhibits featuring some of Joyce's personal effects, photographs and portraits of people who show up in *Ulysses,* and different editions of Joyce's books. Temporary exhibits delve into different aspects of Joyce's life and work.

Location: 35 N. Great Georges St., Dublin 1 (see map p. 154). ☎ 01-878-8547. www.jamesjoyce.ie. Bus: 3, 10, 11, 11A, 13, 16, 16A, 19, 19A, 22, or 22A. Admission: €4.50 ($5.20) adults, €3.50 ($4.05) seniors, students, and children under 10. Open: Monday through Saturday from 9:30 a.m. to 5 p.m., Sunday from 12:30 to 5 p.m. Suggested visit: 1 to 1½ hours.

✔ **The National Museum of Decorative Arts and History (Collins Barracks):** This well-designed museum, housed in 18th-century army barracks, exhibits some of Ireland's finest decorative objects. Galleries are organized by theme — Scientific Instruments, Irish Period Furniture, Irish Silver, and so on — and feature engaging descriptions of the history of the various items. My favorite exhibit is the Curator's Choice, which comprises 25 diverse objects chosen by the museum's curators because of the intriguing stories that they tell. Fashion buffs won't want to miss "The Way We Wore," an exhibit displaying Irish fashions over the past 250 years.

Location: Collins Barracks, Benburb Street, Dublin 7 (see map p. 154). ☎ 01-677-7444. DART: Connolly Station. Bus: 25, 25A, 66, 67, 90. Admission: Free. Open: Tuesday through Saturday from 10 a.m. to 5 p.m., Sunday from 2 to 5 p.m. Suggested visit: 2 hours.

✔ **Old Jameson Distillery:** Take an interesting guided tour through part of Jameson's now-unused Bow Street distillery. You can watch a short film about Irish whiskey and follow the life of this spirit from raw materials through distillation to finished product. The tour finishes off with a blind whiskey tasting for a lucky handful of volunteers and a dram of Jameson's for all other visitors of legal age. On the bottom floor of the distillery, keep an eye out for Smithy the cat, who kept the distillery mouse-free. The Distillery store sells all kinds of Jameson whiskeys and whiskey products, including some addictive whiskey fudge.

Location: Bow Street, Dublin 7 (see map p. 154). ☎ 01-872-5566. DART: Connolly Street. Bus: 67, 67A, 68, 69, 79, 90. Admission: €7.95($9.15) adults, €5.75 ($6.60) students and seniors, €3 ($3.45) children. Open: Daily from 9 a.m. to 6 p.m. (last tour at 5:30 p.m.). Suggested visit: 45 minutes.

## More parks (And a zoo!)

✔ **Garden of Remembrance:** This small, peaceful park is dedicated to the men and women who died in pursuit of Irish freedom from British rule during the 1916 uprising. Near the entrance is a still reflecting pool with a mosaic at its bottom depicting broken weapons — symbols of peace. Farther back, the large statue near the fountain portrays the myth of the Children of Lir, who were turned into swans by their selfish and cruel stepmother. The park's location is significant — it is where several leaders of the 1916 Easter rebellion were held overnight before being taken to Kilmainham Gaol and put to death.

Location: The north end of Parnell Square at the top of O'Connell Street, Dublin 1 (see map p. 154). Open: Daily during daylight hours. Admission: Free. Suggested visit: 15 minutes.

✔ **Phoenix Park and Zoological Gardens:** This is Europe's largest enclosed city park — five times the size of London's Hyde Park. You can drive through it, but if the weather's nice, don't pass up the chance to walk, because Phoenix Park is more than just a green spot for picnic lunches: Enclosed within it are the homes of Ireland's president and the U.S. ambassador. The Zoological Gardens is the world's third-oldest zoo and houses a wide variety of animals, from lions to red pandas. Other sights include the Papal Cross, where Pope John Paul II said Mass to a million Irish in 1979, and Ashton Castle, a 17th-century tower house that's now the visitors' center. Originally a deer park, the area is still home to many deer.

Location: Park Gate, Conyngham Road; Phoenix Park Visitor Centre, Dublin 8 (see map p. 154). Visitor Centre ☎ **01-677-0095**, Zoological Park ☎ **01-677-1425**. To the Park: Bus 37, 38, or 39 to Ashtown Cross Gate. To the Zoo: Bus 10, 25, or 26. Admission: Free to park; to zoo €7.50 ($8.65) adults, €5.25 ($6.05) students, €4 ($4.60) under 17. The park is open from 9:30 a.m. to 5:30 p.m. daily from late March to May and the month of October; from 9:30 a.m. to 6:30 p.m. daily from June to September; and from 9:30 a.m. to 4:30 p.m. Saturday and Sunday from November to mid-March. The zoo is open Monday through Saturday from 9:30 a.m. to 6:00 p.m., Sunday from 10:30 a.m. to 6:00 p.m. Closes at sunset in winter. Suggested visit: 2½ hours.

## More cathedrals and churches

✔ **St. Ann's Anglican Church:** In this church, the writer of the creepy novel *Dracula*, Irishman Bram Stoker, married Florence Balcombe, witty playwright and Oscar Wilde's first love. Wolfe Tone, the famous rebel, was also married here. Highlights are the gorgeous stained-glass windows and ornate plasterwork.

Location: Dawson Street, Dublin 2 (see map p. 154). ☎ **01-676-7727.** DART: Tara Street Station. Bus: 10, 11A, 11B, 13, 20B. Admission: Free. Open: Monday through Friday 10 a.m. to 4 p.m. Suggested visit: 30 minutes.

✔ **St. Audoen's Church:** There are actually two churches of the same name off of Cook Street, but you're looking for the smaller and older of the two. St. Audoen's is situated right next to the only remaining gate of the Old City, which was built in 1214. The only surviving medieval church in Dublin, St. Audoen's features a doorway from 1190; a 13th-century nave; and three of the oldest church bells in Ireland, cast in 1423. A nicely done exhibit explains the history of the church, and tour guides who take you through the church itself really know their stuff.

Location: Cornmarket (off High St.; see map p. 154) ☎ **01-677-0088.** Admission: €1.90 ($2.20) adults, €1.20 ($1.40) seniors, €.70 (80¢) students and children. Open: June through September daily from 9:30 a.m. to 5:30 p.m. (last tour at 4:45 p.m.). Suggested visit: 40 minutes.

✔ **St. Michan's Church:** Unless you plan to make your next vacation a tour of the ancient pyramids, this may be your best chance to see actual mummies. It's hard to believe, but the combination of cool temperatures, dry air, and methane gas at this location preserves bodies, and the vaults below the church contain the remains of such people as Henry and John Sheares, leaders of the Rebellion of 1798, and a Crusader. The church itself is also worth a look, boasting an organ believed to have been played by Handel, and detailed wood carvings of instruments above the choir area.

Location: Church Street, Dublin 7 (see map p. 154). ☎ **01-872-4154.** DART: Tara Street Station. Bus: 34, 70, or 80. Admission: €3.50 ($4.05) adults, €3 ($3.45) seniors and students, €2.50 ($2.90) under 12. Open: November through March 16 Monday through Friday from 12:30 to 3:30 p.m. and Saturday from 10 a.m. to 12:45 p.m.; March 17 through October Monday through Friday from 10 a.m. to 12:45 p.m. and from 2 to 4:30 p.m., and Saturday from 10 a.m. to 12:45 p.m. Suggested visit: 30 minutes.

### *Green on green: Dublin's top golfing spots*

Check out Chapter 4 for a countrywide golf itinerary, or enjoy these courses near Dublin:

✔ **Portmarnock:** This links course has been home to several major championships. It's a natural golf course, incorporating the rugged landscape of the region rather than being purpose-built.

Location: Portmarnock, County Dublin (see map p. 169). ☎ **01-846-2968.** www.portmarnockgolfclub.ie. Par: 72. Fees: €165 ($190) weekdays, €190 ($219) weekends. Visitors welcome every day except Wednesday.

✔ **Royal Dublin:** Situated on manmade North Bull Island in Dublin Bay, only 6.4km (4 miles) from the center of Dublin, this is a championship course that has offered exciting play amid great scenery for more than 100 years. The links are located along the seaside.

Location: North Bull Island, Doillymount, Dublin 3 (see map p. 169). ☎ **01-833-6346.** www.theroyaldublingolfclub.com. Par: 72. Fees: €100 ($115) Monday, Tuesday, and Thursday; €115 ($132) Friday. Visitors welcome Monday, Tuesday, Thursday, and Friday.

## Attractions around County Dublin

Fry Model Railway Museum **3**
Glasnevin Cemetery **6**
James Joyce Tower and Museum **7**
Malahide Castle **3**
National Botanic Gardens **6**
Newbridge House and Park **1**
Portmarnock Golf Course **4**
Royal Dublin Golf Course **5**
St. Margaret's Golf Course **2**

✔ **St. Margaret's:** One of the hosts of the Irish Open, this is a relatively new, challenging, and exciting inland course of the highest standard, with an infamously difficult finishing hole.

Location: Stephubble, St. Margaret's, County Dublin (see map p. 169). ☎ **01-864-0400.** www.stmargaretsgolf.com. Par: 73. Fees: €65 ($75) weekdays, €80 ($92) weekends. Visitors welcome daily.

## *Attractions a little out of town*

Dublin Bus (☎ 01-873-4222) runs two great tours that cover the outlying areas of Dublin. The *Coast and Castle Tour* travels north and covers the fishing villages of Dublin Bay, the coastline, and Malahide Castle. It leaves at 10 a.m. daily. The *South Coast Tour* covers the port towns of Dun Laoghaire and beautiful Dalkey, Killiney Bay, and the Wicklow Mountains. It leaves at 11 a.m. and 2 p.m. daily. Tours depart from 59 Upper O'Connell St., Dublin 1. Prices for both are €20 ($23) adult, €10 ($12) under 14.

Check the "Attractions Around County Dublin" map for the location of these sights.

✔ **James Joyce Tower and Museum:** This tower was made famous in the first scene of *Ulysses,* in which Joyce has his main character, Stephen Dedalus, stay here with the character Buck Mulligan. Located on a rocky beach in the quaint town of Sandycove, the tower was built with 11 others in 1804 as protection against a possible invasion by Napoleon. Joyce actually did stay in the tower with his friend Oliver St. John Gogarty (who inspired the fictional Mulligan) at the start of the century, and now the place is officially known as Joyce Tower. It houses such Joycean effects as letters, a walking stick, and a cigar case. Lovers of Joyce and *Ulysses* will have a great time here; less enthusiastic fans may be disappointed by the small size of the exhibit and may want to stick to the James Joyce Centre (reviewed in "More cool things to see and do," earlier in this chapter).

Location: Sandycove (see map p. 169). ☎ 01-280-9265. DART: Sandycove Station. Bus: 8. Admission: €6.25 ($7.20) adults, €5.25 ($6.05) students and seniors, €3.75 ($4.30) under 12. Open: April through October Monday through Saturday from 10 a.m. to 1 p.m. and from 2 p.m. to 5 p.m., Sunday from 2 to 6 p.m. Other times by arrangement. Suggested visit: 1 hour.

✔ **Malahide Castle:** This castle was witness to the longevity of one of Ireland's great and wealthy families, the Talbots, who resided here from 1185 to 1973. The architecture of the house is varied, and period furniture adorns the rooms. There's a large collection of Irish portraits, many from the National Gallery. The Great Hall chronicles the Talbots with portraits of family members. One tragic legend tells of the morning of the Battle of the Boyne in 1690, when

14 members of the family shared a last meal; by the end of the battle, all had been killed. The grounds are spectacular; be sure to check out the Botanic Gardens. Kids will have a great time at the Fry Model Railway Museum (see the next review) located on the castle grounds.

Location: Malahide (see map p. 169). ☎ **01-846-2184.** Irish Rail: Malahide Station from Connolly Station. Bus: 42. Admission: €6.25 ($7.20) adults, €5.25 ($6.05) seniors and students, €3.75 ($4.30) under 12; combined tickets available with Fry Model Railway Museum (see next review). Open: April through October, Monday through Saturday from 10 a.m. to 5 p.m., Sunday from 11 a.m. to 6 p.m.; November through March, Monday through Friday from 10 a.m. to 5 p.m., Sunday from 11 a.m. to 5 p.m. Suggested visit: 1½ hours.

✔ **Fry Model Railway Museum:** Located on the grounds of Malahide Castle (see the previous review), the Fry Model Railway Museum will entertain kids of all ages. This unique collection of handmade trains spans the history of train travel in Ireland and runs over an area covering 2,500 square feet, with stations, bridges, trams, buses, and a mini representation of the River Liffey. The collection was assembled by Cyril Fry, a railway engineer during the 1920s and 1930s.

Location: Malahide Castle (see map p. 169). ☎ **01-846-3779.** Irish Rail: Malahide Station from Connolly Station. Bus: 42. Admission: €6.25 ($7.20) adults, €5.25($6.05) seniors and students, €3.75 ($4.30) children; combined tickets available for castle and museum. Open: April through September, Monday through Saturday from 10 a.m. to 5 p.m., Sunday from 2 to 6 p.m. Suggested visit: 1 hour.

✔ **National Botanic Gardens:** With a huge plant collection (more than 20,000 species) this is a must for anyone who has a green thumb (or aspires to have one). Highlights include a rose garden, an alpine area, and an arboretum. The huge greenhouses (called *glass houses* in Ireland) shelter tropical plants and other exotic species.

Location: Glasnevin, Dublin 9 (see map p. 169). ☎ **01-837-7596.** Bus: 13, 19, 134. Admission: Free. Open: April to October Monday through Saturday from 9 a.m. to 6 p.m., Sunday from 10 a.m. to 6 p.m.; November through March Monday through Saturday from 10 a.m. to 4:30 p.m., Sunday from 10 a.m. to 4:30 p.m. Suggested visit: 45 minutes.

✔ **Newbridge House and Park:** Walking around Dublin, you see plenty of examples of Georgian exteriors, but here's your chance to see a fine Georgian interior. Each gorgeous room in the manor house features original furniture and objects. The extensive park grounds are home to a kid-friendly animal farm.

Location: Donabate (see map p. 169). ☎ **01-843-6534.** Irish Rail: Donabate Station from Connolly Station. Bus: 33B. Admission: €4

($4.60) adults, €3 ($3.45) seniors and students, €2 ($2.30) under 12. Open: April through September, Tuesday through Saturday from 10 a.m. to 1 p.m. and 2 p.m. to 5 p.m., Sunday from 2 p.m. to 6 p.m.; October through March, Saturday and Sunday from 2 p.m. to 5 p.m. Suggested visit: 1½ hours.

## Seeing Dublin by guided tour

If you want something more independent than the guided tours listed below, check out one of the Dublin Tourism Board's many self-guided tours of the city. The **Rock 'n' Roll Trail** focuses on contemporary Irish musicians such as U2, Sinead O'Connor, and Chris de Burgh; the **Georgian Trail** covers five 18th-century squares, surrounded by period homes; the **Old City Trail** concentrates on the medieval area of Dublin; and the **Cultural Trail** covers the city's impressive architecture. Maps are available at the **Dublin Tourism Board** on Suffolk Street. You can also get the information online at www.visitdublin.com/tours/walkingtours.asp. Give yourself an afternoon for each tour.

### Jameson's Dublin Literary Pub Crawl

Literature has never been more fun! Two excellent Irish actors perform humorous tidbits by Dublin's best-known writers as they guide you to pubs of literary fame and other interesting stops. You'll be laughing hysterically by the end of the tour — and not just because of the numerous pints you've consumed. There's a chance to win some prizes at the end (including some Jameson-related), so pay attention. Arrive by half an hour before the tour begins to get your tickets.

*Tours generally run every evening at 7:30 p.m. and Sun at noon during the summer (April–Nov) and Thur–Sun at 7:30 p.m. and at noon on Sun in the winter (Dec–March). Purchase tickets ½ hour in advance at The Duke (Duke St., off Grafton), where the tour begins. Information:* ☎ *01-670-5602. Be sure to call, because times sometimes change.* www.dublinpubcrawl.com. *Price:* €*10 ($12) adults,* €*8 ($9.20) students. The crawl lasts about 2 hours and 15 minutes.*

### Historical Walking Tours of Dublin

Walk this way for an interesting historical look at the city and at Ireland at large. On the Original Tour, nicknamed the "Seminar on the Street," Trinity history students and graduates give a relatively in-depth account of Irish history as they guide you to some of the city's most famous sites, including Trinity, the Old Parliament House, Dublin Castle, City Hall, Christ Church, and Temple Bar. This tour is likely to thrill history buffs and anyone interested in the details of Irish history, and may bore anyone looking for short anecdotes. During the summer, the company adds three special tours: Piety, Penance & Potatoes, a sexual history of Ireland; The Gorgeous Mask, a look at architecture and society; and A Terrible Beauty, a tour focusing on the birth of the Irish state (1916–1923).

*Original Tours: Daily at 11 a.m. and 3 p.m. Apr–Sept, daily at noon Oct–March. Special tours: Daily at noon May–Aug (call to see which days each special tour runs). Leaves from the front gate of Trinity College on College St., Dublin. Information:* ☎ *01-878-0227.* www.historicalinsights.ie. *Price:* €10 ($12) adults, €8 ($9.20) students, seniors, and children.

## Hop On Hop Off Bus Tours

I highly recommend this tour, which is perfect if you want some guidance but also want the freedom to take as much time as you want checking out the sights. Pretty much every attraction the city has to offer is at one of the bus stops, and there's commentary throughout. The tour takes 1 hour and 15 minutes if you just ride the bus straight through, but you can, as the name says, hop on and hop off, stretching the tour out to a whole day. Some attractions offer discounts for people taking this tour.

*All tours leave from Dublin Bus, 59 Upper O'Connell St., Dublin 1.* ☎ *01-873-4222.* www.dublinbus.ie. *Bus runs daily 9:30 a.m.–6:30 p.m. (a bus stops at each stop every 12 minutes from 9:30 a.m.–5:30 p.m. and every 30 minutes from 5:30–6:30 p.m.) Price:* €12.50 ($14) adults, €11 ($13) students and seniors, €6 ($6.90) children under 14.

## Traditional Irish Musical Pub Crawl

This pub crawl is a fabulous experience for anyone even remotely interested in Irish music. Two excellent musicians guide you from pub to pub, regaling you with Irish tunes and songs; cracking many a joke; and filling you in on the instruments used in Irish music, the history of the music, and the various types of tunes and songs. The musicians who present this tour care deeply about Irish music and create an experience that is as authentic as possible. Get thee to the phone or Internet to order tickets, or show up early at the pub to assure yourself of a space on the tour.

*Tours leave from Oliver St. John Gogarty's Pub in Temple Bar (corner of Fleet and Anglesea streets).* ☎ *01-475-3313.* www.discoverdublin.ie. *Tours take place May–Oct daily 7:30 p.m., Nov and Feb–April Fri and Sat at 7:30 p.m. Arrive early or book ahead. Price:* €10 ($12) adults, €8 ($9.20) students and seniors.

## Viking Splash Tours

Two things make this 75-minute tour stand out from the competition: First, you're riding around in a World War II amphibious vehicle (called a *duck*) that at one point leaves the normal tourist trail to sail along the Grand Canal. Second, the Viking theme doesn't just color the historical information related along the tour; all riders are given Viking helmets and encouraged to roar at "rival" tour groups. Kids, I promise, will not be bored.

*All tours leave from Bull Alley beside the gardens of St. Patrick's Cathedral, around the corner from the tour's ticket office and gift store at 64–65 Patrick St., Dublin 8.* ☎ *01-707-6000.* www.vikingsplashtours.com. *Runs daily every half hour 10 a.m.–5 p.m. from June 16 to August 31, runs Tues–Sun roughly every half hour Feb 10–April 30 and in Nov. Price:* €14.50–€15.95 ($17–$18) adult, €7.95–€8.95 ($9.15–€10) child under 13 (the higher prices apply on weekends in Jun and all of Jul and Aug).

## Suggested one-, two-, and three-day sightseeing itineraries

If you just have **one day** and really want to pack the sightseeing in, I recommend taking the **Hop On Hop Off Bus Tour** (see the preceding section with that title) so that you can see as many attractions as possible in the most efficient way.

Take in **Trinity College** and the **Book of Kells** (see the listing in the "The top attractions" section, earlier in the chapter) first and then wander around the excellent shopping areas of Grafton Street and Nassau Street.

Grab lunch at **Beshoff** (see the previous "Dublin's Top Restaurants A to Z")or **Nude** (covered in the earlier "Lunch on the move" section), and picnic in **Merrion Square** (see "The top attractions"). In the afternoon, visit the nearby **National Museum** and **National Gallery** (both in the preceding "The top attractions" section).

Treat yourself to a delicious dinner at the **Mermaid Café** (listed in "Dublin's Top Restaurants A to Z, " earlier in the chapter) before meeting up with the **Traditional Irish Musical Pub Crawl,** outlined in the previous "Seeing Dublin by guided tour" section. If you're still craving more traditional music after the pub crawl, end your day at the **Cobblestone** (see the "Traditional Irish music venues" section, later in the chapter ).

If you have **two days,** follow the itinerary for day one. On the morning of the second day, take the **Historical Walking Tour** (see the earlier "Seeing Dublin by guided tour" section). Then head over to the **Chester Beatty Library** (in the preceding "The top attractions" section) to gaze at the gorgeous books and art housed within.

Eat lunch in one of the pubs recommended in the "Pub grub" section and then head out to see **St. Patrick's Cathedral, Dublinia,** and the **Guinness Store** (all outlined in the "The top attractions" section). Drop into the **Queen of Tarts** (see the listing in "Dublin's Top Restaurants A to Z") for an afternoon treat on your way back to Temple Bar.

Stroll Temple Bar, and have dinner at **Elephant & Castle** (listed in the "Dublin's Top Restaurants A to Z" section) before joining up with the **Jameson's Literary Pub Crawl** (outlined in the "Seeing Dublin by guided tour" section).

If you have **three days,** follow the itineraries for days one and two. On your third day, after breakfast, make your way to the north side of the River Liffey, and walk up O'Connell Street., stopping to take pictures of the monuments lining the street and picking up a few pieces of fruit on Moore Street.

Get your fill of literary Dublin with a visit to the **James Joyce Centre** and the **Dublin Writers Museum,** which has a great little café for lunch. (Both are listed in the "More museums" section.)

After lunch, head over the **Ha'Penny Bridge** to take the guided tour of **Dublin Castle** (both described in "The top attractions"); then walk over to Temple Bar to leisurely explore the shops, galleries, and pubs. You may want to indulge in dinner at **The Tea Room** (listed in the "Dublin's Top Restaurants A to Z" section) before heading off to see a show at the famous **Abbey Theatre,** described in the upcoming "Checking out Dublin's excellent theater scene" section.

# Shopping in Dublin

Dublin is the shopping capital of Ireland. Within the city limits, you can easily find all sorts of famous Irish items, including Donegal tweed, Waterford Crystal, Belleek china, and Claddagh rings. The nearby map locates the shopping meccas.

## Locating the best shopping areas

There are three main shopping areas in Dublin. The first, on the north side of the River Liffey, is the **Henry Street–Mary Street area,** off O'Connell St. You can find reasonably priced goods, especially clothing, at the malls and stores in this area. **Moore Street,** just off the main shopping drag, offers a daily open-air market with plenty of the freshest (and cheapest) fruits and vegetables in the city. This is where you'll hear the perfected lilt of the vendors hawking their wares — a Dublin attraction in its own right.

The **Grafton Street area** on the south side of the River Liffey offers a variety of shopping options. Bustling Grafton Street itself is lined with trendy big-name clothing stores and is home to **Brown Thomas,** Ireland's ultra-fashionable department store. The side streets off Grafton are home to upscale and funky boutiques and stores. Nearby Nassau Street is the place to find the best in Irish crafts, from sweaters to crystal.

If you're looking for the funkiest fashions, jewelry, art, and music, head to the **Temple Bar area.** The hottest new places to shop in these parts are on Cow's Lane.

If your idea of shopping consists mostly of pampering yourself, the **Powerscourt Townhouse Shopping Centre,** 59 S. William St., Dublin 2 (☎ 01-679-4144), is for you. This restored Georgian townhouse is home to a variety of shops ranging from clothes boutiques to antique stores.

## Finding Ireland's best wares

Ireland is known the world over for its handmade products and fine craftsmanship, and Dublin, as Ireland's commercial center, is a one-stop source for the best of Irish products.

## Dublin Shopping

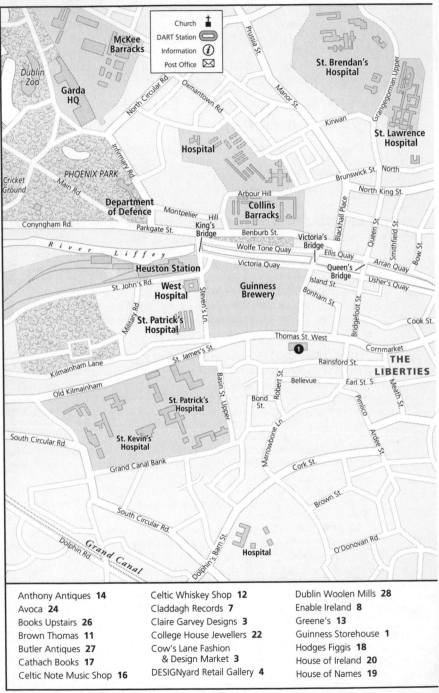

Anthony Antiques **14**
Avoca **24**
Books Upstairs **26**
Brown Thomas **11**
Butler Antiques **27**
Cathach Books **17**
Celtic Note Music Shop **16**

Celtic Whiskey Shop **12**
Claddagh Records **7**
Claire Garvey Designs **3**
College House Jewellers **22**
Cow's Lane Fashion
  & Design Market **3**
DESIGNyard Retail Gallery **4**

Dublin Woolen Mills **28**
Enable Ireland **8**
Greene's **13**
Guinness Storehouse **1**
Hodges Figgis **18**
House of Ireland **20**
House of Names **19**

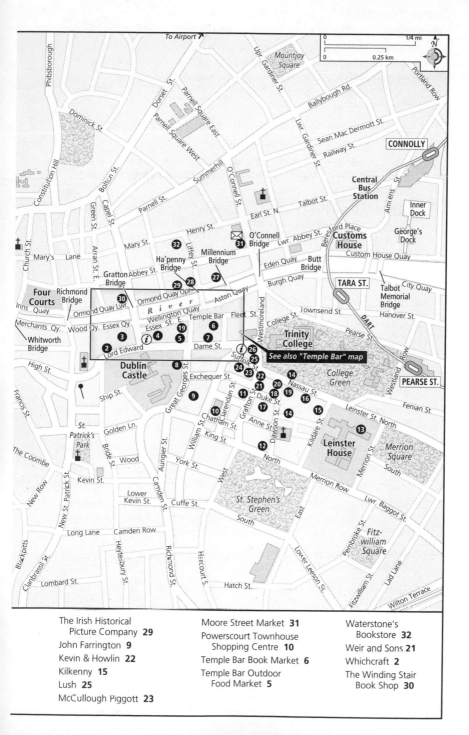

## Antiques

Dublin offers two main areas of concentration for antique dealers: **Francis Street** (between Thomas Street West and the Coombe) and **Dawson and Molesworth streets** (between St. Stephen's Green and Trinity College). The following places are some of your best bets for quality and value:

- ✔ **Anthony Antiques,** 7 Molesworth St., Dublin 2 (☎ **01-677-7222**), specializes in late 19th-century furniture and brass.

- ✔ **Butler Antiques,** 14 Bachelor's Walk, Dublin 1, along the north quays (☎ **01-873-0296**), offers a great variety and some good bargains.

- ✔ **The Irish Historical Picture Company,** 5 Lower Ormond Quay, Dublin 1 (☎ **01-872-0144**), is a vast treasure trove of photographs documenting the life of Ireland since the invention of the camera in every region and theme you can imagine.

## Books

Like any section of a city that surrounds a college campus, there are loads of good bookstores near Trinity College. You can find works of Irish writers here that may be hard to find at home.

- ✔ **Books Upstairs,** 36 College Green and Dame Street, across from the Trinity College front entrance, Dublin 2 (☎ **01-679-6687**), has a comprehensive collection of Irish fiction and nonfiction, a sizable gay and lesbian selection, and some fiction bargains.

- ✔ **Cathach Books,** 10 Duke St., off Grafton Street, Dublin 2 (☎ **01-671-8676**), sells rare editions of Irish literature, plus old maps of Ireland.

- ✔ **Greene's,** 16 Clare St., Dublin 2 (☎ **01-676-2544**), was mentioned in Joyce's *Ulysses* and boasts a huge Irish literature section and a giant secondhand selection.

- ✔ **Hodges Figgis,** 56-58 Dawson St., Dublin 2 (☎ **01-677-4754**), is Ireland's top independent bookstore, offering a wide selection of books. There's a nice café on the first floor.

- ✔ **Waterstone's,** Jervis Centre, Mary Street, Dublin 1 (☎ **01-679-1415**), is pretty much the Barnes & Noble of the Emerald Isle.

- ✔ **The Winding Stair Book Shop,** 40 Ormond Quay, Dublin 1 (☎ **01-873-3292**), is a Dublin treasure, with a great selection of new and used books, and a fabulous little cafe that overlooks the Liffey.

## Clothes

You don't have to go all the way to the Aran Islands or Donegal for authentic Irish knitwear. Here are some Dublin shops where you can find the real deal, plus a few places for less traditional items.

✔ **Avoca,** 11-13 Suffolk St. (☎ 01-677-4215), sells the Irish-designed and -made Anthology line of clothes, with all the vivid colors and funky lace, beads, and ribbons that a twenty- or thirtysomething girl could want, plus it offers all sorts of household goods and clothes for hip babies (like a onesie that says *It girl*).

✔ **Claire Garvey Designs,** 6 Cow's Lane, Dublin 2 (☎ 01-671-7287), is where fairy queens would buy their clothes. Garvey creates shimmery, sheer pieces, many with lace-up bodices and beads. Looking like a goddess doesn't come cheap, though.

✔ **Dublin Woolen Mills,** 41 Lower Ormond Quay, Dublin 1, on the north end of the Ha'Penny Bridge (☎ 01-677 5011), has everything from traditional sweaters to kilts, shawls, and scarves.

✔ **Enable Ireland,** South Great Georges Street, Dublin 2 (next to Juice; ☎ 01-478-2763), sells used clothes from silver vinyl pants to flowery girls' dresses. All profits go to Enable Ireland, which helps people with disabilities lead independent lives.

✔ **Kevin & Howlin,** 31 Nassau St., Dublin 2 (☎ 01-677-0257), sells authentic hand-woven tweed jackets and hats for men and women.

## Crafts and jewelry

If you're in the market for Irish crafts and jewelry, point yourself in the direction of Nassau Street, on the edge of Trinity College, which is lined with shops selling Irish items. Also see "Souvenirs and gifts," later in this chapter.

✔ **Brown Thomas,** 92 Grafton St., Dublin 2 (☎ 01-605-6666), stocks Irish fashion and giftware.

✔ **College House Jewellers,** 44 Nassau St., Dublin 2 (☎ 01-677-7597), stocks gorgeous Celtic-style jewelry and has a comprehensive collection of Claddagh jewelry, from classic to modern.

✔ **DESIGNyard Retail Gallery,** 12 E. Essex St., Dublin 2, along Temple Bar's main thoroughfare (☎ 01-677-8453), stocks exquisite and generally affordable contemporary Irish-designed jewelry, textiles, glass, and earthenware.

✔ **John Farrington,** 32 Drury St., Dublin 2 (☎ 01-679-1899), is a good bet for vintage jewelry, from Georgian silver earrings to Victorian lockets.

✔ **Weir and Sons,** 96 Grafton St., at Wicklow Street, Dublin 2 (☎ 01-677-9678), sells fine jewelry, Waterford Crystal, silver, leather, and watches in elegant showcases.

✔ **Whichcraft,** Lord Edward St., Dublin 2 (☎ 01-670-9371), offers a range of contemporary Irish crafts and jewelry. The last time I was there, I was struck by the twilight-colored Martin Branche pottery. Also check out their gallery in Cow's Lane.

# This little traveler went to market

One of the best ways to experience Dublin is to hit the markets. Here are some of the best:

✓ **Cow's Lane Fashion & Design Market**, Cow's Lane, Old City, Temple Bar, is heaven for those who love hip, handmade clothing and jewelry. Every Saturday from 10 a.m. to 5:30 p.m.

✓ **Moore Street Market**, Moore St., is a bustling market full of vendors selling fresh vegetables, fruits, and flowers. Many vendors still hawk their wares in a lilting, singsong voice reminiscent of the Molly Malones of the past. Monday through Saturday from 9 a.m. to 5 p.m.

✓ **Temple Bar Book Market**, Temple Bar Square, is a smallish outdoor used-book market. Grab some lunch at the outdoor food market, and browse through the offerings. Every Saturday and Sunday 10 a.m. to 6 p.m.

✓ **Temple Bar Outdoor Food Market**, Meetinghouse Square in Temple Bar, with entrances on East Essex and Eustace streets, Dublin 2 (☎ 01-677-2255), is an orgy of Irish gourmet and organic food, including delicacies such as Chez Emily's chocolates, Llewellyn Apple Farm's cider, and Noirin Kearney's breads. Every Saturday from 10 a.m. to 5 p.m.

## *Irish music and musical instruments*

If you fell in love with the sounds of the traditional session you heard at the pub last night, head to one of these stores to pick up a CD, or even a tin whistle or *bodhrán* (*bow*-rahn; a goatskin drum) of your very own.

✓ **Celtic Note Music Shop**, 12 Nassau St., Dublin 2 (☎ 01-670-4157), is a great place to find any type of Irish music, from traditional to contemporary rock. Prices here are slightly lower than at Claddagh Records. They often host free midday in-store concerts by hot traditional Irish bands.

✓ **Claddagh Records**, 2 Cecilia St., Temple Bar, Dublin (☎ 01-677-0262), sells the best traditional Irish and world music CDs. The staff here is exceedingly knowledgeable, so this is the place to go if you're not sure what you're looking for.

✓ **McCullough Piggott**, 25 Suffolk St., Dublin 2 (☎ 01-677-3138), sells all sorts of instruments and the tutorial books and CDs that help you play them.

## *Souvenirs and gifts*

Also see the recommendations in "Crafts and jewelry," earlier in this chapter.

✔ **Celtic Whiskey Shop,** 27–28 Dawson St., Dublin 2 (☎ 01-675-9744), sells everything from the best-known brands of whiskey, such as Bushmills, to rare bottlings from distilleries that have closed their doors. They host tastings in the store each day to whet your palate.

✔ **Guinness Storehouse,** St. James's Gate, Dublin 8 (☎ 01-408-4800; www.guinness-storehouse.com), stocks all things Guinness, from posters and slippers to clocks and candles.

✔ **House of Ireland,** 37 Nassau St., at the corner of Dawson Street, Dublin 2 (☎ 01-671-1111), is one-stop shopping for authentic Irish goods such as Waterford Crystal, china, hand-knit Aran sweaters, and more.

✔ **House of Names,** 26 Nassau St., Dublin 2 (☎ 01-769-7287), creates and sells wall shields and plaques, clothing, and jewelry with the crest, coat of arms, and motto of most European family names. Here's hoping you have one of those cool dragons on your coat of arms.

✔ **Kilkenny,** 5-6 Nassau St. (☎ 01-677-7066), boasts original Irish designs, including glass, knitwear, jewelry, and a large selection of gorgeous pottery.

✔ **Lush,** 166 Grafton St., near the entrance to Trinity College (☎ 01-677-0392), is not particularly Irish, but when your giftees open their packages of colorful homemade soaps, bubble baths, shampoos, and more, they won't care. All the items here look good enough to eat, and you probably *could* eat them, because they're all made with as many natural ingredients as possible. And who can resist a store that hacks individual slices of soap off huge slabs?

# Hitting the Pubs and Enjoying Dublin's Nightlife

James Joyce put it best in *Ulysses:* "Good puzzle would be cross Dublin without passing a pub." With more than 1,000 pubs in the city (the "Dublin Nightlife" map helps locate them), there's something to suit everyone, whether your taste runs to Victorian pubs with globe lights and polished mahogany bars or to local watering holes with worn couches and clocks that read the wrong time.

## Hitting the pubs

### The Brazen Head
#### Dublin 8

The Brazen Head claims to be the oldest pub in Dublin. That may or may not be true, but certainly, many a pint has been pulled here since its opening in 1661 (an older pub, from 1198, stood on this site before the "new" pub was built). The unusual name comes from a story about a bold woman

## Dublin Nightlife

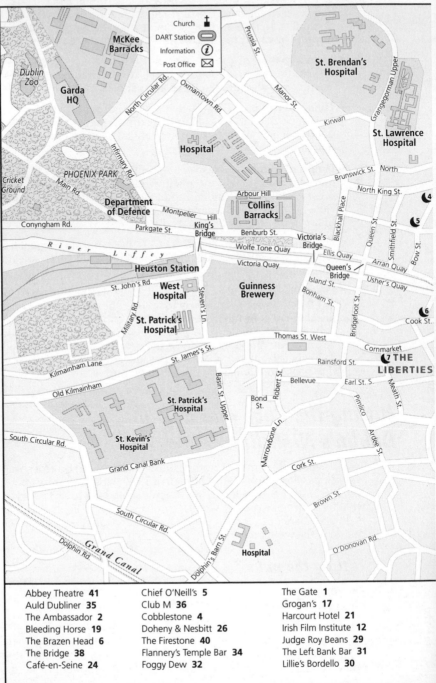

| | | |
|---|---|---|
| Abbey Theatre **41** | Chief O'Neill's **5** | The Gate **1** |
| Auld Dubliner **35** | Club M **36** | Grogan's **17** |
| The Ambassador **2** | Cobblestone **4** | Harcourt Hotel **21** |
| Bleeding Horse **19** | Doheny & Nesbitt **26** | Irish Film Institute **12** |
| The Brazen Head **6** | The Firestone **40** | Judge Roy Beans **29** |
| The Bridge **38** | Flannery's Temple Bar **34** | The Left Bank Bar **31** |
| Café-en-Seine **24** | Foggy Dew **32** | Lillie's Bordello **30** |

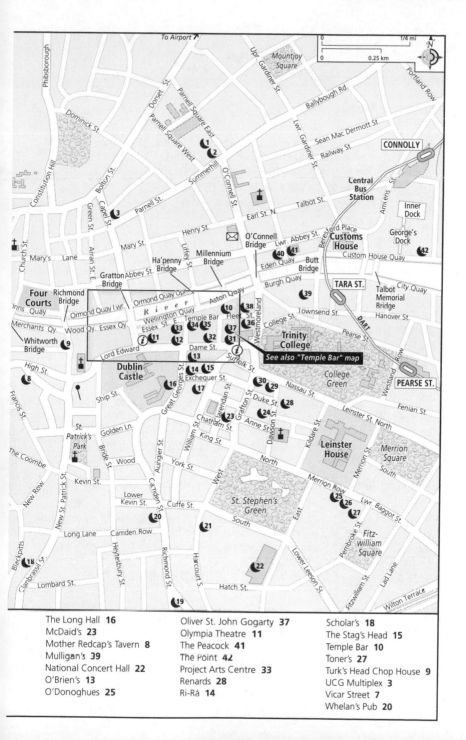

The Long Hall **16**
McDaid's **23**
Mother Redcap's Tavern **8**
Mulligan's **39**
National Concert Hall **22**
O'Brien's **13**
O'Donoghues **25**

Oliver St. John Gogarty **37**
Olympia Theatre **11**
The Peacock **41**
The Point **42**
Project Arts Centre **33**
Renards **28**
Ri-Rá **14**

Scholar's **18**
The Stag's Head **15**
Temple Bar **10**
Toner's **27**
Turk's Head Chop House **9**
UCG Multiplex **3**
Vicar Street **7**
Whelan's Pub **20**

who was so curious during one of the country's many rebellions that she stuck her head out of the window — only to have it chopped off! Though it's a bit touristy, it's a beautiful pub, lit by lanterns.

*20 Lower Bridge St.* ☎ *01-679-5186. Bus: 78A, 79, 90.*

### Doheny & Nesbitt
**Dublin 2**

A poster-child of Victorian pubs, "Nesbitt's" boasts *snugs* (cozy compartments), dark wood, and bartenders full of wisdom. The clientele is heavy on lawyers, economists, and politicians.

*5 Baggott St. Lower.* ☎ *01-676-2945. Bus: 10, 11, 11A.*

### The Firestone
**Dublin 1**

Located across from the Abbey Theatre, this pub used to be called "The Plough," in tribute to Sean O'Casey's play *The Plough and the Stars*. The Firestone is an unpretentious Dublin pub frequented by locals, perfect for a pint before or after a show at the Abbey.

*28 Lower Abbey St.* ☎ *01-874-0971. Bus: 29A, 31, 31A, 31B, 32, 32A, 37, 38, 42A, 42B, 51A, 70, 70X, 130.*

### Grogan's
**Dublin 2**

This small, unpretentious pub is filled with artists, writers, and assorted characters. The walls are covered with works by local artists. You're sure to meet some interesting folks here.

*15 S. William St.* ☎ *01-677-9320. Bus: 16, 16A, 19, 19A, 65, 65B, 83, 112.*

### The Long Hall
**Dublin 2**

Rumored to have the longest bar in the city, The Long Hall is a gorgeous, ornate specimen of a pub. There's a vast array of antique clocks, Victorian lamps, a mahogany bar, and plenty of snugs to get lost in. It backs up to Dublin Castle, so stop in on your way.

*51 S. Great George's St.* ☎ *01-475-1590. Bus: 50, 50A, 54, 56, 77.*

### McDaid's
**Dublin 2**

Attention, writers and literature-lovers: This was bad-boy playwright Brendan Behan's favorite watering hole, and the pub is still known as the place to go for the latest on literary news in Dublin.

*3 Harry St., off Grafton St.* ☎ *01-679-4395. Bus: 10, 11, 13B, 14, 14A, 15, 15A, 15B, 15C.*

## Café-en-Seine: The anti-pub?

Though it's called a pub, **Café-en-Seine**, 40 Dawson St., Dublin 2 (☎ 01-677-4369), looks like it was flown over intact from 19th-century Paris. This incredibly popular spot has a gorgeous Art Deco interior, with a glass atrium, brass chandeliers, murals, and large mirrors. You can get light bites, pastries, and coffees by day and wine, beer, and cocktails by night. The crowd can be a bit snooty, making for excellent people-watching.

### Mulligan's
Dublin 2

This is an authentic old Dublin pub and favorite watering hole for the journalists of the nearby *Irish Times* newspaper. JFK drank here as a young European correspondent for the Hearst newspapers in 1945 and again when he visited as president. It's mentioned in *Ulysses,* and locals say it serves one of the best pints of Guinness in town.

*8 Poolbeg St. (off south quays near O'Connell Bridge).* ☎ *01-677-5582. Bus: 5, 7, 7A, 7X, 8.*

### Scholar's
Dublin 8

The spacious bar at Scholar's, a restored all-boys National School, has a giant screen that offers a perfect view from any seat of the latest football (read: soccer), rugby, hurling, or Gaelic football matches.

*Donovan's Lane, off Clanbrassil St., below St. Patrick's Cathedral.* ☎ *01-453-2000.*

### The Stag's Head
Dublin 2

The Stag's Head is a Victorian classic, with gleaming rich auburn wood, frosted globe lamps, and stained-glass windows. It's popular with Trinity students, journalists, and theater folk. Try to score a seat in the small, opulent room on the right in the rear. And stick around if you get hungry — the food here is terrific.

*1 Dame Court.* ☎ *01-679-3701. Bus: 21A, 50, 50A, 78, 78A, 78B. Look for the mosaic stag head inlaid into the sidewalk on Dame St., pointing the way.*

### Toner's
Dublin 2

This is a great, old, authentic Dublin pub with a high *craic* (fun) factor. You'll find everyone from older folks enjoying a drink to boisterous rugby fans celebrating their team's victory.

*139 Baggott St. Lower.* ☎ *01-676-3090. Bus: 10.*

## Pulling an all-nighter: Late-night bars

Still up for some partying after last call (at the shocking hour of 11:30 p.m.)? I recommend the following extended-hours pubs:

- ✔ **Bleeding Horse**, 24–25 Camden St., Dublin 2 (☎ 01-475-2705).

- ✔ **The Bridge**, 11 Westmoreland St. (directly below O'Connell Street Bridge), Dublin 2. ☎ 01-670-8133.

- ✔ **The Foggy Dew**, 1 Upper Fownes St., Temple Bar, Dublin 2. ☎ 01-677-9328.

- ✔ **Judge Roy Beans**, 45 Nassau St. (across from Trinity College), Dublin 2. ☎ 01-679-7539.

- ✔ **O'Brien's**, 40 Dame St., Dublin 2. ☎ 01-677-8816.

- ✔ **Turk's Head Chop House**, Parliament Street, Temple Bar, Dublin 2. ☎ 01-679-9701.

- ✔ **Whelan's Pub**, 25 Wexford St., Dublin 2. ☎ 01-478-0766.

## Taking in some music

Dublin has a hot music scene, featuring everything from jazz to rock to traditional Irish music.

### Traditional Irish music venues

In addition to visiting the pubs below, I suggest the **Traditional Irish Music Pub Crawl** (listed in "Seeing Dublin by guided tour," earlier in this chapter).

- ✔ **Chief O'Neill's**, Smithfield Village, Dublin 7 (☎ 01-817-3838), is a big airy pub that hosts excellent traditional music sessions.

- ✔ **Cobblestone**, 77 North King St. at Red Cow Lane (☎ 01-872-1799), a dark pub filled with instruments and photographs of traditional Irish musicians, hosts a lively mostly-Irish crowd and friendly sessions each night, with some exceptional musicians. No fuss, no show, no hip location — just the best traditional Irish music in Dublin. This is the real thing. Call before going, because this place may be closing soon.

- ✔ **Flannery's Temple Bar**, 47 Temple Bar, Temple Bar, Dublin 2 (☎ 01-497-4766), is a cozy pub with Victorian globe lights and an eclectic array of objects. Irish music is on tap daily.

- ✔ **Harcourt Hotel**, 60 Harcourt St., Dublin 2 (☎ 01-478-3677), hosts great traditional sessions every day except Sunday.

- ✔ **Mother Redcap's Tavern**, Back Lane, Dublin 8 (☎ 01-453-8306), could be the set for a movie about Dublin in the 1700s. The stone-walled pub features wood beams; shelves lined with a variety of antiques; and old paintings, newspaper clippings, and prints of

Dublin. You can hear traditional music on many nights (call to confirm), with the liveliest session held each Sunday starting in the
early afternoon.

✔ **O'Donoghues,** 15 Merrion Row, Dublin 2 (☎ 01-676-2807), mostly
hosts traditional Irish ballad singers. The dark pub is a bit touristy,
but you'll also find a good many locals enjoying themselves.

✔ **Oliver St. John Gogarty,** 58 Fleet St., Temple Bar, Dublin 2 (☎ 01-
671-1822), is a popular pub is named for surgeon, wit, and writer
Oliver St. John Gogarty, who was the model for Buck Mulligan, a flip
character in *Ulysses*. The interior screams Irish pub, with its decor
of old books and bottles and portraits of traditional Irish music
greats. The pub is always packed with travelers from all over the
world, and you find live Irish music seven nights a week starting at
9 p.m., plus Saturdays at 4:30 p.m. and Sundays from noon to 2 p.m.
Check out the great lunch buffet.

### Rock, jazz, and other music venues

Dublin is not all jigs and reels all the time. The hopping live-music scene
encompasses rock, jazz, country, folk, blues, classical, and more. The
venues listed here consistently offer fantastic concerts:

✔ **The National Concert Hall,** Earlsfort Terrace, Dublin 2 (☎ 01-475-
1666), is Dublin's best venue for classical music performances.

✔ **Olympia Theatre,** 72 Dame St., Dublin 2 (☎ 01-677-7744), puts on
Midnight at the Olympia shows from midnight to 2 a.m., featuring
rock, folk, country, and just about anything else you can think of.

✔ **The Point,** Eastlink Bridge, North Wall Quay (☎ 01-836-3633), is
Dublin's top venue for internationally known rock and folk acts,
seating up to 6,000 people in arena seating.

✔ **Vicar Street,** 58-59 Thomas St., Dublin 8 (☎ 01-454-5533; www.
vicarstreet.com), is a small concert venue with seating. It hosts
excellent (and often well-known) rock, jazz, folk, and traditional
music.

✔ **Whelan's,** 25 Wexford St., Dublin 2 (☎ 01-478-0766), has a cozy
wooden interior; a nice atmosphere; and a great lineup of well-
known rock, folk, and traditional musicians.

## Clubbing your way through Dublin

As in most European capitals, clubbing is taken seriously in Dublin,
and dress is pretty important, especially at the trendiest, most popular
clubs — don't be surprised it you're turned away because of jeans or
sneakers. Often, there are cover charges (usually between €5/$5.75 and
€25/$29), and you could need to show an ID. Clubs usually open just
when buses stop running (about 11:30 p.m.), so expect to take a cab
back to your hotel.

Here are some of the best clubs in Dublin:

- ✓ **Club M,** Blooms Hotel, Angelsea Street (☎ 01-671-5408), packs 'em in Tuesday through Sunday for sweaty, all-night, deejayed dance parties. This place has a reputation as a pickup joint.

- ✓ **Lillie's Bordello,** Adam Court off Grafton Street (☎ 01-679-9204), is still one of the hottest Dublin clubs after ten years, with a lipstick-red interior and the members-only (you can pay to be a member) "Library" room.

- ✓ **Renards,** 35–37 S. Frederick St. (☎ 01-877-5876), pulls in celebrities and locals alike with three floors of bars, dancing, and frequent live jazz.

- ✓ **Ri-Rá,** 1 Exchequer St. (☎ 01-677-4835), fills up every night with dancers getting down to funk, jazz, and other grooves.

## Checking out Dublin's excellent theater scene

Dubliners have long held theater in high reverence, and the city has a thriving theater scene that encompasses everything from the plays of Synge to new multimedia projects.

Ireland's most famous playhouse, the **Abbey Theatre,** 26 Lower Abbey St., Dublin 1 (☎ 01-878-7222), is best known for staging superb productions of works by some of Ireland's best-loved playwrights, including Sean O'Casey and J. M. Synge. The Abbey's sister theater, **The Peacock,** 26 Lower Abbey St., Dublin 1 (☎ 01-878-7222), boasts excellent productions of new plays. The **Gate,** 1 Cavendish Row, Dublin 1 (☎ 01-874-7483), does a beautiful job with European, Irish, and American classics and new plays. The theater is particularly lauded for its productions of Samuel Beckett's work. **Project Arts Centre,** 39 E. Essex St., Dublin 2 (☎ 01-881-9613), is the place to go for new and experimental theater. Call the theaters or check the *Irish Times* newspaper for details about shows.

## Going to the movies

Or, as the Irish say, "the cinema." There are lots of places to catch a flick in Dublin. **The Ambassador,** Parnell St., Dublin 1 (☎ 01-872-7000), plays only one film at a time in an old-fashioned theater complete with a balcony and red curtain that opens to a huge screen. **UCG Multiplex,** midway down Parnell Street in Parnell Center, Dublin 1 (☎ 01-872-8400), is a streamlined and very modern multiplex, with 12 screens showing the latest commercial movies. The **Irish Film Institute (IFI),** 6 Eustace St., Temple Bar, Dublin 2 (☎ 01-679-3477), shows up-and-coming Irish independent cinema, European exclusives, and classics. A place for true film buffs, the IFI is as hip as it gets. There are a cafe, a lively bar, and a book and video/DVD shop on the premises (note that Irish videos and DVDs come in a different format than in the U.S., and most American VCRs and DVD players can't play them).

# Fast Facts: Dublin

## Area Code

The area code for Dublin city and county is 01. Dial the area code only if you're calling Dublin from outside the city. If you're calling from outside the country, you can drop the 0.

## American Express

There is a full-service American Express office, American Express International, at 41 Nassau St., Dublin 2 (☎ 1890-205-511).

## Currency Exchange

Currency exchange is indicated by the sign Bureau de Change. You can exchange money at travel agencies, hotels, and some post offices, but the best rates are to be found at banks. If you have American Express traveler's checks, you can exchange them without paying any commission at the AmEx office, 41 Nassau St., Dublin 2 (☎ 1890-205-511).

## Dentists

Contact the Eastern Health Board Headquarters, Dr. Steeven's Hospital, Dublin (☎ 01-679-0700), if you need emergency dental work.

## Doctors

Usually, your hotel or B&B is able to get you an appointment with its house doctor. The American Embassy, 42 Elgin Rd., Ballsbridge, Dublin 4 (☎ 01-668-8777), can provide you a list of doctors. The Eastern Health Board Headquarters, Dr. Steeven's Hospital, Dublin (☎ 01-679-0700), can also arrange a doctor visit. Also see "Hospitals."

## Embassies and Consulates

United States, 42 Elgin Rd., Ballsbridge, Dublin 4 (☎ 01-668-8777); Canada, 65 St. Stephen's Green, Dublin 2 (☎ 01-478-1988);

United Kingdom, 31 Merrion Rd., Dublin 4 (☎ 01-205-3700); Australia, Fitzwilton House, Wilton Terrace, Dublin 2 (☎ 01-676-1517).

## Emergencies

Dial ☎ 999 for police, fire, or ambulance.

## Hospitals

The two best hospitals for emergency care in Dublin are St. Vincent's Hospital, Elm Park, Dublin 4 (☎ 01-269-4533), on the south side of the city; and Beaumont Hospital, Beaumont Road, Dublin 9 (☎ 01-837-7755), on the north side.

## Information

Dublin Tourism (☎ 01-605-7700; www.visitdublin.com) runs four walk-in visitor centers around the center of the city. The largest and best is on Suffolk Street, Dublin 2. The others are at the Arrivals Hall at the Dublin airport; at Exclusively Irish, at O'Connell St., Dublin 1; and at Baggott Street Bridge, Baggott Street, Dublin 2.

The trendy Temple Bar district has its own information Web site at www.temple-bar.ie. Some good Web sites for Dublin include www.visitdublin.com and www.softguides.com/dublin.

## Internet

Dublin has a number of Internet cafes, including Central Cyber Cafe, 6 Grafton St., Dublin 2 (☎ 01-677 8298).

## Maps

Good maps are available at the Dublin Tourism Centre, Suffolk Street, and online through the Tourism Centre's Web site at www.visitdublin.com/maps.

## Newspapers/Magazines

The major newspaper in Ireland is *The Irish Times* (www.ireland.com). The best events listings are found in *In Dublin* and *Event Guide* (www.eventguide.ie), and www.hotpress.com. *Where: Dublin* is geared to travelers and features restaurant, shopping, and entertainment information.

## Pharmacies

Hamilton, Long, & Co., 5 O'Connell St., Dublin 1 (☎ 01-873-0427), and O'Connell Pharmacy, 21 Grafton St., Dublin 2 (☎ 01-874-1464), are two central pharmacies with extended hours.

## Police

Dial ☎ 999 in case of emergencies. You can contact the police headquarters at Phoenix Park, Dublin 8 (☎ 01-666-0000). Police in Ireland are known as Garda or Gardai (*Gard-ee*) or The Guards.

## Post Office

The General Post Office (GPO) is located on O'Connell Street, Dublin 1 (☎ 01-872-6666). Its hours are Monday through Saturday 8 a.m. to 8 p.m., Sunday 10 a.m. to 6 p.m. Branch offices, called An Post and noted with green storefront awnings, are generally open Monday through Saturday from 9 a.m. to 6 p.m.

## Safety

Late-night crime is not uncommon, so don't walk back to your hotel alone after pub closing time (11:30 most nights); get a taxi. Be especially careful around O'Connell Street and its side streets after the pubs close.

## Smoking

Smoking is not permitted in most public buildings,and is banned in restaurants and bars. Most hotels and some B&Bs offer smoking rooms. Currently, about one-third of Irish adults are smokers, though this number is on the decline.

## Taxis

To get a taxi in Dublin, go to a taxi rank,or hail a cab by sticking out your arm. If you need to call a cab, try Cab Charge (☎ 01-677-2222), Co-op (☎ 01-676-6666), or VIP Taxis (☎ 01-478-3333).

## Weather

Phone ☎ 1550-122-112 for weather information.

# Chapter 12

# Easy Trips North of Dublin: Counties Meath and Louth

● ● ● ● ● ● ● ● ● ● ● ● ● ● ● ● ● ● ● ● ● ● ● ● ● ● ● ● ● ● ● ● ● ● ● ● ● ● ● ● ●

*In This Chapter*
▶ Exploring a 5,000-year-old tomb
▶ Visiting the Hill of Tara
▶ Trying out water sports in the Irish Sea
▶ Hanging out on a working farm

● ● ● ● ● ● ● ● ● ● ● ● ● ● ● ● ● ● ● ● ● ● ● ● ● ● ● ● ● ● ● ● ● ● ● ● ● ● ● ● ●

Collectively, Counties Meath and Louth are known as the ancient land of the Celts. They're the country's hot spots for visiting prehistoric sites, such as ancient burial mounds and areas where the old Irish high kings held court.

**County Meath** has some of the most important ancient religious and political attractions in Ireland — the prehistoric tombs of **Newgrange** and **Knowth** and the **Hill of Tara.** The heart of the area is the River Boyne, home of the famous Battle of the Boyne, in which Protestant William of Orange defeated Catholic King James II, changing the course of Irish history. This region has been fought over by the country's many invaders, and all of those invaders, from the Normans to the English, have left their mark here. The history-rich towns of **Kells, Slane,** and **Trim** (with minor attractions including Slane Castle and Trim Castle) are the best places to stay.

What **County Louth** lacks in big tourist attractions, it makes up for in history and the charm of small towns such as **Dundalk** and **Drogheda** (pronounced *draw*-da). These towns are the stomping grounds of legends such as Cuchulainn (pronounced coo-*cul*-in), Queen Maeve, and the great warrior Finn MacCool (see Chapter 2 for more information on these mythical characters). The most beautiful area of Louth is the far northern area, encompassing the **Cooley Mountains** and **Peninsula** and the charming heritage town of **Carlingford,** which overlooks the Irish Sea.

You can easily take day-trips from Dublin to both counties, which you may well think of as one destination because they're so complementary. But I list a few good hotels in case you want to set up camp for a while.

## Counties Meath and Louth

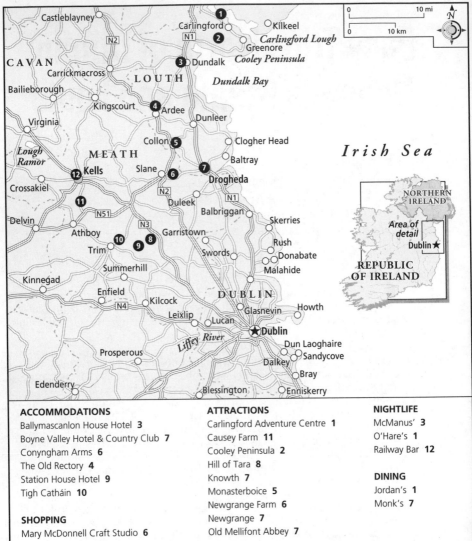

**ACCOMMODATIONS**
Ballymascanlon House Hotel **3**
Boyne Valley Hotel & Country Club **7**
Conyngham Arms **6**
The Old Rectory **4**
Station House Hotel **9**
Tigh Catháin **10**

**SHOPPING**
Mary McDonnell Craft Studio **6**

**ATTRACTIONS**
Carlingford Adventure Centre **1**
Causey Farm **11**
Cooley Peninsula **2**
Hill of Tara **8**
Knowth **7**
Monasterboice **5**
Newgrange Farm **6**
Newgrange **7**
Old Mellifont Abbey **7**

**NIGHTLIFE**
McManus' **3**
O'Hare's **1**
Railway Bar **12**

**DINING**
Jordan's **1**
Monk's **7**

# Getting To and Around Meath and Louth

Most visitors to Louth and Meath arrive by car, often on a day-trip from
Dublin. Take the N2 north toward Slane and the N3 toward Navan and Kells.

You can get to most major towns and attractions from these routes — just follow the signs. If you're heading directly to Louth from Dublin, take the N1 north toward Drogheda, Dundalk, and Newry. Most major towns and attractions are along that route. To get to the Cooley Peninsula from Dundalk, take the R173, which loops to the town of Newry.

**Irish Rail** (☎ 01-836-6222) has stops in the County Louth towns of Drogheda and Dundalk from Dublin.

**Bus Éireann** (☎ 01-836-6111) has year-round routes to Navan, Kells, Slane, Drogheda, Dundalk, Carlingford, and other smaller towns throughout the area.

**Mary Gibbons** organizes an excellent bus tour of Meath from Dublin (see "Exploring Meath and Louth: The Top Attractions," later in this chapter, for details).

# Spending the Night in Meath and Louth

For locations, see the "Counties Meath and Louth" map.

## Ballymascanlon House Hotel
### $$$   Dundalk, County Louth

You can't beat staying in an authentic Victorian mansion for a moderate price. This house retains an old-world ambience, and rooms are decorated with antiques and Victorian touches. This is a great place for sporty folks — there's an 18-hole course on the grounds, and a leisure center boasts a pool, a gym, a Jacuzzi, tennis courts, and more. The hotel also features a bar that hosts Irish music on the weekends.

☎ *042-955-8200. Fax: 042-937-1598.* www.ballymascanlon.com. *Rates:* €150–€160 ($173–$184) double. AE, DC, MC, V.

## Boyne Valley Hotel and Country Club
### $$$   Drogheda, County Louth

Though it's in Louth, this hotel is a great starting point for touring the sites of Newgrange, Knowth, and Mellifont Abbey (all located in nearby Meath). Beautiful gardens and woodlands surround the elegant house and make for a pleasant stroll or a great view from the large atrium. All rooms are spacious and have been smartly refurbished. Amenities include a pool. The fish dishes served in the restaurant are as fresh as it gets; they're prepared from the catch of the Boyne River.

☎ *041-983-7737. Fax: 041-983-9188.* www.boyne-valley-hotel.ie. *Rates:* €152 ($175) double. AE, DC, MC, V.

### Conyngham Arms
$$$  Slane, County Meath

Located near Newgrange and Knowth, the mid-19th-century, inn-style Arms is a good base from which to explore the Boyne Valley. The service at this family-run hotel is personable and friendly, and the four-poster beds are a nice touch. You'll think you're staying in a B&B rather than a hotel. The pub grub in the bar is excellent.

☎ *800-44-UTELL, from the U.S., or 041-988-4444. Fax: 041-982-4205.* www. conynghamarms.com. *Rates: €120–€140 ($138–$161) double. MC, V.*

### The Old Rectory
$$  Ardee, County Louth

You won't find a better deal for your euro than this lovely traditional B&B, which is the picture of Irish hospitality. Hostess Janie Jennings will likely welcome you in with hot tea and homemade scones with gooseberry jam made from berries grown in her garden. Her son Paul loves to chat up the guests, and the rooms are comfortable, with large beds and bathrooms. Don't sleep in; the yummy breakfasts go above and beyond continental fare, with hot cereals, fresh fruit, and special concoctions from the kitchen.

*Kells Rd.* ☎ *041-685-3320.* www.ardeeoldrectory.com. *On the N2 or take the R173 from Dundalk. Rates: €64 ($74) double. No credit cards.*

### Station House Hotel
$$$  Kilmessan, County Meath

Located near the Hill of Tara, this unique hotel was once a railway junction building and uses the old ticket office, luggage room, platforms, engine sheds, and signal box for various hotel functions. The rooms are comfortably furnished, the price is right, and the theme is interesting.

*Take the N3 from Dublin to Dunshaughlin, turn left at end of village, and follow signposts for Kilmessan.* ☎ *046-90-25-239. Fax: 046-90-25-588.* www.thestationhouse hotel.com. *Rates: €120–€180 ($138–$207) double. AE, DC, MC, V.*

### Tigh Catháin
$  Trim, County Meath

This Tudor-style country cottage offers three luxuriously large bedrooms simply decorated in a sweet country style. But you won't be spending much time in them if the weather's nice, because the cottage also boasts pretty gardens and a grassy backyard.

*Longwood Rd. Off R160, about 1km (⅔ mile) oustide Trim.* ☎ *046-943-1996.* www.tigh cathaintrim.com. *Rates: €58–€66 ($67–$76). No credit cards.*

# Dining Locally in Meath and Louth

Locations are indicated on the "Counties Meath and Louth" map.

### Jordan's
**$$$   Carlingford, County Louth   SEAFOOD/IRISH**

Located in a renovated stone warehouse, this restaurant overlooking Carlingford's harbor has excellent dishes made from locally and organically grown ingredients. The interior is classic — ornate wall fixtures, white tablecloths, and fresh flowers — the service top-notch, and the atmosphere casual. You can't go wrong ordering one of their award-winning fish dishes.
*Newry St.* ☎ *042-937-3223. Main courses: €15–€23 ($17–$26). MC, V. Open: Daily 6–10 p.m.*

### Monk's
**$   Drogheda, County Louth   ECLECTIC**

This delightful cafe, located by a river, is the place to go for a filling, delicious breakfast or lunch. They have a huge menu, encompassing breakfast dishes, paninis, sandwiches, fajitas, pastas, and salads. The Cajun salad and the Mexican chicken sandwich are favorites.
*North Quay.* ☎ *041-984-5630. Main courses: €4–€9 ($4.60–$10) MC, V. Open: Mon–Sat 8:30 a.m.–6 p.m., Sun 10:30 a.m.–5:30 p.m.*

# Exploring Meath and Louth:
# The Top Attractions

The knowledgeable Mary Gibbons narrates superb bus tours of Meath, visiting (and going into) Newgrange and the Hill of Tara, and driving along the beautiful and historical Boyne River and through the village of Slane. For information and reservations, call **Newgrange Tours** at ☎ **01-283-9973,** or visit www.newgrangetours.com. Tours cost €35 ($40) for adults, €30 ($35) for students, and leave Monday through Friday from Dublin.

### Newgrange and Knowth (via Brú na Bóinne Visitor Centre)
### Donore, County Meath

A relatively new visitor center combines two of the best prehistoric sites in Ireland into a historic and archeological stop well worth your time (allow about four hours to see everything). The center provides access to the passage-tombs of Newgrange and Knowth, and contains many interpretive displays about the rich history of the Boyne Valley, as well as a must-see audiovisual that provides an excellent introduction to the tombs. The visitor center is the only way to access Newgrange and Knowth; purchase tickets there and take the minibus shuttle to the sites. Arrive early to ensure a ticket — this is a very popular site, and tickets are limited.

Newgrange is a huge, impressively intact round mound — 200,000 tons of earth and stone covering a magnificent and well-preserved 5,000-year-old burial chamber. Take a walk around the tomb to see the ancient stone carvings – spirals, diamonds, and other geometric shapes. No one knows what these designs symbolize, but there are numerous theories, from the conjecture that they are mathematic symbols to the theory that they may have been produced under the effects of hallucinatory drugs. Over the entrance stone to Newgrange is an opening that allows light to slowly creep into the burial chamber during the five days surrounding the winter solstice, filling the room with a warm, golden glow for about 15 minutes. You enter through a low arch and make your way Indiana Jones–style down the long and narrow stone passage to the cool, dark central burial chamber, where you see more stone carvings and may be party to a very special surprise (no hints; you have to go see for yourself).

Knowth is a tomb of similar size to Newgrange, used from the Stone Age through the 1400s. Still undergoing excavation, Knowth has even more beautifully decorated stones surrounding the tomb. You can see the entrance passageway, but you can't enter the chambers. Therefore, if you have to choose between Newgrange and Knowth, I recommend Newgrange — there's more to see. But if you can, see both.

Finally, if you'd like to get on the waiting list to be in the Newgrange chamber during the winter solstice, bring your 2013, 2014, or 2015 datebook — the list is at least nine years long.

*Off N51, Donore, east of Slane. Off N1 from Drogheda or N2 from Slane.* ☎ *041-988-0300. Admission: Centre and Newgrange: €5.50 ($6.35) adults, €4.25 ($4.90) seniors, €1.50 ($1.75) students and children. Centre and Knowth: €4.25 ($4.90) adults, €2.75 ($3.15) seniors, €1.50 ($1.75) students and children. Centre, Newgrange and Knowth: €9.75 ($11) adults, €7 ($8.05) seniors, €4.25 ($4.90) students and children. Open: June to mid-Sept daily 9 a.m.–7 p.m., May and mid- to late- Sept daily 9:00 a.m.–6:30 p.m.; March, April, and Oct daily 9:30 a.m.–5:30 p.m.; Nov–Feb daily 9:30 a.m.–5:00 p.m. Restricted access for people with disabilities. Suggested visit: 4 hours.*

## *Other Cool Things to See and Do*

✔ **Biking part of the Táin Trail Cycling Route:** This cycling route, 589km (365 miles) long in total, goes past some of the major historical sights in Louth. For more information, call the **Dundalk Tourist Office** (☎ 353-42-933-5484).

✔ **Carlingford Adventure Centre** (Carlingford, County Louth): This place offers great outdoor activities — windsurfing, kayaking, and sailing on Carlingford Lough, and trekking and rock climbing in the Cooley Mountains.

Location: Thosel Street, Carlingford, County Louth. ☎ 042-937-3100. www.carlingfordadventure.com. By car: R173 from Dundalk, on the Cooley Peninsula. Open: Year-round.

✔ **Causey Farm:** Want to get your hands dirty while having some old-fashioned Irish fun? The Causey Farm gives you the opportunity to make your own brown bread and scones, cut up some turf in a bog, learn some set dancing and Irish Gaelic, see a sheepdog demonstration, and have a traditional dinner. You spend the day learning, dancing, singing, and eating like a local in days of yore. *Note:* The experience runs only for groups, so it is essential that you call in advance to find out when a group is coming and then join with them. Bring lunch,

Location: Fordstown, Navan, County Meath. ☎ 046-94-34-135. www.causeyexperience.com. Located 7.3km (4½ miles) from Kells off the Kells-Athboy Road. Cost: €25 ($29) per person. Open: Call in advance to find out days and times. Suggested visit: All day.

✔ **Cooley Peninsula, Louth:** This peninsula offers a great scenic drive with impressive views of the Irish Sea and Carlingford Lough (pronounced lock). At one point, the road actually passes through the mountainside. The peninsula is the mythic home of legendary heroes, namely Cuchulainn and Finn MacCool. Dotted along the drive are *dolmen* (Neolithic tombs), forests, mountains, rivers, and quaint fishing villages. The largest village, Carlingford, is a good place to stop for a stretch and to see the ruins of King John's Castle or to visit the Holy Trinity Heritage Centre. Carlingford Lough, across which lies Northern Ireland, is a natural fjord from the Ice Age. Drive the route in a few hours, or hike along Tain Trail out of Carlingford in an afternoon.

Location: Outside Dundalk, County Louth. By car: R173 loops around the Peninsula, off N1 outside Dundalk. Suggested visit: 3 hours.

✔ **Hill of Tara:** The hill of Tara is known as the royal seat of the Irish high kings, who presided over a lively national assembly held every three years to pass laws and resolve disputes. The last assembly was held in 560 A.D., and it is said that 242 kings were crowned on the hill. This site takes some imagination to enjoy, because the only remnants of this pre-Christian political center are mounds and depressions where buildings once stood, plus a few old building stones. A late-Stone Age passage tomb also exists on the site. Take advantage of a guided tour (available on request, so just ask) and the audiovisual in the visitors' center to get a better feel for the site. There are dazzling views from the hill.

Location: South of Navan off the main Dublin road (N3), County Meath. ☎ 046-90-25-903 mid-May–mid-Sept or ☎ 041-988-0300 mid-Sept–mid-March. From Dublin, take the N3 toward Navan, and look for signs beginning about 15km (9 miles) before reaching Nacan.

Near the village of Kilmessan. Admission: €2 ($2.30) adults €1.25 ($1.45) seniors, €1 ($1.15) students and children. Open: Mid-May to mid-Sept daily 10 a.m.–6 p.m. Last admission 45 minutes before closing. Suggested visit: 45 minutes.

✔ **Monasterboice:** Throughout Meath and Louth you see more Celtic high crosses than you can shake a stick at. Beginning in the tenth century, these crosses were decorated with biblical scenes. It's thought that the crosses were used as teaching tools to help the illiterate better understand the Bible. Two such remarkable ninth-century decorated High Crosses are the highlights of the sixth-century Monasterboice monastery, which was founded by St. Buithe, a follower of St. Patrick. Muiredach's Cross, one of the best examples of the popular Celtic crosses, depicts the Last Judgment and Old Testament scenes. The other cross (sometimes called the West Cross) is one of the largest in Ireland. There are also the remains of a round tower and church ruins.

Location: Off the main Dublin road (N1) near Collon, County Louth. By car: N1 from Dublin. Cost: Free. Open: Daylight hours. Suggested visit: 30 minutes.

✔ **Newgrange Farm:** This is your average working Irish farm turned tourist attraction. The friendly Redhouse family gives a tour of the farm, livestock, garden, and 17th-century buildings. You can hold a baby chick, watch a threshing machine in action, see a horse get a new pair of shoes, pet a donkey, and more. This attraction is definitely one for the kids, but adults can enjoy themselves as well and maybe learn a few pointers for the herb garden at home. If you can, try to be here for the Sheep Derby (the jockeys are teddy bears), on Saturdays at 3 p.m.

Location: Off N51, Slane, County Meath. ☎ 041-982-4119. Admission: €6 ($6.90) per person, €5 ($5.75) per person in a family. Open: Easter–Aug daily 10 a.m.–5 p.m. Suggested visit: 1½ hours.

✔ **Old Mellifont Abbey:** Founded by St. Malachy in 1142, Mellifont was the first Cistercian monastery in Ireland. This historic house of worship was suppressed by Henry VIII, then became a pigsty (literally), and later was the headquarters for William III during the Battle of the Boyne. The site is a peaceful and tranquil place. The unique octagonal *lavabo* (a washing trough for religious ceremonies) remains intact, along with several of the abbey's arches, all set along the River Mattock. The visitor center contains examples of masonry from the Middle Ages.

Location: Tullyallen, Drogheda, County Louth. ☎ 041-982-6459. Admission: €2 ($2.30) adults, €1.25 ($1.45) seniors, €1 ($1.15) students and children. Open: May to Sept daily 10 a.m.– 6 p.m. Last admission 45 minutes before closing. Suggested visit: 1 hour.

# Shopping

Mary McDonnell creates beautiful quilts, cushions, jewelry, leather items, and more — many inspired by Celtic legends and design — at **Mary McDonnell Craft Studio,** 4 Newgrange Mall, Newgrange Mall Studio, Slane, Meath (☎ 041-982-4722). The shop displays work by other local artists as well, many also inspired by ancient Celtic art. The shop is closed Monday.

# Hitting the Pubs

The "Counties Meath and Louth" map shows the locations of the following pubs.

### McManus'
**Dundalk, County Louth**

This family-run establishment is like three pubs in one. The Music Bar often hosts spontaneous traditional music sessions that keep your feet tapping. On cold days, make your way to the back Kitchen Bar, an intimate room with brick interior and a warm cast-iron stove. The Secret Beer Garden's outdoor seating area has coal and turf fires burning year-round, as well as the occasional barbecue.

*Seatown Place,* ☎ *042-933-1632.*

### O'Hare's
**Carlingford, County Louth**

As part-grocery, part-pub, O'Hare's is a dying breed of places that combine a local watering hole with a neighborhood convenience store. But this popular place brings in the tourists for another unique attraction: the leprechaun in a glass case. (Judge its authenticity for yourself.) The pub also features traditional music on Wednesdays. The pub grub is good, but the house specialty — oysters — is a must-try. Simply scrumptious. This is The Corrs' (from Dundalk) favorite Louth pub.

*Coming from Dundalk, take the first left off the main road and stay to the right until you see the beer garden. It may be easier to park on the main road and walk to the pub.* ☎ *042-937-3106.*

### Railway Bar
**Kells, County Meath**

This charming pub (known locally as Jack's) is full of warmth and character; it fills up quickly, but fear not: It has a conservatory that opens to a large walled garden out back to handle the overflow. Hearty food is served.
☎ *046-40-215.*

# Fast Facts: Counties Meath and Louth

### Area Codes

042 and 046 for Meath, 042 and 041 for Louth.

### Emergencies/Police

Dial ☎ 999 for all emergencies.

### Genealogical Resources

In Meath, contact the Meath Heritage Centre, Mill Street, Trim (☎ 046-94-36-633). In Louth, contact MC Research Service, Seabank, Castlebellingham, Dundalk (☎ 042-937-2046).

### Hospitals

Louth County Hospital is on Dublin Road in Dundalk (☎ 042-933-4701).

### Information

For visitor information in Meath, go to the Drogheda Tourist Office, Headfort Place (behind the town hall), Drogheda (☎ 042-984-5684). For visitor information in Louth, go to the tourist office at Jocelyn Street, Dundalk (☎ 042-933-5484), open year-round. They can also provide reservation services.

### Internet Access

WriteAccess Cyber Café is at 49 Narrow West St. in Drogheda (☎ 041-980-1533).

### Post Office

Clanbrassil Street, Dundalk, Louth (☎ 042-933-4444).

# Chapter 13

# Easy Trips South of Dublin: Counties Wicklow and Kildare

. . . . . . . . . . . . . . . . . . . . . . . . . . . . . . . . . . . .

## In This Chapter

▶ Wandering through some of Ireland's most beautiful gardens
▶ Exploring the Wicklow Mountains
▶ Making a pilgrimage to the home of Irish racing
▶ Discovering the history of Kildare at a pub

. . . . . . . . . . . . . . . . . . . . . . . . . . . . . . . . . . . .

*I*mmediately south of bustling Dublin, you find the beginnings of all that famous Irish green. While County Wicklow's people trim all that lush greenery into beautiful gardens, County Kildare's citizens tend to feed theirs to the horses — the county is home to dozens upon dozens of horse farms, as well as many racetracks, including Ireland's best, the Curragh.

## County Wicklow

County Wicklow is known as *The Garden of Ireland,* and it's easy to see why. The county begins just barely out of Dublin's limits, but immediately the cityscape gives way to rural roads and stunning scenery. Wicklow's eastern coast is studded with resort areas and harbor towns, where you can have a fine seafood dinner and stay in a family-run guesthouse to experience Ireland's famed hospitality. (The "Counties Wicklow and Kildare" map points out locations.) But it's County Wicklow's inland that amazes. To really get a feel for the area, take a walk on a stretch of the **Wicklow Way,** a signposted walking path that follows forest trails, sheep paths, and county roads from just outside Dublin all the way to Clonegal (a total of about 130km/80 miles), passing through quaint villages along the way.

## Counties Wicklow and Kildare

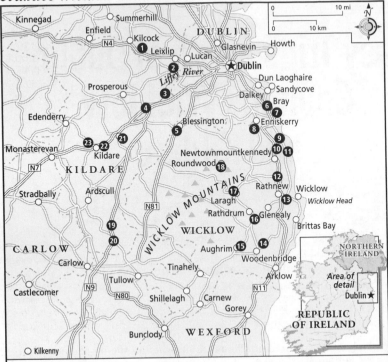

**ACCOMMODATIONS**
Annagh Lodge Guesthouse **21**
Barberstown Castle **3**
Druids Glen Marriott Hotel **10**
Glendalough Hotel **17**
Hunter's Hotel **13**
Kilkea Castle Hotel & Golf
  Club **20**
Noreen Malone's B&B **4**
Slievemore **11**
Tinakilly Country House
  & Restaurant **13**
Tudor Lodge **16**

**DINING**
Avoca Handweavers
  Tea Shop **14**
Bel's Bistro **11**
Harbour View **4**
The Hungry Monk Wine Bar **11**
The Moone High Cross Inn **19**
Moyglare Manor **1**
Red House Inn **21**
The Roundwood Inn **18**
Tree of Idleness **6**

**ATTRACTIONS**
Avondale House and
  Forest Park **16**
Blessington Adventure
  Centre **5**
Brennanstown Riding
  School **6**
Castletown House **2**
The Curragh **21**
Devil's Glen Holiday Village &
  Equestrian Village **12**
Glendalough Round Tower
  and Monastery **17**
Irish National Stud and
  Japanese Gardens **22**
Kildare Country Club **3**
Killruddery House
  and Garden **7**
Meeting of the Waters **16**
The Moone High Cross **19**
Mt. Usher Gardens **6**
National Sea Life Centre **6**
Powerscourt Estate Gardens **8**
Powerscourt Waterfall **8**
Russborough House **5**

Steam Museum **3**
Sugar Loaf Mountain **8**
Wicklow Mountains National
  Park **17**

**SHOPPING**
A La Campagne **13**
Avoca Handweavers **14**
Fisher's of Newtownmount-
  kennedy **9**
Irish Pewter Mill **19**
Kildare Woolen Mills **22**
The Woolen Mills
  Glendalough **17**

**NIGHTLIFE**
Cartoon Inn **16**
The Manor Inn **4**
The Meetings **15**
Old Court Inn **13**
Philip Healy's **13**
Silken Thomas **23**

## Getting to and around County Wicklow

If you're arriving by car, take the N11 (which becomes M11 periodically) south from Dublin toward Arklow. You can turn off along this route to reach most major towns and attractions. The **Irish Rail's** Dublin (Connolly Station)–Rosslare Harbour train line (☎ **01-836-6222;** www.irishrail.ie) has stations in Bray, Greystones, Wicklow, Rathdrum, and Arklow. Dublin Area Rapid Transit (DART) extends as far as Greystones. **Dublin Bus** (☎ **01-872-000;** www.dublinbus.ie) runs from City Centre to Dun Laoghaire and the Bray DART station. **Bus Éireann** (☎ **01-836-6111;** www.buseireann.ie) travels year-round between Bray, Wicklow, Arklow, Rathdrum, and Avoca.

## Spending the night in County Wicklow

### Druids Glen Marriott Hotel
**$$$–$$$$  Newtownmountkennedy**

This hotel, beautifully situated between the Irish Sea and the Wicklow Mountains, has the distinction of being the first Marriott Hotel in Ireland, in case you're a fan of the chain. Built to five-star specifications, the rooms are larger than most, and the hotel has every amenity you can think of, plus a few you probably wouldn't, such as a whirlpool, solarium, and steamroom in the pool area and its own Enterprise Rent-a-Car desk. If you're a golfer, you'll appreciate the location — on the 400-acre Druid's Glen Golf Resort.

*From Dublin, take the N11 national route toward Wexford. Turn off toward Newtownmountkennedy and follow the signs to Druids Glen.* ☎ *01-287-0800. Fax: 01-287-0801.* www.marriotthotels.com. *Rates: €145–230 ($167–$265) double. AE, DC, MC, V.*

### Glendalough Hotel
**$$$  Glendalough**

Occupying a woody area overlooking the ruins of the monastery complex at Glendalough, this 1800s hotel is the perfect launching point for an exploration of Glendalough and the Wicklow Mountains National Park. The public rooms are beautifully furnished with antiques. The good-size, pastel bedrooms are nothing to write home about, but you'll probably be exploring the area the whole day anyway. The traditional Irish dishes served in the dining room are excellent and fresh, and the Glendalough Tavern has some of the best pub food you'll find in a hotel, including a wonderful lamb stew.

*On the 755. Take the R755 off the N11.* ☎ *0404-45-135. Fax: 0404-45-142. Rates: €130–€170 ($150–$196) double. AE, DC, MC, V. Closed Jan.*

### Hunter's Hotel
**$$$  Rathnew**

This family-run hotel is one of Ireland's oldest coaching inns, offering views of breathtaking gardens and nearby mountains. Rooms are huge, with attractive art. Irish dishes, such as Wicklow lamb with fresh vegetables from the hotel's gardens, are served in the restaurant. Blazing fires and antique furniture add to the charm.

*Newrath Bridge. Take the N11 from Dublin and take a left in Ashford village by the bridge and opposite Ashford House pub. Hunter's is 2km (1½ miles) from Ashford.* ☎ *0404-40-106. Fax: 0404-40-338.* www.hunters.ie. *Rates: €180 ($207) double (see Web site for specials). AE, MC, V.*

### Slievemore
**$$$   Greystones**

You could spend all day gazing at Greystone's pretty harbor from Slievemore, an impeccable, whitewashed B&B run by a pleasant couple. Rooms are bright, spacious, and sweet, with sparkling-clean bathrooms (all rooms are en suite except the single, which has a private bathroom outside the room). A delicious and filling breakfast is served in the back conservatory, where you can watch robins flit by as you munch your bacon. It's an easy walk to Slievemore from the DART station, so you don't even need a car to enjoy this darling seaside town and this excellent B&B.

*The Harbour. Follow signs south out of Bray to Greystones village.* ☎ *01-287-4724. Rates: €130–€140 ($150–$161) double. No credit cards.*

### Tinakilly Country House and Restaurant
**$$$$   Rathnew**

This country-house hotel brings together everything you've heard about the grandeur and friendliness of Ireland. Staying here may strain your budget, but when your every whim is being catered to, and you're relaxing in your charming room, you'll be happy you splurged. The hotel is an impressive Victorian mansion filled with antiques and nautical memorabilia. Most rooms have four-poster or canopy beds and overlook the mountains, the Irish Sea, or carefully tended gardens. The cherry on top is Brunel, a wonderful restaurant serving fixed-price dinners (€46/$53) featuring modern cuisine that takes advantage of the freshest ingredients.

*Take the R750 off the main Dublin-Wexford Road.* ☎ *0404-69-274 or 800-525-4800 from the U.S. Fax: 0404-67-806.* www.tinakilly.ie. *Rates: €204–€238 ($235–$274) double. AE, DC, MC, V.*

### Tudor Lodge
**$   Laragh**

This B&B boasts simple, tidy, spacious rooms; a cozy living room; and a patio and terrace that offer views of the surrounding green hills. With a central location in the Wicklow Mountains, the house is a convenient spot to hang your hat while exploring the area.

☎ *0404-45-554.* www.tudorlodgeireland.com. *Rates: €70 ($81) double. MC, V.*

## Dining locally in County Wicklow

In addition to the choices below, see Tinakilly Country House and Restaurant, and Glendalough Hotel in the previous section.

### Avoca Handweavers Tea Shop
$   Avoca   ECLECTIC

If you thought this little eatery was just a decent place to get some tea and baked goods while blowing your budget on Avoca's beautiful woven items, think again. Located in the back of the shop, this cheerful cafe serves some divine lunch choices, from salads, soups, and sandwiches to main courses such as smoked trout and honey-glazed ham. The low lunch prices make it easy to justify buying that extra woollen throw.

☎ *0402-35105. Main courses: €4–€9 ($4.60–$10). MC, V. Open: Daily 8:30 a.m.–6 p.m.*

### Bel's Bistro
$–$$   Greystones   ECLECTIC

Local families and groups of friends fill this casual, modern spot for lunches, leisurely after-work drinks and snacks, and dinners. This is the kind of menu that you don't have to think too hard about — no tomato foams or tapenades; just simple, well-prepared food such as burgers, blackened chicken pasta, fish and chips, and Thai chicken curry. I'm a big fan of the mushroom tart with leek-and-garlic sauce. The bright interior is stylishly decorated with high-backed pine chairs and small contemporary paintings, but the patio out front is the place to be on a nice day.

*Church Rd.* ☎ *01-201-6990. Main courses: €7.50–€19 ($8.65–$22). MC, V. Open: Daily noon–10 p.m.*

### The Hungry Monk Wine Bar
$$$–$$$$   Greystones   ECLECTIC

Excellent wines, glowing candles, dark wood furnishings, and simple hearty food are the catalysts for the convivial atmosphere at this place. Clink your wineglasses over plates of simply prepared fish, stew, or perhaps the excellent Monk Burger, a thick hunk of hamburger cooked with herbs and topped with gherkins. Keep your eyes peeled for the various works of art with monks as their subject. Groups may want to reserve early in order to snag the large, candelabra-lit table. If you feel like a more formal meal, head upstairs to the Hungry Monk's fancier restaurant.

*Church Rd.* ☎ *01-287-5759. Reservations recommended. Main courses: Restaurant courses €15–€32 ($17–$37), wine bar courses €6–€18 ($7–$21). M, V. Open: Restaurant is open Wed–Sat 7–11 p.m., Sun 12:30–8 p.m; downstairs wine bar is open Mon–Sat 5– 11 p.m., Sun 4–9 p.m.*

### The Roundwood Inn
$$$ Roundwood SEAFOOD/IRISH/ECLECTIC

Forget about greasy fish and chips; the Roundwood Inn offers seafood that will knock your socks off, including a platter of salmon, oysters, lobster, and shrimp. In addition, you'll find beautifully prepared Irish and Continental dishes, from a succulent steak to Irish stew. If you want a cheaper meal or a bite to tide you over between meals, check out the terrific pub grub in the bar. The inn was built in the 18th century and is furnished with dark wood and an open fireplace. Service could be nicer, but the food makes up for that.

*Main St. Out of Bray take the R755 to Roundwood.* ☎ *01-281-8107. Reservations recommended for dinner. Main courses: €15–€23 ($17–$26). AE, MC, V. Open: Wed–Sat noon–10 p.m., Sun 1–2:30p.m.*

### Tree of Idleness
$$$ Bray GREEK/CYPRIOT

This is one of Ireland's best Greek restaurants, offering well-prepared standards from moussaka to *keftedes* (Greek meatballs). The seafront dining room is always hopping and full of chatting, laughing patrons.

*Seafront.* ☎ *01-286-3498. Main courses: €19–€24 ($22–$28). AE, MC, V. Open: Tues–Sun 7:30– 11 p.m.*

## Exploring County Wicklow

Here are some of the best ways to enjoy the emerald landscape of County Wicklow.

### Organized tours

Because Wicklow is so close to Dublin, a number of operators offer bus tours, and others take advantage of the area's beauty to offer such interesting options as horseback tours.

### Bus Éireann Bus Tour

Bus Éireann offers day-tours of the Wicklow area from Dublin. The **Glendalough and Wicklow Panorama Tour** (€30/$35 adults, €28/$32 students and seniors, €20/$22 children, not including attraction admission) runs from mid-April through October, covering the south coast of Dublin, Wicklow Mountains, Powerscourt, Roundwood, Laragh, and Glendalough.

*When and where: All tours leave from the main station, on Store Street behind the Customs building. Information: Bus Éireann.* ☎ *01-836-6111. Call for schedule information.*

### Wild Wicklow Tour

This fun day tour, in a small Mercedes coach that goes where the big and bulky buses can't, packs in many of the highlights of Wicklow. First, you visit the beautiful seaside town of Dalkey, home to Bono, Enya, and many of

Ireland's other rich and famous; then move on to Avoca Handweavers, which sells colorful woolen items and funky clothing, as well as delicious lunches. Next, you hit Wicklow's top attraction, the enchanting sixth-century monastic settlement of Glendalough, before stopping for a pub lunch. Your day ends with a visit to Sally Gap, which has stunning views of the surrounding mountains, and Lough Tay, a quietly magnificent mountain lake. I particularly recommend this tour because the guides are friendly, fun, and informative, and allow you time to explore a bit on your own.

*The full-day tour leaves from the Dublin tourist office and picks up at various hotels around Dublin (tell them where you're staying, and they'll tell you the closest pickup point).* ☎ *01-475-3313.* www.DiscoverDublin.ie. *Price:€28 ($32) adults, €25 ($29) student or child. Advance reservations recommended.*

## The top attractions

### Glendalough Round Tower and Monastery
**Glendalough**

This secluded, leafy site, centered on two peaceful lakes, has been a sacred one since the sixth century, when St. Kevin founded a monastery here. The area flourished as a community of learning for almost 900 years, with the sounds of theories and ideas bouncing off the majestic trees and stone buildings. The entire complex was sacked by Anglo-Norman invaders in the 14th century, and most of the buildings were destroyed. However, you can still explore many ruins around the Upper and Lower lakes, including the remnants of a seventh- to ninth-century cathedral; a graveyard full of beautifully designed Celtic crosses; and the highlight, a stunningly-preserved 31m (103-ft.) round tower capped with a belfry. Drop into the well-done visitor center to get a sense of the context of this site. I highly recommend the peaceful walk from the Lower Lake to the less-visited Upper Lake.

*Glendalough.* ☎ *0404-45-325. By car: N11 to R755 from Dublin, R752 to R755 from Wicklow. Admission:€2.75 ($3.15) adults, €2 ($2.30) seniors, €1.25 ($1.45) children and students. Open: Mid-Oct–mid-March daily 9:30 a.m.–5 p.m., mid-March–mid-Oct daily 9:30 a.m.–6 p.m. Last admission 45 minutes before closing. Suggested visit: 1½ hours.*

### Mt. Usher Gardens
**Ashford**

More than 5,000 species of plants from all over the world populate these informal gardens, located along the River Vartry. These 20 acres, which started as a humble potato patch in 1860, have blossomed into a wild ocean of flowers, trees, meadows, and waterfalls, with small suspension bridges crossing the river, and birds and wildlife flitting above and through the exotic greenery. The spot where a mini suspension bridge spans a little waterfall just may be one of the most romantic spots in Ireland. Also on the premises are a tearoom and a courtyard filled with shops.

*Off the main Dublin-Wicklow road (N11), look for the signs.* ☎ *0404-40-116. Admission: €6 ($6.90) adults, €5 ($5.75) seniors, students, and children 5 to 12. Open: March 5–Oct daily 10:30 a.m.–6 p.m. Suggested visit: 1½ hours.*

# The ideal picnic spot

Just beyond Avondale House is the famed **Meeting of the Waters,** where the Avonmore and Avonbeg rivers come together. This spot is so beautiful, it inspired Thomas Moore to write: "There is not in the wide world a valley so sweet / as the vale in whose bosom the bright waters meet." Pack some fruit, bread, and cheese and head to this spot, 5km (3 miles) south of Rathdrum heading toward Arklow on the R752 (which becomes the R755 as you leave Rathdrum).

### *National Sea Life Centre*
### Bray

This highly interactive aquarium follows the route of a river from its origin to its ocean destination, bringing you face to face with thousands of seawater and freshwater creatures along the way. Kids will have a ball following an adventure trail with puzzles and games, using touch screens and picking up ocean dwellers at the touch tank. The feedings, talks, and demonstrations by the aquarium's staff are worth planning your visit around.

*Strand Rd. on the boardwalk.* ☎ *01-286-6939.* www.sealife.ie. *DART: The center is a 10-minute walk from the Bray Station. Admission: €8 ($9.20) adults, €6 ($6.90) seniors and students, €5.50 ($6.35) children. Open: Mon–Fri 11 a.m.–5 p.m., Sat and Sun 10 a.m.–6 p.m. (call to confirm hours during the winter). Suggested visit: 2 hours.*

### *Powerscourt Estate Gardens*
### Enniskerry

These gardens are the finest in Wicklow County, which is saying a lot, because the county is known for its abundance of exceptionally beautiful gardens. First laid out from 1745 to 1767, the gardens were redesigned in Victorian style from 1843 to 1875. The gardens have many different facets, among them a wooded glen graced with a stone round tower that was modeled on Lord Powerscourt's dining-room pepper pot, a magical moss-covered grotto, a formal Italianate area with a circular pond and fountain presided over by sculptures of winged horses, and a walled garden where blazing roses cling to the stone. Don't miss the moving pet cemetery, with sweet monuments to various pets owned by the Powerscourt family, from faithful dogs to a particularly prolific dairy cow. I recommend following the route around the entire estate, which should take you a good hour to two hours. Skip the tour of the house; it's not very interesting. Powerscourt Waterfall is down the road (see "Other cool things to see and do," later in this chapter).

*Off the main Dublin-Wicklow Road (N11). By car: Take the N11 out of Dublin (it becomes the new motorway M11) and follow signs for the garden. By bus: 44 from Dublin to Enniskerry, or Alpine Coach (☎ 01-286-2547) from the Bray DART station to the gardens. ☎ 01-204-6000. Admission: Garden only: €6 ($6.90) adults, €5.50 ($6.35) students and seniors, €3.50 ($4.05) children under 16; House only: €2.50 ($2.90) adults, €2.20 ($2.55) students and seniors, €1.60 ($1.85) children under 16. Open: Daily 9:30 a.m.–5:30 p.m. Closed for the two weeks prior to Christmas. Suggested visit: 2 hours.*

## Wicklow Mountains National Park
### Glendalough

This park, covering nearly 20,000 hectares (50,000 acres), encompasses forest, hills, and large mountain bogs, and protects such wildlife as the rare peregrine falcon. The park centers on beautiful Glendalough (reviewed earlier in this section) and includes Glendalough Valley and the Glendalough Wood Nature Reserve. The visitor center at the Upper Lake offers information on hiking in the park, including route descriptions and maps, and organizes free nature walks, usually on Wednesday at 11 a.m. and 2 p.m. (but call to confirm times). A tough stretch of the Wicklow Way (described in the next section, "Outdoor activities"), runs through the park. In May and October, the park hosts two-day walking festivals.

*Take the N11 to R755 from Dublin; the R752 to R755 from Wicklow. The Information Point is located by Upper Lake, R756 off R755. ☎ 0404-45-425. Park admission: €2.75 ($3.15) adults, €1.25 ($1.45) students and children. Open: May–Aug daily 10 a.m.–6 p.m., April and Sept Sat and Sun 10 a.m.–6 p.m.; closed for the rest of the year. Suggested visit: 1 to 3 hours.*

## Outdoor activities

Also see the description of Wicklow Mountains National Park (earlier in this chapter) and Sugar Loaf Mountain (in the next section, "Other cool things to see and do").

- **Blessington Adventure Centre:** This company offers canoeing, kayaking, sailing, and windsurfing on the sparkling Blessington Lakes. It also runs horseback rides.

   Location: Adventure Centre Pier, Blessington (off N81). ☎ 045-86-5092. Prices vary. Open: Daily 10 a.m. to 5 p.m.

- **Brennanstown Riding School:** Everyone from beginners to advanced riders can take advantage of the indoor and outdoor riding facilities here. The best option is a ride or pony-trek through the scenic Wicklow countryside.

Location: Brennanstown Riding School, Hollbrook, Kilmacanogue, near Bray. ☎ 01-286-3778. Take the DART to Bray. Prices vary, depending on activity.

✔ **Devil's Glen Holiday Village & Equestrian Village:** Devil's Glen offers all sorts of horse-related activities, from jumping lessons to hunting jaunts to pony-trekking. The complex includes thousands of acres of woodland and boasts self-catering accommodations, so you can jump from the saddle into a shower.

Location: Devil's Glen, Ashford, County Wicklow. ☎ 0404-40637. www.devilsglen.ie. Prices vary, depending on activity; treks cost €25 ($29). Open: Daily (call for times).

✔ **The Wicklow Way:** This 122km (76-mile) trail extends from Marlay Park in County Dublin to Clonegal in County Carlow, running through forests, over hills, around bogs and farms, along country roads and old stone walls, and through charming villages high in the Wicklow Mountains. You can walk the whole trail in five or six days, staying in towns along the way, or just drop in for a day hike. The walk from the Deerpark parking lot near the River Dargle to Luggala is a gorgeous day-hike option, as are the hikes between the towns of Tinahely, Shillelagh, and Clonegal. You can get information on hikes at Wicklow Mountains National Park (described in the previous section) or any Wicklow tourist office. Check out the Wicklow Trail Sheets, available at Wicklow tourist offices, for shorter hikes.

A daily Bus Éireann bus runs from Dublin and Waterford to Bunclody near the County Carlow end of the trail, and local buses run from Dublin to Marlay Park.

## Other cool things to see and do

✔ **Avondale House and Forest Park:** Built in 1779 and set in a lush forest valley, this house was the birthplace and home of one of Ireland's great leaders, Charles Stewart Parnell (1846–1891), who fought for Irish home rule and for land reform. The Georgian house has been restored beautifully and features original furniture and a museum illustrating Parnell's life and career. The grounds are lovely, and you're free to explore along a number of well-marked nature trails, including a pretty 5½ km (3½-mile) walk along the river. Avondale is a center of Irish forestry, and its grounds have served as a model of forest preservation for the country.

Location: Rathdrum. ☎ 0404-46-111. Take N11 to R752 to Rathdrum crossroads, and follow signs to the house. Admission: House €5 ($5.75) adults, €4.50 ($5.20) seniors and students under 12; Parking fee: €5 ($5.75); Park: free. Open: Mid-March, April, Sept, and Oct Tuesday to Sunday 11 a.m. to 6 p.m.; May through Aug daily 11 a.m. to 6 p.m. (last admission 5 p.m. at all times). Suggested visit: 1½ hours.

✔ **Killruddery House and Garden:** Killruddery is the oldest surviving formal garden in Ireland, laid out in the 1680s in the French style of the time. Highlights are the outdoor theater, exotic shrubs, orangerie featuring Italian statues, and pond. The gardens are certainly the draw here, but the grand Elizabethan-revival house is also worth a visit. The house has been in the family of the Earls of Meath since 1618 and features a stunning conservatory.

Location: Off the main Dublin-Wicklow Road (N11), Killruddery. ☎ 01-286-2777. Admission: House and garden €6.50 ($7.50) adults, €4.50 ($5.20) seniors and students, €2.50 ($2.90) children. Garden only: €4.50 ($5.20) adult, €3.50 ($4.05) seniors and students, €1.50 ($1.75) children. Open: Garden is open May–Sept daily 1–5 p.m. and April weekends 1–5 p.m.; house is open May, June, and Sept daily 1–5 p.m. Suggested visit: 1½ hours.

✔ **Powerscourt Waterfall:** This pretty waterfall, located in a leafy glen, is Ireland's highest. On a nice day, get some ice cream, and enjoy the view. Don't expect solitude; there are usually a handful of visitors here at any given time.

Location: Off the main Dublin-Wicklow Rd. (N11), Enniskerry. ☎ 01-204-6000. Admission: €4 ($4.60) adults, €3.50 ($4.05) students, €3 ($3.45) children. Open: Daily 9:30 a.m. to 7 p.m. in summer and 10:30 a.m. until dusk in winter.

✔ **Russborough House:** This house, built in the mid-1700s in the Palladian style, is home to the world-famous Beit Collection of paintings, which includes pieces by Gainsborough, Reynolds, Rubens, and Guardi. The furnishings of the house — including tapestries, silver, bronzes, porcelain, and ornate furniture — are also works of art. The grounds are open for exploration, and there are a restaurant, a shop, and a children's playground.

Location: Off N81, Blessington. ☎ 045-86-5239. From Dublin, take the N7 to Naas, and pick up the R410. The house is located where the R410 meets the N81. Admission: €6 ($6.90) adults, €4.50 ($5.20) seniors and students, €3 ($3.45) children under 12. Open: April and Oct Sun and bank holidays 10:30 a.m. to 5:30 p.m., May through Sept daily 10:30 a.m. to 5:30 p.m. (last admission 5 p.m.). Suggested visit: 1 hour.

✔ **Sugar Loaf Mountain:** There are spectacular views from the top of Sugar Loaf Mountain. The climb is pretty easy, and you can get to the top in under an hour. You'll be happy you did — on a clear day, you can see all the way to Wales!

Location: Near Kilmacanogue. Take R755 off N11.

## Shopping in County Wicklow

Wicklow is known for pottery and knitwear. The **County Tourism Office in Wicklow** (☎ 0404-20-070) puts out a publication called the *Pottery Trail,* with a full list of pottery, crafts, and knitwear locations throughout the county.

In Wicklow Town, **A La Campagne,** Main Street (☎ 0404-61-388), offers unique items, including gifts, kitchenware, pottery, and glass; plenty of artsy objects, such as candles and holders; and Irish country pottery. The owner, Stephen Falvin, is often on hand to help pick out a gift or advise on choices. **Avoca Handweaver,** Avoca Village (☎ 0402-35-105), is the oldest handweaving mill in Ireland (dating to 1723) and sells colorful knitwear, including tweed and knit clothing and blankets; beautiful trendy/bohemian clothing; and a wide range of fine Irish crafts. There is also an outlet store in Kilmacanogue, near Bray (☎ 01-286-7466). Located in a converted schoolhouse, **Fisher's of Newtownmountkennedy,** in a big pink building on R765, off N11, Newtownmountkennedy (☎ 01-28-9404), has tons of men's and women's clothes and accessories, both elegant and country-casual, plus cool items like hip flasks and pool cues. **The Woolen Mills Glendalough,** in Laragh, on the R755 (☎ 0404-45-156), is housed in an old farmhouse and sells Irish handcrafts including pottery, glass, jewelry, and handknits.

## Hitting the Pubs

### Cartoon Inn
**Rathdrum**

Make sure you don't snort Guinness through your nose as you laugh at the cartoons on the wall of this pub, many of which were drawn by famous cartoonists. Ireland's annual Cartoon Festival is held in Rathdrum in early summer. Food is served during lunchtime.

*28 Main St.* ☎ *0404-46-774.*

### The Meetings
**Vale of Avoca**

Nestled in the beautiful Vale of Avoca, The Meetings is a Tudor-syle pub that's popular with visitors to Wicklow. You can get good pub grub all day and listen to traditional music on weekend nights. Plus, when the weather's warm, you can sit outside on the patio and take in the view. It's clearly geared to tourists, but that's not necessarily a bad thing. After all, how many pubs provide a Bureau de Change and a craft shop?

☎ *0402-35-226.*

### Old Court Inn
**Wicklow**

You can't miss this pub — it's bright yellow and sits at the center of town. Inside, it's quiet, cozy, and warm, with overstuffed booths. If you visit during chillier times, you can enjoy blazing fireplaces.

*Main St. near the courthouse.* ☎ *0404-67-680.*

### Philip Healy's
**Wicklow**

This unpretentious spot is where locals meet for a leisurely drink and chat. The high ceilings make it feel open and airy, but the pub has plenty of nooks to settle into if you want to have a quiet conversation.

*Main St.* ☎ *0404-67-380.*

## Fast Facts: County Wicklow

### Area Codes
County Wicklow's area codes (or city codes) are 01, 0404, 0402, and 045.

### Emergencies/Police
Dial ☎ **999** for all emergencies.

### Information
For visitor information and help reserving accommodations, go to the tourist office in Fitzwilliam Square, Wicklow (☎ 0404-69-117; www.wicklow.ie), open year-round. They can also provide reservation services.

### Internet
BrayNet Internet Café (☎ 01-286-1520) is in the Star Leisure Centre on the Bray Seafront in Bray.

### Hospital
The main hospital is in Wicklow (☎ 0404-67-108).

## County Kildare

Welcome to horse country. A land of gentle hills and open grasslands, County Kildare is home to hundreds of stud farms. And, of course, one needs a place to race all these fine horses, so the county boasts three large racetracks, including the Curragh, where the Irish Derby is held each year. (The "Counties Wicklow and Kildare" map can help you pinpoint locations.)

## *Getting to and around County Kildare*

By car, take the N7 from Dublin or Limerick to get to Kildare, or take N4 to Celbridge and then use R403. **Irish Rail** (☎ **01-836-6222**) has daily service to Kildare town, and **Bus Éireann** (☎ **01-836-6111;** www.bus eireann.com) services Kildare, Straffan, Newbridge, and other towns throughout the area.

## *Spending the night in County Kildare*

### *Annagh Lodge Guesthouse*
$$ **Newbridge**

The modern Annagh Lodge has pluses, such as a sauna and in-house movies, that you don't generally find in a country guesthouse. You may be surprised at the level of pampering. Bedrooms are luxurious and modern. This is a great location if you're interested in outdoor activities — eight golf courses and fishing are all within a close drive.

*Naas Rd. Take the N7 from Dublin to Newbridge.* ☎ *045-43-3518. Fax: 045-433-538.* www.annaghlodge.ie. *Rates:* €*100 ($115) double. MC, V.*

### *Barberstown Castle*
$$$ **Straffan**

This lavish hotel is made up of several different parts: a 13th-century castle keep, a 16th-century construction, a Georgian country house, and a 20th-century addition. Rooms are elegant, with antiques and reproductions and sumptuous fabrics.

*From Dublin, take the N7 to Kill, where you turn for Straffan; from the west, take N4 to Maynooth, where you turn for Straffan.* ☎ *800-323-5463 in the U.S. or 01-628-8157. Fax: 01-627-7027.* www.barberstowncastle.ie. *Rates:* €*170–*€*200 ($196–$230). AE, DC, MC, V. Closed Jan and Feb.*

### *Kilkea Castle Hotel and Golf Club*
$$$$ **Castledermot**

Keep an eye out for the 11th Earl of Kildare, who is said to haunt this medieval castle, built around 1180. The decor here evokes the Middle Ages, with medieval banners and coats of armor, but the luxurious bedrooms, with chandeliers and dark wood furnishings, top anything that King Arthur and his compatriots would be used to. You can amuse yourself all day on the grounds here, which include an 18-hole golf course, an indoor pool, fishing, tennis, archery, and other sporty pursuits.

☎ *0503-45-156. Fax: 0503-45-197.* www.kilkeacastlehotelgolf.com. *Rates:* €*200–*€*300 ($230–$345) double. AE, DC, MC, V.*

### Noreen Malone's B&B
**$  Naas**

This is the kind of B&B you'd love to move into. Noreen Malone's comfortable house is a welcome departure from the sometimes-impersonal nature of hotels. The exquisitely manicured lawn hints at the clean and nicely decorated rooms and dining area. The town of Naas is just a five-minute walk away, and the price of this lovely stay-over can't be beat.

*Sallins Rd. Take the N7 from Dublin to Naas.* ☎ *045-89-7598. Rates: €66–€70 ($76–$81) double. No credit cards.*

## Dining locally in County Kildare
Also see "Hitting the pubs," later in this chapter.

### Harbour View
**$$–$$$  Naas  IRISH**

The food here is home-cooked, wholesome, delicious, and served in hearty portions. Don't let the nondescript exterior fool you; one foot in the door, and you'll know you're in for a meal that will keep you going all day long or satisfy you after a day spent exploring.

*Limerick Rd. Take the N7 from Dublin to Naas.* ☎ *045-87-9145. Main courses: €12–€20 ($14–$23). AE, DC, MC, V. Open: Daily 7:30–10 a.m. and noon to 9:30 p.m.*

### The Moone High Cross Inn
**$–$$  Moone  PUB GRUB**

Take a seat, and enjoy the friendly atmosphere at this authentic pub, which serves shrimp; salmon; duck; steak; shepherd's pie; and other simple, delicious, well-prepared dishes. Be sure to check out the decor, consisting of old photographs and all sorts of local curios.

*Bolton Hill; 7½ km (5 miles) south of Ballytore.* ☎ *059-862-4112. €6.50–€25 ($7.50–$28) (most in the low teens). MC, V. Serves food Mon–Sat 8:30 a.m.–9:45 p.m., Sun 8 a.m.–8:45 p.m.*

### Moyglare Manor
**$$$$  Maynooth  FRENCH**

Plan nothing else for the evening, because dinner in this formal and romantic dining room is a long and luxurious experience. The cuisine is classic French, with such dishes as pork stuffed with herbs, plaice in champagne sauce, and the very popular crab croquettes. The fresh vegetables served alongside the meal are fresh from the manor's garden. Service is terrific.

*29km (18 miles) west of Dublin on the N4.* ☎ *01-628-6351. Prix-fixe lunch €35 ($40), prix-fixe dinner €55 ($63). AE, DC, MC, V. Open: Daily 12:30–2:30 p.m. and 7:30–9 p.m.*

### Red House Inn
$$$–$$$$   Newbridge   IRISH/MEDITERRANEAN

Set in a country house, this award-winning restaurant offers Irish food with a Mediterranean influence. There are all sorts of dishes, from lamb and beef to fish to vegetarian options. The monkfish is especially popular.

*On the N7 between Naas and Kildare. ☎ 045-43-1657. Reservations recommended. Main courses: €20–€27 ($22–$31). AE, DC, MC, V. Open: Tues–Sat 6:30–10 p.m., Sun 6:30–9:30 p.m.*

## Exploring County Kildare
Houses and gardens and horses, oh my! This section lists the top sights in County Kildare.

### The top attractions

#### Castletown House
**Celbridge**

This stately house was built in the early part of the 18th century for William Connolly, then the Speaker of the Irish House of Commons. Its grandeur is staggering, and it remains a standout in Irish architecture. The mansion was built in the Palladian style, a Renaissance style meant to copy the classicism of ancient Rome. The interior is decorated with Georgian furnishings, and the main hall and staircase are covered with intricate plasterwork. Run by the state and open to the public, the house is worth the drive — about 16km (10 miles) northeast of Naas. Access is by guided tour only.

*From Dublin, take the N4 west, picking up the R403 several miles out of the city. Located on the R403 just before you reach the village of Celbridge. By bus: 67 and 67A from Dublin. ☎ 01-628-8252. Admission: Required guided tours €3.50 ($4.05) adults, €2.50 ($2.90) seniors and students, €1.25 ($1.45) children. Open: Mid-April–Sept Mon–Fri 10 a.m.–6 p.m., Sat and Sun 1–6 p.m.; Oct Mon–Fri 10 a.m.–5 p.m., Sat and Sun 1–5 p.m; Nov Sun 1–5 p.m; closed Dec–mid-April. Suggested visit: 1½ hours.*

#### The Curragh
**Newbridge**

This racetrack, the country's best-known, is often referred to as the Churchill Downs of Ireland. You can catch a race here at least one Saturday a month from March to October. In late June, the Curragh is host to the famous Irish Derby.

*On the Dublin-Limerick road. Take the N7 from Dublin or Naas. By train: Daily service into Curragh. Bus Éireann(☎ 01-836-6111) offers a round-trip bus from Dublin. ☎ 045-44-1205. www.curragh.ie. Admission: €15 ($17) for most races, €20–€50 ($23–$58) for the Derby. Call ahead for upcoming dates. Races usually begin at 2 p.m.*

## Irish National Stud and Japanese Gardens
### Tully

One of the foremost horse breeding grounds in the country, the National Stud is consistently ranked as one of Ireland's top-20 tourist attractions. Visitors can see the majestic horses being groomed and exercised, and during spring, they can ooh and aah over the mares with their foals. Check out the Horse Museum, with exhibits on racing, hunting, and show jumping, plus the skeleton of the famed horse Arkle, who won several racing victories in the 1960s.

On the same grounds are the striking Japanese Gardens, which boast bonsai, bamboo, and cherry trees. The gardens portray the journey of life, starting with birth and ending at eternity, which is represented by a Zen rock garden.

*Take N7 from Dublin or Naas. By train: Daily service into Kildare Railway Station.* ☎ *045-52-1617. Admission: €8.50 ($9.80) adults, €6.50 ($7.50) seniors and students, €4.50 ($5.20) under 12. Open: Feb–mid-Nov daily 9:30 a.m.–6:00 p.m. Suggested visit: 3 hours.*

## More cool things to see and do

✔ **Kildare Country Club (K-Club):** This 18-hole championship golf course was designed by Arnold Palmer himself, and you certainly pay for the privilege of golfing here.

Location: 27km (17 miles) west of Dublin in Straffan. ☎ **01-601-7300.** www.kclub.ie. Par: 72. Fees: €265 ($305) for 18 holes from May to Sept; €185 ($213) in Oct; and €115 ($132) from Nov to April.

✔ **The Moone High Cross:** This 1,200-year-old high stone cross boasts beautiful carvings of Celtic designs, as well as biblical scenes.

Location: Moone. On the southern edge of Moone village, signposted off N9.

✔ **Steam Museum:** Anyone with an interest in steam locomotion will enjoy this museum, housed in a restored church. There is a collection of 18th-century locomotive engines that includes Richard Trevithick's Third Model of 1797, the oldest surviving self-propelled machine in existence. Another room contains stationary engines from the Industrial Age. You can find plenty of steam-locomotion literature in the shop. If it's nice out, check out the 18th-century walled garden.

Location: Off the Dublin-Limerick Road (N7), Lodge Park, Straffan, near Celbridge. ☎ **01-627-3155** summer, ☎ **01-628-8412** winter. By car: Take the N7 from Dublin or Naas. By train: Daily service into Kildare Railway Station. Admission: €6 ($6.90) adults, €5 ($5.75) seniors, students, and children. Open: April, May, and Sept Sun 2:30–5:30 p.m., June through Aug Tues to Sun 2 to 6 p.m. Suggested visit: 2 hours.

## Shopping in County Kildare

Like many other woolen mills in the country, **Kildare Woolen Mills,** 6 Academy St., Kildare (☎ 045-52-0190), offers traditional Irish clothing: sweaters and tweeds, as well as local crafts and gifts. It has a convenient location right in town. The **Irish Pewter Mill,** on the N9, Timolin, Moone (☎ 0507-24-164), is a 1,000-year-old pewter mill boasting a full selection of original pewter jewelry, as well as a collection of tableware. If you arrive in the morning, you can watch craftsmen casting the works sold here.

## Hitting the pubs

Also see The Moone High Cross Inn, reviewed in "Dining locally in County Kildare," earlier in this chapter.

### The Manor Inn

Naas

This warm and inviting pub is a great place to discover the area's history. Pictures and mementos throughout reflect local color and Kildare pride. There's enough information to keep your interest while you wait for some delicious pub grub to come your way. Kids love the children's menu.

*On N7, where the N7 meets the N9, 25 Main St. South.* ☎ *045-89-7471.*

### Silken Thomas

Kildare

Silken Thomas is an entertainment complex with three bars (including a warm and welcoming thatched-roof, oak-beamed pub and a glistening Victorian-style hangout), a restaurant, and a state-of-the art disco. Fortify yourself with some of Silken Thomas's delicious pub grub, including steaks, sandwiches, and soups. The pub's name comes from a member of the Fitzgerald family known for wearing luxurious clothing and being accompanied by standard-bearers carrying silken banners.

*The Square.* ☎ *045-52-2232.*

# Fast Facts: County Kildare

### Area Codes

Kildare's area codes (or city codes) are 01, 045, 053, and 0507.

### Emergencies/Police

Dial ☎ **999** for all emergencies.

### Genealogical Resources

Contact the Kildare Heritage and Genealogy Co. in Newbridge, Kildare (☎ 045-433-602).

**Hospital**

Naas General Hospital (☎ 045-897221) is in Naas.

**Information**

The tourist office in Kildare (☎ 045-52-2696), on The Square, is open mid-May to September. Outside of those times, contact the Wicklow tourist office (see the "Fast Facts: County Wicklow" section ) .

**Internet**

The CyberX Internet Cafe (☎ 01-629-1747) in Maynooth has Internet access and printing capabilities.

# Chapter 14

# The Southeast: Counties Wexford, Waterford, Tipperary, and Kilkenny

● ● ● ● ● ● ● ● ● ● ● ● ● ● ● ● ● ● ● ● ● ● ● ● ● ● ● ● ● ● ● ● ● ● ● ● ● ● ● ● ● ● ● ● ●

## In This Chapter

▶ Traveling back in time at the Irish National Heritage Park
▶ Discovering the wonders of the Hook Peninsula
▶ Touring the Waterford Crystal Factory
▶ Visiting Ireland's version of The Rock (the Rock of Cashel, that is)
▶ Exploring the medieval streets and buildings in Kilkenny

● ● ● ● ● ● ● ● ● ● ● ● ● ● ● ● ● ● ● ● ● ● ● ● ● ● ● ● ● ● ● ● ● ● ● ● ● ● ● ● ● ● ● ● ●

*W*exford, Waterford, Tipperary, and Kilkenny are among Ireland's Southeast counties (see "The Southeast" map) and are often referred to as the sunny Southeast because they generally enjoy more sunshine than the rest of the country. This area is not full of Ireland's greatest hits; instead, the region offers myriad lesser-known but just as intriguing attractions and activities — such as strolling through tiny fishing villages in Wexford, watching the famous Waterford Crystal being created in Waterford, wandering the medieval streets of Kilkenny, or exploring the Rock of Cashel in Tipperary, to name a few.

## County Wexford

County Wexford is one of the unsung treasures of Ireland, offering myriad peaceful beaches; rolling hills; winding rivers; great traditional music; and, in my opinion, some of the friendliest people in all of Ireland. If you're looking for don't-miss attractions, you may find Wexford disappointing, but if you're interested in wandering along beaches and down the streets of fishing villages, chatting with locals, hearing excellent impromptu Irish music, and visiting a number of very well-done museums, such as the Irish National Heritage Park, you're in for a treat.

The county's largest town is Wexford Town (see the map of the same name), a sweet and pretty harbor town that attracts Ireland's yuppies for weekend trips (lots of chi-chi clothing stores stand amidst the main street's cute bakeries and pubs). Along with Enniscorthy, Wexford Town is a great place to base yourself for an exploration of the county.

County Wexford was the heartbeat of the 1798 rebellion, when Irish rebels took a brave stand against the strong arm of the Brits, and it was at Vinegar Hill, near Enniscorthy, where 20,000 rebels were massacred by English cannons, effectively ending that rebellion. You encounter a ferocious pride in Irish freedom in these parts.

## Getting to and around County Wexford

If you're driving from Dublin, take the N11 (which becomes M11 periodically) or the N80 south to Enniscorthy and Wexford Town; from Wexford Town, take the N25 west to New Ross. Most attractions are along the route between Wexford Town and New Ross. A fast and cost-effective shortcut across Waterford Harbour between Passage East, which is about 16km (10 miles) east of Waterford City, and Ballyhack, about 32km (20 miles) southwest of Wexford Town, is provided by **Passenger East Car Ferry** (☎ **051-38-2480**). The ferry runs April to September Monday through Saturday from 7 a.m. to 10 p.m., Sunday from 9:30 a.m. to 10 p.m.; October to March, Monday to Saturday from 7 a.m. to 8 p.m., Sunday from 9:30 a.m. to 8 p.m. Fares are €6.50 ($7.50) one-way and €9.50 ($11) round-trip for a car and passengers, €1.50 ($1.75) one-way and €2 ($2.30) round-trip for foot passengers. Bicycles are permitted.

The Dublin (Connolly Station)-Rosslare Harbour line of **Irish Rail** (☎ **01-836-6222;** www.irishrail.ie) has stations in Rosslare, Wexford, and Enniscorthy. **Bus Éireann** (☎ **01-830-2222;** www.buseireann.ie) travels year-round to Wexford, Enniscorthy, Rosslare, New Ross, and other towns throughout the area.

Ferries connect Britain and Rosslare Harbour, which is 19km (20 miles) south of Wexford Town. **Stena Line** (☎ **053-33-11-5;** www.stenaline. co.uk) has passenger and car ferries from Fishguard, Wales, to Rosslare Harbour Ferryport. **Irish Ferries** (☎ **053-33158;** www.irishferries.ie) has service from Pembroke, Wales, to Rosslare. Irish Ferries also makes trips between Rosslare and the French towns of Le Havre and Cherbourg.

Walking is the best way to get around County Wexford's towns. Even the largest town, Wexford, is easily walkable.

## The Southeast

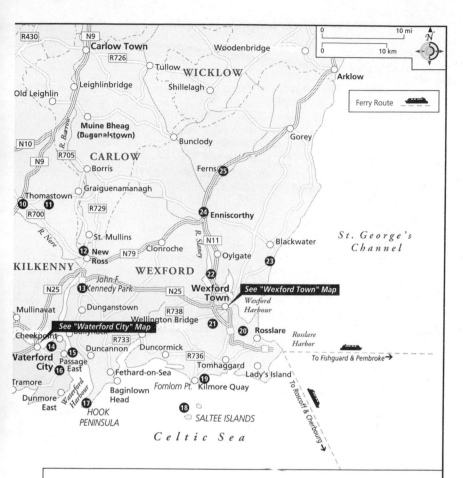

**ACCOMMODATIONS**
Clone House **25**
Cullintra House B&B **11**
Ferrycarrig **22**
Foxmount Country House **15**
Kelly's Resort Hotel **20**
Legends Guesthouse & The Kiln **3**
Riverside Park Hotel **24**
Samuels Heritage B&B **16**

**DINING**
Angela's Wholefood Restaurant **8**
Ballyrafter House **6**
Chez Hanz **3**
The Galley Cruising Restaurant **12**
The Tannery **26**

**ATTRACTIONS**
Brú Ború Heritage Centre **3**
Cahir Castle **7**
Curracloe Beach & Trail **23**
Dunmore Cave **1**
Enniscorthy Castle and Wexford
    Country Museum **24**
Holy Trinity Church & Medieval
    Walls **4**
Hook Peninsula **17**
Irish National Heritage Park **22**
Jerpoint Abbey **10**
John F Kennedy Arboretum **13**
Johnstown Castle Gardens & Irish
    Agricultural Museum **21**
Kilmore Quay **19**
Lismore Castle Gardens **6**
Mount Juliet Golf Course **10**

The National 1798 Visitor
    Centre **24**
Rock of Cashel **3**
Saltee Islands **18**

**SHOPPING**
Nicholas Mosse Pottery **2**
Tipperary Crystal Designs **9**

**NIGHTLIFE**
Antique Tavern **24**
Jack Meade's **14**
Ronald Reagan Pub **5**

## Spending the night in County Wexford

### Clone House
**$$ Enniscorthy**

This 250-year-old farmhouse, set in the picturesque countryside, feels like a quiet getaway spot, so it's almost a surprise to realize that it's also close to golf, beaches, and area attractions. Rooms are furnished with antiques. The best things about this place are the comfy beds and the Breens, the lovely couple who run the house. They're wonderfully knowledgeable about the area and gladly help you decide where to go and what to see.

*Ferns, off the N11 between Enniscorthy and Gorey.* ☎ *054-66-113. Fax: 054-66-225. Rates: €70–€80 ($81–$92) double. No credit cards. Closed November through April.*

### Ferrycarrig
**$$$–$$$$ Ferrycarrig**

This hotel has a stunning location, perched over the River Slaney estuary. The rooms are bright and modern, the facilities (including a health club, indoor pool, and two waterside restaurants) are unbeatable, and the staff is friendly and warm. Plus there's not a bad view in the house.

*Ferrycarrig Bridge. Take N11 from Wexford toward Enniscorthy.* ☎ *053-20-999. Fax: 053-20-982.* www.griffingroup.ie. *Rates: €130–€245 ($150–$282) double including dinner. AE, DC, MC, V.*

### Kelly's Resort Hotel
**$$$ Rosslare**

Situated along a 5-mile stretch of sandy beach, this family-run hotel is truly a resort accommodation. You'll be spoiled by the two pools, indoor and outdoor tennis courts, sauna, and squash courts — though you may not feel as if you're in the Emerald Isle as you sip cocktails on the beach. Rooms are simple, bright, and clean; the resort restaurant serves terrific fare; and nighttime entertainment is on offer. Rates include all three meals each day. The resort is not far from the ferry terminal.

*Take N25 about 16km (10 miles) south from Wexford Town to Rosslare.* ☎ *053-32-114. Fax: 053-32-222.* www.kellys.ie. *Rates: €125–€185 ($144–$213) double. AE, MC, V.*

### McMenamins Townhouse
**$$ Wexford Town**

You'll feel at home immediately at this welcoming Victorian B&B, run by sweet and charming Kay and Seamus McMenamin, who offer what just may be Ireland's best breakfast. The good-size bedrooms are furnished eclectically, with some antiques and some modern touches. The linens are scented with lavender, and the beds are so comfortable that you'd be tempted to sleep in each morning if it weren't for the scent of Kay's gourmet breakfast downstairs. A former restaurant owner and chef, Kay treats her guests to an array of breakfast choices,

## Wexford Town

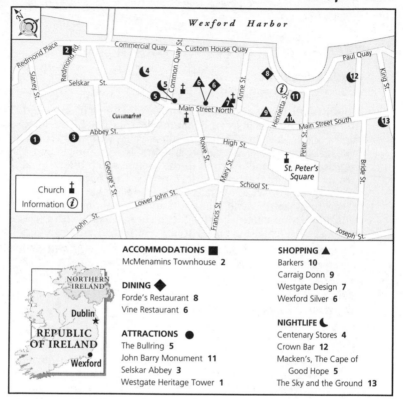

**ACCOMMODATIONS** ■
McMenamins Townhouse **2**

**DINING** ◆
Forde's Restaurant **8**
Vine Restaurant **6**

**ATTRACTIONS** ●
The Bullring **5**
John Barry Monument **11**
Selskar Abbey **3**
Westgate Heritage Tower **1**

**SHOPPING** ▲
Barkers **10**
Carraig Donn **9**
Westgate Design **7**
Wexford Silver **6**

**NIGHTLIFE** ☾
Centenary Stores **4**
Crown Bar **12**
Macken's, The Cape of
    Good Hope **5**
The Sky and the Ground **13**

from fresh-caught fish to light-as-a-cloud pancakes dusted with sugar. All dishes are accompanied by a range of sides, including homemade marmalade made with whiskey, oranges, and brown sugar; and thick, tangy homemade yogurt. The B&B is in Wexford Town, about a five-minute walk from the bus and train station, so it's perfect for those without a car.

*3 Auburn Terrace.* ☎ *053-46-442. Off Redmond Road in Wexford Town. Rates:* € *90 ($104) double. V.*

### Riverside Park Hotel
$$–$$$ **Enniscorthy**

Built in 1998, Riverside Park Hotel is situated on the banks of the River Suir. The hotel's beautiful brick-and-glass wall and round tower are difficult to miss as you're coming into or leaving town. Rooms are warm, bright, and cheerful, with great views. Sporty folks will be in heaven here — the hotel offers reduced greens fees on area courses and a range of watersports, from canoeing to windsurfing.

*The Promenade.* ☎ *054-37-800.* Fax: *054-37-900.* www.riversideparkhotel.com. *On the N11 just outside Enniscorthy. Rates: €89–€166 ($102–191) double. AE, DC, MC, V.*

## Dining locally in County Wexford

### Forde's Restaurant
$$$   Wexford Town  NEW IRISH

This inventive restaurant has taken Wexford Town by storm, placing in the top 100 restaurants in Ireland in both 2003 and 2004. The quiet room looks as though it were decorated by hip royalty, with dramatic wine-colored walls, standing cast-iron candle holders, ivory candles, and mirrors. The hip/dramatic theme extends to the menu, which offers local meats and produce with interesting modern twists. One potato side dish is folded into a spring-roll wrapper, and another is baked in parchment paper with cream and herbs. Menu standouts include salmon wrapped in seaweed with white wine sauce, crab beignets, chicken cakes with ginger and garlic, and a steak fillet with a brie fritter. Service is attentive and unobtrusive.

*Crescent Quay.* ☎ *053-23-832.* Main courses: *€16–€27 ($18–$31). DC, MC, V. Reservations recommended. Open: Mon–Fri 6–10 p.m., Sat 6:30–10 p.m., Sun 12:30– 9:30 p.m.*

### The Galley Cruising Restaurant
$$-$$$$   New Ross  IRISH

Picture this: You're cruising along a glassy river, taking in the picturesque shoreline. You wander in from the outdoor deck to sit down to a beautifully prepared five-course meal featuring fresh local produce. What could be more relaxing? Lunch and tea cruises are two hours long, and dinner cruises are between two and three hours long. You have two or three options for each course, with the emphasis on Continental favorites such as chicken stuffed with cheese and served in a white wine sauce, and salmon bathed in hollandaise. Dress is casual.

*New Ross Quay.* ☎ *051-42-1723. West on N25 from Wexford. Cost of cruise: €20 ($23) lunch, €10 ($12) afternoon tea, €38 ($44) dinner. MC, V. Reservations required. Cruises depart June–Aug daily at 12:30 p.m. (lunch), 3 p.m. (afternoon tea), and 7 p.m. (dinner). Cruises may go out in April or May if there is enough interest. Call and ask. You can also pay just for the cruise if you don't wish to eat. Without food, prices are €10 ($12) lunch, €8 ($9.20) tea, and €15 ($17) dinner.*

### Vine Restaurant
$$   Wexford Town  THAI

This Thai restaurant came up again and again when I asked people in Wexford about their favorite place to eat. You can chow down on all sorts of Thai specialties in a beautiful high-ceilinged room with funky decor. You can't go wrong with any of the dishes flavored with Thai herbs and spices; the duck with tamarind is particularly delicious.

*109 N. Main St.* ☎ *053-22-388. €15–€18 ($17–$20) DC, MC, V. Tues–Sun 6:30–about 10:30 p.m.*

## Exploring County Wexford

John Bayley, who has a degree in local history, leads excellent 1 ½ hour walking tours of Wexford Town. Tours usually leave from the Westgate Heritage Tower, right near **Selskar Abbey,** at 10:30 a.m. and 2:30 p.m. Monday through Saturday (but you should call ☎ **053-46-506** to confirm), and cost €4 ($4.60) adults and €2.50 ($2.90) seniors and students.

You can watch the farmland drift by during a lunch, afternoon tea, or dinner cruise on the Barrow River, offered by The Galley Cruising Restaurant (reviewed in the previous section). If you don't wish to eat on the ship, you can just pay for the tour itself: Without food, prices are €10 ($11.50) lunch, €8 ($9.20) tea, and €15 ($17.25) dinner. Lunch and tea cruises are two hours long, and dinner cruises are between two and three hours long.

### The top attractions

#### Enniscorthy Castle and Wexford County Museum
**Enniscorthy**

This Norman castle, built in the beginning of the 13th century, now houses thousands of artifacts that illustrate the agricultural, military, ecclesiastic, maritime, and industrial history of this area. The extensive collection of military memorabilia from the 1798 and 1916 uprisings is a highlight.

*Castle Hill. North of Wexford off the N11 or east of New Ross off the N30.* ☎ *054-35-926. Admission: €4.50 ($5.20) adults, €3.50 ($4.05) students and seniors, €1 ($1.15) children. Open: Apr–Sept daily 10 a.m.–5:30 p.m.; Oct–Nov and Feb–Mar 2–5p.m. Dec and Jan Sun only 2–5 p.m. Suggested visit: 45 minutes.*

#### The Hook Peninsula

There's so much to see on this small foot of land in southwest County Wexford that it's worth spending the afternoon driving and walking the lovely Slí Charman (Wexford's Coastal Pathway) to the end and back, provided you have the time and it's the peak season (a few places close for the winter). Highlights include the richly ornamented ruins of **Tintern Abbey** (which Wordsworth fans will be familiar with), near Saltmills, with its walled gardens, fortified bridge, and maze of ancient paths (€2/$2.30 adults, €1.30/$1.50 seniors, €0.80/92¢ children and students); **Ballyhack Castle** (☎ 051-38-9468), with displays on the Crusades (€1.30/$1.50 adult, €0.50/58¢ children and students); **Slade Castle,** an amazing fortress ruin near the **Hook Lighthouse** (☎ 051-397-055), one of the oldest lighthouses in Europe; **Duncannon Fort** (☎ 051-38-9454), built to fend off attacks from the Spanish Armada; and the magnificent ruins of **Dunbrody Abbey** (3km/ 4 miles beyond Duncannon).

*Tintern Abbey, Ballyhack, and Duncannon are off R733. To get to Hook Head, go south toward Fethard on R734 from New Ross. Park in Fethard, and walk the coastal path to Slade Castle, the Lighthouse, and even on to Duncannon. Suggested visit: Varies, depending on the distance you go, but give it a couple of hours or more.*

## Irish National Heritage Park
**Ferrycarrig**

Set on 36 acres, this intriguing living-history park traces the region's history from its earliest Stone Age settlements through the Celtic, Viking, and Norman periods. The 16 historical sites feature re-creations of castles, boats, homes, and the landscape during each period, bringing the past off the pages of books and into three dimensions. Exhibits are hands-on, making this a great place for kids. Try to get a tour of the grounds with head guide Jimmy O'Rourke.

*Off the Dublin-Wexford road (N11). A few miles west of Wexford off the N11 at Ferrycarrig. ☎ 053-20-733. Admission: €7 ($8.05) adults, €5.50 ($6.35) students and seniors, €4 ($4.60) children ages 12 to 18, €3.50 ($4.05) children ages 4–12, €17.50 ($20) family. Open: Daily 9:30 a.m.–6:30 p.m (last admission 5 p.m.); time subject to changes in the off season. Suggested visit: About 2 hours.*

## John F. Kennedy Arboretum
**New Ross**

Plant-lovers will enjoy meandering down self-guided trails through gardens featuring more than 4,500 species of trees and exotic shrubs from five continents.

*Off Duncannon Rd. (R733). ☎ 051-388-171. Admission: € 2.75 ($3.15) adults, €2 ($2.30) seniors, €1.25 ($1.45) child or student. Open: Oct–Mar daily 10 a.m.–5 p.m., Sept and April daily 10 a.m.–6:30 p.m., May–Aug daily 10 a.m.–8 p.m. Last admission 45 minutes before closing. Suggested visit: 1 ½ hours.*

## Johnstown Castle Gardens and Irish Agricultural Museum
**Wexford Town**

The fairytale gardens here offer 20 hectares (50 acres) of trees and flowers, plus lakes, hothouses, and ornamental structures. On the grounds is a museum focusing on the important role of farming in Wexford's history, with exhibits on farm transport, dairy farming, and farmhouse furniture, and a comprehensive look at the potato and the Famine.

*Johnstown Castle Estate, Bridgetown Road, off Wexford-Rosslare Road (N25). A couple miles east of Wexford off the R733. ☎ 053-42-888. Castle grounds admission (only charged May–Oct): €4 ($4.60) per car, or €2 ($2.30) per adult pedestrian, €.50 (60¢) student and child pedestrian. Museum admission: €6 ($6.90) adults, €4 ($4.60) students and children, €20 ($23) family. Gardens open: Daily 9 a.m.–5 p.m. Museum open: June– Aug Mon–Fri 9 a.m.–5 p.m., Sat and Sun 11–5 p.m.; Apr, May, and Sept–Nov Mon–Fri 9 a.m.–12:30 p.m. and 1:30–5 p.m., Sat–Sun 2–5 p.m.; Nov–March Mon–Fri 9 a.m.–5 p.m. Suggested visit: 2 hours.*

## Kilmore Quay and the Saltee Islands

The first thing you notice about this picture-postcard fishing village is its row of whitewashed thatched cottages. You can arrange for an angling trip (contact Dick Hayes of Enterprise at ☎ 053-29-704); visit **Kehoe's Pub** (☎ 053-29-830), the center of Kilmore Quay's social life and a museum of fascinating marine artifacts discovered on various dives; and take a trip to the **Saltee Islands**, Ireland's largest bird sanctuary. For more information on the area, call ☎ 053-299-22.

*On R739, 22km (14 miles) south of Rosslare.*

## Selskar Abbey
**Wexford Town**

The story behind this ruined abbey is oddly romantic: Our tale begins when Alexander de la Roche left his fiancée behind to join the Crusades. Hearing that he had been killed, his fiancée became a nun. However, de la Roche was very much alive and was so grieved at the state of affairs upon his return that he joined an Augustinian order, and founded and endowed the abbey at Selskar. If only they'd had cellphones! It is said that Henry II did penance at the abbey for having Thomas à Becket beheaded. Near the abbey are the ruins of a Church of Ireland church from the 1800s. When the congregation at this church merged with a nearby congregation, the church roof was removed so that no rent would be required on the building.

*Westgate St. You are free to roam around the site when the gates are unlocked. If gates are locked, let someone at the Westgate Heritage Center know, and they will open them for you. Suggested visit: ½ hour.*

## Wexford Wildfowl Reserve
**Wexford Town**

This national nature reserve, located in amusingly named North Slob, draws many species of ducks, swans, and other waterfowl. About 10,000 Greenland white-fronted geese call the area home during the winter. Blinds and an observation tower are set up for birders, and the reserve has a visitor center with an audiovisual show and exhibits.

*North Slob just 4.8km (3 miles) east of Wexford Town. ☎ 053-23-199. Admission: Free. Open: Apr 16–Sept daily 9 a.m.–6 p.m.; Oct–Apr 15 daily 10 a.m.–5 p.m. Suggested visit: 1–1½ hours.*

## More cool things to see and do

  ✔ **The Bullring:** The first declaration of an Irish Republic was made here in 1798, and a statue memorializes the men who fought for Irish independence at that time. The name of the area comes from the bloody sport of bull-baiting that took place here in the 17th century. There is a weekly outdoor market here from 10 a.m. to 4:30 p.m. Friday and Saturday.

Location: Off Quay Street, Wexford Town. Suggested visit: A few minutes.

✔ **Curracloe Beach and a Cycling Trip:** This beach is where the opening scenes of *Saving Private Ryan* were filmed. It is home to many migratory birds and is a popular swimming destination during the summer. A nature trail leads you through the sand dunes here. From Wexford, the road up through Curracloe to Blackwater makes an excellent day-long bike trip. Visit **Hayes Cycle Shop,** 108 S. Main St. (☎ 053/22-462) to rent a bike and get directions.

Location: The beach is 11km (7 miles) northeast of Wexford Town on the R742. Information: Wexford County Council. ☎ 053-42-211.

✔ **John Barry Monument:** "Who's John Barry?", you ask. No less than the father of the American Navy! Barry bravely went to the colonies and signed up for the Revolutionary War to fight against the British. He was captain of the famous ship the *Lexington* and in 1797 was appointed by George Washington as commander-in-chief of the brand-spanking-new U.S. Navy.

Location: Crescent Quay, Wexford Town. Suggested visit: Enough time to give him a salute and snap a photo.

✔ **The National 1798 Visitor Centre:** The story of the United Irishmen's first rebellion against the British is told in multimedia pomp at this small but interesting museum. The museum engages visitors with objects, an audiovisual presentation, and interactive computer programs. If it's nice outside, this is a great place for a picnic.

Location: Mill Park Road, Enniscorthy. ☎ 054-37-596. Fax: 054-37-198. www.iol.ie/~98com/. On the N30 and N11 next to Vinegar Hill. Admission is €6 ($6.90) adults, €3.50 ($4.05) students and children. Open Monday through Saturday from 9:30 a.m. to 5 p.m., Sunday from 11 a.m. to 5 p.m. Suggested visit: 1 hour.

✔ **Westgate Heritage Tower:** Before exploring Wexford Town, you may want to stop by this heritage center, housed in one of the five original gate towers along the Viking city walls. A well-done film, *In Selskar's Shadow,* relates the rich history of Wexford Town, and a gallery on the first floor sells beautiful handcrafted gifts made by Wexford artisans. Craftspeople work in the tower, and you may be able to visit their workshops.

Location: Westgate Street, Wexford Town. ☎ 053-46-506. The film costs €3 ($3.45) adults, €1.50 ($1.75) students. Open April to December 24 from 10 a.m. to 6 p.m., and Jan 2 through March from 10 a.m. to 5 p.m. Suggested visit: 1 hour.

## Shopping in County Wexford

**Barkers**, 36–40 S. Main St., Wexford Town (☎ 053-231-59), sells Waterford Crystal, china, and local and international crafts. Far from the Aran Islands,

**Carraig Donn,** 3 S. Main St., Wexford Town (☎ 053-23-651), nonetheless specializes in authentic Aran knitwear — sweaters mostly, but also accessories such as scarves and hats. **Westgate Design,** 22 N. Main St., Wexford Town (☎ 053-23-787), offers a large selection of Irish crafts, from wool clothing to pottery to jewelry. A family of silver- and goldsmiths run **Wexford Silver,** 115 N. Main St., Wexford Town (☎ 053-21-933), which sells finely crafted pieces that make perfect gifts or keepsakes. Also see Westgate Heritage Tower, in the previous section.

## Hitting the pubs in County Wexford

### Antique Tavern
**Enniscorthy**

A black-and-white Tudor-style exterior makes this place easy to find. Inside, the dark and cozy pub is full of antiques. Check out the famous memorabilia that lines the walls, from weapons used during the 1798 Rebellion to farm equipment. The outdoor balcony is nice when the weather's pleasant. *14 Slaney St.* ☎ *054-33-428.*

### Centenary Stores
**Wexford Town**

This Victorian-style pub serves excellent bar food and hosts entertainment almost every evening. *Charlotte St.* ☎ *053-24-424.*

### Crown Bar
**Wexford Town**

The oldest pub in Wexford Town, the Crown was formerly a stagecoach inn and is full of memorabilia. The comprehensive collection of antique weapons includes dueling pistols and pikes from the 1798 Rebellion. Locals pop in to hear and dish town gossip. *Monck St.* ☎ *053-21-133.*

### Macken's, The Cape of Good Hope
**Wexford Town**

As you venture into Wexford's famous Bullring area, you're sure to do a double-take when you see Macken's: The awning over the entrance advertises a bar, undertaker, and grocery. And it's no joke — you can have a pint, pick up a loaf of bread, and make funeral arrangements in one convenient stop! Irish rebels made Macken's a popular meeting place over the centuries, and mementos from their struggles line the walls. Definitely a place like none other. *The Bullring.* ☎ *053-22-949.*

### The Sky and the Ground
**Wexford Town**

This simply-decorated, homey pub, which was the winner of Les Routiers' Traditional Irish Music Pub of the Year award in 2003, is the hot spot for Wexford's traditional music scene. Take a seat, nurse a pint, listen to great trad, and chat with the locals — you'll feel like you were born and raised in Wexford.

*112 S. Main St.* ☎ *053-21-273.*

# Fast Facts: County Wexford

**Area Codes**

County Wexford's area codes (or city codes) are 051, 053, 054, and 055.

**Emergencies/Police**

Dial ☎ 999 for all emergencies.

**Genealogical Resources**

Contact the Genealogy Centre, Yola Farmstead, Tagoat (☎ 053-31-177; Fax: 053-32-612; www.irishroots.net/Wexford.htm).

**Hospital**

Wexford General Hospital is on New Town Road, Wexford (☎ 053-42-233).

**Information**

For visitor information, go to the tourist office at Crescent Quay, Wexford (☎ 053-23-111, open year-round). It can also provide reservation services. Seasonal offices (open June through Sept) are in Enniscorthy at the Town Centre (☎ 054-34-699) and Rosslare Harbour Terminal Building (☎ 053-33-232). Another great source is the Web site www.wexford tourism.com. For telephone directory assistance, dial ☎ 1190.

**Post Office**

The main post office is on Anna Street, Wexford (☎ 053-22-587).

# Visiting County Waterford and Waterford City

Waterford City is the oldest town in Ireland, founded by Viking invaders in the ninth century. You would think that this would make the city an intriguing place to explore, but aside from the Waterford Treasures museum and the historic area surrounding Reginald's Tower, there isn't a whole lot to see in the city (the Waterford Crystal Factory is outside the city).

The main reasons to come to this county are to take the superb tour of the Waterford Crystal Factory and to ramble around the county's lovely coastal villages and ethereal inland mountains.

## Waterford City

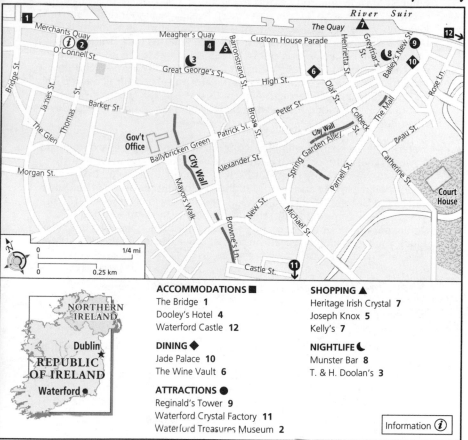

*River Suir*

**ACCOMMODATIONS** ■
The Bridge **1**
Dooley's Hotel **4**
Waterford Castle **12**

**DINING** ◆
Jade Palace **10**
The Wine Vault **6**

**ATTRACTIONS** ●
Reginald's Tower **9**
Waterford Crystal Factory **11**
Waterford Treasures Museum **2**

**SHOPPING** ▲
Heritage Irish Crystal **7**
Joseph Knox **5**
Kelly's **7**

**NIGHTLIFE** ☾
Munster Bar **8**
T. & H. Doolan's **3**

Information ⓘ

# Getting to and around Waterford City

If you're driving, take N25 from Cork and the south, N24 from the west, N19
from Kilkenny and points north, the N11 to the N30 to the N25 from Dublin,
or N25 from Wexford. Lismore is off the N72. A fast and cost-effective route
across Waterford Harbour, between Passage East, County Waterford (16km/
10 miles east of Waterford), and Ballyhack, County Wexford (32km/20 miles
west of Wexford), is provided by **Passenger East Car Ferry** (☎ **051-38-2480**).
See "Getting to and around County Wexford," near the beginning of this chapter, for more details.

**Irish Rail** (☎ 051-873-401; www.irishrail.ie) serves Waterford at Plunkett Station, located next to the Ignatius Rice Bridge. **Bus Éireann** (☎ 01-87-9000; www.buseireann.com) travels year-round to Waterford, Lismore, and other major towns in County Waterford. In Waterford City, buses arrive at Plunkett Station, next to the Ignatius Rice Bridge. Bus Éireann also has a tour bus out of Dublin that covers the River Barrow and the Waterford Crystal Factory. It leaves Connolly Station, Dublin's main bus terminal, at 9 a.m. and returns at 9 p.m. The tour is offered only on Thursdays June 10 through August. Cost is €45 ($52) adults, €35 ($40) children 15 and under. The cost includes lunch and a boat tour of the River Barrow.

Waterford is an easily walkable city. Stroll up the Quays toward Reginald's Tower, take a right, and you're in the heart of town. You need a car to get out to the Waterford Crystal Factory, though, unless you take a taxi (available in the city and mostly found at Plunkett Station on the Quay; call **Rapid Cabs** at ☎ 051-85-8585 or Metro Cabs at ☎ 051-857-157 if you need one to pick you up; the fare should be around €10/$11.50). If you're parking your car here, buy parking disks at local shops near the block you're parking on or at the tourist office. Hotels in the city center generally have their own parking areas.

## Spending the night in County Waterford

### The Bridge
$ Waterford City

This hotel overlooking the River Suir is one of the oldest in Waterford, but it has been updated to provide every modern comfort. The Bridge is what an old Irish hotel should be: It's run like a tight ship by the Treacy family but has a friendly, jovial atmosphere. Bedrooms are spacious and bright, and two in-house restaurants are reliable places to get a good meal.

*1 The Quay. Take The Quay to the foot of the Ignatius Rice Bridge.* ☎ *051-87-7222. Fax: 051-87-7229.* www.bridgehotelwaterford.com. *Rates: €49–€65 ($56–$75) double. AE, DC, MC, V.*

### Dooley's Hotel
$$$ Waterford City

This family-run hotel offers bright, generic hotel rooms right in the center of Waterford City. Service is top-notch. The hotel's pub serves tasty, budget-friendly meals, and the Continental cuisine at the hotel's New Ship restaurant is filling and well-prepared.

*The Quay, near the clock tower.* ☎ *051-87-3531. Fax: 051-87-0262.* www.dooleys-hotel.ie. *Rates: €200 ($230) double. AE, DC, MC, V.*

## Foxmount Country House
**$$   Passage East**

This 17th-century B&B is only 15 minutes away from Waterford City, but you'll feel as though you're in the middle of nowhere — in a good way. The imposing ivy-covered house sits on a large stretch of stunningly landscaped grounds with grand trees, flowers, and a paddock where four horses and a donkey reside. The house is located on a working dairy farm, so you may catch a glimpse of a herd of cows. Want to relax? Head out to the peaceful herb garden at the back of the house. Looking to stretch your legs? Ramble down one of the dirt roads, past emerald pastures. Rooms, which have beautiful views, are spacious and elegantly furnished with antiques, and the large bathrooms feature comfortable tubs. Cordial hostess Margaret Kent serves a bang-up breakfast; I especially enjoyed the porridge with honey, brown sugar, and exceptionally fresh cream, and the tasty scrambled eggs. Head down the road for a pint at Jack Meade's pub (reviewed in "Hitting the pubs in County Waterford," later in this section), which looks as if it was transplanted from Middle Earth.

*Passage East Rd. Take Dunmore East Rd. from Waterford City for 6km (3½ miles) until you reach a fork where you see a garage. Take the left fork toward Passage East, and keep right at the next junction. Turn right just before Jack Meade's pub, beside the bridge.* ☎ *051-87-4906. Fax: 051-87-4308. Rates: €110 ($127) double. No credit cards.*

## Samuels Heritage B&B
**$   Ballymacode**

This beautiful family home is set on 30 acres of farm and garden land overlooking the River Suir. The rooms are all nonsmoking and en-suite; televisions are available upon request. It's within close proximity to beaches and four 18-hole golf courses. You can enjoy your breakfast outdoors if the weather's nice.

*Dunmore Rd. Take Cork Rd. from city center 5km (3 miles) to Dunmore. The B&B is beyond the Regional Hospital and Orpens Pub, on the left.* ☎ *051-87-5094. Rates: €64 ($74) double. MC, V.*

## Waterford Castle
**$$$$   Balinakill**

Staying in this castle is like living a fairytale. Located on a private island in the River Suir (accessible only by the castle's car ferry), only 3.2km (2 miles) from Waterford City, the Norman castle and its Elizabethan-style wings are filled with tapestries, large stone fireplaces, antiques, and oak-paneled walls. All of the richly decorated rooms have stunning views. The staff is warm and friendly.

*The Island.* ☎ *051/878-203. Fax: 051-879-316.* www.waterfordcastle.com. *Rates: €190–€506 ($219–$582) double. AE, MC, V.*

## Dining locally in County Waterford

In addition to the places I list in this section, you can combine your dinner with a river cruise aboard The **Galley Cruising Restaurant.** Although you catch the boat on the River Barrow in New Ross, County Wexford (see the review in "Dining locally in County Wexford," earlier in this chapter), the trip takes you down to the River Suir and through County Waterford.

### Ballyrafter House
$$$$ Lismore SEAFOOD

Local fishermen recommend Ballyrafter House, so you know you can expect good seafood here. The casual restaurant has a great view of the riverside Lismore Castle, and it's the little touches, such as fresh-cut flowers from the garden and the many photographs of smiling fishermen and their big catches, that make this place so memorable. The smoked Blackwater salmon is delicious and is one of the most popular dishes.

*Right on the N72 in Lismore.* ☎ *058-54-002. From Waterford or Cork, take the N25 to the N72 at Dungarvan. Main courses: €28 ($32) prix-fixe for lunch; €44 ($51) prix-fixe for dinner. AE, DC, MC, V. Open: Feb–Nov daily 1–2:30 p.m. and 7:30–9 p.m.*

### Jade Palace
$$-$$$ Waterford City CHINESE

Jade Palalce offers authentic, mouthwatering Cantonese and Szechuan in downtown Waterford. This is the kind of place where you tell the manager what you think you'd like and let him decide for you. And then you'll likely stuff yourself silly using your choice of silverware or chopsticks. The steamed fish with ginger is excellent.

*3 The Mall, next to Reginald's Tower in the city center.* ☎ *051-85-5611. Main courses: €11–€21 ($13–$24). AE, MC, V. Open: Mon–Fri 12:30–2:30 p.m., Sun 1–3 p.m., daily 5:30 p.m. to midnight.*

### The Tannery
$$$-$$$$ Dungarvan NEW EUROPEAN

This stylish, contemporary restaurant was an operating tannery until 1995. The kitchen is wide open so patrons can watch innovative chef Paul Flynn in action. Flynn adds unique twists to whatever dish he's cooking, such as the roast rump of lamb with spiced carrot, tomato, and chickpea risotto or the roast monkfish with red-pepper butter and basil-infused crushed potatoes. The interior is minimalist — white dishes on unadorned light-wood tables.

*10 Quay St. From Waterford or Cork, take the N25 to Dungarvan.* ☎ *058-45-420. Main courses: lunch €13–€15 ($14–$17), dinner €16–27 ($18–$31), Sun lunch and early-bird dinner €25 ($29). AE, DC, MC, V. Open: Tues–Fri 12:30–2:30 p.m. and 6:30–10 p.m., Sat 6:30–10:30, Sun 12:30–2:30 p.m., Sun dinner during peak season (call to confirm).*

## The Wine Vault
$$ **Waterford City** SEAFOOD

A must-stop for wine enthusiasts, the Vault has more than 150 selections, and given the warm, casual atmosphere here, you may be tempted to set up shop in Waterford until you've gone through all of them. This cavernous yet cozy stone-walled restaurant incorporates a house that was built in the 15th century and was probably owned by the mayor of the city at the time. The brick vaulting dates from the 1800s, when the Gallweys, a family of wine merchants, used the building. Everything on the menu is fresh and delicious, and the seafood is exceptional. The fresh mussels, the seafood paella, and the catch of the day are particular standouts. Even if you don't come for dinner, you can stop by to pick up a bottle of wine at the Vault's shop.

*Lower High St.* ☎ *051-85-3444.* www.waterfordwinevault.com. *Main courses: €12–€18 ($14–$21). AE, V. Open: Mon–Sat 12:30–2:30 p.m., 5:30–10:30 p.m.*

# Exploring County Waterford: The top attractions

Waterford Tourist Services' award-winning **Walking Tours of Historic Waterford** (☎ 051-87-3711) leave year-round daily from the Waterford Treasures Museum at 11:45 a.m. and 1:45 p.m. and from the Granville Hotel, on Meagher Quay, at noon and 2 p.m. Cost is €5 ($5.75).

You can cruise the calm and brackish waters of the River Suir estuary for a relaxing tour of the countryside. Cruises leave May to October daily at 3 p.m. from Waterford Harbour, next to the Custom House Parade. The price is €10 ($12), including tea and a snack. Call ☎ 051-42-1723 to book.

For guided hikes in Waterford County, contact Viking Trekking Company (☎ 051-844-480; www.vikingtrekking.com). For self-guided hikes and walks, visit Waterford City's tourist office (see "Fast Facts: County Waterford," at the end of this section) to pick up route maps.

## Lismore Castle Gardens
**Lismore**

The two gardens here (upper and lower) are wonderfully varied, with riotously bright blossoms, apple trees, and a kaleidoscope of roses, all set against the backdrop of a still-occupied 12th-century castle. Because this is an inhabited castle, you can't tour the inside of the castle (however, if you've come into some money, you can stay in the castle when the duke is not in residence). The magical yew tree walk in the lower garden is where Edmund Spenser is said to have written the *Faerie Queen*. Be sure to budget enough time to see the upper garden, which is bigger than the lower garden and boasts a thriving vegetable plot. This is a lovely place for a picnic.

*Lismore.* ☎ *058-54-424. Admission: €5 ($5.75) adults, €4.50 ($5.20) seniors and students, €2.50 ($2.90) kids 16 and under. Open: April, May, Sept, and Oct daily 1:45–4:45, and June–Aug 11 a.m.–4:45p.m. Suggested visit: 1½ hours.*

# By Hook or by Crooke

Waterford is the only city in Ireland that was spared Oliver Cromwell's brutal and bloody 1649 attack, though not through lack of effort. He attempted to invade Waterford from two routes, through Hook Head and Crooke Village — neither of which is a direct or easy way to enter Waterford. Both tries failed. This event was the genesis of the phrase "by hook or by crook" — when one resorts to unconventional and extreme tactics to get something done.

### *Reginald's Tower*
**Waterford City**

Recently restored to its medieval appearance and furnished with appropriate medieval artifacts, this small but significant landmark in the heart of Waterford City is worth the three-story climb to the top. The tower was built by a Viking governor in 1003 and is Ireland's oldest standing building in continuous use. It has been used in many different capacities — as a mint, a fortress, a prison, and an air-raid shelter. It is said that Norman leader Strongbow married Celtic Aiofe (Eva) here, beginning a bond between the Norman invaders and the native Irish.

*The Quay.* ☎ *051-304-220. Admission: €2 ($2.30) adults, €1.25 ($1.45) seniors, €1 ($1.15) students and children. Open: April–Oct 10 a.m.–6 p.m. (last admission at 5:15 p.m.), Nov–Mar Wed–Sun 10 a.m.–5 p.m. (last admission 4:15 p.m.). Suggested visit: 30 minutes.*

### *South East Coastal Drive*

This well-marked drive takes you along the coast through the beautiful seaside towns of Tramore, Dunmore, and Passage East. Along the way, you encounter meandering rivers and tiny fishing villages. If you'd like to bike this route, rent a bike from **Wright's Cycle Depot Ltd.,** Henrietta St., Waterford (☎ 051-874-411). The route, about 80km (50 miles), begins as you cross the bridge from Youghal on the N25 and ends in Tramore.

*The end points of the route are Youghal and Tramore. Out of Youghal, take the N25; out of Tramore, take the R675.*

### *The Vee Drive*

This winding 18km (11-mile) drive leads you through the lush Knockmealdown mountains up to a stunning viewpoint of the farmland laid out like a quilt below and the glowing Galtee mountains beckoning in the distance. The Vee Gap viewpoint, at the highest point of the drive, opens onto a variety of walking trails. Look for the parking lot and a sign mapping out the trails.

*The endpoints of the signposted Vee drive are Lismore and Clogheen From Lismore, take the R668 or the R669 (hook up to the R669 via the N72). From Clogheen, take the R668.*

### Waterford Crystal Factory
**Kilbarry**

What makes crystal shine brighter than regular glass? It's a lead oxite called *litharge*. You'll be able to spout off this fact and many more after a fascinating tour of the Waterford Crystal Factory, where you can watch the factory's craftspeople as they go about their daily work. You'll be shown every step of the meticulous process that goes into the creation of world-renowned Waterford Crystal, from the blowing of the molten glass to the engraving, which is done using a rotating copper wheel. You also get the opportunity to ask questions and get up close to the action as a master craftsperson cuts or engraves a piece. Talk about a stressful job: The Waterford Crystal Factory has a six-step screening process for every piece that's made. About 45% of pieces are destroyed for minor flaws, and only perfect pieces of crystal make it out of the factory, which is why you'll never see Waterford seconds. The glass blowers and craftspeople get paid only for perfect pieces. Along the tour, you have a chance to see some unique crystal pieces, including hefty sports trophies. After the tour, stop in the Waterford Crystal Gallery to stock up; pieces cost about the same here as they do in most stores, so the main attraction is the vast selection.

*From Waterford, take the main road to Cork (N25); the factory is 8km (5 miles) outside town on the right.* ☎ *051-33-2500. Tours: €7.50 ($8.65) adults, €6.50 ($7.50) seniors, €3.50 ($4.05) students, free for kids under 12 Open: March–Oct tours daily 8:30 a.m.–4:15 p.m., showroom daily 8:30 a.m.–6 p.m.; Nov–Feb tours Mon–Fri 9 a.m.–3:15 p.m., showroom daily 9 a.m.–5 p.m. Suggested visit: 2 hours.*

### Waterford Treasures Museum
**Waterford City**

This exceedingly well-done museum, housed in a gorgeously restored granary, presents artifacts that illustrate the history of Waterford from the arrival of the Vikings almost 1,000 years ago up to the present. High-tech interactive audiovisuals, including a ride on a Viking ship, are engaging and entertaining, and the objects here are true treasures, from the sword of King Edward IV to a variety of crystal items.

*Merchant's Quay.* ☎ *051-304-500. Admission: €6 ($6.90) adults, €4.50 ($5.20) seniors and students, €3.20 ($3.70) children, free for children under 5. Open: Apr–Sept Mon–Sat 9:30 a.m.–6 p.m., Sun 11 a.m.–6 p.m.; Oct–Mar Mon–Sat 10 a.m.–5 p.m., Sun 11 a.m.–5 p.m. Suggested visit: 2–3 hours.*

## Shopping in Waterford City

In addition to the choices listed here, you may want to pay a visit to the **Waterford Crystal Factory** store (reviewed in the previous section). **Heritage Irish Crystal,** 67–68 The Quay, Waterford City (☎ **051-875-1787**) is the town's other maker of authentic, hand-blown crystal; it's not as big or famous as Waterford Crystal, but pieces are of excellent quality. Established in the 18th century, **Joseph Knox,** 4 Barronstrand St., Waterford City (☎ **051-875-307**), stocks jewelry with Celtic designs, linen, and china but is especially known for having the best selection of crystal in the city. At 150 years old, **Kelly's,** 75–76 The Quay, Waterford City (☎ **051-87-3557**), is one of the oldest businesses in town, selling crafts, linens, Aran sweaters, Waterford Crystal, and Belleek pottery.

## Hitting the pubs in County Waterford

### Jack Meade's
**Ballycanavan**

This cozy, low-ceilinged pub with crackling fireplaces is located under a stone bridge a few miles out of town and is well worth the drive. Locals tell stories in the bar, and the pub serves great food. During the summer, point yourself in the direction of the banner reading "BBQ," where you'll find excellent steaks, garlicky mushrooms, and other treats, all cheerfully served at picnic tables.

*Checkpoint Rd., Halfway House.* ☎ *051-850-950.*

### The Munster Bar
**Waterford City**

The Munster (also known as Fitzgerald's) is superbly decorated with Waterford Crystal, antique mirrors, and wood walls taken from the old Waterford toll bridge. This place is a favorite with Waterford locals. Traditional music often kicks up on weekend nights.

*Bailey's New St.* ☎ *051-87-4656.*

### T. & H. Doolan's
**Waterford City**

The oldest tavern in Waterford, Doolan's has long been considered one of the best establishments in the area. The black-and-white 18th-century pub opens onto a pedestrian street in the center of town and has excellent traditional music sessions most nights, plus warm fires, delicious pub grub, warm welcomes, and a cheerful crowd. Oh, and the stout is perfect as well. What does the T. & H. stand for? That's for you to find out.

*32 George's St.* ☎ *051-87-2764.*

# Fast Facts: County Waterford

**Area Codes**

County Waterford's area codes (or city codes) are 051, 052, and 058.

**Emergencies/Police**

Dial ☎ **999** for all emergencies.

**Genealogical Resources**

Contact the Waterford Heritage Survey, Jenkins Lane (St. Patrick's Church), Waterford (☎ 051-87-6123).

**Hospital**

Holy Ghost Hospital is on Cork Road, Waterford (☎ 051-37-4397).

**Information**

For visitor information, go to the tourist office at 41 The Quay (☎ 051-87-5788), open Monday to Saturday from April through October, and Monday to Friday November through March.

**Internet Access**

Voyager Internet Cafe, Parnell Court, Parnell Street (☎ 051-84-3843), has Internet access and printing capabilities.

**Post Office**

The main post office is on Parade Quay, Waterford City (☎ 051-874-444).

# Roaming in County Tipperary

With miles and miles of velvety green farmland, warm and friendly welcomes, and a handful of historical sites, it's a wonder that County Tipperary isn't on more visitors' itineraries. The county and its towns are certainly not bustling in any way whatsoever, but that's what makes this place so special: It's the fantasy of a quiet, rolling, green Ireland come true. Because there are a limited number of attractions, one or two days should suffice here, unless you're looking for a long getaway retreat.

## Getting to and around County Tipperary

If you're coming by car, take the N8 from Cork or Dublin (via N7) to Cashel and Cahir. Take the N24 from Limerick or Waterford to Tipperary and Cahir. **Irish Rail** (☎ 01-836-6222; www.irishrail.ie) serves Tipperary, Cahir, and Carrick-on-Suir; and **Bus Éireann** (☎ 01-830-2222; www.buseireann.ie) travels year-round to Tipperary, Cahir, Cashel, and Carrick-on-Suir, as well as other major towns in County Tipperary.

## Spending the night in County Tipperary

### Legends Guesthouse and the Kiln
$$ **Cashel**

This small, comfortable guesthouse looks out onto the Rock of Cashel and offers simple, good-size rooms and bathrooms. The real draw, though, is the restaurant, the Kiln, which serves modern European dishes that sparkle with flavor. After dinner, you can waddle upstairs to your bedroom.

*Near the junction of R660 and the N8, traveling in the direction of Holycross.* ☎ *062-61292. Rates: €110 ($127). MC, V.*

## Dining locally in County Tipperary

Also see Legends Guesthouse and the Kiln, in the previous section.

### Angela's Wholefood Restaurant

$ **Clonmel** **INTERNATIONAL**

Angela's Wholefood Restaurant offers scrumptious, substantial fare at remarkable value. The blackboard menu may include custom-made breakfast omelets, spicy Moroccan lamb stew, savory tomato-and-spinach flan Provençal, homemade soups and sandwiches made to order, and an array of delicious salads. The food is vibrant, fresh, and appreciated by the bustling patrons who line up with trays in hand, from barristers (in garb) to babysitters.

*14 Abbey St.* ☎ *052-26-899. Breakfast menu €2.50–€5 ($2.90–$5.75); lunch menu €2.50–€9 ($2.90–$10). No credit cards. Mon–Fri 9 a.m.–5:30 p.m., Sat noon to 5 p.m.*

### Chez Hanz

$$$ **Cashel** **FRENCH**

This is French cuisine at its finest, and it is served in a gorgeous Gothic structure that began life as a chapel. From the black-and-white uniformed waitstaff to the artistic presentation of the dishes, everything is professional and elegant. The portions are generous, and the famous Cashel blue cheese finds its way into many dishes. All the dishes are top-notch, especially the seafood offerings, such as seafood cassoulet and fresh mussels in a chive sauce.

*Just look for the giant rock; The restaurant is located below it.* ☎ *062-61-177. Main courses: €14–€28 ($16–$32). MC, V. Open: Tues–Sat 6:30–10 p.m. Closed Jan and Sept 5–12. Reservations required.*

---

# Quite a long way to Tipperary

While you're moseying around and hitting the pubs, you're likely to hear the song "It's a Long Way to Tipperary," a happy yet plaintive tune about an Irishman in England missing his home. The song was actually composed by Englishman Jack Judge — a man who'd never been to Ireland in his life! He chose the town's name for his song simply because it rhymed well. The song is perhaps best known by Americans as the tune that the cast of *The Mary Tyler Moore Show* sang as they left the station for the last time.

## Exploring County Tipperary: The top attractions

**Cashel Heritage Tram Tour** provides tours of Cashel's historic sites, as well as entry to the Cashel Heritage Centre and Bolton Library. The train leaves from the Heritage Centre (see the upcoming listing for the Brú Ború Heritage Centre), and you can hop on and off where you please. It operates June through September, Tuesday through Saturday, from noon to 6 p.m. For more information, call ☎ 062-62-511. Tickets cost €3.75 ($4.30) adults, €2 ($2.30), for students.

### The Rock of Cashel
**Cashel**

Sure, this limestone outcropping is big, but even so, you may be wondering, "What's so important about the rock of Cashel?" Well, first of all, it was the seat of the kings of Munster from about A.D. 360 to 1101 and was probably also a center of Druidic worship at this time. Legend places St. Patrick in Cashel in about A.D 432 for his famous explanation of the Holy Trinity. He is said to have shown the pagans a shamrock to illustrate the relationship of the Father, Son, and Holy Ghost. Legend also has it that this is the place where St. Patrick converted the local king, King Aenghus, and baptized him. In the 11th century, Ireland's most important high king, Brian Boru, was crowned king of Ireland here (which explains the presence of the Brú Ború Heritage Centre nearby — see the next listing).

At the summit of the rock, you can explore the shell of the 13th-century St. Patrick's Cathedral, which was gutted in a fire set by Cromwell's troops. You can also visit the 92-foot-high round tower, which is well-preserved. Don't miss the Romanesque Cormacs Chapel, located on a dramatic outcrop, which is decorated with carved beasts and human figures. The unique St. Patrick's Cross (a replica — the original is in the museum) has the carved figure of St. Patrick on one side and Jesus on the other. The roofless cathedral is the largest building on the Rock and was never restored after Cromwell's men set fire to it (along with the villagers hiding inside). An interpretive center, housed in the beautifully restored Vicar's Choral, has great views for photos, contains stone carvings and silver religious artifacts, and offers a 15-minute audiovisual display. Guides from the center are happy to lead you around the rock and relate the history of the site.

*Take N8 from Dublin or N74 east from Tipperary to Cashel. ☎ 062-61-437. Admission: €5 ($5.75) adults, €3.50 ($4.05) seniors, €2 ($2.30) children and students. Open: Mid-March to mid-June daily 9 a.m.–5:30 p.m.; mid-June to mid-Sept daily 9 a.m.–7 p.m.; mid-Sept to mid-Oct daily 9 a.m.–5:30 p.m.; mid-Oct to mid-March 9 a.m.–4:30 p.m. Suggested visit: 1 ½ hours.*

### Brú Ború Heritage Centre
Cashel

Located next to the Rock of Cashel, the Heritage Centre's central attraction is its theater, which resonates with the sounds of well-played traditional Irish music on most nights. An exhibit relates the intriguing history of Irish music (the only connection between this place and Brian Boru is that Boru was a harper). In addition to the theater and exhibit are a restaurant and a comprehensive computerized genealogical research center.

*Take N8 from Dublin or N74 east from Tipperary to the Rock of Cashel.* ☎ *062-61-122. Admission: Free to center; evening performances are €15 ($17) adults, €9 ($10) kids; performances with dinner are €40 ($46) adults and €20 ($23) kids. Open: Mid-June–mid-Sept daily 9 a.m.–11:30 p.m., shows Tues–Sat at 9 p.m.; mid-Sept–mid-June Mon–Fri 9 a.m.–5 p.m. Suggested visit: ½ hour if you're not seeing a show, a few hours if you are.*

### Cahir Castle
Cahir

This was a defensive castle from the 13th to 15th centuries and is one of Ireland's largest and best preserved. It sits on an island in the middle of the River Suir. The walls and towers are in excellent condition, and the interior is fully restored. The 20-minute audiovisual presentation is interesting, covering the history of the castle and of the region's other historic sites. Engaging guided tours of the castle grounds are available (the tour does not enter the castle, so be sure to see the inside of the castle either before or after your tour). Attention, movie buffs: The castle was used as the set for John Boorman's film *Excalibur.*

*Off the N8 from Cashel or Cork or the N24 from Tipperary.* ☎ *052-41-011. Admission: €2.75 ($3.15) adults, €2 ($2.30) seniors, €1.25 ($1.45) students and children. Open: Mid-March to mid-June and mid-Sept to mid-Oct daily 9:30 a.m.–5:30 p.m.; mid-June to mid-Sept daily 9 a.m.–7 p.m.; mid-Oct to mid-March daily 9:30 a.m.–4:30 p.m. Last admissions 45 minutes before closing. Suggested visit: 1 hour.*

### Holy Trinity Church and Medieval Walls
Fethard

Sitting along the River Clashawley, the small town of Fethard (population: under 1,000) claims the most complete circuit of medieval town walls in Ireland. Enter the walled inner city at the cast-iron gateway on Abbey Street, which opens into the pretty churchyard of Holy Trinity. The heather-strewn views of the valley are best from the top of one of the towers, and the castle-like church itself is a fine example of medieval construction.

*Take the small road connecting Cashel and Windgap east from Cashel or go north off the N24 to Fethard. No telephone. Admission: Free. Open: No official hours, but the Abbey Street gate of the town wall is often locked. During normal business hours, you can get a key from Whytes grocery store, just a few doors down on Main Street. And if the church is closed, and you want to enter, you can get a key from Dr. Stoke's office, at the eastern end of Main Street. Suggested visit: 2 hours.*

## Shopping in County Tipperary

A band of rebel craftsmen left Waterford Crystal in 1988 to start **Tipperary Crystal Designs,** Carrick-on-Suir (☎ 051-64-0543), where they produce top-quality items, just as they did under their former label. These folks are so good that they're the only Irish crystal producer to supply prestigious Tiffany & Co. The shop is located off N24, next to the Dovehill Castle.

## Hitting the pubs in County Tipperary

### Ronald Reagan Pub
**Ballyporeen**

Pints are pulled with a special trickle-down tap method that seems to have staved off the inflationary cost of beer at this pub that is, in fact, named after the former U.S. president. In 1984, Ronnie visited Ballyporeen, home-town of his great-grandfather, and the pub/gift shop/shrine has photos of the historic visit on the walls, as well as mementos for sale. The pub is more hype than hops, but an interesting stop.

*Main St, The Square.* ☎ *052-67-133.*

# Fast Facts: County Tipperary

**Area Codes**

County Tipperary's area codes (or city codes) are 051, 052, 062, and 067.

**Emergencies/Police**

Dial ☎ **999** for all emergencies.

**Genealogy Resources**

Contact the Brú Ború Heritage Centre, Rock of Cashel (☎ 062-61-122; Fax: 062-62-700),

or the Tipperary Family History Research Centre (☎ 062-80-555).

**Information**

The Clonmel Tourist Office, Sarsfield St. (☎ 052-22-960) is open year-round Monday to Saturday 9:30 a.m. to 5:30 p.m. Seasonal offices are open June to August Monday through Saturday at Castle Street in Cahir (☎ 052-41-453) and at the Town Hall in Cashel (☎ 062-61-333).

# County Kilkenny

You may want to polish up your old armor and rev up your trusty steed, because Kilkenny City in County Kilkenny is one of the best-preserved medieval towns in Ireland, crowned by the majestic 12th-century Kilkenny Castle. The compact city (see the "Kilkenny City" map) sometimes seems to overflow with tourists during the high season, but you can always get a breath of fresh air in the Kilkenny countryside. You also may want to save some space in your luggage, because Kilkenny County is one of the craft capitals of Ireland, with stores selling items from one-of-a-kind gold bracelets to richly colored pottery.

## Kilkenny City

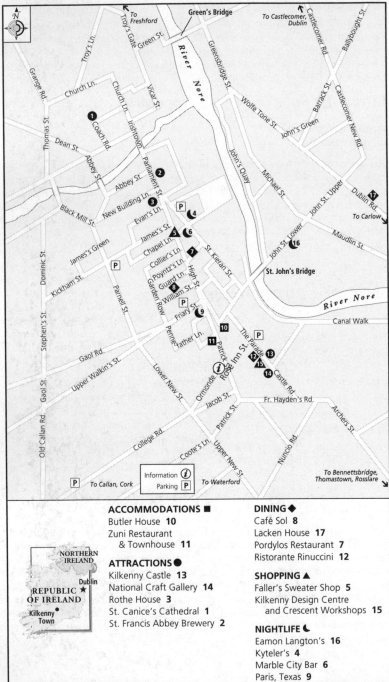

To Freshford
Troy's Ln.
Troy's Gate
Green St.
Green's Bridge
To Castlecomer, Dublin
Castlecomer Rd.
Ballybought St.
Greenbridge St.
River Nore
Grange Rd.
Thomas St.
Church Ln.
Church Ln.
Coach Rd.
Irishtown
Vicar St.
Wolfe Tone St.
John's Green
Barrack St.
Castlecomer New Rd.
Dean St.
Abbey St.
Parliament St.
John's Quay
Michael St.
John's St. Upper
Dublin Rd.
❶
Abbey St.
❷
New Building Ln.
❸
Black Mill St.
Evan's Ln.
P
☾❹
James's Green
James's St.
Chapel Ln.
❺ ❻
Collier's Ln.
❼
John St. Lower
John St. Upper
To Carlow
Maudlin St.
Dominic St.
Kickham St.
Parnell St.
P
Poyntz's Ln.
Garden Row
Guard Ln.
❽
William St.
St. Kieran St.
High St.
❶❻
St. John's Bridge
River Nore
Stephen's St.
Friary St.
P
❾
Canal Walk
Penne...
father Ln.
❶❶
❶❷❶❺
Patrick St.
Rose Inn St.
The Parade
P
❶❸
❶❹
Castle Rd.
Gaol Rd.
Upper Walkin's St.
Lower New St.
Ormonde
ⓘ
Jacob St.
Fr. Hayden's Rd.
Archers St.
Old Callan Rd.
Gaol St.
College Rd.
Coote's Ln.
Patrick St.
Upper New St.
Nuncio Rd.
P
To Callan, Cork
Information ⓘ
Parking P
To Waterford
To Bennettsbridge, Thomastown, Rosslare

NORTHERN IRELAND

Dublin

REPUBLIC ★
OF IRELAND

Kilkenny Town

**ACCOMMODATIONS ■**
Butler House **10**
Zuni Restaurant
& Townhouse **11**

**ATTRACTIONS ●**
Kilkenny Castle **13**
National Craft Gallery **14**
Rothe House **3**
St. Canice's Cathedral **1**
St. Francis Abbey Brewery **2**

**DINING ◆**
Café Sol **8**
Lacken House **17**
Pordylos Restaurant **7**
Ristorante Rinuccini **12**

**SHOPPING ▲**
Faller's Sweater Shop **5**
Kilkenny Design Centre
and Crescent Workshops **15**

**NIGHTLIFE ☾**
Eamon Langton's **16**
Kyteler's **4**
Marble City Bar **6**
Paris, Texas **9**

## Getting to County Kilkenny

By car, take the N9 or N78 south from Dublin and points north and east; the N9/N10 north from Waterford or Wexford; the N8 and N76 from Cork and the southwest; and the N7 or N77 from Limerick and the west. **Irish Rail** (☎ **01-836-6222;** www.irishrail.ie) serves Kilkenny City and Thomastown. **Bus Éireann** (☎ **01-836-6111;** www.buseireann.ie) travels year-round to Kilkenny City and other towns in County Kilkenny and also has a tour bus out of Dublin covering Kilkenny City, Jerpoint Abbey, and the Nore Valley. It leaves Connolly Station, Dublin's main bus terminal, at 9:30 a.m. and returns at 7:00 p.m. every day except Wednesday June through September.

## Spending the night in County Kilkenny

### Butler House
### $$$   Kilkenny City

Not many places could pull off modern abstract artwork hanging on the walls at the same time that Georgian-era designs grace the plastered ceilings, but ivy-covered Butler House does it with style. Built in the 1770s as part of the Kilkenny Castle Estate, Butler House effortlessly blends the traditional elements of the building with contemporary design. Rooms are spacious, soothing, and airy; each is decorated uniquely, and many feature cream and deep orange colors. Bathrooms are sparkling and up-to-date. Try to book a room overlooking the formal courtyard gardens, with a view of the castle, which is lit up at night. The staff here is thoughtful and friendly, always happy to recommend an area restaurant or attraction to suit you. The location is excellent, right next to the castle and Kilkenny Design Centre, and a short walk from most other Kilkenny City attractions.

*16 St. Patrick St.* ☎ *056-77-22-828. Fax: 056-77-65-626.* www.butler.ie. *Rates: €125–€200 ($144–$230) double. AE, DC, MC, V.*

### Cullintra House B&B
### $$   Inistioge

This 250-year-old farmhouse, set among trees and farmland, seems a million miles from everything, even though it's just about 6 miles from Jerpoint Abbey and close to Kilkenny. Furnished elegantly with well-chosen colors and antiques (your host, Patricia Cantlon, is an artist), the house has a bohemian air. Relax by the fireplace in the living room with one of the many cats, meander around the garden, or stroll down to the River Nore. There's a conservatory where you can make tea and watch local foxes milling around out back, and nature trails lead from the house. Your host goes the extra distance to make you feel at home. The excellent homemade candlelit dinner, featuring fresh Irish fare such as salmon and farmhouse cheeses, is a study in living well — guests often feast, chat, and laugh until the crack of dawn.

*The Rower. Take R700 south from Kilkenny or north from New Ross.* ☎ *051-42-3614.* http://indigo.ie/~cullhse. *Rates: €60–€80 ($69–$92) double, dinner €30 ($35). MC, V accepted with 3% charge.*

### Zuni Restaurant & Townhouse
$$$   **Kilkenny**

If you're overdosed on ornate, cluttered Victorian bedrooms, rush your-
self to Zuni for an antidote of clean, Asian-inspired minimalist decor. The
13 guest rooms here are simply furnished in black, white, and deep red, and
boast beds that make you want to sleep late. The location is fabulous — less
than a five-minute walk to Kilkenny's main thoroughfare. The hotel's sleek
restaurant is one of the hottest eateries in Kilkenny, serving lively dishes
from all over the world, from tempura to Moroccan lamb. The friendly,
helpful staff is willing to go above and beyond to make your stay pleasant —
when I left my globetrotting stuffed elephant in one of the rooms, they sent
it out to me in Dublin the very next day.

*29 Patrick St.* ☎ *056-772-3999. Fax: 056-775-6400.* www.zuni.ie. *Rates: €100–€180
($115–$207) double. AE, MC, V.*

## Dining locally in County Kilkenny
Also see Zuni Restaurant & Townhouse in the previous section and
Kyteler's Inn in "Hitting the pubs in County Kilkenny," later in this chapter.

### Café Sol
$   **Kilkenny City   INTERNATIONAL/MEDITERRANEAN**

This bright, cheerful, casual spot serves homemade food all day, starting with
fresh scones in the morning, segueing into hearty soups and sandwiches
for lunch, and ending the day with innovative dishes such as the delicious
roasted organic goose with stuffing.

*6 William St.* ☎ *056-77-64-987. Main courses: €4–€10 ($4.60–$12). MC, V. Open:
Mon–Sat 10 a.m.–5:30 p.m.; Wed–Sat 7–10 p.m.*

### Lacken House
$$$$   **Kilkenny City   NEW IRISH/INTERNATIONAL**

Settle down in this beautiful Victorian house for New Irish cuisine made with
intriguing fresh ingredients. Though there is an à la carte menu, I recom-
mend springing for the prix-fixe dinner, which may include nettle-and-fish
soup with a fried crab claw as a starter and an innovative main course
such as South African ostrich fillet with sweet potato puree, pineapple
salsa, and wasabi crème fraiche.

*On the Dublin Rd. just east of town.* ☎ *056-77-61-085. Reservations required. Main
courses: €50 ($57) 5-course dinner, a la carte €24–27 ($27–$31). AE, DC, MC, V. Open:
Tues–Sat 7–10:30 p.m.*

### Pordylos Restaurant
$$–$$$   **Kilkenny City   INTERNATIONAL**

A concierge at a Kilkenny hotel told me two of the hotel's guests loved
Pordylos so much that they ate dinner there all eight nights of their stay.

And I believe it. Warm and romantic, with wood-beamed ceilings, 16th-century stone walls, and hanging plants, Pordylos invites long, lingering meals and rambling conversation. You can discourse over dishes that draw from cuisines all over the world, such as plump mussels bathed in a lemongrass, coconut, and green curry brew; tagliatelli pasta with blackened Cajun chicken, bacon, garlic, onion, tomatoes, and cream; and vanilla risotto with spinach, pine nuts, wild mushrooms, and mascarpone.

*Butter Slip. ☎ 056-77-70-660. Reservations recommended. Main courses: €14–€22 ($16–$25). AE, MC, V. Daily 5:30–10:30 p.m.*

### Ristorante Rinuooini
**$$–$$$   Kilkenny City   ITALIAN**

Step through the door of this restaurant, and be transported to Italy. The romantically lit room is dominated by two large Renaissance portraits and features Italianate mirrors, alabaster fixtures, and wooden wine racks built into the wall. Service is formal, and guests are nicely dressed. The Italian fare is fresh and full of flavor, and the pasta is obviously homemade — it puts dried pasta to shame. The menu runs from traditional pasta dishes to fish and meat offerings such as calves' liver in a cream sauce with brandy. I recommend the baked bruschetta, which is served hot; the well-spiced, generous meatballs; and the Tortelloni al Pomodoro, crescent-shaped pasta stuffed with ricotta cheese and spinach, served with a chopped tomato, basil, garlic, and white wine sauce.

*Number 1, The Parade opposite Kilkenny Castle. ☎ 056-77-61-575. Reservations required. Main courses: €15–€25 ($17–$29). AE, DC, MC, V. Open: Daily 12:30–2:30 p.m. and 6–10:30 p.m.*

## Exploring County Kilkenny

**Pat Tynan** leads walking tours through the medieval streets of Kilkenny, relating the history of the area and some local lore. A highlight is a little visit to one of the city's old jail cells. This is a great way to get a sense of the layout of Kilkenny City and a grasp of this region's history. Tours leave from the Kilkenny Tourist Office, located in the Shee Alms House in Rose Street. Departure times are mid-March through October Monday through Saturday at 10:30 a.m., 12:15 p.m., 3:00 p.m., and 4:30 p.m., Sunday at 11:15 a.m. and 12:30 p.m.; and November through mid-March Saturdays only at 10:30 a.m., 12:15 p.m., and 3:00 p.m. Tours cost €6 ($6.90) for adults, €5.50 ($6.35) students and seniors. Call ☎ 087-265-1745 to reserve your spot.

### The best attractions

If you're lucky enough to be in Kilkenny on a Tuesday, swing by the market on The Parade leading up to Kilkenny Castle. Sausages, smoked fish, fresh vegetables, baked goods, and other treats are all there for the buying, and the grounds at Kilkenny Castle are perfect for picnicking.

Also see the **Kilkenny Design Centre,** in "Shopping in County Kilkenny," later in this chapter.

## Dunmore Cave
**Ballyfoyle**

An underground river formed these large limestone caverns, which boast some of the most beautiful formations in Ireland. The cave was the site of a Viking massacre in A.D. 928, and Viking artifacts are on display. Guided tours lead you down into the earth and across catwalks that traverse the caverns.

*Castlecomer Rd. (N78) in Ballyfoyle (not Dunmore Village, as the name may imply), 11km (7 miles) north of Kilkenny.* ☎ *056-77-67-726. Admission: €2.75 ($3.15) adults, €2 ($2.30) seniors, €1.25 ($1.45) students and children. Open: Mar–mid-June and mid-Sept–Oct daily 10 a.m.–5 p.m.; mid-June–mid-Sept daily 9:30 a.m.–6:30 p.m; Nov–Feb Sat and Sun and bank holidays 10 a.m.–4:30 p.m. Last admission 45 minutes before closing times. Inaccessible for wheelchairs. Suggested visit: About 1 hour.*

## Kilkenny Castle
**Kilkenny City**

This 12th-century medieval castle, which was remodeled in Victorian times, cuts quite the storybook-castle profile and is the principal attraction in the town of Kilkenny. Surrounded by 50 acres of grounds, including rolling parklands, a riverside walk, and formal gardens, the castle was home to the distinguished Butler family from the late 14th century to the mid-20th century. Guided tours of the castle take you through restored rooms, where you learn a bit about the Butler dynasty as you admire the period furnishings (rooms are decorated as they were in the 1830s). A highlight of the tours is a visit to the 45m-long (150-ft) Long Gallery, which houses portraits of the Butler family and has a beam ceiling gorgeously decorated with painted Celtic lacework. The castle's Butler Gallery hosts modern art exhibits. Tours fill up fast, so get to the castle early to sign up for one. And be sure to stop by the play area if you have kids.

*The Parade.* ☎ *056-77-21-450. Admission: €5 ($5.75) adults, €3.50 ($4.05) seniors, €2 ($2.30) students and children. Open: Apr–May daily 10:30 a.m.–5 p.m., June–Aug daily 9:30 a.m.–7 p.m., Sept daily 10 a.m.– 6:30 p.m., Oct–March daily 10:30 a.m.–12:45 p.m. and 2–5 p.m., Suggested visit: 1½ hours.*

## Jerpoint Abbey
**Thomastown**

This Cistercian abbey is considered one of the best-preserved monastic ruins in the country. It houses Celtic crosses and unique stone carvings of knights and dragons. There's a ton to see as you tiptoe through the graveyard and 15th-century cloister grounds. The small visitors' center provides information about the history of the carvings and abbey.

*Off the Waterford Road (N9. ☎ 056-77-24-623. The abbey is off the N9. Admission: €2.75 ($3.15) adults, €2 ($2.30) seniors, €1.25 ($1.45) children. Open: March–May daily 10:30 a.m.–5 p.m., June–mid-Sept daily 9:30 a.m.–6 p.m, mid-Sept–Oct daily 9:30 a.m.– 5:30 p.m., Nov daily 10 a.m.–4 p.m. Last admission is always 1 hour before closing time. Closed Dec–Feb except for prearranged groups. Suggested visit: 1 hour.*

### St. Canice's Cathedral
**Kilkenny**

This 13th-century church has a beautiful Gothic interior, restored after Cromwell stabled his horses here and destroyed many of the windows, tombs, and monuments in 1650. Check out the four colors of marble used on the floor (green from Connemara, red from Cork, gray from Tyrone, and black from Kilkenny) and the sculpted knight-and-lady effigies on the memorials that pepper the cathedral. The round tower on this site was built around A.D. 849, and you can climb the 167 steps that lead to the top of the tower; it's worth some huffing and puffing for the phenomenal views.

*Off St. Canice's Place and Coach Road. ☎ 056-77-649-71. Admission: €3 ($3.45) adults, €2 ($2.30) seniors and students, children under 12 free. Open: Easter–Sept Mon–Sat 9 a.m.–1 p.m. and 2–6 p.m, Sun 2–6 p.m.; Oct–Easter Mon–Sat 10 a.m.–1 p.m. and 2–4 p.m., Sun 2–4 p.m. Suggested visit: 45 minutes.*

## More cool stuff to see and do

✔ **Mount Juliet Golf Course:** Mount Juliet was host of the Irish Open from 1993 to 1995. The lakes and waterfalls make a picturesque backdrop to this course, called the Augusta of Europe and voted the best inland course in Ireland.

Location: On the N9 Waterford-Dublin Road, Thomastown, County Kilkenny. ☎ 056-77-73-000. Par: 72. Fees: From €75 ($86) midweek, from €90 ($104) weekends, with some reduced early-bird and sunsetter rates.

✔ **National Craft Gallery:** If you enjoy innovative crafts and design, pay a visit to this gallery, where changing themed exhibitions (from glass to metalwork) showcase the best new creations from Irish and international artists.

Location: Castle Yard (across from Kilkenny Castle), Kilkenny, County Kilkenny. ☎ 056-77-61804. www.craftscouncil-of-ireland.ie. Admission: Free. Open January to March Monday through Saturday from 10 a.m. to 6 p.m, April through December daily from 10 a.m. to 6 p.m. Suggested visit: ½ hour.

✔ **Rothe House:** This example of a middle-class home circa 1594 includes an exhibit of clothing from that period and Kilkenny artifacts. Also on site is a genealogical research center.

Location: Parliament St., Kilkenny, County Kilkenny. ☎ 056-77-22-893. Admission: €3 ($3.45) adults, €2 ($2.30) seniors and students, €1 ($1.15) children. Open March to October Monday through Saturday from 10:30 a.m. to 5:00 p.m. and Sunday from 3 to 5 p.m.; November to February Monday through Saturday from 1 to 5 p.m. Suggested visit: 45 minutes.

✔ **St. Francis Abbey Brewery:** This brewery produces **Smithwick's,** a thick red ale, and — of all things — Budweiser.

Location: Parliament St., Kilkenny, County Kilkenny. ☎ 056-77-21-014. Free admission. Open for video screenings and tastings June to August Monday through Friday at 3 p.m.

## Shopping in County Kilkenny

County Kilkenny is a center for crafts and design, and the town of Bennettsbridge (6km/4 miles south of Kilkenny City on the R700) is a focal point. Here and in surrounding locations, you find the workshops of potters, woodworkers, glassblowers, and other craftspeople. If this interests you, be sure to pick up the *Kilkenny Craft Trail* brochure from the tourist office, which will give you details for and directions to a number of workshops.

One of the most popular workshops you'll find in Bennettsbridge is **Nicholas Mosse Pottery** (☎ 056-77-27-505). Expert potter Mosse uses the River Nore to produce the electricity to fire his pots, and each piece is hand-thrown. The earthenware clay pottery, sold as individual pieces or in sets, is hand-painted with charming country themes such as flowers, fruits and vegetables, and farm animals. The shop also sells Nicholas Mosse glassware and linens, plus furniture, jewelry, and other items from some of Ireland's best craftspeople. Be sure to check out the *seconds* (slightly imperfect pots) upstairs for good deals.

In Kilkenny Town, **Faller's Sweater Shop,** 75 High St., (☎ 056-77-70-599), stocks all sorts of tasteful knitwear, from fishermen sweaters to cloaks. And ladies and gentlemen, hold on to your credit cards, because **Kilkenny Design Centre,** Castle Yard, Kilkenny (☎ 056-77-22-118), is a stockhouse of Ireland's best handcrafted items, including pottery, linen, jewelry, glassware, clothing, fine art, and leatherwork. Be sure to visit the many craft workshops in the converted stables behind the Design Centre, where you can watch craftspeople at work as you browse.

## Hitting the pubs in County Kilkenny

### Eamon Langton's
**Kilkenny City**

This place is a deserved four-time winner of the National Pub of the Year award. It has all the hallmarks of a classic Victorian pub, from a beautiful fireplace to globe lamps. Head out to the garden area in back on nice days.

*69 John St.* ☎ *056-77-65-133.*

### Kyteler's Inn
**Kilkenny City**

This 650-year-old coaching inn is named for Dame Alice Kyteler, who ran the place in the 17th century. Kyteler, who buried four husbands, was accused of witchcraft. She fled to England, but her maid was not so lucky — she was burned at the stake. The cozy upstairs bar is always buzzing with conversation and live music. Downstairs, good pub grub is served in a medieval cellar featuring the original stone walls and columns. You may be graced by the presence of Ms. Kyteler herself — a life-size doll sits in one of the cellar windows, so make sure she doesn't slip anything into your stew.

*27 St. Kieran's St.* ☎ *056-77-21-004.*

### Marble City Bar
**Kilkenny City**

Even if you don't stop for a drink at this friendly, welcoming pub, check out the gorgeous facade of wrought iron, brass, and carved wood, all lit by gas lamps.

*66 High St.* ☎ *056-77-62-091.*

### Paris, Texas
**Kilkenny City**

Round up your friends, and head on down to this spacious saloon straight out of the American West. This place is always hopping and often hosts excellent traditional Irish music.

*92 High St.* ☎ *056-77-61-822.*

## Fast Facts: County Kilkenny

### Area Codes
County Kilkenny's area codes (or city codes) are 056 and 051.

### Emergencies/Police
Dial ☎ **999** for all emergencies.

### Genealogy Resources
Contact the Kilkenny Archaeological Society, 16 Parliament St., Rothe House (☎ 056-77-22-893).

### Information
For visitor information and accommodations reservations, go to Shee Alms House, Rose Inn Street, Kilkenny (☎ 056-77-22-893).

### Internet
Compustore, Unit 12, Market Cross Shopping Centre, High Street, Kilkenny (☎ 056-71-210), has Internet access plus printing capabilities.

### Post Office
The Kilkenny District Post Office is at 73 High St., Kilkenny (☎ 056-21-813).

# Part IV
# Counties Cork and Kerry

The 5th Wave  By Rich Tennant

"Let me ask you a question. Are you planning to kiss the Blarney Stone, or ask for its hand in marriage?"

## In this part . . .

**C**ork City (Chapter 15) is a happening big city with the soul of a small town. It has a fabulous selection of restaurants, a vibrant arts scene, proximity to many attractions, and some very friendly locals — what more could you want in a city?

The south and southwest counties certainly have their share of natural beauty, with the gorgeous beaches and seascapes of West Cork (Chapter 15), the peaceful woodlands and lakes of Killarney National Park (Chapter 16), and the stunning mountains, cliffs, beaches, and sea views of the Ring of Kerry and the Dingle Peninsula (both in Chapter 16).

# Chapter 15

# County Cork

$C$ounty Cork (see the nearby map) occupies the eastern half of Southern Ireland and has the country's second-largest city (Cork City); one of its most beautiful golf courses (at the Old Head of Kinsale); a host of historical sights; and, bar none, the most famous rock on the island: the Blarney Stone. Pucker up!

Many travelers breeze into Cork City, look around, stop at Blarney Castle on the way out for a quick smooch, and then head right for Killarney. Big mistake. The stretch of coast from the lovely seaside town of Kinsale to the tip of Bantry Bay is just too beautiful to pass up. And East Cork is a gentle land that boasts several wonderful guesthouses; the pretty harbor town of Cobh; and some great attractions, including Fota Wildlife Park. Stick around a while.

## Cork City and East County Cork

The first thing you notice about Corkonians is that they have a fierce pride in their city, which they have nicknamed "The People's Republic of Cork." And they should be proud of Cork; It manages to have a small-town, friendly feel while offering everything that a large city should, including a lively arts scene and quite a few fabulous restaurants. East County Cork is home to popular attractions such as the Blarney Stone and Castle and Fota Wildlife Park, and the sweet seaside town of Cobh. (The "Cork City" map can help you with locations.)

### Getting to Cork City and east County Cork

To get to **Cork City** by car, take the N25 west from Waterford, the N20 south from Limerick, or the N22 east from Kilkenny. The towns of east County Cork are located off the N25. If you're coming to Cork City from

## County Cork

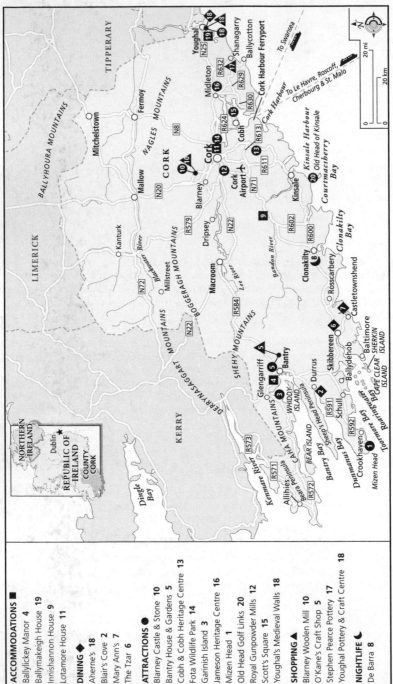

the east, you can save lots of time by taking the **Carrigaloe-Glenbrook Ferry** (☎ 021-481-1485) between Cobh on the east side of the bay and Ringaskiddy (16km [10 miles] south of Cork) on the west side. The scenic trip takes only about five minutes and runs year-round, 7:15 a.m. to 12:30 a.m. daily. The cost is €5 ($5.75) round-trip or €3 ($3.45) one-way.

**Irish Rail** (☎ 1850-366-222; www.irishrail.ie) serves Cork City, Fota, and Cobh regularly; and **Bus Éireann** (☎ 021-50-8188; www.buseireann.ie) serves Cork City, Cobh, Youghal, and other cities throughout County Cork daily. The main bus depot is located at the **Travel Centre,** Parnell Place, Cork.

You can travel right to Cork from Britain and France as well. **Swansea Cork Ferries** (☎ 021-427-1166; www.swansea-cork.ie) sails to Cork from Swansea, Wales. **Brittany Ferries,** 42 Grand Parade, Cork (☎ 021-427-7801; www.brittany-ferries.com), sails from Roscoff, in France, to Cork.

## Getting around Cork City

Cork City is best seen by foot, because most of the smaller roads and alleys are open exclusively to pedestrian traffic. In addition, the city can be confusing to find your way around in by car, specifically because the city's River Lee forks and winds, and creates two sets of *quays* (wharves or piers). Although roads are not as narrow as in most towns, the one-way streets can be frustrating when you're carried across a bridge you didn't mean to cross or you see where you want to go but can't quite seem to get there.

 If you do have a car, either park at your hotel if it's convenient or park when you get downtown, and see the city by foot. Parking in Cork City runs on a disc system. You can purchase disks at small shops on each block. Or you can make use of a multistory parking garage at Lavitt's Quay or Merchant's Quay or find one of several parking lots. Most of the attractions and shopping lie on the island between the two tributaries. **St. Patrick's Street** is the city's hub for shopping, and **Oliver Plunkett Street** is the main place for a Cork City pub-crawl. If you end up needing a taxi in town, call **Taxi Co-op** (☎ 021-427-2222).

It's best to have a car for getting to and from attractions and towns in east County Cork. Car-rental companies in Cork City include Avis (☎ 021-428-1111). **Bus Éireann** (☎ 01-836-6111) operates local service around Cork City to neighboring towns like Blarney, Cobh, and Fota. Most buses leave from the Parnell Place Bus Station. If you need a taxi in the outlying towns, call **Castle Cabs** (☎ 021-38-2222) in Blarney and **Harbour Cabs** (☎ 021-481-4444) in Cobh.

## Cork City

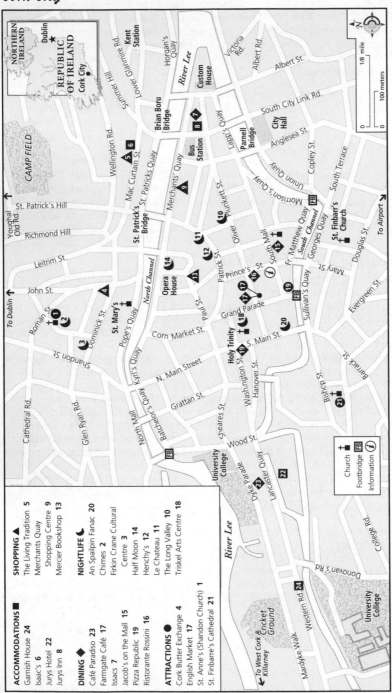

## Spending the night in Cork City and east County Cork

### Ballymakeigh House
**$$  Killeagh**

This is one of my favorite accommodations in all of Ireland. A quiet, casual, beautifully managed farmhouse, it's the kind of place that makes you feel that all is right with the world, especially as you gaze at the blue dusk settling on the dairy cows in the field. The soothing, comfortable bedrooms feature knotty-pine furniture; luxurious comforters; and well-chosen, eclectic art — my room had a painting of the tropics and a large photograph of the Golden Gate Bridge. And then there's the food. Oh, wow. Your warm and friendly hostess, Margaret Browne, happens to be a professional gourmet cook. Her breakfasts are delicious, and if you book before 5 p.m., she will create a glorious six-course dinner for you, using the freshest of local ingredients, including flowers from around her property. Don't miss the dinner — it may turn out to be the best meal of your whole trip. This is a fantastic place for couples looking for a romantic escape.

*Killeagh. The house is 9.5km (6 miles) west of Youghal off the N25; look for the signs.* ☎ *024-95-184. Fax: 024-95-370. Rates: €100–€110 ($115–$127). V.*

### Garnish House
**$$  Cork City**

This townhouse B&B is the best in the city. The large rooms are sweet, soothing, and stylish, boasting brightly painted walls, beds that are an ocean of white sheets and blankets, a bowl filled with fresh fruit, and another bowl with flowers floating in it. Breakfasts are amazing — you'd need a full year of mornings to sample every single treat that friendly hostess Hansi Lucey offers, and I'm willing to bet that you'll make multiple trips to the buffet. The B&B is about a 20-minute walk from the heart of Cork City. Check out the beautiful wood-framed photos of Ireland that decorate the house.

*Western Rd.,.* ☎ *021-427-5111. Fax: 021-427-3872.* www.garnish.ie. *Rates: €80–€100 ($92–$115). Free parking. AE, DC, MC, V.*

### Isaac's
**$–$$  Cork City**

Rustic charm, a great location, and a courtyard garden featuring a beautiful waterfall are the highlights of this comfortable hotel. The rooms are uniquely decorated and comfortable. The two- and three-bedroom apartments are an excellent deal if you're traveling with several people.

*48 MacCurtain St.* ☎ *021-450-0011. Fax: 021-450-6355.* www.isaacs.ie. *Rates: €96–€115 ($110–$132) double. AE, MC, V.*

### Jurys Hotel
**$$$ Cork City**

As at all the jewels in the Jurys Hotel crown, the service here is professional and efficient, and the rooms are modern and cookie-cutter standard, with dark woods and quality fabrics. And as at most Jurys Hotels, the clientele are often businesspeople. The enclosed grounds — featuring a walking path, pool, and outdoor sunbathing — make this hotel a standout.

*Western Rd. Take Lancaster Quay from the city center; it becomes Western Rd.* ☎ *021-425-2700. Fax: 021-27-4477. www.jurysdoyle.com. Rates: €158–€203 ($182–$233) double. AE, DC, MC, V.*

### Jurys Inn
**$$ Cork City**

The service is par for the course, and the modern rooms are comfortable, but there's nothing exceptional about Jurys Inn — except the low price and the excellent location, within a few minutes of the city center. A flat rate for up to three adults or two adults and two children in a room makes this a good deal for traveling families.

*Anderson's Quay between the Custom House and bus station at the mouth of the north channel.* ☎ *021-494-3000. Fax: 021-427-6144. www.bookajurysinn.com. Rates: €71–€79 ($82–$91) up to three adults or family of four. AE, DC, MC, V.*

### Lotamore House
**$$ Tivoli**

This 20-room Georgian-manor-turned-guesthouse is just over 3.2km (2 miles) away from the center of Cork City (you need to have a car), but its sloping grounds make it feel much more rural. Public rooms are beautifully furnished with antiques and portraits, and a grand staircase leads up to bedrooms that have gorgeous old dark-wood furniture and high ceilings. The house has a bit of a moody, echo-y feel to it, perfect for reading a mystery novel on a rainy night. The staff is friendly and helpful.

*Off the Dublin/Waterford Rd. (N8/N25). East off the main road to Waterford (N25).* ☎ *021-82-2344. Fax: 021-82-2219. Rates: €130 ($150) double. AE, MC, V.*

## Dining locally in Cork City and East County Cork

### Aherne's
**$$$ Youghal SEAFOOD**

This port-town restaurant has a reputation for serving the freshest and tastiest seafood in this part of the country. Don't expect a lot of fanciness and formality with your dishes: The chef is more concerned about taste than presentation. New Englanders may never order cod back home again after having it at Aherne's. The seafood chowder is unmatched as well. If you're really hungry, go for the award-winning six-fish, four-shellfish platter.

*163 N. Main St. Take the main road to Waterford (N25) then turn off onto Main St.* ☎ *024-92-424. Main courses: €16–€21($18–$24). AE, DC, MC, V. Open: Daily noon–10 p.m.*

### Café Paradiso
$$$   Cork City   VEGETARIAN

Before you even sit down, you feel the vibe. This bright and electric restaurant is filled with books and toys and a certain . . . energy. Then there's the food, a vegetarian's nirvana with an eclectic and fresh menu offering dishes such as roasted tomato soup with basil pesto, mushroom fritters fried in ginger butter, gingered sweet potato spring rolls with sesame cabbage, panfried couscous, and feta-and-almond cake with arribiata sauce. For dessert, try the rich fudge cake with orange sauce. Is your mouth watering yet? After you dine, you can purchase *The Café Paradiso Cookbook* and try out the recipes at home.

*16 Lancaster Quay. Just beyond Wood St., down the south channel of the river, across the street from Jurys Hotel.* ☎ *021-27-7937. Main courses: €21–€22 ($24–$25). AE, MC, V. Open: Tues–Sat 12:30–3 p.m. and 6:30–10:30 p.m.*

### Farmgate Café
$   Cork City   IRISH

This casual little cafe is located on an indoor balcony overlooking the bustling English Market (reviewed in the following section, "The top attractions"). It serves up excellent, rib-sticking traditional Irish food, including some specialties specific to County Cork, such as tripe and drisheens (blood sausages). The Irish stew is wonderful, as are the lighter dishes, such as quiches and sandwiches. This is a great place to get a taste of Cork food and the Corkonians themselves as locals frequent the place.

*English Market.* ☎ *021-427-8134. Main courses: MC, V. Open: Mon–Sat 9 a.m.–5 p.m.*

### Isaacs
$$–$$$   Cork City   INTERNATIONAL/PIZZA

An informal restaurant that's trendy but doesn't act like it, Isaacs is an amalgam of contemporary and traditional — much like Cork City itself. Located in a converted Victorian warehouse with a vaulted ceiling, Isaacs has red-brick walls adorned with local art pieces, as well as a chatty evening crowd. The international cuisine, from salads to burgers to pizzas, is reliably delicious.

*48 MacCurtain St. Above the north channel; take a right off of St. Patrick's Hill.* ☎ *021-450-3805. Main courses: €14–€22 ($16–$25). AE, DC, MC, V. Open: Mon–Sat 10 a.m.–10 p.m., Sun 6:30–9:30 p.m.*

### Jacob's on the Mall
**$$$**  **Cork City**  **INTERNATIONAL**

From the crisp vegetable-and-duck confit spring roll to the penne pasta with basil pesto, bacon, leeks, peas, and pine nuts, this restaurant creates simple yet sophisticated dishes that let each fresh, flavorful ingredient shine. The chef takes advantage of seasonal local produce, so choosing a dish that's in season (such as wild salmon from mid-June through July) is an excellent idea. The setting is an interesting mix of old and new, with colorful contemporary paintings hanging on a rough stone wall and hanging planters with trees reaching their limbs toward the skylights in the high ceiling.

*30A South Mall.* ☎ *021-425-1530. Main courses: €16–€30 ($18–$35). AE, MC, V. Open: Mon–Sat 12:30–2:30 p.m. and 6:30–10 p.m.*

### Pizza Republic
**$**  **Cork City**  **PIZZA/ITALIAN**

Sometimes in life, you come to a point where you just want a really good pizza, and Pizza Republic delivers (so to speak). This big, casual, American-diner-esque space, with comfortable chairs and modern art (check out the stained-glass pizza), fills up with families, university students, and boisterous groups of friends. The selection of excellent pizzas is vast, with some very innovative creations that incorporate local foods, such as the West Cork pizza, with Clonakilty black pudding, sautéed leeks, and rosemary roast potatoes; and the delicious Naturally Smoked Pizza, with tomato, smoked sausage, mozzarella, and smoked Gubbeen (a sharp Cork cheese). Vegetarians will love the Hot Spinach Pizza, with goat cheese, hot chiles, spinach, and tomato. The menu also offers pastas and salads.

*97–98 S. Main St.* ☎ *021-427-99-69. Main courses: €8.95–€13 ($10–$15). AE, MC, V. Open: Daily noon–11 p.m.*

### Ristorante Rossini
**$$–$$$**  **Cork City**  **ITALIAN**

Quintessentially Italian, down to the elegant blue plates and matching blue candles dripping over chianti bottles, this charming and authentic restaurant is located down one of the side streets off Oliver Plunkett Street. The pasta is homemade by the chef, and you can't go wrong with the specialty *Italia de la Casa* — pasta and seafood with the chef's own sauce creation. If you don't have a pleasant meal here, you just don't like Italian food, period.

*34 Princes St. between Oliver Plunkett St. and South Mall.* ☎ *021-427-5818. Main courses: €16–€23 ($18–$26). AE, DC, MC, V. Open: Mon–Sat noon–3 p.m. and 6–10:30 p.m.*

## Exploring Cork City and east County Cork

Bus Éireann (☎ 01-836-6111) offers half-day day tours of Cork City and Blarney (where you have an option of staying and taking another bus later) on an open-top bus. Tours leave from and arrive at Parnell Place in Cork City. They depart daily at 10:30 a.m. and return at 1:30 p.m. Prices are €9 ($10) for adults, €7 ($8.05) for students and seniors, and €5 ($5.75) for children.

### The top attractions

### Blarney Castle and Stone
#### Blarney

To kiss or not to kiss, that is the question. Yes, it's touristy, but there is a satisfaction that comes from kissing a hunk of rock that's famous across the world, and there is a fun camaraderie with your fellow kissers as you wait in line. The Blarney Stone, located at the top of the ruins of a 15th-century castle (after a fair amount of climbing up narrow, twisting stairways), allegedly imparts eloquence, or *the gift of gab,* to those daring enough to contort upside down from the parapet walk and kiss it. It's a real feat to lean back into nothing and tip your head to kiss the smooth rock — it may even be a little frightening to people afraid of heights (or germs). It's customary to tip the guy who holds your legs, and you may want to give it over *before* he holds you over the faraway courtyard. Blarney is one of the most fortified castles in Ireland — its walls are 5.5m (18 feet) thick in some parts. You can climb through the ruins of the castle, exploring various rooms (including the "murder holes") along the way. Don't leave Blarney without seeing the castle grounds, with their pretty gardens. If you have no intention of puckering up and have explored (or will explore) other castle ruins, a trip out here is probably not worth the time.

*Off the N20 north of Cork City, heading toward Limerick. By bus: You can catch a Bus Éireann round trip to the castle from the bus station in Cork, at Parnell Place.* ☎ *021-438-5252. Admission: €7 ($8.05) adults, €5 ($5.75) students and seniors, €2.50 ($2.90) children 8 to 14. Open: June–Aug Mon–Sat 9 a.m.–7 p.m., Sun 9:30 a.m.–5.30 p.m.; May and Sept Mon–Sat 9 a.m.–6:30 p.m., Sun 9:30 a.m.–5:30 p.m.; Oct–April Mon–Sat 9 a.m. to dusk, Sun 9:30 a.m. to dusk. Not accessible by wheelchair. Suggested visit: 2 hours.*

### Cobh and Cobh Heritage Centre
#### Cobh

Cobh (pronounced *cove*) is a lovely seaside town, and a ramble by the harbor and through the streets, with their vividly colored buildings, is a great way to spend a morning or afternoon.

## This is no blarney: The origins of blarney

Wondering just where the old "gift of gab" lore stems from? Well, we've all heard some blarney in our lives, but the person who did it best (and first) was the charismatic Lord of Blarney, Cormac McDermot McCarthy. When Queen Elizabeth asked all Irish lords to effectively sign over their land to the crown, McCarthy was determined not to. For every demand the queen made, he responded with eloquent letters that claimed undying loyalty and dripped with flattery, although he had no intention of giving in to her demands. After receiving yet another crafty letter, the queen, exasperated, proclaimed, "This is all Blarney. What he says, he rarely means." So today, anyone who uses a lot of eloquence and empty phrases and playfully deceives or exaggerates is said to be talking *blarney*.

Cobh Harbour was the main point of departure for thousands of starving Irish on their way to the United States during the Great Famine and for convicts being sent to Australia. It was also the last port of call for the ill-fated *Titanic* and *Lusitania*. This heritage center, located in a beautiful restored railway station, uses objects, dioramas, text, and sound to relate the stories of these ships and their connections with Cobh. The highlight is the life-size replica of the inside of a ship full of convicts. You can almost feel the waves battering the hull. This whole exhibit will be particularly interesting to those whose relatives emigrated through Cobh.

*Cobh Railway Station.* ☎ *021-481-3591. Admission: €5 ($5.75) adults, €4 ($4.60) seniors and students, €2.50 ($2.90) children,. Open: May–Oct daily 10 a.m.–6 p.m (last admission 5 p.m.), Nov–Apr daily 10 a.m.–5 p.m. (last admission 4 p.m.). Suggested visit: 1 hour.*

### English Market
**Cork City**

This pretty, old-world, stone-floored food market, dating from 1786, is one of the best in Ireland. The market was damaged by fire in 1980, but it has been beautifully renovated, featuring the original cast-iron fountain, columns, and railings. All sorts of meat, vegetables, fruits, sweets, breads, and prepared foods are sold here, and the market is famous for its alley full of sparkling fresh fish. Of the many stalls, locals recommend Arbutus and the Alternative Bread Co. for bread, Kay O'Connell's Fish Stall for fish, On the Pig's Back for sausages and meats, and O'Reilly's for Cork specialties such as tripe and drisheen. This is the perfect place to get the makings of a picnic, and Bishop Lucey Park, a little green park at Grand Parade, is a great spot to have your picnic. If the weather gods are not cooperating with your picnic plans, the Farmgate Café (reviewed in the previous section, "Dining locally in Cork City and East County Cork") is the next-best thing.

*Between Grand Parade and Princes St. Entrances on Patrick St., Grand Parade, Oliver Plunkett St., and Princes St. Open: Mon–Sat 9 a.m.–6 p.m. Suggested visit: ½ hour.*

### Fota Wildlife Park
**Carrigtwohill**

This place is not Irish in the least, but it's a fascinating attraction, where more than 70 species of exotic wildlife roam relatively freely (except the cheetahs — for both your safety and theirs). Giraffes nibble on leaves, peacocks strut their stuff, zebras nuzzle one another, and maras (guinea-pig-type animals from Argentina) bounce along everywhere. Highlights are the families of monkeys, who love to hoot and show off their amazing acrobatics on rope "vines." Panels with text explain where the animals came from and how they live, always with an eye to conservation (the park does a lot of breeding for conservation), and excellent talks are offered from time to time. An open-air train circles the park, but you'll see more by walking. Admission to the wildlife park also includes free admission the Fota Arboretum, with its collection of temperate and subtropical plants and trees.

*Cork Harbour. 16km (10 miles) from Cork City toward Cobh off the N25.* ☎ *021-81-2678. Admission: €9.50 ($11) adults, €6 ($6.90) students, seniors, and children under 16, €38 ($44) for 2 adults and up to 4 children. Open: Mon–Sat 10 a.m.–6 p.m (last admission 5 p.m.), Sun 11 a.m.–5 p.m. (last admission 4 p.m.) Suggested visit: 2 hours.*

### St. Anne's (Shandon Church)
**Cork City**

Until 1986, when they were repaired, each of the four clock faces on the tower of St. Ann Shandon, on Church Street, gave a different time, earning it the nickname "The Four-Face Liar." You can climb the bell tower for the city's best view. And there's an added attraction: You get to ring the bells yourself. The church was undergoing renovations as this book went to press, but it should be open by the time the book is published.

*Church St.* ☎ *021-450-4906. Admission: €3 ($3.45) adults, €2 ($2.30) seniors and students. Open: Mon–Sat 8:30 a.m.–6 p.m. Suggested visit: 20 minutes.*

### St. Finbarre's Cathedral
**Cork City**

This cathedral was built on the site of a monastery and university created by St. Finbarre, Cork City's founder, around A.D. 650. Interesting highlights of the *cruciform* (cross-shaped) cathedral include the one-of-a-kind underground church organ, zodiac symbols on the stained glass, and gilded ceilings. You'll get more out of your visit to this French Gothic–style Protestant cathedral if you take the short informative tour.

*Dean St.* ☎ *021-496-3387. Admission: Free, tour €3 ($3.45) adults, €1.50 ($1.75) children. Open: Apr–Sept Mon–Sat 10 a.m.–5:30 p.m.; Oct–March 10 a.m.–12:45 p.m. and 2–5 p.m. Suggested visit: 30 minutes.*

## Other cool things to see and do

✔ **Jameson Heritage Centre:** Journey through the history of Irish whiskey. You'll see an interesting audiovisual presentation and parts of this restored 18th-century distillery, including the largest pot still in the world, able to hold an intoxicating 30,000 gallons. The modern distillery here (entrance is not permitted) is the largest in Ireland, producing many different whiskies, including Jameson and Tullamore Dew. At the end of the tour, you get to sample some of the smoothest whiskey ever made. The souvenir shop sells everything from shot glasses to bottles of the Water of Life.

Location: Distillery Road, off Main Street, Midleton. ☎ **021-461-3594.** Off the N25, east of Cork City and west from Youghal. Admission costs €7 ($8.05) adults, €5.75 ($6.60) seniors and students, and €3 ($3.45) children. Open daily from 10 a.m. to 6 p.m. Suggested visit: 1¼ hours.

✔ **Royal Gunpowder Mills:** Between 1794 and 1903, these mills — the largest of their type in Europe — manufactured and supplied gunpowder to European armies. The mills were so important that when Napoleon threatened the United Kingdom (which then included Ireland), the British government sent an envoy to control and protect the mills. Today, you can look around the restored buildings and take in a film and exhibits about gunpowder production in County Cork.

Location: Right off the N22 in Ballinollig (look for the signs). ☎ **021-487-4430.** Only five minutes west of Cork on N22 toward Killarney. Admission costs €4 ($4.60) adults, €3 ($3.45) students and seniors, and €2.50 ($2.90) children. Open April through September daily from 10 a.m. to 6 p.m. Suggested visit: 1 hour.

✔ **Scott's Square:** This is an impressive and sobering memorial to the 1,195 people who died aboard the *Lusitania* when it was hit by a German torpedo off the Irish coast in 1915. The sinking prompted America's entry into World War I.

Location: Cobh Harbour, on the square right by the water. Suggested visit: A couple of minutes.

✔ **Youghal (Medieval Walls):** This lovely little port town is worth a stop to get out, stretch your legs, and see what Dublin might have looked like if it hadn't become the capital of the country. Like Dublin, Youghal (pronounced *yawl*) was settled by the Vikings and later fortified by the Normans, who built a wall around the city, half of which still stands. As you make your way from the main Water Gate along the old wall, you see several towers (originally built close enough to allow guards to shout to one another) and the main arched gate, called Cromwell's Arch because it's believed Oliver Cromwell ended his bloody English campaign here. Don't miss the restored Clock Gate (formerly Trinity Gate) at the southern entrance to the town, once the execution site and prison. Guided tours are offered by the Youghal Heritage Centre, which also offers a film relating the town's history and has guides to the wall for sale.

You may want to top off your stop in Youghal with a trip to the town's long, sandy stretch of beach, located right past the town center.

Location: Youghal Heritage Center, Market Square (☎ 024-20170). The film costs €1.50 ($1.75), tours are €3.50 ($4.05). Open June to mid-Sept daily from 9:30 a.m. to 7 p.m., mid-September to May Monday through Saturday from 9:30 a.m. to 5:30 p.m. Youghal is on the N25 east of Middleton. Suggested visit: 2 hours.

## Shopping in Cork City and east County Cork

Cork is a diverse city for shopping. From the highbrow stores on Patrick's Street to the eclectic mix of small retail shops along Oliver Plunkett Street, you can find everything from designer clothing and linen to gourmet cheese and homemade crafts. Cork's only mall, the **Merchants Quay Shopping Centre,** home to 40 shops and the upscale department stores Roches and Marks & Spencer, is on Patrick's Street. Cork also has two main markets. The **Cork Butter Exchange** (John Redmond St.) is a cobblestone rotunda housing many craft workshops and summertime music sessions; Antiques can be found along **Paul's Lane,** off Paul Street. Also see the English Market, reviewed in "The top attractions," earlier in this chapter.

The **Blarney Woolen Mill,** near Blarney Castle, off the N20, Blarney (☎ 021-438-5280), is the original in a string of famous stores. The stores sell everything from crystal to tweed and, of course, sweaters. The **Living Tradition,** 40 MacCurtain St., Cork City (☎ 021-450-2040), offers a large variety of *bodhráns* (Irish drums), tin whistles, and sheet music, and an excellent selection of traditional Irish music CDs. **Mercier Bookshop,** 5 French Church St., Cork City (☎ 021-427-1346), sells a wide selection of titles, from Irish history to cult fiction. It also stocks the complete collection of the Cork-based Mercier Press, Ireland's oldest independent publishing house. **Stephen Pearce Pottery,** on the R629, Shanagarry (☎ 021-464-6807), is the place to go for the popular and unique handmade white-and-terra-cotta earthenware that you see all over, plus hand-blown Simon Pearce glass, linen, and jewelry. **Youghal Pottery and Craft Centre,** Foxhole (☎ 024-91-222), has one of the largest selections of pottery styles under one roof, and specializes in the colorful and unique smoke-fired Raku pottery. It stocks knitwear, crafts, and gifts as well. Foxhole is just a little beyond Youghal on the N25.

## Nightlife and pubs

The **Firkin Crane Cultural Center,** John Redmond St. (☎ 021-450-7487), presents all sorts of contemporary dance. The **Triskel Arts Centre,** Tobin Street (off Main St.; ☎ 021-427-2022), offers theater, contemporary and traditional Irish music, opera, and readings. Opera, dance, and concerts make up the schedule at the **Cork Opera House,** Emmet Place (☎ 021-427-0022).

For night owls, the **Half Moon,** in the Cork Opera House, Emmet Place (☎ 021-427-0022), stages blues, jazz, and pop bands from 11 p.m. to 3 a.m.

If pub-hopping is more your thing, try one of the following:

### An Spailpin Fanac

Open fireplaces, plenty of brickwork, and traditional music Sunday through Thursday make An Spailpin one of the best pubs in town. It's also one of the oldest pubs in Cork and is located opposite the Beamish Brewery, which should give you a good idea what you should order.
*28 S. Main St. ☎ 021-427-7949.*

### Chimes

This is a popular working-class pub and the best place to watch a football or hurling match on the telly. I suggest you drink the local beers: smooth Murphy's or sharp Beamish. Foot-stomping traditional music is usually on tap on weekends.
*27 Church St. ☎ 021-430-4136.*

### Henchy's

A *snug* (a separate room where women were once relegated to drink), a mahogany bar, polished brass, and stained glass characterize this elegant classic pub.
*40 Saint Luke's St. ☎ 021-450-7833.*

### Le Chateau

Centrally located in the heart of Cork and built more than 200 years ago, this labyrinthine Victorian-decorated pub with an inexplicably French name is one of the oldest and most-favored places in town. City memorabilia is featured prominently in the many sections and snugs. The Irish coffee is legendary.
*93 Patrick St. ☎ 021-27-0370.*

**The Long Valley**

This wonderful watering hole is one of the most popular in Cork, known for excellent (and giant) sandwiches and great conversation. A long bar stretches the length of the room, and historic photos line the walls.

*10 Wintrop St., at the corner of Oliver Plunkett St. across from the General Post Office.* ☎ *021-472-2144.*

# Fast Facts: Cork City and East County Cork

### Area Codes

Cork City and East County Cork's area codes (or city codes) are 021, 022, and 024.

### Emergencies/Police

Dial ☎ **999** for all emergencies.

### Genealogy Resources

Mallow Heritage Centre, 27–28 Bank Place, Mallow (☎ 022-21-778).

### Hospital

Cork Regional Hospital is on Wilton Road (☎ 021-54-6400).

### Information

For visitor information, go to the Cork Tourist Office, 42 Grand Parade (near Oliver Plunkett St.), Cork (☎ 021-427-3251).

### Internet

You can check email and surf at IDOT Café, Gate Multiplex, North Main Street (☎ 021-427-3544).

### Post Office

The General Post Office in Cork is on Oliver Plunkett Street (☎ 021-27-2000).

# Kinsale and West County Cork

You can feast on some of the finest cuisine in Ireland (especially seafood) in the charming and popular port city of **Kinsale** (see the nearby map), which is known as the Gourmet Capital of Ireland. Between meals, wander the winding streets, browse through some terrific little shops, and stroll around the sheltered harbor.

**West County Cork** looks like a magazine advertisement for Ireland, with its fishing villages, cozy pubs (many with excellent music), and awe-inspiring cliffs and craggy coastline.

## Getting to Kinsale and west County Cork

To get to Kinsale by car, take the R600 south from Cork or the R605 south from Inishannon. The N71 links Cork to most of the major towns in west County Cork. **Bus Éireann** (☎ **01-836-6111**) travels year-round to Kinsale, Bantry, and other major towns in West County Cork.

## Kinsale

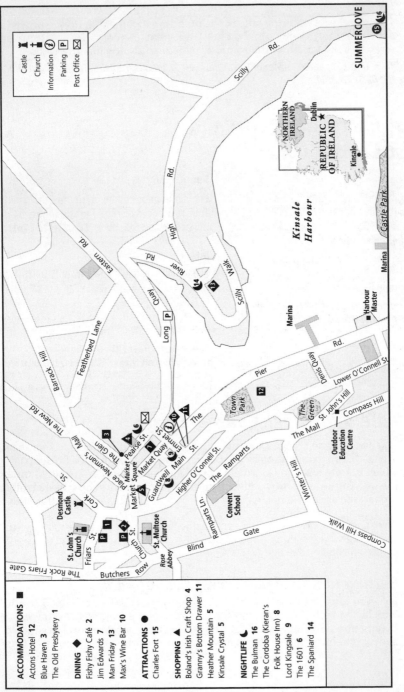

**Castle** ⚔
**Church** ✝
**Information** ⓘ
**Parking** P
**Post Office** ⊠

ACCOMMODATIONS ■
Actons Hotel 12
Blue Haven 3
The Old Presbytery 1

DINING ◆
Fishy Fishy Café 2
Jim Edwards 7
Man Friday 13
Max's Wine Bar 10

ATTRACTIONS ●
Charles Fort 15

SHOPPING ▲
Boland's Irish Craft Shop 4
Granny's Bottom Drawer 11
Heather Mountain 5
Kinsale Crystal 5

NIGHTLIFE ☾
The Bulman 16
The Cordoba (Kieran's
  Folk House Inn) 8
Lord Kingsale 9
The 1601 6
The Spaniard 14

# Spending the night in Kinsale and west County Cork

### Actons Hotel
**$$–$$$  Kinsale**

Three-story Actons Hotel has exceptional amenities, such as an indoor heated pool, a gym, a sauna, a steam room, an outdoor tub, a jacuzzi, a children's pool, and a solarium. The modern rooms boast giant beds. Pay the extra €20 ($23) for a sea view overlooking Kinsale's beautiful harbor and yachting marina — it's worth it. The outdoor breakfast is another nice feature.

*Pier Rd. From the direction of West Cork (Clonakilty), take the N71 to R605.* ☎ *021-477-2135. Fax: 021-477-2231.* www.actonshotelkinsale.com. *Rates: €150–€270 ($173–$311) double. AE, DC, MC, V.*

### Ballylickey Manor
**$$$$  Ballylickey**

One of the few great accommodations overlooking Bantry Bay, this 17th-century manor house boasts an outdoor heated pool and a private fishing area. The five rooms in the manor house and seven cottages around the pool are all decorated in simple country style, and all offer wonderful views of the bay or mountains and the manor's beautiful lawns and gardens.

*Bantry Bay. From Bantry Town, go 4.8km (3 miles) north on the N71 toward Glengarriff. Ballylickey Manor is on the left, facing the water.* ☎ *027-50071. Fax: 027-50-124.* www.ballylickeymanorhouse.com. *Rates: €204–€340 ($235–$391) double. AE, DC, MC, V. Closed Nov–mid-Apr.*

### Blue Haven
**$$$  Kinsale**

There's nothing fishy about this award-winning small hotel, located on the site of Kinsale's old fish market, near the heart of town. The contemporary rooms are bright and uniquely furnished with local crafts, and the staff is friendly and welcoming.

*3–4 Pearse St. Pearse St. becomes Long Quay at the harbor.* ☎ *021-77-2209. Fax: 021-77-4268. Internet:* www.bluehavenkinsale.com. *Rates: €100–€188 ($115–$216) double. AE, DC, MC, V. Closed Jan.*

### Innishannon House Hotel
**$$–$$$  Innishannon**

Innishannon House boasts of being "the most romantic hotel in Ireland." Although the romance pretty much depends on you, the top-shelf wine cellar, fine dining, woodland walks, river's-edge locale, rose garden, and rooms with Irish country-house decor undoubtedly help things along. Boating and private salmon and trout fishing are available.

*Take the N71 west from Cork and east from Clonakilty to Innishannon.* ☎ *021-477-5121. Fax: 021-77-5609.* www.innishannon-hotel.ie. *Rates: €158–€212 ($182–$243) double. AE, DC, MC, V. Closed Nov–mid-March.*

### The Old Presbytery
$$ Kinsale

The uncluttered rooms here are the picture of casual comfort, with beds that are a mass of embroidered white pillows and blankets, unvarnished farmhouse-chic furniture, and large windows. Just to make sure you're totally relaxed, many of the rooms have claw-foot tubs or Jacuzzis (just ask when you book). The staff is warm and friendly, and the guesthouse has a perfect location within a few minutes of the heart of town yet away from the tour-bus hustle and bustle.

*43 Cork St.* ☎ *021-477-2027. Fax: 021-477-2166.* www.oldpres.com. *Rates: €95–€150 ($109–$173). AE, MC, V. Closed Nov–Feb.*

## Dining locally in Kinsale and west County Cork

### Blair's Cove
$$$$ Darrus INTERNATIONAL

For starters, let's talk about the starters — a host of delicious options, arranged buffet-style for you to pick and choose among. Then come the main-course options, mostly fish and meat, all grilled to perfection. And finally, the piano becomes a dessert tray, with a vast array of to-die-for sweet delectables. The Cove is on the water and has an open terrace for summer dining. During the off season, you can have a romantic meal in the candlelit stone barn.

*Barley Rd. 1.6km (1 mile) from Durrus on the road to Barleycove.* ☎ *027-61-127. Reservations recommended. Full dinner €48 ($55), buffet and dessert €38 ($44). MC, V. Open: Apr–June and Sept–Oct Tues–Sat 7:15–9:30 p.m., July–Aug Mon–Sat 7:15–9:30 p.m.*

### Fishy Fishy Café
$$ Kinsale SEAFOOD

Looking for the freshest seafood in town? The shop counter filled with glistening fresh fish and shellfish should indicate that you're in the right place, as should the large metal sculptures of fish and crabs that grace the casual sea- and sky-blue room. The chef handpicks the best of the day's catch each morning and then serves them up in classy but simple dishes that let the flavor of the fish shine. The open-face crab sandwich and the chowder are excellent, but I recommend going for it and polishing off the seafood platter, a banquet of smoked and fresh salmon, mussels, oysters, crab, and langoustines. Don't miss the chickpea spread served with the bread. The secret is out, and they don't take reservations, so come early or late to avoid the crowds — and note that they're only open for lunch.

*Guardwell, next to St. Multoge Church.* ☎ *021-477-4453. Main dishes: €12–€18 ($14–$21). No credit cards. Daily noon–3:45 p.m.*

### Jim Edwards
**$$  Kinsale  PUB GRUB-SEAFOOD**

This cozy bar, with polished wood and nautical decor, serves up mouth-watering, uncomplicated dishes such as rack of lamb, seafood chowder, mussels with garlic crumbs, steaks, and possibly the best crab claws with garlic butter in all of Ireland. There's a popular candlelit restaurant upstairs, but I recommend hanging out in the bar with a pint and some of this superior pub grub.

*Market Quay off Emmet Place.* ☎ *01-477-2541. Main courses: €4–€17 ($4.60–$20). AE, MC, V. Open: Daily 10:30 a.m.–11 p.m.*

### Man Friday
**$$–$$$$  Kinsale  CONTINENTAL-SEAFOOD**

Maybe it's the lantern-style lamps casting a warm glow on the wood-and-stone interior, or maybe it's the cozy banquettes, but something makes you want to linger over dinner at this buzzing romantic restaurant. Maybe it's just that you want to keep eating the fresh, skillfully prepared dishes. The black sole cooked on the bone melts in your mouth, and the steak au poivre is juicy and full of flavor. You'll be licking the shells if you order the mussels stuffed with buttered breadcrumbs and garlic for starters. But then you'd be missing out on the deep-fried brie with plum and port sauce. . .

*On the Scilly Road.* ☎ *021-477-2260. Main courses: €20–€28 ($22–$32). AE, MC, V. Open: Mon–Thurs 6:30–9:30 p.m., Fri–Sat 6:30–10:30 p.m.*

### Mary Ann's
**$$$–$$$$  Skibbereen  SEAFOOD**

Although this place is a traditional 150-year-old pub, Mary Ann's doesn't just serve up the old standards of pub grub. Located in the pleasant small town of Castletownshed, this (along with the Fishy Fishy Café mentioned earlier) is known as *the* place to go for top-notch seafood in West. Popular dishes include fillet of sole with Mornay sauce glaze, scallops meunière, and deep-fried prawns. Also delicious and popular are the local West Cork cheeses.

*Castletownshed. Take the N71 to Skibbereen and go 8.1km (5 miles) south on the Castletownshed Rd. (R596).* ☎ *028-36-146. Main courses: €15–€20 ($17–$23). MC, V. Open: Daily 12:30–2 p.m. and 6–9 p.m.*

### Max's Wine Bar
$$–$$$ **Kinsale** **CONTEMPORARY IRISH**

A meal in this small and unassuming townhouse restaurant, located in the heart of Kinsale, is one of the best gourmet dining experiences you'll have in the area — as a columnist in the *Irish Independent* wrote, "No visit to Kinsale is complete without a visit to Max's." The scallops poached in vermouth and cream are heavenly, and the rack of lamb with red wine and rosemary sauce is unforgettable.

*Main St. ☎ 021-477-2443. Main courses: €18–€26 ($210–$30). MC, V. Open: Daily 12:30–3 p.m. and 6:30–10:30 p.m. Closed Nov–Feb.*

### The Tzar
$$–$$$ **Skibbereen CONTINENTAL-PUB GRUB**

This is a real local's pub, where the regulars go in back of the bar to get their own drinks if the bartenders are occupied. The interior feels like a living room, with plaid curtains and pictures of great sports moments, and you often find a crowd following a game on the television in back. The menu is full of well-done pub classics, including excellent fish and chips, plus some trendy surprises such as a mixed leaf salad with beets, goat cheese, and balsamic vinaigrette. Try the fried local Gubbeen cheese with chile jam. There is a fancier restaurant upstairs, but the bar has much more atmosphere.

*Bridge St. ☎ 028-23-562. Main dishes: €7.95–24 ($9.15–$26). MC, V. Open for food: Daily 12:30–3 p.m. (2:30 p.m. in winter) and 6–9:30 p.m. (9 p.m. in winter).*

## Exploring Kinsale and west County Cork: The top attractions

**Bus Éireann** (☎ 01-836-6111) runs a tour to the town of Bantry, where you depart for a cruise to Cape Clear Island. Tours are given on Saturdays and leave Parnell Place in Cork City at 9:30 a.m., returning at 9:45 p.m. Price is €24 ($28) adults, €20 ($23) seniors and students, and €15 ($17) children.

The **Old Head Golf Links** (☎ 021-477-8444; www.oldheadgolflinks. com) is a brand-new, challenging course located on a stunning outcrop of land surrounded by the Atlantic Ocean, just south of Kinsale. Par is 72, and greens fees are €250 ($288) for 18 holes.

Mizen Head and the Beara Peninsula offer great biking. You can rent a bike from **Roycroft's Stores** (☎ 028-21-235) in Skibbereen.

If you'd like to get out on the water in Kinsale on a *ketch* (a small sailboat), contact **Shearwater Cruises** (☎ 023-496-10).

## Bantry House and Gardens
Bantry

This mostly Georgian house was built in 1750 for the earls of Bantry. The stately home and exquisite Italian gardens overlook Bantry Bay, and every room contains unique tapestries, furniture, and art from around the world. Highlights include the Rose Room, Dining Room, and Rose Garden. If you fall in love with this pleasant brigadoon (and have deep pockets), you can stay overnight in the expensive (€220–€240/$253–$276 per night) B&B. (Call for more information.)

*On N71 between Glengarriff and Skibbereen.* ☎ *027-50-047.* www.bantryhouse. ie. *Admission: €10 ($12) adults, €8 ($9.20) seniors and students, free for kids under 14. Open:Mid March Oct daily 9 a.m.–6 p.m. Suggested visit: 2 hours.*

## Charles Fort
Kinsale

One of Ireland's largest forts, Charles Fort is a star-shaped fortification constructed in the late 17th-century. To get here, you can take the Scilly Walk, a path that curves along the harbor and through woodlands from Kinsale, offering beautiful views of the water. James Fort (1602) is across the river.

*Summer Cove. Scilly Rd. or coastal walk (signposted and called Salmon Walk from Kinsale) starts at Perryville House.* ☎ *021-477-2263. Admission: €3.50 ($4.05) adults, €2.50 ($2.90) seniors, €1.25 ($1.45) students and children. Open: Mid-March to Oct daily 10 a.m.–6 p.m., Nov to mid-March daily 10 a.m.–5 p.m. Restricted access for the disabled due to uneven terrain. Suggested visit: About 1 hour.*

## Garinish Island

This little island is an amazing sight — an Italian garden of rare trees and shrubs set along walkways and pools, and all sitting out in the sea on an uninhabited 37-acre island. Before the owner brought over hundreds of tons of topsoil to grow the exotic plants, the island was bare rock. Half the fun is the short journey getting there on one of the small ferries that serve the island.

*The Blue Pool Ferry (☎ 027-63-333) leaves from the harbor in Glengarriff every half-hour or so and takes 15 minutes to reach the island. Round-trip is €7 ($8.05).* ☎ *027-63-040. Admission: €3.50 ($4.05) adults, €2.50 ($2.90) seniors, €1.25 ($1.45) children and students. Open: June Mon–Sat 10 a.m.–6:30 p.m., Sun 11 a.m.–6:30 p.m.; July–Aug Mon–Sat 9:30–6:30 p.m., Sun 11:30–6:30 p.m.; May and Sept Mon–Sat 10 a.m.–6:30 p.m., Sun noon to 6:30 p.m.; Apr Mon–Sat 10 a.m.–6:30 p.m., Sun 1–6:30 p.m.; March and Oct Mon–Sat 10 a.m.–4:30 p.m., Sun 1–5 p.m. Closed Nov–Feb. Suggested visit: 1½ hours, including ferry trip.*

### Mizen Head

The Visitor Centre and the Fog Signal Station on the very tip of this point are exciting additions to an already popular spot, where you get priceless views of the wild Atlantic waves and the jagged rocks of Ireland's southwesternmost point. You can traverse the famous suspension bridge over craggy cliffs and sea, and climb to the top of Mizen Head. The lightkeeper's house and engine room have been converted into a museum about lightkeepers and the flora and fauna of Mizen Head; the video about lightkeeping is interesting, but the museum itself is a little down at the heels. Set down as far as you can go on the Bantry Peninsula, Mizen Head seems a little out of the way, but the drive from the east is gorgeous, all beautiful beaches and green hills.

*Mizen Head. From Skibbereen, the drive is about an hour. Take the N71 to the R592 in Ballydehop to the R591 in Toomore and follow the signs for Mizen Head. (You don't really know you're on the R591. You begin seeing signs for Mizen back in Skibbereen, and you basically just follow the signs to get there.)* ☎ *028-35-115 or 028-35-591. Admission: €3.50 ($4.05) adults, €2.25 ($2.60) students and seniors, €1.75 ($2) under 12, free for under 5, €9 ($10.35) family of two adults and three children. Open: June–Sept daily 10 a.m.–6 p.m.; mid-March to May and Oct daily 10:30 a.m.–5 p.m.; Nov to mid-March Sat–Sun 11 a.m.–5 p.m. Suggested visit: 30 minutes.*

## Shopping

**Boland's Irish Craft Shop,** Pearse Street, Kinsale (☎ 021-477-2161), offers a variety of items: Aran vests, Kinsale smocks, ceramic sheep, and miniature paintings. **Granny's Bottom Drawer,** 53 Main St., Kinsale (☎ 021-477-4839), sells traditional linen and lace: pillowcases, placemats, tablecloths, and more, all handwoven with delicate care. **Heather Mountain,** 15 Market St. (☎ 021-477-3384), sells a good selection of Aran sweaters and other Irish-made clothing. **Kinsale Crystal,** Market Street (☎ 021-477-4993), sells faceted crystal pieces that positively glow. **O'Kane's Craft Shop,** Glengarriff Road, Bantry (☎ 027-50-003), offers the best of everything: pottery by Nicholas Mosse and Stephen Pearse; glass by Jerpoint Glass Studio; silver jewelry by Linda Uhleman; plus candles, leatherwork, baskets, and more.

## Hitting the pubs

Also see The Tzar, reviewed in "Dining locally in Kinsale and west County Cork," earlier in this chapter.

### The Bulman

This pub offers a stunning view of Kinsale Harbor, excellent seafood dishes, a warm stone interior, crackling fires, and great traditional Irish music on most nights. What more could you want?

*On Scilly Rd. on the way to Charles Fort from Kinsale.* ☎ *021-477-3359.*

### The Cordoba (Kieran's Folk House Inn)

Who doesn't come to Kieran's? This place is popular with both locals and visitors (a rare combination in itself), as well as with the angling and diving crowds. Small but vivacious, it really kicks up on the weekends, when live music is featured. If you're hungry, try one of the Bacchus Brasserie's delicious dishes (it's only open April to Oct).

*Guardwell.* ☎ *021-477-2382.*

 ### De Barra

From top to bottom and inside and out, everything about this lovely traditional pub is authentic. The musicians hail from the local Irish-speaking area (called a *Gaeltacht*), and the decor is hand-painted signs and old-fashioned whiskey jars. People come from far and wide to enjoy the ambience of one of County Cork's finest pubs.

*Main St.* ☎ *023-33-381.*

### Lord Kingsale

A classic black-and-white-exterior pub, Lord Kingsale is a romantic little spot, with small snug areas, live music in weekends, and even poetry readings. Delicious home-cooked food is served all day long, and a comfortable, lived-in atmosphere draws a pleasant, subdued crowd.

*4 Main St.* ☎ *021-477-2371.*

### The 1601

The front bar is essentially a memorial to the town's most famous battle, and the back bar doubles as an art gallery. The pub-grub menu is always changing, but the locals assure me that it never falls short of superb. Modern and traditional music plays on Mondays and Tuesdays. The Irish lost the Battle of 1601, but this great bar reminds us who won the war.

*Pearse St.* ☎ *021-477-2529.*

 ### The Spaniard

The best part of the Spaniard is the outdoor seating that overlooks the harbor. Inside are cozy turf and log fires and traditional, jazz, folk, and blues music. This fisherman-theme pub is built over the ruins of a castle and named in honor of Don Juan del Aquila, commander of the Spanish fleet and ally to the Irish during the Battle of Kinsale in 1601.

*Scilly Rd.* ☎ *021-77-2436.*

## *Fast Facts: Kinsale and West County Cork*

### Area Codes

Kinsale and West County Cork's area codes (or city codes) are 021, 027, and 028.

### Emergencies/Police

Dial ☎ **999** for all emergencies.

### Information

A seasonal tourist office in Kinsale, on Pier Road (☎ 021-477-2234; www.kinsale.ie), is open March through November. In Skibbereen, there is a tourist office at North Street (☎ 028-21-766) that's open year-round.

### Internet

Finishing Services Internet Bureau, 71 Main St., Kinsale (☎ 021-477-3571), offers Internet access.

# Chapter 16

# County Kerry

. . . . . . . . . . . . . . . . . . . . . . . . . . . . . . . . . . . . . . . . .

## In This Chapter

▶ Exploring beautiful Killarney National Park

▶ Taking in the cliffs, sea, and mountains of the Ring of Kerry

▶ Walking, biking, or driving around the gorgeous Dingle Peninsula

▶ Hanging out (perhaps with a dolphin) in funky Dingle Town

. . . . . . . . . . . . . . . . . . . . . . . . . . . . . . . . . . . . . . . . .

County Kerry, shown on the nearby map, is not nicknamed *The Kingdom* for nothing. The county encompasses some of the most famous and stunning natural sights in Ireland, including the Ring of Kerry, the Dingle Peninsula, and Killarney. You'll find sea cliffs, rolling green hills, charming seaside villages, and aquamarine lakes. This area has long been one of the centers of Gaelic culture — many people speak Gaelic as their first language here, and the traditional Irish music and crafts scenes are thriving. Sound like a place you'd like to go? A lot of other people think so, too, making County Kerry one of the most-visited areas in Ireland. During the summer, the towns of Killarney and Kenmare swarm with visitors. If this is not your thing, my advice is to plan your vacation for the spring or fall — or, even better, take some turns off the well-trodden tourist trails. I provide some off-the-beaten-track options in this chapter, such as a mountain drive on the Dingle Peninsula and a hidden farmhouse off the Ring of Kerry.

## Killarney and Killarney National Park

Though Killarney itself doesn't have a ton of attractions, it makes an excellent base for exploring gorgeous Killarney National Park and for beginning or ending your tour of the Ring of Kerry. Killarney swarms with visitors in the summer, meaning that you can get everything you need, but you'll need to wait in line with everyone else visiting the area. The "Killarney" map can help you with locations.

### Getting to Killarney

To get to Killarney by car, take the N21 southwest from Limerick or the N22 northwest from Cork. From the Ring of Kerry and West Cork, take the N70. To get to Tralee from Killarney, take the N22 north. To continue on to Dingle, take the N86 from Tralee. The tip of the Dingle Peninsula

## County Kerry

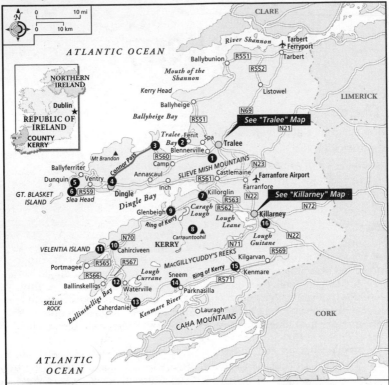

| ACCOMMODATIONS | DINING | SHOPPING |
|---|---|---|
| | | |

**ACCOMMODATIONS**
Alpine House **4**
Blackstones House **8**
The Captain's House **4**
Carhoomeengar
  Farmhouse **15**
Foley's **15**
Greenmount House **4**
Oakley House **1**
The Park Hotel Kenmare **15**
Pax House **4**
Scarriff Inn **13**
Sea Shore Farm **15**
Slea Head Farm **6**
Towers Hotel **9**

**DINING**
Beginish Restaurant **4**
The Blue Bull **14**
d'Arcy's **15**
Doyle's Seafood Bar **4**
The Forge Restaurant **4**
Out of the Blue **4**
Packies **15**
Purple Heather **15**

**ATTRACTIONS**
Ballybunion Golf Club **5**
Blasket Centre **5**
Derrynane House National
  Historic Park **13**
Fungie the Dolphin boat
  docks **4**
Kerry Bog Village Museum **9**
Killarney National Park **16**
Seafari Scenic and Wildlife
  Cruises **15**
The Skellig Experience **11**
Tralee Golf Club **2**
Waterville Golf Links **12**

**SHOPPING**
Annascaul Pottery **4**
Brian de Staic **4**
Cleo **15**
Dingle Bodhráns **4**
Nostalgia **15**
Quills Woolen Market **15**
West Kerry Craft Guild **4**

**NIGHTLIFE**
Bianconi **7**
Caitin Baiters **10**
Dick Mack's **4**
The Dingle Pub **4**
Natterjack **3**
O'Flaherty's **4**
The Point Bar **10**

can be driven via the R559, beginning and ending in Dingle. **Irish Rail** (☎ **064-31-067;** www.irishrail.ie) serves Killarney from Dublin, Limerick, Cork, and Galway. Trains arrive daily at the Killarney Railway Station, Railway Road, off East Avenue Road. **Bus Éireann** (☎ **064-34-777;** www.buseireann.ie) comes into Killarney from all over Ireland. The bus depot is next to the train station.

## Getting around Killarney

This compact town is entirely walkable. The **Tourist Trail** takes you past the highlights of the town: Just follow the signs, or get a pamphlet about the trail at the tourist office (see "Fast Facts: Killarney," later in this chapter, for the address). If you have a rental car with you, I recommend just parking it at your hotel until you're ready for a day-trip to Killarney National Park. Most accommodations offer free parking for guests, but there's also street parking and parking lots. During the day you need to display a parking disc in your car; discs are available at shops and hotels. There's no bus service within the town, but you can get a taxi at the taxi rank on College Square. For taxi pick-up, call **Dero's Taxi Service** (☎ **064-31-251**) or **O'Connell Taxi** (☎ **064-31-654**). For information on getting around Killarney National Park, see "Exploring Killarney National Park," later in this chapter.

## Spending the night in Killarney

### Arbutus Hotel
$$$ **Killarney**

This hotel in the center of town has a traditional Irish feel to it, with cozy chairs arranged around a turf fire in the lobby. Rooms (especially those on the second floor) are large and tastefully furnished. The downstairs Buckley's Pub has an oak-paneled bar, and local opinion says that the bartenders there pull the best pint of Guinness in town. Good traditional music fills the air nightly. The Arbutus is a family-run hotel (three generations of the Buckley family have pitched in since the hotel was opened), and the entire staff is friendly and willing to help with anything.

*College St. From Main St., turn onto Plunkett St. (it only goes one way). Plunkett becomes College, and the hotel is at the roundabout where College meets Lewis Rd.* ☎ *064-31-037. Fax: 064-34-033.* www.arbutuskillarney.com. *Rates: €130–€220 ($150–$253) double. AE, DC, MC, V.*

### Great Southern Hotel Killarney
$$$ **Killarney**

With its manor-house style, the Great Southern doesn't look like part of a chain, even though it is (the Great Southern Hotel company owns and operates nine properties). The Victorian decor in the public rooms is polished and ornate, with detailed plasterwork, chandeliers, and inviting fireplaces. The rooms are large and traditionally furnished, and overlook the

## Killarney

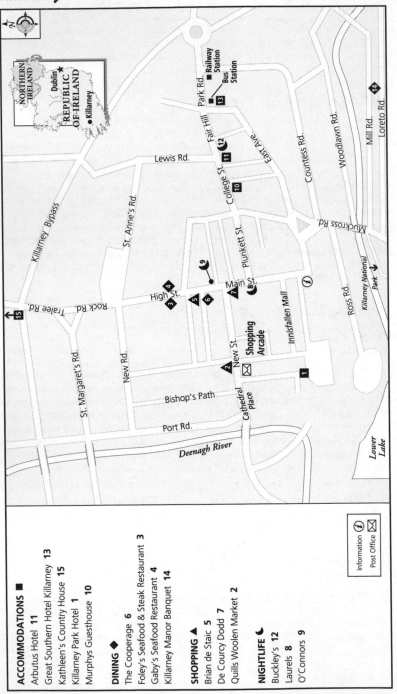

**ACCOMMODATIONS** ■
Arbutus Hotel **11**
Great Southern Hotel Killarney **13**
Kathleen's Country House **15**
Killarney Park Hotel **1**
Murphys Guesthouse **10**

**DINING** ◆
The Cooperage **6**
Foley's Seafood & Steak Restaurant **3**
Gaby's Seafood Restaurant **4**
Killarney Manor Banquet **14**

**SHOPPING** ▲
Brian de Staic **5**
De Courcy Dodd **7**
Quills Woolen Market **2**

**NIGHTLIFE** ☾
Buckley's **12**
Laurels **8**
O'Connors **9**

ⓘ Information
⊠ Post Office

hotel's lush, gorgeously landscaped 8-hectare (20-acre) grounds. The hotel has an abundance of amenities, including a leisure center with pool and Jacuzzi, a cocktail bar, and a new full-service spa. You'll feel completely isolated from the world, even though the hotel's just a short walk from the center of town.

*Railway Rd., off East Avenue Rd. between the railway station and the Tourist Office.* ☎ *850-38-38-48 or 064-31-262. Fax: 064-31-642.* www.gshotels.com. *Rates: €120–€200 ($138–$230) double. AE, DC, MC, V.*

## Kathleen's Country House
### $$ Killarney

This is the top choice for those who are country mice rather than city mice. Kathleen's is located about 1.6km (1 mile) out of Killarney, on large grounds filled with gardens. The bright, recently renovated rooms are furnished with antique furniture and original contemporary art. Kathleen herself is warm, friendly, and always willing to help.

*Madam's Height, Tralee Rd. (N22).* ☎ *064-32-810. Fax: 064-32-340.* www.kathleens.net. *€95–€130 ($109–$150) double. AE, MC, V. Closed mid-Nov–early March.*

## Killarney Park Hotel
### $$$$ Killarney

Every inch of this luxurious hotel is a study in old-world elegance. This is the place for people who want comfort, class, and refinement. The Victorian-style lobby has many plush couches and armchairs surrounding open fires, and there's a fully stocked library where you can plan out your day over a cup of tea. The Garden Bar maintains the country-house style, with wood everywhere and strategically placed fireplaces and snugs, and breakfast is served in a vaulted dining room complete with large oil portraits and plush, high-backed chairs. Guest rooms are spacious and tastefully furnished with antiques and attractive fabrics. This hotel is definitely worth a splurge. Kids are welcome, and a few family rooms are available.

*Kenmare Place between the railway station and the Cineplex.* ☎ *064-35-555. Fax: 064-35-266.* www.killarneyparkhotel.ie. *Rates: €240–€360 ($276–$414) double. AE, DC, MC, V.*

## Murphys Guesthouse
### $$ Killarney

The rooms here, though clean and large, are pretty generic. But you're not paying for top-of-the-line interior design here; you're paying for a superb location. The hotel is in the heart of town and is conveniently located right above an excellent pub, so at the end of the night, after a few pints and some traditional music, you can crawl upstairs to your bed. Service is helpful and professional.

18 College St. Go through the roundabout and down College St. ☎ *064-31-294.* Fax: 064-31-294. www.murphysbar.com. *Rates: €90–€100 double. ($104–$115). AE, DC, MC, V.*

## Dining locally in Killarney

### The Cooperage
$$ **Killarney** NEW IRISH

This hip, urban eatery looks like it could have come out of New York or London, and the creative cuisine does justice to the modern surroundings. The menu runs the gamut from vegetarian options to steak options, but the stars here are the wild game and seafood dishes, including such offerings as venison, pheasant, and sea trout.

Old Market Lane, off High St. ☎ *064-33-716.* Reservations recommended. Main courses: €14–€22 ($16–$25). MC, V. Mon–Sat 12:30–3 p.m., Mon–Thurs 6:30–9:30 p.m., Fri–Sat 6:30–10 p.m., Sun 4–9:30 p.m.

### Foley's Seafood & Steak Restaurant
$$$ **Killarney** SEAFOOD-IRISH

The elegant black-and-white exterior of Foley's is a good indicator of the classy interior. Though it's primarily a seafood restaurant, the meat dishes are very good too. The menu changes all the time, but look for the duck or pheasant and the steak with garlic butter. Foley's also serves several excellent vegetarian dishes. Whatever you choose, be sure to take advantage of the homemade brown bread. The wine list here boasts more than 200 selections.

23 High St. ☎ *064-31-217.* Main courses: €16–€25 ($18–$29). AE, DC, MC, V. Open: 12:30–3 p.m. and 5–11 p.m.

### Gaby's Seafood Restaurant
$$$$ **Killarney** SEAFOOD

The finest seafood in Killarney is served here. Gaby's is well known for its lobster dishes, but the Kerry shellfish platter takes the cake (or maybe the crab cake?), with prawns, mussels, lobster, scallops, and oysters. The rustic brickwork and wooden floors make for pleasant surroundings. The excellent food is complemented by the diverse wine list from Gaby's cellar. You're practically guaranteed a great meal — in fact, you may be so satisfied that you won't mind what it costs you.

27 High St. ☎ *064-32-519.* Main courses: €25–€30 ($29–$35). AE, DC, MC, V. Open: Mon–Sat 6–10 p.m. Closed late Feb to mid-March and Christmas week.

### Killarney Manor Banquet
$$$$ **Killarney IRISH**

"Lord and Lady Killarney" cordially invite you to a 19th-century-style five-course banquet in their 1840s manor. The food is quite good, and the entertainment — a program of song, dance, and ballads — is even better. The mansion is beautifully situated, overlooking Killarney.

*Loreto Rd. about 3km (2 miles) out of town. ☎ 064-31-551. Reservations required. AE, DC, MC, V. Open nightly April–Oct. Dinner is served at 7:45 p.m. Entertainment begins at 9 p.m. The cost is €40 ($46) for dinner and entertainment, €15 ($17) for entertainment only.*

## Exploring Killarney

Killarney is basically a fine place to sleep and eat while absorbing the majestic beauty of nearby Killarney National Park. The few interesting attractions in Killarney Town include St. Mary's Cathedral on Cathedral Place, off Port Road and St. Mary's Church on Church Place, across from the tourist office, but mostly you find good restaurants, lodgings, and pubs and an assortment of shops selling souvenirs of the leprechaun-sitting-on-a-horseshoe-holding-a-shamrock variety.

The **Killarney Tourist Trail** takes you to the highlights, keeping you on track through a series of signposts. The tour begins at the Killarney of the Welcomes Tourist Office at the Town Centre Car Park on Beech Road (☎ 064-31-633) and takes about two hours if you walk at a leisurely pace.

## Exploring Killarney National Park

Killarney National Park (see the nearby map) is a place of sapphire lakes studded with grass-covered islands, heather-covered mountains towering above bogs, lush forests filled with rhododendron, and paths leading through rocky gaps threaded with ribbons of stream. A well-defined (but occasionally dippy and curvy) road winds through part of the park past the three main lakes, but much of the land is accessible only by hiking, biking, horseback-riding, or riding in a horse-drawn jaunting car. If you decide to drive along the road, make time to stop at the various viewpoints, and park your car to take some short walks into the park. Without stopping, the drive takes just over an hour, but you should give it at least half a day, because there's so much to see.

The main entrance and visitor center is at **Muckross House** (☎ 064-31-440). Admission to the park is free, and the park is open during daylight hours.

### Exploring the park by foot, bicycle, or horseback

If you're looking to explore on your own, pick up *Simple Pocket Maps for Walkers and Cyclists in Killarney* at the Killarney of the Welcomes

## Killarney National Park

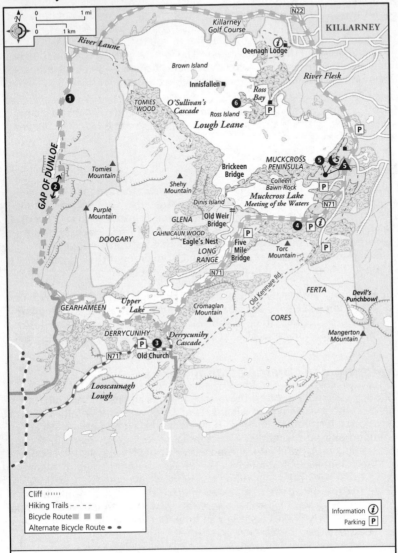

**ATTRACTIONS** ■
The Gap of Dunloe **2**
Kate Kearney's Cottage **1**
Ladies View **3**
Muckross House & Gardens **5**
Muckross Traditional Farms **5**
Ross Castle **6**
Torc Waterfall **4**

**SHOPPING** ▲
Mucros Craft Centre **5**

**NIGHTLIFE** ☾
Molly Darcy's **5**

office or the Killarney Tourist office at Town Hall (see "Fast Facts: Killarney," later in this chapter). These concise color maps guide you into some of the area's hidden and delightful scenery.

✔ **By foot:** There are four signposted trails in the park, including the 2.4km (1.5-mile) Blue Pool Nature trail, which winds through woodlands and past a small lake; the Old Boat House Nature Trail, which travels half a mile near Muckross Lake; the 2.4km (1.5-mile) Mossy Woods Nature Trail, which takes you through woods along low cliffs; and the 4.8km (3-mile) Arthur Young's Walk, which takes you through forest and along the Muckross Peninsula. The visitor center at Muckross House can provide maps of the trails.

✔ **By bicycle:** You can rent a bicycle at **David O'Sullivan's Cycles,** Bishop Lane, New Street (☎ 064-31-282).

✔ **By horseback:** You can hire a horse from **Killarney Riding Stables,** N72, Ballydowney (☎ 064-31-686), or **Muckross Riding Stables,** Mangerton Road, Muckross (☎ 064-32-238).

## Joining an organized tour

If you want to add some structure to your explorations, check out the organized tours in the following list:

✔ **Dero's Killarney National Park Bus Tour:** This three-hour bus tour takes you to all the highlights of Killarney National Park, including Ross Castle, Muckross House and Gardens, Torc Waterfall, Aghadoe, and the Gap of Dunloe.

Where and when: May to September daily at 2:30 p.m. (call to confirm). Departs from Dero's Tours office at 7 Main St., Killarney. Information: ☎ 064-31-251. Price: €15 ($17.25) per person.

✔ **Gap of Dunloe and Lakes of Killarney Tour:** This is a terrific, though touristy, way to see the spectacular Kerry mountains up close and personal. A bus takes you to **Kate Kearney's Cottage,** which was once an inn run by famed local beauty Kate Kearney and is now a craft shop. From there, a horse or a pony cart takes you through the beautiful Gap of Dunloe. You lunch at Lord Brandon's Cottage and then hop on a boat for a tour of the Lakes of Killarney. Finally, you stop at Ross Castle before taking a bus back to town. It takes a full day and really is an adventure.

Where and when: Runs May through September (call for times). Information: 7 High St. ☎ 064-30-200. Price: €18 ($21) per person for bus and boat (plus a small fee for lunch).

✔ **Jaunting-Car Tour:** These horse-drawn buggies are as much a part of Killarney as the lakes and mountains. The drivers will take you through the town or as far as the Gap of Dunloe, and they go into Killarney National Park as far as Muckross House and Torc Waterfall. The drivers are characters, and pretty persuasive — even if you had no intention of taking one, you could find yourself bouncing in the back of a buggy with a blanket snug around your legs. This adventure is best undertaken in the off season, when the Gap of Dunloe is quieter and, thus, much more magical.

Where and when: You can find jaunting cars all over town — or, rather, they'll find you. If you want to book in advance, call Tangney Tours at ☎ 064-33-345, though you won't have a problem finding a car in town on a moment's notice. Price: It's not as though the carts have cab meters, so ask the tourist office or your hotel what to expect. The going rate is €35 to €55 ($40–$63) per car (up to four people can be taken in one car). To be on the safe side, have the driver quote a price before heading out.

✔ **M.V. Pride of the Lakes Waterbus Tour:** This tour takes you around Lough Leane, Killarney's largest lake, in a luxurious passenger cruiser.

Where and when: Tours leave from the pier at Ross Castle, from March to October at 11 a.m., 12:30 p.m., 2:30 p.m., 4 p.m., and 5:15 p.m. and last about an hour. ☎ 064-32638. Price: €8 ($9.20) adults, €4 (4.60) children.

If you get a yen to do the golf thing while you're in the midst of all this green, visit the **Killarney Golf and Fishing Club.** Home of the 1991 and 1992 Irish Open Championship, this course is nestled among the beautiful Lakes of Killarney and below the majestic Macgillycuddy's Reeks Mountains. It's on Mahony's Point, Killarney (☎ 064-31-034; www.killarney-golf.com). Par is 72, and the greens fees are €75 ($86) for two of the three courses and €50 ($58) for the other. Visitors are welcome every day but Sunday.

## Touring Killarney National Park

### Gap of Dunloe

This breathtaking valley is bound on either side by craggy glacial rocks and soaring cliffs, and passes streams and lakes of a deep blue. The gap is accessible only by horse-and-cart, by foot, on horseback, or by bicycle (see the previous two sections for tips on how to traverse the gap). The best time to take the journey is during the off season, when a quiet peace descends on an area that can be overcrowded during July and August.

### Ladies View

Ladies View looks out on an exhilarating panorama of the surrounding mountains and the three lakes. How did it get its name? In the 1800s, Queen Victoria of England made a trip to Killarney and took her entourage through what is now the National Park. The queen's ladies-in-waiting were so overcome with the view from this particular spot that they stopped to gaze at the surroundings.

*Off N71 near the Upper Lake.*

## Muckross House and Gardens

This Victorian mansion is one of Ireland's finest stately manors. The decor and furnishings of the upper part of the home illustrate the lifestyle of the mid-19th-century gentry. The basement portrays the harsher environment that the domestic servants endured. A craft center here houses artisans working at traditional crafts such as weaving, bookbinding, and pottery making. The beautiful gardens are known for their rhododendrons and azaleas. Unfortunately, there is restricted accessibility for the disabled.

*Take Kenmare Road (N71) out of Killarney.* ☎ *064-31-440.* www.muckross-house. ie. *Admission: Muckross House and Gardens alone are €5.50 ($6.35) adults, €4.25 ($4.90) seniors, €2.25 ($2.60) children and students. Combined ticket for house, gardens, and traditional farms (see the next review) are €8.25 ($9.50) adults, €6.25 ($7.20) seniors, €3.75 ($4.30) children and students. Open: Mid-March–June and Sept–Oct daily 9 a.m.–6 p.m.; July–Aug daily 9 a.m.–7 p.m.; Nov–mid-March daily 9 a.m.–5:30 p.m. Suggested visit: 1½ hours.*

## Muckross Traditional Farms

Turn off your cellphone, forget that you stayed in a hotel with electric lighting last night, and immerse yourself in the world of 19th-century rural Ireland. Farms of three sizes (small, medium, and large) occupy the pretty grounds and are populated by folks in period dress who go about their daily tasks: milking cows, cutting hay, gathering eggs from the chickens, harvesting potatoes, baking bread, and so on. You also find a carpenter's workshop, a saddler's workshop, and a blacksmith's forge, all in operation. You are invited to step inside the farmhouses to enjoy home baking in front of the turf fires, to join the farmers in their tasks, and to watch the craftsmen at work. And of course, you are welcome to ask the farmers and workers any questions you may have. The farm, housekeeping, and workshop labor is carried out with such skill and nonchalance that even the most cynical visitors should feel as though they've somehow been transported to a country village in the 19th century.

*Take Kenmare Road (N71) out of Killarney.* ☎ *064-31-440.* www.muckross-house. ie. *Admission: Farm admission alone is €5.50 ($6.35) adults, €4.25 ($4.90) seniors, €2.25 ($2.60) children and students. Combined ticket for traditional farms with the house and gardens (see the previous review) are €8.25 ($9.50) adults, €6.25 ($7.20) seniors, €3.75 ($4.30) children and students. Open: June–Sept daily 10 a.m.– 6 p.m.; May daily 1–6 p.m.; mid-March–April and Oct Sat–Sun 1–6 p.m. Suggested visit: 1 to 2 hours.*

## Ross Castle

This fortified castle was built by the O'Donoghue chieftains, probably during the 15th century, and was the last stronghold in the province of Munster to surrender to Cromwell in 1652. What remains today is a huge tower house, surrounded by a wall with four smaller towers at each corner — clearly, fortification was a priority. Inside the tower is an admirable collection of furniture from the 16th and 17th centuries. The castle sits on a peninsula that projects into Lough Leane, Killarney's largest lake. The *M.V. Pride of the Lakes* (see the previous section, "Joining an organized tour") and other boats leave to explore the lake from the castle. The boat tour to Innisfallen Island, where you can see monastery ruins, is particularly magnificent. You can also take a pretty lakeside walk between Killarney Town and the castle.

*Ross Rd. ☎ 064-35-851. Head south from town on Ross Road. Admission: €5 ($5.75) adults, €3.50 ($4.05) seniors, €2 ($2.30) children and students. Open: March 5–14 Tues–Sun 9:30 a.m.–5:30 p.m., mid-March–May and Sept–mid-Oct daily 9:30 a.m.– 5:30 p.m., June–Aug daily 9 a.m.–6:30 p.m.; mid-Oct–mid-Nov Tues–Sun 9:30 a.m.– 4:30 p.m. Suggested visit: 1 hour.*

### Torc Waterfall

This powerful waterfall is just off N71, near Muckross House and Gardens. You can see the waterfall after a short walk on the lower path, but climb the stone stairs for an even better view of the falls and the surrounding mountains.

*Take the lower path from Muckross House.*

## Shopping in Killarney

**Avoca Handweavers,** Molls Gap (in Killarney National Park off the N71; ☎ 064-34-720), has a huge selection of sweaters and tweeds for men and women. You also find unique pottery, jewelry, and crafts, as well as plenty of souvenirs. The handcrafted jewelry at **Brian de Staic,** 18 High St. (☎ 066-33-822), ranks among the most respected in Ireland. Goldsmith de Staic is renowned for his work, which captures the best of Celtic design. **De Courcy Dodd,** 68 New St. (☎ 064-31-351), sells antiques of all kinds, for everyone from serious collectors to hobbyists. **Mucros Craft Centre,** Muckross House (☎ 064-31-400), features all sorts of Irish crafts. If you're in the market for sweaters and handknits, **Quills Woollen Market,** 3 New St. (☎ 064-32-277), is the place for you. From cardigans to pullovers, you find the finest Irish knitwear here.

## Hitting the pubs

Also see Killarney Manor Banquet (reviewed in "Dining locally in Killarney," earlier in this chapter) for a nighttime entertainment option.

### Buckley's
**Killarney**

Locals say this pub pulls the best pint of Guinness in town. The interior is oak-paneled, and turf fires burn, making it cozy and welcoming. As the story goes, publican Tim Buckley spent some time in New York but in the 1920s returned to Ireland because he deeply missed his hometown. He created this pub to combine all the great things he missed about Ireland while in the United States; maybe that's why it exudes Irish comfort. Pub grub is served all day, and you can find traditional music every night during the summer.

*College St. ☎ 064-31-037.*

# Irish slang translation: Yer man

If you tour around Ireland for a while, you'll probably hear people referring to *yer man* (as in, "I was talking to *yer man* the other day . . ."). You may well wonder who this incredibly popular person is. Well, he's the fella Americans call *this guy* (for example, "I was talking to this guy the other day . . .") and British call "this bloke". You may also hear yer man's feminine counterpart, *yer won.*

## Laurels
**Killarney**

If you stick around until the music begins at 9 p.m., you'll understand why Con O'Leary's place has been dubbed "The Singing Pub." Irish ballad singers are booked every night, making for a convivial, jovial atmosphere. *Main St. ☎ 064-31-149.*

## Molly Darcy's
**Killarney**

This cozy, traditional pub with stone walls, a beamed ceiling, and a thatched roof is the perfect place to hunker down with a pint. *Muckross Rd. In the Muckross Hotel complex across from Muckross House. ☎ 064-34973.*

## O'Connors
**Killarney**

Wood from floor to ceiling, stools and tables low to the floor, and beautiful stained glass characterize this friendly pub, which has been run by the O'Connor family for three generations. Good soup and sandwiches are served all day. *7 High St. ☎ 064-31-115.*

# Fast Facts: Killarney

**Area Code**

Most numbers have the area code 064.

**Emergencies/Police**

Dial ☎ 999 for all emergencies.

**Genealogical Resources**

Visit the Killarney Genealogical Centre, Cathedral Walk, Killarney.

## Hospital

Killarney Community Hospital is on St. Margaret's Road (☎ 064-31-076).

## Information

For visitor information, go to Killarney of the Welcomes Tourist Office, on Beech Road (☎ 064-31-633), open year-round. A great resource is the free publication *Kerry Gems,* which includes useful information such as maps, events, and entertainment. It's available at most hotels and guesthouses in town.

## Internet Access

The funky Rí-Rá Internet Café is on Plunkett Street (☎ 064-38-729), and there is free Internet access at Killarney Library, on Rock Road (☎ 064-32-655).

## Post Office

The Killarney Post Office (☎ 064-31-051) is on New Street.

# The Ring of Kerry and the Iveragh Peninsula

The Ring of Kerry, a 176km (110-mile) circuit around the Iveragh Peninsula, is one of the most popular routes in Ireland. And there are good reasons for its renown: The winding route provides thrilling, dramatic views of the sea and the high inland mountains, and passes through a succession of charming villages, each with its own unique points of interest.

See the Cheat Sheet at the front of this book for a map of the Ring of Kerry.

## Getting to and around the Ring of Kerry

By car, take the N70 south from Tralee or the N71 southwest from Killarney. A car is the best way to get to the Ring of Kerry and the best way to see it all. **Bus Éireann (☎ 064-34-777)** has limited service from Killarney to Cahersiveen, Waterville, Kenmare, and a few other towns on the Ring. In addition, Bus Éireann runs a Ring of Kerry day trip from Cork (see the introductory text in "Exploring the Iveragh Peninsula and the Ring of Kerry," later in this chapter).

The Ring of Kerry is short enough to drive in a single day, but there are lots of things to see and do throughout the peninsula, and there are many places to spend the night, so I recommend taking two days for the drive.

## Spending the night on the Iveragh Peninsula and the Ring of Kerry

### Blackstones House
$ Glencar

You may feel as though you're staying in a friend's house at this cozy farmhouse B&B, located in the mountains next to a rushing river. There are no locks on the bedroom doors, and guests can snuggle up with a book and a pot of tea in the family living room or hang out with one of the dogs while sitting at the picnic table in front of the house. Rooms are modern and have a ski-lodge feel to them, with knotty-pine furniture and original watercolors. All rooms have spectacular views of the swift river that runs through the property (fishing equipment is available at the house), backed by rounded mountains. Hiking opportunities abound, and there are several golf courses nearby, though the isolated location won't suit you if pub-crawling is a priority. Your hosts, Padraig and Breda Breen, are sweet, friendly, and helpful.

*Outside Glencar off the Killorglin Rd.* ☎ ***066-976-0164.*** *Rates: €60 ($69) double. No credit cards. Closed Nov–March.*

### Carhoomeengar Farmhouse
$   **Kenmare**

This is a gem of a farmhouse B&B. John and Maureen Harris have restored this pretty yellow-trimmed home into a warm and welcoming respite after touring the Ring of Kerry. The rooms are nice enough (small, but cute and homey in a grandmotherly sort of way), the house is full of antiques, and the views of Kenmare Bay are lovely. A golf course is nearby, so you can practice your swing. The extensive breakfast menu boasts delicious organic farm produce, and the grounds host some rare breeds of poultry, but the main draw is an excellent price for what you get: a little bit of home.

*Carhoomeengar East. About 6km (4 miles) from Kenmare on the N71.* ☎ ***064-41-987.*** *Rates: €55–€64 ($63–$74) double. No credit cards. Open Easter through Sept.*

### Foley's
$$   **Kenmare**

This small B&B has everything: location, food, music, drink, and comfort, all for a reasonable price. Set in the heart of Kenmare, Foley's is located within walking distance of golf, horseback riding, and fishing. The downstairs pub is cozy and welcoming, and has excellent traditional Irish music most nights.

*Henry St. where the N70 and N71 meet.* ☎ ***064-42-162.*** *Rates: €75–€100 ($86–$115) double. MC, V.*

### The Park Hotel Kenmare
$$$$   **Kenmare**

This grand hotel is beautifully situated, with lawns running down to Kenmare Bay and gorgeous views of the Caha Mountains in the distance. And that's just the outside. The interior is all luxury, all the time, with open fireplaces, high ceilings, rich upholstery, and stunning antiques. Spacious rooms are decorated with sumptuous fabrics and Victorian or Georgian furnishings, and some even boast canopy or four-poster beds. Service is warm and welcoming. The hotel's restaurant serves excellent modern Irish cuisine.

*On the R569 in Kenmare, past the golf club.* ☎ *800-323-5463 in the U.S. or 064-41-200. Fax: 064-41-402.* www.parkkenmare.com. *Rates: €260–€395 ($299–$454). AE, DC, MC, V. Closed Nov–Dec 22 and Jan 3–March.*

### Scarriff Inn
### $$    Caherdaniel

You get a fantastic view of Derrynane Harbor from this family-run inn, located on the Ring of Kerry and offering a perfect place to rest your weary head after a long day of sightseeing. A seafood restaurant offers full meals or just nibblers and even has a bar. If you decide to stay for a while, you can explore the countryside from here. Whether it's fishing, diving, or plain relaxation you're looking for, this is a fine spot to set up camp.

*Caherdaniel.* ☎ *066-947-5132. Fax: 066-947-5425.* www.scarriff-inn.com. *To get there: On the N70. Rates: €70–€100 ($81–$115) double. MC, V. Closed Nov–Feb.*

### Sea Shore Farm
### $$    Kenmare

The selling point of this spacious farmhouse is the unbelievable view of the luminous Bay of Kenmare and the mountains of the Beara Peninsula beyond, visible through the large windows and sliding doors in most rooms. The style of the spacious, uncluttered rooms is sort of a country twist on standard modern hotel decor, with flowery quilts and antique-style furniture. The house is a five- or ten-minute drive from the town of Kenmare, but it feels much more secluded, especially when you ramble down to the empty seashore. Host Mary Patricia O'Sullivan is friendly, helpful, and full of tips about the area.

*Tubrid (right outside Kenmare).* ☎ *064-41-270. From Kenmare, take the N71, make a left on N70 and then take another left turn at the sign for Sea Shore Farm. Rates: €90–€120 ($104–$138). MC, V. Closed mid-Nov–Feb.*

### Towers Hotel
### $$–$$$    Glenbeigh

This elegant hotel is a great place to spend the night after the first leg of your drive around the Ring. Sandy beaches and lofty mountains are just a short walk away, and fishing and golfing are nearby. The hotel's classy restaurant creates superb seafood dishes, and the traditional pub draws locals, so even if you just go in for a bite, you get to see a real slice of this part of Kerry.

*Glenbeigh.* ☎ *066-976-8212. Fax: 066-976-8260. Right off the N70, between Killarney and Cahirsiveen. Rates: €100–€120 ($115–$138) double. AE, DC, MC, V. Closed Nov–March.*

## Dining locally in Kenmare and along the Ring

### The Blue Bull
**$$  Sneem   SEAFOOD-IRISH**

This roadside pub, decorated with old black-and-white prints of Kerry, is known throughout the county for its fresh seafood, so you can't go wrong with the seafood platter. It also serves steaks, hearty soups, and other classic Irish fare, including an excellent Irish stew. Stick around after dinner for some Irish music.

*South Square. On the Ring of Kerry, 24km (15 miles) west of Kenmare. ☎ 064-45-382. Main courses: €10–€20 ($12–$23). AE, DC, MC, V Open for bar food daily 11 a.m.– 8 p.m., for restaurant menu March–Oct daily 6–10 p.m.*

### d'Arcy's
**$$$  Kenmare   IRISH**

Get ready for real gourmet Irish food, prepared with fresh ingredients by a talented chef. This is the kind of food that's changing stereotypes about Ireland's culinary capabilities — it's not just meat and potatoes anymore. Highlights are baked sea trout in puff pastry with smoked salmon and loin of Kerry lamb with eggplant, tomato, and garlic. The kitchen is happy to accommodate vegetarians. The dining room has a big, open fireplace that creates a welcoming, cozy atmosphere.

*Main St. ☎ 064-41-589. Reservations recommended. Main courses: €20–€28 ($23–$32). MC, V. Open: Daily 6:30–10 p.m. Closed Jan–mid-March.*

### Packies
**$$$  Kenmare   IRISH/NEW IRISH**

This hip, cheerful restaurant, with stone walls displaying contemporary local art, serves up delectable dishes that range from traditional Irish to modern, internationally influenced fare. The simple crab claws in garlic butter will have you licking your fingers, and more-adventurous dishes, such as plaice with orange, lime, and cilantro, may have you licking your plate.

*Henry St. ☎ 053-41-508. Reservations recommended. Main courses: €14–€25 ($16–$29). MC, V. Easter–mid-Nov Tues–Sat 6–10 p.m.*

### Purple Heather
**$  Kenmare   HAUTE PUB**

Here's something different: hearty, delicious pub grub with a haute-cuisine edge. This centrally located eatery is perfect for a light meal or snack and is guaranteed not to be ordinary. Tasty seafood salads, vegetarian omelets, soups, and platters piled high with farmhouse cheese are just some of the offerings.

*Henry St. ☎ 064-41-016. Main courses: €4–€17 ($4.60–$20). No credit cards. Open: Mon–Sat 11 a.m.–7 p.m.*

## Exploring the Iveragh Peninsula and the Ring of Kerry

In addition to taking in the glorious views the Ring of Kerry offers around every bend, history and natural history buffs should enjoy the sights in these sections.

### The top attractions

The tip-top attractions of the Ring of Kerry are the drive itself, with all of its breathtaking panoramas, and exploring the rest of the peninsula by car, bike, or foot. I highly recommend driving the Ring yourself if you don't mind winding roads and the occasional monster tour bus hogging the road.

The Ring is usually driven counterclockwise, beginning in Killarney or Killorglin and going around to Kenmare. During the peak tourist season, you'll encounter a good number of other drivers along this route. So if you want to avoid the crowds, begin in Kenmare and go clockwise — that way, you'll be going against the traffic. Another way to beat the tour buses is to hit the road before they do — buses leave Killarney and Killorglin at 9 or 10 a.m.

If you take the standard counterclockwise route and start in **Killorglin,** known as the gateway to the Ring, the next town you come to is **Glenbeigh,** which is partially surrounded by mountains. At **Rossbeigh,** you first catch sight of the Atlantic, and then comes the town of **Cahirsiveen. Portmagee** is a pretty fishing harbor where you cross the bridge to **Valentia Island. Ballinskelligs** is a *Gaeltacht,* or Irish-speaking area, that has an Irish college where children can attend summer classes to learn the language. You may be able to see the steep Skellig rocks in the ocean from here.

**Waterville,** the next town on the Ring, is known as a fishing resort but has plenty of other sporting attractions to divert you from the drive. In beautiful **Caherdaniel,** you can see the home of Daniel "The Liberator" O'Connell, and nearby **Castlecove** is loaded with sandy beaches. The lovely village of **Sneem,** filled with vividly colored buildings, has mountain and river scenery and is a haven of peace and quiet. **Parknasilla** benefits from the Gulf Stream and has a (comparably) warm climate and even subtropical plants. Finally, the Ring of Kerry ends in the charming, picturesque town of **Kenmare,** where you'll enjoy fine hotels, restaurants, shopping, and pubs.

Now, some insider advice: Yes, the Ring is spectacular, but it is only a small part of the Iveragh Peninsula. I highly recommend taking some of the local interior roads through the mountains and hills that make up the center of the peninsula, particularly in the area around gorgeous

Caragh Lake. It's amazing how untouched this area is. Instead of tour buses, you may encounter a farmer leading his herd of cows down the road to a different pasture. And you certainly encounter incredible mountain scenery. All you need is a good driving map.

Driving is the best way to explore this area, but if the idea of curvy roads and gigantic tour buses strikes fear in your heart, check out the **Bus Éireann Ring of Kerry Day Tour** (☎ 01-836-6111). Unfortunately, the buses don't stop very often, but you still get the incredible views. Tours leave from the Cork Bus Station at 10 a.m. and return at 10 p.m. They operate May through September on Mondays, Wednesdays, Fridays, and Sundays, and cost €24 ($28) for adults, €20 ($23) for seniors and students, and €15 ($17) for children.

### Derrynane House National Historic Park
Caherdaniel

This home was where the Great Liberator, Daniel O'Connell, lived for most of his life. O'Connell was a lawyer and politician who fought for the repeal of anti-Catholic laws. O'Connell's former home is now a museum displaying many personal artifacts; don't miss the interesting 25-minute video on his life. The house sits on gorgeous grounds along the coast and boasts extensive gardens.

*Right off the Ring, in Caherdaniel. You see a sign 1 mile north of Caherdaniel for parking.* ☎ *066-9475-113. Admission: €2.75 ($3.15) adults, €2 ($2.30) seniors, €1.25 ($1.45) students and children. Open: Nov–March Sat and Sun 1–5 p.m., Apr and Oct Tues–Sun 1–5 p.m.; May–Sept Mon–Sat 9 a.m.–6 p.m., Sun 11 a.m.–7 p.m. Suggested visit: About 1 hour.*

### Seafari Scenic and Wildlife Cruises

A cruise aboard this covered and heated boat, which holds up to 150 people, is the best way to see peaceful Kenmare Bay and the castles, manor houses, and megalithic monuments that line its shores. The guides on this two-hour cruise provide interesting commentary on local geology and history and are experts at spotting the dolphins, sea otters, gray seals, and water birds that frequent the bay. During the high season, try an evening music cruise and purchase your food and drink on board.

*Leaves from Kenmare Pier (next to the Kenmare suspension bridge), Kenmare.* ☎ *064-83-171. Price: €20 ($23) adults, €15 ($17) students, €10 ($12) children under 12. Frequent departures daily May–Oct 4.*

### The Skellig Experience
Valentia Island

The two Skellig rock islands, Skellig Michael and Little Skellig, jut steeply out of the sea about 14km (8 miles) from the Iveragh Peninsula. This heritage center, located on beautiful Valentia Island, has excellent exhibits and audiovisuals explaining the natural and human history of the Skelligs. You find out about the lives and work of the early Christian monks who created their monastery on Skellig Michael, discover the history of the Skellig lighthouse and its keepers, and find out about the intriguing bird and plant life of the Skelligs. The highlight of the visit is the 1½ hour cruise around the islands. Note that the water is often very choppy, so if you left your sea legs at the hotel, you can visit the Skelligs virtually through a 15-minute audiovisual tour.

*Skellig Heritage Centre. Take the R565 to Portmagee and Valentia Island. The Heritage Centre is just across the bridge from Portmagee as soon as you cross over onto Valentia Island.* ☎ *066-947-6306. Admission: Exhibit and movie €4.50 ($5.20) adults, €4 ($4.60) seniors and students, €2 ($2.30) children under 12; exhibit, movie, and cruise €22 ($25) adults, €19 (22) seniors and students, €12 ($14) children under 12. Open: April–Oct 10 a.m.–6 p.m. Closed Nov–March. Suggested visit: 2 hours.*

### Skellig Michael Boat Trip and Exploration

This fabulous adventure begins with a 45-minute boat ride to the larger of the Skellig Islands, Skellig Michael. Once there, you can ascend the steep steps that lead up to the monastery, which was founded in the 6th or 7th century and flourished until the 12th or 13th century. Among the ruins of the monastery complex, you'll find a church, a number of small beehive-style huts, and two oratories. The thousands of nesting gannets on Little Skellig and the many puffins on nearby Puffin Island are quite a sight.

*The trip takes about 45 minutes and averages €35 ($40) per person. Ferries usually run only in the high season (April–Sept) and depart between 9 a.m. and noon. For a ferry from Ballinskelligs, contact Joe Roddy (☎ 066-9474-268); from Valentia Island, call Des Lavelle (☎ 066-947-6124); from Portmagee, call O'Keefe's (☎ 066-947-7103).*

### Other cool things to see and do

- ✔ **Kerry Bog Village Museum:** This collection of thatched-roof cottages illustrates life in Kerry in the 1800s. It has a blacksmith's forge and house, a stable, a dairy house, a laborer's house, a turf-cutter's house, a thatcher's house, and a tradesman's house. Plenty of freshly cut turf is lying about. Dug out from bogs, turf was once the main fuel for heating houses. Inside the dwellings are authentic furnishings from across County Kerry.

  Location: Ring of Kerry Road (N70), Glenbeigh. ☎ 066-976-9184. Follow signs from the village of Glenbeigh. Admission: €4 ($4.60) adults, €2 ($2.30) students, €1.25 ($1.45) children. Open: March through November daily from 9 a.m. to 6 p.m. Suggested visit: 1½ to 2 hours.

- ✔ **Walking the Kerry Way:** This long-distance hike of 202km (125 miles) leaves from and returns to Killarney and includes a circuit of the Iveragh Peninsula.

Pick up maps at a tourist office in Killarney or Kenmare (see "Fast Facts: The Iveragh Peninsula and the Ring of Kerry," later in this chapter).

✔ **Waterville Golf Links:** If you're craving some golf, visit Waterville — golf course to the stars. It's scenic, overlooking the Atlantic, and it's where Sean Connery plays when he's in Ireland. It's a par-71 course.

Location: Newrath, Waterville. ☎ **066-974-102.** Greens fees are €125($144).

## Shopping

Plenty of small craft shops dot the Ring of Kerry, but the best shopping is in the town of Kenmare. You find a variety of specialty shops and souvenir stores and plenty of what the town is known for — Kenmare lace.

**Cleo,** 2 Shelbourne St., Kenmare (☎ **064-41-410**), sells stylish women's clothes and is noted for its colorful tweed and linen items. **Nostalgia,** 27 Henry St., Kenmare (☎ **064-41-389**), stocks the finest collection of the famed Kenmare lace in tablecloths, bed linens, doll clothes, and more. **Quills Woolen Market,** corner of Market and Main streets, Kenmare (☎ **064-32-277**), has a fine selection of Irish crafts such as Aran sweaters, Donegal tweeds, and Irish linen. If you're a bargain-hunter, check out the Quills outlet store (☎ **064-45-277**) at South Square in Sneem, which is about 20km (12 miles) from Kenmare along the Ring of Kerry.

## Hitting the pubs

### Bianconi
### Killorglin

Bianconi offers good Irish lunches, including smoked salmon and oysters. There's music most evenings, and you can count on a friendly welcome from the staff.

*Right on the N70 near where it meets the N72.* ☎ *066-61-146.*

# The Puck Fair

For three days during the second week of August, Killorglin explodes into a fiesta of music, drinking, storytelling, and general merrymaking during the Puck Fair. A billy goat is crowned King Puck, and the ribbon-bedecked goat presides over the festivities from a high pedestal. The origins of this celebration stretch far back — it is thought to have originated as a pagan festival in honor of Lugh, the Celtic sun god. When I asked a Killorglin gent whether he had taken part in the festivities for all three days, he replied "Aye, and three nights."

### Caitin Baiters
**Cahirsiveen**

This thatched-roof pub is as authentic as they get, and inside, you enjoy hearty food and a well-pulled pint, both at reasonable prices. Some nights (it's hit-or-miss), there are music sessions.

*Kells Bay. From the town's main street, follow the turnoff to Kells Bay; it's on that little road.* ☎ *066-947-7614.*

### The Point Bar
**Cahirsiveen**

If the weather's good, this is the place to be. Sitting outside on the patio, sipping a pint and looking out at the water, is simply idyllic. The bar also serves plenty of good, fresh seafood dishes from 12:30 to 3:00 p.m. and 6:30 to 9:30 p.m.

*On the road to Renard Point (off the Ring road), just a minute or two from the N70.* ☎ *066-947-2165.*

# Fast Facts: The Iveragh Peninsula and the Ring of Kerry

### Area Codes
Most numbers on the Ring of Kerry have the area codes 064 or 066.

### Emergencies/Police
Dial ☎ 999 for all emergencies.

### Hospital
Kenmare Community Hospital can be reached at ☎ 064-41-088.

### Information
For visitor information, go to the Kenmare Tourist Office at Market Square (☎ 064-41-233).

### Internet
You can access the Internet at Kenmare Library (☎ 064 -41-416).

# Tralee and the Dingle Peninsula

Don't tell the Irish Tourism Board, but I think that the Dingle Peninsula is even more beautiful than the Iveragh Peninsula and the Ring of Kerry. While the Ring is dramatic, the Dingle Peninsula has a gentler beauty in parts (though, like the Iveragh Peninsula, it also boasts awe-inspiring views of wave-pounded cliffs) and is less clogged with visitors. Long sandy beaches, stunningly green hills divided by old stone walls, extraordinary pre-Christian ruins, craggy cliffs, and a large *Gaeltacht* (Irish-speaking area) — what more could you want? I have a special

*Tralee*

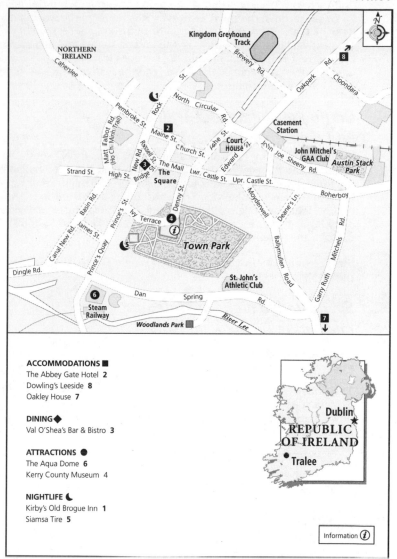

**ACCOMMODATIONS** ■
The Abbey Gate Hotel **2**
Dowling's Leeside **8**
Oakley House **7**

**DINING** ◆
Val O'Shea's Bar & Bistro **3**

**ATTRACTIONS** ●
The Aqua Dome **6**
Kerry County Museum **4**

**NIGHTLIFE** ☾
Kirby's Old Brogue Inn **1**
Siamsa Tire **5**

Information *(i)*

place in my heart for the sweet and funky town of Dingle, with its many shops, restaurants, and galleries, and its beautiful views of Dingle Harbor.

You may want to begin your exploration of the Dingle Peninsula (just north of the Ring of Kerry) in **Tralee,** the quaint town known as the

*Gateway to Kerry.* Tralee (see the nearby map) is the capital town of County Kerry; it's a pleasant place to stay overnight, but there is not a lot to see or do in the town. However, it is home of the world-famous **Rose of Tralee Pageant,** the highlight of the annual Festival of Kerry. The festival lasts for five days at the end of August and includes concerts, street entertainment, and horse races leading up to the beauty-talent contest that names the Rose (call the festival office at ☎ 066-712-1322 for more information).

## Getting to and around Tralee and the Dingle Peninsula

If you're coming by car from Dublin, follow signs for N7 south to Limerick and then get on the N21 or N69 (Coast Road) to Tralee. From the Ring of Kerry and points south, take N70 to Tralee. From Killarney, Cork, and the east, take N22. Trains to Tralee arrive at the railway station on John Joe Sheehy Road (☎ 066-712-3522). Buses arrive in Tralee daily from all over Ireland at the Bus Éireann (☎ 066-712-3566) depot on John Joe Sheehy Road.

**Bus Éireann** also provides service to Dingle Town daily; the depot is on Upper Main Street.

## Spending the night in Tralee and on the Dingle Peninsula

### The Abbey Gate Hotel
**$$$   Tralee**

The Abbey Gate is a great all-in-one place. The hotel is elegant, the rooms are spacious, and everyone's extremely helpful. To sweeten the deal, just downstairs is the good Vineyard Restaurant, which uses fresh local produce to whip up Irish and European meals. In addition, there is a pub, The Old Market Place, that boasts open fires and a cozy atmosphere — a nice stop after dinner and before climbing up to bed.

*Maine St.* ☎ *066-712-9888. Fax: 066-712-9821.* www.abbeygatehotel.com. *Rates: €110–€160 ($127–$184) double. AE, DC, MC, V.*

### Alpine House
**$–$$   Dingle Town**

People rave about this guesthouse. The sizable, bright rooms offer all sorts of perks, such as tea- and coffeemaking facilities, hair dryers, direct-dial phones, and central heating (sure beats huddling next to a radiator on chilly days!). Plus you have use of a roomy guest lounge and can enjoy the hospitality of the O'Shea family. The heart of Dingle Town is just a two-minute walk away, and the views of Dingle Bay are splendid.

*Mail Rd.* ☎ *066-915-1250. Fax: 066-915-1966.* www.alpineguesthouse.com. *Off the main road (N86). Rates: €60–€80 ($69–$92) double. AE, MC, V.*

### The Captain's House
$$ **Dingle Town**

The name of the game here is hospitality, so this is the place to stay if you are craving a genuine welcome. The B&B has an excellent location, right in the middle of Dingle, and offers cozy, sparkling-clean rooms. Breakfast is terrific, featuring homemade marmalade, local cheeses, and other delights, and is served in a room overlooking the award-winning gardens.

*The Mall.* ☎ *066-915-1531. Fax: 066-915-1079. Rates: €90 ($104) double. AE, MC, V. Closed Dec–March.*

### Dowling's Leeside
$ **Tralee**

Once upon a time, I waited until the last minute to make reservations for my stay in Tralee and called the first B&B I could find. And lo and behold, this cozy place became one of my favorite accommodations in Ireland. Maura Dowling is a friendly, down-to-earth, generous hostess, and she has an artist's eye for interior decoration. Bedrooms are bright and cheerful, decorated with original paintings and country-style pine furniture. Antiques furnish the large sitting room, and breakfast is served in a glass-walled conservatory filled with plants. It's like staying with a particularly domestic friend. The town of Tralee is about 15 minutes away.

*Oakpark. Off the N69 Ferry route.* ☎ *066-712-6476. Fax: 066-712-6476. Rates: €54–€60 ($62–$69). AE, DC, MC, V. Closed Nov–mid-Feb.*

### Greenmount House
$$–$$$ **Dingle**

Beware: The views of Dingle Bay and Dingle Town from this modern lodging may cause you to delay your day's plans in favor of lingering over breakfast or relaxing in the sitting room. Though the house doesn't have many rooms, it feels more like a small hotel than a B&B, with spacious rooms (those in the bungalow building have sitting areas and balconies), large bathrooms, upscale modern furniture, and extremely comfortable beds. Service is kind and professional, but if you're looking for a lot of warmth and helpful hints from your hosts, you may be better off at The Captain's House or Alpine House. Breakfast is amazing in both scope and quality — be sure to try some of the mouthwatering cheeses from the buffet. The main streets of Dingle Town are about a 10- or 15-minute walk away.

*John St.* ☎ *066-915-1414. Fax: 066-915-1974.* www.greenmount-house.com. *Rates: €75–€150 ($86–$173). MC, V.*

### Oakley House
### $  Ballymullen

If you don't mind being just barely outside Tralee, try this gorgeous guest-house. It's a grand restored period house with tons of character and charm. Tralee is less than a ten-minute walk away, and the house is close to beaches, golf, and horseback riding. The guest lounge has tea- and cof-feemaking facilities and television. Rooms are very homey — you feel as though you're staying in a house rather than a hotel. The Bennises, who run the house, are certain to make you feel welcome.

*Ballymullen, south of Tralee along the N70.* ☎ *066-712-1727.* Fax: 066-712-1727. To get there: Right on the N70. Rates: €60–€64 ($69–$74) double. MC, V.

### Pax House
### $$  Dingle Town

The first thing that you notice about this place is the view — it's spectac-ular. Overlooking the water, with mountains looming in the distance, Pax House will tempt you to just lounge around on the comfortable balcony all day. Inside, everything's meticulously decorated, and the rooms are gorgeous. A gourmet breakfast welcomes you in the morning.

*Upper John St.* ☎ *066-915-1518.* Fax: 066-915-2461. www.pax-house.com. *Rates:* €100–€140 ($115–$161) double. MC, V. Closed Nov–March.

### Slea Head Farm
### $  Dunquin

Located on a working farm, this cozy B&B is situated in a rural area between Ventry and Dunquin. The panoramas surrounding the house are pure, gorgeous Ireland: cows and sheep grazing on emerald-green grass, a maze of old stone walls creeping up a gentle hill, and a ruined stone house next door. And the finest views are reserved for travelers whose bedroom windows look out onto the nearby sea and the famed Blasket Islands. Rooms are cozy and cute, with homey touches such as stuffed animals perched on the furniture. The Irish-speaking family who runs the B&B is warm and welcoming.

*On road between Ventry and Dunquin.* ☎ *066-915-6120.* www.sleaheadfarm.com. *Rates:* €60–€64 ($69–$74). MC, V. Closed Nov–March.

## Dining locally in Tralee and on the Dingle Peninsula

Visiting a place right on the water pretty much promises you'll find plenty of good seafood, and the restaurants on the Dingle Peninsula won't fail you. From elegant to simple, the dishes in these parts are delicious.

### Beginish Restaurant
#### $$$   Dingle Town   SEAFOOD

Though meat and vegetarian dishes are on the menu, seafood is the star at this classy, elegant restaurant. For your setting, choose between the cozy dining room with a huge fireplace, the serene conservatory looking out on a little garden, or a table in the garden itself when it's warm enough. Then you have the tough task of deciding among such imaginative French-influenced dishes as lobster Thermidor or cod on thyme-scented potatoes. And your final decision: one (or more?) of the hundred or so bottles of wine on the wine list.

*Green St. ☎ 066-915-1588. Main courses: €13–€21 ($14–$24). AE, DC, MC, V. Open: Wed–Sun 12:15–2:30 p.m. and 6–10 p.m. Closed Nov–Easter.*

### Doyle's Seafood Bar
#### $$$–$$$$   Dingle Town   SEAFOOD

If you're looking for lobster, look no further — Doyle's won't disappoint. Here, when you have the specialty of the house, you pick it out of a tank in the bar. Or you can go for some variety with the popular seafood platter, a plate brimming with sole, lobster, salmon, oysters, and crab claws. The menu depends on the fresh seafood caught daily by local fishermen, so although you can't always depend on a certain dish, you can be sure whatever you get will be fresh. The dining room is cozy, with plenty of brick and stone — you may feel like you're eating in someone's wide-open kitchen.

*4 John St. ☎ 066-915-1174. Reservations required. Main courses: €19–€30 ($22–$35). MC, V. Open: Mon–Sat 6–10 p.m. Closed mid-Dec to mid-Feb.*

### The Forge Restaurant
#### $$   Dingle Town   IRISH-CONTINENTAL

This popular restaurant is a family haven. The prices are reasonable, and there's a special menu for kids. The menu covers seafood, meat, and vegetarian dishes, and all meals are made with fresh local produce. You can't go wrong with a nice steak.

*Holyground Rd., just up from Main St. ☎ 066-915-2590. Main courses: €11–€21 ($12–$24). AE, DC, MC, V. Open: Wed–Mon noon–3 p.m. and 6–9:30 p.m. Closed Nov through March.*

### Out of the Blue
#### $$   Dingle Town   SEAFOOD

The official name of this place is Out of the Blue Fresh Fish Seafood Only Restaurant, because it serves only dishes that once swam or crawled through the nearby briny deep (though it also offered a vegetarian plate

# Unbeatable ice cream

I would consider moving to Dingle Town just for **Murphy's Ice Cream**, Strand Street, Dingle (☎ **066-915-2644**). The Murphy brothers opened their store in 2000 with a quest to create the perfect ice cream, and I'd say they're well on their way to attaining their goal. The smooth ice cream is made with top-quality ingredients: Kerry cream and milk (thank those cows the next time you drive past them), and the best natural flavorings, such as Madagascar and Organic Mexican Vanilla in the vanilla ice cream, real Champagne and peaches in the Bellini sorbet, Jamaican Rum in the rum raisin, and so on. You may want to go for one of the distinctly Irish flavors, such as Irish-cream ice cream, black-currant-and-Guinness sorbet, or brown-bread ice cream. After intense menu research, the delicious, caramel-tinged honeycomb ice cream has emerged as my favorite.

while I was there). A little pompous, maybe, but Out of the Blue is allowed to be egotistical, because it serves the best seafood in Dingle Town. The chalkboard menu changes daily because the restaurant builds its dishes around the catches of the day. Preparations, such as skate (ray wings) with caper butter and haddock on tomato sauce, are relatively simple and allow the flavor of the fish to sparkle. The garlic crab claws are unbelievable. The restaurant itself has a Mediterranean feel , with simple pine tables; bright blue, yellow, and red walls and ceiling; and oil paintings of fish and the sea gracing the walls.

*Waterside.* ☎ *066-915-0811. Reservations recommended for dinner; not accepted for lunch. Main courses: €9.50–€20 ($11–$23). MC, V for orders over €50 ($58); otherwise cash only. Open: Daily 12:30–3 p.m. and 6–9:30 p.m. Closed Dec–March 17.*

### Val O'Shea's Bar & Bistro
$   Tralee   IRISH

Looking for some hearty, real Irish food? Look no further. The chefs focus on creating traditional Irish meals at a high standard, and they offer some great vegetarian selections, too. Expect delicious soups and salads that will fill you up and excellent fresh seafood dinners. Despite the full bar and a fairly extensive wine list, it's not exactly a chi-chi place — you'll be comfortable with the whole family, and you won't drop too large a chunk of change on your meal.

*6 Bridge St., in the center of town.* ☎ *066-712-1559. Main courses: €5.50–€13 ($6.35–$14). MC, V. Open: Mon–Sat 12:30–2:30 p.m. and 6:30–10 p.m.*

## Exploring Tralee and the Dingle Peninsula: The top attractions

Like the Ring of Kerry, the big attraction of the Dingle Peninsula is driving, biking, or hiking your way around, taking in all the scenery. I recommend starting in **Castlemaine** and taking the coastal road (R561 or R559) toward Dingle Town. Along the way, you may want to pay a visit to **Inch Beach,** a long sandy beach with the Atlantic waves on one side and curvy, sea-grass-covered dunes on the other. It's a strange sight to stand on the dunes looking at the vast Atlantic in one direction and grazing cows and sheep in the other. Move on toward **Dingle Town,** which is a great place to spend a night or two before driving the Slea Head Tour.

From Dingle Town, take the gorgeous 48km (33-mile) **Slea Head Tour,** a round-trip circuit that takes you along the south coast, up the west end of the peninsula and then back to Dingle Town. The highlight of the route is **Slea Head,** which features towering cliffs with incredible views of the Atlantic ocean and the **Blasket Islands,** sandy beaches (the waters are not safe for swimming), and archeological remains. Also along the route is the village of **Dún Chaoin** (Dunquin), the heart of the Dingle *Gaeltacht* (Irish-speaking area), with its striking views of the Blasket Islands; and the **Gallarus Oratory,** a well-preserved seventh- or eighth-century Christian church located east of the town of Ballyferriter. Adventurers may want depart from the Slea Head Drive at Feothanagh, driving east (and up) on narrow mountain roads through **Connor Pass,** where you have a thrilling panoramic view of the entire peninsula, and then down to the picture-postcard fishing villages of **Cloghane** and **Brandon.** From there, you can drive east past unspoiled sandy beaches, cute fishing villages, and farmland. *Note:* Only confident drivers should attempt the Conner Pass route, as it's winding and steep.

### The Aqua Dome
**Tralee**

If your kids don't think they've been on vacation if they haven't gotten a chance to submerge themselves in water, this indoor water park is the place to go. Kids can splash around in the kiddie pools, fly down sky-high slides, and battle raging rapids — all under one roof. Meanwhile, adults can relax in the sauna dome, which has two saunas, a steam room, a cool pool, and a sun bed. The main pool is for the whole family, and next door

## For archeology buffs

**Sciuird Tours Bus and Walking Tour** (☎ 066-915-1937) offers an excellent two- or three-hour expert-guided tour exploring four or five monuments from the Stone Age to the Middle Ages. You'll take a bus among the sights, which are scattered along the Peninsula, and do some light walking. Tours leave daily at 10:30 a.m. as long as at least six people have booked (14 is the maximum). Tours are €20 ($23) per person. Call for information on departure location; pick-up is often available from Dingle Town accommodations.

is an over-16-only health suite (which is really just a spot with hot tubs and a relaxing place to read the paper). There's also a mini-golf course and remote-controlled trucks and boats.

*Dingle Rd. Next to the steam railway heading out of town. ☎ 066-712-8899. Admission: €10 ($12) adults, €9 ($10) children, and free for children under 3. Open: June Mon–Fri 10 a.m.–10 p.m., Sat and Sun 11 a.m.–8 p.m.; July–Aug daily 10 a.m.– 10 p.m.; Sept–May Mon, Wed, and Fri 10 a.m.–10 p.m., Tues and Thurs 12:30–10 p.m., Sat–Sun 11 a.m.–8 p.m. Suggested visit: As long as you like!*

### Blasket Centre
### Dunquin

This heritage center, on the tip of the Dingle Peninsula, celebrates the Blasket Islands, which lie a few miles from the mainland. Great Blasket, the largest of the islands, was home to a Gaelic-speaking community until the 1950s. Photographs, a video presentation, and other exhibits illustrate the lives of the Blasket Islanders, who farmed and fished for sustenance and have a rich storytelling and musical tradition. Much of the museum focuses on the literary achievements of the Blasket Islanders — several autobiographies and collections of Blasket Island tales were published with great success. The exhibits are very heavy on text, so younger children may be bored. There are incredible views of the islands through the large windows in the center.

*Village of Dunquin (right off the R559). ☎ 066-915-6444. Admission: €3.50 ($4.05) adults, €2.50 ($2.90) seniors, €1.25 ($1.45) children and students. Open: Easter–June daily 10 a.m.–6 p.m.; July–Aug daily 10 a.m.–7 p.m.; Sept–Oct daily 10 a.m.–6 p.m. Closed Nov–Easter. Suggested visit: 1 ½ hours.*

### Fungie the Dolphin
### Dingle

Dingle's most famous resident, Fungie the Dolphin, is a friendly, playful dolphin who has been hanging out around the waters of Dingle Bay since 1984. He's not in captivity, so theoretically, he could take off for bluer waters at any time, but he's stuck around for more than two decades, so odds are good that he's in Dingle to stay. Fungie seems to love playing with humans, and if you take boat tour to see him (there are separate trips for swimmers and nonswimmers), you will likely be treated to a display of arcing jumps and up-close encounters as Fungie swims alongside the boat. Plus you'll have wonderful views of serene Dingle Bay. If you're up for it, I recommend going whole-hog and renting a wetsuit and snorkel gear so that you can play with Fungie in the water. Floating peacefully in the blue water of Dingle Bay and seeing this winsome creature eye-to-eye are worth the initial shock of climbing into the cool water.

*The Pier. ☎ 066-915-2626 for boat trips; ☎ 066-915-1967 for wetsuit hire and swimming trips. Call to pick up a wetsuit and make reservations **the day before** for swimming trips. Cost: For boat trip: €12 ($14) adults, €6 ($6.90) children under 12; for* *swimming trip: €25 ($29) for adults, €15 ($17) for children under 12 if they're swimming, free for children under 12 if they're not swimming; wetsuit €25 ($29). You can buy tickets for the boat ride at a kiosk at the pier. Call for times.*

### Kerry County Museum
**Tralee**

Kerry's history, starting 7,000 years ago, unfolds before you at this well-done heritage center. Exhibits cover everything from myths and legends of the county to local music to Gaelic football. The highlight just may be the theme-park style ride that takes you through a life-size exhibit of Tralee of the Middle Ages, enhanced with sounds and even smells of the time.

*Ashe Memorial Hall, Denny St. ☎ 066-712-7777. Admission: €8 ($9.20) adults, €6.50 ($7.50) students, €5 ($5.75) children. Open: Jan–March Tues–Fri 10 a.m.–4:30 p.m., Apr and May Tues–Sat 9:30 a.m.–5:30 p.m., June–Aug daily 9:30 a.m.–5:30 p.m., Sept–Dec Tues–Sat 9:30 a.m.–5 p.m. Suggested visit: 1½ to 2 hours.*

## Outdoor activities

Try some of these activities to get you out into the bracing Dingle air:

- **Biking:** You can rent bikes from Foxy John's, Main Street, Dingle (☎ 066-915-1316). The most popular bike route is the Slea Head route (see the preceding section, "Exploring Tralee and the Dingle Peninsula: The top attractions").

- **Golfing:** On Sandhill Road, you find **Ballybunion Golf Club** (☎ 068-27-611; www.ballybuniongolfclub.ie), a seaside club with two excellent 18-hole, par-71 courses. The Old Course is the more challenging of the two, and the newer course was fashioned by the legendary Robert Trent Jones. Greens fees are €110 ($127) for the old course and €75 ($86) for the new, or €135 ($155) to play both on the same day. Visitors are welcome on weekdays. The par-71 **Tralee Golf Club,** located at West Barrow, Ardfert, in Tralee (☎ 066-713-6379; www.traleegolfclub.com), is the original European Arnold Palmer–designed course. This course is staged before an amazing backdrop, boxed in by river, the sea, and the crumbling castles of Ardfert. Greens fees are €130 ($150). Visitors are welcome every day except Wednesday and Sunday.

- **Horseback riding:** Mountain and beach rides are available through **Dingle Horse Riding** (☎ 066-915-2018).

- **Walking:** The Dingle Way leaves from Tralee and makes a 153km (95-mile) circuit of the peninsula. For day-hikers, there is a beautiful stretch between Dunquin and Ballyferriter, and the ascent to Mount Brandon's summit, though difficult, is spectacular. Get your hands on The Dingle Way Map Guide (available at tourist offices and shops in the area) before you begin.

# Irish folk theater

**Siamsa Tíre: The National Folk Theatre of Ireland**, Town Park, Tralee (☎ 066-712-7276; www.siamsatire.com), performs theater that celebrates the rich dance, music, and folklore traditions of Ireland.

Past performances have included beautiful theatrical and musical retellings of the Irish myths of the Children of Lir and Oisín's Return to Tír na nÓg (the land of eternal youth), as well as an enchanting performance about life on a small farm long ago.

## *Shopping*

Dingle Town is home to many artists, making it a fabulous place to buy contemporary fine art as well as crafts. In addition, there are some great pottery shops along roadsides throughout the Dingle Peninsula; just drop in when you come across them.

**Brian de Staic,** Studio Shop at The Wood, Dingle, and outlet store on Green Street, Dingle (☎ 066-915-1298), offers unique handcrafted gold jewelry. Many of the pieces incorporate Celtic designs. **West Kerry Craft Guild,** Main Street, features works by an assortment of Dingle craftspeople. **Annascaul Pottery,** Green Street (in the back of the little courtyard; ☎ 066-9157-186), sells crafts from handmade pottery to exquisite "paintings" made with dried flowers. If you're in the market for a *bodhrán,* a traditional Irish drum, or if you just want to see how they're made, drop into **Dingle Bodhráns,** An Clós, Green Street (☎ 087-245-7689).

## *Hitting the pubs*

The Dingle Peninsula, and Dingle Town in particular, is a great place for music. Drop into most any pub during the summer, and you'll hear tin whistles, fiddles, pipes, and other instruments going strong.

### *Dick Mack's*
### Dingle Town

Undoubtedly one of Ireland's quaintest pubs, Dick Mack's retains an aura of times gone by — years ago, pubs often doubled as providers of other essential services; this one doubled as a cobbler's shop, and one side of the place still holds the leatherworking tools of the late owner. There are a great little snug at the end of the bar side and an authentic back room that once served as the kitchen. Apparently, when Tom Cruise and Nicole Kidman stayed in Dingle while filming *Far and Away,* they fell in love with the place. Many other stars have stopped in for a pint — there's even a little walk of fame outside.

*Green St.* ☎ *066-915-1960.*

### The Dingle Pub
**Dingle Town**

Facing the harbor and easily distinguished by the green-and-white shamrock outside, this place is just what it sounds like: the pub that represents Dingle. The inside of the pub is much like Dingle itself: It seems as though nothing's changed in generations, and you can relax in the laid-back atmosphere. Stop in for a pint and a talk with the locals.

*Main St., at the harbor.* ☎ *066-915-1370.*

### Kirby's Old Brogue Inn
**Tralee**

This bright-yellow alehouse has dubbed itself "your landmark in Tralee." Given the great atmosphere and food, it probably will be. Its quaint exterior gives way to a wonderful old pub inside, where you'll hear traditional Irish music and jazz in the summers and where you can nosh on glorified pub grub all day — steaks and seafood barside are quite a treat.

*Rock St.* ☎ *066-712-3221.*

### Natterjack
**Castlegregory**

This pub hearkens back to days of old, and it's a perfect place to stop in for a bite and a refreshing pint after the drive to the north end of the peninsula. This old-fashioned place concentrates more on good music and food than on the latest trend in decor. It offers a children's menu and a beer garden in summertime.

*The West End.* ☎ *066-713-9491.*

### O'Flaherty's
**Dingle Town**

You can count on the music in O'Flaherty's to be good — the owner frequently performs. Check out the posters and clippings that line the walls to get a real feel for Dingle Town. Everything about this place screams *authentic,* and the locals who frequent it often chat in Irish Gaelic. It's big and open, and because of the stone-flagged floor, it doesn't exactly get cozy until it gets full. Stop in for a real taste of Ireland.

*Bridge St.* ☎ *066-915-1983.*

# *Fast Facts: Tralee and Dingle Peninsula*

### Area Code

The main area code for Tralee and Dingle is 066.

### Emergencies/Police

Dial ☎ **999** for all emergencies.

### Hospital

In Tralee, the Tralee General Hospital is on Killarney Road (N22) (☎ 066-7126-222). In Dingle, the Dingle District Hospital is on Upper Main Street (☎ 066-9151-455).

### Information

For visitor information in Tralee, go to the Tralee Tourist Office at Ashe Memorial Hall, Denny Street, Tralee (☎ 066-712-1288), which is open year-round. The Dingle Tourist Office is on Main Street, Dingle (☎ 066-915-1188).

### Internet

DingleWeb, Lower Main Street, Dingle (☎ 066-52-477), has Internet-access and printing capabilities.

# Part V
# The West and the Northwest

The 5th Wave  By Rich Tennant

We've been through the thin and the thick of it
So lost that we're thoroughly sick of it
   Our errors so far
   Leave us in Erin go braugh
It's Limerick, the town that we're looking for.

# *In this part . . .*

**Y**ou can't beat the West and Northwest for their sheer diversity of landscapes. In Clare (Chapter 17), take in the steep Cliffs of Moher, plummeting down to the sea; the rocky moon-scape of the Burren, studded with a rainbow of wild-flowers; and the county's sandy beaches. Up in County Galway (Chapter 18), explore the wild lakes, bogs, mountains, and beaches of Connemara, and gaze out at peaceful Galway Bay. Mayo (Chapter 19) offers heather-covered islands, beaches, and a continuation of the Connemara landscape of bogs, cliffs, and mountains, while travelers to Sligo (Chapter 19) will find lakes, beaches, and woodlands, many connected in some way with poet W.B. Yeats. If you want to get way off the well-trodden track, head up to wild, sparsely-populated County Donegal (Chapter 20) and explore the craggy coast-line, towering cliffs, sandy beaches, and impressive mountains of the region.

And I haven't even mentioned the cities and towns in these parts. Westport in County Mayo (Chapter 19) is one of the most charming, bustling, and picturesque towns in Ireland. Sligo Town (Chapter 19), a friendly town with a healthy arts scene, is an ideal base for exploring sights associated with Yeats. Limerick (Chapter 17) has shed its image of dilapidation, and offers some excellent historic sights, restaurants, and pubs, while Ennis is a small town with winding medieval streets and a fair share of traditional Irish music. And Galway City (Chapter 18) may turn out to be your favorite city in Ireland, with its beautiful location on the shores of Galway Bay and Lough Corrib, its tremendous selection of excellent restaurants, and its thriving pub and traditional Irish music scenes.

# Chapter 17

# Counties Limerick and Clare

. . . . . . . . . . . . . . . . . . . . . . . . . . . . . . . . . . . . . . . . . .

## In This Chapter

▶ Taking an *Angela's Ashes* walking tour in Limerick City

▶ Gazing at art from classical times to today in the Hunt Museum

▶ Gawking at the views from the sheer Cliffs of Moher

▶ Walking through the rocky, flora-filled plain of the Burren

▶ Becoming a banquet guest at a castle

▶ Hearing excellent traditional Irish music

. . . . . . . . . . . . . . . . . . . . . . . . . . . . . . . . . . . . . . . . . .

*F*or years, Counties Limerick and Clare (see the nearby map) were the first places visitors to Ireland saw, because all international flights used to go to Shannon airport in County Clare. Nowadays, Dublin airport has snagged a lot of that business, but whether you fly in directly or visit as part of the typical clockwise swing from Dublin south through Cork and Kerry and then up to Galway, Limerick and Clare are worth a stop. The two counties boast great natural beauty (the rocky plain of the Burren is a must-see), magnificent castles, loads of music (Clare in particular), and a handful of intriguing museums and historical sights.

## County Limerick: Limerick City and Adare

County Limerick has never exactly been the tourist hub of the country, but many visitors to Ireland pass through at some point. Those who have read Frank McCourt's *Angela's Ashes* often picture **Limerick City** (shown in the nearby map) as a town wracked with poverty, unemployment, alcoholism, and rain — lots of rain. "Out in the Atlantic Ocean," McCourt writes, "great sheets of rain gathered to drift slowly up the River Shannon and settle forever in Limerick. . . . The rain drove us to the church — our refuge, our strength, our only dry place. . . . Limerick gained a reputation for piety, but we knew it was only the rain."

## Counties Limerick and Clare

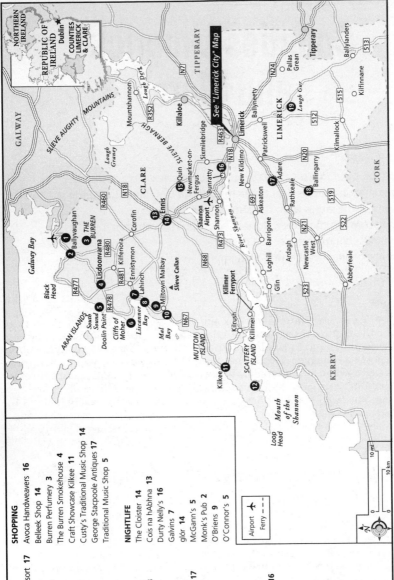

**ACCOMMODATIONS**
Adare Manor Hotel & Golf Resort **17**
Aran View House Hotel **5**
Berry Lodge **10**
Bunratty Castle Hotel **16**
Carrabawn House **17**
Dunraven Arms Hotel **17**
Queens Hotel **14**
Shamrock Inn Hotel **7**
Stella Maris **11**

**DINING**
Barrtrá Seafood Restaurant **8**
Berry Lodge **10**
Bruach na hAille **5**
Cruises Pub **14**
The Inn Between Restaurant **17**
The Mustard Seed **18**
The Wild Geese **17**

**ATTRACTIONS**
Adare Heritage Centre **17**
Aillwee Cave **1**
Bunratty Castle & Folk Park **16**
The Burren **2**
Burren Exposure **1**
Cliffs of Moher **6**
Dolphinwatch Boat Tour **12**
Eamon de Valera statue **14**
Knappogue Castle **15**
Lahinch Golf Club **7**
Lahinch Sea World **7**
Lough Gur **19**
Poulnabrone Dolmen **3**

**SHOPPING**
Avoca Handweavers **16**
Belleek Shop **14**
Burren Perfumery **3**
The Burren Smokehouse **4**
Craft Showcase Kilkee **11**
Custy's Traditional Music Shop **14**
George Stacpoole Antiques **17**
Traditional Music Shop **5**

**NIGHTLIFE**
The Cloister **14**
Cois na hAbhna **13**
Durty Nelly's **16**
Galvins **7**
glór **14**
McGann's **5**
Monk's Pub **2**
O'Briens **9**
O'Connor's **5**

Airport ✈
Ferry – – –

The whole west of Ireland does get its fair share of rain, but you'll be surprised to see how different in all other respects the Limerick of today is from the Limerick McCourt remembers from his youth. In recent years, the city has been pulling itself up from near dilapidation and is becoming a bustling place with a crop of great restaurants and good shopping, plus an excellent museum and several historic sights. Some places in the city still fit McCourt's description, but these are becoming fewer and fewer, as funky cafes open up in previously boarded-up buildings, and so on. A stroll along the River Shannon offers a striking vista of the city, and the imposing sight of **King John's Castle** is never far from view. Limerick City still isn't a destination city, like Dublin, Cork, Belfast, and Galway are, but it is worth a stop for a day or two if you're in this area.

With its main street of thatched-roof cottages, narrow streets, and ivy-covered churches, the pretty little town of **Adare** looks like a set for a movie about old Ireland. The town is clearly geared for tourism, and you find no lack of fellow travelers enjoying the little shops, excellent restaurants, and handful of historic sights. You don't need more than a morning or afternoon, or at most a day, to explore.

## Getting to County Limerick

**Shannon International Airport** (☎ 061-47-1444; www.shannonairport. com), located on the N19, off the N18, south of Ennis and 24km (15 miles) west of Limerick City, receives direct flights from North America, the Continent, and Britain (see Chapter 6 for more information). Rental-car company desks are located at Shannon airport's Arrivals Hall. All the major car-rental companies listed in Chapter 7 are represented there. **Bus Éireann** (☎ 061-31-3333; www.buseireann.ie) offers service from Shannon to the Limerick Railway Station.

### Getting to and around Limerick City

If you're coming by car, Limerick City can be reached by the N20 from Cork, N21 from Tralee, N24 from Tipperary, N7 from Dublin, or N18 from Ennis and Galway.

**Irish Rail** (☎ 061-31-5555; www.irishrail.ie) services Limerick City from Dublin, Cork, Killarney, and other cities throughout Ireland. Trains arrive at Colbert Station, Parnell Street, Limerick. **Bus Éireann** (☎ 01-836-6111; www.buseireann.ie) has daily service to Limerick City (Colbert Station, Parnell St.) and most towns in County Limerick.

Limerick City is best seen on foot. Park near King John's Castle (for free!), and hoof it from sight to sight. (Parking elsewhere in Limerick City requires disks that can be purchased at local shops.) A car is your best way of getting to the major attractions throughout the county, though Limerick has local bus service that covers the city's suburbs, running

## Limerick City

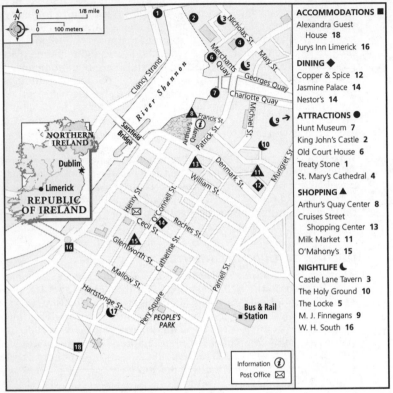

**ACCOMMODATIONS ■**
Alexandra Guest House **18**
Jurys Inn Limerick **16**

**DINING ◆**
Copper & Spice **12**
Jasmine Palace **14**
Nestor's **14**

**ATTRACTIONS ●**
Hunt Museum **7**
King John's Castle **2**
Old Court House **6**
Treaty Stone **1**
St. Mary's Cathedral **4**

**SHOPPING ▲**
Arthur's Quay Center **8**
Cruises Street Shopping Center **13**
Milk Market **11**
O'Mahony's **15**

**NIGHTLIFE ☾**
Castle Lane Tavern **3**
The Holy Ground **10**
The Locke **5**
M. J. Finnegans **9**
W. H. South **16**

Information *(i)*
Post Office ✉

from Colbert Station on Parnell Street, and Bus Éireann has service to other parts of the county. You can also catch a cab at Colbert Station or call **Top Cabs** (☎ 061-32-8011).

### Getting to and around Adare

By car, take N21 southwest from Limerick City. **Bus Éireann** (☎ 01-836-6111) runs through Adare. The town itself is completely walkable.

## Spending the night in Limerick City and Adare

### Adare Manor Hotel and Golf Resort
**$$$$** **Adare**

If nothing but the very best will do, this is the place for you. This tremendous castle-like manor house is one of the most beautiful properties in Ireland. There is nothing subtle about it — the structure was designed to reflect a variety of Irish and English homes admired by the first owners, the Lord and Lady Dunraven. It is an amalgam of styles, with turrets, 52 chimneys, and stone gargoyles gracing its exterior. The public rooms are breathtaking, especially the giant hall inspired by the Hall of Mirrors at Versailles. Opulent fabrics, hand-carved woodwork and stone, and gorgeous views of a river characterize the private rooms. And I haven't even mentioned the 840-acre grounds. The perfectly-groomed emerald grounds boast a Robert Trent Jones–designed golf course, a trout-filled river, formal French gardens, sweeping parklands, and majestic trees. A spa on the premises provides all sorts of relaxing treatments.

*Off the N-21.* ☎ *061-396-566. Rates: €215–€680 ($247–$782). Rates do not include breakfast. AE, DC, MC, V.*

### Alexandra Guest House
**$  Limerick City**

This elegant Victorian house sits in a row of classy homes just a few minutes' walk from the city center, on Limerick's main street. Rooms are big and comfortable, and there's a guest lounge where you can relax and enjoy a cup of tea or coffee. The lovely couple who run the guesthouse are happy to organize day tours. Another nice treat, if you've had your share of Irish breakfasts, is the healthy-meal option.

*O'Connell Ave. Take O'Connell St. south from the city center; O'Connell Ave. is an extension of O'Connell St.* ☎ *061-31-8472. Fax: 061-40-0433. Rates: €58–€64 ($67–$73) double. MC, V.*

### Carrabawn House
**$$  Adare**

Attention to detail and warm hospitality are the cornerstones of this luxurious guesthouse. It's not a thatched-roof cottage, but it is a comfortable, roomy house that you're sure to feel welcome in. It's right on Adare's main road, putting all of County Limerick's attractions within easy reach. Rooms are fully equipped with conveniences: television, phone, hair dryer, and tea and coffee. Be sure to check out the beautiful gardens.

*Killarney Rd. (N21).* ☎ *061-39-6067. Fax: 061-39-6925. Rates: €70–€90 ($81–$104) double. MC, V.*

### Dunraven Arms Hotel
**$$$  Adare**

Other hotels are going to seem like roughing it after you stay in the luxurious Dunraven Arms, built in 1792 and across the street from the well-preserved thatched cottages of little Adare, often called the prettiest village in all of Ireland. The charm of the village is carried into the hotel, where the Old World lives on. Rooms are exquisite, with beautiful antique furniture and even a dressing room. Modern-day does seep into some parts, though: There are a pool, steam room, and gym for guests' use.

*Main St. (N21).* ☎ *800-44-UTELL, from the U.S.; 061-39-6633. Fax: 061-39-6541.* www. dunravenhotel.com. *Rates: €150–€190 ($173–$219) double. AE, DC, MC, V.*

### Jurys Inn Limerick
#### $$$   Limerick City

This hotel is your standard, comfortable place to stay, and though the rooms are rather nondescript, the location is great — in the heart of the city. Best of all, though, kids stay free. This is one of the few places in Ireland that charge a flat room rate for up to three adults or two adults and two children, so if there are more than two of you, it's a great value. There are an informal restaurant, a pub, and a nearby public parking lot.

*Lower Mallow St. In the city center, just over the Shannon Bridge (N18).* ☎ *061-32-7777. Fax: 061-32-6400.* www.jurys.com. *Rates: €132–€182 ($152–$209) double. AE, DC, MC, V.*

## Dining locally in Limerick City and Adare

### Copper and Spice
#### $–$$   Limerick City   INDIAN AND THAI

This cool, modern restaurant does a bang-up job with both Thai and Indian standards and novel twists on these dishes, such as the monkfish curry with tandoori-roasted eggplant, tomatoes, and onions. The chef uses spices boldly to complement the flavors of the meat, fish, or vegetables. Large abstract paintings with fiery colors hang on the wall, small teardrop-shaped lamps dangle from the ceiling, and hammered-copper glasses and pitchers grace the tables. There are a number of excellent vegetarian

---

# The Irish coffee of champions

Every year, the best Irish coffee-makers duke it out for the title of Champion of Champions. The Championship takes place in Foynes, in County Limerick, in mid-July during a three-day festival complete with a smattering of festivities such as music, dancing, and a regatta. See www.irishcoffeefestival.com for more information.

In case you want to practice to compete, here's the basic recipe:

1. Warm a stem glass.

2. Add two teaspoons of sugar and a splash of whiskey.

3. Fill almost to the top with hot black coffee, and stir well.

4. Pour lightly whipped cream on top.

options here, including the okra with crunchy spiced onions. The €22.50 ($26) 3-course meal is quite a deal.

*2 Cornmarket Row. ☎ 061-313-620. Main courses: €8.25–€15 ($9.50–$17). AE, MC, V. Open: Daily 5–10:30 p.m.*

### The Inn Between Restaurant
$$–$$$   Adare   SEAFOOD-IRISH

The Inn Between, a cheery yellow thatched-roof cottage nestled in a row of other cottages, offers more than backdrop for great pictures. You also find good food and a bright, homey atmosphere. If you're good and hungry, try the always satisfying Inn Between burger, served with fries and home-made relish. If you're looking for something a little less hands-on, you can find plenty of more-upscale meals. The inn is particularly proud of its fish dishes. In the warm months, you can sit out back in a lovely courtyard.

*Main St. (N21). ☎ 061-39-6633. Main courses: €12–€20 ($14–$23). AE, DC, MC, V. Open: All year Thurs–Mon 7–9:30 p.m.; summer also 12:30–2:30 p.m.*

### Jasmine Palace
$–$$$   Limerick City   CHINESE

This is the finest Chinese food I found in the Limerick area, with standard Chinese dishes from General Tso's chicken to Peking Duck done beautifully. Not only is the food fantastic, but the crisp table linens and dim lighting also make for a nice atmosphere. A word to the wise: If you're really hungry, get some soup as a starter, because service can be slow.

*O'Connell Mall, O'Connell St. Between Cecil and Roaches streets in the city center. ☎ 061-41-2484. Main courses: €9.95–€18 ($11–$21). AE, DC, MC, V. Open: Mon–Sat 5 p.m. to midnight, Sun 1 p.m. to midnight.*

### The Mustard Seed
$$$$   Ballingarry   NEW IRISH

The surroundings are gorgeous enough to distract your attention, but even endless gardens, a splashing fountain, and a beautiful country manor can't take away the impact of the food at The Mustard Seed. You'll spend a bit more than at many other places mentioned in this book, but you'll get a true gourmet meal in return. Organic vegetables (from the restaurant's own garden), fruits, and cheeses are the foundation of the meals, which range from intriguing meatless entrees to savory poultry dishes, such as the honey-glazed chicken. The atmosphere is calm and gracious.

*Newcastlewest Rd., Echo Lodge. From Limerick City, take the N21 southwest to Adare, and then the R519 south to Ballingarry. ☎ 069-68-508. Main courses: €54 ($62) prix fixe. AE, MC, V. Open: Daily 7–9:30 p.m. Closed Sun and Mon in winter.*

### Nestor's
**$–$$$$ Limerick City INTERNATIONAL**

The brass rails and wood paneling found throughout this exceptional restaurant hint at the classy atmosphere and tasteful menu you find here. Whether you choose the traditional restaurant or Cafe Bar, you get friendly service and delicious, varied food. The restaurant features steaks (the house specialty), Tex-Mex, and pizza, and the cafe serves simple fare such as soups and sandwiches. After 8 p.m., you can often enjoy musical accompaniment (most often traditional Irish sessions) with your dinner. Kids should find something they like with all the variety on this menu.

*O'Connell St. in the city center.* ☎ *061-31-7334. Main courses: €10–€23 ($12–$26). AE, DC, MC, V. Open: Daily noon to 11 p.m.*

### The Wild Geese
**$$$$ Adare NEW IRISH**

Just to give you an idea of the kind of restaurant this is, when the gracious server came around with the bread basket, in addition to the usual white and wheat rolls, we were offered banana rolls, which turned out to be excellent. The chef here is not afraid to use his locally sourced ingredients with a sense of fun and daring. The menu changes, but expect main courses such as a breast of corn-fed chicken stuffed with brie and sun-dried tomatoes, wrapped in pancetta and served with a wild-mushroom risotto, and appetizers such as the onion-and-parmesan tartlet studded with raisins. The interior is simple and candlelit, and the mood is convivial.

*Rose Cottage, Main St.* ☎ *061-396-451. Main courses: two-course fixed-price dinner €30 ($35), three-course fixed-price dinner €36 ($41). AE, DC, MC, V. Open: Tues–Sat 6:30–10 p.m., Sun 6:30–9 p.m.*

## Exploring Limerick City and Adare

Limerick City has enough interesting sights to make a full day of sightseeing. Adare really only has one major attraction — the Heritage Centre — but it's a lovely place to wander.

### Joining an organized tour

The popular *Angela's Ashes* **Walking Tour** covers many sights mentioned in Frank McCourt's book. Tours leave daily at 2:30 p.m. from the tourist office at Arthur's Quay. Book by calling ☎ **061-327-108** or ☎ 087-635-3648. Tours cost €10 ($12).

Join experienced tour guides for an informative and interesting 90-minute **historical walking tour** covering many of Limerick's most interesting historical sights. Tours leave from the tourist office on Arthur's Quay daily at 11:00 a.m. and 2:30 p.m. Price is €8 ($9.20) per person. You can book at ☎ **061-317-522** or just show up.

If you'd rather see the town on your own, pick up the well-done Tourist Trail walking tour map at the visitor center.

The **Adare Heritage Centre** (reviewed in the next section) offers walking and bus tours of the area from July to September (call for times).

## Seeing the top attractions

### Adare Heritage Centre
**Adare**

This museum does a nice job of presenting the tumultuous history of Adare through displays, text, and audiovisuals. The highlight is the model of Adare during the Middle Ages; various areas light up in sync with a 20-minute narration. A 20-minute video also presents the town as it is today — which is interesting, but I suggest you spend the time seeing the real thing instead. Stop into the craft and knitwear shops on the premises, and pop into the cafe for some fresh-baked bread. Books are available if you want to learn more about the area. This place should give you a sense of what else you want to see in and around town.

*Main St.* ☎ *061-39-6666. Admission: €5 ($5.75) adults, €3.50 ($4.05) seniors, students, and children. Open: Daily 9:30 a.m.–5 p.m.. Suggested visit: 1 hour.*

### Hunt Museum
**Limerick City**

Located in Limerick's beautifully refurbished Custom House, this museum's art collection was generously donated by the Hunt family and includes many world-class pieces that occasionally go out on loan to international exhibitions. The range of art is extremely wide, with Picasso and da Vinci sculptures; medieval paintings, jewelry, and crystal; Egyptian, Greek, and Roman pieces; and a great deal of Irish art from as far back as prehistoric times. The fabulous shop in the lobby sells classy souvenirs, and the museum restaurant serves light meals.

*The Custom House, Rutland St. Next to Arthurs Quay on the River Shannon.* ☎ *061-31-2833. Admission: €6 ($6.90) adults, €4.75 ($5.45) students and seniors, €3 ($3.45) children. Open: Mon–Sat 10 a.m.–5 p.m., Sun 2–5 p.m. Suggested visit: 2 hours.*

### King John's Castle
**Limerick City**

This impressive fortress on the banks of the River Shannon was the brain-child of King John, who commissioned it in 1210, and whose name will forever be linked with it in the public mind (even though its real name is Limerick Castle). Clearly a place built to keep people out rather than hold court or host lavish parties, this castle is one of the finest examples of a fortified Norman structure in Ireland. Fierce war defenses sit in the court-yard (how often do you get to manhandle a real battering ram?), and you can get a great view of the city from the corner towers. The interior has been completely restored. To get a complete understanding of the castle's function over the centuries, check out the interpretive center. Models, displays, and graphics combine to explain the past, and the show *The Story of Limerick* explains the turbulent history of this city in an interesting way.

*Nicholas St. East of the Thomond Bridge, at the corner of Nicholas and Castle streets.* ☎ *061-41-1201. Admission: €6.15 ($7.10) adults, €5 ($5.75) seniors and students, €3.80 ($4.35) children. Open: Daily 9:30 a.m.–6 p.m. (last admission at 5 p.m.). Suggested visit:1½ hours.*

### Lough Gur
#### Southeast of Limerick City

If you're at all interested in prehistoric times, Lough Gur will strike your fancy. There are burial mounds, a wedge tomb, and the highlight: the 4,000-year-old Great Stone Circle. Evidence shows this Stone Age settlement was occupied from Neolithic times to medieval times, and what's left is now this archeological park of sorts. An interpretive center is housed in authentic-looking Stone Age huts right on the location of the original settlement. Inside are models of unearthed tools, weapons, and pottery, plus audiovisual displays. There are regular walking tours of the area, but I recommend exploring on your own.

*Lough Gur. 11km (7 miles) southeast of Limerick City off the N24 and R513.* ☎ *061-36-1511. Museum admission: €4.20 ($4.85) adults, €2.80 ($3.20) seniors and students. Park open year-round. Visitor Center open mid-May–Sept daily 10 a.m.–6 p.m. Suggested visit: 45 minutes.*

### More cool things to see and do

- **St. Mary's Cathedral:** Built in the 12th century, this is the oldest building in Limerick City. The rounded Romanesque doorway is a remnant of the original church. Inside are many beautiful 15th-century carvings in black oak. Mass is said daily.

  Location: Bridge Street, one block south of King John's Castle on Nicholas Street, Limerick. ☎ **061-310-293.** Donation: €1.30 ($1.50). Open June to September, Monday through Saturday from 9 a.m. to 5 p.m.; October to May, Monday through Saturday from 9 a.m. to 1 p.m.

- **Treaty Stone:** This noble slab of limestone is reportedly where the Treaty of Limerick was signed in 1691, ending the bloody Siege of Limerick led by Protestant William of Orange, who defeated Catholic King James II.

  Location: Across the Thomand Bridge, facing King John's Castle across the Shannon, Limerick.

# Remembering the Colleen Bawn trial

The famous Colleen Bawn trial occurred more than a century ago, but it could be in any of today's newspapers. The case involved the body of a young woman found on the banks of the Shannon. Turns out she was a servant girl, and her murderer was a wealthy landowner. The high-profile case was tried right here in Limerick's **Old Court House**, on Bridge Street across from St. Mary's Cathedral, and people came from far and wide to follow it. A public hanging followed, in the center of the city. But the sad fate of Colleen Bawn resonated among people across the country, and a play was written about the case. An opera followed suit, but it was renamed *The Lilly of Killarney* — apparently, Limerick didn't make for a sexy-enough set.

## Shopping

Limerick, like nearly all of Ireland's major cities, is a hub of shopping for the surrounding region. The main city thoroughfares, **O'Connell Street** and **William Street,** are lined with small shops and department stores. You won't find a load of places that sell souvenirs; the shopping here is vast and varied, but it mainly suits the needs of the people who live here.

Limerick City has two major shopping areas — one old and one new. The **Milk Market** (corner of Wickham and Ellen streets) is a restored medieval marketplace. Bordered by the original city walls, this quaint area offers country produce on Saturdays and local arts and crafts on Fridays. From Monday to Saturday, stalls and open-fronted shops make up the market, selling all sorts of products, including secondhand clothes and books. Most of city's real shopping gets done at the **Arthur's Quay Centre,** a modern mall in the heart of town. Inside this open, multistoried mall are 30 stores and places to eat. Locals also shop at **Cruises Street Shopping Center,** a complex of more than 50 retail outlets. **O'Mahony's,** 120 O'Connell St., Limerick, (☎ 061-41-8155) has a great selection of books, maps, and stationery so you can catch up on your Joyce or write friends back home in style.

In **Adare,** on the main street, Michelina and George Stacpoole sell sophisticated, brightly colored knitwear; great old Irish prints and postcards; old and rare books; and a vast selection of antiques in **George Stacpoole Antiques** (☎ 061-396-409; www.georgestacpooleantiques.com).

## Hitting the pubs

### Castle Lane Tavern
**Limerick City**

This beautiful tavern's decor (a medieval re-creation, in sort of a Disney way) is so detailed and authentic-looking you may be tempted to summon the barmaid with a hearty "Beer, wench!" — but I don't recommend it. I do suggest you grab a drink and maybe some soup or a sandwich and settle into one of the comfortable sunken benches or stools. The tavern is right next to King John's Castle and just down a cobbled alleyway. The whole area gives the pleasant feeling of being in a time warp.

*Nicholas St. next to St. John's Castle.* ☎ *061-31-8044.*

### The Holy Ground
**Limerick City**

Welcome to the world's only bar in a graveyard. That's right, a corner of the Holy Ground backs up to an old graveyard, and a section of it actually sits in it. It was once the home of the graveyard's *sexton* (or keeper) but was later transformed into a pub (and later still, it was featured on the television program *Ripley's Believe It or Not*). It's a thrill to go in, have a pint, and be able to say you drank in a graveyard, but that's about the only draw. It's pretty cramped (a few notches above cozy), and although regulars are used to tourists eagerly filing in, they're not always ready to open up to a chat. But don't let that stop you; it's a rare opportunity to (legally) be part of something so macabre and weird.

*1 Church St., south off John's Square.* ☎ *061-41-2583.*

### The Locke
**Limerick City**

Dating back to 1724, The Locke is one of Limerick City's oldest and best pubs, and it has a great location, too. It sits right on the bank of the river, amid some of the city's oldest landmarks: the Old Custom House (now the Hunt Museum) and the Old Court House. When weather permits, there's seating across the street on the quay. Inside, you can warm up at the open fires and listen to traditional music every Tuesday and Sunday night. Hot, home-cooked food is available.

*3 George's Quay.* ☎ *061-413-733.*

### M. J. Finnegans
**Annacotty**

Beautifully decorated in an old-world style, this pub combines elegance with homey comforts. Inside, you'll be surrounded by brickwork, wood, stone, and almost distracting vintage decor. If you're hungry, you're in luck; the food is above the usual pub-grub standards, and steaks and seafood are a specialty. There's seating outside when the weather permits. Finnegans is just outside Annacotty on the main Dublin Road.

*Dublin Rd. Take the N7 east from Limerick City.* ☎ *061-33-7338.*

*W. H. South*
**Limerick City**

Made famous by Frank McCourt's *Angela's Ashes,* this pub still basks in the glory bestowed by the Pulitzer Prize–winning author. The walls bear witness to newspaper accounts of the local uproar that occurred when the book was published (many Limerick natives objected to the negative light it cast on their city). Of course, there are also those who consider McCourt the local boy who made good. Star element aside, South's is a gorgeous pub, all wood, marble bar, and snugs, and always buzzing with people. During the day, hot and delicious lunches are served; the soup is consistently good.

*The Crescent, O'Connell St. ☎ 061-31-8850.*

# Fast Facts: County Limerick

**Area Codes**

County Limerick's area codes (or city codes) are 061, 063, 068, and 069.

**Emergencies/Police**

Dial ☎ **999** for all emergencies.

**Hospital**

St. John's Hospital (☎ 061-41-5822) is on St. John's Square, Limerick.

**Information**

For visitor information in Limerick City, go to the tourist center at Arthur's Quay, Limerick (☎ 061-31-7522). In Adare, visit

the Adare Heritage Center, on Main Street (☎ 061-396-666).

**Internet**

In Adare, you can use the Internet at Farriers Internet Café, on Newcastle West (☎ 061-396-163). In Limerick City, hit Netlink Internet Cafe, Sarsfield Street, right near the Sarsfield Bridge (☎ 061-467-869).

**Post Office**

The General Post Office is on Post Office Lane, off Lower Cecil Street, Limerick (☎ 061-31-4636).

# County Clare

County Clare often gets lost somewhere between the dazzle of Counties Galway and Kerry, but people who skip this county are missing out on some of Ireland's finest scenery and attractions. Clare doesn't boast any large cities, but it's dotted with quaint towns and villages that serve nicely as stopovers and starting points for sightseeing. The narrow streets of **Ennis,** the main town in the county, are bustling and lively. Pubs throughout the region offer excellent traditional Irish music. The county boasts two completely restored and furnished castles from the Middle Ages. And then there are the gorgeous and varied natural offerings of County Clare, from the rocky, plant-filled **Burren** to the sheer **Cliffs of Moher.**

## Getting to and around County Clare

**Shannon International Airport** (☎ 061-47-1444), located on the N19, off the N18, about 24 km (15 miles) south from County Clare's main town of Ennis and 24km (15 miles) west of Limerick, welcomes direct flights from North America, England, and other locations in Ireland. See Chapter 6 for more information on the airport.

If you're coming by car, take the N18 north from Limerick or south from Galway to Ennis. Rental-car company desks at Shannon airport's Arrivals Hall represent all the major car-rental companies listed in Chapter 7. **Shannon Ferries** (☎ 065 905-3124; www.shannonferries.com) runs a car ferry connecting Tarbert, County Kerry, with Killimer, County Clare, bypassing Limerick. It runs April to September Monday to Saturday from 7:00 a.m. to about 11:30 p.m., and Sunday from about 9:00 a.m. to about 11:30 p.m. From October to March it runs Monday to Saturday from 7:00 a.m. to about 7:30 p.m., and Sunday from about 10:00 a.m. to about 7:30 p.m. It costs €13 ($15) one-way, €20 ($23) round-trip. Ferries leave Killimer every hour on the hour and Tarbert every hour on the half-hour.

**Irish Rail** (☎ 065-6840-444; www.irishrail.ie) serves Ennis at the Ennis Rail Station on Station Road. All routes run through Limerick. **Bus Éireann** (☎ 01-836-6111; www.buseireann.ie) travels year-round to Ennis, Ballyvaughan, Doolin, Kilkee, and most towns in County Clare.

## Spending the night in County Clare

### Aran View House Hotel
$$–$$$ **Doolin**

Built in 1736, this gorgeous Georgian house overlooks some of Ireland's most fabulous vistas — you can see the Cliffs of Moher and the Aran Islands from here. Rooms are big and tastefully decorated, and the house sits on 100 acres of farmland. The restaurant (fish is the specialty) is comfortable and full of atmosphere, and the staff is sweet and helpful.

*Coast Rd. On the road to the Cliffs of Moher; R487 northwest from Lahinch or southwest from Lisdoonvarna.* ☎ *065-707-4061. Fax: 065-707-4540.* www.aranview.com. *Rates: €100–€160 ($115–$184) double. AE, DC, MC, V. Closed Nov–March.*

### Berry Lodge
$$ **Annagh, Miltown Malbay**

This is a must-stay for any serious gourmet. Originally a well-known cooking school, this 17th-century country house near the sea now offers surprisingly inexpensive accommodation as well. The rooms are simple and colorfully decorated, but the real draw of the place is the food, grown and caught locally. You'll want to have dinner at the Lodge and even consider taking one of the cooking classes — special weekend rates combine rooms with classes. Views of farmlands and sea are spectacular.

*From Kerry, take the car ferry from Tarbert to Killimer. Take the N67 into Quilty village; take the third turn right and then take the first right into Berry Lodge.* ☎ *065-708-7022. Fax: 065-708-7011.* www.berrylodge.com. *Rates:* €74–€80 *($85–$92) double. AE, MC, V.*

### Bunratty Castle Hotel
**$$$   Bunratty**

This bright-yellow Georgian hotel is in the center of Bunratty village, with the famed pub Durty Nelly's just across the street. The hotel is only a few years old, and all rooms are tastefully decorated in traditional Irish style, with dark woods and floral bedspreads. Rooms have every convenience, including air conditioning — pretty rare in Ireland. Everyone is friendly and willing to help. County Clare's top sights are only a short drive away. Kathleen's Irish pub is pleasant and serves food, and you're likely to run across plenty of people to chat with.

*On the Shannon/Limerick road (N18).* ☎ *061-70-7034.* www.bunrattycastle hotel.com. *Rates:* €140–€180 *($161–$207) double. AE, DC, MC, V.*

### Queens Hotel
**$$–$$$   Ennis**

Everything about this hotel is perfectly charming. Old-world hospitality reigns, and the style is traditional Irish. From here, in the center of Ennis, all of County Clare's sights are only a stone's throw away. The bedrooms are completely decked out, with TV, video player, and radio. At the famous Cruise's Pub and Restaurant (which adjoins the hotel), you find excellent home-cooked Irish food and traditional music nightly.

*Abbey St.* ☎ *065-682-8963. Fax: 065-682-8628.* www.irishcourthotel.com. *Rates:* €90–€200 *($104–$230) double. AE, DC, MC, V.*

### Shamrock Inn Hotel
**$$   Lahinch**

This little hotel, located in the heart of the pretty seaside resort town of Lahinch, is pleasant and charming. Rooms are attractively decorated, with pastels and colorful bedspreads, and have a TV, hair dryer, and tea and coffee. The restaurant is cozy, relaxing, and popular with locals, offering a variety of home-cooked dishes. Food is served in the pub during the day, and at night, good Irish music fills the room.

*Main St.* ☎ *065-708-1700. Fax: 065-708-1029.* www.atlantichotel.ie. *Rates:* €101–€112 *($116–$129) double. AE, MC, V.*

### Stella Maris
**$$  Kilkee**

This small, family-run guesthouse located in the heart of town perfectly reflects the quaintness of Kilkee. You can sit by the open peat fires inside or out on the veranda overlooking the bay. The staff is friendly and welcoming. The bar features traditional music and hearty, home-cooked food.

*O'Connell St. Take the N67 south from Ennistymon or N68 southwest from Ennis.* ☎ *065-905-6455. Fax: 065-906-0006. Rates: €90–€130 ($104–$150) double. AE, MC, V.*

## Dining locally in County Clare
Also see Berry Lodge, reviewed in the previous section.

### Barrtrá Seafood Restaurant
**$$–$$$  Lahinch  SEAFOOD**

This small and homey restaurant is down a wee farm road and overlooks Liscannor Bay. The friendly staff serves some of the freshest lobster, oysters, mussels, and salmon on the west coast, all prepared with simple and innovative sauces, spices, or herbs that highlight the taste of the fish, such as the delicious haddock with lime and ginger. The wine list is extensive, and the desserts, such as the gin-and-tonic sorbet, are creative and delicious.

*Off the N67. Go 3.2km (2 miles) south of Lahinch on the Lahinch/Miltown Malbay coast road (N67) until you see the small road to the restaurant.* ☎ *065-708-1280. Reservations required. Main courses: €18–€24 ($21–$28), prix-fixe dinner €35 ($40), early-bird dinner €20 ($23). AE, MC, V. Open: July and Aug daily 5–10 p.m.; Feb–April and Oct Thurs–Sun 5–10 p.m.; May, June, and Sept Tues–Sat 5–10 p.m.*

### Bruach na hAille
**$$–$$$  Doolin  SEAFOOD**

This cottage-like restaurant offers a simple, delicious menu. Local, incredibly fresh seafood is the highlight, and it's prepared creatively. Don't miss the baked seafood au gratin or filet of sole in cider with shellfish cream sauce. Non-fish-lovers have options too.

*Drive through Doolin north along the coast road (R479) 1.6km (1 mile).* ☎ *065-707-4120. Main courses: €16–€25($18–$29). MC, V. Open: April–Oct daily 6–9:30 p.m.*

### Cruises Pub
**$–$$  Ennis  IRISH**

The staff at this cozy, authentic pub is the living embodiment of Irish hospitality, and it serves up a wide range of well-done dishes, from superb lamb stew to excellent pizzas and calzones to salmon with lemon-dill sauce, plus a selection of vegetarian dishes. The interior is dim and traditional, with beautiful carved wood; open fireplaces; tin signs on the wall; and shelves filled with old and weathered miscellany, from jugs and bottles to books. There's top-quality traditional Irish music most nights.

*Abbey St.* ☎ *065-684-1800. Main courses: €7.20–€15 ($8–$17). AE, DC, MC, V. Open: Sun–Thurs noon to midnight, Sat and Sun noon–1 a.m.*

## Exploring County Clare

Several bus companies run tours of the Burren, the Cliffs of Moher, and other attractions in Clare out of Galway City. For details on the various tours, call or visit the Galway Tourist Office (also known as Ireland West Tourism or Aras Fáilte) at Victoria Place, in Eyre Square, Galway City (☎ 091-53-77-00; www.westireland.travel.ie). Healy's (☎ 091-77-0066) is the current favorite for touring the area; it departs from the Galway tourist office daily during the summer and a few times a week during the off season (call for schedules).

### The top attractions

#### Aillwee Cave
**The Burren**

A guide takes you down into this vast cave, where you see ancient stalagmites and stalactites, cross bridges that span frighteningly deep chasms, and get wet standing near the crashing underground waterfall. And you'll be taken into the eerie hibernation chamber of the brown bear that used to inhabit this area. When you're back above ground, you can shop in the many craft shops selling minerals, fossils, and handmade gifts. There's a dairy where you can watch cheese being made and a tearoom where light snacks are served.

*Off the R480 south of Ballyvaughan.* ☎ *065-707-7036. Admission: €8 ($9.20) adult, €6.50 ($7.50) seniors and students, €4.50 ($5.20) children. Open: March–mid-Nov daily 10 a.m.–5:30 p.m. Suggested visit: 1 hour.*

#### Bunratty Castle and Folk Park
**Bunratty**

This formidable castle, built in 1425 and pillaged many times over, is one of Ireland's biggest attractions. It's one of the most authentic medieval castles in the country, and great care has been taken to ensure that the interior is as it was in the 15th century, with furnishings and tapestries that replicate the era. Great halls and tiny stairways characterize the castle, and the dungeon is so eerie that you just may get a serious spook unless you bring someone down there with you. On the castle grounds is the Bunratty Folk Park, an excellent re-creation of a 19th-century Irish village. You can poke your head into farmhouses, a blacksmith's forge, and a watermill, and go down a typical village street that has it all: post office, school, pawn shop, doctor's house, printers, hardware shop, and a real pub where you can stop in for a bite and a drink. At night, Bunratty Castle hosts huge medieval banquets (see the nearby sidebar "Feasting at a castle!").

*On the N18 north of Limerick. The short exit ramp off the N18 takes you to the entrance of the castle.* ☎ *061-360-788. Admission: €10 ($12) adults, €7.95 ($9.15) seniors and students, €5.60 ($6.45) children. Open: Daily 9:30 a.m.–5:30 p.m. Suggested visit: At least 2 hours.*

### The Burren
**Northwest County Clare**

Don't miss this amazing phenomenon — a vast expanse of limestone, as far as the eye can see, that's home to a variety of unique plants and animals. The name *Burren* comes from the Irish *bhoireann,* for "a barren, rocky place," and the "rocky" designation is totally accurate. Instead of bogs and pastures, you find boulders, little lakes and streams, and expansive fields of stone. "Barren" is not really accurate, though; because the limestone covers a maze of underground caves, water seeps up through cracks in the rock, supporting a wide and spectacular variety of plants, including species that usually thrive only in the Arctic or Mediterranean. Lizards, badgers, frogs, and numerous birds call the Burren home. In addition, 26 species of butterflies have been seen here, including one that's indigenous to the area: the Burren Green. Despite the lack of soil, humans lived in the area from the neolithic period through medieval times, leaving behind a variety of structures from dolmens (burial monuments) to churches. From various spots on the Burren, you get views of Clare and Galway Bay. The best way to explore the Burren is by walking. You can either set off on your own on part (or all) of the 42km (26-mile) Burren Way (you can get an information sheet on the trail from any tourist office in the area) or join a guided tour. The hands-down best guided tours are those by **Christy Browne** (☎ 065-708-1168; call ahead to book and find out details), a renowned scholar of the Burren, who covers the history, folklore, animal and plant life, and the geology of the area. The Burren is at its most colorful, with tons of wildflowers, in May and June, but you'll find a variety of flora year-round. You may want to park and begin your exploration of the Burren at Burren Exposure (see the next review).

### Burren Exposure
**Ballyvaughan**

This excellent multimedia center presents a fascinating, clear, succinct introduction to the natural and social history of the Burren. I highly recommend visiting if you're planning to explore the area.

*Galway Rd. (N76), 0.4km (¼ mile) north of Ballyvaughan.* ☎ *065-707-7777. Admission: €5 ($5.75) adults, €3.50 ($4.05) seniors and students. Open: March–Nov 9 a.m.–6 p.m.*

## The Cliffs of Moher

 *Spectacular* doesn't begin to describe the view from these breathtaking cliffs. At places, they rise more than 213m (700 feet) above the crashing Atlantic and stretch for miles in both directions. On the highest cliff is O'Brien's Tower, which was built in the 1800s as a viewing point for tourists. From the tower, you can see the Clare coast; the Aran Islands; and, on a clear day, mountains as far away as Kerry and Connemara. When it's sunny, the cliffs take on a purple hue (hence, the Purple Cliffs of Moher of story and song), and when the wind and rain blow in, it can be a bit harrowing up there. There's a lovely little shop and tearoom in the visitor center. The cliffs can be very touristy, so be prepared for Irish fiddlers in the parking lot and so on.

 *Be extremely careful when walking along the cliffs!* There are no rails separating you from the rocks far below, and sometimes, wind gusts can push you around, so take extreme care when approaching the edges. Watch kids carefully, too.

*Off the R478 on the Atlantic coast. Take the R487 northwest from Lahinch or southwest from Lisdoonvarna.* ☎ *065-708-1171. Free admission to cliffs. Admission: O'Briens Tower €1.50 ($1.75) adult, €0.80 (90¢) children.; parking: €1.25 ($1.45). Open: Cliffs are always accessible. Open: Visitor center daily 9:30 a.m.–5:30 p.m.; O'Brien's Tower May–Sept daily 9:30 a.m.–5:30 p.m. Suggested visit: 45 minutes.*

## Knappogue Castle
### Quinn

This imposing 15th-century castle has seen its share of history. Built by the McNamaras, it was the pride of the tribe, which dominated the area for 1,000 years. But the stronghold had its troubles, too. In the 1700s, Cromwell's troops occupied the castle for ten years, and during the War of Independence in the 1920s, revolutionary forces camped within its walls. The castle has been extraordinarily refurbished, and the interior is overflowing with 15th-century antiques and period furnishings. This castle also hosts a medieval banquet.

*Just off the Ennis-Killmury road (R469) southeast from Ennis.* ☎ *061-36-0788. Admission: €4.20 ($4.85) adults, €2.80 ($3.20) seniors and students, €2.40 ($2.75) children. Open: May–Oct daily 9:30 a.m.–5:30 p.m. (last admission 4:30 p.m.). Suggested visit: 1 hour.*

 ## Lahinch Sea World
### Lahinch

This fascinating Atlantic aquarium will entertain all ages. You come face to face with creatures from the Irish coast, such as sharks, lobsters, rays, and Conger eels. Kids love the touch pool, where they can feel starfish, anemones, and other underwater life. There are a fisherman's cabin, a lobster breeding station, and regular feeding sessions. Want a chance to swim like the fishes? Lahinch Sea World also has a huge indoor heated pool, Jacuzzi, sauna, and kiddie pool. The souvenir shop is well stocked, and the cafe serves light meals and snacks.

*The Promenade. West of Ennistymon on the N67.* ☎ *065-708-1900. Admission: Aquarium only €6 ($6.90) adult, €6 ($6.90) seniors and students, €5 ($5.75) children under 16, €3 ($3.45) 2-4. Open: Daily 10 a.m.–9 p.m. Suggested visit: 2 hours.*

### Poulnabrone Dolmen
**The Burren**

These structures are ancient burial monuments dating back 6,000 years. They're a prominent aspect of the Burren, and more people photograph this landmark than almost any other in Ireland. Go on — stand under the humongous stone and pretend you're holding it up.

*The Burren. Off R480 south from Ballyvaughan.*

## More cool things to see and do

✔ **Lahnich Golf Club:** High elevations at this club provide amazing views of sea and valley. Watch your ball — local goats are known to cross the fairway. There are two 18-hole courses here: the Old Course (par 71) and the Castle Course (par 70).

Location: Lahnich Golf Club, Lahnich, County Clare (☎ 065-708-1003). Fees are €110 ($127) for the old course, €50 ($58) for the castle course. Visitors are welcome daily.

✔ **Dolphinwatch Boat Tour:** This fun and informative two-hour boat trip takes you out among a resident group of friendly bottleneck dolphins. The boat is equipped with a hydrophone, so you can listen to dolphins communicate underwater.

Location: The trip leaves from the port village of Carrigaholt daily April through October, weather permitting. You must book ahead for July and August trips (☎ 065-905-8156); call the morning of the trip to book during other months. The tour costs €18 ($21) adults, €9 ($10) children 16 and under; children 2 and under ride free.

✔ **Eamon de Valera Statue:** Eamon de Valera, Irish freedom fighter, president, and prime minister, is honored with a bronze statue in Ennis. De Valera was born in New York; his American citizenship kept him from facing the firing squad after his part in the Easter Rising of 1916. Find out more about Irish history in Chapter 2.

Location: Ennis town park, off Gort Road (R352).

# Feasting at a castle!

Bunratty and Knappogue castles both stage fun (albeit touristy) **medieval banquets,** complete with a feast of food and lively entertainment.

At Bunratty, the evening features a delicious feast (eaten with your hands, of course), period music and song, and mugs of honey mead. The banquet at Knappogue celebrates the women of Celtic Ireland, both historical and mythical — queens, saints, and sinners. The entertainment involves storytelling, singing, dancing, and music, all masterfully done.

Bunratty also hosts **Traditional Irish Nights,** which aim to replicate a night in a thatch-roofed cottage of old Ireland. You'll dine on Irish stew, brown bread, and apple pie with cream, and then listen to live foot-tapping Irish music.

Reservations are required for all of these events; call ☎ **061-360-788.** The banquets cost €48 ($55), and the Irish night costs €52 ($60).

## *Shopping*

**Avoca Handweavers,** Bunratty (off the N18 north of Limerick; ☎ **061-36-4029**), sells the famous handwoven clothing and accessories from the Avoca Mill in County Wicklow, in addition to Avoca's more trendy line. **Belleek Shop,** 36 Abbey St., Ennis (☎ **065-682-9607**) is the best store in the area for Waterford Crystal; Irish tweed; and, of course, Belleek pottery — that thin white pottery decorated with shamrocks. They have top-notch customer service. The oldest perfumery in Ireland, **Burren Perfumery,** Carron (☎ **065-708-9102**), uses local flora to create unique fragrances. To get there, take the R480 to the Carron turnoff; the shop is located just north of town. **The Burren Smokehouse,** Lisdoonvarna, (☎ **065-707-4432**), is a gourmet store selling the finest smoked Irish Atlantic salmon, trout, mackerel, and eel. You can watch the process of smoking at the visitor center. **Craft Showcase Kilkee,** O'Connell Street, Kilkee ☎ **065-905-6141**), sells crafts from ceramics and sheepskin rugs to Celtic jewelry and baskets — all as authentic and traditional as you'll find. The store is on the main Kilkee-Kilrush Road, on the right from Kilkee city center. The **Traditional Music Shop,** Doolin, (☎ **065-7074-407**), is one of the best shops in the area for Irish instruments (like an authentic tin whistle), plus a large variety of Irish music on CD and cassette — a little traveling music for the rental car! Another terrific traditional music shop is **Custy's Traditional Music Shop,** 2 Francis St., Ennis (☎ **065-682-1727**).

## Nightlife in County Clare

If you've ever wanted to try Irish set dancing (a partnered form of dance that resembles American square dancing), get yourself over to **Cois na hAbhna,** Gort Road (☎ **065-682-0996**) on a Wednesday night. After a performance of music, song, and dancing, Dick O'Connell teaches traditional *ceili dancing* (ceili is pronounced *kay*-lee) from 8:30 to 11:30 p.m. Call to confirm, as times and venue may change.

Ennis's fabulous new performing arts complex **glór,** Friar's Walk, Ennis (☎ 065-684-3013; www.glor.ie), offers music, theater, dance, and visual arts. This place books many of the finest traditional Irish music legends, so be sure to find out which musicians are performing while you're around.

### Hitting the pubs

Also see the excellent **Cruises,** in "Where to dine in County Clare," earlier in this chapter.

### The Cloister
**Ennis**

This pub sits next to the famed Ennis friary, and in the summer, you can sit outside within arm's length of the landmark. Inside, the pub is comfortable and homey, and pub grub is served all day.

*Abbey St. in the center of town.* ☎ *065-682-9521.*

### Durty Nelly's
**Bunratty**

No trip to Clare is complete without a stop in this world-famous pub. Since 1620, this tavern has been a thirst-quencher for everyone from the guards who once protected Bunratty Castle to the tourists who explore it today. The interior looks like it hasn't changed over the centuries, with sawdust-strewn floors, low lighting from lanterns, and traditional music sessions that commence at any time in any room of the pub. There's seating outside for nice days, and a pretty good restaurant is upstairs.

*Next to Bunratty Castle. Take N18 north from Limerick.* ☎ *061-36-4861.*

### Galvins
**Lahinch**

You won't be able to sit still in this interesting pub — there's too much to see. Don't worry — they're used to people wandering around with a pint and looking at the pictures that line the walls. It's a great place to hear music, and musicians passing through the area often drop in to play.

*Church St. in the center of town.* ☎ *065-81-045.*

### McGann's
**Doolin**

This Doolin pub has excellent traditional Irish music and well-pulled pints of Guinness, and is often less packed than O'Connor's (reviewed later in this section).

*Lisdoonvarna Rd.* ☎ *065-707-4133.*

### Monk's Pub
**Ballyvaughan**

A taste of the old world is retained at Monk's, where peat fires burn and rustic furnishings invite you to take a seat. It's right on the water, and good pub grub is served all day. Music fills the air most nights.

*Take the R476 to the R480 north from Ennis.* ☎ *065-707-7059.*

### O'Briens
**Miltown Malbay**

This is the cutest pub in all of Ireland. It is just larger than a walk-in-closet — room enough for one bench, two bar stools, a 4-foot bar and a single Guinness tap (don't worry — the pints are full-size). Joe Murray runs the place and keeps things shipshape.

*Main St. No phone.*

### O'Connor's
**Doolin**

If the prospect of hearing Irish music plays any part in your choice of pubs, O'Connor's is for you. This is one of the premier spots in the country for traditional sessions, and fans travel from all over to hear them. The same family has run this combination pub and market for more than 150 years. The pub sits amid a row of thatched fisherman cottages and really comes to life at night. If this proves too packed, head up to McGann's (reviewed earlier in this section).

*Off the N67 west of Lisdoonvarna.* ☎ *065-707-4168.*

# Fast Facts: County Clare

**Area Codes**

County Clare's area codes (or city codes) are 061 and 065.

**Emergencies/Police**

Dial ☎ **999** for all emergencies.

**Genealogy Resources**

Contact the Clare Heritage Centre, Church Street, Corofin (☎ 065-683-7955).

**Hospital**

Ennis Hospital is on Galway Road (☎ 065-682-4464).

## Information

For visitor information, go to the Ennis Tourist Office Authors Road, Ennis (☎ 065-682-8366), open year-round. It's south of town on N18.

## Internet

MacCools Internet Cafe, Brewery Lane, Ennis (☎ 065-682-1988), and Kilrush Internet Cafe, The Monastery, Kilrush (☎ 065-51-061), have Internet access and printing capabilities.

## Post Office

The General Post Office is on Bank Place, Ennis (☎ 065-682-8976).

# Chapter 18

# County Galway: Galway City, the Aran Islands, and Connemara

● ● ● ● ● ● ● ● ● ● ● ● ● ● ● ● ● ● ● ● ● ● ● ● ● ● ● ● ● ● ● ● ● ● ● ● ● ● ●

## In This Chapter

▶ Hearing some great traditional Irish music in Galway City
▶ Dining in the best restaurants in the West
▶ Visiting the peaceful Aran Islands, bastions of tradition
▶ Exploring the vast boglands and mountains of Connemara
  (and meeting some sweet Connemara ponies!)

● ● ● ● ● ● ● ● ● ● ● ● ● ● ● ● ● ● ● ● ● ● ● ● ● ● ● ● ● ● ● ● ● ● ● ● ● ● ●

County Galway (shown in the nearby map) is a winning combination of the fun and bustle of Galway City with its great music, pubs, restaurants, and shops; the wild and breathtaking mountain-and-bog landscape of Connemara; the peaceful Aran Islands; picturesque small towns; and one of the largest Gaeltachts (Irish-speaking regions) in the country.

## Galway City

Buzzing Galway City serves as a gateway to the rest of the county. It's a fabulous city to explore, with a youthful university population; a robust contemporary (and often avant-garde) arts scene that keeps getting stronger; loads of traditional Irish music; and a great variety of both trendy and traditional places to eat, sleep, drink, and shop. Plus, the city has a gorgeous location, set on peaceful Galway Bay, which is home to a number of swans, and the River Corrib, a favored fishing location. The only thing that Galway City doesn't have is major sights within the city; there are places to visit, but there aren't any must-see attractions. The medieval center of the city is so tiny that you'll know your way around in no time. The "Galway City" map can help you find restaurants, hotels, and other attractions.

## County Galway

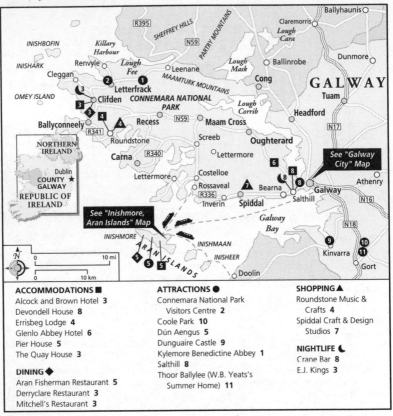

R395
SHEFFREY HILLS
N59
PARTRY MOUNTAINS
Ballyhaunis ○
Claremorris ○
Lough Cara
INISHBOFIN
Killary Harbour
INISHARK
Renvyle ○
Lough Fee
Leenane ○
Lough Mask
Ballinrobe ○
Dunmore ○
Cleggan ○
MAAMTURK MOUNTAINS
Cong ○
GALWAY
❷
Letterfrack
OMEY ISLAND
❸
Clifden ○
CONNEMARA NATIONAL PARK
Lough Corrib
Tuam ○
❸
Headford ○
Ballyconneely ○
❸
❹
Recess ○
N59
Maam Cross ○
N17
R341
NORTHERN IRELAND
Roundstone ○
Screeb ○
Oughterard ○
See "Galway City" Map
Carna ○
R340
Lettermore ○
❻
Dublin
COUNTY GALWAY ★
Costelloe ○
❽
❽
Athenry ○
REPUBLIC OF IRELAND
Lettermore ○
Rossaveal ○
❼
Bearna ○
❽
Galway ○
R336
Salthill ○
N16
Inverin ○
Spiddal ○
See "Inishmore, Aran Islands" Map
Galway Bay
N18
INISHMORE
A R A N   I S L A N D S
INISHMAAN
❾
❿
Kinvarra ○
⓫
❺
INISHEER
Gort ○
N
0        10 mi
❺
❺
0      10 km
Doolin ○

| ACCOMMODATIONS ■ | ATTRACTIONS ● | SHOPPING ▲ |
|---|---|---|
| Alcock and Brown Hotel **3** | Connemara National Park | Roundstone Music & |
| Devondell House **8** | Visitors Centre **2** | Crafts **4** |
| Errisbeg Lodge **4** | Coole Park **10** | Spiddal Craft & Design |
| Glenlo Abbey Hotel **6** | Dún Aengus **5** | Studios **7** |
| Pier House **5** | Dunguaire Castle **9** | |
| The Quay House **3** | Kylemore Benedictine Abbey **1** | **NIGHTLIFE** ☾ |
| | Salthill **8** | Crane Bar **8** |
| **DINING** ◆ | Thoor Ballylee (W.B. Yeats's | E.J. Kings **3** |
| Aran Fisherman Restaurant **5** | Summer Home) **11** | |
| Derryclare Restaurant **3** | | |
| Mitchell's Restaurant **3** | | |

It's said that Christopher Columbus made his last European stop here before setting sail on his famous trip for the New World. Although most people don't arrive by galleon these days, tourism is still huge. However, there's little that's tacky about Galway City, and one gets the sense that the city caters to visitors and locals equally — they certainly don't roll up the sidewalk when the tourists go home. Inside the city veneer is the heart of a small town, with all the hospitality and approachability that implies.

## Getting to and around Galway City

**Aer Lingus** (www.aerlingus.com) has daily service from Dublin into Galway Airport, in Carnmore (☎ **091-75-5569;** www.galwayairport. com). The best way to get into town from the airport is by taxi, which should cost about €16 ($18).

If you're driving to Galway City, take the N18 from Limerick, the N4 and N6 from Dublin, or the N17 from Sligo. If you'd like to rent a car in Galway, try **Budget** (☎ 090-662-7711), on Eyre Square.

**Irish Rail** (☎ 1850-366-222; www.irishrail.ie) pulls into Ceannt Station, near Eyre Square, in the center of Galway, from Dublin and other points. **Bus Éireann** (☎ 011-836-6111; www.buseireann.ie) also travels to Ceannt Station. The private coach service **CityLink** (☎ 091-56-4163) travels between Galway and Dublin for a better price than Bus Éireann.

 Galway City is best seen on foot. The town is compact, and the heart is pedestrian-only, so a car wouldn't do you much good. If you do take a car into the city, know that parking in Galway City requires disks that you can purchase at local shops. Galway has a great local bus service that covers the city's suburbs, running along Eyre Square out to Salthill and the coastal towns. Call ☎ 091-56-2000 for information. You can pick up a taxi on Eyre Square or by calling a taxi company such as **Galway Taxis** (☎ 091-56-1112) or **Cara Cabs** (☎ 091-563-939).

Anchored by **Eyre Square** (*Eyre* is pronounced *air*), which is undergoing major reconstruction that should be complete by the time you read this, the city's picturesque main streets stretch down to the harbor.

## Spending the night in Galway City

 ### Brennans Yard Hotel
**$$–$$$   Galway City**

If you're looking for the hippest hotel in Galway City, stop right now, because you've found it. Right in the heart of the action, near the city's famous Spanish Arch, this hotel occupies a renovated warehouse and has sleek, contemporary decor in both its public spaces and its uncluttered, pine-furnished bedrooms. The staff is also hip — and friendly and knowledgable to boot.

*Lower Merchant's Rd.* ☎ *800-44-UTELL or 091-568-166. Fax: 091-568-262. Rates:* €105–€145 ($121–$161). AE, DC, MC, V.

 ### Devondell House
**$   Galway City**

Berna Kelly should run a school for aspiring B&B hosts and hostesses. Warm and welcoming, she greets every guest with a tea tray filled with home-baked treats and is happy to help you plan your days in Galway and the surrounding area. Her home is cozy and sparkling clean, and rooms are homey and comfortable, with patchwork quilts and crisp Irish linens. You may not want to make any sightseeing plans for the morning because

## Galway City

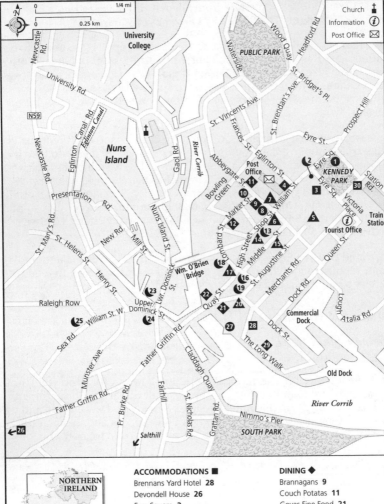

**NORTHERN IRELAND**

Galway City ★

**REPUBLIC OF IRELAND**

**ATTRACTIONS** ●
Browne Doorway **1**
Collegiate Church of
  St. Nicholas **12**
Lynch Memorial Window **10**
Lynch's Castle **8**
Spanish Arch **27**

**ACCOMMODATIONS** ■
Brennans Yard Hotel **28**
Devondell House **26**
Eyre Square **3**
Galway Great Southern Hotel **30**

**SHOPPING** ▲
Design Concourse Ireland **20**
Eyre Square Shopping Centre **5**
Kennys Bookshop and Galleries **14**
MacEocagain/Galway
  Woolen Market **14**
Mulligan **15**
P. Powell & Sons **6**
Thomas Dillon's **17**
The Treasure Chest **7**

**DINING** ◆
Brannagans **9**
Couch Potatas **11**
Goyas Fine Food **21**
Kirwan's Lane **21**
Maxwell McNamaras **4**
McDonagh's Seafood
  House **22**
Nimmo's Wine Bar **29**

**NIGHTLIFE** ☾
Crane Bar **25**
Druid Theatre Company **16**
The Kings Head **13**
Monroe's Tavern **24**
The Quays **19**
Róisín Dubh **23**
Skeff Bar **2**
Tíg Neachtain **18**

Berna's incredible breakfast, which is served at two tables so that you can chat with your fellow guests, invites lingering. The options are endless, from delicious stewed pears, plums, rhubarb, and other fruits to a comprehensive cheese plate to fruit smoothies. And that's just the preamble to the main course! The house is about a 20-minute walk from the heart of Galway City and is within walking distance of the seafront.

*47 Devon Park, Lower Salthill.* ☎ *091-528-306. Rates: €80 ($92) double. No credit cards. Open Feb–Oct.*

### Eyre Square
$$ **Galway City**

This is a classic Irish hotel, with loads of dark wood and a pub downstairs. The location is terrific, right near the bus and railway stations and the heart of Galway's restaurant, shopping, and pub scenes. Rooms, decorated in simple and standard hotel style, are spacious and well maintained.

*Forster St.* ☎ *091-56-9633. Rates: €100 ($115) double. MC, V.*

### Galway Great Southern Hotel
$$$–$$$$ **Galway City**

This is Galway's poshest address. Rooms on one of the higher floors of this incredibly refined hotel offer views of the entire city and beyond. From the rooftop hot tub, you may fool yourself into thinking you can see all the way to Canada! The hotel, centrally located near Galway's main streets, was built in 1845 and is an exquisite example of Victorian style. The spacious lobby and sitting rooms have high ceilings and are furnished with crystal chandeliers and marble from the nearby hills of Connemara. The spacious rooms are elegant, boasting both Victorian antiques and modern amenities such as TVs with Internet access. There are special low rates for children, and a babysitting service is available. If you're looking for fine dining, book a table at the Oyster Room. For a more relaxed meal and a warm atmosphere, stop into O'Flaherty's Pub.

*15 Eyre Sq.* ☎ *850-38-38-48 or 091-56-4041. Fax: 091-56-6704.* www.gshotels.com. *Rates: €120–€200 ($138–$230) double. AE, DC, MC, V.*

### Glenlo Abbey Hotel
$$$$ **Galway City**

Located about 3.2km (2 miles) outside Galway, this 1740s manor house is the picture of gracious living. The house is surrounded by peaceful grounds, including its own nine-hole golf course, and the interior is furnished with luxurious fabrics, antiques, and hand-carved furniture. The spacious guestrooms boast Georgian furnishings, marble bathrooms, and pastoral views. Check out the Pullman Restaurant, which serves meals in two retired *Orient Express* cars.

*Bushy Park.* ☎ *091-526-666.* www.glenlo.com. *Rates: €225–€350 ($259–$403). AE, MC, V.*

## Dining locally in Galway City

You can find a great meal in any of the restaurants listed in this section. But if you're in the mood for something sweet, try **Goyas Fine Food,** 2–3 Kirwan's Lane (☎ 091-567-010), which offers up incredible cakes and tarts, along with generous mugs of tea, coffee, and hot chocolate, in an airy, sky-blue-ceilinged café. Try the orange Madeira, or the fudge cake, or the baked cheesecake, or . . .

### Brannagans
$$–$$$   Galway City   INTERNATIONAL-ECLECTIC

Versatility is at the heart of this little restaurant, where the menu spans the globe. You're practically guaranteed to find what you're craving, whether it's steak, pizza, pasta, seafood, Indian, Cajun, or Asian cuisine. The best thing about it is that it's all done surprisingly well. The fajitas are especially good, with plenty of meat and sautéed veggies to cram into warm tortillas. The atmosphere is cozy, with brick and pine, and gives you the feeling that you're in someone's spacious kitchen.

*36 Upper Abbeygate St. near Lynch's Castle.* ☎ *091-56-5974. Main courses:€10–€23 ($12–$26). MC, V. Open: Mon–Wed 6 p.m.–10:30 p.m., Thurs–Sun 5–10:30 p.m.*

### Couch Potatas
$   Galway City   BAKED POTATOES

This casual baked-potato joint is constantly bustling with chatty twenty- and thirty-somethings. Sit down at one of the wood tables in the white-walled, wood-ceilinged restaurant, and select your spud. There is something to please everyone (as long as you like potatoes), from the Venice By Night, a potato filled with tuna, corn, peppers, tomato sauce, onions, mushrooms and mozzarella cheese, to the Nora Barnacle, a potato stuffed with strips of chicken breast and served with a creamy garlic sauce. There are a few nonpotato appetizers and salads, but I can't imagine why you'd come here for anything but a potato. Be sure to check out the sketches of potatoes engaging in various activities (get your mind out of the gutter!) while you wait for your order. The casual atmosphere and fun meal choices make this a great place for families.

*Upper Abbeygate St.* ☎ *091-561-664. Main courses: €6–€7.75 ($6.90–$8.90). No credit cards. Open: Daily noon–9:30 p.m.*

### Kirwan's Lane
$$$   Galway City   CONTINENTAL-NEW IRISH

Not only do I recommend this upscale, candlelit restaurant, but so does the entire group who sat next to me; They couldn't stop raving about the food and proclaimed their meal the best they had eaten in Ireland. The décor on the lower floor is modern and Scandinavian-looking, while the upper floor is painted with vivid reds and yellows. Dishes use the freshest of ingredients, and some successfully borrow Indian and Asian spices, condiments, and cooking techniques, such as the Indian-spiced chicken with honey, roast parsnips, tandoori mashed potatoes, and Asian black-bean cream. Other dishes are straight-up Irish; I recommend the melt-in-your-mouth Connemara lamb with braised garlic potatoes and a rosemary jus. The several vegetarian dishes are very classy, including a brochette of smoked tofu, eggplant, and wild mushrooms with satay sauce. Save room for the heavenly French chocolate cake served with pistachio ice cream.

*Kirwan's Lane — the small lane next to McDonagh's Restaurant, off Quay St.* ☎ *091-568-266. Reservations recommended. Main courses: €18–€28 ($21–$32). AE, MC, V. Open: Daily 6–10 p.m., and Mon–Sat 12:30–2:30 p.m.*

### *Maxwell McNamaras*
**$$   Galway City   IRISH-CONTINENTAL-AMERICAN**

Serving the good people of Galway since 1016, McNamara's is an institution. Waiting for dinner was never so interesting — with so much history to this comfortable and tasteful place, you're bound to get caught up reading the back of the menu. I'm not sure whether it's true that Columbus brought a McNamara burger with him when he set sail for the New World, but it makes for good conversation. (And who knows? Maybe he did. After all, the food is quite good.) You find plenty of traditional dishes on the menu, but the Mixed Grill stands out as even more decadent than usual: lamb cutlet, sausage, bacon, burger, black-and-white pudding, tomato, and mushrooms. Irish dishes, seafood, and creative pasta dishes round out the menu, and the children's menu will make even the pickiest eater happy. The drink list is vast, with liqueurs, coffee drinks, draft beer, and an extensive wine list.

*Off Eyre Sq., on the corner of Williamsgate and Eglinton streets.* ☎ *091-56-5727. Main courses: €7.95–€21 ($9.15–$24). AE, DC, MC, V. Open: Mon–Sat 9 a.m.–10 p.m., Sun 2:30–10 p.m.*

### *McDonagh's Seafood House*
**$–$$$$   Galway City   SEAFOOD**

Fish doesn't get fresher or better than at this popular place. The McDonaghs, who've been at it for four generations, have had plenty of practice in the trade. The day's catch is personally inspected and chosen before it comes in the door. You can decide exactly how you'd like your fish cooked, whether it's salmon, trout, sole, or one of many other options. Shrimp and lobsters come the way the sea made them: in the shell. If you're looking for something simple and quick, stop by the fish-and-chips shop in the front of the restaurant.

*22 Quay St., beside Jurys Inn, near the Spanish Arch.* ☎ *091-56-5001. Main courses: €8–€34 ($9.20–$39). AE, DC, MC, V. Open: Daily noon to 10:30 p.m.*

### Nimmo's Wine Bar
**$$–$$$   Galway City   NEW IRISH**

This atmospheric restaurant serves some of the best food in Ireland. Though I've never had dinner at an eccentric sea captain's home, I imagine that it would be a lot like dining on the first floor at Nimmo's (there is a fancier upstairs section of the restaurant, but I recommend the lower wine-bar level). Located on the fast-flowing River Corrib, Nimmo's is cozy and romantic, with worn wooden floors and plaster walls, weathered glass bottles and nautical objects, faded black-and-white photographs of ships, and brightly colored candles gracing the eclectic tables. The menu uses fresh, local ingredients and complements them with inventive preparations, spicing, and sauces inspired by cuisines all over the world. The dishes change all the time, but if it's on the menu, try the salmon and brill with a veil of creamy Thai curry sauce, served with perfectly steamed vegetables; I also loved the goat cheese in phyllo with sweet chile-and-lime dressing.

*Long Walk, through the Spanish Arch.* ☎ *091-561-114. Reservations recommended. Main courses: €11–€24 ($12–$27). MC, V. Tues–Sun 6–10 p.m., Fri and Sat also noon–3 p.m.*

## Exploring Galway City: The top attractions

Galway doesn't have any don't-leave-Ireland-without-seeing-it attractions; it's more of a place to wander around, shop a little, and enjoy the fabulous restaurant and nightlife scenes.

The compact heart of Galway is a pedestrian area that begins west of Eyre Square. The main street here starts as William Street at Eyre Square and then changes names many times before hitting the River Corrib.

### Browne Doorway

Looking pretty odd at the head of Eyre Square, the Browne Doorway is a towering stone archway that's connected to nothing. For more than 75 years it's stood there, and it will continue to stand, even though the Square is undergoing a complete overhaul as this book goes to press. Dating from 1627, the doorway comes from an old mansion on Lower Abbeygate Street, and it has the coats of arms of the families Browne and Lynch.

*Located on the northwest side of Eyre Square.*

### Collegiate Church of St. Nicholas

Columbus is rumored to have prayed in this well-preserved medieval church, built in 1320, before setting sail for the New World. You'll find beautiful stone carvings, gargoyles, and the tomb of a Crusader here.

*Lombard St.* ☎ *091-564-648. Admission free. Tours €3 ($3.45; call for reservations). Daily 9 a.m.–5:45 p.m.*

## Searching for Galway's mermaids

Mermaids show up frequently in Irish folklore, often representing something alluring but dangerous. According to legend, if you happen to see a mermaid sitting on a rock, it means bad luck is coming your way. So don't stare out at the rocks too long!

You can look as long as you like at the mermaid depictions around town, though. Galway supposedly has more representations of mermaids than any other place in Ireland. Check out the mermaids in the window of the Collegiate Church of St. Nicholas in the center of town.

### Lynch's Castle (now AIB Bank)

If this isn't the first castle you've seen in Ireland, you may expect something . . . well, larger. This 14th-century home of the legendary Lynch family was restored and now houses a bank, though you can still marvel at the coats of arms and the Spanish-style stonework on the exterior.

*Abbeygate St. Upper between Shop and Market streets.*

### Lynch Memorial Window

James Lynch FitzStephen, unyielding magistrate and mayor of Galway, earned his place in dictionaries when he condemned and executed his own son (convicted of murder) in 1493 as a demonstration that the law does not bend even under family ties. That's where we get the word *lynch*. The Lynch Memorial Window commemorates this event. It's set into a wall just above an ornate Gothic doorway on Market Street.

*Market St. one block northwest of Eyre Sq.*

### Salthill

This fun little resort strip is Ireland's closest thing to the United States' Coney Island in its heyday. It makes for a fun day with the family. Walk along the boardwalk, eat fast food, play arcade games, and visit the Leisureland amusement park.

*Take the R336 west from Galway for about 3km (2 miles).*

### Spanish Arch

The Spanish Arch was built in 1584 so that the crews of Spanish ships could pass their cargoes of wine and brandy into Galway without actually entering the city.

*Between Wolfe Tone Bridge and the Long Walk, at the mouth of the River Corrib.*

## Taking short side trips from Galway City

### Coole Park
#### Gort

The house and grounds here were once home to Lady Gregory — writer, friend of many an Irish luminary, and cofounder of Dublin's Abbey Theatre. The grounds are now a park, with red deer, red squirrels, and badgers, among others animals. There are beautiful nature trails, a lake, and lush gardens. One of the most interesting parts of the park is the *Autograph Tree,* which bears the carved initials of such famous people as George Bernard Shaw; Oliver St. John Gogarty; Sean O'Casey; and W. B. Yeats, Lady Gregory's friend and partner in the Abbey. In the restored courtyard are a visitor center, a place to buy light snacks, and picnic tables.

*Take the N6 out of Galway to the N18; north of Gort, follow the signs.* ☎ *091-63-1804. Admission: €2.75 ($3.15) adults, €2 ($2.30) seniors, €1.25 ($1.45) children and students. Open: Apr–May and Sept daily 10 a.m.–5 p.m., June–Aug daily 10 a.m.–6 p.m. Suggested visit: 1 or 2 hours.*

### Dunguaire Castle
#### Kinvarra

How better to tell the story of a castle's rich history than to show it? Each floor of Dunguaire (dun-*gware*) Castle reflects a different and very colorful time in its history. It's been perfectly restored, and the interior is one of the finest in its class, with furnishings that interestingly mirror the time. According to legend, the castle was built on the site of the Palace of Guaire, sixth-century king of Connaught, and that's where the name comes from. Later, it was owned by Oliver St. John Gogarty, poet, surgeon, and satirical model for Buck Mulligan, one the characters of James Joyce's *Ulysses.* Although born in Dublin, Gogarty lived mostly in Connemara. The view of Connemara and Galway Bay from the top of the battlements is awe-inspiring. The castle is also the setting for excellent medieval-style banquets (book in advance).

*From Galway City, take the N6 to N18; turn right on the N67 and follow it to Kinvarra.* ☎ *091-637-108. Admission: €3.50 ($4.05) adults, €2.50 ($2.90) seniors, €2 ($2.30) children and students. Open: May–Oct daily 9:30 a.m.–5:30 p.m. Suggested visit: 1½ hours.*

### Thoor Ballylee (W. B. Yeats's Summer Home)
#### Gort

This stone tower was poet W. B. Yeats's summer home. Yeats wrote many works here, including "The Winding Stair" and "The Tower," both inspired by this building. The view from the battlements takes in Galway's lush fields and forests. An audiovisual tour and museum are dedicated to Yeats's life and work, and the tower has been restored to look just like it did when the poet lived there in the 1920s. The gardens and a picnic area make for a gorgeous lunch stop when the weather's nice.

*Off the Limerick-Galway Road (N18) in Gort.* ☎ *091-64-1436. Admission: €5 ($5.75) adults, €4 ($4.60) seniors and students, €1.35 ($1.55) children. Open: Easter–Sept daily 10 a.m.–6 p.m. Suggested visit: 1½ hours.*

## Shopping in Galway City

Galway City is home to lot of shops, and you're bound to find items to suit your taste as you stroll around the heart of the city. **Eyre Square Shopping Centre,** lined by old stone walls, has more than 50 shops and an antique market under one glass roof. A great item to buy in Galway is a Claddagh ring — you know, the ones with two hands clasping a heart below a crown. The design originated in the Galway area, and you find numerous stores selling these rings. **Thomas Dillon's,** 1 Quay St., near the Spanish Arch (☎ 091-566-365), claims to be the original maker and is worth a stop for its small Claddagh museum, even if you aren't in the market for a ring.

**MacEocagain/Galway Woolen Market,** 21 High St., (☎ 091-56-2491), specializes in Aran handknits and other knitwear, linen, lace, sheepskins, and jewelry. **Kennys Bookshop and Galleries,** Middle and High streets (☎ 091-56-2739), is a Galway institution, housing an excellent collection of Irish literature and history (including secondhand and antiquarian books), fine art by local artists, prints, and maps. The staff is exceedingly knowledgeable and happy to locate the difficult-to-find stuff. **Design Concourse Ireland,** Kirwan's Lane (☎ 091-566-016), sells gorgeous pottery, as well as other contemporary Irish handcrafts. **The Treasure Chest,** 31–33 William St., (☎ 091-563-862), has just about every Irish gift item you could want under one roof — Waterford Crystal, Royal Tara china, Belleek china, Claddagh rings, Aran knitwear, linen, and more. For the widest selection of Irish music CDs, hit **Mulligan,** 5 Middle St. Court (off Middle St.; ☎ 091-564-961). And if all those CDs inspire you to play, you can pick up Irish (and other) instruments and

## The Claddagh ring

Claddagh rings feature two hands holding a heart, which is topped by a crown. The hands symbolize friendship, the crown symbolizes loyalty, and the heart represents love.

According to tradition, the wearer wears the ring on the ring finger of the left hand with the crown pointing toward the fingertips to show he or she is in love or married. If, on the other hand, the heart is pointing toward the fingertips the wearer is said to be unattached. Traditionally, the ring serves as an engagement or wedding ring.

The name comes from Claddagh, the oldest fishing village in Ireland, located on the west bank of the Corrib Estuary in Galway. In Gaelic, *An Cladach* means "flat, stony shore."

instruction books from the terrific staff at **P. Powell & Sons,** The Four Corners, William Street (☎ 091-562-295).

## Enjoying Galway City nightlife

Galway has some excellent theater and live music that you can take in before hitting one of the pubs listed in this section. **Róisín Dubh,** Dominick Street (☎ 091-586-540; www.roisindubh.net) books spectacular bands and singers, from traditional Irish musicians to singer–songwriters to alternative country bands to jazz groups. The **Druid Theatre Company,** Chapel Lane (☎ 091- 568-617; www.druid theatre.com), presents inventive performances of 20th-century Irish and European plays.

For information on what's going on in pubs, clubs, theaters, and more, pick up a free copy of *XPOSED Weekly Entertainment Guide,* available around town. This is the best place to figure out which of Galway's several clubs are hot at the moment.

### Crane Bar

This is arguably the best place in Galway City for traditional Irish music. Casual sessions take place every night with some of the best musicians in town. The decor is nothing special, but it won't matter once you get carried along on the current of jigs and reels.

*2 Sea Rd., Salthill, less than a mile out of Galway City.* ☎ *091-587-419.*

### The Kings Head

The Middle Ages live on in The Kings Head, with original medieval fireplaces and windows. It's all or nothing here, and every bit of the place looks the part of a pub from the 1500s. There's history galore associated with this place, and a chat with the barkeep will reveal some of its stories. This isn't a cramped, elbow-room pub, either: It's spread over three floors, with a rock or pop band usually on the first floor during the week, a jazz session on Sundays, and an Irish session on Saturdays. Take your picture sitting on the throne next to the downstairs fireplace and enjoy some of the great pub grub.

*15 High St.* ☎ *091-56-6630.*

### Monroe's Tavern

Feeling footloose? Monroe's regularly packs the place every Tuesday night (after 9:30 p.m.) for *set dancing* — a partnered form of Irish dance that resembles American square dancing. And every night features live traditional Irish music — whirling reels keeping a fast, sweaty pace as onlookers shout out in a frenzy of good *craic* (fun). And the crowd isn't all tour-bus shutterbugs; the tavern is most popular with locals. Set in an old house with low ceilings and timber floors, it may seem large for a pub, but it needs the room so that you can get your jig on. During the day, you should stop in for a bite: Monroe's actually specializes in organic fare — delicious!

*Dominick St.* ☎ *091-58-3397.*

### The Quays

No trip to Galway is complete without a stop at this lively pub, a city institution since the 1600s. The stone interior was once the inside of a medieval French church and boasts beautiful details such as stained glass and carved wood. Good music, mostly of the traditional Irish ilk, is on tap every night. The pub grub is quite tasty.

*Quay St. and Chapel Lane.* ☎ *091-56-8347.*

### Skeff Bar

This pub is a good place for conversation. It incorporates all different kinds of decor: Some parts look like an upper-class drawing room, with elegant couches, coffee tables, and Persian rugs; other parts are distinctly Irish pub, with low stools or tall booths. Fireplaces, intricate ceiling work, and stained glass give the place a posh feel. Staircases throughout lead to more bars upstairs. The American food (burgers, chicken fingers, and so on) is good, and there's often a DJ on weekends.

*Eyre Sq.* ☎ *091-56-3173.*

### Tíg Neachtain

This is the real deal. This cozy pub, in a building that dates from the Middle Ages, is filled with old snugs that have seen infinite pints of Guinness and been party to countless late-night conversations. There is music here most nights, ranging from traditional Irish to Cajun to jazz and blues.

*17 Cross St.* ☎ *091-568-820.*

# The Aran Islands

The Aran Islands — Inishmore, Inishmaan, and Inisheer — are havens of traditional Irish culture: Islanders speak Irish Gaelic as a first language. Some residents supplement their tourism income by fishing using *currachs* (small wooden boats), and many live in stone cottages. Most visitors (and there are many, especially during the summer) choose to stay in Kilronan, on Inishmore, the most developed and largest of the islands, where you'll find sandy beaches and **Dún Aengus,** a prehistoric stone fort. The

## Inishmore, Aran Islands

"Inishmore, Aran Islands" map locates the island's attractions. Those craving a bit more solitude should visit Inishmaan, the second-largest island, which also has several prehistoric ruins; or Inisheer, the smallest of the islands, which is filled with farms and meadows of wildflowers from June to August and has several sandy beaches.

For more information on the islands, check out www.visitaranislands.com.

## Getting to and around the Aran Islands

The most common way to get to the Arans is by ferry. **Aran Island Ferries** (☎ 091-56-8903), located at the Galway Tourist Office off Eyre Square, operates ferries that depart from Rossaveal Pier in Connemara (the bus trip from Galway to Rossaveal is included in the price). Prices are €19 ($22) for adults, €15 ($17) for seniors and students, and €10 ($12) for children. The ferries call at each of the islands, with the most popular (and busiest) port being Kilronan, on Inishmore. If you'd rather fly, **Aer Arann Islands** (☎ 091-59-3034; www.aerarannislands.ie) takes off from Connemara airport, about 29km (18 miles) west of Galway City (a bus from the city is available to the airport; just ask when you book), and flies to all three islands; its most popular flights land in Kilronan, on Inishmore. The ten-minute flight is the shortest scheduled flight in the world. Prices are currently around €44 ($51) round-trip for adults, and €25 ($29) round-trip for children. Aran Islands Ferries travels between Inishmore and Inishmaan; if you want to travel between other combinations of islands, you need to travel back to Rossaveal first.

You can't bring your car to the Arans, and there are no car rentals, so when you reach the islands, you have a couple choices: You can rent a bike at **Rothar Arainn Teo,** Frenchman's Beach, Kilronan (☎ 091-61-132), which is what I recommend; Or you can hire a driver and minibus or a bumpy horse and cart (there will be a bunch waiting when you arrive at the islands).

You can also tour the Arans by foot. Walking-tour maps are available at the **tourist office** in Kilronan (☎ 099-61-263). Each route takes a couple of hours.

## Spending the night on the Aran Islands

Each island has several B&Bs; for information, contact the Galway Tourist Office at ☎ 091-53-77-00.

### Pier House
**$$ Lower Kilronan, Inishmore**

On a small island, you're pretty much guaranteed a view of the water from anywhere, but from a room in the Pier House, you get that and more. It's only feet from the harbor; sandy beaches, pubs, and restaurants are all a short walk away; and the ocean breeze makes its way into your room's open window at night. Rooms are quite nice, and it's obvious that great care goes into ensuring a guest's comfort. Plus it's a great value for the price.

☎ *099-61-417. Fax: 099-61-122.* www.galway.net/pages/pierhouse. *Rates: €90–€110 ($104–$127). MC, V. Closed Nov–Feb.*

## Dining locally on the Aran Islands

### Aran Fisherman Restaurant
**$$–$$$ Kilronan, Inishmore SEAFOOD-IRISH**

Having a seafood meal on an island where the main livelihood is fishing is kind of like having a cheese steak in Philly — heavenly. Just a stone's throw from where the seafood comes out of the sea, this restaurant offers shark, lobster, fish, and crab along with meat and vegetarian dishes. Meals come with organic salads made with fresh vegetables grown on the island. If you're in the mood for something lighter, try one of the pizzas. Sitting on the outside patio completes the meal.

*A three-minute walk west from the harbor, on the only road.* ☎ *099-61-363. Main courses: €12–€23 ($13–$26). MC, V. Open: Daily 10:30 a.m.–4 p.m. and 5 p.m.– 10 p.m.*

## Exploring the Aran Islands

The Arans are attractions in and of themselves. Rent a bike (my top recommendation), flag a pony cart or minivan, or lace up your sneakers, then poke around these beautiful islands. The new heritage center, **Ionad Arann**, Kilronan, Inishmore (☎ **099-613-55**), is a good place to begin your visit to the islands. The center offers exhibits and a film investigating the culture, history, and geography of the islands. Admission is €4 ($4.60) for adults, €2.50 ($2.90) for students, and €2 ($2.30) for seniors and children. It's open daily March through October from 11 a.m. to 5 p.m.

### Dún Aengus
**Kilmurvey, Inishmore**

This well-preserved immense prehistoric stone fort stretches over 4.4 hectares (11 acres) and is set on a sheer cliff overlooking the Atlantic Ocean. The fort is composed of three dry-stone walls, set one inside the other. The former use of the fort is still unknown. Views of Connemara, Galway Bay, and the Burren are superb from the innermost wall. Be sure to enter the area through the visitor center.

*7km/4½ miles west of Kilronan.* ☎ *099-61-008. Admission: €2 ($2.30) adults, €1.25 ($1.45) seniors, €1 ($1.15) children and students. Open: March–Oct daily 10 a.m.– 6 p.m., Nov–Feb daily 10 a.m.–4 p.m.*

# Exploring the origins of the Aran sweater

Aran sweaters may be one of Ireland's biggest exports today, but they came from humble beginnings. Originally, the almost-waterproof wool sweaters were knit by the women of the Aran Islands to ensure that the islands' fishermen stayed warm and dry (the waterproofing comes from natural oils from the sheep's skin, which remain on the wool). The wives and mothers of the fishermen created a different pattern for each family. Sadly, one of the reasons that these patterns were created was to help the islanders identify fishermen who had drowned off the dangerous coast.

## Shopping

If you've held out long enough, now's your chance to buy an authentic, often-copied-but-never-reproduced, hand-knit fisherman's sweater on the Aran Islands. Numerous shops sell these sweaters.

# Connemara

The area west of Galway City is known as Connemara. It's a wild and untamed place of still glacial lakes, stands of evergreens, 12 towering mountains (called the Twelve Bens) in the northern area, and endless quiet boglands and granite moorlands in the south. A large part of Connemara is a *Gaeltacht* — an area where you may hear Irish Gaelic being spoken. You also may encounter the rugged little Connemara ponies, the only purebred horses native to Ireland. There are only a few towns of any size in this region. The roughly 1,100-person town of **Clifden** is the unofficial capital of Connemara. Nestled in a valley at the foot of the Twelve Bens mountain range, the town's lively center and excellent location make it a popular base for visitors. A quieter option is **Roundstone,** a bustling little fishing village.

## Getting to and around Connemara

The best way to see Connemara is by driving. Take either N59, the inland route (you'll see signs for the road on Galway City's ring road), or R336, the coastal route.

**Bus Éireann** (☎ 011-836-6111; www.buseireann.ie) serves Clifden and other towns in Connemara.

## Spending the night in Connemara

### Alcock and Brown Hotel
$$–$$$   Clifden

Clifden is a quaint village famous for being near the landing spot of Alcock and Brown, who completed the first transatlantic flight in 1919. It's now a perfect liftoff location for touring the spectacular Connemara National Park, right at your doorstep. The Alcock and Brown Hotel is a wonderful family-run hotel known for its fantastic restaurant, Browns. The inside is modestly and very tastefully furnished, and rooms are spacious. The bar is comfortable and often filled with people relaxing after a day of sightseeing.

*The Square in center of town.* ☎ *095-21-206. Fax: 095-21-842. Rates: €100–€130 ($115–$150) double. AE, DC, MC, V.*

### Errisbeg Lodge
**$  Roundstone**

This peaceful B&B has views of the Errisbeg Mountains and the Atlantic ocean, both of which are close at hand. The B&B has a vast amount of land; proprietors Jack and Shirley King like to say, "We have a national park in our backyard." You can wander among the many wildflowers, encountering sweet Connemara ponies, and then stroll the smooth, sandy beaches. Rooms are simple and clean, with pine furnishings, king-size beds, and colorful comforters. The Kings are incredidbly warm, friendly, and enthusiastic about sharing this beautiful location with their guests. Kids will love running around the grounds and playing with the ponies.

*Ballyconneely-Roundstone Rd. (R341) 2km west of Roundstone, opposite Gurteen Beach.* ☎ **095-35807**. *Fax: 095-35807. Rates: €75–€80 ($86–$92). No credit cards. Closed Nov–Jan.*

### The Quay House
**$$$  Clifden**

The decor here is certainly not your run-of-the-mill prints of Ireland and Victorian-reproduction tables. Owners Paddy and Julia Foyle have furnished this grand restored harbormaster's house with bold, artistic choices, including zebra, tiger, and other animal skins; dramatic paintings in gilded frames; and glass chandeliers. One wall of the airy conservatory breakfast room is decorated with the lids of silver serving platters. Bedrooms are spacious and individually furnsihed, running from ornate Victorian-style quarters to rooms that look like they belong in a chic hunting lodge in Africa. Seven suites have balconies and small kitchens. Paddy and Julia have a deep knowledge of the area and are always happy to advise visitors on outdoor activities, dining, drives, and so on.

*Beach Rd.* ☎ **095-21-369**. www.thequayhouse.com. *Rates: €140–€165 ($161–$190) double. MC, V. Closed Nov–mid-March.*

## Dining locally in Connemara

### Derryclare Restaurant
**$$–$$$  Clifden  SEAFOOD-IRISH**

Warm and cozy is the name of the game here. Candles in cast-iron holders cast a golden glow on the dark, shiny wood tables and benches, and weathered signs decorate the walls. The restaurant buzzes with conversation and laughter from a convivial crowd that runs from couples to large families. Dishes are made with the freshest ingredients, simply prepared and boasting some inspired sauces and spices. My salmon steak with fennel butter sauce was wonderful, and the couple next to me were enjoying their braised Connemara lamb shank *au jus*. Enjoy vegetables such as buttery creamed carrots and perfectly steamed broccoli with your meal.

*Market St.* ☎ *095-21-440. Main courses: €11–€22 ($13–$25). MC, V. Open: Daily noon–10 p.m.*

### Mitchell's Restaurant
**$$–$$$    Clifden    IRISH-ECLECTIC**

Hearty, traditional fare is the staple of this restaurant, and thick stews, steaks, and fish dishes stand out. One of the most popular dishes is the Connemara lamb stew, a perfect marriage of fresh lamb and vegetables. Noteworthy lighter meals — seafood pastas, quiche, and salads — are served during the day for about €6 ($6.90). The decor is warm and rustic, with stone and brick walls, a big open fireplace, and local memorabilia throughout. There's also a children's menu.

*Market St., in the center of town.* ☎ *095-21-867. Main courses: €16–€25 ($18–$29). MC, V. Open: Mid-March–mid-Nov noon–10 p.m.*

## Exploring Connemara

You can choose among several guided bus tours of Connemara. I suggest hitting Galway City's tourist office (see "Fast Facts: County Galway," at the end of this chapter), either in person or virtually, to figure out which one suits you. The excellent tour company **Over the Top Tours** is now offering a Connemara Experience tour, with stops at Roundstone and gorgeous Killary Harbour (Ireland's only fjord), lunch in Clifden, a visit to Kylemore Abbey, and other highlights. Tours cost €23 ($26) for adults, and €20 ($23) for students; they depart daily from the Galway Tourist Office at 9:10 a.m., and from the Salthill Tourist Office at 9:20 a.m. Call ☎ 087-259-3467 for information and reservations, or visit www.overthe toptours.com. **Bus Éireann** (☎ 091-56-2000; www.buseireann.ie) **Connemara Bus Tour** takes you through Clifden and includes a stop at Kylemore Abbey, but the focus of the tour is the beautiful mountain scenery. The bus leaves Galway Railway Station at 10 a.m. daily June through September and returns at 5:50 p.m. It costs €22 ($25) adults, €16 ($18) students and seniors, and €13 ($15) for children.

**Corrib Ferries** (☎ 087-283-0799; www.corribcruises.com) offers round-trip cruises on lovely Lough Corrib, Ireland's largest lake. You cruise from Oughterard, in County Galway, to Cong Village, in County Mayo, where you can gaze upon the exterior of the beautiful 13th-century Ashford Castle. Along the way, you stop on Inchagoill Island for a guided tour of the fifth-century ruins there. The cruise options range from a one-hour cruise to a 5½ hour cruise. If you have the time, go for the longer cruise, which gives you ample time to explore quaint Cong village.

**Connemara Walking Center,** the Island House, Market Street, Clifden (☎ 095-21-379), offers a number of well-done guided walks of Connemara. Call for prices (closed in winter).

Bicycling is a great way to explore this area; you can rent bikes from **John Mannion,** Bridge Street, Clifden (☎ 095-221-60).

### Connemara National Park and Visitors Centre
**Letterfrack**

Some of most spectacular scenery in this part of Ireland is contained in this 2,000-hectare (5,000-acre) park. Mountains, bogs, valleys, and forests make up the park, and four of the mountains in the impressive Twelve Bens range are within its boundaries, including Benbaun, the highest of the 12, which reaches 2,400 feet. There are 4,000-year-old prehistoric structures, flowers that grow only here, and a variety of wildlife, from red deer to the sturdy Connemara ponies. The Visitors Centre (on the N59) has exhibits and an audiovisual show on the park, and organizes nature trail walks (call in advance to see when they're being offered).

*Off the Clifden-Westport Rd. (N59).* ☎ *095-41-054 or 095-41-006. Park admission: €2.75 ($3.15) adults, €2 ($2.30) seniors, €1.25 ($1.45) children and students. Open: Park open year-round. Visitor Centre open mid-March–Oct 10 a.m.–5:30 p.m. Suggested visit: Several hours.*

### Kylemore Benedictine Abbey
**Kylemore**

Sitting in a stunning setting at the base of the mountains and on the shores of a lake, this abbey looks like a storybook castle — and it is, in a way. An English tycoon had the gorgeous neo-Gothic building constructed for his adored wife and sold it to the duke and duchess of Manchester upon her death. Several owners later, a group of nuns escaping the horrors of World War I in Belgium took up residence and converted it into an abbey. Today, the nuns also run a girls' boarding school here. You can visit the striking main hall and reception rooms, walk along the lake to the restored neo-Gothic chapel, and visit the magnificent walled Victorian garden. The Abbey is known for its pottery; you can watch it being created and can purchase some in the craft shop. There's also a small restaurant on the grounds.

*On the Clifden-Westport Rd. (N59), east of Letterfrack.* ☎ *095-41-145.* www. kylemoreabbey.com. *Admission: Abbey €4.50 ($5.20) adults, €3.20 ($3.70) seniors and students; garden €4.50 ($5.20) adults, €3.20 ($3.70) seniors and students. Open: Abbey daily 9 a.m.–5:30 p.m. Garden Easter–Sept daily 10:30 a.m.– 4:30 p.m. Suggested visit: About 1 hour.*

## Shopping in Connemara

Owner Malachy Kearns and his staff at **Roundstone Music and Crafts** in **Roundstone** (off Route 59; ☎ 095-35-875; www.bodhran.com) make and sell a large and high-quality selection of *bodhráns* (Irish drums). Malachy Kearns is something of a celebrity: He made the drums for the *Riverdance* ensemble and is even featured on an Irish postage stamp. **The Spiddal Craft and Design Studios,** Spiddal (☎ **091-553-376;** www.spiddalcraft village.com), houses craftspeople who make and sell a variety of crafts, from musical instruments to candles.

## Hitting the pubs

### E. J. Kings
**Clifden**

Almost anyone who's been to Clifden is familiar with E. J. Kings, because when you go, you can't forget it. Always humming, Kings has many floors, and in the high season, music fills the air. Seafood is the feature of the fantastic pub-food menu, but there's also good traditional fare. When it's cold, a welcoming fire warms the pub, and in nice weather, the outdoor patio is the hottest spot. The atmosphere in Kings is relaxed, and you're sure to get a warm welcome from the young, chatty staff.

*The Square.* ☎ *095-21-330.*

# Fast Facts: County Galway

### Area Codes
County Galway's area codes (or city codes) are 091 and 099.

### Emergencies/Police
Dial ☎ **999** for all emergencies.

### Genealogy Resources
Contact the Galway Family History Society West, Venture Centre, Liosbaun Estate, Taum (☎ 091-75-6737).

### Hospital
University College Hospital is on Newcastle Road, Galway (☎ **091-58-0580).**

### Information
For visitor information and reservation services for Galway City and the whole of

County Galway, go to the Galway Tourist Office (also known as Ireland West Tourism or Aras Fáilte), at Victoria Place, in Eyre Square, Galway City (☎ 091-53-77-00; www.westireland.travel.ie), open year-round.

### Internet
The NetAccess Internet Cafe, in the Olde Malte Arcade on High Street (☎ 091-56-9772), has Internet access and printing capabilities.

### Post Office
Galway Post Office is on Eglinton Street, Galway City (☎ 091-56-2051).

# Chapter 19

# Counties Mayo and Sligo

## In This Chapter

▶ Taking in Stone Age monuments in Ceide Fields
▶ Exploring Yeats Country
▶ Touring grand Westport House
▶ Climbing the mountain of Croagh Patrick

*N*orth of County Galway, Counties Mayo and Sligo (see the nearby map) boast some of the most beautiful scenery you can imagine — beaches; bogs; cliffs; and, of course, those green Irish fields.

Many of **County Mayo's** attractions are near the water, either the Atlantic or calm and striking **Clew Bay.** The N5 (and a few smaller roads) take you to the towns of **Westport** (one of the sweetest and liveliest small towns in Ireland); **Castlebar;** and Mayo's largest town, **Ballina.** Venturing out for a drive west on the N59 takes you along twisty roads that lead to some of the most isolated and sparsely populated regions in the country.

Maybe the best compliment given to **County Sligo** comes from the many Irish writers who have fallen in love with the area over the years. Much of the county is known as Yeats Country because of the fondness poet W. B. Yeats had for the place — his last wish was to be buried here. The relatively small county has tributes to the poet in every corner. **Sligo Town** is a walkable big town with several good restaurants and pubs, and a sizable arts scene. South of Sligo Town, **Strandhill** offers sandy beaches for relaxation.

## Getting to and around Counties Mayo and Sligo

If you're driving from Dublin, take the N4 to Sligo Town or the N5 to Castlebar and Westport in County Mayo. From Galway, take the N17 to meet the N5 in County Mayo or straight to Sligo. From Donegal, go south on the N15 to Sligo. **Irish Rail** (☎ 071-916-9888; www.irishrail.ie)

*Counties Mayo and Sligo*

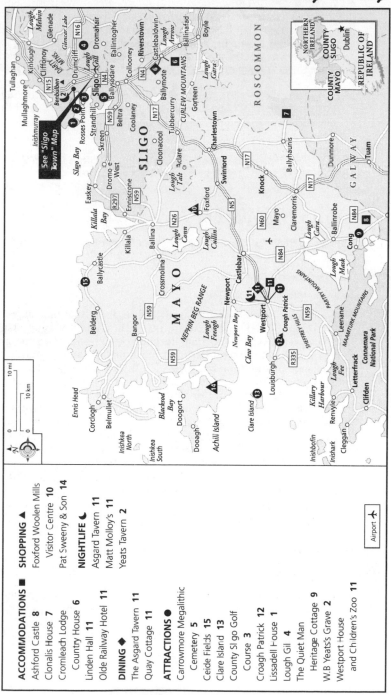

**ACCOMMODATIONS** ■
Ashford Castle **8**
Clonalis House **7**
Cromleach Lodge
 Country House **6**
Linden Hall **11**
Olde Railway Hotel **11**

**DINING** ◆
The Asgard Tavern **11**
Quay Cottage **11**

**ATTRACTIONS** ●
Carrowmore Megalithic
 Cemetery **5**
Ceide Fields **15**
Clare Island **13**
County Sligo Golf
 Course **3**
Croagh Patrick **12**
Lissadell House **1**
Lough Gil **4**
The Quiet Man
 Heritage Cottage **9**
W.B Yeats's Grave **2**
Westport House
 and Children's Zoo **11**

**SHOPPING** ▲
Foxford Woolen Mills
 Visitor Centre **10**
Pat Sweeny & Son **14**

**NIGHTLIFE** ☾
Asgard Tavern **11**
Matt Molloy's **11**
Yeats Tavern **2**

Airport ✈

serves Sligo at Lord Edward Street and also serves Westport, Foxford, Ballina, and Castlebar in County Mayo. **Bus Éireann** (☎ 071-916-0066; www.buseireann.ie) travels year-round to Sligo, Strandhill, Drumcliffe, and other major towns in County Sligo, and to Westport, Cong, Ballina, and other towns in County Mayo. Bus Éireann also has local service between Sligo and Strandhill and Rosses Point in July and August.

**Aer Lingus** (www.aerlingus.com) has daily flights into both Sligo airport (Strandhill, ☎ 071-68-280; www.sligoairport.com) and Knock airport (Charlestown, County Mayo, ☎ 094-67-222; www.knockairport.com).

Taxis in Sligo Town line up on Quay Street. Call **Sligo Cabs** (☎ 071-917-1888) if you need to be picked up.

# Spending the Night

Check out the "Sligo Town" map for locations of attractions there.

### Ashford Castle
**$$$$**   **Cong, County Mayo**

Okay, time for a quiz: What do Fred Astaire, Joan Baez, and Jerry Springer have in common? If you answered that they've all stayed at luxurious Ashford Castle, you are correct. Perched on the banks of sapphire Lough Corrib and surrounded by 350 acres of woodlands and gardens, this castle is a melange of architectural styles. The original building dates from 1228, with a French chateau-style addition added in the 18th century and two Victorian wings added in the 19th century. Inside, the castle is sumptuously decked out with carved oak paneling, crystal chandeliers, gorgeous oil paintings hanging in gilt frames, and lush fabrics. The spacious, bright bedrooms are less extravagant than the public rooms but are still beautifully furnished, with designer fabrics and lovely furniture. Two restaurants serve gourmet menus in opulent period surroundings.

*Take the R346 to Cross, and turn left at the church, going towards Cong. Ashford Castle is on the left side of the road before you reach the village of Cong.* ☎ *094-954-6003. Fax: 094-954-6260.* www.ashford.ie. *Rates: €215–€435 ($247–$500). AE, DC, MC, V.*

### Clonalis House
**$-$$**   **Castlrea, County Roscommon**

Just over the County Mayo border is the Victorian Italianate mansion and ancestral home of the O'Conors of Connacht, descendants of Ireland's last high kings. If you're an O'Conor or O'Connor yourself, you'll find the library and historical heirlooms of particular interest; everyone can enjoy

## Sligo Town

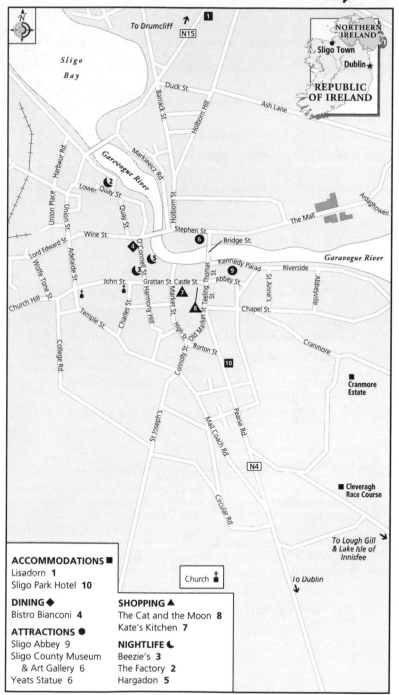

**ACCOMMODATIONS** ■
Lisadorn **1**
Sligo Park Hotel **10**

**DINING** ◆
Bistro Bianconi **4**

**ATTRACTIONS** ●
Sligo Abbey **9**
Sligo County Museum
& Art Gallery **6**
Yeats Statue **6**

**SHOPPING** ▲
The Cat and the Moon **8**
Kate's Kitchen **7**

**NIGHTLIFE** ☾
Beezie's **3**
The Factory **2**
Hargadon **5**

Church ✝

the four-poster beds, beautiful estate grounds, and nearby woods. The caretaker, Pyers O'Conor-Nash, will gladly chat about his family's history or the area attractions over whiskey by the fireplace. The expansive grounds are heaven for kids who like to run and explore. You'll want to have dinner at the manor as well; there are no decent restaurants in the vicinity.

*Take the N60 west from Castlerea or east from Ballyhaunis.* ☎ *094-962-0014.* www.clonalis.com. *Rates: €66–€78 ($76–$90) double. AE, MC, V. Closed Oct–mid-April.*

### Cromleach Lodge Country House
**$$$$   Castlebaldwin, County Sligo**

You won't find much luxury in the western wilds of Ireland — unless you're staying at the Cromleach Lodge, a modern inn overlooking Lough Arrow. Enjoy the view of the lake and its little islands from the glass-walled sun porch or just chill out in your large, posh, comfortable room. The lauded restaurant has local seafood and an excellent prix-fixe seven-course meal, which may very well be the most memorable meal of your trip.

*Take the N4 south from Sligo town toward Boyle to Castlebaldwin.* ☎ *071-91-65-155. Fax: 071-91-65-455.* www.cromleach.com. *Rates: €240–€316 ($276–$363) double. AE, DC, MC, V.*

### Linden Hall
**$   Westport, County Mayo**

This B&B, which is a five-minute walk from the heart of Westport, offers clean, simple, bright rooms with comfortable beds. Your hosts, Maria and Stephen Breen, are friendly and fun, and know the area well. Ask for a room overlooking the wild garden in back.

*Altamount St.* ☎ *098-27005. Rates: €60–€70 ($69–$81) double. No credit cards.*

### Lisadorn
**$   Sligo Town, County Sligo**

This stately home is at the end of a flower-lined drive; a perfect welcome to Sligo's only three-star guesthouse. The place offers amazing hospitality and comfort for the cost, and rooms are large and beautifully furnished. Only five minutes from town and ten minutes from beautiful Rosses Point, Lisadorn is a great location.

*Donegal Rd. From the center of town, take the N15 north.* ☎ *071-91-43-417. Fax: 071-91-46-418. Rates: €44–€64 ($51–$74) double. MC, V.*

### Olde Railway Hotel
**$$$   Westport, County Mayo**

You're sure to have a relaxing time at this 18th-century coaching inn in the heart of Westport, where your comfort is obviously a high priority. Open fires blaze, a glass conservatory overlooks a garden patio, and antique period furniture fills the rooms. There are standard and superior rooms; the latter are much larger and have king-size beds, so they're worth the splurge. This place also serves excellent food. Expect lobster, Connemara lamb, produce from the hotel's vegetable and herb garden, and a vast wine list.

*The Mall in the town center, overlooking the Carrowbeg River.* ☎ *098-25-166. 098-25-090.* www.anu.ie/railwayhotel. *Rates: €120–€150 ($138–$173) double. AE, DC, MC, V. Open Feb–Oct.*

### Sligo Park Hotel
**$$$ Sligo Town, County Sligo**

This is Sligo's most modern lodging, and it's one of those hotels that makes you feel like you're spoiling yourself — especially after you put your travel-weary body back together in the leisure center, which features a pool, steam room, and workout equipment. The hotel sits in well-groomed gardens with scenic countryside all around. The comfortable rooms have large windows overlooking the landscaped gardens.

*Pearse Rd. The N4 becomes Pearse Rd. in town.* ☎ *071-60-291. Fax: 071-69-556.* www.leehotels.ie. *Rates: €110–€194 ($127–$223) double. AE, DC, MC, V.*

# Dining Locally

**Cromleach Lodge** (reviewed in the previous section) offers a wonderful New Irish menu in a dining room with views of the surrounding countryside. You can't go wrong with anything on the menu, which changes but may include such mouthwatering options as breast of free-range duck with onion pureé and plum glaze, and pan-fried wild salmon with a light mustard sauce. The prix-fixe dinner menu is €60 ($69).

### The Asgard Tavern
**$$–$$$ Westport, County Mayo IRISH-STEAKS-SEAFOOD**

This nautical-themed restaurant is right on the water and serves award-winning food. Its filling and hearty lunches, including stews and creamy pasta dishes, are served all day downstairs in the relaxing atmosphere in the pub. Dinner is served upstairs, in the tasteful, candlelit dining room. There, the menu is varied, including creatively prepared steaks and seafood. The Asgard Tavern pub serves exceptional pub food from noon to 3 p.m. and from 6 to 10 p.m. The pub offers music most nights.

*The Quay. Drive west out of Westport and take the Coast Road 1.6km (1 mile).* ☎ *098-25-319. Main courses: €15–€28 ($17–$32). AE, DC, MC, V. Open: Sept–June Mon–Sat 6:30–9:30 p.m.; July and Aug daily 6:30– 9:30 p.m.*

## Bistro Bianconi
**$$–$$$$   Sligo Town, County Sligo   ITALIAN-PIZZA**

The menu at this large, bustling Italian restaurant includes no fewer than six pages full of different kinds of pizza, from a Cajun chicken pizza with sliced peppers and smoked bacon to the Michaelangelo, with mozzarella, caramelized onions, pepperoni, goat cheese, and basil pesto. And that's just the pizza. The bistro also offers steak, chicken, and a wide selection of pastas. Families and groups of friends fill the restaurant, which is decorated in trattoria style, with Roman busts, mosaics, and columns.

*44 O'Connell St.* ☎ *074-914-1744. Main courses: €11–€29 (most in the mid-teens) ($13–$33). AE, DC, MC, V. Open: Mon–Sat 12:30–2:30 p.m. and 5:30–11 p.m.*

## Quay Cottage
**$$$   Westport, County Mayo   SEAFOOD**

This little restaurant overlooks the harbor and is appropriately decked out with nautical treasures. The menu focuses on fresh, simply prepared seafood, such as the flavorful local salmon. There are daily specials and a surprisingly large vegetarian selection.

*On Westport Harbour at the entrance to Westport.* ☎ *098-26-412. AE, MC, V. Main courses: €18–€22 ($21–$25). Open: Daily 6–10 p.m.*

# Exploring Mayo and Sligo

If you are a Yeats fan without a car, luck is on your side, because **JH Transport** (☎ 071-914-2747) offers excellent narrated bus tours of the Sligo area and of sights associated with Yeats. The bus leaves from Sligo; call for times and reservations. The tour costs €14 ($16) for adults and €10 ($12) children 6 to 16; it's free for children 5 and under.

## The top attractions

### Carrowmore Megalithic Cemetery
**Carrowmore, County Sligo**

You may imagine you hear the whispers of generations past as you wander this ancient site of *passage tombs* (burial mounds with entrance passageways) and *dolmen* (tombs composed of one rock lying flat across other standing rocks). This is the largest collection of megalithic tombs in Ireland, and some of the oldest tombs in the country are found here, including one that's estimated to be more than 7,000 years old. A restored cottage houses exhibits and information related to the site.

*Located off the R292 going west out of Sligo Town.* ☎ *071-916-1534. Admission: €2 ($2.30) adults, €1.25 ($1.45) seniors, €1 ($1.15) children and students. Open: Easter–Sept daily 10 a.m.–6 p.m.*

## Ceide Fields
**Ballycastle, County Mayo**

This is the world's most extensive Stone Age monument, with a dwelling area, grazing grounds, and megalithic tombs from 5,000 years ago. Tools and pottery have recently been uncovered and are on display in the interpretive center, which does a nice job of explaining the area with exhibits, a film, and guided tours. Although a bog now covers most of the fields (and you can admire the bog's wild plants and flowers), portions have been cut out to show where the fields were partitioned by stone walls for growing food and grazing animals. The fields back up to some of the most captivating cliffs and rock formations in the country. The interpretive center explains the area's past.

*Take the R314 coastal road north from Ballina, 8.1km (5 miles) west of Ballycastle.* ☎ *096-43-325. Admission: €3.50 ($4.05) adult, €2.50 ($2.90) seniors, €1.25 ($1.45) children and students. Open: Mid-March–May daily 10 a.m.–5 p.m.; June–Sept daily 10 a.m.–6 p.m.; Oct–Nov daily 10 a.m.–5 p.m. Suggested visit: 1 hour.*

## Clare Island
**Clew Bay, County Mayo**

This island is a sanctuary of gorgeous sandy beaches and walking trails. Knockmore Mountain is the heart of the island, and the ruins of Clare Castle and Abbey are nearby. The island is a historian's delight, with huts from the Iron Age and the ruins of a castle that belonged to 1600s pirate queen Grace O'Malley.

*The Pirate Queen ferry (*☎ *098-26-307) runs daily (weather permitting) from Roonagh Quay and costs €15 ($17). Call for times. To get to Roonagh Quay: Follow signs from Louisburgh off the R335. Admission: Just ferry cost. Suggested visit: A few hours.*

## Croagh Patrick
**Murrisk, County Mayo**

According to legend, St. Patrick achieved divine inspiration on this mountain after praying and fasting for 40 days — although I don't suggest staying up there that long, no matter how beautiful the view. On the last Sunday of July, devout Irish Catholics climb the 2,500-foot mountain (some barefoot) in memory of their patron saint. There are stunning views of Mayo and Clew Bay from the mountaintop. The climb takes about two hours and is tough work but not impossible.

*Between Louisburgh and Westport off the R395. Admission: Free. Open: Daylight hours. Suggested visit: A few hours.*

## Drive around Lough Gill
**Drumcliffe, County Sligo**

Serene, azure Lough Gill makes many appearances in Yeats's poems. You may be inspired to jot down a few lines of poetry yourself as you make the

42km (26-mile) drive around this gorgeous lake, stopping to ramble along the nature trails and gaze at the island of Innisfree, made famous in Yeats's poem "The Lake Isle of Innisfree." On the north side of the lake drive, you may want to stop to take a guided tour at the beautiful 17th-century Parke's Castle. The lakeside Hazelwood Sculpture Trail is a splendid walk, passing by a number of wood sculptures (some are being refurbished at the moment, but ideally will be back up by the time you read this). Take along some bread for the ducks and swans.

*1.6km (1 mile) south of Sligo Town. Take Stephen St. in Sligo Town, which turns into N16; turn right onto R286, and follow the signs. Suggested visit: 1½ hours or more, depending on how often you stop.*

### Lissadell House
**Drumcliffe, County Sligo**

W. B. Yeats called Lissadell House "that old Georgian mansion," which is quite the understatement. This grand square stone house was owned by the Gore-Booth family, friends of Yeats. One of the Gore-Booth daughters was Countess Markievicz (she married a Polish count), who took part in the Easter Rising of 1916, was the first woman elected to the British House of Commons, and was the first woman cabinet member in the Irish Dáil. Her sister, Eva, was a poet. A collection of family memorabilia is on display.

*Off the N15 between Sligo and Donegal. ☎ 071-916-3150. Admission: €6 ($6.90) adult, €3 ($3.45) children. Open: June to mid-Sept Tues–Sun 10:30 a.m.–12:15 p.m. and 2–4 p.m. Suggested visit: 2 hours.*

### Lough Gill or Lake Isle of Innisfree Cruise
**Lough Gill, County Sligo**

Relax on the *Wild Rose* boat as you cruise Loch Gill or Innisfree, listening to the vivid poetry of Yeats.

*Cruises leave from Doorly Park Jetty (to get to Doorly Park from Sligo Town, go east on Bridge St. for a mile). ☎ 071-916-4266. Lough Gill cruise: €10 ($12) adults, €5 ($5.75) children over 10; Innisfree cruise: €9 ($10) adults, €5 ($5.75) children over 10. Call for a schedule and to make reservations.*

### Sligo Abbey
**Sligo Town, County Sligo**

This is the city's only surviving medieval building, constructed in the mid-13th century for Dominican monks. Inside are carvings and tomb sculptures. The highlight is the superbly carved high altar from the 15th century, the only one of its kind in a monastic church in Ireland. The abbey burned down in 1414 due to a single lit candle and was damaged again in the 1641 Rebellion. According to legend, worshippers saved the abbey's silver bell from thieves by putting it in Lough Gill; It was retrieved later and is back in the abbey. Legend also says that only those free from sin can hear its toll. The abbey is always cool inside, even in warm weather, so you may want to grab a jacket.

*Abbey St. one block south of Kennedy Parade in the center of Sligo Town. ☎ 071-91-46-406. Admission: €2 ($2.30) adult, €1.25 ($1.45) seniors, €1 ($1.15) children and students. Open: Mid-March–Oct 10 a.m.–6 p.m; Nov–Jan Fri–Sun 9:30 a.m.–4:30 p.m. Suggested visit: 45 minutes.*

### Sligo County Museum, Library, and Niland Gallery
Sligo Town, County Sligo

The Yeats family legacy is the cornerstone of this museum, which features memorabilia of the great poet William Butler and paintings by his brother. Jack. and father. John. The special W. B. Yeats section includes his Nobel Prize for Literature (1923) and first editions of his complete works. Also inside is a small collection of objects from Sligo and all over Ireland, from prehistoric times to the Irish war for independence.

*Stephen St. on the north side of the Garavogue River. ☎ 071-914-2212. Admission: Free. Open: Tues–Sat 10 a.m.–noon and 2–4:50 p.m. Suggested visit: About 1 hour.*

### Westport House and Children's Zoo
Westport, County Mayo

This limestone house, sitting at the head of Clew Bay, is a grand house boasting beautiful original furnishings from the late 18th and 19th centuries. The extraordinary interior boasts high ceilings, a white marble staircase, and a dining room full of antiques and Waterford crystal. The children's zoo is home to ostriches, llamas, camels, and more, and the dungeon now holds video games (how many people can say they've played video games in a dungeon?).

*In the city center. ☎ 098-25-430. Admission: House and zoo €16 ($18) adult, €11 ($13) students, €9.50 ($11) seniors €6.50 ($7.50) children; house only €8 ($9.20), €5 ($5.75) seniors and students, €4.50 ($5.20) children Open: House March Sun 11 a.m.–4 p.m., April–May Sun 2–5 p.m., June daily 11 a.m.–5 p.m., July–Aug Mon–Fri 11 a.m.– 5 p.m., and Sat–Sun 1:30–5:30 p.m. Suggested visit: 2 hours or more.*

## Other cool things to see and do

- ✔ **County Sligo Golf Course:** This course challenges even top players, but dabblers can have fun playing it, too. It's set between striking Atlantic beaches and the hill of Benbulben.

  Location: Rosses Point, County Sligo. ☎ 071-77-186. www.county sligogolfclub.ie. Par: 71. Fees: €60 ($69) weekdays, €75 ($86) weekends. Visitors welcome daily.

   ✔ **The Quiet Man Heritage Cottage:** In the movie *The Quiet Man,*
   American John Wayne comes back to his birthplace in Ireland and
   falls in love with Maureen O'Hara. In the movie, Wayne's character
   tells a local that he was born in the thatched-roof cottage, just
   like the seven generations of his family before him, and the local
   makes a wisecrack about Wayne's buying the place to turn it into a
   tourist attraction. Ironically, you can now visit a replica of the original house — and yes, they do charge a small fee to the tourists.
   Unfortunately, no movie memorabilia remains, so all there is to see
   is the house.

   Location: Circular Road, Cong, County Mayo. ☎ 092-46-089.
   Admission: €3.50 ($4.05) adult, €1.25 ($1.45) children. Open:
   March–Nov daily 10 a.m.–6 p.m. Suggested visit: 30 minutes.

   ✔ **W. B. Yeats's Grave:** Yeats died in France, but in 1948, his remains
   were brought to rest in Sligo — the place he always considered
   home. His grave in the Drumcliffe churchyard is near a beautiful
   Celtic high cross. On the grave itself is an epitaph Yeats wrote:
   "Cast a cold eye on life, on death. Horseman pass by."

   Location: 8.1km (5 miles) north of Sligo on the main Donegal road
   (N15).

   ✔ **The Yeats Statue:** One of the more interesting statues in Ireland is
   a cartoonish likeness of Sligo's famous poet near the banks of the
   Garavogue River, in Sligo Town. Scrawled over his entire figure are
   the words of his own verse.

   Location: On Stephen Street, just across Hyde Bridge in Sligo Town.

## Shopping

The locally famous Foxford wool tweeds, rugs, blankets, and much more
are all at **Foxford Woolen Mills Visitor Centre,** Foxford, County Mayo
(from Westport N5 northeast to N58 north; ☎ 094-56-756). As the name
implies, you can tour the working mill. **Pat Sweeny and Son,** Achill
Sound, Achill Island, County Mayo (follow signs from Louisburgh off the
R335; ☎ 098-45-211), is a fascinating example of a local trading store,
dating back to 1870. It has "everything from a needle to an anchor" and
all the gifts, clothing, fishing gear, food, and petrol in between. **The Cat
and The Moon,** 4 Castle St., Sligo Town (☎ 071-914-3686), sells Irish
handcrafted jewelry, contemporary art, Celtic-inspired home furnishings, and more. Check out the connected art gallery. Stop into **Kate's
Kitchen,** 24 Market St., Sligo Town (☎ 071-914-3022), for picnic food:
meats, cheeses, salads, pâté, homemade bread, Irish chocolates, and
preserves. The store also has soaps and potpourri.

# Hitting the Pubs

Before a Sligo Town pub crawl, you may want to take in a performance at **The Factory** (☎ **071-917-0431**). The performance schedule is diverse, offering everything from West African music to the excellent production of the Sligo-based Blue Raincoat Theatre.

## Beezie's
**Sligo Town, County Sligo**

Pay no attention to the bland exterior of this pub, because the interior is beautiful. Stained glass and fireplaces are located throughout this cozy place. The name pays homage to a woman who would row from her home on Cottage Island to the pub until her death in the 1950s. Live music draws a spirited crowd on Mondays and Thursdays.

*45 O'Connell St.* ☎ *071-43-031.*

## Hargadon
**Sligo Town, County Sligo**

This is the kind of pub that's so interesting to look at, you may not notice the pint in front of you. The superb decor features dark wood walls, stone floors, and lots of colored glass. You have plenty of little snugs to settle into, and you can look at various prints of the city in its early days. The pub used to also be a grocery, and the walls still have shelves with old goods.

*4 O'Connell St.* ☎ *071-917-0933.*

## Matt Molloy's
**Westport, County Mayo**

If you like traditional Irish music, this pub is worth visiting. It was started by the flutist from the famous band The Chieftains, who are often credited with the revival in Irish folk music. The pub is traditionally decorated and pretty roomy, and the back room features music nearly every night.

*Bridge St.* ☎ *098-26-655.*

## Yeats Tavern
**Drumcliffe Bridge, County Sligo**

Just a short walk from the grave of poet W. B. Yeats, this pub is a popular watering hole for locals and visitors alike. Inside, you find plenty of Yeats memorabilia and quotes from his works. This pub features good pub grub at even better prices and sometimes hosts traditional music.

*Go 8.1km (5 miles) out of Sligo Town on the main Donegal road.* ☎ *071-916-3117.*

# Fast Facts: Counties Mayo and Sligo

## Area Codes

071 and 074 for County Sligo; 092, 094, 096, 097, and 098 for County Mayo.

## Emergencies/Police

Dial ☎ 999 for all emergencies.

## Genealogy Resources

Contact the Sligo Heritage and Genealogy Centre, Temple Street, Sligo (☎ 071-914-3728); the Mayo North Heritage Centre, Castlehill, Ballina (☎ 096-31-809); or the South Mayo Family History Research Centre, Main Street, Ballinrobe (☎ 094-954-1214).

## Hospital

Sligo General Hospital is on Malloway Hill (☎ 071-914-2212).

## Information

Tourist offices are located at Aras Reddan, Temple Street in Sligo Town (☎ 071-916-1201; www.northwestireland.travel.ie); and at The Mall in Westport, County Mayo (☎ 098-25-71139; www.visitmayo.com). Both are open year-round.

## Internet

Futurenet Internet Cafe, Pearse House, Pearse Road, Sligo (☎ 071-915-345), has Internet- access and printing capabilities.

## Post Office

Wine Street, Sligo (☎ 071-42-646), and North Mall, Westport (☎ 098-25-219).

# Chapter 20

# County Donegal

## In This Chapter

▶ Touring Glenveagh Castle and its extensive grounds
▶ Staying in a room with a view — of Donegal Bay
▶ Exploring a great and varied art collection
▶ Checking out Europe's highest sea cliffs

County Donegal (shown in the nearby map) has several different faces; the towns on the south side of Donegal Bay are seaside resorts frequented mostly by Irish vacationers, and some, like Bundoran, are pretty tacky. However, above and to the west of Killybegs, the land is stunning and untouched, crowned by the towering sea cliffs at **Slieve League.** The Atlantic Highlands (in the north) and the **Inishowen Peninsula** are wild landscapes, vast and breathtaking, with mountains, woodland, cliffs, and the ever-present crashing of the ocean. There isn't one specific area known for human-made sights; instead, you come across different sights, including a prehistoric fort and a comprehensive art museum, throughout this little-visited corner of the country.

The largest town in the county, **Donegal Town,** is a delightful, walkable village along the River Eske and makes a good point of departure for touring the coast clockwise, passing the **Glenveigh National Park** at the end of your journey. **Ballybofey** is a great starting point for touring the far reaches of the county, including the untamed mountains, coasts, and woodland of the **Inishowen Peninsula.** Any way you go, you'll be surrounded by breathtaking scenery.

## Getting to and around County Donegal

Local flights come into Donegal airport, Carrickfinn, Kincasslagh (☎ 075-48-284; www.donegalairport.ie), located 65km (40 miles) from Donegal Town. If you come by car, you can take the N15 north from Sligo, or the A46 or A47 south from Northern Ireland. **Bus Éireann** (☎ 074-912-1309; www.buseireann.ie) travels year-round to Donegal, Ballyshannon, and other towns in County Donegal. Bus pickup in Donegal is at the **Abbey Hotel,** on The Diamond in the town center.

## County Donegal

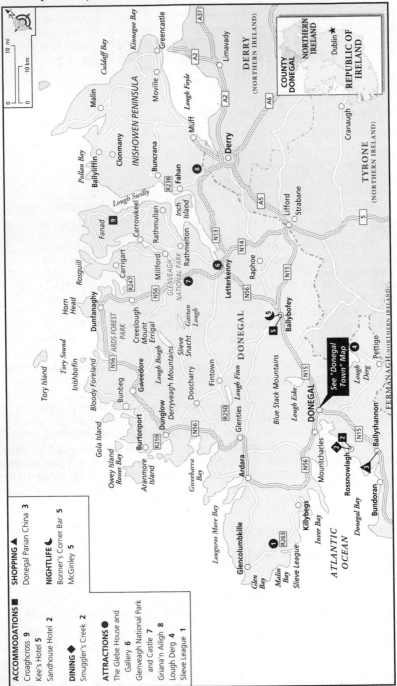

**ACCOMMODATIONS** ■
Croaghcross **9**
Kee's Hotel **5**
Sandhouse Hotel **2**

**DINING** ◆
Smuggler's Creek **2**

**ATTRACTIONS** ●
The Glebe House and
Gallery **6**
Glenveagh National Park
and Castle **7**
Griana'n Ailigh **8**
Lough Derg **4**
Slieve League **1**

**SHOPPING** ▲
Donegal Parian China **3**

**NIGHTLIFE** ☾
Bonner's Corner Bar **5**
McGinley **5**

There's no local bus service, but you can easily walk through and around Donegal Town if you don't have a car. I don't recommend exploring County Donegal without a car or bike (or super sturdy walking shoes and a strong walking stick), because one of the biggest draws is traveling through the natural scenery.

# Spending the Night

The "Donegal Town" map can help with locations.

### Abbey Hotel
**$$$  Donegal Town**

This comfortable hotel has tasteful and spacious rooms — some overlooking Donegal Bay, so be sure to ask about them. The hotel is in the heart of town, and beaches, boating, and horseback riding are all nearby. The comfortable, homey Abbey restaurant is a real treat — not only is the food great, but the decor looks just like a traditional Irish kitchen. There's also a modern-looking bar, the Eas Dun, that serves hot pub grub all day.

*The Diamond, in the town center. ☎ 074-972-1014. Fax: 074-972-3660. Rates: €120–€140 ($138–$161) double. AE, MC, V.*

 ### Croaghross
**$-$$  Portsalon**

Bring extra film, because this B&B has a gorgeous rural setting with views of Lough Swilly. Your hosts, the Deanes, can tell you about the various hikes in the area. The house and rooms are soothing and comfortable; sit down in front of a crackling fire after exploring nearby Glenveagh National Park or the Atlantic Drive. You can't beat the warm and professional service of the Deanes, who make everything look effortless.

*Go north from Letterkenny toward Milford; 1km before Milford turn right on the R246 and follow the signs through Kerrykeel to Portsalon. Turn right at the crossroads in Portsalon and look for the Croaghross sign opposite the golf course. ☎ 074-915-9548. Fax: 074-915-9548. www.croaghross.com. Rates: €70–€100 ($81–$115) double. AE, MC, V.*

### Kee's Hotel
**$$-$$$  Stranorlar/Ballybofey**

This charming historic coaching inn is in the perfect location for exploring Donegal. The staff is warm and friendly, and the rooms are big and comfortable, with views of the grand Blue Stack Mountains. Guests can use the gym and the pool and then relax in front of one of the hotel's open fireplaces. The restaurant serves excellent food, and bikes are available for rent.

## Donegal Town

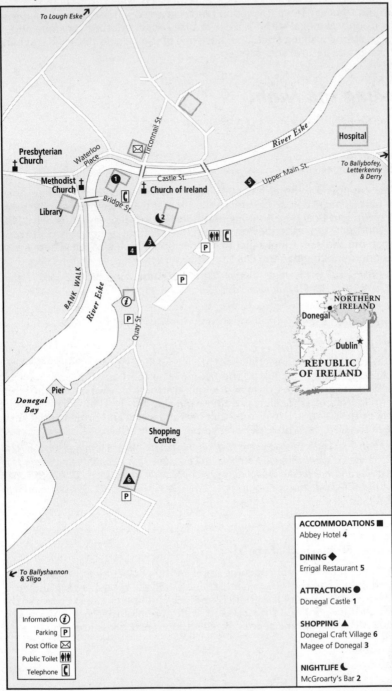

To Lough Eske

Presbyterian
Church

Methodist
Church

Library

Waterloo
Place

Tirconnail St.

River Eske

Hospital

To Ballybofey,
Letterkenny
& Derry

Castle St.

Church of Ireland

Upper Main St.

Bridge St.

BANK WALK

River Eske

Quay St.

Pier

Donegal
Bay

Shopping
Centre

To Ballyshannon
& Sligo

NORTHERN
IRELAND

Donegal

Dublin

REPUBLIC
OF IRELAND

Information *i*
Parking P
Post Office ✉
Public Toilet 👥
Telephone C

**ACCOMMODATIONS** ■
Abbey Hotel **4**

**DINING** ◆
Errigal Restaurant **5**

**ATTRACTIONS** ●
Donegal Castle **1**

**SHOPPING** ▲
Donegal Craft Village **6**
Magee of Donegal **3**

**NIGHTLIFE** ☾
McGroarty's Bar **2**

*Take the N15 northeast from Donegal Town to where it meets the N13.* ☎ *074-913-1018. Fax: 074-913-1917.* www.keeshotel.com. *Rates:* €*100–*€*160 ($115–$184) double. AE, DC, MC, V.*

### Sandhouse Hotel
**$$$–$$$$**    **Rossnowlagh**

This oceanside fishing lodge-turned-four-star hotel boasts a marine spa, an outdoor hot tub, and a panoramic elevator with sea views. When you're not sleeping like a log in your overstuffed bed, you can take a walk along the cliffs, play some golf at one of the three nearby courses, or just take in comforts of the hotel itself — the rooftop garden, warm fires, fresh flowers, and homemade scones and pies. It's worth it to splurge on a room with a view of the Atlantic Ocean and Donegal Bay.

*Rossnowlagh Beach. Off the R231 about 8km (5 miles) northwest of Ballyshannon.* ☎ *071-985-1777. Fax: 071-985-2100.* www.sandhouse-hotel.ie. *Rates:* €*190–*€*260 ($219–$299) double. AE, DC, MC, V.*

# Dining Locally

### Errigal Restaurant
**$**    **Donegal Town**    FISH AND CHIPS (AND MORE)

Fish and chips is the house specialty at this local favorite. Errigal is a family-run restaurant, and the menu is varied enough to appeal to any taste and any budget. It features fish dishes, steaks, chicken curry (which you see on many pub menus), sandwiches, and burgers. Don't look for a light meal here; you'll leave full and satisfied, and with money left in your wallet.

*Upper Main St.* ☎ *074-972-1428. Main courses:* €*5.65–*€*9.35 ($6.50–$11). No credit cards. Open: Mon–Sat 9 a.m.–3 p.m. and 5:30–11 p.m., Sun 3:30–11 p.m.*

### Smuggler's Creek
**$$–$$$**    **Rossnowlagh**    SEAFOOD - IRISH

The view itself is enough to make a meal at Smuggler's Creek memorable. From the conservatory dining room, which sits atop a cliff, you can look out at Donegal Bay, and if your timing's good, you may catch a fantastic sunset. Inside, the stone building is decorated with wooden stools, lobster pots, and porthole windows. Not surprisingly, seafood is a specialty here. What is surprising, considering the low prices, is the gourmet menu. The wild salmon with hollandaise is terrific, as is the rich Smuggler's sea casserole — scallops, salmon, and prawns in a cream sauce. And the steak with trademark Irish whiskey sauce is a treat. Even the bar menu is a notch above, with fresh pâté and garlic mussels amid the usual soup and sandwiches.

*¼ mile off the R231, off the main Sligo-Donegal road (N15). Take the little, no-name side road from the R231 to get closer to the water. Signs won't let you miss the turnoff. ☎ 071-985-2366. Main courses: €10–€25 (lobster is more) ($12–$16). AE, DC, MC, V. Open: Daily noon to midnight.*

# Exploring County Donegal

You can rent bikes to explore Donegal from **Pat Boyle** (☎ 074-972-2515) in Donegal Town, and **Church Street Cycles** (☎ 074-912-6204) in Letterkenny.

## The top attractions

### Donegal Castle
**Donegal Town**

Built in the 15th century by the O'Donnell chieftain, this impressive castle sits beside the River Eske. Inside, lovely furnishings include Persian rugs and French tapestries — 17th-century additions from the last owner, Sir Basil Brooke, who also added an extension with ten gables and a large bay window. Free half-hour guided tours are available.

*☎ 074-9722-405. Admission: €3.50 ($4.05) adult, €2.50 ($2.90) seniors, €1.25 ($1.45) children and students. Open: mid-March–Oct daily 10 a.m.–6 p.m., Nov–Dec Fri–Sun 9:30 a.m.–4:30 p.m. Suggested visit: 1 hour.*

### The Glebe House and Gallery
**Churchill, Letterkenny**

This house was the pride of art collector Derek Hill, and visitors can now view his grand collection. Hill's taste was diverse, and you'll find works by artists from Picasso to Renoir to Jack B. Yeats. The decor of the house is an exhibit in itself, with Islamic ceramics, Japanese art, and priceless wall-paper and textiles. The 1828 building is set amid gardens and woods.

*On the R251 about 18km (11 miles) west of Letterkenny. ☎ 074-913-7071. Admission: €2.75 ($3.15) adult, €2 ($2.30) seniors, €1.25 ($1.45) children and students. Open: Mid-May–Sept Sat–Thurs 11 a.m.–6:30 p.m. Suggested visit: 1½ hours.*

### Glenveagh National Park and Castle
**Churchill, Letterkenny**

This National Park is a stunner, with more than 40,000 acres of wilderness encompassing valleys and glens, pristine lakes, dense woodlands, alpine gardens, and the highest mountain in Donegal: Mount Errigal. In your wanderings, you may come across the herd of red deer that call the park home. The impressive castle here was built in 1870 and modeled after the royal Balmoral Castle in Scotland. Tours take you through the grand rooms, which contain the furnishings left by the last owner, Henry McIlhenny, an

American philanthropist and art collector. Near the castle are spectacular gardens, some featuring exotic plants and flowers. The visitor center has an audiovisual show about the park and information on the various trails.

*Northwest from Letterkenny on the main road to Kilmacrennan (N56). ☎ 074-91-37-090. Admission: €2.75 ($3.15) adults, €2 ($2.30) seniors, €1.25 ($1.45) children and students. Open: Mid-March–early Nov daily 10 a.m.–6:30 p.m. Suggested visit: 3 to 4 hours.*

## Slieve League
### Southwest County Donegal

The movie poster slogan for the cliffs of Slieve League (pronounced sleev *loo*-kra) would read: "If you liked the Cliffs of Moher, you'll love the cliffs of Slieve League." These are the highest sea cliffs in Europe. At Carrick, you can turn off to gaze at their immensity from the Bunglas viewing point and decide if you want to take the challenge and walk the ridge. The hike, which starts at the Bunglas viewing point, is narrow and steep, and requires good balance and good hiking boots.

*View point is off N56 in Carrick. Admission: Free. Suggested visit: A few minutes for the view. The walk takes at least 4 to 5 hours.*

## Other cool things to see and do

- ✔ **Griana'n Ailigh:** The burial site here was created in 1700 B.C., and the stone ring fort was built around A.D. 600. The views of Lough Swilly and Lough Foyle from the battlements of the ring fort are breathtaking. A refurbished old stone church houses an interpretive center explaining the history and myths surrounding the burial ground and fort. You can explore the ancient woods and wetlands nearby.

  Location: Off the N13 northeast from Letterkenny or west from Derry in Burt, Inishowen (☎ 077-68-000). Admission: €3.50 ($4.05). Open daily in summer from 10 a.m. to 7 p.m., in winter daily from noon to 5 p.m. Suggested visit: 45 minutes.

- ✔ **Lough Derg:** Legend has it that St. Patrick spent a Lenten season fasting on one of this lake's tiny islands, and since then, devout Catholics have gone there for penance. Pilgrims must stay awake for three days, eating only one meal a day of dry bread and black tea. Visitors are welcome to visit the island when pilgrimages aren't taking place, and I recommend investing the time in the visitor center to get a real feel for the area's religious and historical import.

  Location: From the Sligo-Donegal Road (N15) take R232 to Pettigo for the visitor center. Admission is free. For trips to the island, you must contact the visitor center in advance (☎ 071-98-61-518). Open April through September. Suggested visit (at the visitor center): 30 minutes.

# Shopping

At **Donegal Craft Village,** on the Ballyshannon-Sligo Road in Donegal Town (☎ 074-972-2015), a collective of artisans create and sell a range of crafts: pottery, jewelry, uilleann pipes (Irish bagpipes), ceramics, batik, and more. At **Donegal Parian China,** on the main Bundoran Road (N15), just south of the town of Ballyshannon (☎ 071-985-1826), you can watch as craftspeople create this thin china, decorated with shamrocks and other Irish plants and flowers, before you purchase items in the shop. **Magee of Donegal,** on the Diamond in Donegal Town (☎ 074-972-2660), is the best source for famous Donegal tweed.

# Hitting the Pubs

### Bonner's Corner Bar
**Ballybofey**

If you're hankering for a pint and some conversation, go to Corner, with its warm and comfortable brick interior. This is a no-nonsense Irish pub, where you can find plenty of friendly locals engaged in lively chats.

*Main St. at Glenfinn St.* ☎ *074-913-1361.*

### McGinley
**Ballybofey**

This pub was recently renovated, but great care was taken to maintain the traditional decor. The bar is huge, with plenty of places to pull up a stool, and the adjoining lounge is spacious and comfortable. You can hear music four nights a week — traditional, as well as an Irish favorite: American country-and-western (honestly, it's extremely popular here). Pub grub is served all day.

*Glenfinn St.* ☎ *074-913-1150.*

### McGroarty's Bar
**Donegal Town**

This wonderful stone building houses a warm, cozy, brightly decorated pub that's chock full of atmosphere. The food is fantastic and varied, and the music ranges from traditional Irish to folksy ballads on Thursday, Friday, Saturday, and Sunday nights.

*The Diamond in the center of town..* ☎ *074-972-1049.*

# Fast Facts: County Donegal

## Area Codes

Area codes (or city codes) are 071, 074, and 077.

## Emergencies/Police

Dial ☎ 999 for all emergencies.

## Genealogy Resources

Contact Donegal Ancestry, Old Meeting House, Back Lane, Ramelton, Letterkenny (☎ 074-51-266; donances@indigo.ie).

## Hospital

Donegal District Hospital is on Upper Main Street (☎ 074-972-1105).

## Information

For visitor information, go to the Donegal Tourist Office, Quay Street, Donegal Town (☎ 074-972-1148; www.donegal.ie).

## Internet

Donegal County Library, Mountcharles Road, Donegal Town (☎ 074-972-1105).

## Post Office

Donegal Post Office, Tirconnail Street (☎ 074-972-1001).

# Part VI
# Northern Ireland

## The 5<sup>th</sup> Wave    By Rich Tennant

# In this part . . .

Northern Ireland has as much splendor and beauty as the Republic with a fraction of the visitors, making it an excellent choice for travelers who don't like crowds. The green folds of the Mourne Mountains (Chapter 23) beg to be hiked, and travelers from all over the world come to clamber over the strange six-sided columns of basalt at the Giant's Causeway (Chapter 22). The North Antrim coast (Chapter 22) is a dramatic landscape of cliffs, beaches, and sea. Farther south, County Fermanagh (Chapter 21) boasts a giant lake with many islands.

In addition to natural beauty, Northern Ireland offers two exciting cities, Belfast (Chapter 22) and Derry (Chapter 21). Belfast has a thriving arts scene, a bunch of excellent new restaurants, and some gorgeous architecture. Being a university town, Belfast also has no lack of places to party, from Old World pubs to trendy clubs. After many years of religious strife, Derry is enjoying peace and is emerging as a city with a lot to offer, including quite a few historical sights, great nightlife, and a growing calendar of theatrical, literary, and musical events.

# Chapter 21

# Counties Derry, Fermanagh, and Tyrone

- - - - - - - - - - - - - - - - - - - - - - - - - - - - - - - - - - - - - - - - - - - -

*In This Chapter*

▶ Exploring Derry's walls
▶ Living in 19th-century Ireland and America: The Ulster American Folk Park
▶ Checking out Belleek china

- - - - - - - - - - - - - - - - - - - - - - - - - - - - - - - - - - - - - - - - - - - -

These three counties, shown on the nearby map, offer diverse attractions. The principal draw of County Derry is Derry City, with its many historical sights, great pubs, and up-and-coming arts scene. The pretty county of Tyrone, with its farmlands, cottages, and gentle mountains, is known mainly for the excellent Ulster American Folk Park. County Fermanagh offers a huge and peaceful lake with 154 islands and the pleasant resort town of Enniskillen.

## Getting to Counties Derry, Fermanagh, and Tyrone

The **City of Derry (Eglinton) Airport** (☎ 028-7181-0784; www.city ofderryariport.com) is 12km (7 miles) from the city and served by **British Airways** (☎ 0345-222-111; www.britishairways.com) and **Ryanair** (☎ 0541-569-569; www.ryanair.com). To get to Derry from the airport, take a cab. The fare is around £10 ($19) to the city center.

To get to Derry by car from Donegal, take the N15 to Strabane and then take the A5 north. To get to Enniskillen from Sligo, take the N16 (which becomes the A4 in Northern Ireland) east. To get to Omagh from Derry or Strabane, go south on the A5; from Enniskillen, go north on the A32. If you're driving from the Republic into Northern Ireland, make sure you notify your rental-car company; extra insurance may be required.

## Counties Derry, Fermanagh, and Tyrone

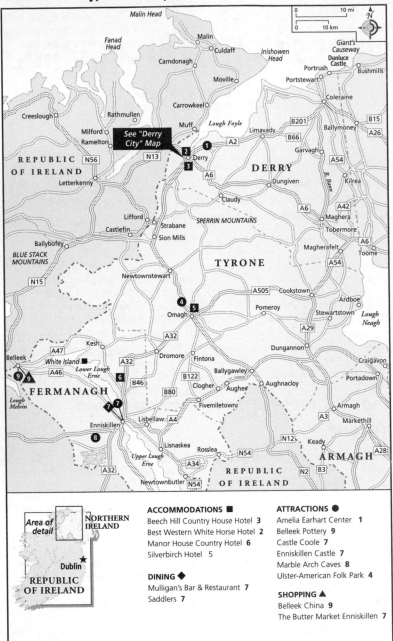

Area of detail

NORTHERN IRELAND

Dublin ★

REPUBLIC OF IRELAND

**ACCOMMODATIONS ■**
Beech Hill Country House Hotel **3**
Best Western White Horse Hotel **2**
Manor House Country Hotel **6**
Silverbirch Hotel **5**

**DINING ◆**
Mulligan's Bar & Restaurant **7**
Saddlers **7**

**ATTRACTIONS ●**
Amelia Earhart Center **1**
Belleek Pottery **9**
Castle Coole **7**
Enniskillen Castle **7**
Marble Arch Caves **8**
Ulster-American Folk Park **4**

**SHOPPING ▲**
Belleek China **9**
The Butter Market Enniskillen **7**

**Northern Ireland Railways** (☎ 888-BRITRAIL or **028-9089-9411;** www.
nirailways.co.uk) services Derry year-round, and **Ulsterbus** (☎ **028-
7126-2261;** www.translink.co.uk) travels year-round to Derry, Omagh,
Enniskillen, and other major towns in Counties Derry, Tyrone, and
Fermanagh.

# County Derry

Inhabited since the sixth century, **Derry City** is one of the oldest cities
in Ireland. This small city has seen its share of turmoil and heartbreak,
from the siege led by Catholic King James' army in 1688, to the many
Irish emigrants who set out from Derry for America in the 18th and 19th
centuries, to the horrors and violence of the Troubles in the 20th century. Things have been basically peaceful in Derry for a while now, and
the city is becoming a fun and vibrant place on its way up, with great
nightlife, a hot cultural scene, and many restored historical sights.

## Spending the night in County Derry

The "Derry City" map can help you locate inns and attractions.

### The Beech Hill Country House Hotel
$$$   Derry City

This elegant 1729 country house is the perfect place for relaxation. Stroll
the gorgeous wooded grounds and then curl up before the fire with a cup
of tea. Or hit the sauna, steam room, or Jacuzzi after working out in the fit-
ness room. About half of the 28 rooms are decorated in Georgian style; the
other half feature modern furnishings. The Ardmore Restaurant serves
locally caught seafood and home-grown seasonal vegetables. The hotel is
just outside Derry City, within easy driving distance of the region's biggest
attractions.

*32 Ardmore Rd. Take the A6 south out of the city toward Belfast and follow the signs.*
☎ *028-7134-9279. Fax: 028-7134-5366.* www.beech-hill.com. *Rates: £79–£90
($146–$167) double. AE, MC, V.*

## Derry or Londonderry?

During the Troubles, what you called the city depended on where you stood politically.
Unionists (who wish to remain under the English crown) called it Londonderry, while
Nationalists (who want to become part of the Republic of Ireland) called it Derry. *Derry*
is the more commonly used name now, through newscasters often try to avert trou-
ble by calling the city "Derry/Londonderry."

## Derry City

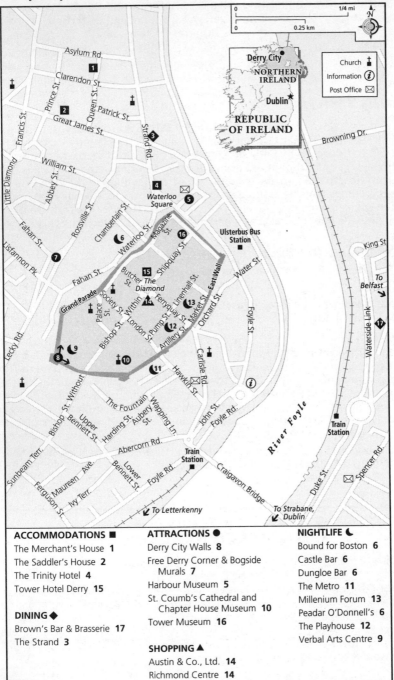

**ACCOMMODATIONS ■**

The Merchant's House **1**
The Saddler's House **2**
The Trinity Hotel **4**
Tower Hotel Derry **15**

**DINING ◆**

Brown's Bar & Brasserie **17**
The Strand **3**

**ATTRACTIONS ●**

Derry City Walls **8**
Free Derry Corner & Bogside
   Murals **7**
Harbour Museum **5**
St. Coumb's Cathedral and
   Chapter House Museum **10**
Tower Museum **16**

**SHOPPING ▲**

Austin & Co., Ltd. **14**
Richmond Centre **14**

**NIGHTLIFE ☾**

Bound for Boston **6**
Castle Bar **6**
Dungloe Bar **6**
The Metro **11**
Millenium Forum **13**
Peadar O'Donnell's **6**
The Playhouse **12**
Verbal Arts Centre **9**

### Best Western White Horse Hotel
**$$  Campsie**

On the main road to the Giants Causeway in County Antrim (see Chapter 22) and only a few minutes from the airport, this hotel is a great hub for venturing out to see the North. The spacious rooms are fabulous, with tasteful wallpaper and pine furniture that gives them a homey country feel, porches that lead out to groomed lawns, and canopy beds in some rooms. Though the hotel is about 8.1km (5 miles) from Derry City, there is frequent bus service. There are fishing and golfing nearby.

*68 Clooney Rd. 8km (5 miles) north of the city.* ☎ *028-7186-0606. Fax: 028-7186-0371. From Derry, take the A2 toward Limavady. Rates: £50–£60 ($93–$111) double. AE, DC, MC, V.*

### The Merchant's House
**$–$$  Derry City**

Owned and run by the same people who do such a fine job with The Saddler's House (see the next review), The Merchant's House is an elegant, beautifully restored Georgian B&B within walking distance of the city center. The home has high ceilings and intricate plasterwork, and the bedrooms are spacious and painted in warm, vivid colors. Flames in the fireplace flicker on the walls of the comfortable parlor. Having breakfast in the polished Georgian dining room, you may think you've slipped back in time.

*16 Queen St.* ☎ *028-7126-9691. Fax: 028-7126-6913.* www.thesaddlershouse. com. *Rates: £40–£45 ($74–$83) double. No credit cards.*

### The Saddler's House
**$$  Derry City**

You'll feel right at home in this cozy Victorian B&B, with its guest common room, selection of books in each bedroom, and tasty breakfasts served in a light-flooded space. Rooms aren't huge, but they're certainly big enough to move around in and charmingly furnished in a way that makes them seem more like rooms in someone's home than rooms in a guest lodging. The location is terrific, within a ten-minute walk of the heart of the city.

*36 Great James St.* ☎ *028-7126-9691. Fax: 028-7126-6913.* www.thesaddlers house.com. *Rates: £45 ($83) double. No credit cards.*

### Tower Hotel Derry
**$$$  Derry City**

This branch of the Irish Tower Hotel chain boasts a terrific location within Derry's medieval walls. The rooms are typical chain-style — nothing fancy, but spacious and comfortable and quite a deal for this rate. The hotel has a gym and sauna, and the staff is always ready to help. The Tower Hotel's central location and business center make it an especially good choice for business travelers.

*Butcher St. just off the Diamond in the center of town.* ☎ *028-713-1000. Fax: 028-713-1234.* www.towerhotelgroup.com. *Rates: £60–100 ($111–185) double. AE, DC, MC, V.*

### The Trinity Hotel
**$$$** **Derry City**

This ultra-elegant hotel almost seems out of place in Derry, contrasting with the medieval look of the city. You'll find it simple yet, despite the reasonable cost, posh. The architecture and materials are modern, but traditional Celtic designs give it a characteristically Irish feel. Although the rooms aren't the most spacious around, the beds are super comfortable, and the furnishings are simple and sleek. Be sure to check out one of the hotel's three bars, especially the stunning Conservatory Lounge.

*22 Strand Rd.* ☎ *028-7127-1271. Fax: 028-7127-1277. Strand Road is just north of the city center and south of Foyle Bridge. Rates: £80–£100 ($148–$185) double. AE, MC, V.*

## Dining locally in County Derry

### Brown's Bar and Brasserie
**$$–$$$$** **Derry City** **NEW IRISH/INTERNATIONAL**

This sleek, modern restaurant, decorated with neutral colors, zebra-print curtains, modern art, and a stalk of bamboo on every table, serves some of the most innovate cuisine in these parts, made with the freshest ingredients. Groups of friends and couples come to feast on sirloin with bacon, mushrooms, Cashel blue cheese, and tomatoes; honey-glazed lamb with mint jus and a tomato, mint, and mozzarella tart; and the fabulous vegetarian Turlu Turlu — leeks, zucchini, and eggplant in a flavorful Middle Easter sauce. Don't miss the "kick-ass olives" appetizer.

*1 Bond's Hill, Waterside.* ☎ *028-7134-5180. Main courses: £8.50–£16 ($16–$30). AE, MC, V. Open: Tues–Fri noon–2:30 p.m., Tues–Thurs 5:30–10 p.m., Fri and Sat 5:30–10:30 p.m.*

### The Strand
**$–$$$** **Derry City** **INTERNATIONAL**

This restaurant, named the Northwest Restaurant of the Year in 2004, has a menu built to please everyone, with everything from soups to an excellent salmon plate, all beautifully prepared. The restaurant reminds me of an American diner — a large space with comfy booths and servers that make you feel well taken care of — though the cuisine is a notch above American diner food on the sophistication front.

*Strand Rd.* ☎ *028-7126-0494. Main courses: £5–£13 ($9.25–$24). AE, MC, V. Open: Mon–Sat noon–3 p.m. and 5–10:30 p.m., Sun 5–10 p.m.*

# Digging into an Ulster Fry

What's the difference between a traditional Irish breakfast in the Republic and an Ulster Fry? Well, along with your fried egg, sausage, bacon, black pudding, fried tomatoes, and toast, you get *soda farls* and *potato cakes*. Soda farls are pieces of soft bread, fluffed with soda and buttermilk; potato cakes are made with mashed potatoes, flour, and butter. They're both fried up with the rest of the breakfast and are delicious.

## Exploring County Derry

Most of the attractions to be seen in County Derry are in **Derry City.** Walking and bus tours are the best way to get to know the city and its complicated background. An excellent walking tour of the city walls is offered by **City Tours** (☎ **028-7127-1996**). Tours leave at 10 a.m. and noon every day from 11 Carlisle St. Another terrific walking tour option is **McNamara's Famous Guided Walking Tours** (call ☎ **028-7134-5335** for schedules, prices, and meeting spots). If walking seems boring, how about touring the city in a horse-drawn carriage? Call ☎ **028-7127-1886** to be picked up anywhere in the city center. Finally, **Hop On Hop Off Bus Tours** (☎ **07080-957-330**) takes you to sights throughout the city. Departures are at 10 a.m., noon, 2 p.m., and 4 p.m. from the Tourist Information Center, which is located at 44 Foyle St. (☎ **028-7126-7284**). Cost is £6 ($11) for adults, £5 ($9) for seniors and students, and £3 ($5.55) for children.

## Amelia Earhart Center
**Ballyarnet**

Amelia Earhart landed in Derry in 1932, becoming the first woman to fly solo across the Atlantic. To find out more about her historic flight, visit the Earhart Center in Ballyarnet.

*4.8km (3 miles) north of Derry City on the A2.* ☎ *028-7135-4040. Admission: Free. Open: Mon–Thurs 9 a.m.–4 p.m., Fri 9 a.m.–1 p.m. Suggested visit: about an hour.*

 ## Derry City Walls
**Derry City**

Derry is one of the few European cities that still have intact city walls. The walls, 7.9m (26 feet) high and about 9.1m (30 feet) thick, were built in 1618 and succeeded in keeping Derry safe from many attacks. In fact, the walls have never been breached, earning Derry the cheeky nickname "The Maiden City." I highly recommend walking the city walls; you can walk the parapet on your own. A few staircases at different points along the walls take you to the top, or you can take one of the excellent tours described in the preceding "Exploring County Derry" section.

## Free Derry Corner and the Bogside Murals

Bogside is one of the Catholic neighborhoods in Derry that has seen the worst of the Catholic–Protestant conflict. In 1969, a local man painted the words "You are now entering Free Derry" on a wall at the corner of Fahan and Rossville streets. The other murals depict events in Derry since 1968, and include, among others, a mural of Annette McGavigan, the first child victim of the Troubles; a mural of a young petrol bomber; and a mural of Bloody Sunday, when 13 civil-rights marchers were shot by British soldiers.

*Bogside area. The best way to see the murals is with the artists who painted them. The artists give tours of the murals from their studio at 7 Meenan Sq. Call ☎ 028-7128-4123 or 028-7137-3842 to arrange a tour.*

## St. Columb's Cathedral and Chapter House Museum
### Derry City

This Gothic Protestant cathedral — named for Saint Columb, founder of Derry — towers above the city walls. It houses many memorials and relics from the 1688 to 1689 siege of Derry, when the city's Protestant population held out against the forces of Catholic King James I for 105 days, helping secure the throne for Protestant King William III. Points of interest include the stained glass that tells the story of the siege, and the tremendous mortar ball that King James fired over the city walls embedded with a note asking the people of Derry to surrender (they refused). The Chapter House Museum displays artifacts of the city's history, including the original keys to the city gates, and shows an audiovisual presentation relating the history of the city.

*London St. ☎ 028-7126-7313. Admission: £1.30 ($2.40) per person. Open: March–Oct daily 9 a.m.–5 p.m.; Nov–Feb daily 9 a.m.–1 p.m. and 2–4 p.m. Suggested visit: 45 minutes.*

## Tower Museum
### Derry City, County Derry

This museum really gets at the heart of Derry history, covering events and daily life from prehistoric times to the present day. It's housed in the O'Doherty Tower, a replica of the 16th-century medieval fort that stood on this spot. The museum is closed as this book goes to press due to the installation of a comprehensive exhibit about the Spanish Armada in Ireland, but there's a good chance renovations will be complete by the time you read this. If not, you can see most of the items from the Story of Derry exhibit at the **Harbour Museum,** Harbour Square (☎ **028-7137-7331**), which is open Monday to Friday from 10:00 a.m. to 1:00 p.m. and from 2:00 p.m. to 4:30 p.m. Admission is free.

*Union Hall Pl.* ☎ *028-7137-2411. Admission: £4.20 ($7.70) adults, £2 ($3.70) seniors and students. Open: Sept–June Tues–Sat 10 a.m.–5 p.m.; July–Aug Mon–Sat 10 a.m.– 5 p.m. and Sun 2–5 p.m. Suggested visit: 1 hour.*

### Shopping in Derry City

The best shopping is found in the inner city, in the **Richmond Centre,** a modern mall facing the Diamond in the center of town and featuring more than 30 shops and boutiques.

The Victorian-style department store **Austin & Co. Ltd.,** The Diamond (☎ 028-7126-1817), is a city landmark, specializing in clothes, perfume, china, crystal, and linens. The coffee shop on the third floor has a great view of the city.

### Nightlife in Derry City

The **Playhouse,** 5–7 Artillery St. (☎ 028-7126-8027; www.derry playhouse.co.uk), presents local, national, and international plays and dance. The **Verbal Arts Centre,** Mall Wall and Stable Lane, Bishop Street (☎ 028-7126-8027), is an incredible place, dedicated to literature in all of its forms. It hosts all sorts of readings, classes, and storytelling events. The **Millennium Forum,** Newmarket Street (☎ 028-7126-4455; www.millenniumforum.co.uk), offers a program of plays, dance, and musicals, including children's shows.

### Hitting the pubs

Want to hear traditional Irish music in Derry? Head to **Waterloo Street,** just outside the city walls in front of Butcher and Castle Gates. Some of the best pubs for informal sessions lie along this route. In particular, the **Dungloe Bar** (☎ 028-7126-7761), **Bound for Boston** (☎ 028-7126-6351), **Castle Bar** (☎ 028-7126-3118), and **Peadar O'Donnell's** (☎ 028-7137-2318) are great places to have a pint.

### The Metro
**Derry City**

Plenty of little alcoves and mementos from across the globe make the Metro an interesting stop. The pub sits in the shadow of Derry's old city walls and serves a mean beef Guinness stew.

*3–4 Bank Pl.* ☎ *028-7126-7401.*

# Counties Fermanagh and Tyrone

Island-studded **Lake Erne** is the centerpiece of County Fermanagh, serving as a destination for boaters and anglers, while County Tyrone is home to what is arguably Ireland's finest outdoor living museum.

## Spending the night in Counties Fermanagh and Tyrone

### Manor House Country Hotel
**$$$$  Killadeas, County Fermanagh**

This Victorian mansion offers wonderful views of Lough Erne. The house is beautifully furnished with antiques, and rooms are traditional with floral fabrics and dark wood furniture. Kids will love the swimming pool and mini-golf course.

*Killadeas is off the B82, north of Enniskillen.* ☎ *028-6862-2211.* www.manor-house-hotel.com. *Rates: £110–£140 ($204–259). AE, MC, V.*

### The Silverbirch Hotel
**$$$  Omagh, County Tyrone**

This hotel, recently renovated and featuring a beautiful atrium, is by far one of the finest in the mid-Ulster region. Although the hotel has become quite modern, it's hidden on the outskirts of Gortin Glen National Park, giving it a timeless, rustic feel. The Buttery Grill is known throughout the area for its top-notch cuisine. The friendly and efficient hotel staff may be the highlight of your stay; someone's always on hand to help out.

*5 Gortin Rd. Just north of Omagh, on the B48.* ☎ *028-8224-2520. Fax: 028-8224-9061.* www.silverbirchhotel.com. *Rates: £78–£92 ($144–$170) double. AE, DC, MC, V.*

# Dining locally in Counties Fermanagh and Tyrone

### Mulligan's Bar and Restaurant
**$$$–$$$$  Enniskillen, County Fermanagh   IRISH-INTERNATIONAL**

This family-run restaurant serves a wide selection that emphasizes local ingredients. Everything that reaches the table is homemade, and it shows. For starters, there are savory pâtés and soups, which make way for tasty seafood dishes like local mussels or salmon and Ulster meat dishes. The atmosphere is inviting and rustic, and there's live music to set the tone for a relaxing meal. Top pick: the Irish stew, which is made with a generous amount of Bushmills whiskey — it may be the best stew you'll ever eat.

*33 Darling St.* ☎ *028-6632-2059. Main courses: £5.50–£15 ($10–$28). MC, V. Open: Mon–Sat 10 a.m.–8 p.m., Sun noon to 8 p.m.*

### Saddlers
**$$–$$$  Enniskillen, County Fermanagh   EUROPEAN**

Horse lovers will delight at the equestrian decor at Saddlers. The food is hearty and varied. You can get salads and steaks, plus barbecued pork ribs, pizzas, and mixed grills. The restaurant sits above the Horse Show bar, a great place for an after-dinner drink.

*66 Belmore St. The Dublin Road (A4) into town becomes Belmore St.* ☎ *028-6632-6223. Main courses: £4.95–£12 ($9–$22). MC, V. Open: Mon–Sat 11 a.m.–11 p.m., Sun noon–10 p.m.*

## Exploring Counties Fermanagh and Tyrone

**Erne Tours, Ltd.** (☎ 028-6632-2882) offers a boat tour of Lower Lough Erne River aboard the 63-seater *Kestrel.* The trip is fully narrated and covers a good deal of the nature and history of the lake. It includes a half-hour stop at Devenish Island, where you can get off and explore some ruins. Trips last just under two hours and depart from Round O Jetty in Enniskillen. Tours operate daily in July and August at 10:30 a.m., 2:15 p.m., and 4:15 p.m.; in May and June on Sunday at 2:30 p.m.; and in September on Tuesday, Saturday, and Sunday at 2:30 p.m. Prices are £7 ($13) for adults, £6 ($11) for seniors, and £4 ($7.40) for children.

The Fermanagh Lakes yield up loads of salmon and trout. **Trevor Kingston,** 18 Church St., Enniskillen (☎ 028-6632-2114), can set you up with information and tackle.

For canoeing, sailing, and windsurfing on the lakes, contact **Lakeland Canoe Centre,** Castle Island, Enniskillen (☎ 028-6632-4250).

### Belleek Pottery Tours
**Belleek, County Fermanagh**

Belleek is Ireland's oldest and most famous pottery works, and on these tours, you can watch highly trained craftspeople create the famous fine bone china and then pick up some of the delicate ivory pottery to take home. In addition to guided tours (given every 20 minutes on weekdays, with the last tour at 3:30 p.m.), there is a museum covering the history of Belleek pottery.

*Main St. Take the A46 northeast from Enniskillen.* ☎ *028-6865-8501. Admission: Free. Tours £4 ($7.40) adults, £2 ($3.70) seniors, £3 ($5.55) children. Visitor center open: April–June and Sept Mon–Sat 9 a.m.–5:30 p.m., July and Aug Mon–Sat 10 a.m.– 6 p.m., Sun noon–6 p.m.; Oct– March Mon–Sat 9 a.m.–5 p.m. Tours: Weekdays from opening until 3:30 p.m., every 20 minutes. Suggested visit: 1 hour (including tour).*

### Castle Coole
**Enniskillen, County Fermanagh**

This 18th-century neoclassical-style house was completely refurbished by the state. Most of the stone fittings and fixtures are from England, and extraordinarily, almost all the original furniture is in place. The opulent State Bedroom has a bed that was specially made for King George IV to use during his 1821 visit to Ireland. Other highlights are a Chinese-style sitting room and gorgeous woodwork and fireplaces throughout. Save some time to explore the surrounding 600-hectare (1,500-acre) woodlands.

*Off the Belfast-Enniskillen Rd. (A4) about 1.6km (1 mile) out of Enniskillen.* ☎ *028-6632-2690. Admission: £3 ($5.55) adults, £1.50 ($2.80) children, grounds £2 ($3.70) per car. Open: Castle hours vary, but usually Easter–May and Sept, Sat–Sun noon–6 p.m.; June Wed–Mon noon–6 p.m., July–Aug daily noon–6 p.m., early Oct 1–5 p.m. Also* *open some weekdays in April; call for details. Castle closed mid-Oct–Easter. Grounds open Apr–Sept 10 a.m.–8 p.m., Oct–March 10 a.m.–4 p.m. Suggested visit: 1 hour.*

### Enniskillen Castle
**Enniskillen, County Fermanagh**

This 15th-century castle, once the stronghold of powerful Irish chieftains, sits majestically in the west end of town, overlooking the River Erne. The castle contains a county museum with exhibits on the area's history, wildlife, and landscape, as well as the museum of the Royal Inniskilling Fusiliers, including their uniforms and weapons. There are also models and figurines depicting old-time castle life.

*Castle Barracks at the west end of town, across Castle Bridge from the A4.* ☎ *028-6632-5000. Admission: £2 ($3.70) adults, £1.50 ($2.75) seniors and students, £1 ($1.85) children. Open: May, June, and Sept Mon and Sat 2–5 p.m. and Tues–Fri 10 a.m.–5 p.m.; July and Aug Sat–Mon 2–5 p.m. and Tues–Fri 10 a.m.–5 p.m.; Oct–April Mon 2–5 p.m. and Tues–Fri 10 a.m.–5 p.m. Suggested visit: 1½ hours.*

### Marble Arch Caves
**Florencecourt, County Fermanagh**

Exploring the Marble Arch Caves is a thrill. Visitors tour the caves on boats that glide on an underground river, while guides point out waterfalls, winding passages, and echoing chambers. The guides are great, giving detailed information about stalagmites and stalactites and the minerals that coat the walls. The tour includes walking sections, but nothing's dangerous or exhausting.

The Marble Arch Caves are hugely popular, so it's wise to book ahead. Also, it gets pretty chilly "down under," so bring a sweater. If there's been heavy rain, the caves occasionally close for safety reasons, so call if there's been bad weather.

*Marlbank Scenic Loop. Off the A35, 19km (12 miles) south of Enniskillen. When you're in the village of Florencecourt, near the border of Northern Ireland and the Republic, there is a loop road that takes you out to the caves, with plenty of signs to point the way.* ☎ *028-6634-8855. Admission: £6 ($11) adults, £4 ($7.40) students and seniors, £3 ($5.55) children under 18. Open: March–June and Sept daily 10 a.m.–4:30 p.m., July–Aug daily 10a.m.–5 p.m. Suggested visit: About 2½ hours.*

### Ulster American Folk Park
**Castletown, County Tyrone**

This immensely interesting outdoor folk park features rebuilt 18th- and 19th-century buildings from Ireland and America, from a Pennsylvania log farmhouse to an Irish-Catholic mass house (a home used as a church). Costumed interpreters are stationed throughout to illustrate and explain life during these times. You begin your tour in Ireland then board a replica of a 19th-century ship bound for America. When you exit, you're in the America of the 18th and 19th centuries. I recommend tagging along with a school group so that you can watch the interpreters role-play everyone from a 19th-century Irish schoolteacher to an American saddler.

The Ulster-American Folk Park has an excellent lineup of events, including American Independence Day celebrations in July, an Appalachian and Bluegrass music festival in September, and a Halloween Festival in October.

*Mellon Road. Off the A5, 4.7km (3 miles) north of Omagh. Look for the signs.* ☎ *028-8224-3292;* www.folkpark.com. *Admission: £4 ($7.40) adults, £2 ($3.70) students, seniors, and children. Open: Oct–March Mon–Fri 10:30 a.m.–5 p.m. (last admission 3:30 p.m.); April–Sept Mon–Sat 10:30 a.m.–6 p.m. (last admission 4:30 p.m.), and Sun 11 a.m.–6:30 p.m. (last admission 5 p.m.). Suggested visit: 2 hours.*

### Shopping in County Fermanagh

The **Butter Market,** on Down Street in Enniskillen (☎ **028-6632-3835**), has studio workshops where craftspeople make and sell all sorts of local items, including ceramic jewelry, screen prints, Celtic-inspired statuary, and leather goods.

# Fast Facts: Counties Derry, Fermanagh, and Tyrone

**Area Code**

The area code (or city code) for Derry, Fermanagh, and Tyrone is 028.

**Emergencies/Police**

Dial ☎ **999** for all emergencies.

**Genealogy Resources**

In County Derry, contact The Genealogy Centre, 14 Bishop St., Derry (☎ 028-7126-9792). In County Tyrone, contact Heritage World, 26 Market Sq., Dungannon (☎ 01868-72-4187).

**Hospital**

Altnagevin Hospital (☎ 028-7134-5171) is on Glenshane Road in Derry.

**Information**

In Derry, go to the tourist office at 44 Foyle St., Derry (☎ 028-7126-7284), open year-round. In County Tyrone, contact the Omagh Tourist Information Centre, 1 Market Street, Omagh (☎ 028-8224-7831). The Fermanagh Tourist Information Centre is located on Wellington Road, Enniskillen (☎ 028-6632-3110).

**Internet**

In Derry City, try Webcrawler Cyber Café, 52 Strand Rd. (☎ 028-7126-8386).

# Chapter 22

# Belfast and County Antrim

· · · · · · · · · · · · · · · · · · · · · · · · · · · · · · · · · · · · · · ·

## In This Chapter

▶ Going back to the early 1900s at the Ulster Folk Museum

▶ Experiencing Belfast's hot nightlife

▶ Climbing on the amazing Giant's Causeway

▶ Bringing out your inner adventurer on a rope bridge

· · · · · · · · · · · · · · · · · · · · · · · · · · · · · · · · · · · · · · ·

*Y*ou get the best of both worlds in this county (shown on the nearby map): an energy-filled city with great dining, lodging, and nightlife options, and the awesome beauty of the cliffs, glens, and ocean of the North Antrim coast.

## Belfast and the Surrounding Area

Belfast (see the map of the same name) is a hopping city, full of university students and, thus, full of hot restaurants and hotels and even hotter clubs and bars. Queens University plays a large role in the arts scene here (both visual and performing), which is becoming bigger and bigger. Belfast is also a beautiful city, with many examples of Victorian, Edwardian, and Georgian architecture.

### Getting to Belfast and County Antrim

Aer Lingus, British Airways, and Virgin Express fly into **Belfast International Airport** (☎ **028-9448-4848;** www.belfastairport.com), about 31km (19 miles) from Belfast. **Belfast City Airport** (☎ **028-9093-9093;** www.belfastcityairport.com) handles flights within the country. To get to the city center from Belfast International Airport, take the Airbus, which leaves every half hour. The fare is £5 ($9.25). From Belfast City Airport, take a cab (the fare should be about £6/$11) or Citybus No. 21.

If you're coming to Belfast from Britain or Scotland, consider the ferry. You can get to Belfast from Stranraer, Scotland, in 90 minutes aboard the **SeaCat** (☎ **08705-523-323;** www.seacat.co.uk). **Norse Merchant Ferries**

## County Antrim

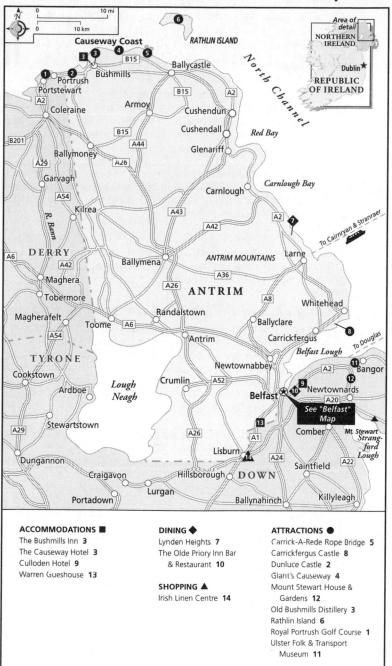

**ACCOMMODATIONS** ■
The Bushmills Inn **3**
The Causeway Hotel **3**
Culloden Hotel **9**
Warren Gueshouse **13**

**DINING** ◆
Lynden Heights **7**
The Olde Priory Inn Bar
   & Restaurant **10**

**SHOPPING** ▲
Irish Linen Centre **14**

**ATTRACTIONS** ●
Carrick-A-Rede Rope Bridge **5**
Carrickfergus Castle **8**
Dunluce Castle **2**
Giant's Causeway **4**
Mount Stewart House &
   Gardens **12**
Old Bushmills Distillery **3**
Rathlin Island **6**
Royal Portrush Golf Course **1**
Ulster Folk & Transport
   Museum **11**

(☎ **0870-600-4321** in Britain, ☎ 01-819-2904 in Ireland; www.norse merchant.com) takes eight hours from Liverpool, and **Stena Sealink** (☎ **08705-707070**; www.stenaline.com) runs fast (1 hr. 45 min.) and slower (3 hr. 15 min.) ferries from Stranraer, Scotland to Belfast. SeaCat also runs from Campbell, Scotland to Ballycastle in County Antrim in July and August.

If you're coming by car from Dublin, take the N1 (which becomes the A1) north to Belfast. To get to the Antrim Coast from Belfast, take the A2, which runs along the entire coast. If you're driving from the Republic into Northern Ireland, make sure you notify your rental-car company, because extra insurance may be required.

**Irish Rail** (☎ **1850-366-222**; www.irishrail.ie) and **Northern Ireland Railway** (☎ **888/BRIT-RAIL** or 028-9089-9411) trains travel from Dublin's Connolly Station to Belfast's Central Station daily and connect many towns in Northern Ireland.

**Ulsterbus** (☎ **028-9033-7004**; www.ulsterbus.co.uk) runs buses to and from towns all over Northern Ireland, including Belfast, Larne, Ballycastle, Bushmills, and several other towns. Ulsterbus also provides service between Belfast and Dublin.

## *Getting around Belfast and the surrounding area*

You can easily navigate Belfast by bus and on foot, so you may want to park your car while you explore or forgo a car altogether. **Citybus** (☎ **028-9066-6630**; www.citybus.co.uk) operates throughout the city. Most buses depart from Donegall Square in the city center. Smartlink multi-journey tickets are available at most newsagents (look for the *Smartlink* sign). If you're going to be moving around the city a lot, it makes sense to buy an all-day ticket.

You can also get around Belfast and the area by bike. **Life Cycles,** 36–37 Smithfield Market (☎ **028-9043-9959**; www.lifecycles.co.uk), rents bikes and provides helmets, locks, and maps. **Irish Cycle Tours** (☎ **066-7128733**; www.irishcycletours.com) will do you one better by renting you a bike and then taking you on a tour of the city.

If you need a cab, look for the **taxi ranks** at Central Station, both bus stations, and at City Hall. The metered cabs in Northern Ireland are standardized London-style black taxis with yellow disks on the windshield. I recommend that you take the standard cabs rather than nonmetered cabs. If you do take a nonmetered cab, ask for the price of the journey when you first enter the cab so that you don't get taken for a monetary ride in addition to a taxi ride.

## Spending the night in Belfast and the surrounding area

 Most Belfast hotels that cater to businesspeople have lower rates on the weekends than they do during midweek. It might be worth it to plan on hitting Belfast over a weekend.

### Ash-Rowan Town House
$$ **Belfast**

This beautiful Victorian row house, on a quiet, tree-lined avenue, is a comfortable and serene place to stay. All four stories are decorated with country-style furniture, Victorian antiques, and fresh flowers from the garden in back. You have a choice of nine different breakfasts here, including the traditional (and filling) Ulster fry.

*12 Windsor Ave. From the city center, follow Bedford St. south past Queen's University and make a right on Windsor.* ☎ *028-9066-1758. Fax: 028-9066-3227. Bus: 69, 70, or 71. Rates: £72–£88 ($133–$163) double. AE, MC, V.*

### Benedicts of Belfast
$$ **Belfast**

Funky, trendy Benedicts is at the center of everything, near some of Belfast's top attractions and hottest eateries and nightspots. Rooms on the second floor are brightly decorated, while rooms on the third floor are sleekly minimalist. The staff is friendly, and the Gothic-style bar and restaurant serve up excellent Continental fare in a lively atmosphere.

*7–21 Bradbury Pl., Shaftsbury Sq. From the Westlink (M1), take Grovesnor Road toward City Hall; go right on Great Victoria St.* ☎ *028-9059-1999. Fax: 028-9059-1990.* www.benedictshotel.co.uk. *Bus: 1, 29, 71, 83, or 84. Rates: £70 ($130) double Mon–Thurs, £60 ($111) double Fri–Sun. AE, MC, V.*

### Culloden Hotel
$$$$ **Holywood, County Down**

The Culloden, located near the Ulster Folk and Transport Museum (described in "Exploring Belfast and the surrounding area," later in this chapter), is a five-star hotel — and it deserves every point on those stars. A former 19th-century mansion, the hotel is surrounded by 4.8 hectares (12 acres) of beautiful, secluded gardens and the picturesque Holywood Hills. Bedrooms are nicely decorated with modern furnishings, but public rooms are filled with stunning antiques, Louis XV chandeliers, and decorative plasterwork. Service is impeccable. Would British Prime Ministers Tony Blair and John Major have stayed here if it wasn't?

*Bangor Rd. On the A2 northeast of Belfast.* ☎ *028-9042-1066. Fax: 028-9042-6777.* www.hastingshotels.com. *Rates: £200–£220 ($370–$407) double. AE, DC, MC, V.*

## Belfast

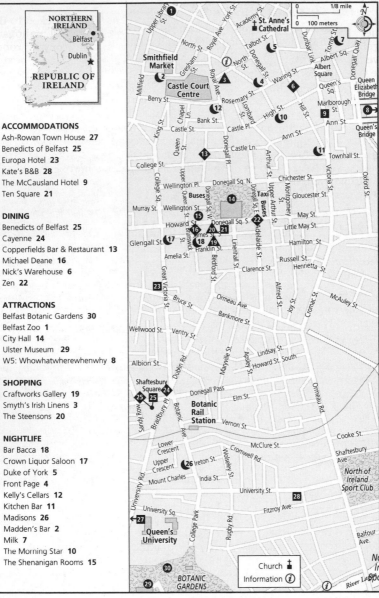

NORTHERN IRELAND

Belfast

Dublin

REPUBLIC OF IRELAND

**ACCOMMODATIONS**
Ash-Rowan Town House **27**
Benedicts of Belfast **25**
Europa Hotel **23**
Kate's B&B **28**
The McCausland Hotel **9**
Ten Square **21**

**DINING**
Benedicts of Belfast **25**
Cayenne **24**
Copperfields Bar & Restaurant **13**
Michael Deane **16**
Nick's Warehouse **6**
Zen **22**

**ATTRACTIONS**
Belfast Botanic Gardens **30**
Belfast Zoo **1**
City Hall **14**
Ulster Museum **29**
W5: Whowhatwherewhenwhy **8**

**SHOPPING**
Craftworks Gallery **19**
Smyth's Irish Linens **3**
The Steensons **20**

**NIGHTLIFE**
Bar Bacca **18**
Crown Liquor Saloon **17**
Duke of York **5**
Front Page **4**
Kelly's Cellars **12**
Kitchen Bar **11**
Madisons **26**
Madden's Bar **2**
Milk **7**
The Morning Star **10**
The Shenanigan Rooms **15**

### Europa Hotel
**$$$–$$$$   Belfast**

The spacious rooms in this world-class high-rise hotel are decked to the nines — huge beds and sofas, luxurious fabrics, and beautiful mahogany furnishings. But you probably won't be spending much time in your room, given the hotel's fabulous location. It's in the heart of Belfast, right next to the Grand Opera House and near the bustling *Golden Mile,* which is lined with historic buildings. The guests here tend to be cosmopolitan and elegant.

*Great Victoria St. From the Westlink (M1), take Grovesnor Rd. toward City Hall; go right on Great Victoria St.* ☎ *028-9027-1066. Fax: 028-9032-7800.* www.hastings hotels.com. *Bus: 02, 03, 04, 05, or Centrelink (100). Rates: £125 ($231) Mon–Thurs, £84 ($155) Fri–Sun, double. AE, DC, MC, V. Breakfast included on weekends only.*

### Kate's B&B
**$$   Belfast**

Step right up, folks, for one of the best deals in town. The seven good-size rooms here are decorated in cozy Victorian style and get a lot of light through their large windows. You can't beat the location near the university, the Botanic Gardens, and loads of funky restaurants and hopping clubs. Proprietor Kate Boyd will fortify you for the day with her "heart attack on a plate" breakfast and help you plan an itinerary for exploring the city.

*127 University St. (east of Westminster St.).* ☎ *028-9028-2091;* katesbb127@ hotmail.com. *Rates: £50 ($93) double. No credit cards.*

### The McCausland Hotel
**$$$–$$$$   Belfast**

This trendy, sophisticated lodging is the definition of a boutique hotel. It's housed in converted 1867 grain warehouses that retain gorgeous architectural details, and it offers incredibly friendly, professional, and personal service. The rooms, decorated in a contemporary style with warm tones, are spacious and designed to anticipate every need, with height-of-comfort beds, minibars (rare in these parts), and heated towel racks. The city center is a five-minute walk away.

*34–38 Victoria St. From the M3, take the Queen's Bridge across the river, and make a right onto Victoria St.* ☎ *028-9022-0200. Fax: 028-9022-0220. Bus: 8, 13, 13B, 21, 155, 160, 161, or Centrelink (100). Rates: £80–£148 ($148–$274). AE, DC, MC, V.*

### Ten Square
**$$$$   Belfast**

The designers of this Asian-style, minimalist hotel in central Belfast wouldn't know the meaning of the word "clutter." Rooms are a study in simple elegance, with vases of fresh flowers, and low beds covered with white comforters. You don't have to go far for nourishment and entertainment, because the hotel is home to three of the hottest Belfast establishments: Porcelain, an Asian fusion restaurant; Red, a hip and buzzing city bar; and China Club, a stylish members-only bar (as a guest, you are automatically a member).

*10 Donegall Sq. South.* ☎ *028-9024-1001. Fax: 028-9024-3210.* www.tensquare.co. uk. *Bus: 82, 83, 84, 85, or Centrelink (100). Rates: £160–£200 ($296–$370) double. AE, MC, V.*

## Dining locally in Belfast and the surrounding area

See also Benedicts of Belfast, mentioned in the previous section.

### Cayenne
**$$$$   Belfast   FUSION**

This wonderful restaurant was one of the first stars in Belfast's constellation of excellent fusion eateries. It's still going strong, serving dishes that combine ingredients in unexpectedly delicious ways, such as the appetizer of cinnamon quail with carrot, honey, and ginger salad. You can't go wrong with any of the main courses, from rabbit with fresh pasta, black olives, rosemary, and pancetta to lobster with black-bean vinaigrette and steamed basmati rice. Service is friendly and professional, and the decked-out crowd is always in high spirits.

*7 Ascot House, Shaftesbury Sq., Belfast.* ☎ *028-9033-1532. Reservations recommended. Bus: 1, 29, 71, 83, or 84. Main courses: £14–£22 ($26–$41). AE, DC, MC, V. Open: Mon–Thurs noon–2:15 p.m. and 6–10:15 p.m., Fri noon–2:15 p.m. and 6–11:15 p.m., Sat 6–11:15 p.m., Sun 5–8:45 p.m.*

### Copperfields Bar and Restaurant
**$-$$   Belfast   IRISH**

Come to Copperfields for a satisfying meal at a good price. The hearty dishes are varied, but the highlights are the excellent steak and fish choices. Specials change daily and are always creative, sometimes borrowing Mexican and Asian influences, and all ingredients are fresh and local. What makes this place so popular, in addition to the food, are the comfy sofas and cozy booths.

*9 Fountain St. From the Westlink (M1), take Divis St. to Fountain St., and turn right.* ☎ *028-9024-7367. Bus: 30, 31, 32, or Centrelink (100). Main courses: £4–£10 ($11–$19). AE, DC, MC, V. Open: Daily 11 a.m.–11 p.m.*

### Michael Deane
**$$$$   Belfast   IRISH**

This upstairs, baroque-looking restaurant is a temple to upscale Irish cuisine, with dishes that you recognize from pub menus around Ireland, prepared with the finest of ingredients and skill. Try the local lamb with goat cheese, ratatouille, wild spinach, aged balsamic vinegar, and red peppers.

*38–40 Howard Pl.* ☎ *028-9033-1134. Bus: 58, 59, 69, 69A, 70, 71, 89, 90, 91, 92, 95, or Centrelink (100). Main courses: 2-course prix-fixe £33 ($61), 7-course prix-fixe £59 ($100), 9-course prix-fixe £59 ($109). AE, DC, MC, V. Open: Wed–Sat 7–10p.m.*

### Nick's Warehouse
$$–$$$$   Belfast   INTERNATIONAL

Set in an old warehouse, this restaurant exudes charm, and despite the size of the place, it feels quite intimate. The service is wonderful (I recommend letting the staff choose something for you if you can't decide). The menu changes frequently and gathers inspiration from cuisines all over the world, but you won't be disappointed with the options, from grilled tuna with sweet-pepper-and-chile salsa to a butternut squash risotto with Jerusalem artichokes and toasted cashews.

*35 Hill St. From the Westlink (M1), take Divis St.; turn left on Skipper St.* ☎ *028-9043-9690. Bus: 8, 13, 13B, 21, 155, 160, 161, or Centrelink (100). Main courses: £7.85–£18 ($15–$32). AE, DC, MC, V. Open: Mon–Fri noon to 2:30 p.m., Tues–Sat 6–9 p.m.*

### The Olde Priory Inn Bar and Restaurant
$–$$   Holywood, County Down   IRISH

This is the most popular place to eat and meet in Holywood, and the eclectic decor and superfriendly staff make it a gem. The head chef, well known in these parts, uses the best produce of the area to create a unique and ever-changing daily-specials board. The menu features many kid-friendly meals. The biggest draw is the Sunday carvery, a feast of meat and other hearty dishes.

*13 High St.* ☎ *028-9042-8164. Main courses: £5–£11 ($9.25–$19). AE, DC, MC, V. Open: Daily 11:30 a.m.–10:30 p.m.*

### Zen
$$   Belfast   JAPANESE

Calling all sushi-holics: You can now get a raw-fish-and-vinegared-rice fix in Belfast, at this hip new restaurant. Bartenders shake martinis behind the glass bar, lit with blue lights, and club-gear-clad twentysomethings strut through the high-ceilinged, dramatic space, which is decorated with carved Japanese wooden screens, black lacquer tables, and a large shiny Buddha. My recommendation is to order a sushi platter or a bunch of sushi rolls. The menu also features an array of cooked Japanese dishes, from vegetable curry to chicken teriyaki.

*55–59 Adelaide St.* ☎ *028-9023-2244. Bus: 58, 59, 69, 69A, 70, 71, 89, 90, 91, 92, 95, or Centrelink (100). Main courses: £8.80–£13 ($16–$24). AE, DC, MC, V. Open: Mon–Fri noon–3 p.m. and 5–11 p.m., Sat 6–11:30 p.m., Sun 1:30–10:30 p.m.*

## Exploring Belfast and the surrounding area

**Citybus Bus Tours** (☎ 028-9032-9808; www.citybus.co.uk) operates 1½ hour tours of Belfast. They depart from late June through September, Monday to Saturday at 11 a.m. from Castle Place (near the big post office). Prices are £5 ($9.25) adults, £4 ($7.40) seniors and children, and £13 ($24) families. The same company also runs a tour of *Titanic*-related sights (call for times). Local experts lead a 90-minute **Old Town of Belfast Walking Tour,** exploring the original city ramparts and relating the city's history. It runs June to October on Saturdays, departing at 2 p.m. from the Tourist Information Centre on North Street (☎ 028-9024-6609). A **Belfast City Center Walk** departs from the same place on Fridays at 2 p.m. from June to October. Both tours cost £4 ($7.40).

### The top attractions

### Belfast Zoo
**Belfast**

This zoo includes a Children's Farm, an island of spider monkeys, an enclosure for primates and other African animals, a Polar Bear Canyon, and pools for penguins and sea lions, to name a few. The zoo houses many endangered animals, and it faces a fantastic view of Belfast Lough. You can have lunch in the Ark Restaurant.

*Antrim Rd. Take Donegall Street from the city center north, and go right on Antrim Road.* ☎ *028-9077-6277. Bus: 45, 46, 47, 48, 49, 50, 51. Admission: April–Sept £6.70 ($12) adult, £3.40 ($6.30) child 4–18; Oct–March £5.40 ($10) adult, £2.70 ($5) child 4–18. Open: April–Sept daily 10 a.m.–7 p.m. (last admission 5 p.m.).; Oct–March 10 a.m.– 4:30 p.m. (last admission 2:30 p.m.). Suggested visit: 2 hours.*

### City Hall
**Belfast**

Modeled on St. Paul's Cathedral in London, Belfast's City Hall was built in 1888 after Queen Victoria conferred city status on Belfast. The building is made of Portland stone, with a central copper dome that rises 52m (173 feet) into the sky and is visible for miles. In front, there are a statue of the queen and a memorial to the victims of the *Titanic*, which was built in a Belfast shipyard.

*Donegall Sq.* ☎ *028-9027-0456, ext. 2618. Bus: 58, 59, 69, 69A, 70, 71, 89, 90, 91, 92, 95, or Centrelink (100). Admission: Free tours of the interior available. Tour times: June–Sept Mon–Fri 11 a.m., 2 p.m., and 3 p.m., and Sat 2:30 p.m. Oct–May Mon–Sat 2:30 p.m. Otherwise by arrangement. Reservations required for all tours. Suggested visit: 45 minutes.*

### Mount Stewart House and Gardens
**Newtownards, County Down**

Though its interior is just grand, with a fabulous entrance hall and the famous George Stubbs painting *Hambletonian,* this impressive 18th-century mansion almost pales in comparison with the spectacular gardens surrounding it. There's a fabulous Shamrock Garden, which has an Irish harp–shaped topiary and a flowerbed shaped like a red hand (the emblem of Ulster) enclosed in a hedge shaped like a shamrock. Spanish and Italian gardens are in the back, and a colorful sunken garden sits in the east yard.

*On the A2 5km (3 miles) southeast of Newtownards, along the Ards Peninsula.* ☎ *028-4278-8387. Admission: House and garden £4.95 ($9.15) adults, £2.35 ($4.35) children. Open: House and garden hours vary month to month, so call for details, but generally, the house is open mid-March–April and Oct Sat–Sun 12–6 p.m.; most weekdays May–Sept noon or 1–6 p.m. Closed Nov–mid-March. Garden open daily year-round at 10 a.m.; closing time varies from 4 p.m. in summer to 8 p.m. in winter. Suggested visit: 1 hour.*

### Ulster Folk and Transport Museum
**Holywood, County Down**

This is one of those attractions that kids and adults both love. This truly excellent museum is composed of two very different parts: In the giant Transport Galleries is a stunning collection of trains, cars, buses, trams, motorcycles, and bicycles, featuring all sorts of gems from a Victorian bicycle to a section of the first railway in Ireland to a DeLorean car (that famous *Back to the Future* vehicle), along with interesting text and displays about the various forms of transportation. A highlight is climbing inside to explore some of the buses, trams, and trains.

The other half of this attraction is an extremely well-done living museum of Ireland in the early 1900s. The museum has re-created a town and a rural area, rebuilding actual period buildings from all over Ireland on this site. Costumed interpreters carry out the tasks of daily life in these buildings — you can watch them cook over an open hearth, spin wool, work metal, print the town newspaper, make lace, and so on; and often, you can try your hand at these activities with them. Don't miss the sweet (in both senses of the word) candy store in the town area. The museum hosts all sorts of events year-round.

*Off the A2, 11km (7 miles) east of Belfast.* ☎ *028-9242-8428. Admission: Folk museum and transport museum individually £5 ($9.25) adults, £3 ($5.55) seniors, students, and children, free for children under 5; combined admission £6.50 ($12) adults, £3.50 ($6.50) seniors, students, and children, free for children under 5. Open: March–June Mon–Sat 10 a.m.–5 p.m., Sat 10 a.m.–6 p.m., and Sun noon to 6 p.m.; July–Sept Mon–Sat 10 a.m.–6 p.m and, Sun 11 a.m.– 6 p.m.; Oct–Feb Mon–Fri 10 a.m.–4 p.m., Sat 10 a.m.–5 p.m. and Sun 11 a.m.–5 p.m. Suggested visit: 3½ hours.*

## Ulster Museum
### Belfast

This is Northern Ireland's national museum, with a hugely diverse collection that ranges from exhibits on local history to ancient artifacts (including treasures from sunken Spanish Armada ships) to a natural-history collection where you can see a skeleton of the extinct great Irish deer. The fourth floor houses an impressive art gallery with works by greats such as Francis Bacon and Henry Moore.

*Stranmillis Rd.* ☎ *028-9038-3000. Bus: 69 or 70. Admission: Free. Open: Mon–Fri 10 a.m.–5 p.m., Sat 1– 5 p.m., and Sun 2– 5 p.m. Suggested visit: 1 hour*

## *Other cool things to see and do*

- ✔ **Belfast Botanic Gardens:** These lovely gardens are home to grassy grounds, a particularly colorful and large rose garden, and one of the first conservatories ever built of castiron and glass.

  Location: Stranmillis Rd., Belfast (☎ **028-9032-4902**). Free admission. Grounds are open daily from 8 a.m. to sunset. The conservatory is open April through September Monday to Friday from 10 a.m. to noon and daily from 1 to 5 p.m.; and October through March Monday to Friday from 10 a.m. to noon and daily from 1 to 4 p.m. Suggested visit: 45 minutes.

- ✔ **Carrickfergus Castle:** During this impressive, well-preserved castle's 800-year history, it grew from a small castle to an unequaled Norman fortress. Tour guides, exhibits, and a fascinating audiovisual presentation really bring the castle's exciting history to life. You'll have fun walking along the parapets and looking out to sea. The castle hosts medieval banquets (call for details and reservations) and, during the first two weeks of August, is home to a lively medieval fair and crafts market.

  Location: Marine Highway, Antrim Street, Carrickfergus, County Antrim (☎ **028-9335-1273**). Admission is £2.70 ($5) adults, £1.35 ($2.50) child and senior citizen, and £7.30 ($13.50) family. Open April through May and September through October Monday to Saturday from 10 a.m. to 6 p.m. and Sunday from 2 to 6 p.m.; June through August Monday to Saturday from 10 a.m. to 6 p.m. and Sunday from 11 a.m. to 8 p.m.; and November through March Monday to Saturday from 10 a.m. to 4 p.m. and Sunday from 2 to 4 p.m. Suggested visit: 2 hours.

- ✔ **W5: Whowhatwherewhenwhy:** This science-and-art complex has a name that evokes the fun of the place. Jutting out over the city's waterfront down at the docklands, this flashy steel-and-neon complex is also home to the Belfast Giants, the city's ice-hockey team. From hands-on lie detectors to moving-tennis-ball art, the place is a wonder for all ages. Be sure to explore the Tomb of Homunculus Hibericus — a cabinet of wonders made with actual bones!

Location: 2 Queen's Quay, Belfast (in the Odyssey Center) (☎ 028-9046-7700; www.w5online.co.uk). To get there, cross Queen Elizabeth Bridge from city center, make the first left, and follow instructions on parking. Bus: 94. Admission is £6 ($11) adult, £4.50 ($8.35) seniors and students, £4 ($7.40) child. Open Monday to Saturday from 10 a.m. to 6 p.m. and Sunday from noon to 6 p.m. Suggested visit: 2 hours.

## Shopping in Belfast

Belfast's City Hall is a perfect landmark for the shopping district, which is just across the street. There, you'll find posh (and expensive) British department stores, Irish shops, and some North American chains.

A wide range of quality Northern Irish crafts fills **Craftworks Gallery,** Bedford House, 16 Bedford St., (☎ 028-9024-4465), and all products are beautifully displayed. You find ceramics, jewelry, hand-painted silk scarves, musical instruments, and more. While you're in the gallery, pick up "Crafts In Northern Ireland," a free brochure that lists various crafts and where to find them. **The Steensons,** Bedford Street (☎ 028-9024-8269), sells celebrated contemporary gold and silver jewelry made by Christina and Bill Steensons. **Smyth's Irish Linens,** 65 Royal Ave. (☎ 028-9024-2232), sells a full stock of Irish linens. Much more than just a shop, the **Irish Linen Centre,** Market Square, Lisburn (about 16km/10 miles from Belfast; ☎ 028-9266-3377), exhibits the history of the famous Ulster linen and conducts handweaving demonstrations — and, of course, sells plenty of Irish linen, from coats to clothes.

## Enjoying nightlife in Belfast

Belfast has a hot and happening nightlife, with lots of club action in addition to the usual pubs.

### Hitting the pubs

Belfast has some of Ireland's finest pubs, many authentically Victorian. The company that produces the famed Bailey's Irish Cream hosts a good **Bailey's Belfast Pub Tour** of the city that covers six of the best, most with traditional music. The tour lasts about two hours and meets Saturday at 7 p.m. May through October at Flannigan's, above The Crown Liquor, at 44 Great Victoria St. Call ☎ 028-9268-3665 to reserve a spot. Tours cost £7 ($13).

### Crown Liquor Saloon

Unquestionably the most famous pub in Belfast, and perhaps the most beautiful in Ireland, the Crown is owned by the state (by the National Trust, to be exact). The traditional interior is gorgeous, with hand-painted tiles, carved wood, brass fittings, and gas lamps — truly a perfect Irish watering hole. You have to try the local Strangford Lough oysters — they're excellent. You may want to find a seat early; The Crown fills up most evenings.

*44 Great Victoria St. ☎ 028-9027-9901. Bus: 82, 83, 84, 85, or Centrelink (100).*

### Kelly's Cellars

Not only is this the oldest continuously used licensed pub in Belfast, but Kelly's was also the popular meeting place for the United Irishmen, who organized the 1798 Rebellion. The name is misleading; Kelly's Cellars is a two-storied building with a stone-floored bar downstairs, decorated with all sorts of memorabilia, and a restaurant upstairs. If you get hungry, try the incredible Black Velvet Steak Pie.

*30 Bank St. ☎ 028-9032-4835. Bus: 80, 81, or Centrelink (100).*

### Madisons

One of the city's newest and most stunning bars, Madisons is named for the modern hotel it's housed in. Using an Art Nouveau theme and sporting a striking copper-and-ceramic bar top, it's a sophisticated and hip gathering place for young professionals and students from the nearby Queens University. There's an over-25 club downstairs that's great for dancing.

*59–63 Botanic Ave. ☎ 028-9050-9800. Bus: 82, 83, 85, 89, 90, 91, or 92.*

### The Morning Star

You have to go down an alley between High and Ann streets to find this historic pub, but you can't miss its striking green-and-red facade, and anyway, it's worth the hunt. The Star serves up the best pint of Caffrey's (Belfast's hometown brew) in town. That's reason enough to go, but the comfortable interior and unique horseshoe bar are attractions as well.

*17–19 Pottingers Entry. ☎ 028-9032-3976. Bus: 8, 13, 13B, 21, 155, 160, 161, or Centrelink (100).*

---

# Best pubs for traditional music

Some of the best pubs in Belfast to get those toes a-tappin' include **Madden's Bar,** Berry Street (☎ 028-9024-4114); the **Duke of York,** 11 Commercial Court, off Lower Donegall Street (☎ 028-9024-1062); **Front Page,** 106–110 Donegall St. (☎ 028-9032-4924); and **Kitchen Bar,** 16 Victoria Sq. (☎ 028-9032-4901).

### The Shenanigan Rooms

It's all about ambience here. Pull up a stool, and rest a pint on a huge old beer barrel. The more sociable can sit at the long medieval feasting tables. It's always jumping here, which probably has as much to do with the great atmosphere as it does with the incredible pub grub.

*21 Howard St.* ☎ *028-9032-3313. Bus: 1A, 1B, 7, 8, 9, 10, 11, 16, 17, 20, 20A, 21, 22, 23, 25, 26, 27, 45, 46, 47, 48, 49, 50, 51, or Centrelink (100).*

## Striking a pose: Club life

### Bar Bacca

This place is full of unpretentious locals hanging out, enjoying good drinks and music from acid jazz to house.

*48 Franklin St.* ☎ *028-9023-0200. Bus: 82, 83, 84, 85, or Centrelink (100).*

### Milk

This is a gorgeous club with gorgeous people, playing hip-hop, house, R&B, funk, classics, and more.

*10–14 Tomb St.* ☎ *028-9027-7447. Bus: 8, 13, 13B, 21, 155, 160, or 161.*

# North Antrim

North Antrim is a place of dramatic beauty, with sheer sea-pounded cliffs, pristine green valleys, and the spectacular weirdness of the Giant's Causeway. Outdoorsy folks will have a ball.

**The Citybus Bus Tours** (☎ **028-9032-9808;** www.citybus.co.uk) runs a variety of tours of Antrim, including tours to the Giant's Causeway.

## Spending the night in North Antrim

### The Bushmills Inn
$$$$ **Bushmills**

The warm glow from a turf fire greets you when you enter this fantastic inn. Then come the grand staircase, cozy oil lamps, and curious antiques that line the halls. The quaint, individually decorated rooms in the Coaching Inn are complemented by the much larger cottage-style rooms in the Mill House on the banks of the River Bush. The round library and the oak-beamed loft will tempt you to skip sightseeing for a day. Don't pass up excellent Irish coffees (made, of course, with premium Bushmills whiskey) by the fire or a superb meal in the dining room. All around, it's an incredible place.

Located on the A2 (called Main St. in Bushmills) on the banks of the Bush River. ☎ *028-2073-2339.* Fax: 028-2073-2048. www.bushmillsinn.com. Rates: £128–£158 ($237–$292) double. AE, MC, V.

### The Causeway Hotel
**$$$   Bushmills**

Located right next to the famed Giant's Causeway, this hotel's view of the spectacular coast cannot be beaten. The rooms are large, but the furnishings aren't remarkable. That won't matter, though, because you'll be on the tip of the Antrim Coast and spending all your time looking at the amazing scenery! This old, family-run hotel dates back to 1836, and although it's been restored and has modern conveniences, it hasn't lost its old-fashioned feel.

40 Causeway Rd. Off the A2; follow signs to Giant's Causeway. ☎ *028-2073-1226.* Fax: 02-2073-2552. Rates: £65–£70 ($120–$130) double. MC, V.

### Warren Guesthouse
**$$   Dunmurry**

Mary Hughes *is* the Warren Guesthouse. She'll pick you up from the airport, take care of your every need, and make sure you're well rested and fed before she sees you off. It's like staying at your mother's house without any of the prying or guilt. The guesthouse is located on the River Ferriaghy and has three spacious luxury rooms (better book ahead) at nonluxury prices — a great place from which to explore nearby Belfast and the Antrim coast.

10 Thornhill Rd. From Belfast, take the A1 south to Dunmurry. ☎ *028-9061-1702.* Fax: 028-9062-0654. www.warrenhouseni.com. Rates: £55 ($102) double.

## Dining locally in County Antrim

### Lynden Heights
**$$$–$$$$   Ballygarry   IRISH**

Situated on the southern end of the Glens of Antrim, this restaurant probably has the best view of any restaurant on the Northern Coast. The staff is friendly and chatty, and the wine list is as good as it is long. Regional dishes like duck, pheasant, and salmon fill the menu, and everything's enhanced by fresh local produce. This is a wonderful stop for anyone driving the coast road, both for a delicious meal and a chance to see the view at leisure. Try the john dory, if it's on the menu.

97 Drumnagreagh Rd. On the Antrim Coast Rd. off the A2 on the B148. ☎ *028-2858-3560.* Main courses: £12–£20 ($22–$37). AE, MC, V. Open: Fri 5–9 p.m., Sat 5–9 p.m., Sun 12:15–8:15 p.m.

## Exploring North Antrim

I highly recommend taking the A2, a spectacular coastal drive along sea-splashed cliffs and by small coastal towns with picturesque harbors. Major attractions along the road include the Giant's Causeway, the Dunluce Castle ruins, and the Carrick-A-Rede Rope Bridge (all reviewed later in this section).

Walkers will want to check out the **Ulster Way,** the **Moyle Way,** and the **Causeway Coast Path;** all three are long-distance hikes, but of course you can do part of any as a day- or half-day hike. Get *Ulster Way: Accommodations for Walkers* at any Northern Ireland Tourism Office for a map of the area and details on nearby accommodations.

**Ardclinis Activity Center,** High Street, Cushendall (☎ **028-2177-1340**), offers outdoor activities from rock-climbing to rafting. Their programs can be a short as a half-day and as long as a week.

If golfing is your bag, you'll certainly want to try **Royal Portrush,** Dunluce Road, Portrush, County Antrim (☎ **028-7082-2311**). There are three excellent 18-hole courses, all of which offer amazing seaside views of the northern Antrim Coast. To get there from Belfast, take the M2 north to Ballymena and then the A26 to Ballymoney. At the roundabout, follow the sign to Portrush (about 16km/10 miles down the road). Par is 72. From April through October, fees are £90 ($167) during the week and £110 ($204) weekends; November through March, they're £50 ($93) at all times. The course is open daily from 9:30 a.m. to noon and 2 p.m. onward. Guests are welcome daily.

### Carrick-A-Rede Rope Bridge
**Larrybane**

Here's one for the Indiana Jones in all of us! This heart-stopping rope bridge, spanning a chasm 18m (60 feet) wide, is not for the fainthearted: It wiggles and shakes underfoot as the sea crashes 24m (80 feet) below, and no matter how brave you are, you're in for a scare (though later you can tell yourself it was a thrilling adventure). There is a 1km (⅔ mile) walk to the bridge.

*Off the B15 (look for the signs). ☎ 028-2073-2143. Admission: £2 ($3.70) adults, £1 ($1.85) children. Open: Mid-March–June and Sept 10 a.m.–6 p.m., July–Aug 10 a.m.–7 p.m. Suggested visit: 30 minutes.*

### Dunluce Castle
**Bushmills**

These gorgeous castle ruins, mostly dating from the late 16th century, perch precariously over the sea (so precariously, in fact, that part of the main house plunged into the sea below in 1639). You can explore at will, discovering ruined fireplaces, round towers, and picture windows that frame the sea and sky, and imagining the lives of the powerful Scottish family that lived in this dramatic place. I recommend getting an information sheet from the visitor center before entering the ruins; it's full of interesting details about the different areas of the ruins.

*Dunluce Rd. Take the A2 about 5.6km (3½ miles) east of Portrush.* ☎ *028-2073-1938. Admission: £2 ($3.70 ) adults, £1 ($1.85) seniors and children. Apr–May and Sept Mon–Sat 10 a.m.–6 p.m. and Sun 2–6 p.m.; June–Aug Mon–Sat 10 a.m.–6 p.m. and Sun noon– 6 p.m.; Oct–March Mon–Sat 10 a.m.–4 p.m. and Sun 2–4 p.m.*

### Giant's Causeway
**Bushmills**

This is one of Ireland's strangest and most awesome sights. The Giant's Causeway is a 4.8km (3-mile) stretch of roughly 40,000 tightly packed, mostly hexagonal basalt rock columns of varying heights — some up to 12m (40 feet) tall — that jut up from the foot of a cliff and eventually disappear under the sea. The experts will tell you the causeway was formed by the quick cooling of an ancient volcanic eruption, but according to legend, Finn MacCool built the causeway as a path across the sea to reach his girlfriend on a Scottish island. (An aside: In 1842, the writer William Thackeray noted in his *Irish Sketch Book,* "Mon Dieu! And I have traveled a hundred and fifty miles to see that?" Just goes to show, even the eighth wonder of the world can't please everybody!) You can either walk or take the shuttle bus to the biggest concentration of columns. Don't worry about missing anything if you take the shuttle bus — most of the columns are located where the bus drops you off.

*Off the A2 along the North Antrim Coast.* ☎ *028-2073-1582. Admission: Parking £5 ($9.25), shuttle bus 70p ($1.30). Open: Daily 10 a.m.–5 p.m. Suggested visit: 1–1½ hours.*

### The Old Bushmills Distillery
**Bushmills**

A thorough and well-guided tour of the world's oldest distillery awaits you at Bushmills. One highlight: a room that's so heady with whiskey fumes the workers have to get a ride home at the end of the day because they've inhaled so much alcohol. (No fear; a couple minutes won't affect you.) The shop has every Bushmills product you can imagine, from fudge to golf towels and, of course, every kind of whiskey the distillery makes. The tour ends with a taste test.

*Main St. On the A2 along the North Antrim Coast.* ☎ *028-2073-1521. Admission: £3.95 ($7.30) adults, £3.50 ($6.50) seniors and students, £2 ($3.70) children. Open: Apr–Oct tours given frequently Mon–Sat 9:30 a.m.–4 p.m. and Sun noon–4 p.m. (last tour at 3 p.m. on all days); Nov–March tours Mon–Sat at 10:30 a.m., 11:30 a.m., noon, 1:30 p.m., 2:30 p.m., and 3:30 p.m., Sun at 1:30 p.m., 2:30 p.m., and 3:30 p.m. Suggested visit: 2½ hours.*

# For the birds: Rathlin Island

Rathlin's strategic position between Ireland and Scotland made it the site of many battles over time.

Today, the tiny, boomerang-shaped island off the coast of Ballycastle is a peaceful place and the home of thousands of seabirds, including puffins, and only about 100 people. Storytelling, song, and music flourish here, and islanders are always happy to welcome visitors.

On the eastern end of the island is Bruce's Cave, where the Scottish King Robert the Bruce hid after being defeated by the English. For information on the ferry schedule, contact the Caledonian MacBrayne ticket office at ☎ **028-2076-9299.**

# *Fast Facts: Belfast and County Antrim*

### Area Codes

The area code (or city code) for County Antrim is 028. From the Republic of Ireland, dial 048.

### Emergencies/Police

Dial ☎ **999** for all emergencies.

### Genealogy Resources

Ulster Historical Foundation, Balmoral Buildings, 12 College Sq. East, Belfast BT1 6DD (☎ 028-9023-9885; www.uhf. org.uk).

### Hospital

The Belfast City Hospital is at 51 Lisburn Rd. (☎ 028-9032-9241).

### Information

For visitor information, go to the Belfast Welcome Center at 47 Donegall Place (☎ 028-9024-6609; www.gotobelfast. com)

### Internet

Check out Revelations Internet Cafe at 27 Shaftesbury Sq. (☎ 028-9032-0337).

### Post Office

The main post office in Belfast is located at Castle Junction, at the top of High Street (☎ 08457-223344 for information).

# Chapter 23

# Counties Down and Armagh

. . . . . . . . . . . . . . . . . . . . . . . . . . . . . . . . . . . . . . . . .

## In This Chapter

▶ Taking in the Mourne Mountains
▶ Exploring St. Patrick's old haunts
▶ Imagining pre-Christian history at a storied fort

. . . . . . . . . . . . . . . . . . . . . . . . . . . . . . . . . . . . . . . . .

The stars of **County Down** (shown in the "Counties Down and Armagh" map) are the velvety green and purple Mourne Mountains. The Mournes are the highest mountains in Northern Ireland, their rounded peaks reaching over 610m (2,000 feet). They are a hiking and walking paradise — the mostly uninhabited mountains are threaded with trails that run from easy riverside strolls to strenuous boulder scrambles. This just may be the Irish and Northern Irish country landscape that you pictured before you got here, with weathered stone walls and farmhouses, sheep gamboling in the folds of the hills, lazy cows, windswept mountain gaps, and winding rivers. The stone Mourne Wall, built between 1904 and 1922, connects the 15 mountain peaks, snaking gracefully over rocky cliffs and up heather-covered crests.

The mountains roll down to the coastal area, where tacky-though-charming seaside towns like Newcastle invite lolling on the sandy beaches, sauntering down the street with an ice cream cone, and rattling the bones of your traveling companions in bumper cars at the many amusement complexes.

Northeast of the Mourne Mountains is the land of St. Patrick, the patron saint of Ireland and Northern Ireland, who planted the first seeds of Irish Christianity here in the fifth century. Born in Britain around A.D. 389 and brought to Ireland as a slave, Patrick spent four years as a shepherd for a Druid. During that time, his spiritual life flourished, and after escaping slavery, Patrick trained for the priesthood, probably in France. He returned to Ireland as a missionary, sure that God was directing him to spread Christianity in the pagan land, and began the task of converting the Irish and establishing churches. St. Patrick's Day (March 17) is a holy day in Ireland. People attend Mass; businesses and schools are closed; and until recently, pubs were closed, too.

## Counties Down and Armagh

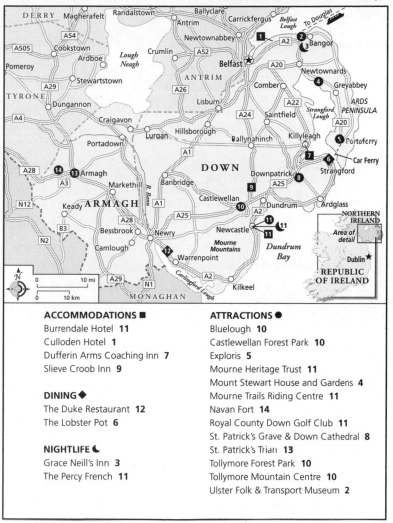

**ACCOMMODATIONS** ■
Burrendale Hotel **11**
Culloden Hotel **1**
Dufferin Arms Coaching Inn **7**
Slieve Croob Inn **9**

**DINING** ◆
The Duke Restaurant **12**
The Lobster Pot **6**

**NIGHTLIFE** ☾
Grace Neill's Inn **3**
The Percy French **11**

**ATTRACTIONS** ●
Bluelough **10**
Castlewellan Forest Park **10**
Exploris **5**
Mourne Heritage Trust **11**
Mount Stewart House and Gardens **4**
Mourne Trails Riding Centre **11**
Navan Fort **14**
Royal County Down Golf Club **11**
St. Patrick's Grave & Down Cathedral **8**
St. Patrick's Trian **13**
Tollymore Forest Park **10**
Tollymore Mountain Centre **10**
Ulster Folk & Transport Museum **2**

South and west of County Down is little **County Armagh,** where the city of Armagh is also heavily associated with St. Patrick, who built a stone church and preached Christianity here. The city is still a religious center, home to the seats of both the Catholic and Anglican archbishops. A visit to Armagh City makes a good day-trip from County Down.

# Getting to Counties Down and Armagh

The nearest airports are in Belfast, which is also the destination for ferries from England and Scotland: See Chapter 22 for information on those methods.

If you're coming by car from Dublin, take the N1 north to Newry (N1 becomes the A1 in Northern Ireland). From Newry, take the A28 to Armagh. To get to the coast from Newry, take the A2 southeast (the A2 runs along the entire coast). If you're driving from Ireland into Northern Ireland, make sure you notify your rental-car company because extra insurance may be required.

**Irish Rail** (☎ 1850-366-222; www.irishrail.ie) and **Northern Ireland Railways** (☎ 888-BRITRAIL or 028-9089-9411) serve Newry, Portadown, Lurgan, Lisburn, and Bangor year-round. **Ulsterbus** (☎ 028-9033-3000; www.ulsterbus.co.uk) travels year-round to Newry, Portadown, Armagh City, and other major towns in Counties Armagh and Down.

# County Down

I include some attractions, accommodations, and restaurants that are actually in County Down in Chapter 22, because they are easy side trips from Belfast, so check that chapter also.

## Spending the night in County Down

### Burrendale Hotel
**$$$   Newcastle**

This modern hotel really has it all. The contemporary rooms, decorated in light colors, are spacious and relaxing. Among the beauty salon, bistro, indoor pool, and bar, there are enough reasons to stay in for the day, but with a sandy beach on the Irish Sea, two large parks, and the Mourne Mountains at the hotel's doorstep, I bet you'll hardly be in your room at all. Locals and visitors alike enjoy the hotel's Vine Restaurant and Cottage Kitchen Restaurant. Golfers will be thrilled with the location: There are 15 courses nearby — including one of the best on the island, Royal County Down. The enormous family rooms accommodate even the most active kids.

*51 Castlewellan Rd.,* ☎ *028-4372-2599. Fax: 028-4372-2328.* www.burrendale.com. *To get there: Off the A2 toward Downpatrick. Rates: £110 ($204) double. AE, DC, MC, V.*

### Dufferin Arms Coaching Inn
**$$   Killyleagh**

This charming inn is located in the shadow of Killyleagh Castle in the little town of Killyleagh, on the road between Downpatrick and Belfast. It has bright, comfortable rooms with beautiful wooden furniture — some rooms even have four-poster beds. The inn is much larger than it looks from the outside, with three pubs, a library, and a guest lounge, plus a restaurant that features Irish cooking and occasionally hosts medieval feasts. Service is warm and friendly.

*31–33 High St. (Killyleagh is off the A20.)* ☎ *028-4482-8229. Fax: 028-4482-8755.* www . dufferincoachinginn.co.uk. *Rates: £65 ($120) double. AE, MC, V.*

### Slieve Croob Inn
**$$   Castlewellan**

If you aren't stirred by the setting of this lodging, restaurant, and bar complex, surrounded by verdant rolling hills, you need to check your pulse. Located where an old farmhouse used to stand, the modern inn has a simple mountain-lodge look to it, with pine furniture, landscape prints, and doors painted forest green. Rooms and bathrooms are ample and sparkling clean. But it doesn't really matter what the rooms look like when there are trails and lanes that virtually begin at the front door, some leading to vistas of Newcastle Bay. The cozy bar and restaurant has gorgeous views; the food is fine as hiking fuel, but it's nothing special. They do, however, make a mean poached egg for breakfast.

*Seeconnell Centre, 119 Clanvaraghan Rd. Look for signs 1.6km (1 mile) north of Castlewellan on the A25.* ☎ *028-4377-1412. Fax: 028-4377-1162. Rates: £65 ($120) double. MC, V.*

## Dining locally in County Down

### The Duke Restaurant
**$$–$$$   Warrenpoint   INTERNATIONAL/NEW IRISH**

Fresh, flavorful produce is at the root of the zingy dishes served at this busy, jovial restaurant. Main courses range from meat dishes to vegetarian options, and the seafood choices, such as grilled turbot with wilted bok choy and prawn bisque cream, are especially delicious.

*Above the Duke Bar, 7 Duke St. Warrenpoint is 9.7km (6 miles) southeat of Newry on the A2.* ☎ *028-4175-2084. Main courses: £9–£14 ($17–$26). Tues–Sun 6–10 p.m.*

### The Lobster Pot
**$$–$$$   Strangford   SEAFOOD-IRISH-EUROPEAN**

Lobster is, not surprisingly, the house specialty here. Plenty of excellent Irish and classic European dishes are served, but seafood is the highlight of the menu. The decor is comfortable and homey, and the service is quick and helpful. When the weather's nice, you can drink your aperitif in the lovely beer garden.

*9–11 The Square.* ☎ *028-4488-1288. Main courses: £9.95–£15.50 ($18–$29). AE, MC, V. Open: Mon–Sat 11 a.m.–9:30 p.m., Sun 12:30–8:30 p.m.*

## *Exploring County Down*

Be sure to lace those walking shoes tightly, because County Down is a playground for nature lovers, with myriad hiking trails; all sorts of outdoor activities; and a dreamy setting of rivers, woods, and purple-green mountains. The Down Cathedral and the Aquarium are excellent rainy-day options.

### *The Mourne Mountains*

In my opinion, the finest way to see this beautiful area is to take a hike along one of the many trails. You can access the Mourne Mountains along the A2, getting off at Newcastle, Kilkeel, Rostrevor, Warrenpoint, or any other town in the area. There is also a road that passes the 15 summits of the mountains.

Be aware that the word *walk* is used instead of *hike* in Ireland and Northern Ireland. Anything from a gentle ramble to a tough scramble over boulders may be called a *walk,* so ask for specifics.

Stop by the **Mourne Heritage Trust,** 87 Central Promenade, Newcastle, County Down (☎ 028-4372-4059; www.mournelive.com), open Monday through Friday 9 a.m. to 5 p.m., before exploring the mountains. They offer all sorts of maps and information, present a series of talks on various facets of the area, and run guided weekend hikes. I recommend picking up the *Mourne Country Outdoor Pursuits Map,* published by the Ordnance Survey of Northern Ireland, which is a detailed topographical map that has many trails marked. I also recommend purchasing *Mourne Mountain Walks,* a packet of ten laminated cards featuring maps and detailed instructions for ten of the area's best hikes.

One of my favorite routes is the **hike to Hare's Gap,** which takes you on a gentle, winding path uphill, with a scramble over large boulders before you reach the gap and a section of the graceful Mourne Wall. There are breathtaking views of the countryside as you ascend, and Hare's Gap is the starting point for a number of other excellent trails that take you higher and deeper into the mountains. Find the route at the parking lot along Trassey Road at the northern foot of Clonachullion Hill. Turn left upon exiting the parking lot, and you see the gate and stile that mark the beginning of the hike. The round-trip hike should take about three-and-a-half hours; good shoes are essential.

Another popular trail leads from the fishing village of **Kilkeel** to the parking lot at the Silent Valley Information Centre to **Silent Valley,** where a section of the Mourne Wall encloses the reservoir that provides water for the residents of County Down. You can pick the route up in Kilkeel or join up at the parking lot in Silent Valley. The walk is easy, leading you through woodlands and moorlands between two giant granite peaks. If you don't wish to walk, you can catch the shuttle bus that travels the route between the Silent Valley Information Centre and the peak of nearby Ben Crom Mountain daily in July and August and on weekends May, June, and September (£ 2/$3.70 adults; 75p/$1.40 kids). To get to Kilkeel, take the A2. To get to the Information Centre parking lot, drive 6.5km (4 miles) north of Kilkeel on Head Road. The **Silent Valley Information Centre** number is ☎ **028-9074-6581,** and the center and grounds are open daily Easter through September from 10:00 a.m. to 6:30 p.m., and October through Easter from 10:00 a.m. to 4:00 p.m.

If you want to improve or develop your hiking skills, **Tollymore Mountain Centre,** Bryansford, Newcastle (☎ **028-4372-2158;** www. tollymoremc.com), offers a range of instructional courses geared to everyone from beginning to experienced hikers.

You can do more than just hike in the Mourne Mountains. Here are some more options for outdoor activities:

- ✔ **Tollymore Mountain Centre,** Bryansford, Newcastle (☎ **028-4372-2158;** www.tollymoremc.com), offers numerous hiking, rock-climbing, canoeing, and kayaking instructional courses in the area, ranging from one day to three days.

- ✔ For information on **canoeing** here and in other areas of Northern Ireland, you can contact the **Canoe Association of Northern Ireland** (☎ **028-7134-3871;** office@cani.org.uk).

- ✔ **Bluelough,** The Grange Courtyard, Castlewellan Forest Park, Castlewellan (☎ **028-4377-0715;** www.mountainandwater.com), is geared more toward fun than skill-building, offering rock-climbing, canoeing, kayaking, hiking, and archery adventures.

- ✔ Little traffic and gorgeous vistas make the Mournes, especially around Castwellan, prime **cycling** territory. **Ross Cycle,** 44 Clarkhill Rd., signposted from the Clough-Castlewellan Road outside Castlewellan (☎ **028-4377-8029**), rents bicycles (you can park and ride or get the bike delivered to you).

- ✔ Point your putter in the direction of the excellent **Royal County Down Golf Club,** 36 Golf Links Rd., Newcastle (☎ **028-4373-3314;** www.royalcountydown.org), a links course full of sand dunes and surrounded by the stunning Mourne Mountains. Visitors are welcome on the Championship course on Mondays, Tuesdays, Thursdays, and Fridays, and on the Annesley links every day except Saturday. Fees for the Championship course are £40 to £45 ($74–$83) during the winter and £95 to £105 ($176–$194) during the summer. Fees for the Annesley links are £12 to £20 ($22–$37) winter and £18 to £28 ($33–$52) summer.

- ✔ The **Mourne Trails Riding Centre,** 96 Castlewellan Rd., Newcastle (☎ **028-4372-4315**), offers horseback riding on local trails.

## Other top attractions in County Down

### Castlewellan Forest Park
**Castlewellan**

This 460-hectare (1,137-acre) wooded park just begs you to stroll around, enjoying the trout-filled lake, wooded paths, and views of a Scottish baronial-style castle on the grounds. The highlight is the gorgeous Annesley Garden and Arboretum, a splendid formally landscaped collection of trees and flowering shrubs from around the world, studded with fountains, ponds, and greenhouses. Don't miss the Peace Maze, the longest and largest hedge maze in the world. Give yourself lots of time — I was in there for a couple of hours. Maybe you should bring breadcrumbs. The Grange Coffee House is a sweet little spot for a light lunch and sells heavenly bite-size apple tarts. There is an area for tent campers and for trailers (called *caravans* in Ireland) if you wish to spend the night.

*Entrance is across from the marketplace in the town of Castlewellan. ☎ 028-4377-8664. Admission: Free for pedestrians, £4 ($7.40) per car. Open: Daily 10 a.m.–sunset. Suggested visit: 2 ½ hours.*

### Exploris
**Portaferry**

Exploris is Northern Ireland's only public aquarium, giving a fish-eye view of life in the Irish Sea with displays of the saltwater environment in Strangford Lough (the lake that Exploris borders) and the environment of the Irish sea. You can watch thousands of specimens of local sea life doing their thing and hang out with the aquarium's popular seals.

*The Rope Walk. On the A2 on the tip of the Ards Peninsula. ☎ 028-4272-8062. Admission: £5.40 ($10) adults, £3.20 ($5.90) children, seniors, and students. Open: Apr–Aug Mon–Fri 10 a.m.–6 p.m., Sat 11 a.m.–6 p.m., and Sun 1–6 pm; Sept–March Mon–Fri 10 a.m.–5 p.m., Sat 11 a.m.–5 p.m., and Sun 1–5 p.m. Suggested visit: 2 hours.*

### St. Patrick's Grave and Down Cathedral
**Downpatrick**

Sitting atop the Hill of Down is Down Cathedral, a small and austere church built in the 18th and 19th centuries in the style of its 13th– and 16th-century predecessors (buildings of religious signficance have stood here for the past 1,800 years). Legend has it that the little churchyard here contains the remains of Ireland's patron saint, St. Patrick. A rock slab with the word *Patric* across it marks the spot. To find out more about St. Patrick and the interesting history of this area, walk over to the **St. Patrick Heritage Centre/Down County Museum** (☎ 028-4461-5218), open June through August Monday through Friday from 10 a.m. to 5 p.m.,

Saturday and Sunday from 1 to 5 p.m.; and September through May Tuesday through Friday from 10 a.m. to 5 p.m. and Saturday from 1 to 5 p.m. (free admission).

*Down Cathedral, 33 Cathedral St. ☎ 028-4461-4922. Admission: Free. Open: Mon–Fri 9:30 a.m.–5 p.m, Sat and Sun 2–5 p.m. Suggested visit: 20 minutes, unless you're also visiting the Heritage Centre.*

### Tollymore Forest Park
Newcastle

A range of wildlife, from foxes to badgers to otters, roams this pleasant 480-hectare (1,200 acre) forest park. Amble along the river, perhaps stopping for a picnic, or break a sweat on one of the mountain trails.

*Tullybrannigan Rd. Follow the signs from B180, 3.2km (2 miles) north of Newcastle. ☎ 028-4372-2428. Admission: Free (parking is £4/$7.40). Open: Daily 10 a.m. until dark. Suggested visit: 1–3 hours, depending on what you want to do.*

## Hitting the pubs in County Down

### Grace Neill's Inn
Donaghadee

Many pubs claim to be the oldest in Ireland, but this one really is. Don't believe me? *The Guinness Book of World Records* says so, and those people know their pubs. The old part of the tavern practically defines what an Irish pub should look like, and even though it's been extended to include a lounge and conservatory, the whole place keeps the old-school style. The pub grub here is great.

*33 High St. (Donaghadee is off the A2, near Bangor). ☎ 028-9188-2553.*

### The Percy French
Newcastle

Drop into this Tudor-style pub for lunch or dinner (they offer a full menu of Irish classics) or just to have a pint and take in the jovial atmosphere.

*Downs Rd. ☎ 028-4372-3175.*

# County Armagh

Tiny County Armagh packs a lot of historical punch, containing the royal, pre-Christian Navan Fort as well as several sights associated with St. Patrick. The attractions in Armagh City are easily seen in a morning or afternoon, so I don't include accommodations or dining options.

### Exploring County Armagh

### Navan Fort
**Armagh**

Located just outside the city of Armagh, Navan Fort once pulsed with pre-Christian religious and royal activity. In myth, it is said that legendary Queen Macha had her palace here and that the great warrior Cuchuliann housed his armies here. Only mounds remain today, but the fascinating exhibits and audiovisuals in the interpretive center bring the history of the area to life.

*The Navan Centre, 81 Killylea Rd. 3km (2 miles) west of Armagh on A28. ☎ 028-3752-5550. Admission: £4.50 ($8.30) adults, £3 ($5.55) students and seniors, £2.50 ($4.65) children. Open: Mon–Sat 10 a.m.–5 p.m., Sun 11 a.m.–5 p.m.*

### St. Patrick's Trian
**Armagh**

This attraction presents the rich religious and secular history of Armagh. Engaging exhibits relate the story of Armagh's earliest roots; the history of St. Patrick, who chose to base himself in Armagh while preaching Christianity; and even the tale of *Gulliver's Travels*, featuring a giant figure of Gulliver among tiny Lilliputians. This is a good place to get a sense of what you'd like to see in town.

*40 English St., off Friary Rd. ☎ 028-3752-1801. Admission: £4 ($7.40) adults, £3 ($5.55) seniors and students, £2.25 ($4.15) students. Open: July–Aug Mon–Sat 10 a.m.–5 p.m., Sun 2–6 p.m.; Sept–Jun Mon–Sat 10 a.m.–5 p.m., Sun 2–5 p.m.*

## Fast Facts: Counties Down and Armagh

**Area Codes**

The area code (or city code) for counties Down and Armagh is 028. When calling from the Republic of Ireland, dial 048.

**Emergencies/Police**

Dial ☎ 999 for all emergencies.

**Information**

For visitor information in Down, go to the tourist office at 74 Market St., Downpatrick, County Down (☎ 028-4461-2233), or on the Central Promenade in Newcastle (☎ 028-4372-222). In Armagh, go to the visitor center at St. Patrick's Trian, at 40 English St. (☎ 028-9442-8331).

# Part VII
# The Part of Tens

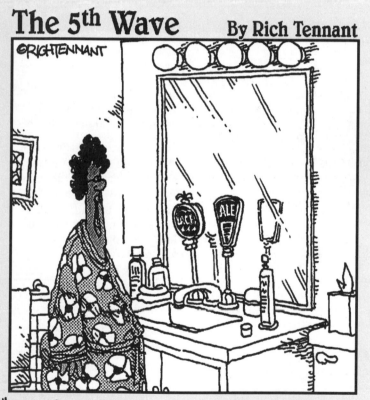

The 5th Wave    By Rich Tennant

©RICHTENNANT

"Douglas, I'd like to talk to you about the souvenirs you brought back from our trip to Ireland."

# *In this part . . .*

*I* give you a couple of fun extras. You can skip this part completely and still have a great trip, or read on for some bonus information.

In Chapter 24, I list ten traditional Irish dishes and beverages that you shouldn't miss, from home-baked brown bread to Guinness.

If you're wondering what to bring home from Ireland, check out Chapter 25. I describe some of the best and most authentically Irish products sold on the island and point you towards the finest places to buy them.

# Chapter 24

# Top Ten Traditional Irish Dishes and Drinks

● ● ● ● ● ● ● ● ● ● ● ● ● ● ● ● ● ● ● ● ● ● ● ● ● ● ● ● ● ● ● ● ● ● ● ● ● ● ● ● ● ● ● ● ● ● ●

## *In This Chapter*

▶ Breaking some brown bread

▶ Digging into a traditional breakfast

▶ Sipping Guinness

● ● ● ● ● ● ● ● ● ● ● ● ● ● ● ● ● ● ● ● ● ● ● ● ● ● ● ● ● ● ● ● ● ● ● ● ● ● ● ● ● ● ● ● ● ● ●

*T*hough most Irish cities now offer everything from sushi to margaritas, you'll have no trouble finding these quintessential delicious Irish dishes and beverages.

## *Apple and Rhubarb Tarts*

The world would be a happier (and plumper) place if everyone sat down a few days a week to a rhubarb or apple tart, served with a cool dollop of fresh cream.

## *Brown Bread*

Earthy wheaten brown bread is the perfect vehicle for creamy fresh Irish butter, as well as the ideal implement for scooping up the dregs of your soup or stew.

## *Guinness*

Does the thick black stuff really need an introduction? See Chapter 2 for more about the lifeblood of Ireland.

## *Hard Cider*

Sweet and refreshing, a glass or pint of cider is the perfect way to cool down on a warm, lazy evening.

# Irish Breakfast

You won't need lunch after chowing down on a traditional Irish breakfast. In its most complete form, the Irish breakfast in the Republic features bacon, eggs, sausages, fried tomatoes, fried mushrooms, black pudding (a sausage that gets its color from pig's or cow's blood), and white pudding (another sausage, but without the blood). You may also find baked beans staring up at you from the plate. In the North, the traditional breakfast plate (called an Ulster Fry) boasts two kinds of breads — soda farls and potato bread — in addition to everything else.

# Irish Farmhouse Cheeses

Smoky Gubbeen cheese from County Cork, creamy Cashel bleu cheese — I could go on and on . . .

# Irish Stew

The cornerstones of hearty, stick-to-your-ribs Irish stew are juicy pieces of lamb, cubed potatoes, and onions, but you could spend a lifetime cataloging the subtle variations in recipes across the country — a sprinkling of parsley in this pub, a handful of carrots in that restaurant, and so on.

# Irish Whiskey

Irish whiskey is different from Scotch whisky in several ways. The malt barley for Scotch is dried using peat smoke, but the malt barley used in Irish whiskey is dried in a warm closed oven, preserving the integrity of the barley flavor. In addition, Irish whiskey is distilled three times, giving it a smoothness that connoisseurs claim is unrivaled.

# Potatoes

It wouldn't be a book about Ireland without mention of the humble tuber that served as a staple on the island for centuries. The Irish have created a number of delicious potato-based dishes, including *champ* (potatoes mashed with milk and green onions or leeks) and *boxty* (grilled potato pancakes).

# Salmon

Irish salmon is glistening, pink, and fresh, and you can find it in a variety of forms, from simple smoked slices to moist fillets bathed in dazzling sauces.

# Chapter 25

# The Top Ten Items to Buy in Ireland

**S**ure, a handful of travelers come back from their trip with nothing more than a few rolls of film and a notebook full of observations and sketches, but most people are a bit more acquisitive than that. Ireland is a wonderful place to indulge your inner shopper, offering a plethora of items (many handmade) that are uniquely Irish.

## China

The Belleek Factory, in Northern Ireland, produces wafer-thin porcelain pieces, often decorated with small painted shamrocks or flowers. You can find Belleek pottery all over Ireland, but the Belleek Factory is a force to be reckoned with, selling the entire line of pottery plus some unique factory-only items (see Chapter 21).

## Crystal

Ireland makes some of the world's finest crystal — pieces that seem to glow and sparkle from within. If Waterford crystal is on your to-buy list, head to the Waterford Crystal Factory, which I talk about in Chapter 14, for the widest selection. Don't dismiss the lesser-know crystal factories; some of them produce crystal that is just as beautiful as Waterford.

# Irish Whiskey

Just think: You can sit back and sip the smooth water of life while recalling your trip to Ireland. If you get to the Old Jameson Distillery (see Chapter 11), you can even have a bottle personalized. Whiskey fudge makes the perfect thank-you present for dog-sitters and plant-waterers.

# Jewelry

Ireland is home to numerous talented silversmiths and goldsmiths, many of whom incorporate ancient Celtic motifs into their designs. One of the most popular souvenirs from Ireland is the Claddagh ring — a ring with two hands clasping a heart that's topped with a crown. Thomas Dillon's, in Galway (see Chapter 18), is one of the best places to find a Claddagh ring.

# Lace

In the 1860s, Poor Clare nuns in Kenmare began teaching local girls to make lace in hopes of helping the struggling economy. The beautiful needlepoint lace is now famous worldwide. In Kenmare, hit Nostalgia for a huge selection of lace (see Chapter 16).

# Linen

You can find the famous snow-white Irish linen in all sorts of forms, from tablecloths to bed sheets to summer dresses.

# Musical Instruments

I can't think of a better souvenir from Ireland than a tin whistle. It's inexpensive, truly Irish, easy to bring home on the airplane, and relatively easy to play (buy a tutor book or tape along with it). If you are more of the percussive type, you may want to look into buying a *bodhrán,* the ancient goatskin frame drum. Roundstone Musical Instruments (in Chapter 18) is *the* place for bodhrán-hunters.

# Pottery

It seems that every road in Ireland bears a sign pointing to a pottery studio. And the amazing thing is that the pieces at most of these places are of the highest quality. Design runs the gamut from the country-style painted pottery of Nicholas Mosse (see Chapter 14) to unglazed modern pieces.

# Irish clothing sizes

The United States and Ireland have different systems for measurements (except for men's shirt and suit sizes, which are the same in both countries). Use the following charts only as guides to steer you toward a near fit — sizes can vary among manufacturers and from store to store.

**Women's Coats and Dresses**

| United States | 4 | 6 | 8 | 10 | 12 | 14 | 16 | 18 |
|---|---|---|---|---|---|---|---|---|
| Ireland | 6 | 8 | 10 | 12 | 14 | 16 | 18 | 20 |

**Women's Shoes**

| United States | 5 | 6 | 7 | 8 | 9 | 10 |
|---|---|---|---|---|---|---|
| Ireland | 4 | 5 | 6 | 7 | 8 | 9 |

**Men's Shoes**

| United States | 7 | 8 | 9 | 10 | 11 | 12 |
|---|---|---|---|---|---|---|
| Ireland | 6 | 7 | 8 | 9 | 10 | 11 |

## Sweaters

You can thank all those sheep for Ireland's beautiful sweaters. There is a breathtaking range of offerings, from chic cashmere turtlenecks to thick oatmeal-colored Aran sweaters. Check the label to determine whether the sweater is handwoven.

## Tweed

Like those battered tweed hats that many farmers wear? You can find them all over Ireland, along with tweed jackets and suits. If you're searching for the perfect tweed, you may want to head up to County Donegal, the birthplace of the famous Donegal tweed, where you'll find tweed-heaven at Magee of Donegal (see Chapter 20).

# Appendix

# Quick Concierge

○ ○ ○ ○ ○ ○ ○ ○ ○ ○ ○ ○ ○ ○ ○ ○ ○ ○ ○ ○ ○ ○ ○ ○ ○ ○ ○ ○ ○ ○ ○ ○ ○ ○ ○ ○ ○ ○ ○ ○ ○ ○ ○

## Fast Facts

### American Express

American Express has an office in Dublin at 41 Nassau St. (☎ 1-890-205-5511). Dial ☎ 1-890-706-706 to report lost or stolen traveler's checks.

### ATMs

ATMs (called *service tills* or *cash points*) are located all over the country, even in the smallest towns. The major networks are Plus (☎ 800-843-7587; www.visa.com) and Cirrus (☎ 800-424-7787; www.mastercard.com).

### Credit Cards

Visa and MasterCard are the most commonly accepted credit cards, followed by American Express, then Diner's Club. If your credit card is lost or stolen, call one of the following emergency numbers from Ireland: For American Express, call collect ☎ 00-1-336-393-1111; for Master Card, call ☎ 1-800-55-7378 in the Republic or ☎ 0800-96-4767 in Northern Ireland; for Visa, call ☎ 1-800-55-8002 in the Republic or 0800-89-1725 in Northern Ireland; and for Diner's Club, call ☎ 303-799-1504 (call collect) from the Republic of Ireland or ☎ 0-800-46-0800 in Northern Ireland.

### Customs

You can't bring firearms, ammunition, explosives, narcotics, poultry, plants and their immediate byproducts, domestic animals from outside the United Kingdom, or snakes into Ireland. Also, you may bring in no more than 200 cigarettes, one liter of liquor, and two liters of wine.

Travelers from European Community countries may bring home as many goods as they like, as long as they are for personal use. For information on U.S. Customs restrictions on what you can bring home from Ireland, read the brochure *Know Before You Go* at www.customs.gov, or request a printed brochure from the U.S. Customs Service, 1300 Pennsylvania Ave. NW, Room 54D, Washington, DC 20229. Canadian travelers can find out about customs by writing for the booklet *I Declare*, issued by Revenue Canada, 2265 St. Laurent Blvd., Ottawa K1G 4KE (☎ 506-636-5064; www.ccra-adrc.com). Australian travelers can obtain a *Know Before You Go* brochure from consulates or Customs offices. For a brochure, write to Australian Customs Services, GPO Box 8, Sydney NSW 2001 (☎ 02-9213-2000; www.customs.gov.au). New Zealanders can get the *New Zealand Customs Guide for Travelers* from New Zealand Customs, 50 Anzac Ave., P.O. Box 29, Auckland (☎ 09-359-6655; www.customs.govt.nz).

### Dentists and Doctors

If you need to see a dentist or physician, ask the concierge or host at your hotel or guesthouse for a recommendation. Otherwise, consult the Golden Pages of the Irish telephone book or the Yellow Pages of the Northern Ireland telephone book, or contact your local consulate for a recommendation. Many emergency rooms have walk-in clinics. Expect to pay for treatment up front and to be reimbursed by your insurance company after the fact.

## Driving

You must have a valid driver's license from your home country to drive in Ireland. The speed limit is 112 kmph (67 mph) on motorways and 100 kmph (60 mph) on open non-urban roads. Speed-limit signs have a red circle with the limit written inside in black. The Irish drive on the left side of the road. For more on driving in Ireland, turn to Chapter 7.

## Drugstores

Drugstores are usually called *chemists* or *pharmacies*. Look under "Chemists — Pharmaceutical" in the Golden Pages of the Irish telephone book or "Chemists — Dispensing" in the Yellow Pages of the Northern Ireland telephone book.

Pack prescription medications (in their original-label vials) in your carry-on luggage. Bring along copies of your prescriptions, in generic form rather than under a brand name, in case you need to get a refill.

## Electricity

The standard electrical current is 220 volts in the Republic of Ireland and 250 volts in Northern Ireland. The Republic uses three-pronged plugs, while the North uses two prongs. If you bring non-Irish appliances, you need both a transformer and a plug adapter (available at many hardware stores and sometimes airports). Many new laptops have built-in transfomers, so check before you buy one.

## Embassies and Consulates

The American Embassy is at 42 Elgin Rd., Ballsbridge, Dublin 4 (☎ 01-668-8777); the American Consulate is at 14 Queen St., Belfast BT1 6EQ (☎ 028-9032-8239). The Canadian Embassy is at 65-68 St. Stephen's Green, Dublin 2 (☎ 01-678-1988); the British Embassy is at 31 Merrion Rd., Dublin 4 (☎ 01-205-3700); and you can find the Australian Embassy at Fitzwilton House, Wilton Terrace, Dublin 2 (☎ 01-676-1517).

## Emergencies

For the Garda (police), fire, ambulance, or other emergencies, dial ☎ **999.**

## Information

See "Where to Get More Information," later in this appendix.

## Internet Access and Cybercafes

Cybercafes and library Internet access are all over Ireland. Check the Fast Facts section of each destination chapter.

## Liquor Laws

You must be 18 or older to be served alcoholic beverages. You can purchase alcoholic beverages by the bottle at liquor stores, pubs displaying *off-license* signs, and most supermarkets. Ireland has very severe laws and penalties regarding driving while intoxicated.

## Maps

If you're driving, a good driving map is essential. My favorite is the Ordnance Survey Ireland's *Ireland Touring Map*. For local maps, the tourism or visitors' offices in each area are your best bet.

## Police

A law enforcement officer is called a *garda,* in the plural, it's *gardai* (pronounced gar-dee) or simply *the guards*. Dial ☎ **999** in an emergency in both the Republic of Ireland and Northern Ireland.

## Post Office

Post offices in the Republic are called *An Post* (www.letterpost.ie for general information) and are easy to spot: Look for a bright-green storefront with the name across it. Ireland's main postal branch, the General Post Office (GPO), is on O'Connell Street (☎ 01-872-6666), in the heart of Dublin. From the Republic, mailing an air-mail letter or postcard costs €.57 (66¢).

In Northern Ireland, post offices are called Post Offices, and the offices and post boxes are bright red. The main post office in Belfast is located at Castle Junction, at the top of High Street (☎ 08457-223344 for information. The cost to send a letter is 39p (72¢).

## Restrooms

Public restrooms are usually called *toilets* and marked with international symbols. Some toilets use the Gaelic words *Fir* (Men) and *Mna* (Women). Gas stations normally do not have public toilets.

## Safety

For many years, violent crimes in Ireland were rare. Unfortunately, that seems to be changing. Though Ireland's large cities are still generally safer than those in the United States, reasonable precautions are needed. It is a good idea to take a taxi back to your hotel after pubs close, especially in Dublin, and be on the alert in deserted areas at night. In addition, leave your passport and other important documents in your hotel room, always lock car doors, and don't carry loads of cash. If you want more detailed information on safety, pick up the brochure *A Short Guide to Tourist Security,* published by the Garda (police) and available at most tourist offices in the Republic. Thankfully, political violence has been on the wane in Northern Ireland since the Good Friday Agreement in 1998. For up-to-date safety recommendations for Northern Ireland, call the U.S. Department of State 24-hour Hotline at ☎ 202-647-5225.

## Smoking

In the Republic, smoking is banned in pubs, restaurants, clubs, stores, public transportation, and taxis. In Northern Ireland, restaurants and pubs tend to be smoky, although some restaurants offer a non-smoking area. Some B&Bs and smaller guesthouses do not allow smoking; check before making a reservation.

## Taxes

Sales tax is called *value-added tax* (VAT) and is often already included in the price quoted to you or shown on price tags. In the Republic, VAT rates vary — for hotels, restaurants, and car rentals, it's 13.5%; for souvenirs and gifts, it's 21%. In Northern Ireland, the VAT is 17.5% across the board.

Travelers can have their VAT refunded for souvenir purchases. For information on VAT refunds, see Chapter 5. If you choose to ship items directly home from the store, your purchase is automatically VAT-free.

## Telephone

To call Ireland from anywhere in the world, dial the international access code (011 from the United States and Canada, 0011 from Australia, 0170 from New Zealand, and 00 from the United Kingdom) and then the country code (Ireland is 353; Northern Ireland is 44), followed by the city code without the initial zero (for example, you dial 1 for the Dublin city code, even though it is listed in this book as 01) and the number. *An exception:* When calling Northern Ireland from the United Kingdom, dial 028 and the local eight-digit number.

Public phones in Ireland take either coins or cards. To make a phone call from a card phone, you must purchase a *callcard* in the Republic or a *phonecard* in Northern Ireland. Both types of cards are available at post offices and newsagents.

The Irish toll-free number for directory assistance is ☎ 11811. From the United States, the (toll) number to call for directory assistance is ☎ 00353-91-770220. For local operator assistance in Ireland, dial ☎ 10 in the Republic and ☎ 100 in Northern Ireland.

To call locally in the Republic of Ireland and Northern Ireland, just dial the number direct. You need to include the city code when calling from town to town in the Republic; in Northern Ireland, you can just dial the eight-digit local number.

To call Northern Ireland from the Republic, omit the country code and dial 048 and then the local eight-digit number. To call the Republic from Northern Ireland, dial 00-353 and then the city code and number.

To make international direct calls from the Republic of Ireland and Northern Ireland, dial the international access code (00), followed by the country code (1 for the United States and Canada, 44 for the United Kingdom, 61 for Australia, and 64 for New Zealand), the area or city code, and then the local number. So to call the U.S. States number 718-000-0000, you'd dial 00-1-718-000-0000.

From the Republic of Ireland, dial ☎ 11818 for international directory assistance and ☎ 114 for operator assistance with international calls. From Northern Ireland, dial ☎ 153 for international directory assistance and ☎ 155 for operator assistance with international calls.

Calling-card access phone numbers are as follows: In the Republic of Ireland, call ☎ 1800-55-0000 for AT&T, ☎ 1800-55-1001 for MCI, and ☎ 1800-55-2001 for Sprint. In Northern Ireland, call ☎ 0500-89-0011 for AT&T, ☎ 0800-89-0222 for MCI, and ☎ 0800-89-0877 for Sprint.

If you plan to call home a lot while in Ireland, you may want to open an account with Swiftcall (toll-free in Ireland ☎ 0800-929-932; www.swiftcall.com). Its rates offer you considerable savings, not only from Ireland to the United States but vice versa. International WORLDLINK (☎ 800-864-8000) offers an array of additional services for overseas travelers, such as toll-free voice-mail boxes, fax, mail, and news services.

### Time Zone

Ireland is five time zones ahead of the eastern United States (when it's noon in New York, it's 5 p.m. in Ireland). Ireland observes daylight saving time.

### Tipping

Most hotels and guesthouses add a service charge to the bill, usually 12.5% to 15%. Always check to see what amount, if any, has been added to your bill. Giving additional cash gratuities is appropriate if you've received exceptional service or if the hotel has charged less than 12.5%. For porters or bellhops, tip €1 ($1.15) per piece of luggage.

For taxi drivers, hairdressers, and other providers of service, tip an average of 10% to 15%.

Tip at least 10% or 15% at a restaurant. However, check to see whether a service charge has been added to the bill before paying. If the service charge has been added, you may want to round up the amount to 15% if you received good service.

It is not customary to tip bartenders at pubs. For waiter service at a bar, leave about €1 ($1.15).

### Weather Updates

The best site on the Web for Ireland's weather forecasts is www.ireland.com/weather.

# *Toll-Free Numbers and Web Sites*

**Air Canada**
☎ 888-247-2262
www.aircanada.ca

**AirlinesAer Lingus**
☎ 800-474-7424 in the U.S.
☎ 01-886-8888 in Ireland
www.aerlingus.com

**American Airlines**
☎ 800-433-7300
www.aa.com

**British Airways**
☎ 800-AIRWAYS
☎ 0870-850-9850 in the U.K.
www.british-airways.com

**British Midland**
☎ 800-788-0555 in the U.S.
☎ 0870-607-0555 in Britain
www.flybmi.com

**CityJet**
☎ 353-1-8700-100 in Ireland
www.cityjet.com

**Continental Airlines**
☎ 800-523-3273
www.continental.com

**Delta Air Lines**
☎ 800-221-1212
www.delta.com

**easyJet**
No U.S. number
☎ (44) 870-6000-000 or
☎ 0871-7500-100 in the U.K.
www.easyjet.com

**Lufthansa**
☎ 800-645-3880 in the U.S.
www.lufthansa.com

**Northwest Airlines**
☎ 800-447-4747
www.nwa.com

**Ryanair**
No U.S. number
☎ 0541-569-569 in the U.K.
www.ryanair.com

**United Airlines**
☎ 800-538-2929
www.united.com

**Virgin Atlantic Airways**
☎ 800-862-8621 in the continental U.S.
☎ 0293-747-747 in Britain
www.virgin-atlantic.com

## *Car-rental agencies*

**Alamo**
☎ 800-462-5266
www.goalamo.com

**Argus**
In Ireland: ☎ 353-1-490-6173
www.argus-rentacar.com

**Avis**
In Ireland: ☎ 353-1-214-281-111
www.avis.com

**Budget**
☎ 800-472-3325
www.budget.com

**Dan Dooley**
☎ 800-331-9301
www.dan-dooley.ie

**Hertz**
☎ 800-654-3131
www.hertz.com

**Murrays Europcar/AutoEurope**
☎ 800-223-5555
www.europcar.ie

**National**
☎ 800-CAR-RENT
www.nationalcar.com

# *Where to Get More Information*

## *National Tourist Information Offices*

The **Irish Tourist Board** (also known as *Bord Faílte*) and the **Northern Ireland Tourist Board** have tons of helpful informational literature; comprehensive B&B, farmhouse, and hotel directories for a nominal fee; and a friendly staff that's eager to answer your questions. The Irish Tourist Board has an excellent Web site at www.tourismireland.com. Its location in the Republic is Baggott Street Bridge, Dublin 2 (☎ 1850-230-3300), and its location in Northern Ireland is 53 Castle St., Belfast BT1 1GH (☎ 028 0032 7888). See the next section for locations around the world. The Northern Ireland Tourism Board also has a great site at www.discovernorthernireland.com. It's located at 16 Nassau St., Dublin 2 (☎ 01-679-1977), in the Republic and at 59 North St., Belfast BT1 1NB (☎ 028-9023-1221), in Northern Ireland.

## *In the United States*

**Irish Tourist Board:** 345 Park Ave., New York, NY 10154; ☎ 800-223-6470 within the United States or 212-418-0800.

**Northern Ireland Tourist Board:** 551 Fifth Ave., Suite 701, New York, NY 10176; ☎ 800-326-0036 within the United States or 212-922-0101.

## *In Canada*

**Irish Tourist Board:** 2 Bloor St. W., Suite 1501, Toronto, ON, M4W 3E2; ☎ 800-223-6470.

**Northern Ireland Tourist Board:** 2 Bloor St. W., Suite 1501, Toronto, ON, M4W 3E2; ☎ 800-576-8174 or 416-925-6368.

## *In the United Kingdom*

**Irish Tourist Board:** 150 New Bond St., London W1Y 0AQ; ☎ 020-7493-3201.

**Northern Ireland Tourist Board:** 24 Haymarket, London SW1 4DG; ☎ 020-7766-9920.

## *In Australia*

**All Ireland Tourism (Republic and Northern Ireland):** 36 Carrington St., Fifth Level, Sydney, NSW 2000; ☎ 02-9299-6323.

## *In New Zealand*

**Irish Tourist Board:** Dingwall Building, Second Floor, 87 Queen St., Auckland; ☎ 0064-9379-8720.

## *Other sources of information*

For more restaurant, accommodation, and attraction options, pick up a copy of *Frommer's Ireland* (Wiley).

# Index